The Politics of International Economic Relations

The Politics of International Economic Relations

SEVENTH EDITION

JOAN EDELMAN SPERO
The Doris Duke Charitable Foundation

JEFFREY A. HART
Indiana University

Australia • Brazil • Japan • Korea • Mexico • Singapore • Spain • United Kingdom • United States

WADSWORTH
CENGAGE Learning

The Politics of International Economic Relations, Seventh Edition
Joan Edelman Spero,
Jeffrey A. Hart

Senior Publisher: Suzanne Jeans

Executive Editor: Carolyn Merrill

Development Editor: David Estrin

Assistant Editor: Katherine Hayes

Editorial Assistant: Nathan Gamache

Associate Development Project Manager: Caitlin Holroyd

Senior Marketing Manager: Amy Whitaker

Marketing Communications Manager: Heather Baxley

Associate Content Project Manager: Sara Abbott

Art Director: Linda Helcher

Production Technology Analyst: Jamison MacLachlan

Senior Print Buyer: Karen Hunt

Senior Rights Acquisition Account Manager, Text: Margaret Chamberlain-Gaston

Text Researcher: Karyn Morrison

Production Service/Compositor: Integra

Rights Acquisition Account Manager, Image: Mandy Groszko

Cover Designer: Mike Stratton

Cover Images: Alex Slobodkin, William Stall, Radu Razvan, and Adam Korzekwa

For product information and
technology assistance, contact us at **Cengage Learning Customer & Sales Support, 1-800-354-9706**

For permission to use material from this text or product, submit all requests online at **www.cengage.com/permissions** Further permissions questions can be emailed to **permissionrequest@cengage.com**

Library of Congress Control Number: 2008942810

ISBN-13: 978-0-534-60274-1

ISBN-10: 0-534-60274-6

Wadsworth
20 Davis Drive
Belmont, CA 94002
USA

Cengage Learning is a leading provider of customized learning solutions with office locations around the globe, including Singapore, the United Kingdom, Australia, Mexico, Brazil, and Japan. Locate your local office at **www.cengage.com/global**

Cengage Learning products are represented in Canada by Nelson Education, Ltd.

To learn more about Wadsworth, visit **www.cengage.com/wadsworth**

Purchase any of our products at your local college store or at our preferred online store **www.cengagebrain.com**

Printed in the United States of America
2 3 4 5 6   19 18 17 16 15

To Alexis, Eva, and Isabella Spero

Contents

PART IV   Implications of the End of the Cold War

10 East–West Economic Relations: From Isolation to Integration   378

Preface

The first edition of *The Politics of International Economic Relations*, published in 1977, was written to fill a void in the study of international relations—the gap between international politics and international economics. Since 1977, that gap has narrowed significantly. International political economy has emerged as a new and increasingly prominent field in political science. Theoretical and empirical analyses of the politics of international economic relations appear regularly in professional books and journals. Although the most important bridge building has come from political scientists, now economists are also including political variables in their analyses and applying economic theory to the study of political behavior. A new and diverse generation of students is being made aware of the interrelationship between economics and politics and is learning to use and integrate the tools of these disciplines.

Much has happened since 1977 to reinforce this academic evolution. Above all, turbulence in the world economy has heightened the political aspect of international economic relations. The persistent problems of the dollar and other international currencies, the many trade disputes between the United States and its major trading partners, crises in world oil markets, and the continuing debt crisis in the Third World have obliged scholars to reexamine the assumptions that separated the disciplines of economics and political science for over a century.

The focus and organization in this book has not changed much since the first edition was published. This edition of *The Politics of International Economic Relations* continues the previously established tradition of separating the discussion into problems faced by developing countries and former communist countries and problems that primarily affect industrialized capitalist countries. In the fifth edition, we added new material that reflected major changes in the international system since the end of the Cold War. Also in the fifth edition, we discussed and tried to explain the increasing pragmatism of domestic and foreign economic policies in many parts of the Third World, but especially in the faster-growing developing countries. Last, the fifth edition added material on the growing gap between the poorest regions of the world and the richest ones.

The sixth edition provided new information about the various monetary crises of the late 1990s, the early years of the World Trade Organization, the continuing rapid growth in foreign direct investment, the integration of the formerly communist countries into the capitalist world economy, and a rethinking of theories of economic development that followed the Asia Crisis of 1997–1998. Finally, the sixth edition explored the relationship between globalization and governance in greater depth than in previous editions.

This seventh edition of *The Politics of International Economic Relations* was completed before the outbreak of the global financial and economic crisis that began in the United States in 2008 and spread throughout the world. That crisis continues to unfold as this book goes to press.

The causes of the crisis, which will long be debated, include imprudent lending by financial institutions, especially U.S. bank lending in the so-called subprime mortgage market; excessive borrowing by financial institutions to support new and risky operations; the creation of complex securitized financial instruments whose risks were not fully understood and that were acquired and traded around the world; outdated and ineffective financial regulation and supervision at a national level; and inadequate systems for global financial management. The consequences of the crisis on global economic stability, prosperity, and equity will unfold in the coming years.

The causes and ramifications of the crisis of 2008 and beyond are not explicitly discussed in this edition. However, many of the complex and interrelated aspects of the upheaval are explained and foreshadowed in *The Politics of International Economic Relations*. For example, this edition discusses the creation of new financial instruments, the globalization of financial markets and financial institutions, and the resulting frequency of global financial crises. It explains the growing interdependence of national economies and the evolution of global financial management systems, as well as the limitations of multilateral governance in a global world. Throughout the study, there is a focus on the need for systemic leadership especially by the United States and the European Union, the critical role of the U.S. economy, and the inability of United States to manage the global system unilaterally. The concluding chapter looks ahead to the need for improved systemic management and reform in a global economy.

Carolyn Merrill, Executive Editor at Wadsworth, shepherded the seventh edition through a more than usually fraught gestation. Her experience and *sangfroid* are much appreciated. David Estrin, the development editor, was cheerful and reliable throughout the process. Thivya Nathan, Katherine Hayes, Sara Abbott, and Michael Lepera saw the book through production. Our thanks to all.

About the Authors

Joan Edelman Spero

Joan E. Spero is currently a Visiting Fellow at the Foundation Center. From 1997 to 2008, Ms. Spero was President of the Doris Duke Charitable Foundation, which makes grants in the performing arts, environmental preservation, medical research and prevention of child abuse.

Ms. Spero served in the U.S. Department of State as Undersecretary for Economic, Business, and Agricultural Affairs (1993–1997) and as Ambassador to the United Nations for Economic and Social Affairs (1980–1981). She was a corporate executive at American Express Company (1981–1993) and an Assistant Professor at Columbia University (1973–1979). Ms. Spero graduated from the University of Wisconsin and holds a master's and doctoral degrees from Columbia University.

Jeffrey A. Hart

Jeffrey A. Hart is Professor of Political Science at Indiana University, Bloomington, where he has taught international politics and international political economy since 1981. His first teaching position was at Princeton University from 1973 to 1980. He was a professional staff member of the President's Commission for a National Agenda for the Eighties from 1980 to 1981. Hart worked at the Office of Technology Assessment of the U.S. Congress in 1985–1986 as an internal contractor and helped write their 1987 report, *International Competition in Services*. He was a visiting scholar at the Berkeley Roundtable on the International Economy from 1987 to 1989. His major publications include *The New International Economic Order* (1983), *Interdependence in the Post Multilateral Era* (1985), *Rival Capitalists* (1992), *The*

Politics of International Economic Relations (5th and 6th editions; with Joan Spero), *Globalization and Governance* (1999; edited with Aseem Prakash), and scholarly articles in *World Politics, International Organization, British Journal of Political Science, New Political Economy,* and *Journal of Conflict Resolution.*

From Management to Governance in International Economic Relations

G overnments have attempted to regulate various aspects of their international economic interactions since the first trader crossed a national border. **International economic regimes** are rules, norms, procedures, and institutions that are intended to achieve common economic goals by constraining the behavior of governments. These regimes range from simple bilateral trade agreements to complex multilateral arrangements such as the World Trade Organization. International regimes can affect the nature and degree of international interaction among members. Regimes are shaped by political factors such as the distribution of power among the players, the degree of shared goals and interests, and the nature of leadership within the system.

International economic systems are clusters of regimes that include, among other things, rules for trade, investment, and monetary flows. In the half-century since the end of World War II, there have been three international economic systems: the **Bretton Woods system**, which prevailed from World War II until 1971; the system of **interdependence** from 1971 to 1989; and, from 1989 to the present, the contemporary system of **globalization**.

BRETTON WOODS

For nearly two decades, the Bretton Woods system was effective in controlling conflict and achieving the common goals of its members. The rules, institutions, and procedures of the system were embodied in three organizations created during and immediately after World War II. Named for the New Hampshire town in which two of the organizations—the **International Monetary Fund (IMF)** and the **World Bank**—were created, the Bretton Woods system consisted of those two organizations plus the **General Agreement on Tariffs and Trade (GATT).** These three institutions have evolved significantly over time but remain cornerstones of international economic governance to the current day.

During the Bretton Woods era, international economic interaction was still limited but growing. In the early years of Bretton Woods, many countries were recovering from the devastation of the war and were in no position to compete internationally. Tariffs, quotas, and exchange controls protected national markets and hampered the international flow of goods and money. International investment was limited and concentrated heavily in raw materials and retailing, not in manufacturing.

The Bretton Woods system rested on three political foundations: the concentration of power in a small number of states, the existence of a cluster of important interests shared by those states, and the presence of a dominant power willing and able to assume a leadership role.[1] The concentration of both political and economic power in the developed countries of North America and Western Europe enabled these countries to dominate the Bretton Woods system. They faced no challenge from the communist states of Eastern Europe and Asia (including the Soviet Union), which were isolated from the rest of the international economy in a separate international economic system. Although the less-developed countries (LDCs) were integrated into the world economy, they had no voice in management because of their political and economic weakness. For much of this period, many developing countries in Africa and Asia were still subordinated within colonial empires. Finally, Japan, weakened by the war and lacking the level of development and the political power of North America and Western Europe, remained outside the management group for much of the Bretton Woods era. As a defeated power, Japan was not initially a member of the Bretton Woods institutions. It joined the IMF and World Bank in 1952 and did not become a member of the GATT until 1954. The concentration of power facilitated the system's management by confining the number of actors whose agreement was necessary to establish new international economic regimes and to carry out management within the agreed upon system.

Management also was made easier by a high level of agreement among the system's powerful members on the goals and means of the international economic system. The developed countries shared a belief in **capitalism** and liberalism and relied primarily on market mechanisms and private ownership. These countries also agreed that the liberal economic system required governmental **intervention**. In the era after World War II, national governments assumed responsibility for the economic well-being of their citizens, and employment, stability, and growth became important objects of public policy. The **welfare state** was a response to the **Great Depression**, which created a popular demand for governmental intervention in the economy, and out of the theoretical contributions of the **Keynesian** school of economics, which prescribed governmental intervention to maintain adequate levels of employment.

The developed countries also favored a liberal international economic system, one that relied primarily on a free market with a minimum of barriers to the flow of private trade and capital. The experience of the Great Depression, in which proliferation of exchange controls and **trade barriers** led to economic disaster, remained fresh in the minds of public officials. Although these countries disagreed on the specific implementation of this liberal system, all agreed that an open system would maximize economic welfare. At the same time, governments recognized that international markets could be unstable and sought to design mechanisms to manage crises and control conflict.

Some governments also believed that a liberal international economic system would lead not only to economic prosperity and economic harmony but also to international peace.[2] One of those who saw such a security link was Cordell Hull, the U.S. secretary of state from 1933 to 1944. Hull argued that

> ... unhampered trade dovetailed with peace; high tariffs, trade barriers, and unfair economic competition, with war ... if we could get a freer flow of trade—freer in the sense of fewer discriminations and obstructions—so that one country would not be deadly jealous of another and the living standards of all countries might rise, thereby eliminating the economic dissatisfaction that breeds war, we might have a reasonable chance of lasting peace.[3]

The common interest in economic cooperation was enhanced by the outbreak of the **Cold War** at the end of the 1940s. The economic weakness of the West, some officials felt, would make it vulnerable to internal communist threats and external pressure from the Soviet Union. Economic cooperation became necessary not only to rebuild Western economies and to ensure their continuing vitality but also to provide for their political and military security. In addition, the perceived communist military threat led the developed countries to subordinate their economic conflict to their common security interests.

The developed market economies also agreed on the nature of international economic management, which would involve the creation and maintenance of a liberal system. This strategy would require the establishment of a stable international monetary system and the reduction of barriers to trade and capital flows so states would have a favorable environment for ensuring national stability and growth. The state, not the international system, bore the main responsibility for national stability and growth. Thus, the members of the system shared a very limited conception of international economic management: regulation of the liberal system by removing barriers to trade and capital flows and creation of a stable monetary system.

Finally, international management relied on the dominant power to lead the system. As the world's foremost economic and political power, the United States clearly was in a position to assume that responsibility of leadership. The U.S. economy, undamaged by war and with its large market, great productive capability, financial facilities, and strong currency, was the dominant world economy. The ability to support a large military force plus the possession of nuclear weapons made the United States the world's strongest military power and the leader of the Western alliance. The European states, with their economies in disarray due to the war, their production and markets divided by national boundaries, and their armies dismantled or weakened by the war, were not in a position to assume the leadership role. Japan, defeated and destroyed, was at that time not even considered part of the management system.

The United States was both willing and able to assume the leadership role. U.S. policymakers had learned an important lesson from the interwar period. The failure of U.S. leadership and the country's withdrawal into **isolationism** after World War I were viewed as major factors in the collapse of the economic system and of the peace. U.S. policymakers believed that after World War II the United States could no longer isolate itself. As the strongest power in the postwar world, the United States would have to assume primary responsibility for establishing political and economic order. With the outbreak of the Cold War, yet another dimension was added to the need for U.S. leadership. Without such leadership, the U.S. government and its allies abroad believed, the economic weakness in Europe and Japan would lead to communist political victories.

Furthermore, the Europeans and the Japanese—economically exhausted by the war—actively encouraged this U.S. leadership role. They needed assistance from the United States to rebuild their domestic production and to finance their international trade. The political implications of U.S. leadership, therefore, were viewed as positive, because political elites in these countries felt that U.S. economic assistance would alleviate domestic economic and political problems and encourage international stability. What the Europeans feared was not U.S. domination but U.S. isolation; the late entry of the United States into both world wars was fresh in their minds.

Throughout the Bretton Woods period, the United States mobilized the other developed countries for management and, in some cases, managed the system alone. The United States acted as the world's central banker, provided the major initiatives in international trade negotiations, and dominated international investment.

This coincidence of a limited degree of international economic interaction combined with favorable political conditions—the concentration of power, the cluster of shared interests, and the leadership of the United States—provided the political capability equal to the tasks of managing the international economy. The Bretton Woods system enabled Europe and Japan to recover from the devastation of the war, established a stable monetary system, encouraged more open trade, finance, and investment, and in turn led to a period of rapid economic growth.

INTERDEPENDENCE

By the 1970s, however, the Bretton Woods system was replaced by a new international economic system characterized by interdependence. Changes in the nature of international economic interaction and a shift in the balance of power among the key players led to a restructuring of the international economic order.

Important economic changes increased the management challenges facing the system. Ironically, it was the very success of Bretton Woods that led to these challenges. Economic growth and ongoing international liberalization combined with innovations in computing and telecommunications technologies led to higher volumes of international economic interaction and growing penetration of national economies by international trade, investment, and monetary flows. The reduction of barriers to trade and capital as well as the revolution in information technologies enabled an expansion in international economic interaction among the developed market economies: larger international capital flows, the growth of international trade, and the development of international systems of production. As a result, national economies became more interdependent and more sensitive to economic policy and events outside the national economy. The problem was heightened because this sensitivity grew at a time when, more than ever, states were expected to ensure domestic economic well-being. Because of the influence of external events, states found it increasingly difficult to manage their national economies. The greatest disruptions were caused by periodic monetary crises that forced dramatic **revaluations** of currencies and disrupted trade.

Interdependence led to two reactions and two different challenges to the underlying liberal consensus on which the system was based. One reaction was to erect new barriers to limit economic interaction and, with it, interdependence. An open international system, in this view, no longer maximized economic welfare and most certainly undermined national **sovereignty** and autonomy. Some critics argued that a continued focus on **tariff** reductions was no longer appropriate in an increasingly tariff-free world economy. **Nontariff barriers (NTBs)** had become deeply embedded in national economic policy, partly as a response to reduced tariffs. Pressures grew not only for new forms of protection and **managed trade**, but also for efforts to strengthen regional **free-trade** groupings such as the **European Economic Community (EEC).** These regional groupings were not on the whole protectionist, although the possibility always existed that new barriers to extra-regional trade and investment flows would be erected even as internal ones were being dismantled.

Another reaction was to go beyond Bretton Woods and the idea of a limited management to new forms of international economic cooperation that would manage interdependence. An open system, according to this viewpoint, maximized welfare but required, in turn, new forms of international management that would assume responsibilities and prerogatives formerly undertaken by the state. These views led to efforts to establish a regular series of international economic summits and attempts (mostly unsuccessful) to coordinate national macroeconomic policies. In the 1980s, new initiatives were taken to upgrade the multilateral trade regime with a new and more ambitious multilateral trade negotiation—the Uruguay Round.

During the period of interdependence, changes in power and leadership also altered political management of the international economic system. Although the developed countries remained the dominant political and economic powers, states outside the group challenged their right to manage the system. In particular, the LDCs sought to increase their access to the management and, thus, to the rewards of the international economic system. In the 1950s and 1960s, most colonies had gained their independence and now sought to improve their economic performance and their influence in the international economic system. Some developing countries took a pragmatic approach to multilateral management, seeking to work within the prevailing regime and to play a greater role within the system. Other developing countries dissented from the liberal foundation of international management, arguing that open monetary, trade, and financial systems perpetuated their underdevelopment and subordination to the developed countries. These countries sought to develop their economies both by protecting themselves from international economic interaction and by trying to make their development a primary goal and responsibility of the system. The oil crisis of the early 1970s led to an effort on the part of these countries to alter the rules of the game and to create what they called a New International Economic Order.

In the 1970s and 1980s, the Soviet Union and the countries of Eastern Europe also sought limited participation in the international economy. Changes in domestic and international policy in the two key communist countries—the Soviet Union and the People's Republic of China—opened up the possibility of greater East-West economic interaction. Gorbachev's **perestroika**, or restructuring, sought to move the Soviet economy more in the market direction and to open up trade, finance, and investment relations with the West. This move had the unforeseen result of hastening the Soviet Union's economic decline and helping to bring about the breakup of the Soviet empire. In contrast, China's economic reforms led to rapid growth. Expectations of political liberalization grew within China until the suppression of the student demonstrations in **Tiananmen Square** in 1989.

More important, power shifted within the group of advanced industrial nations. In the 1960s, Europe experienced a period of great economic growth and dynamism in international trade. Six European countries had united in 1957 to form the EEC, a trading bloc rivaling the U.S. economy and a potential political force. By 1986, the six countries became twelve and the EEC evolved into the European Union (EU), whose goal was not only the elimination of trade barriers and the creation of a **customs union** but also the removal of all barriers to the movement of capital, labor, and services. Japan's **economic development** was even more spectacular. In the 1960s, Japan became a major world economic power and joined the developed countries' condominium. By the 1980s, Japan was a powerful economic competitor to both the United States and Europe.

In the 1970s and 1980s, a weakened dollar and a weakening balance of trade diminished U.S. international economic power. During much of this period, the United States suffered from "twin deficits" in both government spending and the **balance of payments**. At the same time, Europe and Japan became more and more dissatisfied with the prerogatives that leadership gave the United States and increasingly criticized those prerogatives, especially the dollar system and U.S. payments **deficits**. The United States, for its part, was increasingly dissatisfied with the costs of leadership.

The relaxation of security tensions in the early 1970s reinforced the changing attitudes toward U.S. leadership, especially in Europe but also, to a lesser degree, in Japan. **Détente** and the lessening of the perceived security threat weakened the security argument for Western economic cooperation and U.S. leadership. Europe and Japan were no longer willing to accept U.S. dominance for security reasons, and the United States was no longer willing to bear the economic costs of leadership.

Although U.S. dominance was increasingly unsatisfactory for the United States, Europe, and Japan, no new leader emerged to fulfill that role. Europe, although economically united in a common market, lacked the political unity necessary to lead the system. West Germany and Japan, the two strongest economic powers after the United States, were unable to manage the system by themselves and, in any case, were kept from leadership by the memories of World War II.

Because of the growth in international economic interaction and conflicts among the key players, the era of interdependence was characterized by periodic crises and conflict among members. The powerful members of the system sought to address the management problems by developing new mechanisms for multilateral cooperation. They instituted reforms of the Bretton Woods institutions, including a major revision of the international monetary regime and a greater focus on economic development. They also created new cooperative arrangements such as the Group of Seven economic summits to supplement the existing institutional structure. As a result, the period of interdependence ushered in continuing liberalization, the gradual evolution of international economic institutions, and the adaptation of the system to the new level of international economic interaction and the changed balance of power.

GLOBALIZATION

In the 1990s, a third international economic system emerged, one which continues to the present day. This system was, to an important extent, an extension of the era of interdependence. Continued international liberalization combined with improved technologies increased international economic interaction as well as national sensitivity to that interaction. However, important changes fundamentally altered the character of the prevailing system, and the world entered a new era, that of globalization.

The most dramatic changes were political. The end of the Cold War had a profound impact on the international economic system. With the fall of the Berlin Wall and the collapse of communism, the political bases of the global economy shifted dramatically. The great divide between the capitalist and communist worlds and their respective economic systems disappeared. The ideology and practice of capitalism spread to Eastern Europe, Russia, the former Soviet republics, and even to China and Vietnam. Developing countries that had opposed the liberal international economic order chose to join the prevailing consensus. Thus, the system became truly global from a geographical perspective. With differing levels of effectiveness, governments throughout the world adopted capitalist policies: deregulation, **privatization**, and international liberalization. Trade barriers were reduced, exchange controls were removed, and investment bans were eliminated. Former communist countries and developing countries also joined the Bretton Woods institutions and agreed to play by their rules.

This change in economic beliefs and practices was accompanied by significant technological developments. New information technologies increased the capacity and decreased the costs of computing and communication and made possible the ever-increasing internationalization of production and finance. Increasingly, goods, capital, technology, and even people were able to move freely across international boundaries. Globalization led to more open markets for goods and services, to global firms producing and distributing products in multiple markets, and to global financial markets in which currency, debt, and equities were traded 24 hours a day around the globe. The technological revolution of the Internet created further changes in the nature of international trade, investment, and finance.

The impact of globalization was uneven. The speed of economic change accelerated and flows of capital and goods became more volatile, causing rapid and sometimes wrenching changes for hundreds of millions of people. Many countries, companies, and individuals were beneficiaries of globalization. Numerous developing countries in Asia and Latin America prospered because they were able to attract foreign investment and technology and to expand exports. Others, unable to compete on world markets, were left behind. The poorest countries, especially those in Africa, were unable to expand their trade or attract investment; they became even more marginal.

The end of communism in the former Soviet Union and Eastern Europe created new demands on the system for resource flows, economic interaction, and participation in management of the system. Many countries of Eastern Europe made great progress in the transition from communism to capitalism and from isolation to participation in the rules, institutions, and procedures of the international economic system. It was still unclear at the dawn of the twenty-first century whether others, especially Russia and China, would be able to make that transition and become full members of the global economic system.

Globalization also altered the building block of the international system—the sovereign nation state. Globalization further undermined the ability of governments to manage their economies through national economic policies such as interest and **exchange rate** policies. In the period of globalization, the challenge to national policy went beyond economic management. As international economic interaction penetrated more deeply into national economies, it called into question the ability of governments to pursue other national goals such as environmental preservation and labor policies.

Furthermore, because of the geographic spread of the system, states became vulnerable to disruptions from around the world. In particular, financial disruptions originating in developing countries or former communist states threatened economic stability throughout the system. Because the international economic system was not designed to address these global crises, globalization thus further challenged the system of international rules and institutions governing international economic relations.

As in the era of interdependence, two opposing reactions to the new challenges to national sovereignty emerged. Some political actors called for the modernization and expansion of international economic rules, institutions, and procedures. In their view, the advantages of globalization and the inevitability of its progress made it imperative to update the system by expanding international cooperation and rule making. Other political actors, concerned about the economic and political impacts of globalization, called for limitations on international economic liberalization. In their view, globalization served the wealthy, not the poor, and threatened the environment and labor. Many of those opposed to globalization challenged the role of the Bretton Woods institutions as tools of the wealthy countries that did not address the needs of the poor in both developed and developing countries.

Finally, the end of the Cold War and the creation of a global, capitalist economy altered power relationships. The United States emerged as the world's only superpower, able to project its economic, military, political, and even ideological influence around the world. In the economic arena, the continental-sized U.S. economy and U.S. businesses proved to be powerful, flexible, and adaptable to the new, competitive global economy. American technological superiority, particularly its role as the leader in information technology, put U.S. companies in a strong competitive position. Thus, U.S. businesses and financial institutions were able to play a powerful role in international markets. Furthermore, with the collapse of communism and the success of the U.S. economy, American capitalism became the world's standard economic model.

However, power in the economic arena was not as unequal as in the political and security arenas. Balancing the United States was a series of regional economic powers, including the traditional great powers. France, Germany, and the United Kingdom continued to dominate Western Europe. Japan was the economic superpower of Asia. In addition, countries like Brazil, China, and India began to emerge and to vie for economic leadership in their regions.

Economic integration also created new power relationships. The membership of the European Union (EU) grew, creating an economic powerhouse of around 496 million consumers by 2008, **gross domestic product (GDP)** and trade levels roughly equal to those of the United States, common regulatory systems, and a common currency. EU economic integration has become the basis for greater political unity, including plans to develop a common foreign and defense policy as well as military cooperation.

While economic integration in Latin America is far behind that of Europe, regional economic cooperation through **Mercosur** and the Andean Common Market has emerged in a vibrant way in South America. In Asia, the countries of the **Association of Southeast Asian Nations (ASEAN)** agreed on a plan to create a free-trade area in the region. The revival of **regional integration** efforts

TABLE 1.1   International Economic Systems, 1945–Present

Dates	Name of System	Type of Management or Governance
1945–1971	Bretton Woods system	Superpower management
1971–1989	Interdependence	Collective management
1989–present	Globalization	Global economic governance

in the 1980s and 1990s reinforced—rather than undermined—the trend toward open markets and a liberal world economic order.

The dramatic changes that began in the 1990s and continued into the twenty-first century—globalization, American hegemony, and the effects of the end of the Cold War—fundamentally altered the international economic system. Governments sought to respond to the new order by modernizing institutions, rules, and procedures and by developing new techniques to manage crises and pursue common interests. Governments also updated the international trading regime by replacing the GATT with the World Trade Organization (WTO), which held an expanded mandate and broader powers. In addition, they modified the IMF to enable it to respond to new types of financial crises. At the same time, governments sought to respond to their domestic constituents, who expressed concern about the impact of globalization on economic well-being and on other national objectives. The tension between the dynamism and benefits of globalization on the one hand and the threat to national sovereignty and policies posed by globalization on the other hand emerged as a central theme of the era.

CONCLUSION

Since the end of World War II, the world economy has been regulated by three systems (see Table 1.1). During the Bretton Woods system, the establishment of a stable world economy was seen as a management problem for major powers, and particularly for the United States as the world's largest national economy. During the period of interdependence, responsibility for management shifted gradually from the United States to a group of nations including the United States, the wealthier nations of Western Europe, and Japan. The main political problem facing the international economy in the current period of globalization was how new forms of governance would develop and whether they would be able to deal with three key challenges: (1) the continued political responsibility of governments for the economic welfare of their citizens in the face of increased globalization of the world economy, (2) the transition of the formerly communist countries to **democracy** and their full participation in the world economy as capitalist market economies, and (3) the reduction of inequalities within and across nations. If these tasks were not addressed in a way that satisfied the needs of the marginalized nations of the world, these countries would perceive the system to be illegitimate and would continue to provide support for those who wished to destroy it (or to replace it with something else). Thus, as the world moved from the Bretton Woods system, to interdependence, and then to globalization, many of the world's economic elites concluded that it was necessary to move beyond the idea of superpower or collective management of the world economy toward a more ambitious goal—to establish a legitimate governance system. On their success would hinge the future of the world economy.

ENDNOTES

1. On the idea of the need for a leader, see Charles P. Kindleberger, *The World in Depression, 1929–1939* (Berkeley and Los Angeles, Calif.: University of California Press, 1973). Kindleberger's early speculations on this issue have resulted in an enormous number of works on what is now called "hegemonial stability theory (HST)." See the bibliography for citations of these works.

2. Kenneth Waltz, *Man, the State and War* (New York, N.Y.: Columbia University Press, 1969). For a discussion of how liberal ideas motivated U.S. foreign economic policy after World War II, see David P. Calleo and Benjamin M. Rowland, *America and the World Political Economy* (Bloomington, Ind.: Indiana University Press, 1973). For more recent works on this topic, see G. John Ikenberry, "Creating Yesterday's New World Order: Keynesian 'New Thinking' and the Anglo-American Postwar Settlement," in Judith Goldstein and Robert O. Keohane, eds., *Ideas and Foreign Policy: Beliefs, Institutions, and Political Change* (Ithaca, N.Y.: Cornell University Press, 1993); Erik Gartzke, "Kant We All Just Get Along? Opportunity, Willingness, and the Origins of the Democratic Peace," *American Journal of Political Science*, 42(1998), 1–27; and Edward D. Mansfield, *Power, Trade, and War* (Princeton, N.J.: Princeton University Press, 1994).

3. Quoted in Richard N. Gardner, *Sterling-Dollar Diplomacy in Current Perspective: The Origins and Prospects of Our International Economic Order*, expanded ed. (New York, N.Y.: Columbia University Press, 1980), 9.

2

Governing the International Monetary System

The international monetary system is at the center of the international economy. This system provides the framework for trade, investment, and other
economic transactions and payments across international boundaries. Money is
also central to national sovereignty. The ability to issue currency and the accom-
panying ability to influence its value are important prerogatives of national governments and tools of domestic economic policies. This chapter examines how
nations have worked together to create and manage international monetary systems and how governments have sought to balance the need for international
cooperation with the desire to maintain sovereignty over national currencies
and national economies. This chapter explores how those responsible for managing
the system have sought to provide the three central functions of any international
monetary system: adequate **liquidity**, timely **adjustment**, and **confidence** in the
stability of the system.

Just as any national economy needs an accepted currency, the international
economy requires an accepted vehicle for exchange. Unlike national economies,
however, the international economy lacks a central government that can issue
currency and manage its supply. Historically, this problem was solved through
the use of gold and national currencies. In the nineteenth century and first half
of the twentieth century, gold was used to back currencies and to settle international accounts.[1]

In the nineteenth century and early twentieth century, the British pound sup-
plemented gold by serving as a reserve, transaction, and intervention currency.
After World War II, the U.S. dollar became the key international currency.
Dollars were held as reserves by central banks; the dollar became indispensable

for international trade, investment, and finance; and dollars were used to intervene in exchange markets to influence exchange rates.

An international monetary system must also have means for adjusting imbalances in international payments. In national economies, payments imbalances among regions are adjusted more or less automatically through movement of capital and through fiscal and **monetary policies**. In international economic relations, disequilibria in payments can be settled by financing, by changing domestic economic policy to shift trade and investment patterns, by rationing the supply of foreign exchange through exchange controls, or by allowing the currency exchange rate to change. Effective adjustment can be promoted by international cooperation, but successful cooperation depends primarily on implementing domestic policies to achieve international solutions, a politically difficult task.

In the Bretton Woods system, adjustment was based on a **fixed exchange rate** system supplemented by financing, exchange controls, exchange rate changes, and adaptation of national policies. During the periods of interdependence and globalization, a mix of adjustment mechanisms existed. Exchange rates among major members of the system *floated;* that is, they changed frequently in response to market conditions as well as to government intervention. Complementing these **floating exchange rates** were fixed rates among groups of countries, such as the EU, and fixed rates between two countries, as was the case with countries that linked their currencies to the dollar or to other major currencies. Under floating rates, frequent exchange rate changes driven by markets were supplemented by intervention by national authorities in currency markets, financing, and changes in national economic policies.

The tension between international adjustment needs and domestic political requirements is a central dilemma of international monetary relations. For example, it is often necessary but politically difficult to implement policies that reduce governmental budget deficits and **inflation** in order to stabilize a country's exchange rate or to reduce the deficit in its **balance of payments**. Such policies generally result in lower growth rates and higher levels of unemployment in the short term but higher rates of growth and employment in the long term. It is tempting for governments to put off the domestic economic reforms necessary to defend a declining currency or to delay adjustments that might reduce the size of a balance-of-payments deficit because the necessary adjustments are likely to be politically unpopular.

Finally, a stable international monetary system promotes international exchange and economic prosperity, whereas instability disrupts international transactions, threatens financial institutions, and damages domestic economies. A loss of confidence in the system can create economic and political disaster. During the **Great Depression** of the 1930s, for example, competitive exchange rate devaluations, competing monetary blocs, and the absence of international cooperation contributed greatly to economic breakdown, domestic political instability, and war. During the financial crisis of 1997–1998, Asian currencies, financial institutions, businesses, and even governments collapsed and threatened the world economy as a whole. While instability and crises cannot be eliminated in an international monetary system, they can be reduced and managed. Thus, one of the political challenges of international monetary management is to prevent and manage periodic crises and thereby promote systemic stability.

THE BRETTON WOODS SYSTEM

The Original Bretton Woods System

In July 1944, representatives of 44 nations met on an estate in Bretton Woods, New Hampshire, to create a new international monetary order. Their goal was to establish an international economic system that would prevent another economic and political collapse and another military conflict. Their beliefs were that previous monetary systems that relied primarily on **market forces** had proved inadequate and that the world needed a publicly managed international monetary order.[2]

U.S. policymakers involved in creating the new economic order had concluded that the failure of U.S. leadership was a major cause of the economic and political disaster.[3] During World War II, U.S. leaders thus decided that the United States would have to assume the primary responsibility for establishing a postwar economic order. That order would be designed to prevent economic nationalism by fostering free trade and a high level of international interaction. A liberal economic system, ensured by international cooperation, would provide the foundation for a lasting peace. Thus, during two years of bilateral negotiation, the United States and the United Kingdom, the world's leading economic and political powers, drew up a plan for a new system of international monetary management.[4]

The Anglo-American plan, approved at Bretton Woods, became the first publicly managed international monetary order. For a quarter of a century, international monetary relations were stable and provided a basis for growing international trade, economic growth, and political harmony among the developed market economies. The new order was intended to be a system of limited management by international organizations. For the first time in history, two public international organizations, the International Monetary Fund (IMF) and the **International Bank for Reconstruction and Development (IBRD**, also known as the World Bank), were created to perform certain monetary functions for the international system.

The rules of Bretton Woods, set forth in the articles of agreement, provided for a system of fixed exchange rates. Public officials, fresh from what they perceived as a disastrous experience with floating rates in the 1930s, concluded that a fixed exchange rate was the most stable and conducive basis for trade. Thus, all countries agreed to establish the **parity**, or value, of their currencies in terms of gold and to maintain exchange rates within 1 percent, plus or minus, of parity. The rules further encouraged an open system by committing members to the convertibility of their respective currencies into other currencies and to free trade.[5]

The IMF was to be the keeper of the rules and the main instrument of public international management. Under the system of weighted voting, the United States exerted a preponderant influence in that body. IMF approval was necessary for any change in exchange rates, and it advised countries on policies affecting the monetary system. Most important, it could advance credits to countries with payments deficits. The IMF was provided with a fund composed of member countries' contributions in gold and in their own currencies. The original quotas totaled $8.8 billion. In the event of a deficit in the current account, countries could borrow from this fund for up to 18 months and, in some cases, for up to five years.

Despite these innovations in public control, the Bretton Woods agreement emphasized national and market solutions to monetary problems. The Bretton Woods policymakers expected that national monetary reserves, supplemented when necessary by IMF credits, would finance any temporary balance-of-payments disequilibria. The agreement made no provision for the creation of new reserves; new gold production was considered sufficient. In the event of structural disequilibrium, policymakers expected that there would be national solutions—a change in the value of the currency or an improvement by other means of a country's competitive position. The agreement gave few means to the IMF, however, to encourage such national solutions.

The Bretton Woods planners expected that the international economy would recover and the system would enter into operation after a brief transition period of no more than five years. To facilitate postwar recovery, the planners created the World Bank to make loans that would facilitate a speedy recovery and promote economic development.[6]

By 1947, however, it had become clear that the Bretton Woods system was not working and that the Western economic system was on the verge of collapse. World War II had destroyed the European economic system, which had been based heavily on international trade. Its productive capacity had been destroyed or disrupted, its overseas earnings had turned into debts, its shipping was decimated, and its payments deficit was large and growing. Western Europe was faced with vast import needs, not only for reconstruction but also for mere survival.[7]

The Bretton Woods institutions were unable to cope with Europe's problems. The IMF's modest credit facilities were insufficient to deal with Europe's huge needs and, in any case, the IMF could make loans only for current-account deficits, not for capital and reconstruction purposes. The resources of the World Bank, which was designed for capital investment, were woefully inadequate. By

1947, the IMF and the World Bank admitted that they could not deal with the system's economic problems.[8]

The economic crisis of 1947 was directly linked to political problems. Germany lay in ruins economically and politically. The governments of Italy and France, faced with pressures from powerful labor unions, were highly unstable. Britain, partly due to its economic difficulties, was withdrawing from India and Palestine and abandoning its political and security commitments to Greece and Turkey. More important, the Soviet Union seemed willing and able to take advantage of the West's economic plight and political instability to further its aim of territorial expansion in Europe. The Soviet Union had forcibly established communist governments in the countries it occupied at the end of the war— Hungary, Romania, Poland, and Bulgaria—and it had pressured Iran and Turkey for territorial concessions. Communist guerrillas were making significant headway in Greece, and large communist parties in the governments of Italy and France tried to take advantage of labor unrest. In addition, the Soviet Union refused to cooperate with the allies on a postwar settlement for Germany.[9]

U.S. Leadership

Because of these economic and political crises, the United States assumed a greater leadership role in international monetary management. The strength of the U.S. economy, the lessons of the interwar period, and security incentives made U.S. leadership acceptable at home both economically and politically. The Europeans and Japanese also accepted U.S. management. Economically exhausted by the war, they needed U.S. assistance to rebuild their domestic production, finance their international trade, and provide a setting for political stability. Thus, after 1947, the United States began to manage the international monetary system by providing liquidity and adjustment.

By 1947, it was clear that neither gold nor the pound could continue to serve as the world's money. Gold production was insufficient to meet the demands of growing international trade and investment. Because of the weakness of the British economy, the pound was no longer able to serve as the primary world currency. The only currency strong enough to be used to meet the rising demands for international liquidity was the dollar. The strength of the U.S. economy, the fixed relationship of the dollar to gold ($35 an ounce), and the commitment of the U.S. government to convert dollars into gold at that price made the dollar as good as gold. In fact, the dollar was better than gold because it earned interest and could be used for trade and finance.

A major stumbling block to the dollar's emergence as the world's key currency, however, became apparent: a huge dollar shortage. The United States was running huge trade surpluses, and its reserves were immense and growing. For the system to work, this flow would need to be reversed; the United States had to run a payments deficit. That is just what happened.

From 1947 until 1958, the United States encouraged an outflow of dollars, which provided liquidity for the international economy. Dollars flowed out through U.S. aid programs: the Truman plan for aid to Greece and Turkey, aid to underdeveloped countries, and, most important, the **Marshall Plan**, which from 1948 to 1952 gave 16 Western European countries $17 billion in outright grants.[10] U.S. military expenditures in North Atlantic Treaty Organization (NATO) countries and in the Korean War provided another source of dollar liquidity. Thus the dollar became the world's currency, and the United States became the world's central banker, issuing dollars for the international monetary system.

In addition to providing liquidity, the United States managed imbalances in the system. It facilitated short-term adjustment through foreign aid and military expenditures, which helped offset the huge U.S. trade surplus and the European and Japanese deficits. In addition, the United States abandoned the Bretton Woods goal of convertibility and tolerated European and Japanese trade protection and discrimination against the dollar. For example, the United States absorbed large volumes of Japanese exports while accepting Japanese restrictions against U.S. exports. It supported the European Payments Union, an intra-European clearing system that discriminated against the dollar, and it promoted European exports to the United States. Finally, the United States used the leverage of Marshall Plan aid to encourage devaluation of many European currencies to support national programs of monetary stabilization.

To encourage long-term adjustment, the United States nurtured European and Japanese trade competitiveness. Policies for economic controls on the defeated Axis countries were scrapped. Aid to Europe and Japan, including the Marshall Plan aid to Europe, was designed to rebuild productive and export capacity. In the long run, U.S. leaders expected, such European and Japanese recovery would benefit the United States by widening markets for U.S. exports.[11]

The system worked well. Europe and Japan recovered and then expanded. The U.S. economy prospered partly due to the dollar outflow, which led to the purchase of U.S. goods and services. Yet by 1960, the Bretton Woods system was in trouble again.

Multilateral Management Under U.S. Leadership

The economic foundation of the U.S. management of the international monetary system was confidence in the U.S. dollar. This confidence was based on the strength of the U.S. economy, the enormous U.S. gold reserves, and the commitment to convert dollars into gold. But ironically, the system also relied on a process that eventually undermined the very confidence on which the structure was built: the constant outflow of dollars from the United States. The U.S. deficit and the foreign holding of dollars provided sufficient liquidity for international transactions. If, however, the deficit continued, and if outstanding dollar holdings abroad became too large in relation to gold reserves, confidence in the dollar—and thus in the entire system—would be jeopardized.[12]

By 1958, the United States no longer sought a payments deficit. The European and Japanese recoveries were nearly complete. Balances of payments were improving, and official reserves were growing steadily. By the end of 1959, European and Japanese reserves equaled those of the United States. U.S. gold holdings, however,

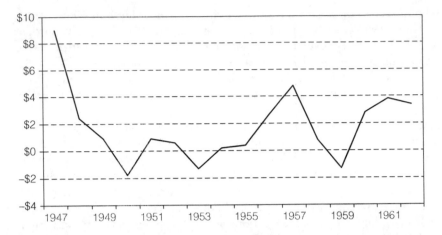

FIGURE 2.1 Balance on Current Account (Balance of Payments) of the United States, 1946–1962, in Billions of Current Dollars

SOURCE: *Economic Report of the President 1989* (Washington, D.C.: U.S. Government Printing Office, January 1989), pp. 424–425.

had fallen and dollars held abroad had risen. In 1960, for the first time, foreign dollar holdings exceeded U.S. gold reserves.[13] Private long-term capital outflow, caused to a great extent by direct investment abroad and foreign military and aid expenditures, contributed to payments deficits (see Figure 2.1).

The first run on the dollar, which occurred in November 1960 when speculators converted dollars into gold, signaled the end of the unilateral system of U.S. management. The dollar system did not collapse. The United States was still able to play a strong leadership role, and the dollar and its economy remained healthy. But the United States could no longer manage the system alone. Henceforth, the United States would be obliged to join in collective management, that is, to seek the cooperation of other members of the system.

At the end of the 1950s, the IMF, largely inactive during the period of U.S. unilateral management, began to play a more important role, largely by lending funds to Europeans and others to finance temporary payments disequilibria. Increases in the fund's quotas at this time facilitated the more active role. The principal functions of monetary management, however, were performed by a multilateral group of the major states. One important new form of multilateral management was central bank cooperation. Since 1930, European central bankers had met together regularly at the **Bank for International Settlements (BIS)** in Basel, Switzerland, but the United States had never become a member and had never participated in their frequent meetings.[14] After the dollar crisis of 1960, however, high officials of the U.S. central bank, the **Federal Reserve**, joined the monthly meetings, although the United States did not join the BIS until 1994.

U.S. participation enabled the Basel group to control important aspects of the international monetary system. The bankers provided *ad hoc* crisis management by supporting currencies that came under pressure. The group also regulated the price of gold. In 1961, the bankers agreed to control gold speculation by centralizing gold dealings through a "gold pool," a mechanism by which the bankers bought gold when it fell below $35 an ounce and sold it when it rose above that limit. The bankers also cooperated in exchange markets and began to play an important role in the burgeoning Eurocurrency market (see next section) by investing, intervening, and accumulating information. Finally, the bankers regularly exchanged information about national policies that affected the international monetary system.

A second management system developed at this time was the **Group of Ten (G-10)**. The Group of Ten was formed in December 1961 when representatives of ten industrial countries—Belgium, Canada, France, Germany, Italy, Japan, the Netherlands, Sweden, the United Kingdom, and the United States—met to create the **General Arrangements to Borrow (GAB)**, a $6 billion fund for exchange rate management that was under the control of the ten members.[15] The G-10 soon became a forum for discussion and exchange of information, a vehicle for negotiating monetary reform, and a mechanism for crisis management. In 1968, for example, the group stopped a dollar crisis and eased pressure on the U.S. gold supply by creating a two-tier gold system: a private market in which the price of gold could fluctuate freely and a public market in which the group agreed to sell one another gold at $35 an ounce.

A series of bilateral arrangements between the United States and other members of the Group of Ten supported this multilateral management system. These arrangements included currency swap arrangements and standby credit lines to be used by central bankers for crisis management; special long-term U.S. bonds denominated in foreign currencies that countries agreed to hold in lieu of converting dollars into gold; and German agreements to purchase U.S. military equipment and to continue to hold large amounts of U.S. dollars to offset the cost of U.S. troops stationed in Germany.[16]

Finally, the United States sought to shore up the system by improving the U.S. balance of payments and by reestablishing confidence in the weakening dollar. Unilateral U.S. efforts included a tax on foreign securities designed to make borrowing in the United States less desirable and thus reduce capital outflows, capital restraints on U.S. foreign investment, the tying of foreign aid to the purchase of goods and services, a decrease in duty-free tourist allotments, and programs to encourage U.S. exports. However, the United States was unwilling to alter its expansionary macroeconomic policies despite the pressures this put on its balance of payments.[17]

Multilateral management mechanisms not only prevented and contained currency crises but also achieved a major reform of the system. In the early 1960s, inadequate liquidity was shaping up to be a crucial problem. Once the United States solved its balance-of-payments problems, as was expected, there would be a liquidity shortage and a need to provide alternative forms of international money. The problem of the future, international monetary policymakers believed, would not be too many dollars but too few.[18]

In 1968, after five years of negotiations by the Group of Ten, an agreement was reached to create **Special Drawing Rights (SDRs)**, artificial international reserve units created by the IMF that could be used to settle accounts among central banks. Significantly, the new form of international liquidity would be managed not by the United States alone but by the Group of Ten jointly, as the Europeans were given veto power on the creation of new SDRs.[19] The $6 billion of the new "paper gold" created was small compared with total world reserves at that time (close to $100 billion in 1970);[20] nevertheless, for the first time in history, the international monetary system had an internationally created and managed asset. Ironically, just at this point the system began to crack. Continuing currency crises in 1967 and 1968 heralded the eventual demise of the Bretton Woods regime and the emergence of a new international monetary system.

FROM BRETTON WOODS TO INTERDEPENDENCE

Financial Interdependence and Pluralism

The emergence of a high level of financial interdependence played a central role in the collapse of the first postwar monetary system. The return to convertibility of the Western European currencies at the end of 1958[21] and of the Japanese yen in 1964 made possible the huge expansion of international financial transactions. Multinational banks became the vehicles for large international financial flows. Beginning in the 1960s, the number of multinational banks increased rapidly. In 1965, only 13 U.S. banks had branches abroad, but, by the end of 1974, 125 did. The assets of the U.S. banks' foreign branches rose from about $9 billion in 1965 to over $125 billion in 1974. Concomitantly, there was an expansion of foreign banks in the United States. The number of foreign branches and agencies in New York City, for example, rose from 49 in 1965 to 92 in 1974. The total assets of these branches and agencies in the same period rose from $5 billion to $29 billion, and by the end of 1974 foreign banks operating in the United States had total assets of $56 billion.[22]

Financial interdependence was also a result of the internationalization of production. Multinational corporations that controlled large pools of liquid assets became sophisticated in moving their capital from country to country to take advantage of **interest rate** spreads or expected exchange rate adjustments. In the 1960s and 1970s, as crises multiplied and risks increased, the movement of such capital became an important part of financial management.[23]

A final source of financial interdependence in this period was the **Eurocurrency** market. Eurocurrencies are national currencies—dollars, marks, francs, pounds, yen—held and traded outside their home country, primarily in Europe. For example, branches of U.S. banks or foreign banks in London accept dollar deposits and lend those deposits in the form of dollars. The Eurocurrency market originated in the late 1950s, primarily with Eurodollars, and grew to huge proportions in the 1960s and 1970s, reaching almost $1 trillion in assets by 1978 (see Figure 2.2).[24] The market flourished largely because it was controlled neither by state regulation nor by constraints of domestic money markets.

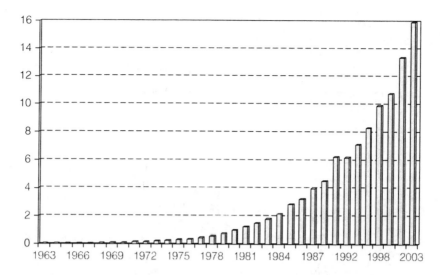

FIGURE 2.2 The Growth of the Eurodollar and Eurocurrency Markets, 1963–2003, in $Trillions

SOURCE: Bank for International Settlements.

Thus, it was able to establish highly competitive interest rates that attracted huge sums. Because the Eurocurrency market consisted largely of short term money, funds in the market were highly mobile and highly volatile.[25]

These new forms of financial interdependence made possible huge international capital flows that put great strain on the international monetary system. In a fixed exchange rate regime, as previously noted, governments facing balance-of-payments disequilibria had several policy alternatives. If the disequilibria were small or short term, governments could finance the imbalances or impose exchange controls. If the disequilibria were structural, governments could either change the value of their currencies—devalue or revalue them—or alter domestic fiscal or monetary policy to restore balance. However, political leaders often were reluctant to take politically risky measures to address structural imbalances. The failure to resolve these disequilibria led to large speculative international capital movements. Efforts to intervene in exchange markets to prevent change were overwhelmed by rapid and massive international financial flows, which made it impossible to maintain the fixed value of currencies within a range of plus or minus 1 percent. Crises developed and governments eventually were forced to alter both exchange rates and national economic policies.

Financial interdependence also interfered increasingly with national economic management, especially with national monetary policy. Interest rates, for example, became a less effective means of managing the national economic system. Low interest rates, used to stimulate an economy, led to an outflow of capital to countries with higher interest rates. Conversely, high interest rates,

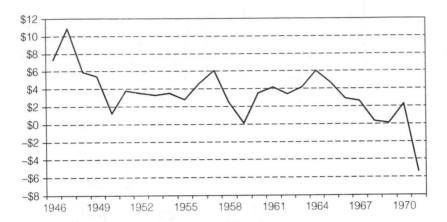

FIGURE 2.3 U.S. Balance of Trade in Goods and Services, 1946–1973, in Billions of Current Dollars

SOURCE: *Economic Report of the President 2001*, p. 392.

used to manage inflation, could be defeated by capital inflows attracted precisely by those higher interest rates.

For a long time, the United States was the one country that was not interdependent in this sense. U.S. national economic policy was not influenced by the international position of the dollar or by financial interdependence. Large capital flows had less effect on the huge U.S. economy than on the smaller European and Japanese economies. Furthermore, as long as other countries absorbed dollar outflows, the United States did not have to take domestic measures to balance international accounts. Thus, in the 1960s the United States was able to avoid restrictive monetary or fiscal policies. Nevertheless, the U.S. economy was constrained by the international monetary system. By the late 1960s, the dollar was overvalued, partly because of inflation induced by expenditures on the Vietnam War and partly because other countries had altered their exchange rates to account for inflation, even though the value of the dollar had not been altered. This overvaluation of the dollar contributed to large investment outflows and led to declining exports and increasing imports, which had an adverse impact on the balance of trade (see Figure 2.3).

The solution for any country, aside from the United States, in this position would have been to devalue the currency or deflate the economy to reestablish a competitive trade position. Neither was politically attractive. The United States was willing to have others revalue but did not want the domestic political problem of devaluing the dollar. Other countries holding vast sums of dollars and enjoying trade surpluses refused to allow a realignment of their currencies. The Europeans and the Japanese demanded instead a deflationary U.S. policy, on the premise that the dollar outflow and the expansion of the U.S. economy were causing inflation abroad.

In addition to interdependence, increased pluralism also affected monetary management. By the end of the Bretton Woods era, the United States was no

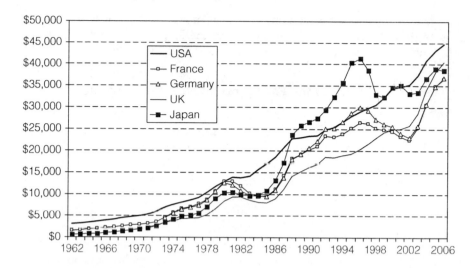

FIGURE 2.4 Per Capita Income in the G-5 Nations, 1962–2006, in Current Dollars, using the Atlas Method

SOURCE: World Bank, *World Development Indicators 2007.*

longer the dominant economic power it had been for almost two decades. Europe and Japan—with higher levels of growth and with per capita income approaching that of the United States—were narrowing the gap between themselves and the United States (see Figure 2.4). A more equal distribution of economic power led to a renewed sense of political power and to increasing dissatisfaction with U.S. dominance of the international monetary system and, in particular, with the privileged role of the dollar as the international currency. The Europeans and Japanese resented the prerogatives that the monetary system provided for the United States. They were concerned that U.S. domestic policies were undertaken with little or no regard for international economic consequences and were critical of the fact that the United States could carry out unlimited foreign expenditures for political purposes—military activities and foreign aid—without the threat of payments constraints. Such prerogatives of U.S. dominance were acceptable to a war-weary Europe and Japan confronting a hostile Soviet Union; they were less acceptable to a recovered and revitalized Europe and Japan faced with a less hostile neighbor.

The continuing decline of the dollar accentuated the problem of maintaining confidence in the system. Despite large and persistent deficits, it had seemed possible until 1965 that the dollar drain might be reduced or eliminated and that confidence in the system could be preserved. But the Vietnam conflict, as well as the refusal of the Johnson administration to pay for both the war and its domestic social programs by increasing taxes, resulted in an increased dollar outflow to pay for the military expenses and in rampant inflation caused by a growing budget deficit, which led to further deterioration in the U.S. balance of payments (see Figure 2.3). By the end of the 1960s, the United States experienced chronic

trade deficits. The recovery of Europe and Japan also made monetary management more difficult. One example of this was the long and difficult negotiation
over SDR reforms, which lasted five years and almost failed several times.[26]

The Nixon Shock and the Emergence of Floating Exchange Rates

By 1970, financial interdependence had grown faster than international management. New problems created by interdependence, including huge international
capital flows, strained the fixed exchange rate system and interfered with national
economic management. Despite the expansion of the bilateral swaps and the creation of new multilateral swaps, the central banks were unable to control the
large currency flows and to contain currency crises while the G-10 was unable
to move on further monetary reform.

Most important, the United States abdicated monetary leadership and pursued a
policy of "benign neglect." Under this policy, the United States let others defend
the existing exchange rate system, permitted a huge foreign dollar buildup, and remained passive during currency crises. The United States also followed its domestic
policies regardless of international consequences and disregarded the inflationary
consequences of the huge dollar outflow in other parts of the system. Furthermore,
the United States no longer sought to mobilize the system for reform.

By late summer 1971, benign neglect was no longer a sustainable policy. In
the spring and summer of 1971, there was a run on the dollar, and, for the first
time in the twentieth century, the United States showed a trade deficit (see
Figure 2.3). The U.S. gold stock declined to $10 billion versus outstanding for-
eign dollar holdings estimated at about $80 billion, inflation was rampant, and
unemployment was widespread. Political problems due to the economic situation led to pressure from all political quarters to do something.

On August 15, 1971, President Nixon—without consulting the other members of the international monetary system—announced a new economic policy:
henceforth, the dollar would no longer be convertible into gold, and the United
States would impose a surcharge of 10 percent on dutiable imports in an effort to
force West Germany and Japan to revalue their currencies.[27] August 15, 1971,
marked the end of the Bretton Woods system.

The shock of August 15 was followed by efforts by the G-10 (under U.S.
leadership) to patch up the system of international monetary management. The
first attempt, reached at the Smithsonian Institution in Washington, D.C., in
December 1971, was an agreement that provided for a 10-percent devaluation
of the dollar in relation to gold, a realignment of other exchange rates, and
greater flexibility in rates that would float within a plus or minus 2.25 percent
of parity, over twice the range of the Bretton Woods agreement.

The Smithsonian agreement was intended to be temporary and to give
the participants time to negotiate long-term reform. In 1972, the **Committee
on Reform of the International Monetary System and Related Issues**
(also called the **Committee of Twenty**) was established within the IMF to reform the international monetary system. Composed of the G-10 plus ten representatives of developing countries, this committee was charged with devising

ways to manage world monetary reserves, establishing a commonly accepted currency, and creating new adjustment mechanisms.

The Smithsonian agreement provided little more than temporary crisis control
and did not solve the fundamental problems of managing financial interdependence.
The increased flexibility in and realignment of exchange rates were insignificant in
the face of differing national policies and huge international capital flows. In addition, the dollar, still the center of the system, remained inconvertible into gold.
Soon massive currency flows led to new pressures on the Smithsonian rates,
and national currency controls to hold back the pressure on the new rates proliferated. By March 1973, all of the major world currencies were floating.
Management was left to the market and in a minor way to central bankers who
intervened in exchange markets on a somewhat cooperative basis to prevent
extreme fluctuations.

The effort of the Committee of Twenty to achieve reform also was unsuccessful. The committee's reform plans centered on a system of stable but adjustable exchange rates and the provision of new forms of international liquidity. But
while the committee debated, massive changes occurred in the international
monetary system. Fixed exchange rates were replaced by floating ones. Inflation
erupted, fueled by U.S. inflation combined with an enormous dollar outflow
and worldwide commodity shortages. Different national rates of inflation made
stability impossible and amplified national desires for floating exchange rates to
enable a degree of isolation from external inflation.[28]

Petrodollar Recycling

Finally, while the committee debated, a handful of oil exporters engineered a
dramatic rise in the price of petroleum (see Chapter 9). Within a year, the
price of oil quadrupled. As a result, huge sums—an estimated $70 billion in 1974
alone—were transferred from the oil-consuming countries, primarily from the
developed market economies, to the oil-producing states.[29] This price change created a major new problem of financial recycling. Under the ideal free-trade
model, the surplus earnings of the oil-producing states would have been
channeled back to the oil-consuming countries in the form of revenue from
the import of goods and services from the oil consumers. But the transfer of
resources to the oil-producing states had been too large for them to absorb.
Despite huge development needs and arms expenditures, these states as a whole
could not take in enough imports to make up for the loss to the consuming
countries. In 1974, the current-account surplus of the oil-producing states was
over $70 billion, and by 1980, a second round of precipitous oil price increases
had pushed it above $114 billion.[30]

Many of the oil-consuming countries could not reduce their oil consumption sufficiently to eliminate the deficits or increase exports sufficiently to cover
the gap. Thus they had to borrow to pay for their deficits, and the only sources
for such borrowing were the countries with surpluses from oil earnings. This was
the recycling problem that, less than a decade later, was transformed into the
developing countries' external **debt crisis** (see Chapter 6).

After 1974, surpluses were recycled primarily through private banks, which accepted the deposits of the oil-exporting countries and lent these funds to the oil-importing countries. Smaller amounts were recycled through government securities, through direct loans and investment by the oil-producing states, and through international institutions such as the IMF and the World Bank, which borrowed from the oil producers and made loans to the oil consumers. The private system, especially the banking system, was the primary monetary manager. Throughout the 1970s, private banks remained the principal recyclers and, in the process, these banks accumulated large Eurocurrency deposits and equally large international loan portfolios. Despite the effectiveness of reliance on the private market, this situation posed certain problems. The role of the private banks in recycling required increasing their ratio of assets (loans) to capital, thus bringing into question the financial stability of the banking system. Furthermore, many developing countries that borrowed heavily from commercial banks eventually were unable to service their loans. By the early 1980s, the resulting debt crisis raised serious questions about the strength of the international financial markets.

The float, inflation, and the monetary consequences of the oil crisis overwhelmed the Committee of Twenty. In January 1974, the committee concluded that, because of the turmoil in the international economy, it would be impossible to draw up and implement a comprehensive plan for monetary reform.[31]

For a year and a half, the world focused on the overwhelming problem of coping with the immediate consequences of the oil shock: inflation, recession, and recycling. Then, in November 1975, heads of government of the major monetary powers—the United States, the United Kingdom, France, West Germany, Japan, and Italy—met at the French chateau of Rambouillet to decide on the framework for a new monetary system. This meeting was the first of what would become regular annual economic summits of the **Group of Seven (G-7)** major industrial powers (see Table 2.1).[32] At the IMF meeting in January 1976, the final details were hammered out in the Second Amendment to the Articles of Agreement of the International Monetary Fund.

The Second Amendment called for an end to the role of gold and the establishment of SDRs as the principal reserve asset of the international monetary system. This amendment legitimized the *de facto* system of floating exchange rates but permitted return to fixed exchange rates if an 85-percent majority approved such a move. In addition, this amendment called for greater IMF **surveillance** of the exchange rate system and management of national economic policies to promote a stable and orderly system.[33]

In reality, the monetary powers had codified the prevailing exchange rate regime. The Second Amendment did not resolve the problem of the dollar: its guidelines for managing exchange rates were undefined, its calls for appropriate national policies and national cooperation with the fund carried little obligation, its mechanisms for institutionalizing cooperation were fragile, and it was implemented in an unstable international economic environment. The Second Amendment signaled the beginning of a period characterized as much by national and regional management as by multilateral management.

TABLE 2.1 **International Economic Summits, 1975–2008**

Date	Location
November 15–17, 1975	Rambouillet, France
June 27–28, 1976	San Juan, Puerto Rico
May 7–8, 1977	London, United Kingdom
July 16–17, 1978	Bonn, West Germany
June 28–29, 1979	Tokyo, Japan
June 22–23, 1980	Venice, Italy
July 20–21, 1981	Ottawa, Canada
June 4–6, 1982	Versailles, France
May 28–30, 1983	Williamsburg, Virginia, United States
June 7–9, 1984	London, United Kingdom
May 2–4, 1985	Bonn, West Germany
May 4–6, 1986	Tokyo, Japan
June 8–10, 1987	Venice, Italy
June 8–10, 1988	Toronto, Canada
July 14–16, 1989	Paris, France
July 9–11, 1990	Houston, Texas, United States
July 15–17, 1991	London, United Kingdom
July 6–8, 1992	Munich, Germany
July 7–9, 1993	Tokyo, Japan
July 8–10, 1994	Naples, Italy
June 15–17, 1995	Halifax, Canada
April 19–20, 1996	Moscow, Russia
June 27–29, 1996	Lyon, France
June 20–22, 1997	Denver, Colorado, United States
May 15–17, 1998	Birmingham, United Kingdom
June 18–20, 1999	Köln, Germany
July 21–23, 2000	Okinawa, Japan
July 20–22, 2001	Genoa, Italy
June 26–27, 2002	Kananaskis, Canada
June 1–3, 2003	Evian-les-Bains, France
June 8–10, 2004	Sea Island, Georgia, United States
July 6–8, 2005	Gleneagles, Scotland, United Kingdom
July 15–17, 2006	St. Petersburg, Russia
June 6–8, 2007	Heilegendam, Germany
July 7–9, 2008	Hokkaido, Japan

SOURCE: University of Toronto, G8 Information Center at http://www.g7.utoronto.ca/.

INTERDEPENDENCE

The system of interdependence was characterized by tension between the demands of the international monetary system for cooperation among the actors on the one hand and national economic and political interests on the other. From 1971 to 1989, national governments wrestled with the balance between multilateral cooperation and national autonomy as they coped with the three challenges of an international monetary system: liquidity, adjustment, and confidence. Cooperative mechanisms, including the IMF and the G-7, were further developed and proved most effective in crisis management. National economic policies were increasingly shaped by interdependence, and countries made numerous efforts to coordinate national policies. However, achieving the level of international cooperation necessary to maintain stability in the world monetary system proved difficult because of domestic political constraints.

Growing Financial Interdependence

In this period, international financial markets continued to grow in size and significance.[34] Most developed countries—the United Kingdom, France, Germany, Canada, Australia, and, to a lesser degree, Japan—relaxed exchange controls, opened domestic markets to foreign financial institutions, and removed some domestic regulatory barriers. As a result of such deregulation, national financial markets became integrated into the global market, which enabled larger amounts of capital to flow more freely across national boundaries.

Revolutions in telecommunications, information processing, and computer technologies made possible a vastly increased volume, speed, and global reach of financial transactions. The growing sophistication of financial players reinforced deregulation and the technological revolution. The concentration of capital in institutions, such as pension funds, mutual funds, money market funds, and insurance companies, reinforced the trend toward sophisticated, global management of large pools of capital. Professional managers of such funds, operating in an environment of volatile prices, exchange rates, and interest rates, were increasingly willing to move money across international boundaries to diversify risk and take advantage of market differentials.[35]

As a result of these multiple forces, global financial markets exploded in size and became a major influence on the floating exchange rate system. World financial flows exceeded trade flows by a factor of at least 30 to 1.[36] By 1992, total cross-border ownership of tradable securities had risen to an estimated $2.5 trillion. Many of these assets were short-term holdings in foreign currencies and securities and were therefore highly liquid investments. Net daily turnover in nine of the major national markets for foreign currency was approximately $600 billion in 1989.[37]

The emergence of a highly integrated world capital market facilitated enormous flows of international funds that responded as much to political risk and interest rate differentials as to trade balances. Thus, for example, high real American interest rates and the search for a political safe haven in the early 1980s attracted a

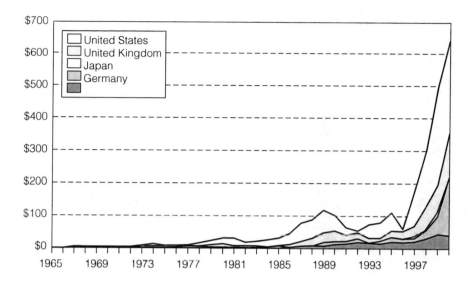

FIGURE 2.5 Inflows of FDI into the Big Five Industrialized Countries, in Billions of Current Dollars, 1965–2006

SOURCE: World Bank, *World Data 1994 CD-ROM* (Washington, D.C.: World Bank, 1994); UNCTAD, *World Investment Report* (New York, N.Y.: UN, various years).

large flow of capital into the United States (see Figure 2.5). These flows maintained, for a few years, the strength of the dollar despite the deteriorating U.S. current-account position and the strengthening trade balances of other industrial countries, particularly Germany and Japan.

Liquidity: The Problem of the Dollar

The interdependent monetary system continued to confront the long-standing dilemma of the dollar. Despite continuing challenges to the dollar's credibility and persistent dissatisfaction abroad with U.S. economic policies, the U.S. dollar survived as the world's major currency. Throughout the 1970s and 1980s, foreign exchange constituted approximately 90 percent of official reserves excluding gold, and the dollar accounted for an average of 70 percent of official holdings of foreign exchange in those years.[38]

The dollar retained its central role despite widespread dissatisfaction both when it was seen as excessively weak (as in the late 1970s) and as excessively strong (as in the first half of the 1980s). As in the Bretton Woods system, the size of the U.S. economy and its highly developed financial markets, as well as U.S. political stability, made it desirable and feasible to use the dollar. The U.S. government continued to support the dollar's role while other countries with strong economies and stable polities were reluctant to allow their currencies to play a central international role. For years, West Germany and Japan, fearing loss of control over their domestic economies, restricted their **capital markets** to make it difficult for foreigners to

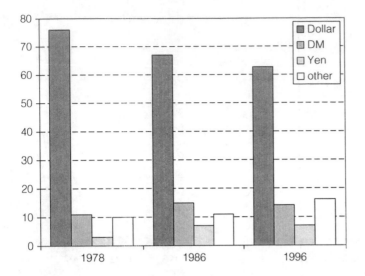

FIGURE 2.6   The Dollar as Percent of Total Official Foreign Currency Holdings, 1978, 1986, and 1996

SOURCE: International Monetary Fund, *Annual Reports,* various years.

hold deutsche marks and yen. Efforts to enlarge the role of SDRs, including changing their valuation and raising interest rates, were unsuccessful.[39]

Nevertheless, there occurred a shift away from the dollar as the exclusive reserve and transaction currency. In 1978, dollars accounted for 76 percent of official holdings of foreign exchange, while deutsche marks accounted for 11 percent and yen for 3 percent. By 1996, the dollar share had fallen to 62.7 percent while the deutsche mark had risen to 14.1 percent and the yen to 7 percent (see Figure 2.6). Holding and using currencies other than the dollar became more attractive in the 1980s as the U.S. balance of payments weakened dramatically, while other countries, particularly Japan and Germany, accumulated payments surpluses.

Furthermore, in the 1980s a number of countries liberalized financial regulations, which made it easier for their currencies to be used and held abroad. Japan, for example, took a number of steps to internationalize the yen: eliminating exchange controls, removing restrictions on Euro-yen activities of Japanese institutions, and increasing access of foreign financial institutions to Japanese capital markets. Importantly, these steps were taken under pressure from the United States to open up financial markets to foreign institutions and to allow the yen to become an international currency, and these steps were negotiated bilaterally with the United States.[40]

Adjustment Under Floating Exchange Rates

Floating exchange rates (as opposed to the fixed rates of Bretton Woods) were a central characteristic of the new international monetary system.[41] Although most

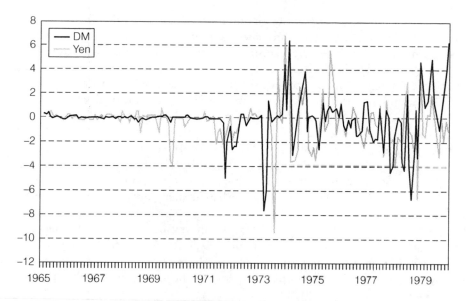

FIGURE 2.7 Volatility in Deutsche Mark (DM) and Yen Exchange Rates with the U.S. Dollar, 1965–1979, Percentage Changes from the Previous Month

SOURCE: *International Financial Statistics CD-ROM* (Washington, D.C.: IMF, January 2002.

of the IMF's members maintained some form of fixed exchange rate, the world's major currencies now floated against one another.[42] Proponents had argued that a float would provide for relative stability and rationality in exchange rates through the stabilizing effect of speculation. Prompt exchange rate changes, these proponents contended, would result in more effective current-account adjustment. Trade deficits and inflation would lead to exchange rate depreciation, increased competitiveness of exports, and decreased competitiveness of imports, and these results would thereby restore the trade balance. A float also would make possible greater autonomy for national policy in an era of interdependence by freeing economic policy from the external balance-of-payments constraints of maintaining a fixed exchange rate.

Floating exchange rates operated effectively in several ways. They did not disrupt international trade and investment, as many critics feared, and trade and investment flourished in this period. Floating rates probably were the only system that could have endured the serious economic shocks of the 1970s and 1980s, including the oil and debt crises. Floating rates also encouraged the long-term movement of exchange rate changes, generally in a direction to correct payments imbalances. However, several serious problems existed with the floating-rate system. Exchange rates were volatile, frustrating a smooth and rapid adjustment process. Most major currencies were subjected to wide and often inexplicable fluctuations, especially in short-term rates (see Figure 2.7). In addition, many countries increased the size of their foreign currency reserves in response to the perceived need to intervene in foreign currency markets to reduce volatility.

Faced with the new realities of interdependence and floating rates, the monetary powers sought to coordinate economic policies in order to achieve long-term stability. The mechanism for this coordination was the G-7. Meeting at the level of heads of state, finance ministers, or deputy finance ministers, G-7 governments sought to influence each other's national policies for the common good of systemic stability. However, national governments were not always willing or able to adjust national economic policies to benefit international economic needs. This was particularly true of the United States, which remained the most important monetary power. U.S. policy was characterized by two conflicting strategies: (1) efforts to improve the functioning of the system through multilateral cooperation, and (2) resistance to the inevitable consequences of interdependence for U.S. domestic economic policy.

From 1977 to 1981, the Carter administration emphasized collective management of international economic relations. A principal objective in the early Carter years was to achieve world recovery from the recession of the mid-1970s through cooperation among the major industrialized countries. The U.S. strategy for global economic growth was based on the "**locomotive theory**," which called for coordinated national economic policies and for countries with payments surpluses—that is, Germany and Japan—to follow expansionary policies that would serve as engines of growth for the rest of the world.

Collective management seemed to achieve some success when Germany, France, and Japan agreed at the Economic Summit in Bonn in 1978 to pursue more expansionary policies, and the United States agreed, as a trade-off, on a program to curb inflation and energy consumption. The agreement seemed to be a major milestone, demonstrating that the world's economic powers were capable of coordinating national economic policies and that the United States could still be the driving force behind multilateral management.[43] However, the 1978 dollar crisis, which immediately followed the agreement, demonstrated that governments, especially the U.S. government, still were reluctant to alter domestic policies for international reasons.

The dollar crisis of 1978 followed a familiar pattern. More rapid growth and greater inflation in the United States than the rest of the world led to trade and current-account deficits, to plummeting confidence in the ability of the United States to pursue stringent economic policies, and to a continuing decline in the dollar. Initially, the United States resisted defending the dollar. Then the government sought to resolve the problem through external policies and limited domestic policies: intervening in foreign exchange markets, doubling the swap network with West Germany, selling SDRs and gold, adopting voluntary wage and price guidelines, and imposing fiscal constraints.

Finally, the United States was forced to take major domestic and international measures. On November 1, 1978, President Carter announced a new economic and dollar defense program that called for a restrictive monetary policy, the mustering of $30 billion in foreign currencies for possible intervention in foreign exchange markets, a policy of active intervention in those markets, and

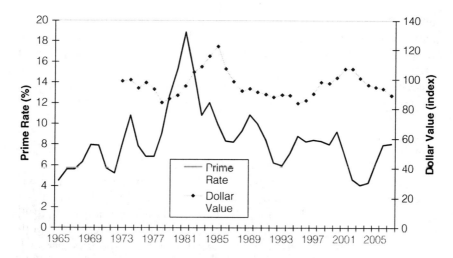

FIGURE 2.8 Interest Rate (Bank Prime Rate) and the Multilateral Trade-Weighted and Inflation-Adjusted Value of the Dollar, 1965–2007

SOURCE: *Economic Report of the President 2008,* http://www.gpoaccess.gov/eop/tables08.html.

an expansion of the sale of U.S. gold.[44] The package was a major departure from previous U.S. policy. For the first time since World War II, the United States altered domestic economic policy for international monetary reasons.

Initially, it seemed that the thrust of U.S. policy was altered permanently and that the United States had accepted its interdependence. The oil crisis of 1978–1979 changed policy concerns from economic stimulation to an emphasis on the control of inflation. When the dollar again came under pressure, the Federal Reserve announced a major new policy designed to bring U.S. inflation under control. Before October 1979, the Fed had concentrated on raising or lowering interest rates through open-market operations and raising or lowering the discount rate, the rate at which the Fed makes loans to member banks, as the principal policies for controlling the supply of money and credit. In 1979, the Fed turned instead to **monetarism**—that is, to managing the growth of the nation's money supply. By focusing on the size and growth of certain monetary aggregates and by responding immediately to changes in the size of those aggregates, the Fed hoped to bring inflation under control and to return stability to the international monetary system.

In particular, the Fed adopted a policy late in 1979 of increasing interest rates by rapidly tightening the money supply, thereby reducing inflation. As a result, the prime rate for bank loans went up from 9.06 percent in 1978 to a peak of 18.87 percent in 1981 (see Figure 2.8),[45] and, while inflation was reduced significantly, these higher interest rates also created a serious recession (i.e., the rate of economic growth decreased and unemployment increased), which thus reduced the chances for reelection for Jimmy Carter.[46]

With the election of Ronald Reagan in 1981, the policy of combining international cooperation with domestic policy changes was altered to U.S.

unilateralism in international monetary relations. Domestically, the Reagan administration combined the tight monetary policy and the monetarist approach (begun in 1979) with an expansionary fiscal policy known as **supply-side economics**.[47]

The United States pursued a tight monetary policy, based on strict adherence to monetary targets, in order to fight inflation. Yet at the same time, the United States raised expenditures, especially for defense, and—according to supply-side theory—reduced taxes in an effort to stimulate savings, investment, and growth.

The United States reverted to economic unilateralism in its international monetary policy. Departing from previous U.S. policies, the Reagan administration officially rejected intervention in foreign exchange markets and ceased efforts to coordinate national economic policies. Although the impact of U.S. policies on the world economy was profound and often disruptive, the United States carried out its abrupt shift and continued to conduct its policies, not only without serious consultation, but also without taking into account the impact of the policies on other countries. The United States also conducted domestic economic policy without taking into account the international repercussions on the U.S. economy.

One element of continuity in the transition from the Carter to the Reagan administrations was the continued stress on the importance of deregulation. A major advocate of deregulation in the Carter Administration was Alfred Kahn, Chairman of the Civil Aeronautics Board from 1977 to 1978. Kahn succeeded in deregulating commercial air fares during his tenure, but more importantly he provided an intellectual basis for bipartisan support for further deregulation. The Reagan administration pursued deregulatory policies with a vengeance, as part of its overall policy of reducing the size of government. The Thatcher government in Britain and the Reagan administration both pushed for deregulation and reduced government spending. The shift away from Keynesian demand-management policies to monetarism in macroeconomic policy, and toward deregulation in meso- or **microeconomic** policy, during this period is sometimes referred to as the rise of neo-liberalism.

There were many beneficial effects of the new U.S. policies: inflation subsided, and, as confidence grew, the dollar turned from a weak to a strong currency. But there were also heavy costs. The tight monetary policy of the United States drove interest rates at home and abroad to unprecedented levels. High U.S. interest rates led to a dollar that was overvalued in trade terms and to dislocations in exchange markets (see Figure 2.8). Short-term capital flowed into the United States to take advantage of high interest rates.

Other developed countries were faced with difficult policy choices: raising their interest rates above the level warranted by their economic situation and thus avoiding an outflow of capital to the United States but dampening growth; keeping rates low and allowing capital to flow to the United States; or imposing capital controls. The decision of most was to avoid capital controls and raise interest rates. But in the end, most countries found themselves with the worst of both worlds: recession as well as capital outflows.[48] The consequences for the

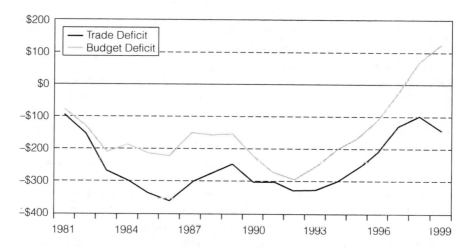

FIGURE 2.9 The Twin (Trade and Budget) Deficits of the United States, 1981–1999, in Billions of Current Dollars

SOURCE: *Economic Report of the President 2001*, pp. 367 and 392.

developing countries were far worse: declining exports and greater debt service costs, the recipe for the debt crisis. The repercussions on the United States also were serious. A high dollar and world recession led to a decline in U.S. exports and massive merchandise trade deficits (see Figure 2.9). The drop in U.S. exports in turn retarded American growth. The monetary system that was supposed to foster trade and investment was now disrupting it.

Stability and Crisis Management

While developed countries had a mixed record in coordinating national policies, they did achieve significant cooperation in crisis management. Crises during the period of interdependence originated primarily in two massive financial imbalances that were not adjusted through market mechanisms and policy coordination: the imbalance between oil-exporting and oil-importing countries and the twin deficits of the United States (see Figure 2.9).

As discussed earlier in the chapter, a rapid increase in bank lending to developing countries was a major solution to the problem of recycling oil-exporting countries' financial surpluses. In the period before 1979, the private system of recycling worked well. Lending helped promote developing countries' productive capacities, maintained their growth, and, in turn, created demand for exports from the developed countries. LDC exports grew along with debt, enhancing these countries' debt service abilities. However, after the second oil crisis of 1979, debtor countries were hit hard by the increase in the price of oil; by restrictive monetary policies in the major industrial countries that led to record-high real interest rates and an increased debt service burden; and by world recession, which led to a plunge in commodity prices and in demand for LDC exports. Nonetheless, banks continued to lend and developing countries continued to borrow, building up a huge debt, which they were increasingly unable to service (see Chapter 6, which discusses international financial flows to developing countries).

A crisis erupted in 1982 when Mexico announced that it was unable to service its debt. Mexico's external debt totaled more than $80 billion and included loans that accounted for a significant percentage of the largest U.S. banks' capital in 1982. And Mexico was just the tip of the iceberg. At the end of 1982, total LDC debt amounted to $831 billion.[49] The world's major private banks had significant exposure in developing countries. Default by the debtor nations thus could have had several serious consequences for the international monetary system: a collapse of confidence in the international banking system, possible illiquidity or insolvency of the banks, dangerous disruption of financial markets and—in a worst-case scenario—world recession or depression.

As will be discussed in greater detail in Chapter 6, the international financial community succeeded in containing the debt crisis of the 1980s through a significant level of cooperation. The resources of the IMF were increased and it assumed the new role of financier and overseer of national economic policies of developing countries. Finance ministries created a new mechanism called the **Paris Club** to negotiate the rescheduling of public debt and the **London Club** to negotiate rescheduling of private debt. Governments also worked with private banks to conduct a series of reschedulings for specific countries.

The debt crisis altered somewhat the U.S. attitude toward international financial cooperation. Despite its unilateralism in exchange rate policy, the United States, as will be seen in Chapter 6, cooperated actively in the management of the debt crisis. The Federal Reserve eased its stringent monetary policy in order to lower worldwide interest rates; the United States became more willing to intervene in limited situations to smooth volatile foreign exchange markets; and, in a reversal of previous policy, the United States supported increases in IMF quotas in order to enable the fund to play a role in debt management.[50]

Unprecedented imbalances among the developed countries created another destabilizing situation. In the 1980s, the United States accumulated two massive and unprecedented deficits—sometimes referred to as the **twin deficits** (see Figure 2.9). A large budget deficit was the result of lowering taxes without reducing government spending. The budget deficit contributed to the trade and balance-of-payments deficits by increasing demand for imports and creating favorable conditions for capital inflows. Other causes of the trade deficit included an overvalued dollar; strong U.S. economic growth in comparison with other developed countries; lower demand in traditional markets for U.S. agricultural exports; the increased competitiveness of foreign companies even as the competitiveness of U.S. industry declined; the rise in protectionist barriers; and the Third World debt crisis, which lowered demand for U.S. exports (see Chapter 3).

The twin deficits of the 1980s called for adjustments in U.S. economic policies, which, as noted previously, were not forthcoming. Instead of adjusting, the United States used its unique position in the international monetary system to finance its deficits. As in the past, the central role of the dollar in the international

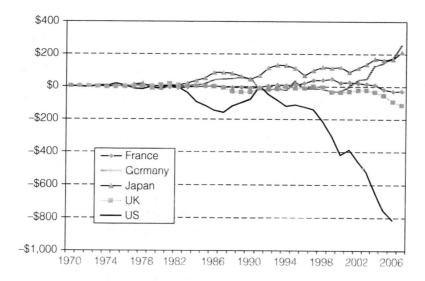

F I G U R E 2.10   Balance of Payments in the G-5 Countries, 1970–2007, in Billions of Current Dollars

SOURCE: World Bank, *World Development Indicators 2001* on *CD-ROM*; OECD.StatExtracts, http://webnet.oecd.org/wbos/Index.aspx.

financial system enabled the United States to more or less automatically finance its deficits through foreign capital inflows. In the 1980s, the amount of such financing dwarfed that of previous years. In 1986, the United States had a positive net international investment at market value of $136 billion. In 1989, the United States became a net debtor with a negative net investment position of $77 billion.[51] Despite the changed U.S. international position, the dollar remained strong for the first half of the 1980s, buoyed by high real U.S. interest rates and the search for a political safe haven.

United States dependence on foreign capital inflows created a serious threat to the dollar, which remained the basis of the international monetary system. At some point, the trade deficit would undermine confidence in the U.S. currency and lead to a decline in the dollar. Furthermore, because much of the capital inflow sustaining U.S. imbalances was short-term, a loss in confidence could lead to a precipitous free-fall of the dollar and a serious shock to the system.

Two mirror images of the U.S. balance-of-payments deficit were the balance-of-payments surpluses of Japan and West Germany (see Figure 2.10). By 1985, Japan had a current-account surplus of $51 billion and Germany a surplus of $18 billion. The Japanese current-account surplus peaked at $86 billion in 1986 but declined to $44 billion by 1990; the German trade surplus rose from $18 billion in 1985 to $48 billion in 1990. Also of growing importance were the growing current-account surpluses of the newly industrialized Asian countries such as Taiwan, which averaged a surplus of around $10 billion per year between 1985 and 1990, and Korea, whose current-account surplus peaked at $14.5 billion in 1988 but returned to deficit in 1990.[52]

By 1985, a serious misalignment in world exchange rates had developed. The dollar had appreciated sharply due to the combination of tight monetary and loose fiscal policies in the United States and to conflicting rather than complementary policies among the major trading partners of the United States. From mid-1980 to mid-1985, the dollar appreciated 21 percent against the yen, 53 percent against the deutsche mark, and 49 percent against the pound.[53] Despite massive U.S. trade deficits, the dollar remained strong because of high U.S. interest rates, a growing U.S. economy, and confidence in U.S. political stability. Exchange markets were highly volatile due to differing national economic performances, the globalization of financial markets, and the absence of coordinated government intervention in exchange markets. In large part because of the overvalued dollar, the U.S. trade deficit reached crisis proportions, politically as well as economically. Protectionist pressures arising from the trade deficit increased, finally forcing the United States to cooperate with other countries in a joint effort to manage exchange rates.

In a secret meeting held on September 22, 1985, at the Plaza Hotel in New York, finance ministers and central bankers from the United States, Japan, the United Kingdom, West Germany, and France, the so-called **Group of Five (G-5)**—the other two members of the G-7, Canada and Italy, were left out—met to coordinate economic policies.[54] The participants agreed to work together on economic matters, especially intervention in exchange markets. The United States pledged to narrow its budget deficit by reducing spending, and the other participants agreed to pursue economic policies that would help ease the imbalances in the world economy and promote healthy growth with low inflation. The **Plaza agreement** was followed by coordinated exchange market intervention and interest rate reductions, which led to a more reasonable exchange rate for the dollar against currencies such as the yen and the deutsche mark and thus all currencies of the European Monetary System (see section below). The Plaza agreement marked the beginning of a new era in monetary management. Finance ministers of the world's monetary powers, recognizing the need to expand policy coordination, began meeting regularly to coordinate exchange rate intervention and to attempt—not always successfully—to coordinate economic policy as well.[55]

The Plaza agreement was significant in another way; it marked the active entry of Japan into the world management system. Before 1985, Japan had been largely a passive member of the management system. Although Japan's economy and international trade had grown dramatically, the yen did not become fully convertible until 1980. By 1985, Japan's economic weight was second only to that of the United States. Japan was the second-largest market economy in the world, used a currency that was increasing significantly in international use, and had amassed a massive financial surplus heavily invested abroad, especially in the United States. Any efforts to stabilize the system and to coordinate economic policies would be meaningless without Japan's participation.

Japan's new strength created new vulnerabilities, including the threat of closure of the trading system because of rising protectionism, especially in Japan's critical U.S. market; the uncertainty of financial investments due to a collapsing dollar; and increasing political pressure on Japan to open its markets, liberalize its financial system, and alter its domestic policies to help manage the world economy. Gradually, although reluctantly, Japan began to respond to its changed economic and political environment. From the time of the Plaza agreement, Japan played an active role in international monetary negotiations and in the efforts to agree on and implement appropriate domestic economic policies. International economic management hinged increasingly on the cooperation of the three big economic powers: the United States, Germany, and Japan.

The new cooperative approach that began with the Plaza agreement was formalized at the May 1986 economic summit in Tokyo. There, the G-7 not only reaffirmed the importance of cooperative intervention in exchange markets but also affirmed that close coordination of domestic economic policies was needed to stabilize the system.[56] The G-7 agreed to monitor the basic economic policies and performance of each country—inflation, interest rates, growth, unemployment, deficits, and trade balance—and to recommend remedial action whenever the policy of one country was thought to be damaging others. The stated goal of the summit was to coordinate domestic economic policies to attain steady growth with a minimum of inflation.

But stated goals and policy action are quite different. International coordination of domestic fiscal and monetary policy remained elusive. While finance ministers and central bankers often agreed on appropriate policies, political constraints—the need for legislative approval and the reluctance to relinquish sovereignty over macroeconomic policy—limited actual coordination. Some steps were taken. In 1986, the United States passed legislation to slow the growth of the U.S. federal budget deficit. Germany and Japan took the limited step of lowering discount rates to stimulate their economies to offset the decline in U.S. growth. But agreement could not be reached on the appropriate levels of U.S. budget-cutting or of growth stimulation in Japan and Germany.

There were also disagreements on the appropriate exchange rate for the dollar. Japan and Germany feared a large decline of the U.S. currency would damage their trade as well as the value of their investments in the United States and argued that a significant dollar decline would upset financial markets. The United States, however, wanted to use the dollar decline to improve the trade imbalance and deflect congressional pressure for protectionist trade legislation and argued that a larger decline of the dollar would not upset capital inflows into the United States, which were needed to finance the trade and budget deficits. As disagreement persisted, cooperation in exchange market intervention broke down and exchange markets became unstable.

In February 1987, the world's monetary powers met at the Louvre in Paris to attempt once again to stabilize the international monetary system. Officials announced to the world that exchange rates had come into the proper relationship, and that the officials would oppose further substantial shifts and would cooperate to stabilize exchange rates at prevailing levels. The participants agreed on informal, flexible, and unannounced target ranges for intervention in exchange markets. At the Louvre, officials again sought to coordinate domestic policies. Germany and Japan agreed to take modest but significant steps to stimulate domestic demand, and the United States reaffirmed its commitment to reduce its budget deficit.[57]

The **Louvre agreement** was both a major step in the effort to establish international economic management and another example of the problem of co-ordinating economic policy. With one important exception, the G-7 did not live up to its stated commitments to coordinate policy. The German government, faced with a public that had an historical fear of inflation, was reluctant to pursue serious stimulative policies, and the U.S. Congress and administration were unable to agree on a significant deficit reduction package. Japan, however, did move toward stimulating domestic demand by pursuing a more expansionary fiscal policy and by reorienting from reliance on export-led growth to development of domestic demand.[58]

As G-7 cooperation disintegrated, private investors, fearing a dollar devaluation, reduced inflows of funds to the United States, which forced central banks to buy dollars to stabilize exchange rates and prevent a crash of the U.S. currency. As a result, the bond market began a severe decline; international equity markets collapsed in October 1987; and the dollar began what seemed like a free-fall, declining 15.6 percent against the yen and 13.4 percent against the deutsche mark from September to the end of December.

The October crisis galvanized the key actors to make domestic economic policy changes. The United States eased monetary policy and Congress passed a limited deficit reduction bill, the Gramm-Rudman-Hollings bill; West Germany and other European countries lowered interest rates; and Japan's cabinet approved a stimulative budget. Finally, in December 1987, the G-7 announced that appropriate steps had been taken to stabilize exchange rates and that there should be no further significant shifts in the value of the dollar. The G-7 implemented massive coordinated action by central banks to stabilize the dollar and to signal their intent to the world. Throughout 1988, the G-7 met regularly and acted effectively to stabilize exchange markets. Cooperation in monetary policy increased and progress was made on the coordination of fiscal policy. Japan, in particular, successfully pursued a stimulative domestic economic policy. The United States made some limited progress in reducing its budget and trade deficit. As a result, exchange rates, including the dollar, stabilized. However, the long-term success of international monetary cooperation of the G-7 continued to depend on the ability of the key monetary actor, the United States, to pursue policies that would reduce its twin deficits.

Europe's Efforts to Build a Regional Monetary System

The **European Monetary System (EMS)**, an ambitious effort at international monetary cooperation, was launched during the period of interdependence.[59] Members of the European Union, with their high level of intra-EU trade and cross-border investments as well as their Common Agricultural Policy, which is based on common prices and relies on stable exchange rates, have an especially strong interest in stabilizing exchange rates among themselves.[60]

Discussions on stabilizing exchange rates in Europe began in the 1960s, shortly after the signing of the Treaty of Rome. Fissures in the Bretton Woods system, along with early achievements in European economic integration, were the main factors behind the initiation of these talks. The talks culminated in the Werner Report of 1970, which set forth detailed plans for monetary union. The recommendations of the Werner report were rendered moot by the collapse of the Bretton Woods system in 1972.

After 1972, the member states agreed to hold their currencies within a 2.25-percent band against one another while allowing this band to move within a 4.5-percent band against the dollar. This arrangement was called the "snake in the tunnel." In addition to the six member states of the European Economic Community (EEC), Britain, Ireland, and Denmark joined the snake in May 1972. Britain and Ireland left the snake in June 1972.

The snake was an attempt to reconstruct an international fixed-rate monetary regime in the face of the collapse of Bretton Woods. It failed to accomplish that goal, however, or even the more limited one of jointly floating the EU member states' currencies against the dollar. Italy left the snake in February 1973 and France left in January 1974. The French returned briefly in mid-1975 only to leave permanently eight months later.

Part of the problem was the way in which the shock of higher world oil prices was transmitted within Europe. Britain became an oil exporter and needed flexibility to adjust its exchange rate to maximize the benefits of increased oil revenues. France was unable to keep inflation low enough to remain in the snake, and Italy was unable to reduce its balance-of-payments deficit sufficiently. These countries needed to devalue their currencies to maintain the international competitiveness of their export-oriented industries.

In December 1978, the Council of Ministers of the European Community (EC) agreed to create a "zone of monetary stability in Europe." This system called for fixed, but adjustable, exchange rates among the members and a floating rate with the outside world; the creation of a **European Currency Unit (ECU)**, a basket of currencies that would serve as a basis for fixing exchange rates, a means of settlement, and a potential future reserve asset; and a network of credit arrangements and plans for a future European Monetary Fund for financing payments imbalances and supporting the fixed rates. The EMS went into effect in March 1979.

At that time, all members of the EMS except the United Kingdom agreed to participate in the **Exchange Rate Mechanism (ERM)** by maintaining fixed exchange rates with 2.25-percent fluctuation margins (except for the Italian lira, which was allowed to fluctuate within a wider 6-percent band). Fixed rates were to be maintained by convergent national economic policies and, when necessary, by intervention in currency markets financed by mutual lines of credit. The United Kingdom's opposition to the ERM was both economic (based on the special role of the pound sterling as an international currency and as the currency of an oil exporter) and political (based on the need to subject its domestic economic policy to international constraints, especially to the policies of West Germany, which had the strongest economy and currency in the EMS).

During the first four years of the EMS, seven realignments of EMS currency values were made. These realignments devalued the lira and the franc relative to the deutsche mark by 27 and 25 percent, respectively. This was a healthy development, given that the initial exchange rates for the lira and the franc probably had been set too high. Indeed, the next four years of the EMS witnessed only four more realignments, and even these were substantially smaller than the previous ones. After 1983, exchange rate variability within the EMS declined substantially, while monetary policies converged on virtually every dimension.[61] From January 1987 until September 1992, no realignments were made within the ERM, while Spain, the United Kingdom, and Portugal joined the ERM, and Finland, Sweden, and Norway explicitly linked their currencies to the ECU.

The success of the EMS, however, was not complete. The European Monetary Fund, which was to have been a quasi-central bank and the institutional framework for the EMS, was not established. In 1989, central bankers agreed to the long-term objective of creating a **European Central Bank (ECB)** but recognized that members would first have to harmonize economic and monetary policies over a period of years.[62] Numerous realignments of rates were made, and fixed rates were made possible by exchange controls on weaker currencies. The Italian lira had wider than 6-percent fluctuation margins. Furthermore, despite growing internal support for EMS membership, the United Kingdom, Greece, and Portugal remained outside the EMS. Nevertheless, by fixing rates and forcing coordination of national economic policies, the EMS produced lower inflation and less misalignment of rates than would have occurred had unguided market forces prevailed. Finally, although the ECU had not, as intended, become a major reserve unit or a means of settlement between EU monetary authorities, it had established a permanent role in international financial markets as a major currency of denomination for banking and securities market transactions.

GLOBALIZATION

Globalization of Financial Markets

The globalization of financial markets grew, in part, out of the same forces that had created financial interdependence. Motivated by a growing consensus on free-market principles, developed countries accelerated the liberalization of domestic financial markets, privatized government-owned financial institutions, and further opened their markets to foreign participants.

Japan, which had retained tight domestic regulatory control and had kept its markets more closed than any other developed country, gradually opened its markets. The U.S. government used bilateral negotiations to pressure Japan to open its financial markets to foreign competition. The United States–Japan **Framework for a New Economic Partnership**, signed by President Clinton and Prime Minister Miyazawa in 1993, was designed to address macroeconomic, sectoral, and structural measures for reducing the U.S. trade and payments deficits with Japan. Negotiations between 1997 and 2001 led to the United States–Japan **Enhanced Initiative** on Deregulation and Competition Policy of the Framework, which included measures on financial services. In addition, the Uruguay Round multilateral trade agreement of 1994 (see Chapter 3) included a protocol on the liberalization of trade in financial services.[63]

These international pressures were reinforced by domestic developments that led Japanese monetary and financial policies to change in important ways. After several decades of rapid economic growth, Japan entered a prolonged period of economic recession and financial crises in the 1990s. The rapid growth of the 1980s led to a speculative boom, asset inflation, and excessive lending by Japanese financial institutions. In the early 1990s, the real estate bubble burst and many Japanese businesses that were protected by government regulation and hindered by out-of-date corporate practices failed to adjust to global competition. The resulting recession had a severe impact on Japanese banks and financial institutions. As prices of real estate and equities collapsed, and as many sectors of the economy faced serious losses, Japanese financial institutions found themselves with growing nonperforming loans, and several institutions went into bankruptcy. The Japanese government was unwilling or unable to take decisive steps to deal with the enormous overhang of bad loans (estimated to be as large as $1 trillion). The weakness in the financial sector in turn aggravated the recession as banks were unwilling or unable to engage in new lending.[64]

The recession in Japan and the collapse of several major financial institutions undermined the opposition of regulators to the foreign acquisition of Japanese financial institutions. In the 1990s, several banks (including the Long-Term Credit Bank) and several securities firms (including Yamaichi Securities) were taken over by U.S. investors. In 1996, Prime Minister Hashimoto, in an effort to respond to new global pressures and to address the problems of the financial sector, announced a plan to deregulate financial markets through a so-called **Big Bang** approach to financial deregulation. Inspired by the British Big Bang of 1985, the goal of Japan's Big Bang was to implement major changes in financial regulations to make financial markets more competitive, accessible, and transparent. Japan's Big Bang eased regulations in the securities, insurance, and banking sectors. Legislation passed in 1998 eliminated controls on foreign exchange trading; deregulated brokerage commissions; permitted financial institutions to trade in new types of securities, such as derivatives; and reduced barriers between investment and commercial banking.[65]

The European Union also took important steps toward financial liberalization. The **Single European Act (SEA)** of 1986 and the **Maastricht Treaty on European Unity** of 1992 committed EU members to dismantling most remaining controls on the movement of capital. The European Council of Ministers issued a new set of directives for banking and investment services. One of these called for coordination of monitoring provisions of credit institutions and harmonization of regulations concerning asset overexposure.[66] Another directive made it possible for credit institutions authorized in one member state to do business in other member states without additional authorizations. In addition, in 1993, the council issued a directive that made it easier for credit institutions authorized in one member state to establish branches in other member states.[67] A new payments system for large transactions, called Trans-European Automated Real-time Gross settlement Express Transfer (TARGET), was established, and a new pan–European reference rate, called the Euro Interbank Offered Rate or Euribor, was set up for comparing floating-rate interest instruments.[68]

The creation of the **Economic and Monetary Union** and a single European currency (the **Euro**) was to have a major impact on the European financial enterprises because of the elimination of revenues from intra–European currency exchange transactions. In anticipation of the creation of a common currency, European banks and other financial institutions began to reorient their strategies around a more open and transparent European financial market. Some of this reorientation took the form of mergers and acquisitions. Some movement also was made toward diversifying financial services, particularly into securitization and derivatives. A new German-Swiss exchange called Eurex was founded in 1998 to handle derivatives exclusively. Its trading volume soon rivaled that of the Chicago Board of Trade. A corporate Euro bond market emerged in the late 1990s. Completely new markets like the Neue Markt in Frankfurt and the Nuova Mercato in Bologna arose to service the demand for venture and start-up capital that European capital markets previously had ignored.

European financial liberalization remained limited to some extent by the continuing role of national governments. While the European Central Bank became responsible for certain key policy decisions, such as when to intervene in world currency markets to support the Euro, national governments continued to be responsible for regulating the financial enterprises that operated within their borders. In addition, national central banks remained influential via their participation in the **European System of Central Banks (ESCB)** in setting European monetary policy goals. Nevertheless, European capital markets were being liberalized rapidly and extensively in the 1990s.[69]

The United States also made important changes to its financial system. That system had been constrained by the **Glass–Steagall Act of 1933**, which had been enacted in response to abuses that allegedly contributed to the Great Depression. Glass-Steagall forbade interstate banking and created barriers among different sectors of the financial system—commercial banks, investment banks, and insurance companies. With the evolution of the financial markets and their globalization, Glass-Steagall became increasingly outdated. Domestic financial institutions lobbied intensely for the removal of the Glass-Steagall barriers. However, due to domestic political gridlock, it proved difficult for many years to do more than gradually revise the Glass-Steagall Act through regulatory reinterpretation. Glass-Steagall was finally replaced with the passage of the Gramm-Leach-Bliley Act in 1999, which made interstate and universal banking possible in the United States.[70]

One of the most significant changes in the era of globalization was the broadening geographic reach of international financial markets. In the 1990s, many developing countries were integrated into global financial markets. As the domestic consensus shifted from government control and protection to free-market policies, many developing countries launched liberalization efforts by reducing exchange rate controls and other barriers to international capital movements and by opening their domestic financial markets to foreign investors.[71] International negotiations also played a role. Mexico, for example, opened its markets as part of the North

American Free Trade Area agreement, and both Korea and Mexico liberalized as part of their accession negotiation when they joined the Organization for Economic Cooperation and Development (OECD). Significantly, the Uruguay Round financial services agreement covered developing countries as well. The new agreement required the developing countries in the WTO to reduce domestic barriers to the establishment of foreign banks after an agreed transition period.

The currencies of most developing countries were linked in some way to one of the major world currencies, a situation that reflected both trade and financial ties. Many Latin American and East Asian countries formally or informally linked their currencies to the dollar, while Eastern Europe and the former European colonies in Africa were tied to European currencies. Interestingly, Japan did not participate in these spheres of influence, although the Japanese government promoted a plan to link the dollar, the yen, and the Euro in a basket of currencies against which emerging countries could peg their currencies.[72]

Finally, the former communist countries became part of the system. The first challenge for these countries was to establish the convertibility of their currencies. Achieving convertibility often resulted in efforts to reduce budgetary and/or balance-of-payments deficits in order to stabilize exchange rates. Some newly independent countries that had relied on the Russian ruble as their domestic currency chose to create new national currencies. All countries set up private banking systems, increased the independence of central banks, liberalized their financial systems, and joined the IMF and the World Bank. The challenges and opportunities connected with these important changes will be discussed in Chapter 10.

China remained a communist country but became a major player in world markets through a combination of domestic economic reforms and decentralization of control over efforts to promote regional economic development. In the 1990s, foreign investment flowed into China in massive amounts to gain access to the Chinese domestic market and to take advantage of low labor costs. Chinese banks remained under the control of the government, for the most part, as did the Chinese currency, the yuan (also called the renminbi). A major dispute between China and the United States over the yuan–dollar exchange rate developed during the second administration of George W. Bush as China's bilateral trade surplus grew even larger than Japan's (see Chapter 10 for details).

Financial institutions from developed countries responded quickly to the new liberalization in developing and former communist countries. As a result, international financial flows increased dramatically (see Chapter 6). The revolution in information technology enhanced this shift in government policy. The global diffusion of information technology has made it possible for people around the world to trade foreign exchange and stocks at any time of the day. The Forex system, for example, allowed individuals or firms to trade in foreign currencies on a 24-hour basis. Similar systems were developed for equity market and futures trading. New regulations allowed the creation of **electronic trading systems**, which gave investors direct access to markets, thereby eliminating or reducing the role of intermediaries like the traditional stock brokerage houses.[73]

The new technology both forced and enabled banks and investment firms to create new financial services to replace revenues that had been lost as a result of reduced trading fees. Computing and communications systems also made it possible to create new, structured financial products such as securitization (i.e., asset-backed securities created out of income streams from credit cards, auto loan payments, and mortgage payments) and various so-called derivatives. A **derivative** is a contract, the value of which depends on (is "derived" from) the price of some underlying asset (e.g., a raw material like petroleum or an equity) or a particular reference rate such as an interest rate or stock-market index like the Dow Jones Index.

Derivatives contracts take two principle forms: futures and options. A futures contract obligates a buyer and a seller to complete a transaction at a predetermined time in the future at a price agreed upon today. An option gives a party a right to buy or sell at a specified price for a stipulated period of time.[74]

Similar changes occurred in other countries such as Japan, Great Britain, and Mexico. As those countries replaced traditional trading floors with electronic trading systems, they realized reduced costs, increased speed of execution, and improved efficiency. Another characteristic of financial globalization was the proliferation of securities markets. Many countries that had not previously had a stock market or other kinds of markets for trading in securities established such markets for the first time in the 1990s. Other countries that already possessed such markets improved or enhanced them.

Financial institutions increasingly became truly global in operations and ownership. A new wave of mergers and acquisitions resulted in the creation of larger banks in the United States, Europe, and Japan. About 400 bank mergers occurred each year in the United States. The number of banking organizations in the United States decreased from approximately 12,300 in 1980 to approximately 7,100 in 1998. The percentage of domestic deposits held by the 100 largest organizations increased from 47 percent in 1980 to nearly 69 percent in 1997.[75] In the 1990s, the number and value of bank mergers and acquisitions in the major industrialized countries increased markedly (see Figure 2.11). Many large banks merged to form even larger banks. As a result, concentration of ownership in the financial services industry rose substantially during this period.[76]

Economic and Monetary Union

One of the central developments in the global system was the creation of the Economic and Monetary Union (EMU). In February 1986, the members of the European Community committed themselves to deepening the integration process by signing the Single European Act (SEA). One of the provisions of the SEA undermined the institutions that had allowed the EMS to operate successfully to that point. The SEA mandated removal of all obstacles to completing the internal market, including capital controls. Capital controls included a broad variety of measures affecting capital markets, including taxes on holdings of foreign currencies and regulations on how foreign currencies could be put to use. Capital controls allowed the central banks of EMS members to prevent speculation against their currencies in anticipation of realignments. Without these controls, in short, it would be impossible to continue with the EMS strategy of periodic realignments.[77]

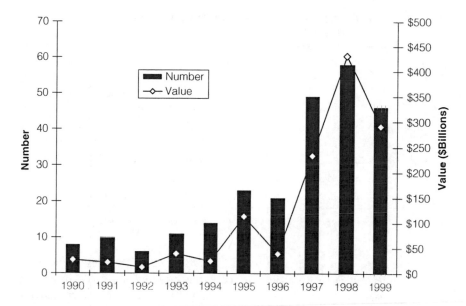

FIGURE 2.11 Number and Value of Bank Mergers and Acquisitions with Value Greater than $1 Billion

SOURCE: Bank for International Settlements, Group of Ten, *Report on Consolidation in the Financial Sector* (Basel, Switzerland: Bank for International Settlements, January 2001).

As part of the process of implementing the SEA, therefore, a committee was appointed under the chairmanship of Jacques Delors, President of the European Commission, to study the feasibility of creating a monetary union for Europe. The Delors Report was published in 1989, beginning a new round of negotiations that culminated in proposals for a three-stage process to achieve an Economic and Monetary Union (EMU) that were included in the Maastricht Treaty on European Unity, signed on February 1992. The key elements of the EMU were to be the liberalization of capital markets, the creation of a European Central Bank (ECB), and the establishment of a single European currency.

Much of the politics of European monetary integration in the early 1990s centered on the preconditions for participation in the monetary union (see Table 2.2). Not all members of the EU could meet the preconditions by the original deadline (December 31, 1996), and it became increasingly clear that the EMU would be composed initially of a subset of EU member-states.[78] In the end, twelve EU members became full participants in the EMU.

In January 1994, the European Monetary Institute was created as a precursor to the formation of the European Central Bank. In January 1995, Austria, Finland, and Sweden joined the European Union, bringing the total number of member-states up to fifteen. In December 1995, the EU began a lengthy campaign to win political support for the establishment of a single currency. The European Central Bank, with the power to set interest rates and manage the money supply, was established on June 1, 1998, in Frankfurt. The last stage of the EMU began on January 1, 1999, when the Euro was introduced as a legal

T A B L E 2.2   Preconditions for Participation in the European Monetary Union

Variable	Target
Inflation	Less than or equal to 1.5 percent over rate of lowest three members
Interest rate on long-term government bonds	Less than or equal to 2 percent above rate of 3 members with the lowest inflation rates
Government deficit/GDP	Less than or equal to 3 percent of GDP
Outstanding government debt/GDP	Less than or equal to 60 percent of GDP
Currency exchange rate	Within ERM band for at least 2 years

SOURCE: *Economic Report of the President* (Washington, D.C.: Government Printing Office, 1994), 247.

currency and the exchange rates between the currencies of the eleven members of the EMU and the Euro were determined. Greece joined the EMU in January 2001. On January 1, 2002, national currencies in the twelve member-states of the EMU were officially replaced by the Euro.[79]

During the first two years of its existence, the Euro depreciated sharply against the dollar and the yen. The ECB tried to stem the Euro's depreciation by raising interest rates. European governments were more concerned about the potential negative effects on growth of higher interest rates than maintaining the value of the Euro. The German government, in particular, supported a weaker Euro because that would increase German exports to the rest of the world. In 2004, the Euro began to appreciate relative to other major currencies. Now the European governments criticized the ECB for failing to cut interest rates. The French government asked the ECB to take growth and unemployment rates, as well as inflation, into account when formulating monetary policy.[80] So far, however, the ECB has focused primarily on restraining inflationary pressures and has been able to limit the influence of euro area governments on its monetary policy decisions.

Adjustment

The size of global private capital markets dwarfed the funds available for G-7 monetary management and reduced the effectiveness of intervention in currency markets. Due to these circumstances, financial authorities in the major countries concluded that intervention was of limited effectiveness and should be used infrequently and only under certain conditions, that is, when a serious misalignment could be altered by joint action. The new financial flows thus made it ever more imperative for countries to pursue sound domestic macroeconomic policies that improved the fundamental health of their economies and thereby promoted international adjustment and stability.

The main instrument of international monetary management in the period of globalization was coordination among G-7 finance ministries and central banks. Most significant was the cooperation and coordination among the Group of Three (G-3)—the United States, Japan, and Germany and subsequently the ECB. The G-7 finance ministers and their deputies met regularly to discuss national policies, urge members to pursue appropriate macroeconomic policies, and recommend structural reforms. Finance ministries and central bankers, especially those of the G-3, were in touch frequently and informally between these regular meetings to discuss market conditions. Ministers also organized opportunistic interventions to influence currency markets. Because national monetary policy had become a key tool of national policy and international adjustment, central bank officials came to play a more significant role in international financial coordination They continued to meet in the G-10 and to coordinate frequently and informally among themselves and with their finance ministries.

In this period, the major countries moved to improve the fundamentals of their economies by reducing budget deficits and inflation and by implementing market reforms. The most significant change occurred in the United States. By the 1990s, the domestic political consensus in the United States had shifted toward a greater willingness to address the problem of the budget deficit and toward a solution to the need for the United States to be competitive in international markets.

In 1993, the newly elected Clinton administration pushed successfully for legislation to reduce the U.S. budget deficit. The administration proposed a short-run economic stimulus package combined with a long-run plan to reduce the deficit by $500 billion over five years in the Omnibus Budget and Reconciliation Act of 1993. Key provisions included a variety of tax increases, reductions in Medicare reimbursements, reductions in discretionary spending, and about $15 billion in stimulus outlays, including the expansion of the Earned Income Tax Credit.[81]

The U.S. economy subsequently experienced a dramatic economic resurgence. Due to deficit reduction legislation and major increases in economic growth, the U.S. budget deficit went from $269.2 billion in fiscal year 1991 to an estimated surplus of $236 billion in fiscal year 2000 (see Figure 2.9).[82] At the same time, as will be seen in Chapter 3, the productivity and international competitiveness of the United States improved. The restructuring of U.S. industry, the emergence of the high technology sector, and active trade liberalization negotiations contributed for a time to an improved trade deficit.

Despite significant movement toward a balanced budget and a rebound of the U.S. economy, the dollar remained weak in the first half of the 1990s while other currencies, especially the yen, were unusually strong. International currency markets had not yet taken into account the improving economic situation in the United States and were influenced by a statement that U.S. Secretary of the Treasury Lloyd Bentsen made suggesting that the United States favored a weak dollar. The result was a record low value of the dollar relative to the Japanese yen in spring 1995 at the time of the Mexican peso crisis (see the section below on the peso crisis). In March and April of 1995, U.S. Treasury Secretary Robert Rubin and his counterparts in Europe and Japan determined that currencies were seriously misaligned, that this misalignment did not reflect

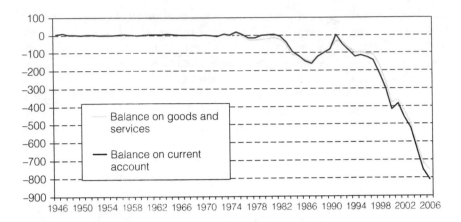

FIGURE 2.12 U.S. Balance of Trade in Goods and Services and Balance on Current Account, 1946–2006, in Billions of Current Dollars

SOURCE: *Economic Report of the President 2008*, http://www.gpoaccess.gov/eop/tables08.html.

the fundamental economic strength of the U.S. economy, and that the time had come for a major intervention to reverse the slide of the U.S. dollar. A series of coordinated interventions in the spring of 1995 led to a rise in the dollar and an improved alignment of major currencies (see Figure 2.13 below).[83]

By the second half of the 1990s the situation in currency markets had reversed: despite a growing trade deficit, the dollar was strong while the yen and Euro were weak (see Figure 2.12). In the 1990s, European countries moved to reduce their budget deficits and reform their economies. These efforts paid off in the form of lower rates of inflation, but price stability came at the expense of lower growth rates and higher unemployment. Despite the improvements in Europe, the renewed dynamism of the U.S. economy gave European firms and investors strong incentives to invest in the United States, contributing further to the strength of the dollar.

Furthermore, the structural problem of the EMU continued. The new European currency was managed by a weak central bank, the weak leader of that institution, and a number of different finance ministries. Throughout 2000 the Euro continued to drop, and, in the fall of that year, it reached a new low. After just 20 months the Euro had lost nearly 30 percent in value against the dollar. Eager to bolster the Euro as well as European monetary integration, the ECB persuaded the United States to join in an intervention to support the Euro in September 2000. The move helped put a floor under the Euro, but it had still not recovered its value by the fall of 2001 (see Figure 2.13). A weak Euro helped European exports but undermined the credibility of the currency and fueled inflationary pressures.

While the United States economy seemed to go from strength to strength, the Japanese economy, which had seemed invincible in the 1980s, hit a brick wall. The bubble economy began to collapse in 1990. Land prices in major

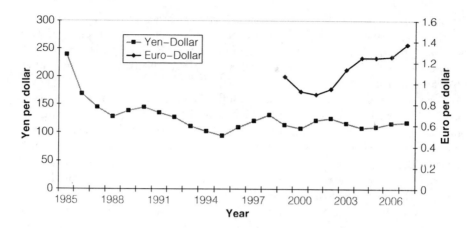

FIGURE 2.13 Yen–Dollar and Euro–Dollar Exchange Rates, 1985–2007

SOURCE: *Economic Report of the President 2008,* http://www.gpoaccess.gov/eop/tables08.html.

Japanese cities began to fall that year and continued to fall through 1994. At the beginning of 1992, prices were down nearly 20 percent from their early 1991 levels. Prices in six major cities fell from approximately 100 percent of nominal GDP at their peak in 1990 to only slightly over 50 percent of nominal GDP at the end of 1993.

Japanese stock prices began to fall in January 1990. Meanwhile, interest rates rose quickly in response to the Bank of Japan's raising of the discount rate. The Iraqi invasion of Kuwait on August 2, 1990, destabilized the stock market further, as investors worried about war, inflation, and higher oil prices. The Nikkei stock index lost 11 percent in a single day before stabilizing.

The share price collapse of 1990 presaged a severe economic downturn that began in the spring of 1991. The overheated economy of the bubble period left Japanese firms holding huge volumes of accumulated stocks in the form of capital investment, household durables, and buildings; and this led to reductions in demand for new goods as the economy adjusted to the changes. The collapse in real estate values and declining competitiveness of many Japanese businesses weakened the loan portfolios of Japanese banks and financial institutions. Bad loan problems in turn contributed to low levels of new lending by financial institutions.

These economic problems were aggravated by a resurgence of the yen against the dollar and other major currencies, which began in the first quarter of 1990 and continued through 1995; after falling to approximately 150 yen to the dollar, the yen strengthened and by the spring of 1995 was trading in the range of 80 to 85. It strengthened considerably during 1996. The high yen placed severe strains on Japan's heavily export-driven economy (see Figure 2.13).

Japan's central bank, the Bank of Japan, loosened monetary policy in the early summer of 1991, as signaled by its decision on July 1, 1991, to lower the discount rate from 6.0 percent to 5.5 percent. A series of further relaxations followed. In September 1993, the Bank of Japan discount rate dropped to 1.75 percent—the lowest since the Bank was founded in 1883. In April 1995, the rate dropped even further, to 1.0 percent. Despite these efforts, growth in money supply remained sluggish.

The Japanese economy continued to suffer during the 1990s from low nominal GDP growth rates. Annual growth had been around 7 percent during the bubble period. It fell beginning in 1990 and by 1991–1993 was close to zero. Profits in the manufacturing sector fell by 24.5 percent in 1991 and 32.1 percent in 1992. Bankruptcies began to rise starting in the latter half of 1990. Failures of real estate firms or of firms engaged in active fund management constituted more than half the corporate bankruptcies in 1991 and 1992.

Among the hardest hit by the collapse of the bubble economy were the commercial banks, especially those which had extended large amounts of real estate financing or which had speculated in the share market boom. Eventually, the losses showed up on the banks' books: reserves for loan losses in the banking sector grew dramatically beginning in 1991. The rate of new lending by banks fell off quickly during 1990 and continued to fall though the first half of the decade. Bond ratings for the ten largest Japanese financial institutions also fell rapidly beginning in 1990 and continued to fall through the first half of the 1990s.[84]

The dollars remained the currency of choice for official reserves through the 1990s and into the first decade of the twenty-first century (see Figure 2.6). The number two and three currencies after the dollar until 2002 were the deutsche mark and the yen, respectively, but the Euro replaced the deutsche mark after 2002 as a reserve currency. By 2007, the Euro's share of official reserves had increased to 26.1 percent.

Some observers were concerned that there could be a sudden movement out of dollars into other currencies, especially Euros, if the U.S. economy were to experience a major downturn or if U.S. economic policy suddenly took a turn toward imprudence. Because the U.S. budget, trade, and balance of payments deficits continued to grow after a short reversal at the end of the 1990s (see Figures 2.9, 2.10, and 2.12), so did the need to finance those deficits through a combination of domestic and foreign borrowing. Both Japan and Germany resumed their earlier pattern of being next exporters to the United States. Japan was displaced by China in 2000 as the largest single contributor to the U.S. trade deficit (see Figure 2.14). Investments in the United States by China and the oil-exporting countries grew in size and importance between 2000 and 2007.

A significant proportion of these investments were managed by **sovereign wealth funds (SWFs)**. See Figure 2.15. A SWF is a state-owned fund composed of financial assets such as stocks, bonds, property, and other financial instruments (including derivatives). In the past, surplus countries held a large proportion of their U.S. investments in bonds issued by the U.S. Treasury. After 2000, the surplus countries began to use SWFs to manage their investments in the United States and elsewhere.[85]

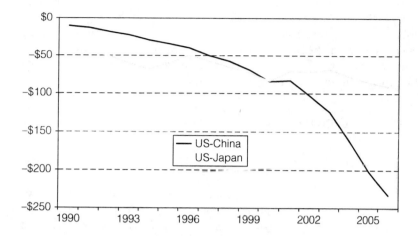

FIGURE 2.14 U.S.-China and U.S.-Japan Bilateral Trade Deficits, in Billions of Dollars, 1991–2006

SOURCE: *Economic Report of the President 2000 and 2008.*

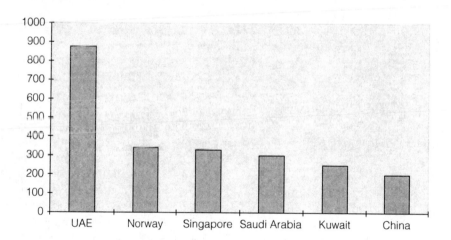

FIGURE 2.15 Largest Sovereign Wealth Funds

SOURCE: Morgan Stanley, September 2007.

CRISIS MANAGEMENT

Beginning in the 1990s and continuing into the twenty-first century, a series of major crises occurred that suggested that globalization might have its limits. Two major types of financial crises that caused problems for the entire system were regional or country-based crises and large bank and other financial institution failures.

The regional and country-based crises included, among others, the European currency crisis of 1992–1993, the Mexican peso crisis of 1994, the Asian financial crisis of 1997–1998, the Russian financial crisis of 1998, and the Argentine crisis of 1999-2002. This series of crises illustrated, in particular, the dangers posed by greater dependence on increased flows of short-term investment capital, especially in parts of the world where the capital flowed out during crises much more rapidly than it flowed in during normal times.

Regional or Country-Based Crises

The European Currency Crisis of 1992–1993   On June 2, 1992, Denmark held a referendum on the Maastricht Treaty to determine whether that country would join the EMU. The treaty was rejected by a slim majority of Danish voters. The politics of European monetary integration were complicated further by the unification of East and West Germany in 1990. Economic decisions made at the time of unification generated inflationary pressures that caused the German central bank, the Bundesbank, to raise interest rates. Higher German interest rates put pressure on the other members of the EMS to either raise their interest rates or unpeg their currencies to prevent an outflow of short-term capital to Germany.

The Danish vote and the German post-unification monetary policy changes led to a round of speculation affecting European currencies and to a series of currency crises in 1992–1993. The first currency to suffer was the Italian lira. Then the three currencies in the wide (6-percent) band of the EMS—the British pound, the Spanish peseta, and the Portuguese escudo—weakened. Pressure mounted again prior to the French referendum on the Maastricht Treaty on September 20, 1992. On August 26, the pound fell to its ERM floor. On September 16, the British and Italian governments withdrew the pound and the lira from the ERM. Other ERM members intervened in support of their currencies, but the lira was devalued by 7 percent against other ERM currencies on September 13 and later was allowed to float. The pressure on the EMS did not end, however. Indeed, it actually intensified until the final crisis effectively ended Europe's policy of pegging exchange rates within narrow bands. After the temporary withdrawal of Germany from the EMS in July 1993, European governments opted to widen the narrow band from 2.25 to 15 percent on August 2, 1993.[86]

The 1992–1993 crises illustrated the problems of managing a fixed exchange rate system in the face of political uncertainty and high international capital mobility.[87] Nevertheless, the commitment to European monetary union remained strong. Most EU member states viewed monetary integration as a key step in both the political and economic processes of European integration. The predictability and simplicity of a fixed or single currency would facilitate trade and investment flows within the EU. A unified European market, in turn, was seen as integral to promoting Europe's competitiveness in the global marketplace, especially vis-à-vis the United States and Japan. Thus large European firms that operated in more than one European country actively supported monetary integration, and many political leaders argued that national interests could best be realized in a united Europe.[88]

The Mexican Peso Crisis of 1994–1995   The Mexican peso crisis demonstrated that problems in an emerging market such as Mexico could threaten the world's financial system, and that the world lacked mechanisms to prevent and manage such crises. In the early 1990s, Mexico seemed to have found the recipe for economic development. Domestic deregulation and privatization combined with liberalization of trade and investment led to rapid growth and a massive inflow of foreign direct and portfolio investment. Unlike the 1980s, flows to Mexico and other emerging markets took the form not of bank lending but of borrowing from the world's rapidly growing securities markets. But in 1994 economic mismanagement in Mexico, especially the maintenance of an overvalued currency and excess dependence on short-term capital inflows, combined with several political shocks, including an uprising in the south, the assassination of the leading presidential candidate, and the kidnapping of a prominent businessman, led to a collapse of confidence. Funds that had flowed so easily into Mexico now fled, and the peso collapsed. The Mexican crisis led to significant pressures on the currencies and financial systems of other Latin American countries, most notably Argentina and Brazil, and disrupted markets from India to South Africa. From there, the crisis threatened financial markets worldwide.

To prevent further disintegration of the Mexican economy and the possible attendant political instability, the U.S. government stepped in with a $20 billion support package for Mexico and pressed members of the Bank for International Settlements to make available another $10 billion. The IMF agreed to an unusually large loan of $17.8 billion in return for an agreement by Mexico to implement a stiff stabilization program. Supported by this international safety net, the Mexican government implemented stringent fiscal and monetary policies that stabilized the exchange rate but caused a serious recession and weakened the domestic financial system. Stringent domestic policies and multilateral lending by the World Bank and IMF also shored up the Argentine financial system.[89]

Having experienced in such a dramatic way the vulnerabilities created by the new global financial flows, the G-7 developed a plan at the 1995 economic summit in Halifax, Nova Scotia, for crisis prevention and management. The G-7 proposed that the IMF pursue more ambitious surveillance policies to prevent future crises. The G-7 also called for greater transparency—greater disclosure of financial and economic information—on the part of IMF member states. In addition, the G-7 recommended the formation of an IMF Emergency Financing Mechanism and a doubling of General Arrangements to Borrow (GAB) within the IMF to ensure that such funds would be adequate for the management of future crises. Finally, the G-7 called for further study of how international debt could be restructured to prevent future crises. In the 1980s, the IMF, together with key central banks, the main lending banks, and the debtor country's government, could renegotiate debt. In the 1990s, an anonymous global financial securities market became a key actor, and it proved difficult to incorporate in debt negotiations. The challenge to the international monetary system was to invent new ways of restructuring debt in this new environment.

The Asian Financial Crisis of 1997–1998   A second global financial crisis began in 1997 in Thailand and quickly spread throughout Asia to the Philippines,
Malaysia, Indonesia, and Korea. The contagion threatened Taiwan, China, Hong
Kong, and even Japan, and also spread to other emerging markets. In 1998, an
aftershock in Russia spread to Brazil and elsewhere in the global system. Stock
markets around the world, including those in the United States, gyrated and debt
markets dried up.

The roots of the Asian financial crisis lay in the Asian economic miracle of the
1980s. High savings rates, a strong work ethic, high levels of education, significant
capital investment, responsible macroeconomic policies, and export-oriented trade
strategies led to high growth rates, a significant improvement in standards of living,
and a broadening distribution of wealth. In the 1990s, as discussed previously,
these so-called **Asian tigers** began to liberalize their capital markets.

Unfortunately, these strong economies had weak financial systems. Because
of close links between banks, governments, and corporations—a situation known
as **crony capitalism**[90]—bank lending often was directed to favored institutions
without adequate attention to their financial soundness and sometimes based on
corrupt practices. In large part because of this practice, and also because banks
lacked the culture and practice of risk management, lending and rates did not
accurately reflect risk. Financial institutions also were poorly regulated and supervised. Reporting and disclosure were inadequate, and there was no oversight of
bad loan portfolios. The corporations in these countries also suffered from a culture of debt. Low-cost credit was available due to high savings rates and loose
banking practices, and balance sheets were thus heavily laden with debt, which
was often short-term debt.

Asian government policies also contributed to the crisis. In an effort to contain inflation, Asian governments had tied their exchange rates to the dollar. As
the dollar became stronger after 1995, Asian currencies became overvalued.
Overvaluation plus the linkage with the dollar encouraged excessive international borrowing in dollars by corporations and financial institutions that
expected the continuation of prevailing exchange rates. The dollar linkage also
hurt competitiveness when the dollar strengthened while the yen and Chinese
renminbi weakened, leading to large current-account deficits in a number of
Asian countries. Governments also allowed their economies to overheat.
Finally, governments removed capital controls and liberalized financial systems
without strengthening financial regulation and the domestic banking system.

Global financial markets also played a role in the crisis. In the 1990s, international financial institutions—much like the banks in the 1970s and 1980s—
were attracted to the emerging Asian markets, which were growing rapidly,
pursuing sound macroeconomic policies, and offering higher interest than those
in developed countries. In 1996, over $250 billion in private capital flowed into
emerging markets, compared with $20 billion in 1986.

By mid-1997, the economic vulnerabilities in Asia became more evident to
these lenders. Export growth of the tigers was threatened by a decline in demand
from Japan, which was in recession; strong competition from China, which had
devalued its currency in 1994; and a strong dollar, to which their currencies were

tied. In some countries, businesses and banks faced immediate financial problems. Furthermore, several political uncertainties needed to be faced: a weak government in Thailand, uncertainty about the stability of the political system in Indonesia, and an upcoming presidential election in Korea.

The crisis began with a loss of confidence in the Thai baht. On July 2, 1997, Thailand was forced to allow its currency to float. However, international authorities did not foresee the firestorm that would ensue. Indeed, the United States declined to take special action and allowed the IMF to handle the Thai crisis. The IMF quickly provided liquidity and negotiated standby agreements that called for restrictive macroeconomic policy designed to calm markets. Nevertheless, the contagion spread rapidly in what was probably an overreaction by international markets. Significant IMF support to all affected countries (with the exception of Malaysia) was unable to stem the tide. On July 11, the Philippines was obliged to let its currency float, in August the Indonesian rupiah began to float, and by the end of 1997 most Asian currencies—with the exception of China's renminbi, which was not convertible and which had been devalued earlier—had been significantly devalued. The crisis threatened Japan and China and posed the danger of a worldwide collapse of financial markets.

The principal crisis manager was the IMF. It provided liquidity to countries that were experiencing stress on their financial systems, insisted on austerity programs in debtor countries as a way to calm international investors, and pressed for structural reforms within borrowing countries (see Chapter 6). As will be seen, these IMF policies led to significant criticism of the IMF itself. IMF austerity programs were accused of aggravating the crisis and causing social and political dislocations, while IMF structural reforms were criticized for intruding on national prerogatives. Nevertheless, the IMF action helped provide liquidity to the debtor Asian countries and was eventually a key factor in stemming the crisis.[91]

As the crisis threatened to spread in late 1997 and early 1998, the United States stepped in to support and complement the role of the IMF. The United States mobilized other lenders (including the World Bank and the Asian Development Bank) and other countries (like Japan) to put pressure on borrowers to back up IMF policy recommendations, and helped to shape international negotiations to restructure bank debt. By early 1998, international action had managed the liquidity problem and stopped the financial implosion. Then, in August, the Russian ruble collapsed.

The Russian Financial Crisis of 1998   Russia experienced severe economic problems in its transition from communism to capitalism beginning in 1989 (see Chapter 10). One of those problems was tax collection. Because of political opposition to the enforcement of existing tax laws, the government was unable to cover its current expenditures with tax revenues and was forced to finance government deficits by borrowing from abroad. The Russian government issued treasury bills denominated in dollars to attract foreign investors. However, as economic and tax collection problems persisted, speculation grew about the future devaluation of the ruble. Speculators believed, rightly, that the Russian government would be unable to honor its commitments to pay interest on the dollar-denominated bonds. As a result, investors began to withdraw their funds rapidly from the Russian bond market.

On August 17, 1998, Russian Prime Minister Sergei Kiriyenko's government decided to float the ruble and default on $40 billion of the dollar-denominated treasury bills. The government also announced a unilateral and legally dubious 90-day moratorium on payments by Russian entities on their foreign obligations. President Boris Yeltsin fired Kiriyenko on August 23 and replaced him with former Prime Minister Victor Chernomyrdin in a move intended to calm the country and to reassure international investors. Sergei Dubinin, head of the Russian Central Bank, resigned three weeks later. By that time, the ruble had fallen from around 6 rubles to the dollar on August 17 to about 11.[92]

The Argentine Crisis of 1999–2002   In 1991, Argentina pegged its currency, the austral, to the dollar, as part of a larger and mostly successful effort to reduce inflation. The austral was replaced with the peso in 1992, but the peso remained pegged to the dollar. During the 1990s, Argentina experience a series of budget deficits which the government financed by borrowing at home and abroad. Its public external debt grew, there was speculation about a possible devaluation of the peso, and IMF efforts to get the Argentine government to reduce its budget deficit did not succeed. In 1999, when Brazil devalued its currency, the real, and the dollar declined against the Euro, there was a spike in Brazilian exports to Argentina and a rapid reduction in Argentine exports to Brazil and Western Europe that sent the economy into a tailspin. Three years of deep recession followed. Finally, the peso was allowed to float against the dollar, resulting in rapid devaluation. Argentine exports recovered and the economy began to grow again.[93]

The lessons of these crises were several. First, the crises in Mexico, Russia, and Argentina illustrated the dangers connected with seeking stability by pegging one's currency to the dollar. An unwillingness to float and devalue the currency in the context of speculative pressures to do so in the short term led to instability and drastic downturns in the economy in the long run. Second, the rapid outward movement of capital in each of these crises suggested that there might be a need for a return to some form of capital controls, perhaps targeted specifically at reducing short-term outflows.[94] Third, some economists were critical of the way that the IMF handled the Asia Crisis and argued that the IMF's austerity policies were not appropriate where there were serious international contagion effects and a regional crisis of confidence leading to a credit crunch.[95]

Crises Involving Banks and Other Financial Institutions

The second category of crises involving banks and other financial institutions included the collapse of the Barings Bank, an old and well-established British bank, in 1995, major losses incurred by Long-Term Credit Management (a **hedge fund**) in 2000, major losses at Société Générale (a French bank) in 2007, and the subprime mortgage crisis in 2007–2008.

These private financial crises all involved new financial instruments (see above discussion of structured products) made possible by computing and communications technology and by the deregulation of global financial markets. Barings was brought down by trading conducted by a small team of employees in a Singaporean futures market (SIMEX) speculating on the movement of the Nikkei index, an index of stock prices on the Tokyo Stock Exchange. The lead trader hid his losses in a phony account until they grew to over 300 million pounds. The bank collapsed when the losses were finally revealed.[96]

Long-Term Credit Management (LTCM) almost collapsed when a complicated mathematical algorithm developed for bond arbitrage suddenly began to produce heavy losses. Several large international banks had loaned major amounts LTCM during its early years suddenly viewed LTCM as a risky borrower and therefore reduced their exposure. LTCM's capital base shrank accordingly to the point where remaining investors began to panic. The bailout of LTCM in 1988 by the Federal Reserve Bank of New York was carried out in the name of preventing an international investment crisis.[97]

In early 2008, Jerome Kerviel, an employee of Société Générale, engaged in unauthorized trading involving arbitrage between equity prices and equity derivatives that resulted in a $7 billion loss for the bank. The bank's management had not been monitoring the trades adequately, but Kerviel and his collaborators had concealed their actions (once again) by creating phony accounts. The bank survived, but not without shaking up global financial markets that were dealing with the problems created by the decline in U.S. real estate prices, which was in turn caused by problems in the markets for subprime mortgages and mortgage-backed securities (see below).

The Subprime Mortgage Crisis

In 2007 and 2008, the collapse of a massive market in mortgage-backed securities led to a financial crisis that included the collapse of a venerable American investment bank (Bear Stearns), serious losses at numerous U.S. and European financial institutions, and a freezing of credit markets globally. The crisis originated in the United States with an asset bubble which had multiple, complicated, and interrelated causes. Low interest rates in the United States and excessively easy lending practices led to massive borrowing to finance the building and purchase of homes. The financing of mortgages—especially mortgages to borrowers with low credit ratings—was made possible by lax lending standards and poor risk management by financial institutions. The funds to finance these mortgages was made possible by new credit instruments created by banks which packaged subprime (i.e., low credit-rating) mortgages with higher quality mortgages which were then sold and traded globally.[98]

Numerous institutions and investors in the United States, Europe, China, the Middle East, and elsewhere bought and traded these mortgage-backed financial instruments. Mortgage lenders began to look in desperation for people who did not already have a mortgage. They relaxed standards for the granting of mortgages. Some fraudulently exaggerated the assessed values of homes in order to secure larger mortgage fees for mortgages that they knew their customers could not afford. People seeking loans no longer had to demonstrate that they had sufficient income to pay them back. Banks left the business of actually servicing mortgages to secondary mortgage holders, who in turn sold their mortgages to companies that aggregated large numbers of mortgages to create new mortgage-backed securities.

None of the new players in the mortgage market—the non-bank lenders, the secondary mortgage holders, and the companies offering mortgage-backed securities—were subject to surveillance by the Federal Reserve. This lack of supervision may have been the result of explicit decisions made by Federal Reserve Chairman Alan Greenspan and his successor, Ben Bernanke, to leave the mortgage markets alone. Nevertheless, a large number of borrowers and especially subprime borrowers could no longer service their mortgages, foreclosure rates went up, owners of mortgage-backed securities belatedly realized that they were engaging in a highly risky form of investment so funding dried up, and housing prices collapsed. Commercial banks, investment banks, and insurance companies, which had created, bought, and/or traded these instruments, suffered huge losses.

The consequences were systemic and global. A crisis in confidence spread throughout financial markets, financial institutions lost confidence in and stopped trading with each other, and many financial markets simply froze. The crisis threatened the real economy as financial institutions pulled back on lending to businesses and consumers. Fear of recession led to a major decline in equity markets.

The crisis was managed by the U.S. Federal Reserve and other central banks of developed countries. Beginning in 2007, the U.S. Federal Reserve lowered interest rates to provide liquidity to the banking system (thereby aggravating the decline of the dollar), opened its discount lending window to securities firms and vestment banks as well as commercial banks, and facilitated the takeover of Bear Sterns by the large commercial bank J.P. Morgan Chase.

Looking ahead, the key central banks sought ways to improve their national regulation to reduce the risk of another similar crisis and began to revisit international agreements, which were intended to prevent crises in the global financial system. Most important were the Basel agreements done through the BIS, which set common standards and required banks to hold capital reserves against various types of risky financial assets.

The first Basel Accord, or Basel I, was the result of a round of deliberations by central bankers in 1988 at a meeting in Basel, Switzerland, that resulted in the publication of a set of minimum capital requirements for banks by the Basel Committee on Banking Supervision. The Basel II Framework, first published in June 2004, was intended to promote a more flexible approach to capital supervision, one that encourages banks to identify the risks they may face, today and in the future, and to develop or improve their ability to manage those risks.[99] The frequency of crises in the 1990s led to a call for major reforms, for a new "international financial architecture" to predict and head off future crises.[100]

Preventing Future Crises

The financial crises of the 1990s revealed serious structural problems regarding the safety and soundness of the global financial system. Many problems lay within countries. Borrowing countries faced corruption, insufficient bank regulation and supervision, and inadequate fiscal policy. Private financial institutions from both lending and borrowing countries confronted inadequate risk assessment and risk management.

To prevent future crises, international markets would need more and better information about the debt exposure of countries and institutions, while borrowing countries would need to improve their financial supervision and regulation. To manage future crises, the IMF would need greater resources, and the system would need better mechanisms for restructuring securities debt.[101]

After the Mexican and Asian crises, a number of systemic reforms were implemented. In addition, debtor countries began to implement financial and economic reform, often under the supervision of the IMF. The IMF created new, higher standards for disclosure of financial information by members and began providing more information about member countries' economic and financial situation to the public. Attention also was given to creating international standards for supervision and regulation of financial institutions. In 1998, the Group of Ten developed its Core Principles for Effective Banking Supervision, which covered **licensing**, methods of banking supervision, and cross-border banking. The crisis also led to new mechanisms for crisis management. In 1997 and 1998, two new facilities were created in the IMF: the Emergency Financing Mechanism, which enabled the IMF to respond more quickly to extraordinary financing requests in return for more regular scrutiny; and the Supplementary Reserve Financing Facility, which enabled the IMF to lend at premium rates in short-term liquidity crises. The IMF also received access to greater resources through a capital increase and the **New Arrangements to Borrow (NAB)**.

The General Arrangements to Borrow permitted the IMF to borrow funds from 11 industrialized countries when needed. The NAB, which was established in the wake of the peso crisis because of the concern that substantially greater resources would be needed to respond to future crises, expanded the list to 25 countries. The 1995 international economic summit of the G-7 in Halifax, Nova Scotia, recommended doubling the amount available to the IMF through the GAB. Accordingly, the IMF's Executive Board decided to establish the NAB on January 27, 1997.[102]

Despite these international and national reforms, many gaps in the system of crisis prevention and management remained. Most important, the ability and willingness of debtor governments to implement national reforms and the ability of the IMF to press for implementation were weak. In addition, many countries refused to share financial information with the IMF or to allow the IMF to make public the information given to it. International principles covering bank supervision and regulation did not address issues of securities firms and securities markets. Furthermore, the system had no mechanisms for restructuring debt.

Government authorities continued to wrestle with how to stabilize the system without confronting the problem of **moral hazard**.

The idea of moral hazard comes from the insurance industry:

> Moral hazard is the risk that a contract will change the behavior of one or both parties. If I cover you for all of your mistakes, then you will likely assume more risk than is optimal for both of us.[103]

For this reason, most insurance companies only partially cover the expenses of recovering from damages and make the insured responsible for the remainder so that the insured has an incentive to reduce risk. Some analysts have claimed that bailouts of countries suffering from crises also create moral hazard and that therefore some uncertainty should always exist about bailouts to prevent the taking of unnecessary risks. This idea also has been applied to the global debt crisis.

There is no shortage of proposals for fixing the international financial system. Ambitious proposals such as creating a world central bank or a world bankruptcy court proved politically impossible and economically unworkable. However, a number of smaller steps—improving the ability of the IMF to act before a crisis erupts, fostering greater cooperation among national regulators, and developing techniques for restructuring debt across national boundaries—offered the promise of improving the safety and soundness of the financial system.

GLOBAL MONETARY GOVERNANCE IN THE TWENTY-FIRST CENTURY

Whether states will muster the political will and skill to govern the global monetary system remains to be seen. Gone are those simpler days when the United States, along with the United Kingdom, could draw up a constitution for a world monetary order. In a world where monetary power is more widely dispersed, governance will depend not on the preferences of a dominant power but on the negotiation of several key powers, primarily the United States, the European Union, and Japan. Governance also will depend on incorporating new economic powers that may emerge in the twenty-first century, such as China, India, and Brazil. While monetary power is now more widely dispersed, it is not equally dispersed. The United States still remains the most powerful monetary actor and, without an active U.S. role within the multilateral system, effective governance is impossible.

Governance also will be complicated by conflicts between globalization and national sovereignty. Managing globalization requires the coordination of national economic policies and the imposition of international discipline over policies that traditionally have been the prerogative of national governments. The experience of the European Monetary System and the efforts of the G-7 to coordinate policy indicate both the need for and the difficulty of achieving such coordination. Numerous ideas for achieving coordination and stability have been proposed, ranging from managed floats to formulas for fixing exchange rates to a return to a modified gold standard or a standard based on a basket of commodities. Ultimately, these ideas all depend on the ability of countries to pursue sound economic policies at home and to achieve international coordination when needed. Indeed, some analysts believe that such coordination is impossible and that discipline and management are best left to the marketplace.

In a multilateral system, improvement in governance will be slow. Success will depend on trial and error and the development of common norms as opposed to formal agreements, as in the days of Bretton Woods or even the Second Amendment. Such a process is not necessarily bad, as formal agreements often do not work as planned. The Bretton Woods agreement, for example, never operated as the United States intended. But in the Bretton Woods period, a dominant power was ready and able to step in to establish new rules for regulating conflict. Today, although the United States is still necessary, it is not sufficiently dominant to fulfill its earlier role. The danger in the present multilateral system is that with incomplete governance, crises may go unregulated, cumulate, and become far more difficult and costly to resolve.

It is possible—although by no means certain—that the most powerful actors in the world monetary system will develop the means not only of crisis management but also of crisis prevention. The consensus among them on the need for cooperation and joint management persists in word if not always in deed. The leaders of the industrialized nations have repeatedly stressed the necessity of cooperating to maintain economic prosperity and political stability. Mechanisms for consultation and policy coordination still operate, but what will be done to deepen global governance remains to be seen. A more central question in some respects is: Will the consensus on the desirability of promoting freer monetary flows in the world economy persist in the face of growing complications of globalization?

ENDNOTES

1. Barry Eichengreen, *The Gold Standard in Theory and History*, 2nd edition (New York, N.Y.: Routledge, 1997); Barry Eichengreen, *Golden Fetters: The Gold Standard and the Great Depression, 1919–1939* (New York, N.Y.: Oxford University Press, 1996); and Giulio M. Gallarotti, *Anatomy of an International Monetary Regime: The Classical Gold Standard, 1880–1914* (New York, N.Y.: Oxford University Press, 1995).

2. See Robert Triffin, *The Evolution of the International Monetary System: Historical Reappraisal and Future Perspectives* (Princeton, N.J.: International Finance Section, Department of Economics, Princeton University, 1964); Stephen V. O. Clarke, *Central Bank Cooperation, 1924–1931* (New York, N.Y.: Federal Reserve Bank of New York, 1967); Eric Helleiner, *States and the Reemergence of Global Finance: From Bretton Woods to the 1990s* (Ithaca, N.Y.: Cornell University Press, 1994); and Anthony M. Endres, *Great Architects of International Finance: The Bretton Woods Era* (New York, N.Y.: Routledge, 2005).

3. See Charles Kindleberger, *The World in Depression 1929–1939* (Berkeley and Los Angeles, Calif.: University of California Press, 1986).

4. See Richard N. Gardner, *Sterling-Dollar Diplomacy in Current Perspective: The Origins and Prospects of Our International Economic Order* (New York, N.Y.: Columbia University Press, 1980), Chapters 1 and 2; and G. John Ikenberry, *After Victory: Institutions, Strategic Restraint, and the Rebuilding of Order After Major Wars* (Princeton, N.J.: Princeton University Press, 2000).

5. Richard N. Gardner, Chapters 3–5, 7; J. Keith Horsefield, ed., *The International Monetary Fund, 1945–1965: Twenty Years of International Monetary Cooperation*, vol. 1 (Washington, D.C.: International Monetary Fund, 1969), 10–118.

6. Edward S. Mason and Robert E. Asher, *The World Bank Since Bretton Woods* (Washington, D.C.: Brookings Institution, 1973), 11–13.

7. See United Nations Economic Commission for Europe, *A Survey of the Economic Situation and Prospects of Europe* (Geneva, Switzerland: United Nations, 1948); and United Nations Economic Commission for Europe, *Economic Survey of Europe in 1948* (Geneva, Switzerland: United Nations, 1949).

8. Mason and Asher, *World Bank Since Bretton Woods*, 105–107 and 124–135.

9. See John Lewis Gaddis, *The Cold War: A New History* (London, UK: The Penguin Press, 2006).

10. Greg Behrman, *The Most Noble Adventure: The Marshall Plan and the Time When America Helped Save Europe* (New York, N.Y.: The Free Press, 2007).

11. For example, see Walter LaFeber, *The American Age: U.S. Foreign Policy at Home and Abroad*, vol. 2, 2nd ed. (New York, N.Y.: Norton, 1994), 479–482.

12. See Robert Triffin, *Gold and the Dollar Crisis: The Future of Convertibility* (New Haven, Conn.: Yale University Press, 1960).

13. International Monetary Fund, *International Financial Statistics* (Washington, D.C.: IMF, Supplement 1972), 2–3.

14. The Bank for International Settlements was a consortium of European central banks originally establised in 1930 to implement a plan for rescheduling German reparations and to provide a forum for central bank discussion. The BIS now includes representatives of the central banks from other industrialized regions. See James C. Baker, *The Bank for International Settlements: Evolution and Evaluation* (Westport, Conn.: Quorum Books, 2002) and Gianni Toniolo, *Central Bank Cooperation at the Bank for International Settlements 1930–1973* (New York, N.Y.: Cambridge University Press, 2005).

15. Switzerland joined in 1964, which made the Group of Ten in fact a group of eleven.

16. Gregory Treverton, *The Dollar Drain and American Forces in Germany: Managing the Political Economies of Alliances* (Athens, Ohio: Ohio University Press, 1978).

17. G. L. Bach, *Making Monetary and Fiscal Policy* (Washington, D.C.: Brookings Institution, 1971), 111–150.

18. See Walter S. Salant et al., *The United States Balance of Payments in 1968* (Washington, D.C.: Brookings Institution, 1963).

19. Stephen D. Cohen, *International Monetary Reform, 1964–1969* (New York, N.Y.: Praeger, 1970); and Fritz Machlup, *Remaking the International Monetary System: The Rio Agreement and Beyond* (Baltimore, Md.: Johns Hopkins University Press, 1968).

20. International Monetary Fund, *Annual Report 1972* (Washington, D.C.: IMF, 1972), 28.

21. This was convertibility for nonresidents. Full convertibility came in 1961.

22. Richard A. Debs, "International Banking" (address delivered to the tenth annual convention of the Banking Law Institute, New York City, May 8, 1975), 3.

23. Sidney M. Robbins and Robert B. Stobaugh, *Money in the Multinational Enterprise: A Study in Financial Policy* (New York, N.Y.: Basic Books, 1973); and Lawrence B. Krause, "The International Economic System and the Multinational Corporation," *The Annals*, 403 (September 1972): 93–103.

24. There are many theories regarding the origins of the Eurodollar market. For example, see Paul Einzig, *The Euro-Dollar System: Practice and Theory of International Interest Rates*, 4th ed. (New York, N.Y.: St. Martin's Press, 1970); and Geoffrey Bell, *The Eurodollar Market and the International Financial System* (New York, N.Y.: Wiley, 1973).

25. Now almost as important as Eurocurrency markets for generating international flows of short term investment were the enormous pools of capital that were invested by the managers of equity and fixed-income assets funds, which were called "mutual funds" in the United States. See further discussion of this below.

26. By the time an agreement was reached, the problem of a dollar shortage, which it had been intended to solve, had been transformed into a dollar glut.

27. On the crisis, see Susan Strange, "The Dollar Crisis 1971," *International Affairs*, 48 (April 1972): 191–215; and Joanne Gowa, *Closing the Gold Window: Domestic Politics and the End of Bretton Woods* (Ithaca, N.Y.: Cornell University Press, 1983).

28. Committee on Reform of the International Monetary System and Related Issues (Committee of Twenty), *International Monetary Reform: Documents of the Committee of Twenty* (Washington, D.C.: International Monetary Fund, 1974), 8.

29. International Monetary Fund, *Annual Report 1975* (Washington, D.C.: IMF, 1975), 12.

30. International Monetary Fund, *Annual Report 1983* (Washington, D.C.: IMF, 1983), 21.

31. Committee on Reform, *International Monetary Reform*, 216, 219.

32. See George de Menil and Anthony M. Solomon, *Economic Summitry* (New York, N.Y.: Council on Foreign Relations, 1983); Robert D. Putnam and Nicholas Bayne, *Hanging Together: The Seven-Power Summits* (Cambridge, Mass.: Harvard University Press, 1984); and Joseph P. Daniels, *The Meaning and Reliability of Economic Summit Undertakings, 1975–1989* (New York, N.Y.: Garland, 1993).

33. International Monetary Fund, *Proposed Second Amendment to the Articles of Agreement of the International Monetary Fund: A Report by the Executive Directors to the Board of Governors* (Washington, D.C.: IMF, March 1976).

34. On internationalization, see *Recent Innovations in International Banking* (Basel, Switzerland: BIS, April 1986); Maxwell Watson, Donald Mathieson, Russell Kincaid, and Eliot Kalter, *International Capital Markets: Developments and Prospects* (Washington, D.C.: International Monetary Fund, February 1986); and Maxwell Watson, Russell Kincaid, Caroline Atkinson, Eliot Kalter, and David Folkerts-Landau, *International Capital Markets: Developments and Prospects* (Washington, D.C.: International Monetary Fund, December 1986).

35. Excellent documentation of this trend can be found in Barry Eichengreen, *International Monetary Arrangements for the 21st Century* (Washington, D.C.: Brookings Institution, 1994), 65–66.

36. See *World Financial Markets*, September/October 1987; and Robert Wade, "Globalization and the State: What Scope for Industrial Policies," in Susanne Berger and Ronald Dore, eds., *Convergence or Diversity? National Models of Production and Distribution in a Global Economy* (Ithaca, N.Y.: Cornell University Press, 1996).

37. Eichengreen, *International Monetary Arrangements*, 60; *BIS 71st Annual Report* (Basel, Switzerland: BIS, 2001), 98.

38. International Monetary Fund, *Annual Report 1987* (Washington, D.C.: IMF, 1987), 58, 60.

39. *Ibid.*, 58.

40. See Edward J. Lincoln, *Japan:Facing Economic Maturity* (Washington, D.C.: Brookings Institution, 1988), 210.

41. For example, see Group of Thirty, *The Problem of Exchange Rates: A Policy Statement* (New York, N.Y.: Group of Thirty, 1982); Henry C. Wallich, Otmar Emminger, Robert V. Roosa, and Peter B. Kenen, *World Money and National Policies* (New York, N.Y.: Group of Thirty, 1983); and John Williamson, *The Exchange Rate System* (Cambridge, Mass.: MIT Press, 1983).

42. For statistics on this, see Benjamin J. Cohen, *The Geography of Money* (Ithaca, N.Y.: Cornell University Press, 1998), 65.

43. For discussion on the 1978 agreement, see de Menil and Solomon, *Economic Summitry*, 23–29, 47–48.

44. The restrictive monetary policy consisted of a record increase in the discount rate from 8.5 to 9.5 percent and the imposition of a reserve requirement on certificates of deposit. The "war chest" included enlarged swaps with the central banks of West Germany, Japan, and Switzerland; the issuance of U.S. Treasury securities denominated in foreign currencies; a drawdown in IMF reserves; and the sale of SDRs.

45. *Economic Report of the President* (Washington, D.C.: Government Printing Office, 1994), 352.

46. Helleiner, *States and the Reemergence of Global Finance*, 131–135. On monetarism, see Milton Friedman and Anna Jacobson Schwartz, *A Monetary History of the United States 1867–1960* (Princeton, N.J.: Princeton University Press, 1963), the twelfth volume of a series, Studies in Business Research, published by the National Bureau of Economic Research.

47. See Bruce R. Bartlett, ed., *The Supply Side Solution* (Chatham, N.J.: Chatham House, 1983); Victor A. Canto et al., *Foundations of Supply-Side Economics: Theory and Evidence* (New York, N.Y.: Academic Press, 1983); Lawrence Robert Klein, *The Economics of Supply and Demand* (Baltimore, Md.: Johns Hopkins University Press, 1983); and Paul Krugman, *Peddling Prosperity: Economic Sense and Nonsense in the Age of Diminished Expectations* (New York, N.Y.: Norton, 1994), ch. 3.

48. See Kenneth King, *U.S. Monetary Policy and European Responses in the 1980s*, Chatham House Paper 16 (London, UK: Routledge, 1982); and Sylvia Ann Hewlett, Henry Kaufman, and Peter B. Kenen, eds., *The Global Repercussions of U.S. Monetary and Fiscal Policy* (Cambridge, Mass.: Ballinger, 1984).

49. See World Bank, *World Debt Tables* (Washington, D.C.: World Bank, 1988).

50. On the Paris and London Clubs, see http://www.clubdeparis.org/en/; Barry Eichengreen and Richard Portes, *Crisis? What Crisis? Orderly Workouts for Sovereign*

Debtors (London, UK: Center for Economic Policy Research, 2001); and Lex Rieffel, *Sovereign Debt Restructuring: The Case for Ad Hoc Machinery* (Washington, D.C.: Brookings Institution Press, 2003).

51. *Economic Report of the President* (Washington, D.C.: Government Printing Office, 1995), table B-103. Net international investment is calculated by subtracting the value of assets owned by foreign firms and individuals in the United States from the value of assets owned by U.S. firms and individuals abroad. The value of these assets can be calculated either on the basis of original cost or on current market value. The figures reported here are based on current market value.

52. Jürgen von Hagen and Michele Fratianni, "The Transition to Monetary Union and the European Monetary Institute," *Economics and Politics*, 5 (July 1993): 167–168; and Wayne Sandholtz, "Choosing Union: Monetary Politics and Maastricht," *International Organization*, 47 (Winter 1993): 1–39.

53. U.S. Department of Commerce, *U.S. Trade Performance in 1985 and Outlook* (Washington, D.C.: Government Printing Office, 1986), 105–106.

54. Eichengreen, *International Monetary Arrangements*, 98.

55. The text of the Plaza Agreement can be found at http://www.g8.utoronto.ca/finance/fm850922.htm.

56. The G-7 included the United States, Japan, Germany, the United Kingdom, France, Canada, and Italy. Annual economic summits of the G-7 usually included representatives of the European Union. After 1991, Russia would join to form the G-8.

57. Funabashi, 177–210.

58. See *Report of the Advisory Group on Economic Structural Adjustment for International Harmony* (chaired by Haruo Maekawa), submitted to Prime Minister Nakasone on April 7, 1986.

59. See Horst Ungerer et al., *The European Monetary System, 1979–1982*, Occasional Paper No. 19 (Washington, D.C.: International Monetary Fund, 1983); Horst Ungerer et al., *The European Monetary System: Recent Developments*, Occasional Paper No. 48 (Washington, D.C.: International Monetary Fund, 1986); Directorate General for Economic and Financial Affairs, EC, "The Creation of a European Financial Area," *European Economy*, No. 36 (Brussels, Belgium: Commission of the European Community, May 1988); and Daniel Gros and Niels Thygesen, "The EMS: Achievements, Current Issues and Directions for the Future," CEPS Paper No. 35 (Brussels, Belgium: Centre for European Policy Studies, 1988).

60. This argument is made very convincingly in Jeffry Frieden, "Economic Liberalization and the Politics of European Monetary Integration" (University of California, Los Angeles, July 1993, unpublished manuscript). See also Barry Eichengreen and Jeffry Frieden, "The Political Economy of European Monetary Unification," in Barry Eichengreen and Jeffry Frieden, eds., *The Political Economy of European Monetary Unification* (Boulder, Colo.: Westview, 1994); and Jeffry Frieden, "The Impact of Goods and Capital Market Integration on European Monetary Politics," *Comparative Political Studies*, 29 (April 1996): 193–222.

61. See Susan M. Collins and Francesco Giavazzi, "Attitudes toward Inflation and the Viability of Fixed Exchange Rates: Evidence from the EMS," in Michael D. Bordo and Barry Eichengreen, eds., *A Retrospective on the Bretton Woods System: Lessons for International Monetary Reform* (Chicago, Ill.: University of Chicago Press,

1993); Jürgen von Hagen, "Monetary Policy Coordination in the European Monetary System," in Michael U. Fratianni and Dominick Salvatore, eds., *Monetary Policy in Developed Economies* (Westport, Conn.: Greenwood Press, 1993); and Jürgen von Hagen and Michael Fratianni, "Policy Coordination in the EMS with Stochastic Asymmetries," in Clas Wihlborg, Michele Fratianni, and Thomas D. Willett, eds., *Financial Regulations and Monetary Arrangements After 1992* (New York, N.Y.: North Holland, 1991). Von Hagen argues that the EMS dampened inflation rates somewhat but possibly at the expense of lower growth rates. Von Hagen and Fratianni discuss the argument that the main function of the EMS was to better enable its members to absorb shocks from the world economy.

62. European Community, Committee for the Study of Economic and Monetary Union, *Report on Economic and Monetary Union in the European Community* (The Delors Report), (Brussels, Belgium: European Community) April 12, 1989. The European Central Bank would operate alongside the central banks of the EMU members in the European System of Central Banks (ECSB).

63. See the Second Protocol to the General Agreement on Trade in Services at http://www.wto.org/english/tratop_e/serv_e/2prote_e.htm.

64. C. Fred Bergsten, Takatoshi Ito, and Marcus Noland, *No More Bashing: Building a New Japan–United States Economic Relationship* (Washington, D.C: Institute for International Economics, October 2001).

65. See Jennifer A. Amyx, *Japan's Financial Crisis: Institutional Rigidity and Reluctant Change* (Princeton, N.J.: Princeton University Press, 2004).

66. Council Directive 92/121/EEC.

67. Council Directive 93/6/EEC.

68. See http://www.euribor.org/.

69. Jean-Pierre Danthine, Francesco Giavazzi, and Ernst-Ludwig von Thadden, *European Financial Markets after EMU: A First Assessment*, Working Paper 8044, National Bureau of Economic Research, Cambridge, Mass., December 2000. See also Sofia A. Perez, *Banking on Privilege: The Politics of Spanish Financial Reform* (Ithaca, N.Y.: Cornell University Press, 1997); and Sofia A. Perez, "Systemic Explanations, Divergent Outcomes: The Politics of Financial Liberalization in France and Spain," *International Studies Quarterly*, 42 (December 1998): 755–784.

70. For a summary of the provisions of this Act, see http://www.senate.gov/~banking/conf/.

71. John B. Goodman and Louis W. Pauly, "The Obsolescence of Capital Controls? Economic Management in an Age of Global Markets," *World Politics*, 46 (October 1993): 50–82. See also Quan Li and Dale L. Smith, "Testing Alternative Explanations of Capital Control Liberalization," *Review of Policy Research*, 19 (March 2002): 28–52; and Scott L. Kastner and Chad Rector, "International Regimes, Domestic Veto-Players, and Capital Controls Policy Stability," *International Studies Quarterly*, 47 (March 2003): 1–22. We will provide specific examples of this in Chapters 6 and 7.

72. "Stabilizing Asia's Currencies," editorial in the online version of *Mainichi Shimbun*, accessed on October 30, 2001, at http://mdn.mainichi.co.jp/news/archive/200101/17/20010117p2a00m0oa098000c.html.

73. Terrence Hendershott, "Electronic Trading in Financial Markets," *IT Pro* (July/August 2003): 10–14; and Dagfinn Rime, "New Electronic Trading Systems in

Foreign Exchange Markets," in Derek C. Jones, ed., *New Economy Handbook* (New York, N.Y.: Elsevier, 2003), ch. 21.

74. Jan Aaart Scholte, "Global Trade and Finance," in John Baylis, Steve Smith, and Patricia Owens, eds., *The Globalization of World Politics: An Introduction to International Relations*, 4th edition (New York, N.Y.: Oxford University Press, 2008), 461

75. Roger W. Ferguson, Jr., "The Changing Banking Environment and Emerging Questions for Public Policy," Federal Reserve Bank of Minneapolis, June 1998.

76. Bank for International Settlements, Group of Ten, *Report on Consolidation in the Financial Sector* (Basel, Switzerland: Bank for International Settlements, January 2001).

77. Barry Eichengreen, "European Monetary Integration," *Journal of Economic Literature*, 31 (September 1993): 1328.

78. See Geoffrey Garrett, "The Politics of Maastricht," *Economics and Politics*, 5 (July 1993): 105–123. Garrett argues that Germany favors the second path, sometimes called the "two-speed Europe" option.

79. There are currently 15 member states of the EU who use the Euro as their currency. Slovenia joined the euro area in 2007; Cyprus and Malta in 2008. See http://www.ecb.int/bc/intro/html/map.en.html.

80. Thomas Oatley, *International Political Economy: Interests and Institutions in the Global Economy*, 3rd edition (New York, N.Y.: Pearson Longman, 2008), 303.

81. Robert Woodward, *The Agenda: Inside the Clinton White House* (New York, N.Y.: Simon & Schuster, 1994); Jonathan Orszag and Laura Tyson, *The Process of Economic Policy-Making During the Clinton Administration* (Cambridge, Mass.: Center for Business and Government, Kennedy School of Government, Harvard University, June 2001); D. W. Elmendorf, J. B. Liebman, and D. W. Wilcox, *Fiscal Policy and Social Security Policy in the 1990s*, NBER Working Paper, September 2001; and A. J. Auerbach, *The U.S. Fiscal Problem: Where We Are, How We Got Here, and Where We're Going*, NBER Working Paper, April 1994.

82. *Economic Report of the President* (Washington, D.C.: Government Printing Office, 2001), 367.

83. J. Bradford DeLong and Barry Eichengreen, *Between Meltdown and Moral Hazard: The International Monetary and Financial Policies of the Clinton Administration* (Cambridge, Mass. and Berkeley and Los Angeles, Calif.: NBER and the University of California at Berkeley, May 2001).

84. Geoffrey P. Miller, "The Role of a Central Bank in a Bubble Economy," at http://www.gold-eagle.com/editorials/cscb003.html.

85. Brad Setser and Rachel Ziemba, *Understanding the New Financial Superpower—The Management of GCC Official Foreign Assets* (New York, N.Y.: RGE Monitor, December 2007).

86. Eichengreen, *International Monetary Arrangements*, 98.

87. *Ibid.*, 100–101.

88. The arguments made here are consistent with those made by Jeffry Frieden and Wayne Sandholtz in previously cited work. See also Jeffry A. Frieden, "Real Sources of European Currency Policy: Sectoral Interests and European Monetary Integration," *International Organization*, 56 (Autumn 2002): 831–860.

89. For more about the Mexican peso crisis, see W. Max Corden, "The Mexican Peso Crash: Causes, Consequences, and Comeback," in Carol Wise and Riordan

Roett, eds., *Exchange Rate Politics in Latin America* (Washington, D.C.: Brookings Institution, 2001); Sebastian Edwards and Miguel A. Savastano, *The Morning After: The Mexican Peso in the Aftermath of the 1994 Currency Crisis* (Cambridge, Mass.: NBER, 1998); and Jeffrey Sachs, Aaron Tornell and Andrés Velasco, "The Collapse of the Mexican Peso: What Have We Learned," *Economic Policy*, 22 (1996): 15–56, 63.

90. David C. Kang, *Crony Capitalism: Corruption and Development in South Korea and the Philippines* (New York, N.Y.: Cambridge University Press, 2002).

91. On the Asia Crisis, see Frederic S. Mishkin, "Lessons from the Asian Crisis," *Journal of International Money and Finance*, 18 (1999): 709–723; Giancarlo Corsetti, Paolo Present and Nouriel Roubini, "What Caused the Asian Currency and Financial Crisis," *Japan and the World Economy,* 11 (September 1999): 305–373; Stephan Haggard, *The Political Economy of the Asian Financial Crisis* (Washington, D.C.: Institute for International Economics, 2000); Gregory W. Noble, and John Ravenhill, eds., *The Asian Financial Crisis and the Architecture of Global Finance* (Cambridge, Mass.: Cambridge University Press, 2000); T. J. Pempel, *The Politics of the Asian Economic Crisis* (Ithaca, N.Y.: Cornell University Press, 1999); and Shale Horowitz and Uk Heo, eds., *The Political Economy of International Financial Crisis: Interest Groups, Ideologies, and Institutions* (New York, N.Y.: Rowman and Littlefield, 2001).

92. Padma Desai, "Why Did the Ruble Collapse in August 1998?" *American Economic Review: Papers and Proceedings*, 90 (May 2000): 48–52; and Abbigail J. Chiodo and Michael T. Owyang, "A Case Study of a Currency Crisis: The Russian Default of 1998," *Federal Reserve Bank of St. Louis Review*, 84 (November/December 2002: 7–17. The consequences of the Russian crisis will be discussed further in Chapter 10.

93. Michael Mussa, *Argentina and the Fund: From Triumph to Tragedy* (Washington, D.C.: Institute for International Economics, 2002).

94. Jagdish Bhagwati, "The Capital Myth: The Difference between Trade in Widgets and Dollars," *Foreign Affairs*, 77 (May/June 1998): 7–12; and Geoffrey R.D. Underhill and Xiaoke Zhang, "Conclusion: Towards the Good Governance of the International Financial System," in Geoffrey R.D. Underhill and Xiaoke Zhang, eds., *International Financial Governance under Stress: Global Structures versus National Imperatives* (New York, N.Y.: Cambridge University Press, 2003).

95. Joseph E. Stiglitz, *Globalization and Its Discontents* (New York, N.Y.: Norton, 2003).

96. Nicholas W. Leeson and Edward Whitley, *Rogue Trader: How I Brought Down Barings Bank and Shook the Financial World* (Boston, Mass.: Little, Brown, 1996); and Stephen Fay, *The Collapse of Barings* (New York, N.Y.: Norton, 1997).

97. Nicholas Dunbar, *Inventing Money: The Story of Long-Term Capital Management and the Legends Behind It* (New York, N.Y.: Wiley, 2000); Roger Lowenstein, *When Genius Failed: The Rise and Fall of Long-Term Capital Management* (New York, N.Y.: Random House, 2000); Craig Furfine, *The Costs and Benefits of Moral Suasion: Evidence from the Rescue of Long-Term Capital Management*, BIS Working Papers No. 103 (Basel, Switzerland: BIS, August 2001); Bong-Chan Kho, Dong Lee, and Rene M. Stulz, *U.S. Banks, Crises, and Bailouts: From Mexico to LTCM*, NBER Working Paper 7529, (Cambridge, Mass: NBER, February 2000) http://www.nber.org/papers/w7529; and Franklin R. Edwards, "Hedge Funds and the Collapse of Long-Term Capital Management," *Journal of Economic Perspectives*, 13 (Spring 1999): 189–210.

98. Danielle diMartino and John V. Duca, "The Rise and Fall of Subprime Mortgages," *Economic Letter: Insights from the Federal Reserve Bank of Dallas*, 2 (November 2007): 1–8, http://dallasfed.org/research/eclett/2007/el0711.pdf.

99. The Basel II Framework can be found at http://www.bis.org/publ/bcbs107.htm.

100. See Nouriel Roubini and Marc Uzan, eds., *New International Financial Architecture*, vols. I–II (Northampton, Mass.: Elgar, 2005) for an excellent collection of articles on this subject.

101. For details on how the IMF and other international financial institutions pursued these goals in recent years, see World Bank, "International Financial Architecture: A Progress Report," July 12, 2005, http://www.worldbank.org/ifa/.

102. International Monetary Fund, The General Arrangements to Borrow (GAB); The New Arrangements to Borrow (NAB): A Factsheet (Washington, D.C.: IMF, August 2001).

103. http://www.investopedia.com/terms/m/moralhazard.asp. See also Nouriel Roubini and Brad Setser, *Bailouts or Bail-Ins? Responding to Financial Crises in Emerging Economies* (Washington, D.C.; Institute for International Economics, 2004), 74–75.

3

International Trade
and Domestic Politics

Trade policy is the stuff of domestic politics. **Tariffs**, **quotas**, and **nontariff barriers** are familiar issues for a broad range of economic groups, from farmers to manufacturers to labor unions to retailers. Because trade policy often determines prosperity or adversity for these groups, it is also the subject of frequent and often highly charged domestic political conflict.

In the United States, the Constitution accentuates the political conflict over trade policy by giving Congress the power to levy tariffs and regulate foreign commerce while at the same time giving the president authority in foreign policy. Conflict within Congress and between Congress and the executive branch is a central characteristic of U.S. trade policy. Because members of Congress are responsible to their constituents and, therefore, responsive to their economic concerns, there is often pressure within Congress for a trade policy that protects those special interests. Furthermore, the demands of relatively few interest groups directed at Congress may snowball into national trade policy, as occurred with the **Smoot-Hawley Tariff Act** of 1930, the most protectionist law of the century.[1]

While Congress tends to link trade policy with particular domestic interests, the U.S. executive branch often links trade policy with larger foreign policy and foreign economic goals. Thus, for example, since the 1930s, U.S. presidents have advocated open trade as the preferred economic policy, for broad economic and strategic reasons. Presidents, however, must have congressional approval for any agreement to reduce trade barriers. Yet the very process of approval raises the threat of interest group opposition. Presidents have tried to overcome this legislative constraint by asking Congress to delegate authority to the president to conclude trade agreements and to limit the need for subsequent congressional

approval. Since 1934, Congress has regularly delegated such power for specifically limited periods of time and with specific constraints. After the passage of
the Trade Act of 1974, this was called **fast-track authority**.[2] Domestic politici-
zation of trade matters in the United States and throughout the world has been
an important constraint on globalization. In this chapter, we shall examine the
evolution of governance in the international trading system in the face of both
domestic and international political constraints.[3]

THE BRETTON WOODS SYSTEM

The same factors that led to the creation of a managed international monetary
system after World War II also led to the first attempt to create an international
trade regime. **Protectionism** and the disintegration of world trade in the 1930s
created a common interest in an open trading order and a realization that states
would have to cooperate to achieve and maintain that order. Protectionism in
the interwar period led not only to economic disaster but also to international
war. In the postwar era, mechanisms for guarding against such economic nationalism and reducing and regulating restrictions on trade would have to be created.
In the United States, policy was shaped by Secretary of State Cordell Hull, who
was the major advocate of the liberal theory that open trade would lead to economic prosperity and international peace.[4] The interwar experience also led to
the willingness of the United States to lead the system.

The Havana Charter

Conflict within and across nations made it difficult to translate the generally perceived common goals into an international order for more open trade. The conflict between domestic politics and international management began with the
negotiations for the **Havana Charter**, the first attempt to build a global legal
regime for international trade. The charter was an essential part of the plan to
create a new, internationally managed economic system in the postwar era and,
like the rest of that plan, was a product of strong U.S. leadership.

   During World War II, the United States obtained from its allies commitments to a postwar international commercial order based on the freeing of international trade. In 1945, the U.S. government presented a plan for a multilateral
commercial convention to regulate and reduce restrictions on international
trade.[5] The convention offered rules for many aspects of international trade—tariffs,
preferences, quantitative restrictions, subsidies, state trading, international commodity agreements—and provided for an **International Trade Organization (ITO)**,
the analog of the International Monetary Fund in the area of trade, to oversee the
system. In 1947, the Charter for the ITO was signed in Havana.[6]

   Agreement on a new international order for trade, however, was more
difficult to achieve than was agreement on a monetary order. The process of

negotiating a postwar trade regime was very different from that of negotiating the postwar monetary regime. At Bretton Woods, the United States and the United Kingdom dominated the decision making and were able to arrive at an early compromise. The two powers were less able to agree on trade, however, and, in any case, other countries' views had to be taken into account.

At the trade conference in Havana, the less-developed countries in attendance (mostly from Latin America) demanded special trade provisions for the promotion of economic development in the new world trade regime. The Europeans pressed for a system that permitted them to continue their preferential trading arrangements. The British delegation supported proposals for commodity agreements and other methods of stabilizing the export revenues of developing countries. The result was a document quite different from the one envisioned by U.S. negotiators. In the end, the Havana Charter was a complex compromise that embodied in some ways the wishes of everyone, but in the end satisfied no one.[7]

Nevertheless, the charter might have become operational had it not been for domestic politics in the United States. Although the Roosevelt and Truman administrations had been strong advocates of a new trading order and had led the international system through the complex negotiating process, Congress prevented the United States from adhering to the Havana Charter. The traditionally high tariff policy of the Republican party; the opposition of both the protectionists, who felt that the charter went too far, and the liberals, who felt that it did not go far enough toward free trade; and the opposition of business groups that opposed compromises on open trade and at the same time feared increased governmental involvement in trade management coalesced in a majority against the United States' own charter. After delaying for three years, the Truman administration finally decided in 1950 that it would not submit the Havana Charter to Congress, where it faced inevitable defeat. Once the United States withdrew, the charter was dead.[8] Despite a prevailing norm of international cooperation and strong and persistent U.S. leadership, an agreement on international trade proved elusive.

The General Agreement on Tariffs and Trade

The demise of the Havana Charter meant that trade management would be more limited than was originally envisaged. The consensus for an international trading order survived, embodied in the General Agreement on Tariffs and Trade or the **GATT**. It had been signed by attendees of the Havana conference in 1947, to provide a procedural base and establish guiding principles for the periodic multilateral tariff negotiations. In fact, the first trade "round" was held in Geneva in that same year. Intended originally to be a treaty operating under the umbrella of the ITO, the GATT, by default, became the world's trade regime.[9]

The GATT reflected the prevailing agreement on open trade: the economic consensus that open trade would allow countries to specialize according to the principle of **comparative advantage** and thereby achieve higher levels of growth and well-being, and the political consensus that a liberal trading regime would promote not only prosperity but also peace. The major rule for implementing free trade under the GATT was the principle of nondiscrimination. All of the contracting parties—that is, all member states—agreed to adhere to the **most-favored-nation (MFN) principle**, which stipulated that "any advantage, favor, privilege, or immunity granted by any contracting party to any product originating in or destined for any other country shall be accorded immediately and unconditionally to the like product originating in or destined for the territories of all other contracting parties."[10] The only exceptions to this general rule of equal treatment were for existing preferential systems and future customs unions and free-trade associations. A second element of nondiscrimination in the GATT was the provision for **national treatment**, a rule designed to prevent discrimination against foreign products after they enter a country. Under GATT rules, a country must give imports the same treatment as it gives products made domestically in such areas as taxation, regulation, transportation, and distribution.[11]

GATT also established an international commercial code with rules on such issues as **dumping** and subsidies. Dumping is defined as pricing "below normal market price,"[12] although in some nations, like the United States, the definition of dumping in national legislation is more elaborate. Antidumping restrictions are designed to prevent the use of **predatory pricing**, which allows the firms of one country to underprice the firms of other countries in order to increase their market power.[13] **Subsidies** are government payments made to domestic producers to partially offset their costs of producing and selling goods and services. Governments use subsidies to support weak firms just entering a new market as well as older firms suffering from intensified competition. Dumping and subsidies are often attacked politically as "unfair" trade practices, and hence the GATT needed to address this issue by including restrictions on them in the overall regime.[14]

One of the most important rules in the GATT's commercial code prohibited the use of **quantitative restrictions**, such as import quotas, except for temporary balance-of-payments or national security reasons. The GATT also provided a mechanism for resolving disputes under its commercial code. .

There were, however, important departures from these rules. Provisions in the original GATT treaty and amendments made in the 1950s established a separate regime for agricultural trade. GATT rules on agriculture reflected the powerful political influence of agricultural groups and the resultant policies of government intervention to protect domestic prices and producer incomes and to ensure food security. GATT rules reflected, in particular, the domestic agricultural policies of the United States, which pressed for an international regime that would enable the United States to preserve its policy of production controls, **price supports**, export subsidies, and import protection implemented in the 1930s. Thus, for example, export subsidies on primary agricultural products were permitted as long as those subsidies did not interfere with established market shares, a concept alien to GATT rules for trade in other goods. GATT rules facilitated the use of quantitative restrictions in agriculture. In 1955, for example, the United States obtained a waiver under GATT rules that gave it special permission to impose quotas on agricultural products.[15]

There were also important gaps in the coverage of the GATT. Whereas the Havana Charter included provisions for economic development, commodity agreements, restrictive business practices, and trade in services, these were not included in the GATT. In addition, other topics not of great concern at the time, such as relations with state-trading countries, were left undeveloped in the code. These departures from GATT norms and gaps in GATT coverage eventually became a major problem for the management of international trade. Finally, the GATT's institutional mechanisms had important weaknesses. The **dispute settlement mechanism** was lengthy, allowed parties to delay or block decisions, and was not binding.[16]

In addition to establishing trade principles, the GATT provided a set of rules and procedures for what was to be the principal method of trade management in the postwar period: multilateral trade negotiations. The agreement contained a commitment to enter into such negotiations and provided guidelines for them. The most important rule was **reciprocity**, the concept that tariff reductions should be mutually advantageous.[17] Although not part of the original GATT, the **principal supplier procedure** by which negotiations were to take place among actual or potential principal suppliers—those nations accounting for 10 percent or more of a given product in world trade—also became a negotiating rule of the GATT.[18]

From a temporary treaty, the GATT became not only an established commercial code but also an international organization with a secretariat and a director general to oversee the implementation of its rules, manage dispute settlements, and provide a forum and support for multilateral trade negotiations.

U.S. Leadership

Whereas the GATT provided the framework for achieving trade liberalization, the United States put that framework into action. With the coming of the Cold War, Cordell Hull's vision of trade liberalization took on new significance as a key to a prosperous West and to Western security in the face of Soviet aggression. The great postwar economic strength of the United States and the lure of foreign markets were a further reason for U.S. interest in leading trade liberalization.

U.S. leadership was made possible by a new domestic approach to trade policy.[19] In order to avoid the pressure of special interest groups for protection, Congress delegated to the president, for a specific period of time, the authority to reduce tariffs by specific amounts without subsequent congressional approval. This congressional delegation of negotiating authority was periodically renewed throughout the postwar period. Later, when nontariff barriers were negotiated, Congress agreed to consider proposals for their removal without allowing amendments and within a short time frame. This was called the **fast-track negotiating authority**. In addition, Congress created a quasi-judicial system of trade remedies that channeled grievances of specific industries to fact-finding agencies outside the Congress. Finally, the decision-making process in Congress was concentrated in two powerful committees that dominated trade policy and that supported a liberal trading order.[20]

In the two decades following World War II, the United States led the system by helping Europe and Japan rebuild production and by pushing for trade liberalization. In the early years, the Marshall Plan, or the European Recovery Program as it was officially known, was the tool of U.S. leadership in Europe. As we have seen, the United States played a key role in financing international trade and encouraging long-term European trade competitiveness through the Marshall Plan. The United States also used the plan as a lever to encourage regional trade liberalization in Europe. During the war and the immediate post-war period, significant barriers to trade had been erected throughout Europe, which underscored the trade restrictions in effect since the 1930s. The United States pushed actively for the liberalization of trade and payments among Western European countries and, in some cases, made available the funds for such liberalization, even though this conflicted with the larger U.S. goal of non-discrimination on an international basis and even though regional liberalization sometimes involved direct discrimination against the United States.[21]

The United States also took an important leadership role with Japan. During the Occupation, the supreme commander for the Allied forces and his administration directly controlled Japanese trade and the Japanese monetary system. Until the 1960s, the United States helped the recovery and development in Japan by keeping the U.S. market open for Japanese goods while at the same time accepting Japanese protectionist policies, many of which had been instituted under the Occupation. The United States also supported Japanese membership in the GATT and urged the Europeans, unsuccessfully, to open their markets to Japanese exports.[22]

Finally, the United States took a leading role in multilateral trade negotiations. The United States, with the world's largest economy and a huge share of international trade, was the essential motivating force in a series of multilateral trade negotiations. Because the United States was, in many cases, one of the world's principal suppliers, its participation was required under the GATT's negotiating rules. Because the U.S. market was so important, there was little possibility of achieving reciprocity in tariff negotiations without the United States. Most importantly, without U.S. initiatives, the negotiations would probably never have taken place. Initiatives by the United States were responsible for the nine major trade negotiations from the Geneva Round in 1947 to the **Doha Round**, which began in 2001 (see Table 3.1). The U.S. negotiators were necessary participants—mobilizing others, seeking compromises—in the actual negotiations.

Furthermore, throughout the 1940s and 1950s, the United States accepted limited benefits from the trade negotiations. Although tariffs were reduced on a reciprocal and mutually beneficial basis, U.S. trading partners gained more than the United States did. Because of European and Japanese exchange controls that persisted through the 1950s, the trade concessions had a limited effect on U.S. exports. Because the United States did not impose controls, Europe and Japan gained immediate benefits from the tariff reductions. The United States accepted such asymmetrical benefits because of a commitment to European and Japanese recovery, because it expected to benefit from the reductions when the exchange controls were removed, and because it sought to maintain the momentum of establishing a more open trading system.

TABLE 3.1   Multilateral Trade Negotiations

Years	Name of Round	Number of Participants
1947	Geneva	23
1949	Annecy	13
1950	Torquay	38
1956	Geneva	26
1960–1961	Dillon	26
1962–1967	Kennedy	62
1973–1979	Tokyo	102
1986–1993	Uruguay	123
1999–	Doha	152

SOURCE: *Economic Report of the President* (Washington, D.C.: Government Printing Office, 1995), 205; World Trade Organization.

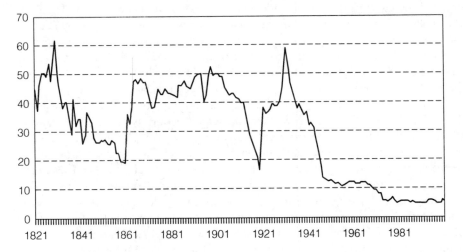

FIGURE 3.1 Average U.S. Tariff Rates on Dutiable Imports, 1821–2000, in Percentages

SOURCE: U.S. International Trade Commission; U.S. Department of Commerce, Bureau of the Census, *Historical Statistics of the United States; and Statistical Abstract of the United States,* various years.

The system worked very well for the developed countries. Most quotas and exchange rate barriers were eliminated. Although restrictions remained in agricultural products, there was substantial liberalization of trade in manufactured products (see Figure 3.1).[23] The resulting rapid growth of world trade was an important source of economic prosperity (see Figure 3.2). The high point of trade management of this period was the Kennedy Round, which culminated in 1967. Although states were unable to reach any significant agreement on agricultural trade, tariffs on nonagricultural products in the developed countries were reduced by about one-third.[24] After the Kennedy Round reductions, tariffs

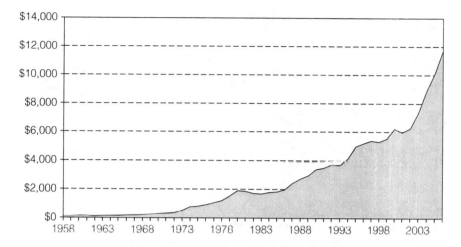

FIGURE 3.2 Growth in World Exports, 1958–2006, in Billions of Current Dollars
SOURCE: International Monetary Fund, *Direction of Trade Statistics Yearbook* (various years).

on dutiable, nonagricultural products were reduced to an average of 9.9 percent in the United States, 8.6 percent in the six EC (European Community) states, 10.8 percent in the United Kingdom, and 10.7 percent in Japan.[25] The overall reduction in tariffs for the first five trade rounds was 73 percent; for the Kennedy Round alone it was 35 percent.[26]

INTERDEPENDENCE

Structural Change and Protectionism

After 1967, however, important changes in the international trading system began to emerge and to undermine the GATT system of management and the liberal international trading order created by the GATT. Over the next two decades, structural changes led to domestic political challenges to international management of trade and to new forms of protection. Governments sought, with only limited success, to stem the tide of protectionism and to modernize the international trading regime. Thus the conflict between national and international approaches to management—the same conflict we have seen in the international monetary system—came to plague international trade management.

As in the case of monetary relations, a central force for change was increased interdependence. Interdependence increased the level of political sensitivity to trade as trade came to affect more sectors and more jobs. After World War II, economic growth, trade liberalization, decreasing transportation costs, and broadening business horizons led to a surge in trade among the developed market economies.[27] Merchandise trade among the developed countries more than quadrupled between 1963 and 1973; increased over two-and-one-half times from 1973 to 1983; and grew more than two times again between 1983 and 1993.[28] From 1960 to 2006,

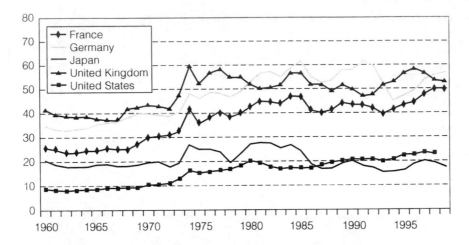

FIGURE 3.3 Trade/GDP in the United States, Britain, Germany, France, and Japan, 1960–1999, in Percentages

SOURCE: World Bank, *World Development Indicators 2001 CD-ROM* (Washington, D.C.: World Bank, 2001): OECD.Stat, http://stats.oecd.org/.

the percentage of GDP derived from trade (exports plus imports) went from 9.6 to 28.2 percent in the United States, from 35.5 percent to 84.7 percent in Germany, and from 14.5 percent to 55.1 percent in France. Trade over GDP remained steady and low in Japan and steady and steady and high in Britain (see Figure 3.3).

The role of trade was even greater in certain sectors. For example, in 1979, 5.5 percent of U.S. consumer goods and 12 percent of U.S. business equipment purchases came from abroad. By 1987, the figures for consumer goods had grown to about 12 percent, whereas foreign business equipment outlays exceeded 40 percent.[29] Interdependence in certain sectors was reinforced by the emergence of the globally organized multinational corportation, which (among other things) sources parts from around the world. One example is the Boeing Company, which produces commercial jetliners. In 1990, 90 percent of the components for Boeing aircraft were built in the United States. By 2001, more than 50 percent of Boeing components were imported.[30]

Another dimension of trade interdependence was the growing convergence of the developed countries' economies. The rapid accumulation of physical and human capital, the transfer of technology, and the growing similarities of wages narrowed the differences in **factor endowments**, which are the basis for comparative advantage and trade. In 1970, for example, labor costs in the United States and West Germany were over twice the labor costs in Japan. By 1986, the costs were roughly equal.[31] Similarly, in 1970, U.S. manufacturing productivity was 58 percent greater than West Germany and 105 percent greater than Japan in 1970. By 1986, these figures had fallen to 20 percent and 2 percent, respectively (see Figure 3.4).[32]

Interdependence and globalization led to more complex forms of specialization and fostered the growth of multinational corporations and **intra-industry trade**. Intra-industry trade is trade that occurs across national boundaries but

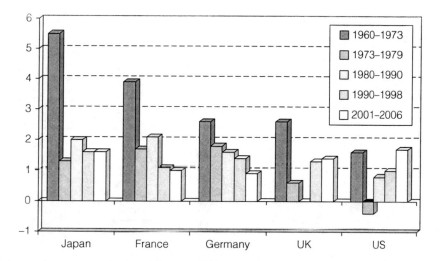

FIGURE 3.4 Multi-Factor Productivity Growth in Five Industrialized Nations, 1960–2006
SOURCE: OECD *Economic Outlook* (various editions); OECD.Stat, http://stats.oecd.org/.

within the same industry. For example, when country X sell auto parts to country Y and country Y sells auto parts to country X.

A second change that increased protectionism pressures was the shift in competitiveness worldwide. Changes in factor endowments altered the competitive positions of several industries in the developed countries, including autos, steel, textiles, shipping, and consumer electronics. In some sectors, especially in industries like textiles and apparel where technology is stable and labor is a major factor in production costs, the shift favored the developing countries. Lags in capital investment in the developed countries plus rising labor productivity, lower labor costs, and aggressive export policies in some of the developing countries led to a shift in manufacturing from the industrialized nations to the **newly industrializing countries (NICs)**, such as Taiwan, South Korea, Mexico, and Brazil.[33] An even bigger shift occurred in the first decade of the twenty-first century when China became one of the preferred sites for manufacturing labor-intensive goods and India began to compete for outsourced business services.

Because of differing levels of investment and research, of management effectiveness and labor productivity, as well as misaligned exchange rates, shifts in relative competitiveness occurred among the major trading countries. The reasons for these shifts became the subject of intense debate. In the United States, for example, the competitiveness debate in the 1980s focused on declining U.S. competitiveness vis-à-vis Japan, which was evidenced by greater Japanese investment per employee, civilian **research and development (R&D)** spending, productivity growth, shares of world trade and production, and average growth of total gross fixed **capital formation**.[34] In the first decade of the twenty-first century, the undervaluation of the Chinese currency, the yuan, resulted in rapid

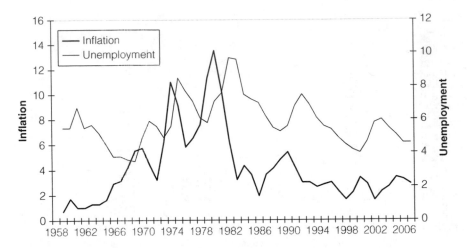

F I G U R E 3.5 Inflation and Unemployment in the U.S. Economy, 1958–2007, in Percentages

SOURCE: *Economic Report of the President 2008.*

growth in Chinese exports of manufactured goods and major trade disputes with the United States and the European Union.

A third change contributing to protectionism was disruptions in the economic system in the 1970s and 1980s. Trade management from the end of World War II until the end of the Kennedy Round took place in an environment of unprecedented growth and stability. From 1960 to 1970, growth in the OECD countries averaged almost 5 percent per year, unemployment stood at 2.7 percent, and the volume of world trade grew at an average annual rate of 8.5 percent.[35] Throughout this period, the U.S. trade balance was strongly positive, providing the basis for a national consensus for liberalizing trade. In such an expanding world economy, economic groups were able to perceive the advantages of cooperation and trade liberalization.

In the 1970s and 1980s, these favorable conditions altered dramatically and contributed to the new protectionism. The 1970s was the era of **stagflation**, slow growth combined with rampant inflation. In the wake of the oil crisis, the developed countries' real GNP growth dropped to 2.7 percent between 1974 and 1979, while their inflation exploded to double digits, reaching a high of 13.4 percent in 1974.[36] Unemployment in the OECD countries increased to an average of 4.9 percent for the period 1974 to 1979.[37] Stagflation increased pressures on governments to adopt beggar-thy-neighbor policies such as trade restrictions (see Figure 3.5).

The floating exchange rate system also contributed to growing protectionism. In the 1970s, monetary problems led to trade measures designed to protect payments balances such as exchange controls and special duties. The breakdown in the system of fixed exchange rates also complicated the process of trade negotiations. In a fixed rate system, negotiators had been able to estimate the impact of agreements on their trade and payments. Under floating rates, such calculations were much more difficult. As a result of these economic changes, the value in dollar terms of world trade grew at an annual average of only 5 percent between 1975 and 1984.[38]

In the early 1980s, deep recession put a brake on trade. Deflationary policies led to a steady decline in inflation from 12.9 percent in 1980 to 2.5 percent in 1986.[39] At the same time, growth came to a halt. The years 1980 to 1982 witnessed the lowest average growth rate—0.73 percent per year—of any three-year period since the end of World War II.[40] Unemployment rose to levels once thought politically unacceptable. By the end of 1983, recession had pushed total unemployment in the OECD countries to a record 8.5 percent.[41] Significantly, unemployment was concentrated in those industries with the highest levels of foreign competition. For example, in December 1982, when total U.S. unemployment reached its peak of 10.6 percent, unemployment in the auto industry stood at 23.2 percent, and in the primary metals (steel) industry, it was 29.2 percent.[42] Because of the recession, world trade stagnated. The growth of the volume of world trade slowed to 1.2 percent in 1980 and 0.8 percent in 1981, and it actually fell by 2.2 percent in 1982.[43]

By the second half of the 1980s, the economic environment for the industrialized countries improved. Growth rates increased somewhat, while inflation rates began to fall.[44] World trade began to resume its expansion (see again Figure 3.2). Because of labor market rigidities, however, unemployment remained high in most of Europe and the United States and persisted as a force for protection. In 1986, unemployment in the developed countries still stood at 8.3 percent, with U.S. unemployment at 7.0 percent, Japanese at 2.8 percent, and the EC at 11.2 percent.[45] In the 1980s, the exchange rate system emerged as a central problem for trade management. As we saw in Chapter 2, the misalignment of exchange rates was a major factor in the emergence of massive trade and payments imbalances. In particular, the overvaluation of the dollar and corresponding undervaluation of the yen and deutsche mark were a major cause of the U.S. trade and balance of payments deficit and the resultant rise in protectionism in the United States.

Interdependence: The European Union   In the 1970s and 1980s, the rise of Japan and the European Union[46] and the relative decline of the United States complicated the system of trade management. Trade problems and a decline in power combined with growing protectionist pressures left the United States less willing and less able to lead the system. At the same time, the EU and Japan were not prepared to assume a leadership role. Absent strong leadership, management where power is more evenly shared proved a major challenge to the system.

In this period, the European Union emerged as the world's largest trading bloc. The EU established a customs union with free internal trade in goods, a **common external tariff**, and a **common agricultural policy**. Trade of EU countries grew rapidly from 24.5 percent of total world trade in 1960 to 41.1 percent in 1990.[47] Trade among EU member states grew even faster. Intra-EU trade as a share of total world trade increased almost threefold, from 8.4 percent in 1960 to 24.4 percent in 1990.[48] Intra-EU trade as a share of total EU member-state trade burgeoned from 34.4 percent in 1960 to 59.5 percent in 1990.[49]

In building this regional trading system, the EU weakened the principle of nondiscrimination basic to the GATT—albeit with the blessing of the United States—and thus some day might pose a challenge to liberalization of the larger international system. As we have argued earlier, however, so far the EU has resisted temptations to favor trade and capital flows within the Union at the expense of flows between the EU and the rest of the world. The continuing political fragmentation of the EU weakened its ability to act as the sole representative of Europe in international affairs, especially in traditional foreign policy areas. But the EU represented all of its member states in trade negotiations and at international economic summits. So it can be argued that the EU, like other regional economic integration efforts (see the section on regionalism below), was still a building block for a liberal international economic order rather than an impediment.

The EU's first goal was to build a customs union with internal free trade and a common external tariff. Such customs unions are permitted as an exception to the GATT/WTO rules of nondiscrimination.[50] The European effort to establish such a union was supported by the United States, which, since the days of the Marshall Plan, actively encouraged a united Europe as a way of strengthening the West. When it looked as if the EU might increase trade discrimination, the United States, by initiating the Kennedy Round, sought to ensure that European integration would remain open and nondiscriminatory. The success of that round suggested that Europe would remain committed to multilateralism and liberalism. However, in the 1970s and 1980s, Europe showed signs of moving in the opposite direction.

The EU's **Common Agricultural Policy (CAP)** blocked imports into the community and artificially stimulated competition in other markets. The EU also entered into new preferential trading arrangements, which were explicitly outlawed under the GATT rule of nondiscrimination. The first was an agreement in 1958 with the then French colonies in Africa. In the 1990s, the EU negotiated preferential agreements with most of the Mediterranean Basin, much of Africa, and even with some developed countries of Western Europe. The Union viewed such agreements as aid to underdeveloped countries and as adjustments for the discriminatory effects of CAP. The enlargement of the EU to its current membership of 27 nation-states created further problems (see Table 3.2). This expansion not only increased the size of the agricultural protectionist regime and the existing preferential system but also became a force for the extension of EU preferences. Some of the European Free Trade Area (EFTA) countries, which for political reasons did not join the EU, as well as many Commonwealth countries, became linked with the EU through preferential trade agreements.

In the 1980s, EU attention focused on the new policy of completing the creation of a **common internal market** by 1992.[51] In 1985, the community announced a plan to remove over 300 nontariff barriers to intra-EU trade rang-

TABLE 3.2   Member States of the European Union as of 2008

Country	First Year of Membership
Austria	1995
Belgium	1957
Bulgaria	2007
Cyprus	2004
Czech Republic	2004
Denmark	1973
Estonia	2004
Finland	1995
France	1957
Germany	1957
Greece	1981
Hungary	2004
Ireland	1973
Italy	1957
Latvia	2004
Lithuania	2004
Luxembourg	1957
Malta	2004
Netherlands	1957
Poland	2004
Portugal	1986
Romania	2007
Slovakia	2004
Slovenia	2004
Spain	1986
Sweden	1995
United Kingdom	1973

ing from harmonizing standards to eliminating delays at borders to allowing cross border sales of services such as banking and insurance to tax harmonization. The thrust of the internal market program was decidedly liberal, based as it was on efforts to remove nontariff barriers to free trade.

However, as Europe worked toward the creation of a unified market, questions began to emerge about its impact on the multilateral trading system. Talk of "Europe for the Europeans" and "**fortress Europe**" raised concerns about increasing barriers to the outside world through, for example, extension of national protectionist policies to the Union as a whole or through harmonization of standards and regulations that would discriminate against non-European goods and services. Other questions concerned treatment of foreign firms that had invested in Europe and whether they would be considered "European" for purposes of cross-border sales of services and for government procurement.

The fears of many Americans in the 1980s about the creation of a "fortress Europe" were probably unjustified. The signing of the Single European Act in 1986 and the Maastricht Treaty in 1992 (see Chapter 2) and continued progress toward the goals established by the two treaties did not result in a more protectionist Europe. Changes in European institutions in the 1980s were aimed at making it easier for Europe to undertake the economic changes necessary for the region to maintain its international competitiveness in the face of growing competition from North America and Asia. The desire of Europe to be a player in markets for high-technology products, however, resulted in some policies— such as the massive subsidies for the European civilian aircraft consortium, Airbus Industrie, and for the European electronics industry—that brought it into conflict with the United States and Japan. In short, the worries about Europe shifted away from concerns about protectionism to complaints about the use of **industrial policies** to favor European enterprises in international competition.[52]

Interdependence: Japan   The rise of Japan as a force in the world economy and world trade also complicated trade management. As late as 1960, Japan was a minor economic power, with only a 3-percent share of world GNP.[53] By 1980, Japan controlled approximately 10.7 percent of world GNP.[54] Behind this rapid change in position was the Japanese economic miracle: an average annual real growth in GNP of 10 percent from 1950 to 1970. Starting from a position of relative technological backwardness, Japan achieved this remarkable growth rate through its ability to absorb and adapt foreign technology, the availability of inexpensive labor due to the movement of people out of agriculture, and heavy investment in manufacturing.[55] Government policies played a central role in the Japanese miracle. Targeted industries, such as steel, oil refining, petrochemicals, automobiles, aircraft, industrial machinery, electronics, and computers, were promoted through tax incentives as well as financing provided by government-owned lending institutions and a huge accumulation of private savings encouraged by government policies.

Export expansion and import restrictions played a central role in government policy. Because of Japan's dependence on imports of raw materials and capital goods essential for growth, government plans and private industry strategies placed heavy emphasis on limiting "nonessential" imports and fostering exports.[56] Government provided industry with significant protection from import competition through tariffs and quantitative restrictions as well as administrative regulations, such as import licensing and import deposits. While the other developed countries were liberalizing trade through multilateral negotiations, Japan retained barriers on virtually all imports. At the same time, tax incentives, export financing assistance, and an undervalued yen encouraged Japanese exports. Finally, the government carefully controlled foreign investment.[57] Thus, in the

1950s and 1960s, Japan created an industrial base heavily biased against imports and oriented toward exports.[58]

After 1973, growth slowed due to the end of the process of technological catch-up, lower investment rates, and other factors, such as slower population growth and rising energy costs. Industrial development shifted from heavy industry, such as steel, to more sophisticated industries, such as automobiles and electronic products.[59] Nevertheless, Japan's average growth rate of 4.3 percent from 1974 to 1985 exceeded that of other industrial economies. In the 1970s, Japanese government policy also changed. Although the government still took a lead role in certain strategic sectors, such as computers, the role of government in industrial development began to decline as Japanese industry reached greater maturity.[60]

Beginning in 1970, Japan gradually liberalized trade policy. Quotas on many goods were eliminated; significant across-the-board tariff cuts were instituted; and the yen began to appreciate. Following the Tokyo Round, Japanese tariff barriers were roughly comparable to those of the United States.[61] Japan's strategy of export promotion, however, not only remained but was reinforced by the oil crises of 1973 and 1978–1979, which accentuated Japan's sense of dependence on and vulnerability to imports of raw materials.

By the 1980s, Japan had become a source of trade friction due to the seemingly chronic Japanese trade surplus. Most visible was Japan's growing imbalance in trade with the United States, its principal trading partner. While the bilateral Japan-EU surplus grew from $9.9 billion in 1980 to $26.5 billion in 1993, its surplus with the United States grew from $7.3 billion in 1980 to $51 billion in 1993.[62]

The principal cause of the massive surplus was an imbalance in macroeconomic policies, particularly between the United States and Japan, which was reflected in capital flows and exchange rates. Japan maintained a high savings rate fostered by government policies, which dated from the era when Japan needed high levels of investment for economic development. However, because of slower economic growth and a policy of government fiscal austerity, there was insufficient demand for these savings within Japan. As the Japanese government eliminated exchange controls and other limits on Japanese outward foreign investment, surplus yen began to flow abroad in response to demand, primarily from the United States. U.S. savings rates were low, while demand for funds in the growing U.S. economy was too high to be satisfied from domestic sources alone. For much of the 1980s, the U.S. government generated huge budget deficits that had to be financed. Japan provided much of that financing. The high value of the dollar against the yen between 1981 and 1985 made Japanese exports more competitive worldwide, especially in the United States.

Differing domestic demand was also an important dimension of the macroeconomic imbalance. As the United States stimulated its economy in the early 1980s, imports of consumer goods increased more than 150 percent from $34.4 billion in 1980 to $87.0 billion in 1987.[63] The Japanese were well positioned to take advantage of this surge in consumer demand. For decades, Japanese manufacturers had concentrated on export-led growth and on developing the U.S. market. Since the 1970s, they had focused on developing products targeted at the U.S. consumer. Japanese automobiles and consumer electronic products, for example, were well designed for the U.S. market, of high quality, and, due to productivity improvements and a declining yen, increasingly price competitive. At the same time, because of slower growth and fiscal austerity, Japanese demand, especially demand for competitive U.S. machine tools and heavy equipment, was restrained.

These macroeconomic differences were accentuated by continuing barriers to imports and to inward foreign investment into Japan. With the exception of agriculture, most Japanese tariff and quota barriers had been removed. However, nontariff barriers deriving from the earlier era of cooperation between government and business remained a problem. Government procurement policies favored Japanese telecommunications and computer manufacturers. Regulation was used effectively to block imports. For example, **patent** approvals were delayed until Japanese producers became competitive. Inspections and approvals by foreign testing agencies were rejected by some ministries, and the process of regulatory approval was often long and not transparent. Industrial targeting, as in the case of computers, was used to discriminate against foreign goods. In addition, private patterns of behavior, such as the so-called *keiretsu* **system**—the preference of Japanese firms for dealing with other Japanese firms in industrial groups characterized by cross-shareholding—and the tendency of large Japanese firms to control their own retail distribution systems formed barriers to foreign access to Japanese markets.[64] Some U.S. multinationals were rich and patient enough to pay the high price of entering and servicing the Japanese domestic market. IBM, Caterpillar, Xerox, McDonalds, ToysRUs, Johnson & Johnson, CocaCola, among others, were successful in establishing a firm foothold in Japan. Some large firms, like Kodak and Motorola, tried to enter the market but were unsuccessful. For those U.S. firms that were smaller or less export-oriented, overcoming these public and private barriers proved especially difficult.

As a result, the bilateral U.S.–Japan trade imbalance soared in the 1980s. Even after the Plaza agreement of 1985 when the value of the dollar relative to the yen began to decline, Japanese surpluses continued to grow. In part this was due to the so-called **J-curve effect**, whereby the impact of a devaluation is initially an increase in a deficit as the cost of goods already contracted for import rises. Persistent devaluations of the dollar from 1985 to 1987 accentuated the J-curve effect and masked the turnaround in the physical volume and yen value of U.S.–Japan trade. Furthermore, the trade impact of dollar devaluation was reduced, because Japanese exporters, dependent on the U.S. market, increased prices less than the magnitude of the dollar devaluation in order to retain their market share. They were able to do this without cutting profit margins too much because of continuous improvements in production and distribution technologies.[65]

The political consequence of the Japanese trade surplus was increasing trade friction between Japan and its trading partners. Pressures grew for pro-

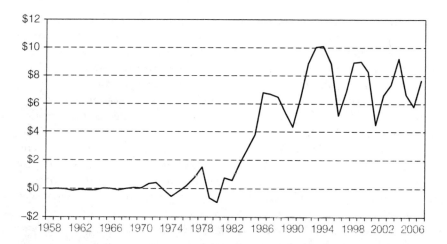

FIGURE 3.6   Japanese Balance of Trade in Billions of Current Dollars, 1958–2006
SOURCE: OECD.Stat., http://stats.oecd.org/.

tection against Japanese imports and for action to open Japanese markets. In the West, the Japanese surpluses were often attributed not to macroeconomic imbalances but to **unfair trade practices** by Japan. Protectionist pressures were accentuated by the traditional Japanese export strategy of capturing market share. This strategy led to swift penetration of certain foreign markets, which led to equally swift foreign political reaction in such powerful sectors as semiconductors, telecommunications equipment, and automobiles. Finally, the slow process of decision making in Japan, where consensus must be formed before action is taken, exacerbated growing Western criticism of Japan as a free rider in the system.[66]

Growing Western exasperation seemed unfounded in Japan. From a Japanese perspective, the country had moved far and fast under Western prodding to liberalize trade. Under heavy pressure, Japan had opened up a variety of protected markets, such as telecommunications, cigarettes, beef, citrus, and airport construction. It had taken steps toward liberalization of its financial markets, opening the securities and trust banking business to foreigners.[67] Furthermore, Western governments subjected Japan to numerous highly protectionist **Voluntary Restraint Agreements (VRAs)**.[68] In the mid-1980s, under pressure from the West and from a revalued yen, Japan stimulated domestic demand and reduced its trade surplus somewhat. After the Plaza agreement, net exports measured in terms of physical volume and net receipts in yen declined (see Figure 3.6). Imports from the developing countries increased dramatically. As seen from Japan, foreign profligacy, especially U.S. macroeconomic policy and declining Western productivity and competitiveness, were the root of the problem.[69]

Interdependence: The United States   Finally, one of the most important developments in the 1970s and 1980s was the erosion of U.S. dominance of the international trading system and the related decline in U.S. support for a multilateral trade regime. While the United States remained the world's largest economy and largest trading power, it was no longer overwhelmingly preponderant as it was in the first two postwar decades. In 1950 the United States accounted for 26.1 percent of trade among developed market economies (which would have been 80 percent or more of world trade); by 1990 the United States accounted for only 11.6 percent of world trade.[70] Furthermore, after 1970 the United States began to experience what seemed to be chronic trade and balance of payments deficits. The huge and traditional (since 1893) U.S. trade surplus turned in 1971 into a persistent and growing deficit (see again Figure 2.11). The traditional U.S. surplus with Japan turned into deficit in 1965, and its traditional surplus with Western Europe diminished and, depending on the relative macroeconomic situation, periodically became a deficit.

The erosion of U.S. trading dominance was accentuated by interdependence. Between 1970 and 1990, trade as a percentage of U.S. GNP rose from 8.7 percent to 21.5 percent (see Figure 3.3).[71] Interdependence was a new condition for the United States. In contrast with Europe and Japan, whose economies had long been dependent on trade, international trade had been important but not vital to the United States because of its vast continental market. As the United States faced more competition at home and abroad, the political consensus for a multilateral, open trading regime led by the United States began to erode.

The decline of U.S. trade preponderance and the swelling trade deficit raised questions about U.S. international competitiveness. The ability of countries to compete in foreign trade depends on productivity, which, in turn, depends on investment in both physical and human capital as well as on research and development. While much of the deterioration of the U.S. trading position in the 1980s was attributable to the overvalued dollar, there were deeper problems created by several decades of sluggish **productivity growth**. Even though U.S. exports rebounded and regained some world market share following the devaluation of the dollar in 1985, the United States maintained a chronic balance-of-trade deficit during the 1980s.

Several indicators suggested a relative decline in U.S. competitiveness. While the United States retained the highest absolute level of productivity, it had lost ground relative to competitors. **Total factor productivity**—output per combined units of labor and capital—in the U.S. business sector grew more slowly than that of other industrialized countries after the 1960s (see Figure 3.4).[72] Between 1972 and 1987, investment in relation to GDP increased only 3.1 percent in the United States—less than half the G–7 average of 7.1 percent—while in Germany it rose 33 percent, and in Japan, 24.6 percent.[73] While overall research and development expenditures in the United States kept pace with those of other developed countries, much of that expenditure was for military purposes. Nondefense research and development spending relative to GDP in the United States increased only 3 percent between 1970 and 1992, while that of Germany increased 31 percent and that of Japan 55 percent. In terms of patenting activity, the United States also lost ground. Between 1963 and 1977, for example, 72.3 percent of the patents awarded in the United States were of U.S. origin; by 1991, this figure was only 53.4 percent.[74] Not all evidence suggested a U.S. decline, however. Average labor costs increased in Japan and Germany from 1980 levels, while declining in the United States.[75] Furthermore, U.S. industry adapted to changing competition by increasing automation, downsizing, mergers, and streamlining operations. While the United States lost some of its relative position in this period with respect to Japan, Western Europe, and the Asian NICs, in absolute terms U.S. competitiveness remained strong.

Finally, in the 1970s and 1980s, U.S. support for multilateralism was further undermined by changes in domestic politics.[76] A series of congressional reforms weakened the power of the committees that had virtually exclusively controlled U.S. trade policy. The growing importance of nontariff barriers imbedded in a variety of national policies meant that these committees could no longer claim exclusive jurisdiction over trade issues. In addition, a quasi-judicial system established by the Congress, called the **International Trade Commission**, which was supposed to manage trade grievances, began to break down both under the weight of increasing numbers of **antidumping petitions** and because a series of presidents often rejected the commission's recommendations as leading to protectionism. The pressures then spilled back to the Democratic Congress, which came to feel that the Republican administration was rigid and uncooperative on trade policy. The result was increasing efforts by Congress to reform U.S. trade law to reduce presidential discretion and to oblige retaliation against countries found in violation of international trade agreements.[77]

As a result of these changes, domestic pressures for protection increased and became increasingly effective. As trade problems developed, more industries organized into special interest groups to put pressure on Congress and the executive for relief from foreign competition. Beginning in the late 1960s, following the Kennedy Round, vulnerable industries such as textiles, steel, electronics, and shoes began to put strong pressure on Congress to alleviate import competition. In 1970, organized labor officially shifted its policy from support for free trade to active lobbying for protection. Proposals for sectoral protectionist legislation increased in Congress and put pressure on the president to negotiate bilateral agreements outside the GATT to avert legislated quotas and tariffs. At the same time, U.S. industries facing barriers to market access abroad increasingly turned to the U.S. government for help in breaking down foreign barriers. As markets became increasingly global, many high-technology, export-oriented industries, such as the semiconductor and super-computer industries, chafed under restrictions on access to foreign markets. Their goal was to use access to U.S. markets as bargaining leverage to open up foreign markets.[78]

As the trade problem deepened and spread from sensitive industries to the entire economy in the 1980s, many U.S. industry, labor, and political leaders came to believe the United States was no longer benefiting from the system and was being subjected to unfair treatment by its trading partners and by the trading regime. Japan, in particular, was singled out as a country that benefited from the liberal trading order and access to U.S. markets while maintaining barriers to its own market.[79] Proposals for broad-based protectionist legislation increased in Congress. In 1988, Congress enacted omnibus trade legislation, which tightened U.S. trade law to

give the president less discretion in case of unfair trade practices by foreign competitors and to require the executive branch to identify and achieve changes in the
policy of countries that have unfair trade practices.[80]

In response to persistent congressional pressures, the Reagan, Bush, and Clinton
administrations sought nonlegislative ways to resolve trade conflicts: voluntary
export restraint agreements as in automobiles; negotiations to open overseas markets,
such as the **Market Opening Sector Specific (MOSS)** talks, the **Structural
Impediments Initiative** and the Framework for a New Economic Partnership
between the U.S. and Japan; and aggressive use of the U.S. trade provisions, which
authorizes the U.S. government to retaliate against countries deemed not to be
allowing U.S. exports fair market access.[81] Finally, the United States negotiated
a broad-based bilateral trading agreement with Israel in 1986 and a major agreement with Canada in 1987. The **U.S.–Canada Free Trade Agreement**,
which was signed in 1988, reduced a number of trade and investment barriers
between the two countries, established rules on trade in services, and put in place
a new dispute settlement mechanism between the two countries.[82]

An Old Issue: Agriculture

In the 1980s there were still important sectors that had not yet been brought
under GATT rules and process. One was agriculture. As we have seen, agriculture was subject to a separate GATT regime and did not benefit from the liberalization process of the postwar era.

National agricultural policies of most developed countries remained interventionist and protectionist. Since the 1930s, the U.S. government intervened in
domestic agricultural markets to maintain agricultural prices and the income of
U.S. farmers. It supported domestic prices by purchasing surplus commodities,
production controls, and deficiency payments, and further managed the domestic
market through export subsidies and import quotas. Japan's government, led by a
political party that depended heavily on electoral support from farmers and
also motivated by a deep concern for food security resulting from wartime
shortages, had widespread import restrictions to maintain domestic agricultural
prices above world price levels and to provide farmers with incomes comparable to
nonfarmers.

The European Union maintained farm incomes through its Common
Agricultural Policy (CAP). The CAP established common, artificially high
internal prices, which it maintained through the purchase of surpluses and a flexible external tariff on agricultural imports, which ensured that imported products
were more expensive than domestic products and that imported products could
only assume the slack that the EU producers could not fill. Because the CAP had
no production controls, high prices for agricultural products generated large food
surpluses, which were exported with the help of export subsidies.[83]

Although protection was extensive, the exemption of agriculture from the rules
of international trade did not become a serious problem until the 1980s. Conflict
was limited because agricultural trade grew steadily, driven by economic growth,
rising incomes, and improved diets. However, in the 1970s, burgeoning popula-

tions, inappropriate agricultural policies in developing countries and the Eastern bloc, unfavorable weather conditions, and overall global inflation led to a dramatic rise in the demand for food imports and in the price of agricultural products. Rising prices and expected long-term food shortages led both importing and exporting countries to increase production.[84] Favorable market conditions combined with government encouragement resulted in soaring food production.[85]

As production increased, world demand for agricultural products declined. Per capita food consumption grew at a slower rate; supply far outdistanced demand; world commodity markets collapsed; and agricultural producers in many developed countries faced the worst economic crisis since the 1930s. Governments that protected their domestic markets and maintained high domestic prices through a combination of domestic price supports, purchase of excess supplies, and import protection found themselves with growing mountains of surplus commodities.

To reduce these surpluses, governments increased export subsidies and dumped agricultural products on the already strained international market. Export subsidies further depressed prices and had a serious negative effect on exporting countries such as Canada, Australia, and a number of developing countries that had relatively less intervention at home and that now faced greater competition abroad.[86] The budgetary costs of the agricultural trade war were also high. The costs of the CAP, estimated at $60 billion in 1986, created a budget crisis in the EU. United States expenditures for price and income support rose sixfold from 1982 to 1986, when they surpassed $26 billion.[87] Conflicts over agricultural policy increased. Even Japan, a large net importer of agricultural products, was criticized as never before for its protectionist policies.

GATT was unable to restrain the agricultural trade war, because domestic agricultural programs and export subsidies received special treatment under its rules. The combination of trade war and budgetary costs led countries for the first time in the postwar period to consider seriously multilateral negotiations that would change the GATT regime for agriculture and lead to reform of domestic agricultural policies.

The New Protectionism

The result of structural changes in the global trading economy was a surge in new protectionist policies in developed countries. The new protectionism took several forms. One form was nontariff barriers (NTBs) to trade. In part, the NTB problem grew out of the very success of the GATT. The GATT had been designed to liberalize trade by removing quotas and tariffs. With the success of such liberalization in manufactured products, the major remaining barriers to trade were nontariff barriers such as government procurement policies, customs procedures, health and sanitary regulations, national standards, and a broad range of other laws and regulations that discriminate against imports or offer assistance to exports. Regional policy, agricultural policy, and consumer and environmental protection are other examples of nontariff measures that have trade-distorting consequences.

The success of the GATT in trade liberalization actually increased the use of nontariff barriers. Because governments could no longer use tariffs and quotas as tools of national economic policy, they tried to insulate the domestic economy from international competition through a variety of national policies. States used subsidies and tax preferences to help ailing industries, such as steel and shipbuilding. They provided a variety of incentives for the development of new, technologically sophisticated industries, such as aerospace and computers. They also used a combination of tax and financial incentives as well as requirements for local content, export performance, and technology transfer for foreign investors.

Countries now had to reduce nontariff trade barriers to maintain what had already been achieved, let alone continue the process of liberalization. However, the control of nontariff barriers was far more difficult than the regulation and removal of tariffs and quotas. Such policies were usually an integral part of national economic and social policies. Because they were often carried out for reasons other than trade protection, NTBs had traditionally been considered national prerogatives not subject to international negotiation. Nontariff barriers also posed practical negotiating problems. Because NTBs took many different forms and because many different governmental bodies had authority over them, it was not possible to use the same kinds of negotiating techniques that had proved successful in reducing tariffs.[88] The reduction of nontariff barriers required international agreements to coordinate and harmonize a broad range of policies, for which the GATT offered few guidelines.[89]

Another form of the protectionism that followed the reductions in tariffs negotiated in GATT trade rounds were voluntary restraint agreements (VRAs), also known as **voluntary export restraints (VERs)**. VRAs were developed as a response to pressure for protection from import-sensitive industries. The GATT provided three principal forms of recourse for industries hurt by imports. If foreign competitors were dumping—that is, selling goods abroad at prices below the cost of production—countries were allowed to impose a duty to offset the dumping. Although antidumping laws were well developed both domestically and internationally, action could take a long time, and proving dumping cases could be difficult. The GATT also permitted countries to impose duties to offset foreign subsidies of exported products. Finally, the GATT permitted certain emergency measures known as **safeguards**. The GATT permitted governments to impose restrictions on fairly traded imports if an unforeseen surge in imports resulting from a trade concession caused or threatened serious injury to a domestic industry. Such safeguards had to be applied to all countries; protection had to be limited in time and be gradually removed; and importing countries had to adopt meaningful adjustment policies.

For several reasons, however, safeguards were rarely invoked directly. They had to be applied to all countries, whereas governments preferred to target certain suppliers for import controls. The GATT also required the importing country to grant compensatory concessions to all affected exporting countries. Furthermore, GATT did not clearly define "serious injury" and offered inadequate guidance—for example, on consultative procedures, duration, and adjustment—for implementing and regulating safeguards. Thus, governments turned increasingly to VRAs, which were outside the GATT framework.[90] They also increasingly moved toward the use of national antidumping laws, which were designed to be consistent with GATT rules for safeguards, to compensate for the absence of clear GATT rules in this area.

Under such agreements, which were usually bilateral and sometimes secret, low-cost exporters "voluntarily" restricted sales to countries where their goods were threatening industry and employment. There was a long history of such agreements. In the 1950s and 1960s, for example, the United States negotiated a number of voluntary **export controls** with Japan and many LDCs, under which exporters restricted their sales in the U.S. market. Two agreements—the **Long-term Textile Arrangement** of 1962 and the subsequent **Multi-Fiber Arrangement** of 1974—were negotiated multilaterally and within the GATT context (see Chapter 7). These earlier agreements were unusual steps, exceptions to normal GATT procedures. In the 1970s and 1980s, however, VRAs became an accepted mode of trade regulation.[91] VRAs proliferated in various sectors— textiles, steel, automobiles, electronics, and footwear—and covered trade among the industrial nations themselves.

In the United States, the typical pattern was a surge of imports, followed by massive filings of unfair trade actions, followed by pressure on Congress for protectionist legislation, followed, in turn, by a negotiated voluntary export restraint agreement as a way to reduce imports without resolving the legal cases and without legislating protection.

Steel was the first major industry subjected to VRAs among developed market economies. In 1968, faced with surging imports and under pressure from proposed legislation to limit steel imports, the Johnson administration negotiated VRAs with the European Union and Japan, which set specific tonnage limits on each for their steel exports to the United States.[92] In 1978, in response to new surges of imports and large number of antidumping cases, the Carter administration instituted the **trigger price mechanism (TPM)**, which established a "fair value" reference price for steel based on Japanese production costs. All European and Japanese imports entering the United States below that price were presumed to be dumped and were subject to a fast-track antidumping investigation. By 1982, due to a rise in the dollar and renewed import competition, the TPM was on the rocks. Numerous trade actions against foreign producers and proposed legislation to cut imports forced the Reagan administration to negotiate VERs with not only the EU, Japan, and Australia but also Argentina, Brazil, Mexico, Korea, and South Africa.[93]

In the 1980s, VRAs among developed countries grew. The most important industry to be added to the list was automobiles, which account for 15 percent of world manufactured goods exports.[94] A surge in Japanese exports led to legal and political pressure to keep Japanese automobiles out of Western Europe and the United States. The first VRA on automobiles was in 1976 between the United Kingdom and Japan. The following year, France negotiated an agreement with Japan. In 1981, in response to proposed legislation to limit Japanese imports, the Reagan administration and Japan agreed to a VER. Agreements with West

Germany, Canada, the Netherlands, Belgium, and Luxembourg followed.[95] By the latter half of the 1980s, VRAs had spread to high-technology sectors.

The GATT regime became increasingly irrelevant in the face of the new protectionism. The GATT had been designed to manage import restrictions, especially quantitative restrictions and tariffs, not nontariff barriers and voluntary export controls. Furthermore, countries often preferred politically negotiated bilateral solutions to the GATT's multilateral rules and procedures. Finally, with increasing government intervention in the economy, shifting comparative advantage and surplus capacity in many sectors, and frequent departures from GATT rules, many policymakers and analysts began to argue for a regime based on managed trade, not on the GATT principle of open trade. A managed-trade regime would recognize the reality, indeed the desirability, of government intervention in national economies to decide comparative advantage and intergovernmental agreements to shape international trade flows.[96] Proposals for such a regime ranged from an outright advocacy of tariff barriers as a tool of national policy[97] to proposals for global negotiations to allocate world production[98] to a set of regimes based on varying levels of government intervention, anywhere from managed trade in surplus sectors to free trade in the advanced sectors.[99]

The Tokyo Round

The Tokyo Round, the seventh round of multilateral trade negotiations, began in 1973 and ended in 1979. It attempted to respond to the changed international trading system and to start the process of trade reform. It was the result of a U.S. initiative launched after the dollar crisis of 1971. Begun in 1973 in the midst of the oil crisis, deep recession, and rising protectionism, it took place in an economic and political environment less propitious than that of earlier trade negotiations. Nevertheless, its goals were more ambitious than those of earlier rounds. Previous negotiations sought to lower quotas and tariff barriers, primarily on nonagricultural products, and to implement GATT goals and rules. The Tokyo Round continued the pursuit of tariff reduction and also tried to regulate uncharted areas of international trade such as nontariff barriers; safeguards (i.e., the use of unilateral measures such as voluntary export restraint agreements); tropical products, which were of interest to developing countries; agriculture; and several other sectors in which there were still unresolved problems.

In April 1979—six-and-a-half years after the first meeting in Tokyo—the multilateral trade negotiations were concluded.[100] Some of the goals of the participants had been achieved: tariffs on manufactured products were reduced; codes on certain nontariff barriers (NTBs) were drawn up; and changes were made in the application of GATT rules to the LDCs (see Chapter 7). Other efforts collapsed, including the liberalization of trade in agriculture and, most critically, the effort to regulate safeguards.

The most important outcome of the Tokyo Round was the progress made on regulating nontariff barriers to trade. The Tokyo Round agreement included several new codes that significantly modified the GATT system by extending trade management to nontariff barriers to trade. For example, the **Code on Subsidies and Countervailing Duties** was a step toward dealing with anti-dumping laws and national industrial policies. The code recognized subsidies on manufactured products (but not raw materials) as nontariff barriers to trade. It allowed countries unilaterally to impose countervailing duties when a **subsidy** led to a material injury in the importing country and, with authorization from the other signatories, to impose such duties if subsidies led to injury to exports in third markets. The **Code on Government Procurement** recognized govern-ment purchasing policies as nontariff barriers (NTBs) and set rules for giving equal treatment to both national and foreign firms bidding for contracts from official entities. Although the number of government agencies covered by the code was small, it established an important precedent. Other codes covering product standards and customs valuation and licensing established rules for regu-lating these NTBs. The NTB codes not only established rules but also provided for surveillance and dispute settlement mechanisms. Each code set up a commit-tee of signatories, some of which had powers only to consult (i.e., to oversee) and some of which were given dispute settlement authority.[101]

Despite the new departure signified by the NTB codes, there remained impor-tant limits to their effectiveness. Because the NTB codes applied only to the signato-ries, they diverged for the first time from the GATT principle of most-favored-nation status (MFN) or nondiscrimination. Whereas the developed countries signed and rat-ified the codes, most of the developing countries were not convinced of their value and chose not to sign, thus leaving themselves open to discrimination that was legal under the GATT's rules. The codes were also incomplete. The Code on Subsidies and Countervailing Duties, for example, did not specify which forms of government intervention beyond direct export subsidies were to be considered trade barriers.[102] Even more serious was the failure to reach agreement on a safeguards code to bring rapidly proliferating VRAs under multilateral management. The pivotal, unresolvable issue in the safeguards negotiations was selectivity, the desire of some GATT contract-ing parties, most importantly the EU, to target safeguards measures instead of applying them in a non discriminatory manner.[103]

The efforts to extend trade management to include agriculture also met with little success. The negotiations were unable to reconcile two opposing views of the purpose and nature of international control in agriculture. The United States, because of its competitive advantage in agriculture, advocated liberalization of agricultural trade including the modification of the European Union's CAP. The EU, in contrast, urged the use of commodity agreements to stabilize world prices and long-term supply and refused to negotiate on the fundamentals of CAP. Japan was also unwilling to liberalize trade in agriculture. The result was thus minimal: an agreement to consult about certain agricultural problems, including those connected with meat and dairy products. The sectoral negotia-tions yielded only one important result: an agreement on civil aircraft that liber-alized trade in this industry. Finally, only limited progress was made on improving the GATT's dispute settlement mechanism. Thus, although the Tokyo Round agreement was an important step, it was only a limited one,[104] and it was to prove inadequate to stem burgeoning protectionist pressures.

GLOBALIZATION

The trading system had been transformed by the forces of globalization. International trade increased dramatically, creating ever greater interdependence. Furthermore, the nature of trade was transformed by increased trade in services and by trade-related intellectual property and new investments in high-technology industries. Globalization created conflicting political demands. On the one hand, there were calls for expansion of trade liberalization and international management of old and new trade issues. On the other hand, many groups demanded protection and a halt to the forces of globalization.

New Forms of Trade

One new form of trade arose from the growing importance of services in the national economies and international trade of the developed countries. **Services**, or **invisibles**, differed from goods in that they could not be stored and, therefore, required some form of direct relationship between the buyer and seller. International trade in services thus required some form of commercial presence in foreign markets. Consumer services were provided directly to retail customers by such businesses as restaurants, hotels, and travel agencies and tended to be produced, sold, and consumed within the same market. Producer services—banking, securities trading, insurance, law, advertising, accounting, data processing—were used in the intermediate production of manufactured goods and other services and were more frequently traded internationally.

In 1998, services accounted for about 65 percent of U.S. GDP and for more than 50 percent of the GNPs in twelve other developed countries.[105] Within the service sector, producer services experienced particularly rapid growth.[106] As the economies of the developed countries matured, services came to play an ever greater role in the production and distribution of goods.[107] During the 1970s and 1980s, services also became a major factor in international trade among developed countries.[108] The liberalization of goods and capital markets created business opportunities for firms trading in services, while the revolution in telecommunications and computer technologies made possible the rapid transmission of data at long distance and enabled services to be offered across national boundaries. In 1990, for example, U.S. exports of services amounted to $137 billion. By 1999, services exports totaled $254.7 billion.[109] Because of problems both in defining services and collecting data, worldwide exports of services were difficult to quantify with any degree of certainty. Many estimates put this figure around $600 billion.[110] Services accounted for between 20 percent[111] and 30 percent[112] of world trade.

Services trade grew despite widespread nontariff barriers. Many service industries, such as telecommunications, banking and insurance, and law and accounting, were highly regulated and often involved state-owned industry. Frequently, national regulation discriminated against foreign services providers by denying access to national markets or by imposing constraints on activities of foreign firms operating in domestic markets. Such barriers included discriminatory treatment of foreign firms in licensing and taxation; policies through which a section of the market was reserved for domestic industry; investment **performance requirements**; discriminatory government procurement; and government monopolies.[113] Barriers to trade in services had not been subject to the process of liberalization, because services were not covered by the GATT regime. Although there were efforts to establish liberalizing rules for such services as insurance in the OECD, by and large services remained outside the international trade regime.

As services grew in importance in the developed countries, service industries—particularly those in the United States and the United Kingdom—began to organize to press governments for adaptation of the trading regime to cover services. In the United States, for example, the service industry successfully pressed for a change in U.S. trade law to make trade rules and remedies applicable to services as well as goods.[114] As a result, services barriers began to receive greater attention in bilateral U.S. trade relations. The service sector in the developed countries also sought successfully to make the inclusion of services in the GATT a goal of the Uruguay Round of multilateral trade negotiations.

Intellectual property was another new trade issue that emerged in the late 1980s.[115] The comparative advantage of many of the most competitive industries of the developed market economies became increasingly dependent on their advanced technology, which was expensive and time-consuming to develop. Such technology could sometimes be easily and quickly copied and used to produce products at a much lower cost than that incurred by the developer, thus undermining the competitive ability of the firm that developed the technology. The cost of computer software, for example, derived largely from developmental costs. Yet such software could often be easily copied and sold at a price far below the cost to the developer. Similarly, the cost of developing pharmaceutical products was high, while drugs could be easily copied, produced, and sold below the cost to the developer.

For this reason, and to encourage the development of technology, most developed countries protect the developer of technology through patent, trademark, and **copyright** laws. However, intellectual property protection differed among the developed countries and frequently was nonexistent in developing countries. As high-technology firms increased in importance in trade and as their concern about intellectual property protection increased, they argued that **piracy**—the illegal copying of audio and video materials and computer software—undermined their ability to compete internationally and, thus, disrupted trade. Because efforts to standardize and expand protection for intellectual property through the **World Intellectual Property Organization (WIPO)** did not lead to common rules and dispute settlement procedures, they and their governments argued that the GATT should be broadened to cover intellectual property issues.

Finally, trade and investment issues began to merge in this period. Some developed countries also pressed for GATT rules to eliminate trade-restrictive and trade-distorting effects of government investment policies and practices.[116] **Trade-related investment measures (TRIMs)** included local content requirements, which required domestic sourcing; licensing requirements, which stipulated that an investor license production locally and often limit the amount of royalties; product mandating requirements, which obliged an investor to supply certain markets with specific products; trade-balancing requirements, which mandated arbitrary export or import levels; and export-performance requirements, which obliged an investor to export a percentage of its production.

The New Regionalism

Another change in the trading system which began in the 1980s was the movement away from multilateralism toward bilateral and regional arrangements. As multilateral reform seemed to stall (see below on the Uruguay Round), many countries turned to alternative trade agreements. The EU, the largest regional trading bloc, continued to expand taking in the former EFTA countries and reaching agreements with many central and eastern European countries on association and possible eventual membership in the EU.

At the same time, the United States moved in the direction of regional agreements for the Americas and the Pacific Rim. In the spring of 1990, President Carlos Salinas de Gortari of Mexico proposed negotiations for a free trade area with the United States. Motivated not just by economic interest but also by the desire for a stable and prosperous southern neighbor, the U.S. government accepted. Negotiations, which also included Canada, began formally in June 1991. The stated aims of the **North American Free Trade Area (NAFTA)** were to "eliminate barriers to trade, promote conditions of fair competition, increase investment opportunities, provide adequate protection for intellectual property rights, establish effective procedures for...[resolving]...disputes, and to further trilateral, regional and multilateral cooperation."[117]

The NAFTA agreement signed in December 1992 was far-reaching. It extended many of the provisions of the U.S.–Canada Free Trade Agreement to Mexico and, in many aspects, went well beyond that earlier agreement. NAFTA provided for the elimination of tariffs and other trade barriers on manufactured goods, including such sensitive products as textiles, autos, and auto parts. It was intended gradually to eliminate tariffs and other trade barriers to agricultural trade. NAFTA also included significant agreements for liberalizing trade in services, including special provisions for land transportation and financial services that had previously been closed to foreign access in Mexico. It provided for a liberal investment regime that included national treatment for North American firms and elimination of performance requirements, and it opened a number of previously reserved sectors to foreign direct investment. The agreement also increased the level of intellectual property protection in Mexico. Finally, NAFTA extended the U.S.–Canadian dispute settlement system to all three countries.[118]

NAFTA expanded the regional orientation of U.S. trade policy. At the same time, the agreement created an incentive for the completion of the Uruguay Round (see below). Furthermore, NAFTA became the opening shot in a major domestic U.S. debate linking trade issues with labor and environmental practices.

As trade with the NICs and other developing countries grew in the 1980s and 1990s, labor unions and their congressional supporters became concerned that labor practices such as the use of child and prison labor, and the denial of organizational rights to unions, gave developing countries a competitive advantage in labor-intensive production at the expense of American workers. Organized labor in the United States, and particularly their representatives in the AFL-CIO, saw linkages between trade agreements and foreign guarantees of labor rights as a way to advance the interests of their members internationally. Others supported this position because they opposed free trade generally and saw the debate over NAFTA as an opportunity to make their views known.[119]

At the same time, environmental groups sought to use the national debate over NAFTA to advance their concerns. Some environmentalists viewed new trade agreements as opportunities to alter the environmental laws and practices of other countries. These environmentalists had previously supported congressional legislation that imposed trade sanctions on countries that violated international agreements for the protection of endangered species.[120]

As a result of the new issues of labor and environment, securing ratification of NAFTA in the U.S. Congress was one of the more difficult tasks undertaken by the Clinton administration in its first year in office. Many in the president's own political party opposed the agreement because of concern about its effect on domestic employment. Others argued that free trade with Mexico would lead to further degradation of the environment, especially along the U.S.–Mexican border. As a candidate in 1992, Governor Bill Clinton had criticized the agreement because it did not include labor and environmental provisions and vowed to negotiate additional agreements to cover these issues. As president in 1993, he reopened negotiations with Mexico and Canada to do so.

In the summer of 1993, the NAFTA agreement was modified to include new side agreements on **environmental and labor practices**. An agreement on the environment provided for the effective implementation of national environmental laws and cross-border cooperation to address pollution problems and to develop and finance border **infrastructure**. Another side agreement on workers' rights provided for the implementation of national labor laws and for cooperation on occupational, health, and safety standards, child labor, labor statistics, labor-management relations, and worker training.[121] Organized labor and some environmental groups continued to oppose even modified agreement, however. Congressional ratification of NAFTA in November 1993 was made possible only by bipartisan support for the agreement.

Following the ratification of NAFTA, a number of countries in the Western Hemisphere sought access to the new trade area. Many countries of Latin America and the Caribbean were already removing trade barriers among themselves. For example, Argentina, Brazil, Paraguay, and Uruguay formed a customs union known as **Mercosur** (Mercosul in Portuguese) and Mexico negotiated free-trade agreements modeled loosely on NAFTA with Colombia and Venezuela. In December 1994, at the Summit of the Americas, a meeting of thirty-four democratically elected leaders of the hemisphere, the participants agreed to work toward a free-trade area of the Americas by the year 2005.[122]

Movement toward regional trade liberalization was also occurring in the Asian and Pacific region. In 1992, the six members of the **Association of South East Asian Nations (ASEAN)**—Brunei, Indonesia, Malaysia, Singapore, the Philippines, and Thailand—committed themselves to create a free-trade area by 2003. Then in 1994, the **Asia Pacific Economic Cooperation (APEC)** Forum, consisting of eighteen countries bordering on the Pacific Ocean, agreed to work toward free trade and investment in the region by 2020.[123]

Bilateralism also increased during this period. The U.S. and Japanese governments negotiated numerous bilateral accords under the MOSS, SII, and Framework agreements. These were multilateralized under the GATT's MFN rules. The EU entered into negotiations for agreements with a number of countries in the Mediterranean region.

As regional and bilateral arrangements proliferated, concern increased that the multilateral system might fragment into preferential trading blocs. While regional and bilateral agreements are appropriate ways to pursue the goal of free trade, they can become exclusive and trade-distorting if they are not constrained by a strong multilateral system. The future direction of the trading system thus depended on the ability of the major trading nations to modernize the GATT and to continue the process of multilateral liberalization.

The Uruguay Round

Because of growing globalization, pressures on the GATT system increased. Departures from GATT rules, such as voluntary export restraints, grew; the agriculture trade war erupted; and trade conflicts became more frequent and more heated. Nevertheless, the postwar political consensus supporting open trade remained alive, if not well. The leaders of the developed countries used economic summit and OECD meetings to reiterate their commitment to open trade principles and to resolving specific conflicts, even as they negotiated managed-trade agreements. New forms of international dialogue were tried. Bilateral meetings, most notably between the United States and Japan, were used to try to resolve specific trade conflicts. Multilateral meetings, such as regular quadrilateral meetings of the United States, Japan, the European Union, and Canada, which came to be known as the **Quad**, were begun to try to resolve systemic issues.

The precarious nature of the multilateral trading regime was revealed in 1982, when the GATT held its first ministerial meeting since the 1973 meeting that launched the Tokyo Round. The agenda of the meeting was ambitious: a review of the Tokyo codes on nontarriff barriers; action on GATT dispute-settlement procedures; continuation of the negotiations on a safeguards code; efforts to bring agriculture under the GATT regime; and consideration of new codes on trade in high technology and services. The government officials attending the meeting pledged only to "make determined efforts" to ensure that their countries' trade policies were consistent with the GATT's rules.[124] Perhaps the most positive result of the ministerial meeting was the widening recognition that the international trading system faced collapse.

The following year, the Reagan administration, aided by the economic recovery in the United States, supported by the Prime Minister of Japan and the GATT secretariat, began a campaign to launch a new round of multilateral trade negotiations. Initially the EU, confronted with severe unemployment and recession, argued that the time was not right. However, in 1985, the world's trade officials agreed to launch a new round of multilateral trade negotiations and established a committee to develop an agenda.

In September 1986, a special session of the GATT contracting parties meeting in Punta del Este, Uruguay, officially launched the negotiations, which came to be known as the Uruguay Round and set a target date of 1990 for their completion. The Uruguay Round negotiations, which began in 1987, marked a new effort by the developed countries to devise new rules and institutions for managing the new global trading system. The ministerial declaration issued at Punta del Este instituted a standstill on new trade-restrictive or distorting measures and called for the elimination by the end of the Uruguay Round of measures inconsistent with the provisions of the GATT. The trade ministers also established fifteen negotiating groups that fell into four broad categories.

One group focused on issues that had been taken up in earlier negotiating rounds, including those (such as tariffs) that had long been on the GATT agenda as well as others (such as subsidies and safeguards) that had not been resolved satisfactorily in the Tokyo Round. Most important, and perhaps most difficult, among these issues were safeguards. As we have seen, the GATT rules on safeguards were ineffective and relatively easy to circumvent through new protectionist measures, such as voluntary restraint agreements (VRAs). Although the 1986 ministerial declaration called for "a comprehensive agreement on safeguards," the political difficulty of reaching such an agreement remained significant. As in the Tokyo Round, the central conflict centered on selectivity. The EU insisted on the need for selectivity. The United States advocated safeguards taken either on a most-favored-nation or "consensual selectivity" basis. The developing countries—for whom the safeguards negotiations were a top priority in the Uruguay Round—strongly advocated the most-favored-nation position.

A second set of negotiations focused on concerns of developing countries, such as tropical products, natural resource–based products, textiles, and clothing. Due to the increasingly active role of the developing countries in the GATT, successful completion of these negotiations was essential to their continued involvement in the GATT system (see Chapter 7).

A third set of negotiating groups had mandates to reform existing GATT rules or mechanisms. Dissatisfaction with existing GATT dispute settlement mechanisms had been mounting for years. Countries were able to delay or block resolution of a dispute; there was no effective mechanism for enforcing decisions or overseeing their implementation; and protection of third countries affected by the dispute was inadequate. The ministerial declaration at Punta del Este instructed the negotiating group on dispute settlement to "improve and strengthen the rules and procedures of the dispute settlement process." Negotiations moved rapidly in this negotiating group due to broad agreement on the need to expedite dispute settlement procedures and to the absence of any significant North-South division. By

the end of 1988, negotiators had agreed on several measures to streamline procedures and speed up decisions in the dispute settlement process. These reforms were
implemented on a provisional basis in 1989.

The negotiations on the **functioning of the GATT system (FOGS)** were
intended to strengthen the role of GATT as an institution. The negotiating
group focused on ways to enhance GATT surveillance of trade policies and practices; to improve the overall effectiveness and decision making of the GATT by
involving ministers; and to strengthen the GATT's relationship with the IMF
and World Bank. Because there was a significant degree of consensus on what
needed to be done, negotiations on FOGS proceeded smoothly. By the end of
1988, agreement was reached on the establishment of a new trade policy review
mechanism to examine and publicize national trade policies on a regular basis.
Negotiators agreed to begin implementing this mechanism in 1989 rather than
wait until the conclusion of the Uruguay Round.

Finally, some groups sought to broaden the scope of the GATT to cover non-
traditional areas. One of the most significant and controversial decisions made at
Punta del Este was the agreement to include the so-called new issues—services,
intellectual property rights, and investment—in the round. The opposition to their
inclusion was led by a small group of developing countries, which feared that
GATT rules developed for the new issues could be used by the industrialized
countries to overwhelm their fledgling industries and to undermine domestic policies that the developing countries considered critical to their national economic
development. They argued that the Uruguay Round should concentrate instead
on unfinished business from the Tokyo Round and on reform in areas where
the GATT had clearly failed to impose adequate international discipline, such as
safeguards, textiles, and agriculture. They also insisted that the GATT was not
the appropriate forum for the new issues that, they argued, came under the purview of other organizations, such as WIPO for intellectual property or the United
Nations for investment.

The industrialized nations stressed the need to modernize the GATT by
broadening its scope to deal with new areas of trade. As in previous GATT
rounds, the United States took the initiative in pushing aggressively for the
inclusion of services, intellectual property rights, and investment in the Uruguay
Round. The EU and Japan supported the U.S. position, but they were not
entirely convinced of the wisdom of increasing the burden on the GATT at a
time when so many longstanding problems had yet to be resolved. They also
shared some of the concerns of the developing countries about the extent to
which GATT rules in the new areas might impinge on their sovereignty in
domestic regulation and government policy. In the case of investment in particular,
they questioned the appropriateness of using the GATT as the forum for management. Finally, while there was a consensus among the developed countries
about the principles that would cover some of the new issues (especially services
and intellectual property), it proved difficult to come to agreement on specific
details of the application of those principles.

Over the years considerable progress was made toward agreement on various
matters under negotiation. Yet, by 1993, the Uruguay Round seemed headed

toward failure. At the beginning of the talks, it looked as if the main conflict would be between the rich and poor nations. But as the 1980s wore on, most of the developing nations moved toward more export-oriented development strategies that depended upon an expansion of overseas markets, which would only be possible with a new trade agreement. At the same time, important lines of cleavage developed among the industrialized nations.

Disagreements over agricultural subsidies were the most contentious and almost resulted in the failure of the Uruguay Round. At the beginning of the Uruguay Round, the U.S. government ambitiously proposed phasing out all direct farm subsidies and farm trade protection within a decade. The **Cairns group**—a coalition of fourteen smaller producing nations from both developed and developing regions (including Argentina, Australia, Canada, Hungary, and Malaysia among others)—advocated a similar approach.[125] Japan opposed the U.S. approach, but generally tried to keep a low profile.

The EU accepted the need to reduce subsidies, but viewed the U.S. proposal as highly unrealistic, advocating instead an approach that would allow it to maintain its Common Agricultural Policy. In fact, the EU was divided internally on the issue of subsidies with France and Germany whose farmers benefited from subsidies aligned against countries like the United Kingdom where agriculture was not a significant part of the economy. Not until 1992 when EU members reached an internal agreement to reduce subsidies were parties able to make progress on negotiations to reduce agricultural subsidies.

Finally, in 1993, the newly elected U.S. president, Bill Clinton, made the completion of the Uruguay Round a high priority for his administration. He asked for and received fast-track negotiating authority from Congress that expired on December 15, 1993. In addition, Clinton administration initiatives in convening a meeting to promote Asia Pacific Economic Cooperation (APEC) in Seattle, Washington, in November 1993 had the desired effect of raising fears in Europe that the United States would proceed without Europe if necessary to secure new arrangements for trade. U.S. initiatives, together with the appointment of Peter Sutherland as the new GATT secretary general, created the impetus for a successful resolution of the remaining differences between the United States and the EU.

Between December 1 and December 15, 1993, negotiations were conducted in earnest for the completion of the Uruguay Round. A number of breakthroughs occurred on contentious issues including agricultural subsidies, audio-visual services (film and television), and financial services. Director General Sutherland then declared the Uruguay Round successfully concluded on December 15. The agreement was signed by delegates from 124 countries on April 15, 1994, in Marrakesh, Morocco, and entered into force on January 1, 1995.

The Marrakesh Agreement

The agreement signed at Marrakesh was a 400-page document accompanied by roughly 22,000 pages of detailed tariff schedules. The agreement established a new entity called the **World Trade Organization (WTO)** in Geneva, which would assume the functions of the old GATT Secretaria, and new procedures including a binding dispute settlement mechanism. The Marrakesh agreement also provided for further cuts in tariffs, significant reductions in agricultural subsidies, elimination of textile and apparel quotas over ten years, new trade rules for services, intellectual property, and trade-related investment.

The most comprehensive of all GATT trade agreements, the Uruguay Round agreement broke new ground in a number of areas. It improved market access in many sectors by reducing tariff and nontariff barriers. The agreement cut tariffs on manufactured products by over one-third. It provided for the gradual elimination of the Multi-Fiber Arrangement (MFA) under which quotas were imposed limiting developing country textile exports to developing countries. The Uruguay Round agreement also expanded the number of agencies and products covered by the government procurement code negotiated in the Tokyo Round.

The agreement also extended the world trade regime to agriculture in a meaningful way for the first time. While many agricultural barriers remained, the agreement improved market access for many agricultural products. It provided for the elimination of quotas and their replacement by tariffs (known as **tariffication**), which in turn could be reduced over time in a straightforward manner. The agreement also established limits on export and agricultural subsidies that distort trade.

The process of rules development begun in the Tokyo Round was expanded. Although the Marrakesh Agreement did not eliminate the use of antidumping laws as a nontariff barrier, it did improve the code on antidumping measures to improve transparency, and suggested new and better methods for measuring the extent of dumping and new procedural rules to prevent the abuse of national antidumping laws. The agreement on **Subsidies and Countervailing Measures (SCM)** significantly improved upon the Tokyo Round code by expanding the list of prohibited practices, increasing the disciplines on subsidies, and broadening the coverage to all GATT members. The Marrakesh agreement also included an **Agreement on Safeguards**, which defined when countries could impose temporary restrictions to deal with surges in imports that threatened serious injury to a domestic industry.

The Uruguay Round also modernized the international trading system by establishing rules for new issues: services, intellectual property, and investment. The agreement applied the traditional rules of international trade, including national treatment and MFN, to services and provided for greater market access in many service sectors, including advertising, accounting, engineering, finance, information and computer services, and tourism.

The **General Agreement on Trade in Services (GATS)** had two parts: the framework agreement containing the general rules and disciplines; and the national "schedules" which listed individual countries' specific commitments on access to their domestic markets by foreign suppliers. Each WTO member listed in its national schedule those services for which it wished to guarantee access to foreign suppliers. All commitments applied on a non discriminatory basis to all other members. There was complete freedom to choose which services to commit. In addition to the services committed, the schedules limited the degree to which foreign services providers could operate in the market. For example, a country making a commitment to allow foreign banks to operate in its territory might limit the number of banking licenses to be granted (a market access limitation). It might also limit the number of branches a foreign bank might open (a national treatment limitation).[126] The hope was that by establishing a formal list of of commitments, there could be a general movement over time through sequential negotiations toward more liberal market access for and more extensive national treatment of foreign firms.

The negotiations on **trade-related aspects of intellectual property rights (TRIPs)** led to the establishment of comprehensive trade rules to protect copyrights, patents, trademarks, and industrial designs. The agreement incorporated national treatment and MFN and dealt with such problems as compulsory licensing. However, to satisfy the developing countries, it allowed for relatively long periods for phasing in the new rules.[127] The agreement on trade-related investment measures (TRIMs) took a first step toward developing international rules on investment. It prohibited measures such as local content, trade balancing, and foreign exchange balancing requirements. The TRIMs agreement was incomplete, however, because even though it did apply national treatment principles, it did not include MFN provisions and did not adequately deal with the important questions connected with the right of establishment and the use of investment incentives.

A number of issues that could not be settled by the end of the Uruguay Round continued to be negotiated after the signing of the Marrakech agreement. In 1997, the Basic Telecommunications and Financial Services Agreements were completed and signed. At the 1998 ministerial meeting in Geneva, WTO members agreed to study trade issues arising from global **electronic commerce**.

New Trade Challenges

Following the conclusion of the Uruguay Round and partly because of its success, the World Trade Organization, the Marrakesh agreement, and subsequent Uruguay Round agreements became the foundation for further globalization of world trade. International and national liberalization of markets combined with the application of new information and computing technologies made international flow of capital, people, and ideas much easier and less expensive. The ability of multinational corporations to operate on a truly global basis was greatly enhanced (see Chapter 4). Developing countries and formerly communist countries joined the global trading system and the WTO (See Chapters 6 and 8). China and Taiwan joined the WTO in 2001 and 2002, respectively, bringing the percentage of the world's population covered by the WTO agreements to 97 percent (see Table 3.3).[128]

A number of important issues on the trade agenda remained unresolved. Despite significant progress, agriculture remained highly protected. Barriers to trade in agriculture were of particular concern to the developing countries

TABLE 3.3   WTO Members Joining Between 2001 and 2007

Country	Year
Armenia	2003
Cambodia	2004
China	2001
Lithuania	2001
Macedonia	2003
Moldova	2001
Nepal	2004
Saudi Arabia	2005
Taiwan	2002
Vietnam	2007

SOURCE: World Trade Organization.

who felt that they had made many concessions and had hoped for reciprocal concessions in agricultural trade. Antidumping and safeguards measures were only partially controlled by the new WTO agreements. The continued diffusion of national antidumping laws would result in inconsistencies and a greater demand for harmonization and dispute settlement at the global level. The WTO's **Dispute Settlement Understandings (DSU)** were more ambitious than those of the GATT and were criticized for being overly legalistic.[129] The agreements on services, intellectual property, and investment measures had gaps in coverage that, according to some critics, needed to be closed.[130]

Furthermore, the significant reduction in tariffs and nontariff barriers as a result of the Uruguay Round exposed a new set of national policies which affected trade flows. One such issue was competition policy. As traditional barriers to trade fell, different national laws and regulations regarding competition or antitrust policy emerged as obstacles to free trade. Despite the reduction of tariffs and other barriers to trade, foreign entrants still faced powerful, even dominant, local competitors who followed practices that restrained trade. Yet there were no international rules or practices regarding competition policy. Definitions of **cartels** and restraint of trade differed significantly from country to country, regulatory structures varied widely, and national remedies differed in effectiveness.

Another new issue was electronic commerce. While electronic commerce moved relatively freely across national boundaries, there were barriers to the open use of telecommunications infrastructure—the hardware and software that made e-commerce possible. A Declaration on Global Economic Commerce was adopted in May 1998 at the Geneva Ministerial Meeting of the WTO. The members of the WTO promised to continue their current practice of not imposing customs duties on electronic commerce. A work program was established by the WTO General Council on September 25, 1998, to deal with this issue.

Another set of unresolved issues concerned the link between trade and social policy, especially environmental and labor policy. Concerns about the relationship between trade and the environment began to surface in the 1980s and, as we have seen, played a role in the negotiations for a North American Free Trade Agreement. Environmentalists expressed concern that liberal international trade regimes could result in **environmental dumping**—that is, the placement of the most environmentally destructive activities in countries with the least restrictive environmental regulations, thus forcing all other countries down to the standard set by the least environmentally conscious countries (also called a **race to the bottom**).[131] They were also concerned that WTO rules interfered with national environmental laws and regulations, which might have a trade distorting impact.

One particular concern is the use of trade measures to restrict the importation of products that were obtained or produced using environmentally undesirable methods of production. The most celebrated example was the attempt by the United States in the early 1990s to restrict the importation from Mexico of canned tuna that had been obtained by the use of nets that many consumers in the United States considered to be harmful to dolphins.[132] The nets in question did not permit dolphins to escape when the tuna were being hauled in. Since U.S. law mandated the use of nets that did not result in unnecessary dolphin deaths and since U.S. producers were not allowed to market tuna caught by the old method in the United States, the legal regime governing domestic tuna products was extended to imported products in the form of a total ban on the sale of those products. The Mexican government protested and took the case to the WTO. The WTO ruled against the United States in this case, provoking some environmentalists to assert that free trade and environmental protection were inherently incompatible.

The key issue at stake in the Dolphin/Tuna cases and other high profile trade and environment cases brought before WTO panels was the question of whether the WTO agreements forbade members to make trade policies that dealt with the method of manufacturing or processing of goods. The legal argument that carried the day for Mexico in the Dolphin/Tuna case was that trade policies should only concern characteristics of the goods and services involved in trade and not the methods by which they were produced. To do otherwise gave too many opportunities to countries that wanted to discriminate against the trade of other WTO members, thus undermining the core goal of nondiscrimination.

More recently, concerns about global climate change caused by the burning of fossil fuels intensified efforts to identify ways in which the trade regime could be modified to encourage reduced emissions of greenhouse gases like carbon dioxide. Measures to address global warming through carbon taxes, carbon offset programs, and the establishment of cap-and-trade systems for emissions of carbon dioxide might be facilitated by appropriate changes in the trade regime. The current regime does not encourage transportation of goods via ocean shipping, the most carbon-efficient method, and does not discourage transportation via air freight, the least carbon-efficent method. As China joins the major polluters, most of whom are industrialized countries, because of its high growth rate and heavy dependence on coal, new agreements on trade might help to reduce the trend toward global warming.[133]

A final set of challenges involved the functioning of the WTO. Like the IMF and the World Bank, the WTO is an **intergovernmental organization** whose members are national governments and whose participants and decision makers are representatives of those governments. A number of **nongovernmental organizations (NGOs)**, including environmental groups like the Sierra Club and the World Wildlife Federation, called for reform of the WTO to make it possible for interest groups to participate along with governments in WTO decisions. These international NGOs argued that the world economy requires a more democratic form of governance, like that in most democratic countries, in which NGOs and other interest groups can lobby for favored policies and participate directly in forums for policy deliberation. Giving interest groups greater access to the WTO, they contend, would bolster democracy by enabling greater citizen participation in governance. Those calling for such reforms argued that global society should develop the same sort of vigorous private sector that fostered democracy at that national level, and that the WTO and other international organizations should adopt policies to permit direct participation by NGOs. Other groups and governments disagreed, arguing that NGOs already had access to decision making through their national governments and national decision processes and that it was appropriate and necessary to maintain the intergovernmental nature of the WTO.[134]

There were also demands for greater transparency in the operations of the WTO. The term "transparency" refers to the ability of citizens to hold government officials accountable for their actions.[135] What this meant in practice was that the WTO was being asked to make documents, including drafts of treaties more widely available to the general public, to hold meetings in forums where the public could at least observe if not participate in the proceedings, and to better publicize the results of meetings and negotiations. Those advocating greater transparency claimed that it was a prerequisite for more democratic governance.[136]

The success of the Uruguay Round led to the mobilization of a variety of antiglobalization groups, mostly based in the North and mostly focusing on environmental and labor issues. The political left embraced the cause of reversing globalization, slowing it down, or at least giving it a more human face. Antiglobalization groups increasingly criticized intergovernmental institutions like the IMF and the WTO which make important decisions regarding the world economy for being insufficiently democratic. Many NGOs wanted some form of direct participation in the deliberations of those organizations rather than relying solely on national governments for the policies they favored. In order to continue the process of liberalization and improving international economic governance, those responsible for shaping the trade system would have to address these issues of governance and legitimation.

Shifting Power Relationships

In the 1990s, the relationship among the three major trading countries evolved. One dramatic change was the resurgence of United States economic power. The restructuring of U.S. industry, the dominance of the United States in the new information and telecommunications technologies, the flexibility of the U.S. econ-

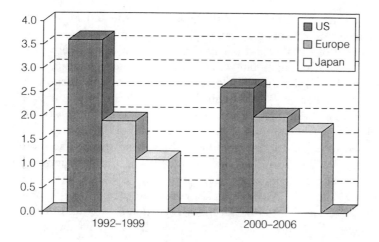

FIGURE 3.7 Average Real GDP Growth Rates in the United States, Europe and Japan, 1992–2006

SOURCE: OECD.Stat., http://stats.oecd.org/.

omy, and its macroeconomic health led to the primacy, if not hegemony, of the United States in international economic relations. The average annual growth rate of real GDP in the United States between 1992 and 1999 was 3.6 percent. This compared quite favorably with an average of 1.9 percent in the EU15 and 1.1 percent in Japan.[137] Between 2000 and 2006, the United States continued to growth more rapidly than the Euro zone and Japan (see Figure 3.7).

In the personal computer (PC) industry, for example, U.S. firms led the world and dominated many related segments including microprocessors, operating systems, and packaged software. U.S. firms held the greatest share of world shipments for PC systems. Among the top ten PC makers, U.S. firms held a 59-percent share of the world market in 1985 and 40 percent in 1995. In microprocessors, most of the high value-added design and engineering activities took place in the United States. U.S. companies controlled about 75 percent of the packaged software industry overall, and virtually 100 percent of the operating system market. The vast majority of PC software was developed in the United States.[138]

At the same time, there was a growing inability of the United States to lead the trading system. Domestic political conflict over the future of trade policy proved the most significant stumbling block. Some constituencies advocated expanded trade liberalization and development of international rules on issues like competition policy and investment, expansion of the WTO to include new members especially China, and development of the WTO's institutional system. Others pressed for greater focus on the new agenda—trade and environment, trade and labor rights. Still others argued that globalization was benefitting the few and needed to have a more human face.

A second change in the trading regime was the economic weakness of Japan. As was discussed in Chapter 2, the Japanese economy entered a period of **stagnation** in the early 1990s that lasted through the decade and spilled into the next millennium. Trade remained a mainstay of the Japanese economy, but fluctuations in the value of the yen and the growing economic competitiveness of other East Asian countries, including China, cut into the growth rate of Japanese exports and forced Japanese multinationals to move production to lower-wage regions (see Chapter 4). Although the Japanese economy improved after 2000, it was no longer seen as a major competitive threat to the rest of the industrialized world.

Europe continued to expand in membership, while trying to become more internally integrated. The EMU was created along with a common currency (although only twelve of fifteen member states joined the EMU at first). Ties with Eastern Europe and the Mediterranean countries were strengthened. Eurosclerosis finally ended in the 1990s but growth remained lower and unemployment higher than in the United States. Still, Europe had a new vitality and a new sense of direction that had been lacking in the 1980s.

International trade politics clearly reflected this shift in power among the developed countries. The United States returned to the kind of leadership in international economic affairs that had typified the period after the end of World War II. One key difference, however, was that it no longer had a high level of domestic agreement on the benefits of free trade. It was no longer possible for the U.S. government to depend on the support of organized labor for further liberalization of trade. There were also many domestic business and environmental groups who opposed further trade liberalization. It was more difficult to obtain approval from Congress for fast-track negotiating authority.

Negotiations for the **Free Trade Area of the Americas (FTAA)** continued at the technical level although the absence of U.S. fast-track authority slowed the negotiations significantly.[139] The APEC process continued but even more slowly following the Asian financial crisis which began in 1997. A number of bilateral free trade agreements were also negotiated. Along with EU agreements with Eastern Europe and the Mediterranean, the U.S. negotiated a free trade agreement with Jordan and Japan with Singapore.

However, the main emphasis of trade policy remained at the multilateral level. This was partly because the Uruguay Round agreement established timetables for negotiation of unresolved issues by WTO members. The so-called **built-in agenda** of the WTO included mandates to complete negotiations on liberalizing agricultural and services trade and to develop rules on government procurement and subsidies by 1999. In addition to fulfilling the Uruguay Round mandates, countries also sought to address the other post-Uruguay Round trade problems including the functioning of the WTO, older trade problems especially anti-dumping practices, as well as the new agenda issues.

It was in the hope of launching a new millennial round to address these issues that trade ministers accepted a U.S. invitation to meet in Seattle, Washington, in December 1999. That ministerial meeting was a political failure. The delegates were unable to agree on a new round of multilateral trade negotiations. The failure of the Seattle meeting was due in small part to what became known as the **Battle in Seattle**, protests staged by antiglobalization groups at the time of the meeting. The groups that demonstrated in Seattle were not a unified movement but a coalition of diverse interests that opposed various aspects of the multilateral system. Some advocated greater attention to environmental issues in the trade regime; others highlighted the negative impact of trade liberalization on poor people and workers. Some wanted to work within the system; others wanted to destroy it.[140]

Examples of radical groups that participated in the Seattle demonstrations were the Rainforest Action Network, the Ruckus Society, Direct Action Network, Mobilization for Social Justice, Corporate Watch, and Fifty Years is Enough. Examples of more mainstream groups that participated in the demonstrations were Public Citizen, the German Green Party, the AFL-CIO, the Teamsters, the Sierra Club, and the Service Employees International Union (SEIU). The extensive media coverage of the violence connected with police efforts to contain the more unruly demonstrators in Seattle led many people to believe that the talks were unsuccessful because of the demonstrations. This was not the case. The Seattle meeting failed mainly because of differences among the WTO members themselves and their resulting inability to agree on an agenda for future negotiations. Negotiators were unable to resolve profound conflicts among the developed countries on issues such as agriculture, tariffs, antidumping, competition policy, and investment. As a result, the developed countries were divided and unable to provide leadership for the meeting.

The Doha Round

The Doha Round was launched at the WTO's Fourth Ministerial Conference in Doha, Qatar, November 8–14, 2001, two months after the Al Qaeda attacks on the World Trade Tower and the Pentagon.[141] The formal name was the Doha Development Round, reflecting the belief of the developing countries that the Uruguay Round had not dealt adequately with issues that concerned them. In the two years following the Battle in Seattle, a number of econometric studies were completed that demonstrated the large potential benefits to the world economy from liberalizing trade in agriculture. There were at least 20 negotiating areas in the Doha Round, but the most prominent ones were agricultural trade liberalization and nonagricultural market access (NAMA). The governments of the industrialized countries wanted lower tariffs on industrial products in the emerging market economies (especially Brazil, China, and India) and were willing to commit to trade liberalization in agriculture to secure these concessions.[142] The end of March 2003, was set as the deadline for reaching agreement on "modalities" (targets, formulas, and timetables) for the round; the round itself was to conclude on January 1, 2005.

The Fifth Ministerial Conference of the WTO was held in Cancún, Mexico, in September 2003. The United States and the EU had reached an agreement on a broad framework for negotiating agricultural trade liberalization, but the G-20 (which included Brazil, China, India, and South Africa) produced a counterproposal excluding developing countries from agricultural liberalization. The industrialized countries wanted to expand the agenda to include competition policies and investment, but the developing countries did not. As a result, the Cancún meeting ended without an agreement. The goal of concluding the round by 2005 was deemed unrealistic.

In July 2004, the members of the WTO agreed on the Doha Work Program.[143] The Work Program set a deadline of July 2005 for completing a draft of the modalities for agriculture. In October 2005, in the hopes of giving the round a boost, U.S. Trade Representative Robert Portman submitted a proposal to reduce agricultural subsidies in the industrialized nations. This was, to some extent, an effort to highlight the fact that subsidies were higher in Europe and Japan than in the United States, a strategem not lost on the Europeans and the Japanese.

The main type of agricultural subsidy used in the United States involves payment to farmers who agree not to grow certain crops. This is done to support price levels by reducing supply. In Europe, the main type of agriculture subsidy involves direct payments to farmers to guarantee minimum prices. In Japan, rice farmers are subsidized through a price support program whereby the government purchases all domestic production at a guaranteed price (that is about eight times the international price) and then sells it to Japanese consumers at lower prices. Because of the great expense of operating this kind of subsidy progam, the Japanese government is forced to maintain quantitative restrictions on imports of rice from abroad. The OECD estimated the aggregate size of agricultural subsidies in 2004 to be around $114 billion in Europe, $60 billion in the United States, and $50 billion in Japan.[144]

In the United States and Europe, the vast majority of funds go to large agricultural concerns, not to small farms, but in all three regions there are strong political coalitions supporting the subsidy programs. Major reforms of the EU's Common Agricultural Policy (CAP) after 2000 reduced the overall size of the CAP and virtually eliminated agricultural export subsidy programs. The EU's internal debate on agricultural subsidies helped to create a better negotiating environment, but in the end the EU did not come forward with a generous proposal to reduce subsidies in the Doha Round. This forced the industrialized countries to admit that the round could not be completed in 2005 as planned.

The WTO Director-General, Pascal Lamy, produced his own draft agreement for discussion at the Hong Kong ministerial meeting which reflected prior disagreements over modalities. This draft was adopted with minor changes in Hong Kong on December 18, 2005.[145] The next modalities meeting took place in Geneva, Switzerland, in July 2006. These talks did not resolve the key issues, despite the fact that the trade promotion authority granted to President Bush under the Trade Act of 2002 was due to expire on June 1, 2007. On July 24, 2006, Pascal Lamy recommended a suspension of the negotiations "to enable serious reflection by participants which is clearly necessary."[146]

The G-4 (the United States, the EU, Brazil, and India) negotiated through the winter of 2006 and the spring of 2007 but still could not reach an agreement. The G-4 negotiations broke down again in Potsdam, Germany, in June 2007. The United States government blamed the governments of Brazil and India for the impasse, while the latter countered that the U.S. had not gone far enough in its proposals to reduce agricultural subsidies to justify concessions on their part on opening their markets to imports.

In February 2008, New Zealand's Ambassador Crawford Falconer, chair of the WTO agricultural negotiating group, released a revised draft agreement on the modalities for agriculture.[147] While a significant number of major differences remained to be resolved, this draft suggested that substantial progress finally had been made. When the WTO ministerial talks resumed in May 2008, there were some who were optimistic that the Doha Round was nearing its conclusion. Others remained pessimistic that the Round would end successfully.[148]

One potential consequence of a failed round would be an increase in bilateral and regional trade agreements. The United States, for example, had bilateral free trade agreements (FTAs) with fourteen countries: Israel, Canada, Mexico, Jordan, Chile, Singapore, Australia, Morocco, the Dominican Republic, El Salvador, Guatemala, Honduras, Nicaragua, and Bahrain. Three FTAs awaiting Congressional approval in 2008 were with Colombia, Panama, and South Korea. FTAs with Peru and Oman were awaiting implementation.[149] The EU had regional trade agreements with the African, Caribbean, and Pacific (ACP) countries—the current one was the **Cotonou Agreement** (see Chapter 7)—and eleven other regions and bilateral trade agreements with thirty–three countries, including the United States, Mexico, Canada, and Japan.[150] During a major trade round, these bilateral and regional agreements are used to establish precedents for the next multilateral regime, but are also seen as insurance in case of the collapse of a round. If the Doha Round collapses, the number of bilateral and regional agreements will increase and the existing arrangements will be deepened.

CONCLUSIONS

The multilateral trade regime represented by the WTO was the result of a series of efforts beginning in the period immediately following World War II to create multilateral institutions to foster an open, liberal trading system. During the Bretton Woods System, these efforts were primarily initiatives of the U.S. government. During the period of interdependence, the rules of the trade regime evolved as trade exapanded and as other countries became serious competitors of the United States in world markets. Despite the challenges of interdependence, the Tokyo Round was successful in expanding and modernizing the trading regime. Similarly, during the period of globalization, the Uruguay Round successfully addressed both old and new challenges, including agriculture, nontariff barriers, new trade issues, and the growing potential for regionalization of world trade. The positive outcomes of the Tokyo and Uruguay Rounds were not a foregone conclusion. Serious differences existed and continue to exist over important issues like agriculture, services, telecommunications, intellectual property, antidumping, and nontariff barriers. The Doha Round and its successors would have to address these issues.

The trade regime was responsible, along with related regimes for the international monetary system and foreign direct investment, for fostering a world economy that was more open and liberal than it had been since the onset of

World War I. Its very success in doing so, however, resulted in a widespread debate over globalization and the rise of new political movements that opposed it. In the next chapter, we will argue that the growth in the power and presence of multinational corporations also made for a more open world economy while intensifying the political debate over globalization.

ENDNOTES

1. E. E. Schattschneider, *Politics, Pressures and the Tariff* (Englewood Cliffs, N.J.: Prentice-Hall, 1935). See also I. M. Destler, *American Trade Politics*, 4th edition (Washington, D.C.: Institute for International Economics, 2005); Fiona McGillivray, *Privileging Industry: The Comparative Politics of Trade and Industrial Policy* (Princeton, N.J.: Princeton University Press, 2004); Philip A. Mundo, *National Politics in a Global Economy: The Domestic Sources of U.S. Trade Policy* (Washington, D.C.: Georgetown University Press, 1999); Robert A. Pastor, *Congress and the Politics of U.S. Foreign Economic Policy, 1929–1976* (Berkeley and Los Angeles, Calif.: University of California Press, 1976); and Stephanie Ann Lenway, *The Politics of U.S. International Trade: Protection, Expansion and Escape* (Marshfield, Mass.: Pitman, 1985).

2. The current term is **trade promotion authority**.

3. The analysis in this chapter concentrates on trade relations among developed market economies. For issues involving the underdeveloped countries, see Chapter 6 of this text; for East-West trade issues, see Chapter 10.

4. See, for example, Richard N. Gardner, *Sterling-Dollar Diplomacy in Current Perspective: The Origins and Prospects of Our International Economic Order* (New York, N.Y.: Columbia University Press, 1980), p. 9; Harold B. Hinton, *Cordell Hull: A Biography* (Garden City, N.Y.: Doubleday, 1942); Michael A. Butler, *Cautious Visionary: Cordell Hull and Trade Reform, 1933–1937* (Kent, Ohio: Kent State University Press, 1998); and Walter LaFeber, *The American Age: U.S. Foreign Policy at Home and Abroad*, vol. 2, 2nd ed. (New York, N.Y.: Norton, 1994), 372–373.

5. U.S. Department of State, *Proposals for the Expansion of World Trade and Employment* (December 1945); and U.S. Department of State, *Suggested Charter for an International Trade Organization of the United Nations* (September 1946).

6. Gardner, *Sterling-Dollar Diplomacy*; Clair Wilcox, *A Charter for World Trade* (New York, N.Y.: Macmillan, 1949). The trade charter was not exclusively an American idea; British planners were also closely involved in the process. See E. F. Penrose, *Economic Planning for the Peace* (Princeton, N.J.: Princeton University Press, 1953).

7. See Gardner, *Sterling-Dollar Diplomacy*, chs. 8 and 17; Wilcox, *A Charter for World Trade*; Committee for Economic Development, Research, and Policy Committee, *The United States and The European Community: Policies for a Changing World Economy* (New York, N.Y.: CED, November 1971); and John H. Jackson, *The World Trading System: Law and Policy of International Economic Relations* (Cambridge, Mass.: MIT Press, 1989), 32–34.

8. Gardner, *Sterling-Dollar Diplomacy*, ch. 17; and William Diebold, Jr., *The End of the ITO* (Princeton, N.J.: International Finance Section, Department of Economics and Social Institutions, Princeton University, 1952).

9. Jackson, *The World Trading System*, 33.

10. Kenneth W. Dam, *The GATT: Law and International Economic Organization* (Chicago, Ill.: University of Chicago Press, 1970), 392.

11. *Ibid.*, 396–397.

12. Peter B. Kenen, *The International Economy*, 3rd ed. (New York, N.Y.: Cambridge University Press, 1994), 247. In the GATT commercial code, dumping is defined as pricing exported goods lower than in the domestic market of the exporting country.

13. **Market power**—usually created by having few or no competitors—allows firms to take advantage of the "rents" (supernormal profits) that accrue to monopoly or oligopoly producers.

14. The GATT commercial code originally addressed only export subsidies, not sub-sidies in general; *Ibid.*, p. 249.

15. Dale E. Hathaway, *Agriculture and the GATT: Rewriting the Rules* (Washington, D.C.: Institute for International Economics, September 1987), 103–113; Judith Goldstein, "The Impact of Ideas on Trade Policy: The Origins of U.S. Agricultural and Manufacturing Policies," *International Organization*, 43 (Winter 1989): 31–71; and Judith Goldstein, *Ideas Interests, and American Trade Policy* (Ithaca, N.Y.: Cornell University Press, 1993).

16. Jackson, *The World Trading System*, 303.

17. For an interesting discussion of the evolution of thinking about reciprocity in U.S. trade policy, see Caroline Rhodes, *Reciprocity, U.S. Trade Policy, and the GATT Regime*, 8–12. See also Robert Keohane, "Reciprocity in International Relations," *International Organization*, 40 (Winter 1986): 1–28.

18. See Richard Blackhurst, "Reciprocity in Trade Negotiations under Flexible Exchange Rates," in John P. Martin and Alasdair Smith, eds., *Trade and Payments Adjustment under Flexible Exchange Rates* (London, UK: Macmillan, 1979), 224.

19. For an analysis of the process of making trade policy during this period, see Raymond A. Bauer, Ithiel de Sola Pool, and Lewis Anthony Dexter, *American Business and Public Policy: The Politics of Foreign Trade* (Chicago, Ill.: Aldine, Atherton, 1972).

20. I. M. Destler, *American Trade Politics: System Under Stress* (Washington, D.C.: Institute for International Economics, 1986), 9–36; and I. M. Destler, *Renewing Fast-Track Legislation* (Washington, D.C.: Institute for International Economics, 1997).

21. William Diebold, Jr., *Trade and Payments in Western Europe: A Study in Economic Cooperation, 1947–1951* (New York, N.Y.: Harper and Row, 1952); Robert Triffin, *Europe and the Money Muddle: From Bilateralism to Near Convertibility, 1947–1956* (New Haven, Conn.: Yale University Press, 1957); Hadley Arkes, *Bureaucracy, the Marshall Plan, and the National Interest* (Princeton, N.J.: Princeton University Press, 1973); Imanuel Wexler, *The Marshall Plan Revisited: The European Recovery Program in Economic Perspective* (Westport, Conn.: Greenwood, 1983); and Daniel Verdier, *Democracy and International Trade: Britain, France, and the United States, 1860–1990* (Princeton, N.J.: Princeton University Press, 1994), 203–213.

22. Robert S. Ozaki, *The Control of Imports and Foreign Capital in Japan* (New York, N.Y.: Praeger, 1972), 5–9; Warren S. Hunsberger, *Japan and the United States in World Trade* (New York, N.Y.: Harper and Row, 1964); and Theodore Cohen, *Remaking Japan: The American Occupation as New Deal* (New York, N.Y.: Free Press, 1987).

23. For example, see Gardner Patterson, *Discrimination in International Trade: The Policy Issues, 1945–1965* (Princeton, N.J.: Princeton University Press, 1966); and Karin Kock, *International Trade Policy and the GATT, 1947–1967*, Stockholm Economic Studies XI (Stockholm, Sweden: Almquist and Wiksell, 1969).

24. John W. Evans, *The Kennedy Round in American Trade Policy: The Twilight of the GATT?* (Cambridge, Mass.: Harvard University Press, 1971), 282. For other studies of the Kennedy Round, see Ernest H. Preeg, *Traders and Diplomats: An Analysis of the Kennedy Round Negotiations Under the General Agreement on Tariffs and Trade* (Washington, D.C.: Brookings Institution, 1970); and Thomas B. Curtis and John R. Vastine, *The Kennedy Round and the Future of American Trade* (New York, N.Y.: Praeger, 1971).

25. Robert E. Baldwin, *Non-Tariff Distortions of International Trade* (Washington, D.C.: Brookings Institution, 1970), 1.

26. *Economic Report of the President* (Washington, D.C.: U.S. Government Printing Office, 1995), 205.

27. Richard N. Cooper, *The Economics of Interdependence: Economic Policy in the Atlantic Community* (New York, N.Y.: McGraw-Hill, 1968), 59–80.

28. *General Agreement on Tariffs and Trade, International Trade, 1986–1987* (Geneva, Switzerland: GATT, 1987), 158; and *General Agreement on Tariffs and Trade, International Trade, 1990–1991*, vol. 2 (Geneva, Switzerland: GATT, 1991), 78.

29. Allen Sinai, "The 'Global' Factor and the U.S. Economy," *Economic Studies Series*, no. 27, Shearson Lehman Brothers (October 6, 1987): 1.

30. Prepared Testimony of Dr. Paul Freedenberg, Association for Manufacturing Technology, Hearing on Establishing an Effective Modern Framework for Export Controls, U.S. Senate Committee on Banking, Housing, and Urban Affairs, February 7, 2001, http://banking.senate.gov/01_02hrg/020701/freeden.htm.

31. Council on Competitiveness, *Competitiveness Index: Trends, Background Data, and Methodology* (Washington, D.C.: Council on Competitiveness, 1988), Appendix II.

32. *Ibid.*

33. See Richard Blackhurst, Nicolas Marian, and Jan Tumlir, *Adjustment, Trade, and Growth in Developed and Developing Countries*, GATT Studies in International Trade, no. 6 (Geneva, Switzerland: General Agreement on Tariffs and Trade, 1978); and William Diebold, Jr., "Adapting Economics to Structural Change: The International Aspect," *International Affairs* (London) 54 (October 1978): 573–588.

34. Paul R. Krugman and George N. Hatsopoulos, "The Problem of U.S. Competitiveness in Manufacturing," *New England Economic Review* (January/February 1987): 22; Organization for Economic Development and Cooperation, *OECD Economic Outlook*, 42 (Paris, France: OECD, December 1987), 41, 178; Stephen Cohen and John Zysman, *Manufacturing Matters* (New York, N.Y.: Basic Books, 1987), ch. 5; and Jeffrey Hart, *Rival Capitalists: International Competitiveness in the United States, Japan, and Western Europe* (Ithaca, N.Y.: Cornell University Press, 1992), ch. 1.

35. *Economic Report of the President* (Washington, D.C.: Government Printing Office, 1988), 373, 374; and GATT, *International Trade, 1986–1987*, 10. Unemployment figures are for the G-7 countries.

36. *OECD Economic Outlook*, 42 (December 1987), 174, 184.

37. *Ibid.*, 190.

38. International Monetary Fund, *World Economic Outlook* (Washington, D.C.: IMF, October 1993), Statistical Appendix, table A21. The figures cited are based on averages of growth in world exports and imports.

39. *OECD Economic Outlook*, 42 (December 1987), 184.

40. *Ibid.*, 174.

41. *Ibid.*, 190.

42. U.S. Department of Labor, Bureau of Labor Statistics.

43. International Monetary Fund, *Annual Report, 1987* (Washington, D.C.: IMF, 1987), 16.

44. *OECD Economic Outlook,* 42 (December 1987), 174, 184.

45. *OECD Economic Outlook,* 42 (December 1987), 5, 28.

46. From this point on, we will be using European Union or its acronym EU to refer to the what was called initially the European Economic Community (EEC) and then later the European Community (EC). The European Union became the official name for the entity in 1992. We will revert to the older names and acronyms wherever that is historically appropriate or where to do otherwise would be confusing.

47. International Monetary Fund, Direction of Trade Annual, 1960–1964; IMF, Direction of Trade Annual, 1970–1974; and Gabriel Stern and Tamim Bayoumi, Regional Trading Blocs, Mobile Capital, and Exchange Rate Coordination, Bank of England, Working Paper Series no. 12, April 1993, 9.

48. *Ibid.*

49. *Ibid.*

50. See Jacob Viner, *The Customs Union Issue*, Studies in the Administration of International Law and Organization, vol. 10 (New York, N.Y.: Carnegie Endowment for International Peace, 1950).

51. See Paolo Cecchini, ed., *The European Challenge, 1992: The Benefits of a Single Market* (Hants, England: Wildwood House, 1988); Lord Cockfield, *White Paper on Completing the Internal Market* (Brussels, Belgium: Commission of the European Community, 1985); Jacques Pelkmans and Alan Winters, *Europe's Domestic Market*, Chatham House paper no. 43, Royal Institute of International Affairs (London, UK: Routledge, 1988); Michael Calingaert, *The 1992 Challenge from Europe: Development of the European Community's Internal Market* (Washington, D.C.: National Planning Association, 1988); Gary Clyde Hufbauer, ed., *Europe 1992: An American Perspective* (Washington, D.C.: Brookings Institution, 1990); David R. Cameron, "The 1992 Initiative: Causes and Consequences," in Alberta M. Sbragia, ed., *Europolitics: Institutions and Policymaking in the "New" European Community* (Washington, D.C.: Brookings Institution, 1992); Wayne Sandholtz and John Zysman, "1992: Recasting the European Bargain," *World Politics,* 42 (1989): 95–128; and Wayne Sandholtz, *High-Tech Europe* (Berkeley and Los Angeles, Calif.: University of California Press, 1992).

52. See, for example, Laura D'Andrea Tyson, *Who's Bashing Whom?: Trade Conflict in High-Technology Industries* (Washington, D.C.: Institute for International Economics, 1992), ch. 5; and Marc Busch, *Trade Warriors: States, Firms, and Strategic-Trade Policy in High-Technology Competition* (New York, N.Y.: Cambridge University Press, 2001), ch. 3.

53. International Monetary Fund, *Direction of Trade Statistics Yearbook, 1994* (Washington, D.C.: IMF, 1994).

54. Based on statistics in the *World Development Report* (Washington, D.C.: World Bank, 1982). World GDP estimates in this source did not include estimates of GDP for the Soviet Bloc countries.

55. See Edward Denison and William Chung, "Economic Growth and Its Sources," in Hugh Patrick and Henry Rosovsky, eds., *Asia's New Giant* (Washington, D.C.: Brookings Institution, 1976), 63–151.

56. Philip H. Trezise and Yukio Suzuki, "Politics, Government, and Economic Growth in Japan," in Patrick and Rosovsky, op. cit., 753–811; and Chalmers Johnson, *MITI and the Japanese Miracle* (Stanford, Calif.: Stanford University Press, 1982).

57. Mark Mason, *American Multinationals and Japan: The Political Economy of Japanese Capital Controls, 1899–1980* (Cambridge, Mass.: Harvard University Press, 1992); and Dennis Encarnation, *Rivals Beyond Trade: America versus Japan in Global Competition* (Ithaca, N.Y.: Cornell University Press, 1992).

58. There is some controversy as to whether the Japanese case represents "export-led" growth or not. On this debate, see Lawrence B. Krause and Sueo Sekiguchi, "Japan and the World Economy," in Patrick and Rosovsky, op. cit., 397–410; and Shigeto Tsuru, *Japan's Capitalism: Creative Defeat and Beyond* (New York, N.Y.: Cambridge University Press, 1993), ch. 3.

59. Edward J. Lincoln, *Japan Facing Economic Maturity* (Washington, D.C.: Brookings Institution, 1988), 14–68.

60. Ezra Vogel, *Comeback Case by Case: Building the Resurgence of American Business* (New York, N.Y.: Simon and Schuster, 1985); and Richard Samuels, *The Business of the Japanese State: Energy Markets in Comparative and Historical Perspective* (Ithaca, N.Y.: Cornell University Press, 1987).

61. C. Fred Bergsten and William R. Cline, *The United States-Japan Economic Problem* (Washington, D.C.: Institute for International Economics, 1987), 53–119.

62. International Monetary Fund, *Direction of Trade Statistics Yearbook 1987* (Washington, D.C.: IMF, 1987), 243, 245; *Direction of Trade Statistics Yearbook 1988* (Washington, D.C.: IMF, 1988), 243; and *Direction of Trade Statistics Yearbook 1995* (Washington, D.C.: IMF, 1995).

63. Bureau of Economic Analysis, *Survey of Current Business* (Washington, D.C.: Department of Commerce, July 1984), 60; and *Survey of Current Business*, May 1988, 11.

64. On this subject, see Ronald Dore, *Flexible Rigidities* (Stanford, Calif.: Stanford University Press, 1986), 79; Michael Gerlach, *Alliance Capitalism: The Social Organization of Japanese Business Networks* (Berkeley and Los Angeles, Calif.: University of California Press, 1989); Marie Anchordoguy, *Computers, Inc. Japan's Challenge to IBM* (Cambridge, Mass.: Harvard University Press, 1989); Robert Z. Lawrence, "Efficient or Exclusionist? The Import Behavior of Japanese Corporate Groups," *Brookings Papers on Economic Activity*, 1 (1991): 311–330; and Laura D'Andrea Tyson, *Who's Bashing Whom?*, 56–57.

65. The U.S. bilateral trade deficit with Japan decreased with the devaluation of the dollar against the yen, especially after 1993, when the Clinton administration adopted a policy of not intervening in currency markets to support the dollar's value against the yen. The trade deficit was cut substantially but still remained high.

66. See Clyde V. Prestowitz, Jr., *Trading Places: How America Allowed Japan to Take the Lead* (New York, N.Y.: Basic Books, 1988); and Karel van Wolferen, *The Enigma of Japanese Power* (London, UK: Macmillan, 1989).

67. C. Fred Bergsten and William R. Cline, *The United States–Japan Economic Problem* (Washington, D.C.: Institute for International Economics, 1987), 53–119.

68. These are generally agreements to restrict exports, called **voluntary export restraints (VERs)**. VERs were used to get around the GATT restrictions on quantitative import restrictions. VRAs were "voluntary" on the part of both the exporter and the importer and therefore did not violate GATT norms of reciprocity, whereas in actuality the effects of the VRAs were virtually indistinguishable from those of unilaterally imposed quantitative import restrictions. That is, they tended to raise the price of the goods subject to VERs in the country of destination because demand remained relatively constant while supply diminished.

69. See Makoto Kuroda, "Japan's Trade Surplus Is Declining Fast," *Amex Bank Review*, 15 (March 24, 1988): 2–3.

70. International Monetary Fund, *International Financial Statistics Yearbook 1985* (Washington, D.C.: IMF, 1985); and World Trade Organization, http://www.wto.org.

71. *International Financial Statistics Yearbook*, 1985; *International Financial Statistics*, April 1988 (Washington, D.C.: IMF 1985 and 1988).

72. *OECD Economic Outlook*, 42 (December 1987): 41.

73. Council on Competitiveness, *Competitiveness Index*, Special Supplement, May 1988, 7.

74. National Science Foundation, National Science Board, *Science and Engineering Indicators* (Washington, D.C.: U.S. Government Printing Office, 1993), 455.

75. *OECD Economic Outlook*, 42 (December 1987): 70.

76. See I. M. Destler, *American Trade Politics: System Under Stress* (Washington, D.C.: Institute for International Economics, 1986).

77. This was the origin of the tightened antidumping and unfair trade laws of the 1970s and 1980s. See Stephen Woolcock, Jeffrey Hart, and Hans van der Ven, *Interdependence in the Postmultilateral Era* (Lanham, Md.: University Press of America, 1985); Richard Boltuck and Robert E. Litan, eds., *Down in the Dumps: Administration of the Unfair Trade Laws* (Washington, D.C.: Brookings Institution, 1991); J. Michael Finger, ed., *Antidumping: How It Works and Who Gets Hurt* (Ann Arbor, Mich.: University of Michigan Press, 1993); and Pietro S. Nivola, *Regulating Unfair Trade* (Washington, D.C.: Brookings Institution, 1993).

78. On the politics of supporters of free trade, see I. M. Destler and John S. Odell, *Anti-Protection: Changing Forces in the United States Trade Politics* (Washington, D.C.: Institute for International Economics, September 1987); and Helen V. Milner, *Resisting Protectionism: Global Industries and the Politics of International Trade* (Princeton, N.J.: Princeton University Press, 1988).

79. Helen V. Milner and David B. Yoffie, "Between Free Trade and Protectionism: Strategic Trade Policy and a Theory of Corporate Trade Demands," *International Organization*, 43 (Spring 1989): 239–272.

80. See Prestowitz, *Trading Places*, op. cit.

81. Tyson, *Who's Bashing Whom?*, 58–66; and Edward J. Lincoln, *Japan's Unequal Trade* (Washington, D.C.: Brookings Institution, 1990).

82. Geza Feketekuty, *International Trade in Services: An Overview and Blueprint for Negotiations* (Cambridge, Mass.: Ballinger, 1988), especially ch. 9.

83. By 1991, the CAP built up surpluses of over 20 million tons of cereals, 1 million tons of milk, and 750,000 tons of beef. Nicholas Hopkins, *Completing the GATT*

Uruguay Round: Renewed Multilateralism or a World of Regional Trading Blocs?, Wilton Park Paper 61 (London, UK: Her Majesty's Stationery Office, 1992), 9.

84. Robert B. Reich, "Beyond Free Trade," *Foreign Affairs* 16 (Spring 1983): 773–804. See also Stephen S. Cohen and John Zysman, *Manufacturing Matters: The Myth of the Post-Industrial Economy* (New York, N.Y.: Basic Books for the Council on Foreign Relations, 1987).

85. See Raymond Hopkins and Donald F. Puchala, eds., "The Global Political Economy of Food," *International Organization,* 32 (Summer 1978): entire issue.

86. Dale E. Hathaway, *Agriculture and the GATT: Rewriting the Rules* (Washington, D.C.: Institute for International Economics, September 1987), 43.

87. See Robert L. Paarlberg, *Fixing Farm Trade: Policy Options for the United States* (Cambridge, Mass.: Ballinger Publishing for the Council on Foreign Relations, 1988), 13–40.

88. See the discussion of "tariffication" in the section above that deals with the Uruguay Round negotiations.

89. See William Diebold Jr., ed., *Bilateralism, Multilateralism and Canada in U.S. Trade Policy* (Cambridge, Mass.: Ballinger, 1988); Jeffrey J. Schott and Murray G. Smith, eds., *The Canada–United States Free Trade Agreement: The Global Impact* (Washington, D.C.: Institute for International Economics, 1988); and Paul Wonnacott, *The United States and Canada: The Quest for Free Trade* (Washington, D.C.: Institute for International Economics, 1987).

90. Robert E. Baldwin, *Non-Tariff Distortions of International Trade* (Washington, D.C.: Brookings Institution, 1970); William Diebold, Jr., *The United States and the Industrial World: American Foreign Policy in the 1970s* (New York, N.Y.: Praeger, 1972), 123–140; J. Michael Finger, H. Keith Hall and Douglas R. Nelson, "The Political Economy of Administered Protection," *The American Economic Review,* 72 (1982): 452–466; Stanley D. Metzger, *Lowering Non-Tariff Barriers: U.S. Law, Practice and Negotiating Objectives* (Washington, D.C.: Brookings Institution, 1974); and Jagdish Bhagwati, *Protectionism* (Cambridge, Mass.: MIT Press, 1988), ch. 3.

91. See 97th Cong., 2d sess., *The Mercantilist Challenge to the Liberal International Trade Order, a study prepared for the use of the Joint Economic Committee,* Congress of the United States, December 29, 1982 (Washington, D.C.: U.S. Government Printing Office, 1982), 8–31.

92. See Brian Hindley and Eri Nicolaides, *Taking the New Protectionism Seriously,* Thames Essay No. 34 (London, UK: Trade Policy Research Centre, 1983); and Michael Borrus, "The Politics of Competitive Erosion in the U.S. Steel Industry," in John Zysman and Laura D'Andrea Tyson, eds., *American Industry in International Competition* (Ithaca, N.Y.: Cornell University Press, 1983).

93. Ingo Walter, "Structural Adjustment and Trade Policy in the International Steel Industry," in William R. Cline, *Trade Policy in the 1980s,* 497–500; Gary C. Hufbauer and Diane T. Berliner, and Kimberly A. Elliot, *Trade Protection in the United States: 31 Case Studies* (Washington, D.C.: Institute for International Economics, 1986), 156, 176; Ingo Walter, "Structural Adjustment and Trade Policy in the International Steel Industry," in Cline, *Trade Policy in the 1980s,* 489.

94. Hufbauer et al., 170–173.

95. General Agreements on Tariffs and Trade, *International Trade 1986–1987,* 29.

96. See Laura D'Andrea Tyson, *Who's Bashing Whom?*; Robert B. Cohen, "The Prospects for Trade and Protectionism in the Auto Industry," in Cline, *Trade*

Policy in the 1980s (Washington, D.C.: Institute for International Economics, 1983), 527–563; and Gary C. Hufbauer et al. 249–262.

97. See Paul R. Krugman, ed., *Strategic Trade Policy and the New International Economics* (Cambridge, Mass.: MIT Press, 1986).

98. This is the view of the Cambridge Economic Policy Group; see their journal, the *Cambridge Economic Policy Review*.

99. Albert Bressand, "Mastering the World Economy," *Foreign Affairs*, 16 (spring 1983): 747–772.

100. Business Roundtable, "Negotiations on International Investment in the Uruguay Round: A Preliminary Statement," March 1988; and U.S. Trade Representative, *Submission of the United States to the Negotiating Group on Trade-Related Investment Measures* (Washington, D.C.: Office of U.S. Trade Representatives, June 1987).

101. See U.S. Senate, Committee on Finance, Trade Agreements Act of 1979, *Report on H.R. 4537 to Approve and Implement the Trade Agreements Negotiated Under the Trade Act of 1974, and for Other Purposes*, 96th Cong., 1st sess. (Washington, D.C.: Government Printing Office, 1979); Stephen D. Krasner, "The Tokyo Round: Particularistic Interests and Prospects for Stability in the Global Trading System," *International Studies Quarterly*, 23 (December 1979): 491–531; and Thomas R. Graham, "Revolution in Trade Politics," *Foreign Policy*, 36 (Fall 1979): 49–63.

102. See U.S. Senate, Committee on Finance, MTN Studies No. 4, *MTN and the Legal Institutions of International Trade*, report prepared at the request of the Subcommittee on International Trade, 96th Cong., 1st sess. (Washington, D.C.: Government Printing Office, 1979).

103. See Gary C. Hufbauer, "Subsidy Issues After the Tokyo Round," in Cline, *Trade Policy in the 1980s*, 327–361.

104. See Alan W. Wolff, "The Need for New GATT Rules to Govern Safeguard Actions," in Cline, *Trade Policy in the 1980s*, 363–391.

105. *Survey of Current Business* (October 2000).

106. David C. Mowery, *International Collaborative Ventures in U.S. Manufacturing* (Cambridge, Mass.: Ballinger, 1988); Steven S. Wildman and Stephen E. Siwek, *International Trade in Films and Television Programs* (Cambridge, Mass.: Ballinger, 1988); Lawrence J. White, *International Trade in Ocean Shipping Services* (Cambridge, Mass.: Ballinger, 1988); Ingo Walter, *Global Competition in Financial Services: Market Structure, Protection, and Trade Liberalization* (Cambridge, Mass.: Ballinger, 1988); Thierry J. Noyelle and Anna B. Dutka, *International Trade in Business Services: Accounting, Advertising, Law, and Management Consulting* (Cambridge, Mass.: Ballinger, 1988); Jonathan David Aronson and Peter F. Cowhey, *When Countries Talk: International Trade in Telecommunications Services* (Cambridge, Mass.: Ballinger, 1988); and Daniel M. Kasper, *Deregulation and Globalization: Liberalizing International Trade in Air Services* (Cambridge, Mass.: Ballinger, 1988).

107. *Economic Report of the President* (Washington, D.C.: Government Printing Office, 1988), 144.

108. See Ronald Kent Shelp, *Beyond Industrialization* (New York, N.Y.: Praeger, 1981); Thomas M. Stanback, Jr., Peter J. Bearse, Thierry J. Noyelle, and Robert A. Karasek, *Services: The New Economy* (Totowa, N.J.: Allanheld, Osmun, 1981); and

Office of Technology Assessment, *Trade in Services: Exports and Foreign Revenues* (Washington, D.C.: Government Printing Office, September 1986).

109. *Survey of Current Business* (October 2000), p. 119.

110. *International Financial Statistics Yearbook, 1987*, 701.

111. Coalition of Service Industries; British Invisibles Export Council, *Annual Report and Accounts 1986–1987* (London, UK: British Invisible Exports Council, 1987), 34.

112. U.S. Department of Commerce, *U.S. Trade: Performance in 1985 and Outlook* (Washington, D.C.: Government Printing Office, 1986), 2.

113. Coalition of Service Industries. Derived from IMF figures by Boston Economic Advisors, Inc.

114. See Spero, "Removing Trade Barriers"; and William Diebold, Jr., and Helena Stalson, "Negotiating Issues in International Services Transactions," in Cline, *Trade Policy in the 1980s*, 581–609.

115. U.S. Congress, *Trade and Tariff Act of 1984*, Public Law 98–573, October 30, 1984.

116. See Keith E. Maskus, *Intellectual Property Rights in the Global Economy* (Washington, D.C.: Institute for International Economics, 2000); Susan K. Sell, *Power and Ideas: North-South Politics of Intellectual Property and Antitrust* (Albany, N.Y.: State University of New York Press, 1998); Robert P. Benko, *Protecting Intellectual Property Rights: Issues and Controversies* (Washington, D.C.: American Enterprise Institute for Public Policy Research, 1987); R. Michael Gadbaw and Timothy J. Richards, eds., *Intellectual Property Rights: Global Consensus, Global Conflict?* (Boulder, Colorado: Westview Press, 1988); and Helena Stalson, *Intellectual Property Rights and U.S. Competitiveness in Trade* (Washington, D.C.: National Planning Association, 1987).

117. *Description of the Proposed North American Free Trade Agreement*, prepared by the governments of Canada, the United Mexican States, and the United States of America, August 12, 1992, 1.

118. Peter Coffey, *NAFTA: Past, Present, and Future* (Boston, Mass.: Kluwer, 1999); Norris C. Clement, *North American Economic Integration: Theory and Practice* (Northhampton, Mass.: Edward Elgar, 1999); and Frederick Mayer, *Interpreting NAFTA: The Science and Art of Political Analysis* (New York, N.Y.: Columbia University Press, 1998).

119. I. M. Destler and Peter J. Balint, *The New Politics of American Trade: Trade, Labor, and the Environment* (Washington, D.C.: Institute for International Economics, 2000).

120. See Edith Brown Weiss and John H. Jackson, eds., *Reconciling Environment and Trade* (Ardsley, N.Y.: Transnational Pulishers, 2001); Gary P. Sampson, *Trade, Environment, and the WTO: The Post-Seattle Agenda* (Washington, D.C.: Overseas Development Council, 2000); Diana Tussie, ed., *The Environment and International Trade Negotiations: Developing Country Stakes* (New York, N.Y.: St. Martin's Press, 2000); and I. M. Destler and Peter J. Balint, *The New Politics of American Trade: Trade, Labor, and the Environment* (Washington, D.C.: Institute for International Economics, 2000).

121. Gary C. Hufbauer and Jeffrey J. Schott, *NAFTA: An Assessment* (Washington, D.C.: Institute for International Economics, 1993).

122. See Randall R. Parrish, *Stability with Hegemony: Brazil, Argentina, and Southern Cone Integration* (Albuquerque, N.M.: University of New Mexico Press, 2000);

Riordan Roett, ed., *Mercosur: Regional Integration, World Markets* (Boulder, Colo.: Lynne Rienner, 1999); and Richard E. Feinberg, *Summitry in the Americas: A Progress Report* (Washington, D.C.: Institute for International Economics, 1997).

123. See Emiko Fukase and Will Martin, *Free Trade Area Membership as a Stepping Stone to Development: The Case of ASEAN* (Washington, D.C.: World Bank, 2001; and John Ravenhill, *APEC and the Construction of Pacific Rim Regionalism* (New York, N.Y.: Cambridge University Press, 2001).

124. See John H. Jackson, "GATT Machinery and the Tokyo Round Agreements," in Cline, *Trade Policy in the 1980s*, 159–187.

125. Diana Tussie, "Holding the Balance: The Cairns Group in the Uruguay Round," in Diana Tussie and David Glover, eds., *The Developing Countries in World Trade* (Boulder, Colo.: Lynne Rienner, 1993).

126. See http://www.wto.org/english/tratop_e/serv_e/gats_factfiction1_e.htm. Accessed on December 22, 2001.

127. Klaus Stegemann, "The Integration of Intellectual Property Rights into the WTO System," *The World Economy*, 23 (September 2000): 1237–1267; and Keith E. Maskus, *Intellectual Property Rights in the Global Economy.*

128. Yang Guohua and Cheng Jin, "The Process of China's Accession to the WTO," *Journal of International Economic Law*, 4 (June 2001): 297–328.

129. It should be noted that the new DSU resulted in a major increase in the number of requests for consultations (when compared with the earlier GATT dispute settlement system). As of the end of 2006, 359 requests for consultation had been made. See Young Duk Park and Georg C. Umbricht, "WTO Dispute Settlement 1995–2000: A Statistical Analysis," *Journal of International Economic Law*, 4 (March 2001): 213–230; and Robert Hudec, "The New WTO Dispute Settlement Procedure: An Overview of the First 3 Years," *Minnesota Journal of Global Trade*, 1 (1999): 1–53; and Henrik Horn and Petros C. Mavroidis, "The WTO Dispute Settlement System 1995–2006: Some Descriptive Statistics," The World Bank, March 14, 2008, http://siteresources.worldbank.org/INTRES/Resources/469232-1107449512766/DescriptiveStatistics_031408.pdf.

130. John H. Jackson, "International Economic Laws in Times that Are Interesting," *Journal of International Economic Law*, 3 (March 2000): 3–14; Judith Goldstein and Lisa L. Martin, "Legalization, Trade Liberalization, and Domestic Politics: A Cautionary Tale," *International Organization*, 54 (2001): 603–632; Claude Barfield, *Free Trade, Sovereignty, Democracy: The Future of the World Trade Organization* (Washington, D.C.: The AEI Press, 2001); Allan Rosas, "Implementation and Enforcement of WTO Dispute Settlement Findings: An EU Perspective," *Journal of International Economic Law*, 4 (March 2001): 131–144.

131. Debora L. Spar and David B. Yoffie, "A Race to the Bottom or Governance from the Top?" in Aseem Prakash and Jeffrey A. Hart, eds., *Coping with Globalization* (London, UK: Routledge, 2000).

132. For the details of the case, see http://www.american.edu/TED/TUNA.HTM. For a discussion of the case, see R. Daniel Kelemen, "The Limits of Judicial Power: Trade-Environment Disputes in the GATT/WTO and the EU," *Comparative Political Studies*, 34 (August 2001): 622–650.

133. See a speech by Pascal Lamy, "Doha Could Deliver Double-Win for Environment and Trade," December 9, 2007, http://www.wto.org/english/

news_e/sppl_e/sppl83_e.htm. See also, Trevor Houser, Rob Bradley, Britt Childs, Jacob Werksman, and Robert Heilmayr, *Leveling the Carbon Playing Field: International Competition and U.S. Climate Policy Design* (Washington, D.C.: Peterson Institute, May 2008), especially ch. 3.

134. An excellent discussion of this issue is in John H. Jackson, "The WTO 'Constitution' and Proposed Reforms: Seven 'Mantras' Revisited" *Journal of International Eocnomic Law*, 4 (March 2001): 67–78. For examples of arguments in favor of democratizing the WTO, see Philip McMichael, "Sleepless Since Seattle: What is the WTO About?" *Review of International Political Economy*, 7 (Autumn 2000): 466–474; and Robert O'Brien, Anne Marie Goetz, Jan Aaart Scholte, and Marc Williams, *Contesting Global Governance: Multilateral Economic Institutions and Global Social Movements* (New York, N.Y.: Cambridge University Press, 2000).

135. Ellen M. Katz, "Transparency in Government: How American Citizens Influence Public Poliy," in Paul Malamud, ed., *Transparency in Government* (Washington, D.C.: U.S. Department of State, n.d.), http://usinfo.state.gov/products/pubs/transgov/.

136. Gabrielle Marceau and Peter N. Pedersen, "Is the WTO Open and Transparent?: A Discussion of the Relationship of the WTO with Non-governmental Organizations and Civil Society's Claims for More Transparency and Public Participation," *Journal of World Trade*, 5 (1999): 5–49.

137. Computed by the authors from data in *OECD Historical Statistics 1970–1999* (Paris, France: OECD, 2001).

138. Jason Dedrick and Kenneth L. Kraemer, *Asia's Computer Challenge: Threat or Opportunity for the United States & the World?* (New York, N.Y.: Oxford University Press, 1988), pp. 58–64.

139. See José Manuel Salazar-Xirinachs and Maryse Robert, eds., *Toward Free Trade in the Americas* (Washington, D.C.: Brookings Institution, 2001).

140. Good evidence for this can be seen in the discussions that occurred at a teach-in organized by the International Forum for Globalization on November 26–27, 1999. For a detailed, pro-demonstrator account of the Seattle demonstrations, see Janet Thomas, *The Battle in Seattle: The Story Behind the WTO Demonstrations* (Golden, Colo.: Fulcrum Books, 2000).

141. See Jeffrey J. Schott, C. Fred Bergsten, and Renato Ruggiero, *The WTO After Seattle* (Washington, D.C.: Institute for International Economics, 2001); Jagdish Bhagwati, "After Seattle: Free Trade and the WTO," *International Affairs*, 77 (January 2001): 15–29; and Gary P. Sampson, *Trade, Environment and the WTO: The Post-Seattle Agenda* (Washington, D.C.: Overseas Development Council, 2000).

142. Dilip K. Das, "Suspension of the Doha Round of Multilateral Negotiations and the Need for Its Rescuscitation," *The Estay Center Journal of International Law and Trade Policy*, 9 (2008): 54.

143. World Trade Organization, *Doha Work Programme*, WT/L/579, August 2, 2004, http://www.wto.org/english/tratop_e/dda_e/draft_text_gc_dg_31july04_e.htm.

144. http://www.centad.org/relatedinfo9.asp.

145. World Trade Organization, *Ministerial Declaration*, WT/MIN(05)/DEC, http://www.wto.org/english/thewto_e/minist_e/min05_e/final_text_e.htm.

146. World Trade Organization, "DG Lamy: time out needed to review options and positions," July 24, 2006, http://www.wto.org/english/news_e/news06_e/tnc_dg_stat_24july06_e.htm.

147. World Trade Organization, Committee on Agriculture, Special Session, *Revised Draft Modalities for Agriculture*, TN/AG/W/4/Rev. 1, http://www.wto.org/english/tratop_e/agric_e/agchairtxt_feb08_e.pdf.

148. For more on the Doha Round, see Dilip K. Das, *The Evolving Global Trade Architecture* (Northampton, Mass.: Edward Elgar, 2007); Kimberly Ann Elliott, *Delivering on Doha: Fram Trade and the Poor* (Washington, D.C.: Institute for International Economics, 2006); Alex F. McCalla and John Nash, eds., *Reforming Agricultural Trade for Developing Countries*, 2 volumes (Washington, D.C.: The World Bank, 2007); and Pitou van Dijck and Gerst Faber, eds., *Developing Countries and the Development Agenda of the WTO* (New York, N.Y.: Routledge, 2006).

149. http://www.ustr.gov/Trade_Agreements/Bilateral/Section_Index.html.

150. http://ec.europa.eu/trade/issues/bilateral/index_en.htm and http://ec.europa.eu/trade/issues/bilateral/regions/index_en.htm.

The Multinational Corporation and Global Governance

A **multinational corporation (MNC)**[1] is "an enterprise that engages in foreign direct investment (FDI) and that owns or controls value-added activities in more than one country."[2] A firm is not really multinational if it just engages in overseas trade or serves as a contractor to foreign firms. There are a number of ways of assessing the degree of multinationality of a specific firm. For example, firms are considered to be more multinational if (1) they have many foreign affiliates or subsidiaries in foreign countries; (2) they operate in a wide variety of countries around the globe; (3) the proportion of assets, revenues, or profits accounted for by overseas operations relative to total assets, revenues, or profits is high; (4) their employees, stockholders, owners, and managers are from many different countries; and (5) their overseas operations are much more ambitious than just sales offices, including a full range of manufacturing and research and development activities.[3]

Multinational corporations finance some portion of their overseas operations by transferring funds from the country of the **parent firm** to the country of the **host firm** (usually an **affiliate** or **subsidiary**, but also possibly a **joint venture** with another firm). This transfer is called foreign direct investment. The purpose of the transfer is to own or control overseas assets. What precisely constitutes control is somewhat problematic. For practical purposes, most collectors of statistics on FDI consider an overseas investment to involve control only when the investor owns 10 percent or more of the equity (total stock) of the affiliate—on the assumption that investors owning less than 10 percent of equity have no control.[4] Even though a group of smaller investors can band together to control a firm, their investments will not generally be included in statistics on FDI. So there is a gray area between genuine FDI and foreign portfolio investment—investment that does not involve direct control over overseas assets.[5]

Foreign direct investment is not a new phenomenon.[6] From the time that people began to trade with one another, they set up foreign commercial operations. Mediterranean traders like the Genoese and the Venetians established banking operations in distant locations as early as 1200 CE to finance the trade which their ships carried. Foreign commercial investment reached a high point in the development of the large mercantile trading companies, such as the British East India Company and the Hudson's Bay Company. Beginning in the eighteenth century, but more importantly in the nineteenth century, there was direct foreign investment in agriculture, mining, and manufacturing as distinct from the earlier forms of commercial investment. By the early 1890s, large U.S. manufacturing firms—like Singer Sewing Machines (the first large multinational corporation), American Bell, General Electric, and Standard Oil, to mention but a few—had large investments abroad. By 1914, according to one study, U.S. direct foreign investment amounted to an estimated $2.65 billion, 7 percent of the U.S. gross national product (GNP) of that time.[7]

In another sense, foreign direct investment *is* a new phenomenon. The nature and extent of international business changed dramatically after 1945. After World War II and during the period of the Bretton Woods system, there was a major expansion in the investments of U.S. firms abroad. The new investments tended to be in manufacturing, whereas previous investments had been in agriculture, banking, retailing, and raw materials. This expansion of U.S. multinational activity was not seriously questioned until the end of the Bretton Woods period.

The activities of U.S.-owned multinational corporations were the focus of much political debate during the period of interdependence. In Latin America, a response to the growing power of U.S. multinationals was a number of attempts to regulate them. A wave of **nationalizations** of raw material MNCs occurred in the 1970s in Latin America and on the part of the OPEC countries (see Chapter 8). In Europe, Japan, and the NICs, the main reaction of governments to the growing power of U.S. MNCS was to favor the growth of indigenous MNCS. The growth of FDI flows and the number of MNCs and MNC subsidiaries remained rapid during this period.

One distinct feature of the period of globalization was the spread of MNCs to many countries that had never had their own MNCs and never hosted an MNC subsidiary. The number of home and host countries and the number and variety of multinational firms increased markedly. In 1994, for example, there were 37,000 multinational parent firms controlling over 200,000 foreign affiliates.[8] By 2006, there were 78,000 MNCs with 780,000 overseas affiliates.[9] The formerly communist countries promoted inflows of FDI after 1989. The result was that globally oriented MNCs of various nationalities were increasingly influential players in the world economy.

During the period of globalization, the controversy over MNCs tended to center around their role as agents of globalization rather than as promoters of U.S. imperial aims. MNCs from Europe and East Asia began to challenge U.S. MNCs in a number of high-technology industries. China and India became much more important as homes and hosts for globally oriented MNCs. MNCs headquartered in Mexico, Brazil, Korea, Taiwan, China, and India began to invest abroad. While the global political system remained largely under the control of the governments of nation-states, as businesses from a variety of regions became more globally oriented, the question of who was to regulate whom and how became an important political issue.

To some extent the globalization of business began with regional expansions and therefore was linked to the construction of stronger regional monetary and trading blocs (see Chapters 2 and 3). If nationally oriented firms could no longer compete successfully with globally oriented ones, then one way for the firms of smaller nation-states to cope with globalization was to promote regional economic integration. However, governments that encouraged regional integration of markets without eventually lowering trade and investment barriers with the rest of the world were promoting regionalization rather than globalization.[10] So, just as in the case of trade, there was some concern about a potential tradeoffs between regionalization and globalization.

In this chapter we will concentrate on factors influencing global FDI flows and the expansion of MNC activities. The largest flows occurred primarily between developed countries, so most of this chapter will be devoted primarily to that subset of countries. In Chapter 8, we will discuss how FDI flows from the industrialized countries to the developing countries increased and how the people and governments of the developing world were dealing with this.

COMMON CHARACTERISTICS OF MNCs

Multinational corporations range from companies that extract raw materials to those that manufacture high-technology products like wide-body aircraft to those that offer financial services such as insurance or banking. These multinational corporations differ not only in what they do but also in how they do it: their level of technology, their organizational structure, and the structure of the market for their products. Nevertheless, certain common characteristics can be used to identify problems created by the rise of the importance of MNCs.

Multinational corporations are among the world's largest firms. In 2006, the top 50 multinationals had revenues over $80 billion. The largest—Wal-Mart—had revenues of over $350 billion in that year (see Table 4.1). The revenues of each

TABLE 4.1 **Top 50 MNCs in 2006 Ranked by Revenues in Billions of Dollars**

Firm	Industry	Home Country	Assets ($Billions)
Wal-Mart	Retail	US	352
Exxon Mobil	Petroleum	US	347
Royal Dutch Shell	Petroleum	Netherlands	319
BP	Petroleum	UK	274
General Motors	Automotive	US	207
Toyota Motor	Automotive	Japan	205
Chevron	Petroleum	US	201
DaimlerChrysler	Automotive	Germany	190
ConocoPhilips	Petroleum	US	172
Total	Petroleum	France	168
General Electric	Heavy Machinery	US	168
Ford Motor	Automotive	US	160
ING Group	Insurance	Netherlands	158
Citigroup	Banking	US	147
AXA	Insurance	France	140
Volkswagen	Automotive	Germany	132
Sinopec	Petroleum	China	132
Credit Agricole	Banking	France	128
Allianz	Insurance	Germany	125
Fortis	Banking	Belgium/Netherlands	121
Bank of America	Banking	US	117
HSBC Holdings	Banking	UK	115
American Intl. Group	Insurance	US	113
China National Petroleum	Petroleum	China	110
BNP Paribas	Banking	France	109
ENI	Petroleum	Italy	109
UBS	Banking	Switzerland	107
Siemens	Information Tech.	Germany	107
State Grid	Utilities	China	107
Assicurazioni Generali	Insurance	Italy	102
J.P. Morgan Chase	Banking	US	100
Carrefour	Retail	France	99
Berkshire Hathaway	Insurance	US	99
Pemex	Petroleum	Mexico	97

T A B L E   4.1   (Continued)

Firm	Industry	Home Country	Assets ($Billions)
Deutsche Bank	Banking	Germany	96
Dexia Group	Banking	Belgium	96
Honda Motor	Automotive	Japan	95
McKesson	Retail	US	94
Verizon Communications	Telecommunications	US	93
NTT	Telecommunications	Japan	92
Hewlett-Packard	Information Tech.	US	92
IBM	Information Tech.	US	91
Valero Energy	Petroleum	US	91
Home Depot	Retail	US	91
Nissan Motor	Automotive	Japan	90
Samsung Electronics	Consumer Electronic	South Korea	89
Credit Suisse	Banking	Switzerland	89
Hitachi	Information Tech.	Japan	88
Societe Generale	Banking	France	84
Aviva	Insurance	UK	83

SOURCE: *Fortune Global 500 2007*, http://money.cnn.com/2007/07/09/magazines/fortune/Explanations_footnotes.fortune/ index.htm.

of the top ten multinational corporations in 2006 were over $168 billion, more than the **gross domestic product (GDP)** of at least 140 countries.[11] Indeed, Wal-Mart's 2006 revenues were larger than the GDP of all but the 21 largest national economies and well ahead of Denmark, Norway, Saudi Arabia, and Poland. These corporate giants also tended to compete in oligopolistic markets. Some were able to dominate markets because of their sheer size, others (even some small- and medium-sized firms) because of their access to financial resources, control of proprietary technology, and/or possession of a special, differentiated product.[12]

Multinational corporations do not simply market their products abroad; they send abroad a package of capital, technology, managerial talent, and marketing skills to carry out production and marketing in foreign countries. In many cases, the multinational's production is truly global, with different stages of production carried out in different regions of the world. Marketing also is often global. Goods and services produced by MNCs are often sold throughout the world. Finally, the largest multinational corporations tend to have affiliates or operations in a sizeable number of countries. One analyst defines a multinational corporation as one with investments in six or more foreign countries and finds that such firms accounted for 80 percent of all foreign subsidiaries of major U.S. corporations.[13]

Joint ventures and licensing are options available to multinationals wanting to do business abroad without being the sole owner of a foreign subsidiary. In a joint venture, the various partners own less than 100 percent of the equity of the joint venture firm. There may be a majority owner with more than 50 percent ownership, or all the owners might be minority owners. The owners typically select a management team made up of representatives of all the owner firms to run the joint venture. Licensing involves the granting of usage rights for intellectual property—for example, **patents**, copyrights, and **trademarks**—in exchange for some sort of payment. In certain countries, joint ventures and licensing are the only avenues available to MNCs who wish to participate in the local economy due to the restrictive inward investment policies of host governments.

Another option for MNCs is the **strategic alliance**. Strategic alliances are partnerships between separate, sometimes competing, companies. When the companies are from different countries, they are called international strategic alliances. The companies are drawn together because each needs the complementary technology, skills, or facilities of the other; nonetheless, the scope of the relationship is strictly defined, leaving the companies free to compete outside the relationship. A strategic alliance may be formally ratified in the form of a joint venture, but companies are increasingly using other ways to work together with other firms. The purposes of these alliances range from joint research and development to designing industry standards to sharing distribution or marketing networks in a way that both benefits the companies and reduces their risks. One of the catalysts for these arrangements has been the rapidity of technological change and the skyrocketing costs of development, especially in high-technology industries. Another has been the perceived need to compensate for disadvantages that individual firms have in competing with larger and more integrated firms or alliances.[14]

Decision making for multinationals tends to be centralized, though management structures vary from company to company, and policy control emanates from the parent company when the international aspects of a firm's business become important. The classic evolution of international investment has been from semi-independent foreign operations to the integration of international operations within a separate international division to the integration of international operations within the whole company. As a result, although multinational corporations have decentralized many decisions to the local level, key decisions involving foreign activities, such as the location of production facilities, marketing and branding strategies, location of research and development facilities, long-range planning, and especially capital investment, tend to be made by the parent company.[15]

Yet another organizational characteristic is the integration of production and marketing on an international scale. Production may take place in different stages in several different countries, and the final product may be marketed in still other countries. The European Ford Escort, for example, includes parts from 15 different countries, which are assembled in the United Kingdom and Germany and then sold throughout Europe. The Apple iPod was designed in the United States and is assembled in China; its components come from the United States, Taiwan, South Korea, and Japan. iPods are sold just about everywhere.[16] Central control and management of the geographically dispersed activities of MNCs are facilitated by modern computing and telecommunications technologies.

Multinationals tend to be mobile and flexible. Some are tied to specific countries by the need to get access to specific assets, such as raw materials of a particular kind, or by a large capital commitment that cannot be shifted easily to another location (e.g., oil wells and refineries located near major oil fields). Others, however, are able to shift their operations easily whenever needed for the purpose of maximizing company profits, markets, security, or survival. As part of their effort to transcend national borders, many multinationals try to create global staffs that are drawn from many countries to serve in yet others. As part of their effort to gain and protect their knowledge in strategically important areas, they recruit skilled personnel and make corporate allies wherever they can find them. Mobility and flexibility are thus increasingly an advantage that globally oriented MNCs have over more locally or even nationally oriented firms.

The special characteristics of multinational corporations can cause conflicts with national governments, because governments are territorially bound and politically committed to defending the interests of their citizens, whereas firms are not territorially bound and are legally committed to defending the interests of their stockholders or stakeholders. Most importantly, multinational corporations may seek goals or follow policies that are valid from the firm's international perspective but are not necessarily desirable from a national perspective.[17] An important contemporary example is the interest of Wal-Mart in obtaining products assembled or manufactured in the low-wage countries like China for sale to consumers in high-wage countries like the United States. Wal-Mart pushes its U.S. suppliers to relocate production to China for this reason, even though the consequences for low-skilled workers in the United States may be quite negative. The policies and goals of multinational corporations may therefore conflict with the policies and goals of the states in which they operate.

There is also a related jurisdictional problem. Multinational corporations operate in many countries and are therefore subject to many different legal jurisdictions. Because no one country is responsible for overall jurisdiction and because jurisdiction can be unclear, a given MNC may have problems deciding what laws it needs to obey and where. Some governments, like the U.S. government, engage in efforts to regulate the activities of U.S. citizens and U.S.-based companies abroad. The U.S. government, for example, has laws against the bribery of foreign officials to secure contracts.[18] The legal name for this kind of regulation is **extraterritoriality** and it is the subject of much criticism on the part of foreign governments. MNCs are generally opposed to extraterritorial regulation for obvious reasons.[19]

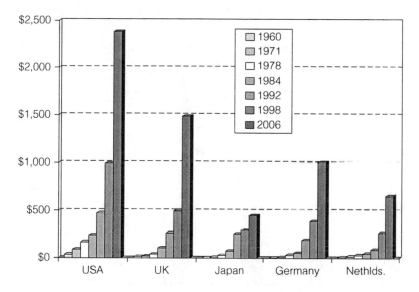

FIGURE 4.1   Outward Stock of Direct Foreign Investment in Billions of Dollars, 1960–2006

SOURCE: UNCTC, *Transnational Corporations in World Development* (New York, N.Y.: UN, 1988); UNCTAD, *World Investment Report* (Geneva, Switzerland: UNCTAD, 1999 and 2007).

TRENDS IN FDI AND OTHER MNC ACTIVITIES

The rapid spread of multinational corporations, and especially of U.S. multinationals, has been characteristic of the contemporary world economy. From 1971 to 2006, the stock of U.S.-owned direct investment abroad measured by book value rose from $86.2 billion to $2.4 trillion. Foreign direct investment by other developed countries, though smaller than U.S. investment, also rose sharply. From 1971 to 2006, the stock of direct investment by Germany rose from $7.3 billion to $1 trillion, that of the United Kingdom from $16.2 billion to $1.5 trillion, and that of Japan from $4.4 billion to $450 billion (see Figure 4.1). The total stock of FDI worldwide was over $12 trillion in 2006.[20]

Total annual outflows of FDI rose from around $12 billion in 1970 to $1.2 trillion in 2006 (see Figure 4.2). Growth in outflows tapered off after the deepening of the world debt crisis in the early 1980s, but resumed after that until 2000 when a major dip in both outflows and inflows occurred that lasted several years. Average annual growth in both outflows and inflows of FDI was over 18 percent in both the 1980s and the 1990s.[21] The aggregate trend in global FDI inflows mirrored that of outflows for the most part (see Figure 4.3). While industrialized nations were by far the main sources of FDI outflows and the main destinations for FDI inflows, developing nations steadily increased their share of both inflows and outflows (see Figures 4.2 and 4.3).

The top 500 MNCs accounted over 90 percent of global FDI and more than half of world trade by the late 1990s. Out of the 500 top MNCs, 441 were headquarted in the developed countries of North America, Western

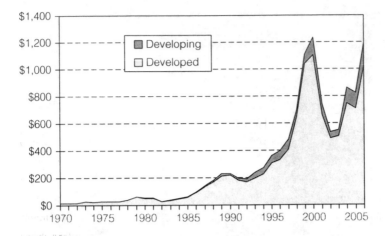

FIGURE 4.2 Outflows of FDI from Industrialized and Developing Nations, in Billions of Current Dollars, 1970–2006

SOURCE: United Nations Conference on Trade and Development, *World Investment Report 2007* (Geneva, Switzerland: UNCTAD, 2007).

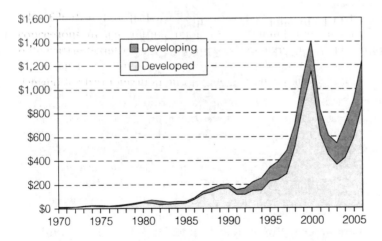

FIGURE 4.3 Inflows of FDI from Industrialized and Developing Nations, in Billions of Current Dollars, 1970–2006

SOURCE: United Nations Conference on Trade and Development, *World Investment Report 2007* (Geneva, Switzerland: UNCTAD, 2007).

Europe, and Japan.[22] Sales of foreign affiliates of MNCs were greater than total world exports, implying that MNCs used FDI as much as or more than they used exports to service overseas demand for their goods and services. In addition, FDI inflows represented 12.6 percent of global gross fixed capital formation in 2006, up from 5 percent in 1990 and 2 percent in 1980, suggesting the growing importance of FDI in world economic growth.[23]

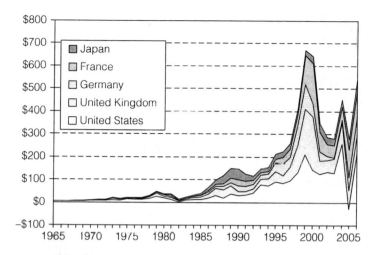

FIGURE 4.4 Outflows of FDI from the Big Five Industrialized Countries, in Billions of Current Dollars, 1965–2006

SOURCES: World Bank, *World Data 1994 CD-ROM* (Washington, D.C.: World Bank, 1994); UNCTAD, *World Investment Report* (Geneva, Switzerland: UNCTAD, 2007).

The FDI outflows and inflows of the five largest industrialized economies have fluctuated widely in recent years. All five large industrialized economies experienced rapid increases in outbound FDI in the 1980s. Japanese outflows, in particular, rose very rapidly in the 1980s and then declined rapidly in the early 1990s (see Figure 4.4). Inflows of FDI into Japan remained low relative to those of other large industrialized countries. FDI inflows into the United States increased rapidly during the 1980s, reflecting the efforts of European and Japanese firms to establish economic beachheads in North America in a time of movement toward a more regionalized world trading system. They rose again in the first decade of the the twenty-first century, partly a consequence of the weakening dollar (see Figure 4.5).

Canada, which traditionally had widespread and high levels of foreign investment, represented the most extreme case of an industrialized country that was dependent on inflows of FDI. Annual inflows of FDI into Canada averaged $979 million between 1982 and 1987. Inflows increased rapidly from $7.6 billion in 1990 to $69 billion in 2006.[24] Part of the reason for the increase in FDI inflows in the last fifteen years was the formation of NAFTA.

Annual inflows of FDI into the European Union averaged $19 billion in 1982–1987. Inflows increased to $109 billion in 1990.[25] In 2006, FDI inflows into the EU reached a level of $566 billion.[26] While the United States was the origin of the largest percentage of non-European FDI inflows, the U.S. share declined steadily in the 1980s and the Japanese share increased rapidly.[27]

Investment in the United States by European and Japanese corporations increased greatly in the 1980s. Whereas, in the early 1960s, the stock of foreign direct investment in the United States was negligible, by 1980 the United States had about $83 billion in foreign direct investment. By 1992 this had grown to $420 billion. In 1970, the inward stock of direct foreign investment

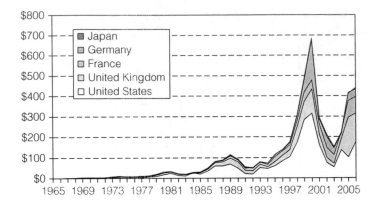

FIGURE 4.5 Inflows of FDI into the Big Five Industrialized Countries, in Billions of Current Dollars, 1965–2006

SOURCE: World Bank, *World Data 1994 CD-ROM* (Washington, D.C.: World Bank, 1994); UNCTAD, *World Investment Report* (Geneva, Switzerland: UNCTAD, 2007).

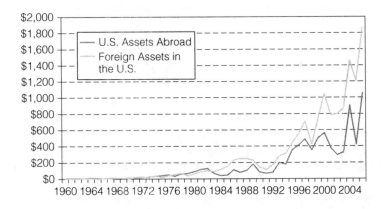

FIGURE 4.6 U.S.-Owned Assets Abroad vs. Foreign-Owned Assets in the United States, in Billions of Current Dollars, 1960–2006

SOURCE: *Economic Report of the President 2007* (Washington, D.C.: U.S. Government Printing Office, 2007).

in the United States was only about 20 percent of the stock of U.S. direct investment abroad. By 1992, that figure was about 86 percent.[28] In the early 1980s, the value of foreign assets in the United States began to exceed the value of U.S. assets abroad (see Figure 4.6), a trend that has continued with some variation to the present.[29]

There were several reasons for the increased interest of foreign corporations in investment opportunities in the United States. One was the increased size and aggressiveness of non–U.S. firms. In the year 2000, for example, of the top 500 MNCs, 148 were based in the European Union and 107 were based in Japan.[30] Another reason was that the decline of the dollar in the 1970s, the late 1980s, and the first decade of the twenty-first century brought down the cost of acquiring U.S. firms, making them more attractive acquisitions for foreign corporations. These circumstances coincided with an uptick in corporate restructuring and downsizing in the United States, which left many companies up for sale, and with the search by U.S. surplus trading partners for safe places to invest their money. A further incentive to invest in the United States was growing trade frictions and protectionist pressures in such vulnerable sectors as electrical equipment and automobiles.[31] Production in the United States guaranteed continued access to the huge U.S. domestic market. And finally, foreign investors were attracted to the U.S. market by the relative political stability of the United States.

One interesting new dimension of foreign investment in the United States was the influx of foreign banks and securities firms, which were attracted to the United States by clients who had already located there, by profits to be made in U.S. financial markets, and by the low cost of acquiring U.S. banks. The growth of Japanese banks was particularly important in the 1980s, keeping pace with the spread of Japanese business and foreign investment. Japan was the world's leading capital exporter by the end of the 1980s, and the United States was one of its favorite sites for investment.

Japanese financial institutions challenged U.S. supremacy in the banking and securities areas. In 1985, Japanese banks overtook U.S. banks as the world's biggest lenders.[32] Although only one of the top ten banks in the world measured by assets was Japanese in 1978, twelve of the top fourteen were Japanese by the end of 1986,[33] and four of the top ten securities firms ranked by capital were Japanese.[34] The assets of Japanese banks grew from 25 percent of the total assets of the largest 50 banks in 1980 to 57 percent in 1989.[35] Even after the bursting of the Japanese economic bubble in 1991, Japanese banks continued to dominate the list of the world's largest banks. Loan activity dropped back, however, especially in important overseas markets like the United States.[36]

Another more recent trend was the growth in **private equity** financing of mergers and acquisitions connected with foreign direct investment. Private equity involves the issuing of shares of businesses that are not publicly traded on a stock exchange. There are a variety of ways that private equity can be used for financing business operations. One of the older and more familiar ones is **venture capital**. In venture capital, a wealthy individual or a group of wealthy individuals provides funds to a "start-up" firm in exchange for financial control in the form of equity. Many of the large semiconductor firms of Silicon Valley started with venture capital funding. Because of the high risk associated with start-up enterprises, the investors require high rates of return on their investments. They expect many of the ventures they invest in to fail, so the ones that succeed have to succeed big in order to justify the investment.

Another form of private equity is the **leveraged buyout (LBO)**. The leveraged buyout is a method for converting a publicly traded firm into a privately held firm by purchasing a controlling interest in the firm. A wealthy individual or group may do this on their own or with bank loans. The rationale for doing this has to be that, by taking a public firm private, the purchaser is increasing the overall value of the assets of the firm. There was a boom in leveraged buyouts in

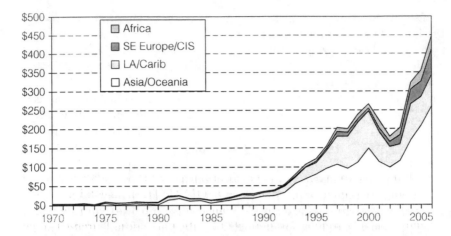

FIGURE 4.7 FDI Inflows into Developing and Transition Economies by Region, in Billions of Dollars, 1970–2006

SOURCE: UNCTAD, *World Investment Report 2007* (Geneva, Switzerland: UNCTAD, 2007).

the 1980s stimulated by the successes of LBO-innovators like Warren Buffett. The passage of the Sarbanes–Oxley Act of 2002, which was designed to correct problems in U.S. corporate governance, allowed for the low interest rates made possible by declining inflation rates after 2000, and a general climate of financial deregulation stimulated the growth of a third form of private equity, the private equity fund. **Private equity funds** were created to pool the risks associated with investments in venture capital and LBO markets.[37] By 2006, $356 billion had been invested in this market, an increase of 25 percent over the previous year.[38] Private equity funds contributed to an uptick in mergers and acquisitions and thereby an increase in flows of FDI internationally between 2000 and 2006.

FDI outflows to the developing world were highly concentrated in Latin America and Asia. These two regions accounted for two-thirds of the total FDI outflows of OECD member countries that did not go to other OECD countries. Between 1985 and 2006, there was a major reduction in Latin America's share of FDI outflows and a major increase in the Asian share (see Figure 4.7). After 2000, FDI began to flow in significant quantities to countries that used to be part of the Soviet Bloc.

To summarize, one of the big changes during the period of interdependence was the increased role of Europe and Japan in generating outflows of FDI. All three major industrialized regions rapidly increased their FDI outflows, but one major industrialized country, Japan, stood out as attracting considerably lower inflows than the others. Europe and the United States considered this to be evidence of significant barriers to FDI inflows in Japan, even though the Japanese government had dismantled most legal barriers. Accordingly, in the 1990s, both the U.S. government and the EU put pressure on the Japanese government and industry groups to open the Japanese economy to inflows of foreign direct investment.[39]

During the period of globalization, the biggest changes in FDI flows were associated with the rapid growth of MNCs from the developing world (especially East Asia), the temporary downturns associated with the Japanese and the dot.com bubbles, and the rise of private equity funds. The generally upward trend in flows was not hindered by the lack of a multilateral investment regime and not helped much by the TRIMs agreement in the Uruguay Round. Something else was driving the trend toward greater flows.

EXPLAINING THE GROWTH IN MNC ACTIVITY

There are a number of theories about the factors that have contributed to the enormous expansion of the MNC activity in the past three decades. Changes in technology and organizational sophistication created the possibility of expansion. The development of new communications technologies, cheaper and more reliable transportation networks, and innovative techniques of management and organization have made possible the kind of centralization, integration, and flexibility that are the hallmark of the successful MNC. But these were merely enabling factors. The question remains as to why we have seen such a great expansion of MNC activity since the end of World War II.

One answer would be to stress the importance of government policies.[40] Some governments—particularly powerful governments like that of the United States—actively encouraged multinational expansion. The progressive elimination of restraints on capital flows made expansion of direct investment possible. The reduction of tariffs made direct investment more attractive. Governments directly subsidized FDI outflows by providing various forms of insurance for international investments. The United States, for example, created the **Overseas Private Investment Corporation (OPIC)** in 1961 to insure U.S. firms against some of the risks involved in direct investment.[41] Canadians and Europeans created incentives to attract inflows of foreign investment.[42] Although the U.S. federal government has not officially courted foreign investment, in recent years states and local communities have taken the lead, even competing with one another for foreign manufacturing plants.[43]

But, again, government policy changes alone would not have resulted in the expansion of MNC activity described above. Foreign investment, after all, is the result primarily of decisions made by private firms. Theories about FDI that do not take into account the firm-level incentives to invest overseas are not likely to be very helpful in explaining the trends described above. We turn, therefore, to a set of theories that deal with this issue.

Horizontal and Vertical FDI and the KK Model

One key distinction in the economics literature on MNCs is between horizontal and vertical FDI. **Horizontal FDI** replicates activities that occur in the home country in a variety of host countries. The purpose of horizontal FDI is to gain access to local markets that might otherwise be inaccessible. **Vertical FDI** fragments production across countries so that different tasks are located according to differences in the relative abundance of **factors of production**. Thus, skilled-labor-intensive activities would occur in skilled-labor-abundant locations and unskilled-labor-intensive activities would occur in unskilled-labor-intensive locations, and so on. Here the purpose of FDI is to minimize production costs so that the firm can be internationally competitive in multiple markets.[44] Horizontal FDI tends to go to relatively wealthy regions of the world, whereas vertical FDI tends to go to developing countries that have abundant labor and low wages or some other factor-based advantage such as an abundance of raw materials or energy.

Since most of the FDI flows are among the industrialized countries and a small proportion of flows are between the industrialized and the developing countries, then one important theoretical question is why there is more horizontal than vertical FDI. A theory that attempts to explain this is James Markusen's knowledge-capital or KK model.[45]

Internalization Theory

Internalization theory contends that firms expand abroad through foreign direct investment in order to "internalize" activities in the presence of market imperfections, just as they expand domestically by building multiple plants and offices for similar reasons. The particular market imperfections that create incentives for internalization are represented in the idea of transaction costs. **Transaction costs** arise when markets produce undesirable results because of various imperfections. For example, when the costs of concluding long-term contracts with an external firm are higher than the costs of establishing a new internal unit to accomplish the same purpose, then it can be said that the market for long-term contracts is imperfect and generates high transaction costs.[46]

There are both natural and artificial reasons for market imperfections. Long-term contract markets are inherently difficult to organize and prone to high transaction costs. Similarly, it is frequently difficult to put an accurate price on technologies when licensing them or otherwise transferring them to another firm. There are problems of asymmetry of information between the buyer and seller that make such markets notoriously tricky. Often sellers require buyers to sign "nondisclosure agreements" to protect their intellectual property before explaining what the technology does in the first place. It is no wonder that buyers often perceive these transactions to have high costs and that they sometimes try to avoid them by creating their own technologies or by buying companies that own the technologies they need (both forms of internalization). Sellers are equally wary, mainly because they do not wish to lose control over knowledge that may provide them with important competitive advantages.

Market imperfections of this sort may be considered artificial to the extent that they are at least partly the result of government policies. Markets for information are frequently faulty, but trade barriers or lax government enforcement of intellectual property rights may also create higher than normal transaction costs for firms considering alternatives to foreign direct investment, and thus may help to motivate them to internalize those costs by investing abroad.[47]

The OLI Model

John Dunning has expanded upon internalization theory by suggesting that three conditions must be met before a firm will be able to compete with local firms despite the disadvantages of being foreign: (1) it must have market power that derives from ownership of some specialized knowledge, (2) it must consider the particular foreign location advantageous for new investments relative to alternative locations including its home market, and (3) it must prefer FDI over exporting and licensing by the usual internalization logic. This expansion on internalization theory is called the **OLI model**, where OLI stands for ownership, location, and internalization.[48]

The OLI model is one of the most widely accepted theories of foreign direct investment.[49] Nevertheless, there are other theories that attempt to explain aspects of MNC behavior and/or MNC/host country relationships that are somewhat different from and not entirely compatible with the either the KK or the OLI model.

Product Cycle Theory

The product cycle theory argues that firms expand abroad when their principal products become "mature" in domestic markets. During the initial or rapid growth stage of product commercialization the firm attempts mainly to respond to domestic demand. As growth tapers off, the firm may begin to look for new sources of demand in export markets. Eventually, domestic demand begins to fall as the market is saturated, new firms begin to challenge the earlier entrants to the market, and the firm looks for ways to protect its revenues and profits by establishing foreign subsidiaries with lower factor costs so as to remain competitive in the home market and/or gain better access to foreign markets. As overall demand for the product moves toward zero, the firm will try to move on to new products or attempt to create new advantages by altering the product (see Figure 4.8).[50] The product cycle theory was designed to explain changes over time in FDI on the part of manufacturing firms, and was never put forward as a general theory of MNCs or FDI. Nevertheless, it adds something to OLI theory by positing a reason for changes over time in firm-specific ownership advantages.

Obsolescing Bargain Theory

A close relative of product cycle theory is the theory of the obsolescing bargain. In obsolescing bargain theory, a firm that has invested in a host country starts with a good bargaining position with the host country's government because of firm-specific advantages such as superior technology, access to capital markets, and access to final product markets. An excellent example of this would be the initial negotiations between American oil companies and host governments in

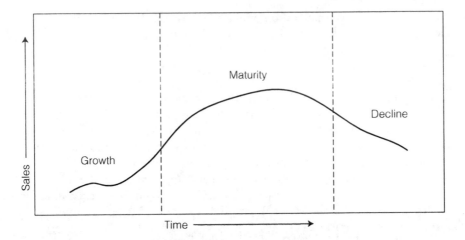

F I G U R E 4.8 Product Cycle Theory

SOURCE: Raymond Vernon, "International Investment and International Trade in the Product Cycle," *Quarterly Journal of Economics*, 80 (May 1966): 190–207.

the Middle East in the 1920s. U.S. firms were able to win favorable "concessions" for the right to drill for petroleum in the new oil fields. Once the firm has made an investment, however, the bargaining advantage may slowly shift to the host country. The technology may mature and become more easily accessible to the host country's firms, and the host country may learn how to gain better access to global capital markets and to final product markets. It then attempts to negotiate more favorable terms with the foreign investor.[51]

Oligopoly Theory

The oligopoly theory of foreign investment contends that firms move abroad to exploit the **monopoly** power they possess through such factors as unique products, marketing expertise, control of technology and managerial skills, or access to capital.[52] In the battle for profits and market share, firms engaged in oligopolistic competition may move abroad as part of their overall competitive strategy. They may move aggressively to exploit a new foreign market in the hope that this action will give them a permanent advantage over their competitors. Conversely, a company whose competitors have just entered a foreign market might be forced to go international defensively, in order to block their opponent's move or at least prevent the competitor from gaining a survival-threatening advantage.

The oligopoly theory is consistent with the OLI model in that the OLI model asserts that a firm must have some sort of market power derived from firm-specific advantages (usually based on the firm's special knowledge). Many oligopolistic industries are populated with precisely this type of firm. What oligopoly theory adds to the OLI model is the idea that the timing of entry into specific foreign markets may depend upon the timing of entry of a given firm's competitors.

The Tariff-Jumping Hypothesis

Another important hypothesis about FDI flows deals with the attempt by MNCs to jump over tariff or nontariff barriers by establishing foreign subsidiaries. The tariff-jumping hypothesis has been used recently to explain the increased willingness of Japanese and U.S. MNCs to invest in Ireland and the United Kingdom to gain access to markets in Western Europe. Because Ireland and the UK are members of the European Union, investing in those two countries may provide improved access to all the members of the EU. As a result, the data appear to indicate that non-European MNCs seem more than usually interested in investing in those two countries. The tariff-jumping hypothesis, again, is consistent with the OLI model because, for example, the existence of the European Union, with its high external tariffs and low internal ones, gives a locational advantage to relatively low-wage countries within the EU.[53]

Barrier jumping is also posited as an explanation for the rapid increase in FDI flows from Japan to the United States. This is particularly true of Japanese investments in automobile production in the United States. The first big jump in Japanese FDI in autos occurred in 1981, the year in which a VER was negotiated to limit Japanese exports. Investments continued during the 1980s on the assumption that the U.S. market would be closed to Japanese imports unless they were replaced with local production. As a result, Japanese production capacity in the United States increased from zero in 1980 to approximately 2.8 million units per year in 2004.[54]

The Importance of the Home Country

More recent theorizing about the behavior of MNCs stresses the importance of the home country. Marked differences in the behavior of MNCs from different home countries—for example, U.S. firms versus Japanese firms—suggest that the way in which the home country structures its domestic economy has an important impact on the way in which domestic firms internationalize their business activities, despite the fact that most economic theories of MNC behavior seem to imply that the home country context should be largely irrelevant. While there is a certain convergence in the behavior of firms from different home countries over time in terms of the way they deal with questions of organizing export activities, local production, R&D, and marketing,[55] firms of different nationalities retain important distinctive characteristics that are strongly affected by the home environment.

For example, Japanese firms belong to confederations of allied firms called *keiretsu*. When Japanese firms go abroad, they try to sustain their ties with other keiretsu firms at home and abroad, even when this might not be entirely rational from a short-term economic perspective.[56] U.S. firms, in contrast, are not as likely to develop long-term relationships with other firms, even though they are quite willing to nurture short-term partnerships. Other systematic differences between U.S. and Asian firms include different average rates of return on foreign assets and debt/equity ratios. For example, Japanese and Korean firms tend to have lower returns on foreign assets and higher debt/equity ratios than U.S. firms.[57]

THE CONSEQUENCES OF MNC ACTIVITY

Modern governments have given high priority to the public policy goals of **economic efficiency**, growth, and improvement in the standard of living. In evaluating the impact of multinational corporations on developed market economies and determining the governance problems raised by multinationals, one must examine the effect of those firms on economic performance. This is not a simple task, however, because it is somewhat difficult to separate out the effects of FDI and other MNC activities from those of other variables on a given country's economic performance. For most macroeconomists, for example, capital investment is capital investment no matter who owns it or where it comes from. It is clear that FDI flows add to the pool of capital available for investment on a global basis. Many empirical studies have demonstrated that there is a positive relationship between increases in FDI flows and economic growth rates in a wide variety of countries.[58] Empirical studies of the impact of increases in FDI inflows, nevertheless, have to consider what might have happened to domestic investment levels in the absence of increased FDI inflows. Similar points could be made about transfers of new technology or efforts to raise the skill levels of local MNC employees.[59]

Proponents of multinational corporations argue that FDI is a mechanism for increasing productivity and stimulating growth. By transferring capital, technology, and know-how and by mobilizing idle domestic resources, multinational corporations (argue their advocates) increase productivity, foster growth, and thereby improve welfare.[60] To be more specific, the potential gains from FDI fall into three main categories. First, FDI may facilitate trade in goods and services by allowing firms to compensate for market imperfections by engaging in international **intrafirm trade**. Second, FDI may increase the productivity of firms that are directly engaged in FDI, especially those that are the recipients of FDI inflows. Third, FDI may generate positive **external economies** that benefit firms and other economic actors that are not directly engaged in FDI.[61]

There are strong indications that increases in FDI flows are associated with rising levels of trade—that FDI is not a substitute for trade but actually helps to generate trade. Even when MNCs invest in overseas production facilities to service foreign markets, for example, some of that overseas investment generates demand for exports from the home country. A hypothetical example would be the establishment of an automobile assembly plant by a U.S. MNC in Belgium. Until the firm locates Belgian (or European) suppliers of automobile components, it is quite likely the firm will continue to purchase components from U.S. companies for its Belgian operations. Even when local suppliers are substituted for initially imported components, there will continue to be a demand for goods and services that the firm thinks it can get only from the home country.

In other words, the same factors that create incentives for FDI also create incentives for intrafirm trade. In 1988, for example, Japanese subsidiaries in the United States purchased over four-fifths of their imports from their parent companies in Japan and exported over three-fifths of their exports to the same companies. In the same year, intracompany trade between U.S. parent firms and U.S.-owned foreign affiliates accounted for over two-fifths of total U.S. imports and over one-third of total U.S. exports.[62] As a result of the increase in FDI flows and MNC activity, a large and growing proportion of world trade in manufactures, perhaps as much as 50 percent, is accounted for by intrafirm trade.[63]

It is possible, however, that external economies are more important than gains from trade, since FDI tends to generate more rapid growth in overseas production and sales than in exports (with some notable exceptions). Measuring the extent of external economies is difficult, and therefore not much research has been undertaken in this area. One method that has been used is to examine changes in productivity, export performance, and research effort of locally oriented domestic firms after the entry of foreign firms.[64] Some additional clues about externality gains can be obtained from analyses of inflows of FDI into specific countries and industries.

For example, suppose that there had never been any Japanese investment in local production of automobiles in the United States and that U.S. auto firms had succeeded in getting higher trade barriers against Japanese firms to reduce competition from Japan. Then consumers would have lost by not being able to purchase the relatively inexpensive but high quality automobiles produced by Japanese firms, and U.S. firms would not have been forced to upgrade the quality of their products and the efficiency of their plants to match those of Japanese producers.[65] The end result would have been a decline in the overall international competitiveness of the U.S. auto industry. Thus Japanese inflows of FDI in automobiles in the 1980s may have been good for U.S. competitiveness. This is called a **demonstration effect** of FDI because the presence of foreign firms demonstrates the advantages of organizing production in a different way.

It is important to remember, however, that the United States generally has low barriers to trade. As a result, incentives for firms located there to become internationally competitive are higher than those for firms located in countries with high barriers to trade. Thus one would not expect FDI inflows into the latter to have positive effects on their international competitiveness. Similarly, one would not expect the externality-based benefits of FDI inflows to be as great in countries with relatively low levels of human capital development as in countries, like the United States, with relatively high levels of human capital.[66] This suggests that there may be a stronger basis for concern about the possible negative effects of FDI inflows in developing countries than in industrialized countries (see Chapter 8). Nevertheless, even in industrialized countries there are important concerns about the effects of MNC activities.

Critics of multinational corporations believe that inflows of FDI may reduce efficiency and stifle growth in host countries. Because MNCs tend to be oligopolistic, they may be able to predate domestic firms, limit their own production, maintain artificially high prices, and thus earn **oligopoly rents**. If the rents are not reinvested locally, but rather are extracted via profit repatriation, then the country might have been better off limiting the entry of MNCs or limiting the **repatriation of profits**, because domestic firms would have been more likely to reinvest such rents domestically. In addition, critics argue that MNCs may actually hinder national growth and economic prosperity by absorbing local capital instead of providing new capital, by applying inappropriate technology, by creating "bad" (low-skill and low-wage) jobs instead of "good" (high-skill and high-wage) jobs, by doing research in the home country instead of in the host country, and by employing expatriate, not indigenous, managers. Most of these criticisms have been tested empirically and most of the available evidence suggests that they are not correct, but there are a few areas where the criticisms seem to have some validity.[67]

Over the years, much research has been devoted to the question of the effects of FDI on economic performance on specific countries or regions.[68] Most studies of the economic impact of multinational corporations on their host developed market economies conclude that their overall effect is positive. The 1981 Caborn report adopted by the Parliament of the European Community, which called for greater regulation of multinational corporations, found that multinational enterprises raise the level of world economic activity and have "favorable impacts on productivity, growth rates and overall level of employment, on the dissemination of new products and processes and also of managerial know-how."[69] Other benefits cited in studies of individual European economies include improvements in balance of payments, research and development, the level of technology, and increased dynamism.[70]

Possible Negative Effects of MNCs

Despite indications of overall benefits from multinational corporations, such investment is not without costs for the host state. Costs are incurred because behavior that is rational for the corporation may be less beneficial to the host country. Several concerns have been revealed in public and private studies.[71] The fear of **technological dependence** is one. Although access to advanced technology is one of the primary economic benefits of multinational corporations for the host developed countries, that access may stifle domestic research and development. The concentration of research and development in the home state may discourage research and development activities in the host state and result in the subordination of the host to technology controlled from abroad. There is a related concern that host states may pay excessive costs for imported technology, because the control of technology by a multinational enables the parent to charge a monopoly **rent** for its use.[72] A similar concern arises concerning management skills. The transfer of managerial talent to host countries can be a source of efficiency and growth, but the use of foreign managers may also deny nationals opportunities to use and develop their skills.

Yet another concern grows out of the multinational corporations' oligopolistic character. The entrance of foreign competitors may stimulate domestic competition and thus encourage efficiency, but it may also reduce competition and threaten existing domestic industries. Even such market dominance by multinational corporations may be beneficial if it brings with it new technologies and other economic efficiencies. But if it does not introduce such improvements, it may decrease efficiency. Special concern is voiced by states when multinational corporations acquire existing national firms. Acquisition may give the firm access to capital, technology, and other resources and thereby improve its performance, but it may simply indicate a transfer of ownership, adding no new efficiencies.

Some concern has been expressed regarding the import orientation of multinational corporations. An official Canadian study, known as the Gray report, found that subsidiaries in Canada preferred to seek supplies and services within the company, as opposed to within the country. This preference for importing from the parent may provide the highest-quality goods and services, but it may retard the development of Canadian manufacturing and service sectors and thus limit the spillover effect that foreign investment has on the rest of the Canadian economy.[73] Other concerns have been voiced regarding export policy. Although the evidence suggests that multinational corporations have an equal or better export record than their domestic counterparts do, the practice of restricting exports and limiting markets of individual subsidiaries is not unknown in multinational corporations. Finally, there is concern connected with the multinational corporations' balance-of-payments impact. The consensus of economists is that balance-of-payments effects of MNCs are minor in comparison with macroeconomic factors such as the growth rate of the economy, changes in exchange rates, and the like; but critics continue to argue that MNCs contribute to trade deficits because of their greater propensity than domestic firms to import needed inputs.[74]

The multinationals' economic impact on host economies is generally positive, and the public generally perceives that positive impact. Yet there are real economic concerns in specific areas. The most important issue for the developed host countries is not whether foreign investment is economically worthwhile but whether it is possible to increase the benefits and decrease the costs associated with foreign direct investment.

For much of the 1960s and 1970s, examination of the effects of multinational corporations focused on the host states, with the implicit assumption that the home state was always the recipient of economic benefits. In the last two decades, however, that assumption has come under fire. Some analysts and influential interest groups in the United States, particularly labor union representatives, believe that U.S. direct foreign investment had a negative effect on the U.S. economy by favoring foreign investment over foreign trade and production in the United States, exporting jobs instead of goods, allowing tax revenues to escape, and impairing domestic economic development by sending capital abroad instead of using it at home. Although these arguments had increasing political significance, several studies of the impact of foreign investment on the U.S. economy revealed that investment had not taken place at the expense of domestic investment, trade, or employment.[75]

Indeed, the politics of multinational corporations within the industrialized countries increasingly involves debates over what should be done to assist domestically owned MNCs to become more internationally competitive. Some political actors favor extensive interventions on the part of the government to promote specific firms and industries—sometimes called industrial policy, but also referred to as technology policy when it involves more focused assistance for the creation and commercialization of new technologies. These proponents often argue in favor of interventions to counter the industrial policies of others, especially Japan and the Asian NICs. Others oppose such interventions as being contrary to the norms of the multilateral trading system, difficult to carry out in the new globalized world economy because the national identity of MNCs is becoming somewhat less clear, and generally ineffective in promoting the interests of the nation.

National Economic Control

A second area of potential conflict between MNCs and governments in developed countries is the interference of multinational corporations in the national control of the economy. As developed states have sought to manage their economies to improve economic efficiency, growth, and welfare, concern about external constraints on that control by multinational corporations has emerged.

The concern with national control is clearly revealed in studies of elite and public attitudes toward foreign investment. In a survey of European public opinion, most of the negative views on multinationals centered on fears that they might erode the national control of the economy.[76] Many respondents saw major differences between U.S. and European multinationals: corporations based in the United States were viewed as typically powerful, dynamic, and well organized but also uncontrollable and morally suspect; whereas multinationals based in Europe were seen as socially committed, humane, and loyal as business partners.[77] Various studies of Canadian attitudes reveal that the most adverse feeling toward multinational corporations involved the loss of control. Canadians generally believe that there is a trade-off between the economic benefit of multinational corporations and their adverse effect on control over national affairs.[78]

The sense of lost control reflects, in part, an intangible feeling that, as a result of foreign investment, decisions crucial to the national economy are made outside the nation. The perception is not that these decisions are adverse, just that they are made elsewhere. The tendency of multinational corporations to centralize decisions in the parent suggests that the fears that decision making shifts from host to investing country are often justified. Interestingly, the intangible fear of loss of decision making may not be related to the level of foreign investment. Canadians, who have a vast amount of foreign investment, are no more concerned than are the English, who have much less. The French, with a low level of investment, on the other hand, evidence a high level of concern. The fear of lost control seems to be related more to different national expectations regarding the need for independence than to the actual threat to that independence.[79]

The fear of lost control of sensitive industries is particularly acute. Countries, including the United States, have always been concerned about foreign ownership of such sectors as communications, transportation, and finance. Increasingly, public officials feel that industries with a large influence on the economy, such as the automotive or petroleum industries, or those in the vanguard of scientific and technological development, such as computers or electronics, should remain under national control.[80] Such concern emerged in the United States in 1987 when the Japanese company, Fujitsu Ltd., tried to acquire an 80-percent share in Fairchild Semiconductor Corporation, a pioneering firm in the industry and a large supplier of computer chips for the U.S. military that had fallen upon bad times. Various U.S. government officials argued strongly that the sale ought to be blocked on national security grounds. Ironically, Fujitsu was proposing to buy the 80-percent share that already belonged to another foreign firm, the French company Schlumberger, Ltd. Apparently the concern of government officials was not simply that it was foreigners who wanted to buy Fairchild, but that it was the Japanese in particular, with whom U.S. semiconductor competition has been particularly fierce. In this case, the issue never came to decision because Fujitsu withdrew its offer as a result of the controversy. Since that time, however, as foreign investment in the United States has increased, public opinion has been wary of foreign investors, especially in the sensitive high-technology industries.

Whereas multinational corporations have often played an important role in achieving national goals, there is a concern that they are less responsive to national economic planning than are domestically owned firms operating primarily in the national market.[81] The concern is, first, that activity rational for an international firm may not be in tune with that planned for the national economy and, second, that the multinational has the capacity to circumvent mechanisms for implementing national plans. Because multinational corporations have access to outside financing, they are not as dependent as domestic industry is on national governmental finance and thus may not respond to governmental incentives to invest in certain industries or certain regions. Because they have fewer links with the national economy and polity, it is feared, multinational corporations are less likely to cooperate voluntarily with national planning goals.

The Gray report, for example, expressed a concern that multinational corporations might interfere with the Canadian government's goal of increasing investment in manufacturing and discouraging overdevelopment of resource extraction. The report pointed out that foreign fabricating and manufacturing firms that integrate vertically backward to obtain secure supplies of natural resources are less likely to respond to Canadian needs and economic capabilities because their raison d'être is shaped heavily by their committed investment elsewhere.[82]

A greater concern is that multinational corporations may evade national taxation. Through its central control of pricing, the multinational corporation can take profits in countries where taxes are low and avoid showing profits and paying taxes in those countries where taxes are high. Because transactions of subsidiaries of the same multinational are not arm's length transactions—that is, not determined by free-market prices—the central decision-making unit can artificially fix the prices of those transactions. These so-called **transfer prices** can be manipulated to minimize taxes.[83] A multinational can, for example, inflate the price of imports or decrease the value of exports among affiliated companies in order to minimize the earnings of a subsidiary in a high-tax country. This issue emerged in the United States when certain states proposed using a **unitary tax** formula for computing state taxes of multinational corporations. The purpose of the unitary tax is to prevent multinationals from manipulating transfer prices to their own benefit. Rather than taxing the company on its state revenues, the state would tax it according to a complex formula based on its world-wide earnings. This provoked a strong reaction, particularly from Japanese and British corporations, who threatened to stop investing in states that used unitary tax formulas.[84]

A controversy over California's unitary tax led to the U.S. Supreme Court's 1994 decision on a lawsuit filed by Barclays Bank of the United Kingdom in 1984 and another by Colgate-Palmolive in 1986 arguing that the California system was unconstitutional. On June 20, 1994, the Court voted 7–2 in favor of California's right to keep the unitary tax. If the Court had voted against California, the state would have had to refund approximately $2 to $4 billion in taxes already collected under the law and return to a system of taxation based on the assumption of "arms length" relationships between MNC parents and local subsidiaries.

The California legislature decided in 1986 and 1993 to modify the unitary tax law to make it elective. State authorities realized that the system was creating disincentives for inflows of new FDI and recognized that it was quite difficult to administer because of wide variations in national accounting practices, fluctuations in international exchange rates, and lack of full cooperation from foreign MNCs in tax audits.[85] So while the ruling of the U.S. Supreme Court paved the way for other states to adopt unitary taxes, California was slowly but surely jettisoning the idea.

Another dimension of interference in national control is in what one author called the "national order."[86] Multinational corporations, it is charged, are less bound by national social codes and economic relationships. Thus the links between business and government that exist in Europe and in Japan and that are a tool for national economic management may be more tenuous and less effective between national governments and foreign multinationals.[87]

Another aspect of the national order is labor-business relations. It has been argued that foreign multinationals have followed labor policies inimical to national labor policies. It has been charged that they are more willing than national firms, for example, to discharge employees and are less willing to consult employees in making decisions that will affect them.[88] Europe is particularly sensitive to this because of its commitment to labor rights and employment protection, but these concerns have also surfaced in the United States. In 1988, the British construction company Beazer tried to buy Koppers, a Pittsburgh-based construction materials and chemicals company. In order to stir up public opposition to the takeover, Koppers' management successfully played up fears that Beazer, as an allegedly insensitive foreign company, would close the plant or fire workers.

Interference by Home Governments of Multinationals

Another dimension of the problem of control is not the threat from the multinational itself but from the multinational's home government to the host country, primarily the threat from the United States to the host countries of U.S. multinational corporations. Such extraterritorial interference occurs when U.S. laws are applied beyond U.S. borders through subsidiaries of the multinational corporation (MNC).[89]

One area of U.S. extraterritorial interference has been through application of U.S. export controls. The Trading with the Enemy Act of 1917, the Export Control Act of 1949, and its successors, the Export Administration Acts of 1969 and 1979, were used by the U.S. government to control dealings of foreign affiliates of U.S. corporations.[90] The Trading with the Enemy Act empowered the president to regulate all commercial and financial transactions by U.S. citizens with foreign countries or nationals in time of war or national emergency. The act was invoked to prohibit all trade with Cuba, North Korea, North Vietnam, and, until recently, China. The Export Control and Export Administration acts gave the executive branch the authority to "prohibit or curtail" all commercial exports, including technical know-how, to communist or other specified countries from U.S. companies or their foreign subsidiaries on the basis of national security, foreign policy, or short supply. Because U.S. courts held the parent firm criminally liable for the acts of its foreign affiliates, there was a great incentive for multinational corporations to cooperate with these U.S. regulations.

There have been cases in which the United States has blocked U.S. subsidiaries' transactions abroad that were legal under the laws of the host country. In 1982, in a highly politicized episode, the United States ordered U.S. multinational corporations operating abroad to comply with a U.S. embargo on the export of high-technology products to the Soviet Union for use in the construction of a natural gas pipeline from the Soviet Union to Western Europe. The sanctions, originally promulgated in December 1981, following the imposition of martial law in Poland, were extended in June 1982 to subsidiaries of U.S. companies abroad and foreign companies working under U.S. license. The embargo applied to technology that had been purchased when there were no controls on exports from the United States. The incident provoked a serious conflict between the United States and its European allies, who saw the U.S. action as a unilateral and retroactive application of extraterritorial jurisdiction. Some European governments issued formal orders requiring the resident companies to honor the contracts, and when the companies complied, the United States imposed penalties on them, including the revocation of all export licenses.[91]

The U.S. government, however, has not always prevailed. Resistance by the French government and courts led the United States to withdraw its restriction on the sale of trucks made in France by a U.S. firm to the People's Republic of China. And after five months, the U.S. decision to extend the pipeline embargo to foreign subsidiaries of U.S. corporations and licenses was reversed following an agreement by the North Atlantic Treaty Organization (NATO) allies to study

East-West trade. Numerous other cases suggest that the U.S. government is often willing to back down when foreign governments insist.[92]

Another area of U.S. (as well as EC and West German) extraterritorial interference has been through antitrust legislation. The Sherman and Clayton acts seek to prevent restraint of competition both within the United States and in U.S. import and export trade. The U.S. courts have asserted a wide-ranging extraterritorial jurisdiction of these laws, including application to the subsidiaries of U.S. multinational corporations. The fact that a U.S. corporation is a parent of a foreign subsidiary has been held sufficient for jurisdiction by U.S. courts. On this basis, the U.S. government has attempted to force, not always with success, disclosure of information by foreign subsidiaries. It has forced U.S. parents to divest themselves of foreign affiliates or to alter the behavior of their affiliates, even though that ownership or behavior was legal under the host country's laws. United States courts, for example, forced a U.S. beer company to divest itself of a subsidiary in Canada and obliged American parents to order their subsidiaries to cease to operate in a radio cartel in Canada, even though this cartel had been approved by the Canadian government.

In another case, U.S. courts claimed jurisdiction in a private antitrust claim against foreign companies joining in a uranium cartel outside the United States and with the expressed consent of their governments. But instead of the defendant firms, the relevant governments, including Canada and the United Kingdom, appeared in court and argued that the United States could not exercise jurisdiction because it had provoked the cartel by embargoing the use of foreign-origin uranium in U.S. nuclear reactors; because the cartel was, as a result, created as a matter of government policy; and because laws outside the United States do not regard cartel formation as unlawful. The court not only rejected these arguments but also criticized the governments for appearing in place of the firms. Largely in reaction to the uranium case, the United Kingdom enacted legislation to block such action by foreign governments.[93]

Finally, there has been intervention through U.S. balance-of-payments policies. In the 1960s, the U.S. government tried to improve its balance of payments by asking U.S. corporations to limit their new foreign investment in developed countries, to increase the amount of foreign investment financed by borrowing abroad, and to increase the return of earnings and short-term assets from their foreign affiliates. This had a serious impact on investment abroad, particularly in Europe, where the policy threatened to dampen economic growth, hurt the balance of payments, and dry up local capital markets when U.S. corporations borrowed on local capital markets instead of borrowing in the United States. The capital restraints were ended in the 1970s following the emergence of the float and the improvement in the U.S. balance-of-payments position. Given the internationalization of capital markets in the 1980s, it is unlikely that similar controls could be imposed today.[94]

The U.S. government also used U.S. multinational affiliates to pressure South Africa to end its **apartheid** policy. The Comprehensive Anti-Apartheid Act of 1986 prevented U.S. companies and their foreign branches from providing new loans to the South African government or engaging in new investment in South Africa. Canada, the European Community, the Commonwealth nations, and the Nordic nations passed similar laws prohibiting new investment, and the Nordic countries and Australia and Canada did not allow new bank loans. Congress considered but did not enact stricter legislation, such as requiring mandatory disinvestment by U.S. multinationals or imposing a full-trade boycott on South Africa.

In addition to federal actions directed at ending apartheid, many U.S. state and local governments took a strong stance against apartheid by enacting partial or total disinvestment policies, prohibiting investment of state-run funds in companies that did business in South Africa, or refusing to make purchases from or give contracts to firms that did business in South Africa. Although the state and local governments were not in a position to mandate that U.S. companies withdraw from South Africa, their laws forced multinationals to choose between their U.S. business and their South African business.

Federal, state, and local laws were successful in inducing U.S. corporations to leave South Africa. From 1984 to 1988, for example, 141 U.S. companies withdrew their equity investments from South Africa (although some of these maintained other economic links). It is unlikely that the actions of the United States or those of the other countries that supported the economic embargo against the South African apartheid regime were responsible by themselves for bringing about the end of apartheid, but it is significant that Nelson Mandela was quick to acknowledge its importance after his election to the presidency of the post-apartheid regime. Also, it is noteworthy that so many governments considered manipulation of their multinationals to be a legitimate means of undermining apartheid in South Africa.[95]

In conclusion, the potential for the home country to interfere with MNC activities abroad is very real. If one considers the volume of transactions carried out by multinational corporations, however, the number of actual threats of home country interference is relatively small. Home governments of industrialized nations appear to have adopted a policy of avoiding interference in the activities of MNC affiliates, except in unusual circumstances.

Multinationals and the National Political Process

One final but important area in which multinational corporations may interfere is in the politics of the home and host states. As with any corporation in the home or host country, the multinational is a potentially powerful political actor that can, and at times does, seek to influence law, public policy, and the political environment. The nature and significance of the multinational corporation's effect on national politics in developed countries are areas that have not been sufficiently examined and about which little is known.

There are several ways in which multinational corporations might attempt to influence politics in host countries. In the most extreme case, they might overthrow an unfriendly government or keep a friendly regime in power. They might intervene in elections through legal or illegal campaign contributions or take action to support or oppose particular public policies. Finally, multinational corporations might influence the national political culture—that is, shape public political values and attitudes. In all of these actions, the firm may act on its own, at the instigation or with the support of the home government.[96]

In the case of Canada, the Gray report, which considered these possibilities, concluded that multinational corporations have little direct impact on Canadian public policy. The influence of foreign investment, according to that study, was in shaping alternatives available to Canadian decision makers. For example, because of the structure of Canadian industry and the fact that some firms are foreign controlled, public policy is limited in its efforts to rationalize industry.[97] The U.S. Senate Subcommittee on Multinational Corporations found that multinational corporations have engaged in legal and illegal payments in developed countries, but the subcommittee did not suggest just how such payments influenced public policy.[98]

Multinational corporations may also affect public policy in the home state. One study of U.S. foreign policy found that the direct influence of any particular corporation is likely to be balanced by countervailing powers, even though corporate groups may shape policy. The most important influence, the study concluded, was the ability of business generally to influence the political consensus from which U.S. foreign policy is drawn. The predominance of the liberal approach to international economic relations is an example of this intangible yet significant influence.[99]

A somewhat different view emerged from the hearings of the Senate Subcommittee on Multinational Corporations held in 1975. These hearings suggested that multinational corporations at times become an important part of the dynamic of U.S. foreign policymaking by initiating demands, providing information, and at times cooperating in the execution of policy. Another impression is that multinational corporations at times follow policies independent of, and perhaps in contradiction to, official governmental policy.[100]

Another effect of multinational corporations on national politics is through their influence on social structure. One study suggested that multinational corporations are altering both national and international class structures, creating new social, economic, and political divisions. According to the study, there is a new class structure emerging that consists of a transnational managerial class favoring a liberal international economic order; a large class of established labor with secure employment and status in their local communities, which has been the primary object and beneficiary of social legislation and economic management; and a group of social marginals that has not been integrated into the new industrial society and that suffers the system's social costs. The study found that this new class structure, shaped by the multinational enterprise, will create new social conflicts not suited to control by presently established institutions.[101]

In conclusion, there has been concern and conflict regarding the multinational corporation. However, the regulation of multinational corporations was not as highly politicized and controversial an issue in the Western system as it was in the Third World, especially after the end of the Bretton Woods period. One reason for this was the adoption of policies to encourage the growth of domestically owned MNCs in Western Europe, Japan, and the NICs. Although some in the West believed that multinational corporations should be managed to maximize benefits, there was a general perception of the importance of international investment and the need to remain competitive with other industrialized nations. The former prime minister of Canada, Pierre Trudeau, offered this explanation:

> I don't worry over something which is somewhat inevitable, and I think the problem of economic domination is somewhat inevitable, not only of the United States over Canada but perhaps over countries of Europe as well ... These are facts of life, and they don't worry me. I would want to make sure that this economic presence does not result as I say in a real weakening of our national identity. I use that general expression too. The way in which I do that is to try and balance the benefits against the dis advantages. It is obvious if we keep out capital and keep out technology, we won't be able to develop our resources and we would have to cut our standard of consumption in order to generate the savings to invest ourselves and so on. ... Each country wants to keep its identity or its sovereignty, to speak in legal terms. It has to instantly make assessments, and when we make assessments it is to try and select those areas which are important for our independence, for our identity.[102]

During the period of globalization, however, leftists and environmentalists in the West would take another look at the MNCs and make them part of their objections to the evils of globalization.

INTERNATIONAL REGIMES FOR FOREIGN DIRECT INVESTMENT

Compared with the control of money and trade, the international governance of FDI has been extremely limited and relatively informal.[103] One reason is that constructing international regimes for FDI has only recently become an issue in international economic relations. The need for monetary and trade orders became clear as a result of the crisis of the 1930s, a crucial impetus for the establishment of the postwar economic regimes. In foreign direct investment, however, no such international crisis and no consensus have arisen in the West. It was not until the 1960s that MNCs became an issue in international politics and even then, they were more important for North-South politics than for relations among the industrialized countries (see Chapter 8). The fear of economic costs and loss of national control caused by the growth in FDI in the industrialized countries has been balanced for the most part by the perception of economic benefits.

One factor shaping these generally positive perceptions of multinational corporations is the dominant liberal philosophy of the governments and globally oriented business interests in the industrialized world. FDI, like other international financial flows and trade, is viewed by these individuals as economically rational and beneficial. The role of large corporations in politics is not seen as dangerous in countries where domestic corporations play such roles. This general receptivity to international capital affects reactions to multinational corporations. The principal dissent comes from labor leaders and from the governments of France and Japan, two countries that were slow to embrace the idea of foreign direct investment and which actively fostered partnerships between the government and domestic firms in the pursuit of national economic development.[104]

Another reason for the limited perceived threat has been the power relationship between the multinational corporations and the governments of the developed countries. In the developed countries, the multinational corporation is not perceived as a major threat to governmental power. Whereas firms can influence economic performance and interfere with a nation's economic management, they cannot undermine the authority of powerful, sophisticated governments. Although multinational corporations control sensitive sectors, they do not, except in Canada, loom so large in the national economy that governments feel they must acquiesce to their strength. Furthermore, Western governments possess not only the expertise—lawyers, accountants, economists, business experts—to regulate multinational corporations but also the confidence that they can devise means for control.

Yet another reason for the limited perception of threat in the West is that virtually all industrialized regions have their own multinational corporations. The position of the governments of the developed market economies as both home and host moderates their desires to restrict multinational corporations, for any restriction would limit the expansion of their own MNCs. Reinforcing this limited concern over foreign investment in the late 1970s and early 1980s was the troubled economic scene in the West, one of the more prominent features of which was a decline in new capital formation. There has thus been a reluctance to question the source of any new capital investment.

A final dimension of the limited threat and lack of international control of multinational corporations is the absence of U.S. interest in such management. Concern about foreign investment in the United States, especially by the Japanese, has been rising. Nevertheless, U.S. perception of a need for management, crucial to the development of a formal regime, has not existed in the field of international investment. The lack of perceived problems for U.S. political and economic systems, the dominant liberal ideology, and the political significance of the large multinational corporations in U.S. politics has made U.S. leadership more interested in promoting than controlling foreign investment.

As multinationals have become more important and better understood, the trend toward liberalizing regulations on multinationals has been echoed throughout the Northern states, as we will see in the following discussions of national, regional, and international management.

National Governance

Most efforts to control multinational corporations in the present international system occur within the host country. Although policy in developed market economies has been receptive to foreign investment, there have been some attempts to regulate foreign corporations to maximize economic benefits and to minimize the loss of control.

The most important form of regulation is the control of initial capital investment. States have sought to restrict key sectors for national investment and to regulate the degree of foreign ownership or control in sectors open to foreign investment. Although all countries have some form of key sector control—transportation, communications, and defense industries are commonly restricted industries—few of the developed market economies have comprehensive regulations or even a clear national policy regarding foreign investment.[105]

For many years, Japan followed a comprehensive, restrictive policy.[106] In investment as well as trade, Japan's public philosophy and governmental policy differ from those of other Western countries. Postwar policy was originally based on the Foreign Exchange Control Law of 1949 and the Foreign Investment Law of 1950, which provided governmental authority to screen all new foreign investment, with a view to limiting that investment, and to prevent the repatriation of earnings and capital of foreign investors. Government policy was highly restrictive. New foreign investment was limited to a few industries, and within those industries, foreign ownership was limited to no more than 49 percent. When purchasing existing industry, foreigners were limited at most to a 20 percent ownership of unrestricted industries and a 15 percent interest in the many restricted industries.

While restricting direct foreign investment, Japan tried to obtain the benefits of multinational corporations by purchasing advanced technology through licensing agreements instead of acquiring technology through foreign control. As a result of these comprehensive, restrictive policies, FDI inflows into Japan have been quite low (see again Figure 4.5). Also, most foreign MNC affiliates are joint ventures in which the foreign partner owns 50 percent or less of the venture.

Starting in 1967, as Japan's balance of payments strengthened and foreign pressure for liberalization increased, Japanese policy changed somewhat. The number of restricted industries was reduced, and 100-percent foreign ownership was permitted in many industries in May 1973. In 1980, the Japanese government passed a new Foreign Exchange Control Law. This legislation liberalized foreign exchange controls, removed formal entry restrictions on foreign direct investment (with the exception of twenty–two industries, including agriculture, forestry, fisheries, mining, petroleum, leather, and leather manufactures) and permitted 100-percent foreign control through new investment or acquisition.

In the mid–1980s, Japan relaxed controls in the financial services sector, allowing foreign institutions to obtain securities and trust bank licenses and encouraging the Tokyo Stock Exchange to open membership to foreigners. There remained a review process through the Committee on Foreign Exchange and Other Transactions in the Ministry of Finance, which evaluated foreign investment according to criteria such as effects on national security, impacts on domestic enterprise in the same or related business, smooth performance of the national economy, reciprocity with the home country of the investor, and the need for approval for capital export transactions. One of the most effective barriers to foreign investment was the keiretsu system, which can effectively restrict inward foreign investment. Many Japanese financial and industrial firms hold each other's stock as part of their *keiretsu* obligations, a policy promoted by the Japanese government since World War II to prevent hostile takeovers of any sort, including foreign acquisitions.[107] Finally, though the Japanese government has allowed some liberalization, it has always retained the power to restrict foreign investment at any time at its own discretion.

On the other hand, the Japan External Trade Organization (JETRO), once an export-promoting organization, has been turned into an investment-attracting organization; and the Japan Development Bank is now providing favorable rates on loans to foreign investors. As a result of liberalization, foreign investment in Japan has risen, although Japan still has very low levels of foreign investment inflow in comparison with those of other OECD countries (see again Figure 4.5).[108] Similarly, the Ministry of Economy, Trade, and Industry (METI) has become a defender of the "internationalization" of the Japanese economy, even while it remains a promoter of the interests of Japanese firms in world trade. METI understands that in order for Japanese exports and outbound foreign investments to expand in the long run, Japan will have to become more open to imports and inbound FDI. Thus METI pushes Japanese business and the rest of the Japanese government in the direction of making it easier for non-Japanese firms and individuals to set up business in Japan.[109]

There is some evidence in recent years that the efforts of JETRO and METI to encourage investment in Japan are succeeding. FDI inflows into Japan increased from zero in 1995 to a peak of $12.7 billion in 1999, only to fall back a bit in 2000 to $8.2 billion.[110] Inflows averaged about $6 billion from 2001 to 2005. When Nissan got into financial difficulties in 1999, the French car maker Renault upped its stake in the Japanese firm to 36.8 percent through a share-swapping arrangement and negotiated an alliance with Nissan that included new investment in Japan for the production and sales of Renault models with marketing support from Nissan. In 1999, Salomon Smith Barney bought a 20-percent stake in Nikko Securities, Japan's third largest securities firm, and also formed a joint venture with Nikko called Nikko Salomon Smith Barney combining the Tokyo operations of Salomon with the Equities, Fixed Income, Research and Investment Banking Divisions of Nikko; and a U.S. firm named Ripplewood organized a consortium to purchase the Long-Term Credit Bank, a bank that had failed as a result of bad loans.[111] DaimlerChrysler purchased a one-third equity share in Mitsubishi Motors in March 2000 when the latter experienced some debt-servicing problems. Boots (the British drugstore chain) and Carrefour (the French department store chain) first entered the Japanese retail marketplace also during this period. Thus, Japan was becoming more open to foreign investment by the end of the 1990s partly as a result of the bubble economy.

Canada also drew up a policy for regulating the inflow of foreign investment in the seventies. The Canadian Foreign Investment Review Act of 1972 established the **Foreign Investment Review Agency (FIRA)** to screen virtually all new direct foreign investment in Canada. Its coverage was comprehensive (including new businesses), most acquisitions, the expansion of existing foreign-owned firms into nonrelated businesses, and change of foreign owner-ship. As a matter of national policy, FIRA refused takeovers in the fields of broadcasting, rail and air transportation, newspapers, nuclear energy, and bank-ing. Evaluation of the benefit to Canada of foreign investment was determined by criteria such as contribution to employment, new investment, exports, pro-cessing of raw materials, purchase of supplies in Canada, access to sophisticated technology, improved productivity, and competition, as well as the degree of Canadian equity participation.

FIRA also insisted that foreign investors fulfill performance requirements in return for permission to invest in Canada. These commitments included import substitution requirements, export targets, research and development expen-ditures to be made in Canada, local equity participation guarantees, and exclusive production-in-Canada arrangements. Many investors were deterred by such requirements from making application to FIRA.[112] Others complied. But FIRA's restrictions brought a negative reaction from the United States, which in 1982 filed a complaint with the GATT, charging that FIRA's performance require-ments were illegal. In 1983, a GATT panel found that Canadian requirements forcing companies investing in Canada to buy a certain proportion of their goods and services in Canada were illegal under GATT but that its export performance requirements were compatible with GATT.[113]

In 1984, the Foreign Investment Review Act was replaced by the Investment Canada Act, which was designed to promote, rather than discourage, foreign investment. Foreign investment is still screened, but only those invest-ments exceeding C$5 million and C$50 million for direct and indirect invest-ments, respectively, are subject to the screening procedure, greatly decreasing the number of foreign investments subject to review. The stated purpose of the review is to ensure that the investment be "of net benefit to Canada."[114] Under the U.S.–Canada Free Trade Agreement signed by the two countries in 1989, U.S. firms were given even greater opportunities for Canadian investment, because indirect acquisitions would eventually be exempted from any review, and the threshold for review of direct acquisitions would be raised.[115] U.S. firms wishing to make major investments in Canada still must have their proposals reviewed (which is not the case for Canadian firms investing in the United States), but the likelihood of rejection has continued to decrease. These develop-ments were reinforced and generalized to include Mexico with the signing of the North American Free Trade Agreement (NAFTA) in 1992.

Other states also screen inbound investment. Britain and France rely on an ad hoc consideration of applications for new direct foreign investment. Investments that might create foreign dominance of an important economic sector, damage national research and development, interfere with official plans for industrial rationalization, or create excessive concentration are reviewed by the appropriate ministries or agencies. There are no formal statutory guidelines for evaluating foreign investment, other than national antitrust and competition laws,[116] but in practice, judgments tend to favor investments that benefit employment, bal-ance of payments, research and development, and exports; create new enterprises instead of acquiring existing firms; encourage national management at both the national and the parent level; and fit in with governmental plans for industrial reorganization.

In general, investment policy in the mid–1960s was restrictive, but since then many countries have become highly receptive to foreign investment.[117] The United Kingdom, for example, has been traditionally favorable to foreign investment, and, under Conservative government after 1979, Britain abandoned any government planning role, preferring to leave investment decisions to the operation of a free market. In 1985 the British government permitted a merger between Westland, a helicopter manufacturer, and the U.S. company United Technologies, despite strong pressure to favor the development of a Euroconsortium to strengthen European air industry cooperation. In 1988, the Swiss chocolate company, Nestlé, was allowed to buy Rowntree (a British candy producer) despite strong nationalistic protests. Nonetheless, even in a fundamentally liberal environment, such as Great Britain's, the desire for a national presence, or even a **national champion** in certain industries, has occasionally prevailed. When British Caledonian Airways was up for sale in 1987, both the Scandinavian carrier SAS and British Air made a bid for control. The government subtly discouraged SAS by declining to guarantee retention of route licenses; the British Air bid succeeded, allowing it to expand significantly its size and route capacity, providing England with a strong national airline carrier to compete in the post–1992 internal market.

U.S. controls on foreign investment have traditionally been limited to the International Investment and Trade in Services Act (IITSA) of 1976, which established a mechanism to monitor foreign investment, and the International Emergency Economic Powers Act of 1977, which empowers the president to block foreign acquisitions of U.S. companies or compel divestiture of an already acquired domestic company if he or she determines there is an extraordinary threat to the national security, foreign policy, or economy. Various other sectoral controls limit foreign investments in areas such as aviation, atomic energy, and communications.

As foreign investment in the United States increased dramatically in the 1980s, more attention was given to regulation. The Bryant Amendment to the Omnibus Trade Bill of 1988, which was defeated, would have required foreign investors to file certain proprietary information with the Department of Commerce for public disclosure. In that same year, an amendment to the Defense Production Act of 1950 (known as the **Exon-Florio amendment** after its sponsors Senator J. James Exon and Representative James J. Florio) extended the scope of the IITSA to prohibit mergers, acquisitions, or takeovers of U.S. firms by foreign interests when such actions are deemed a threat to the national security of the United States. After lapsing for technical reasons in the fall of 1990, the Exon-Florio authority was reinstated in August 1991 and made a permanent part of U.S. law.[118]

The job of implementing the Exon-Florio amendment was given to an interagency committee called the **Committee on Foreign Investment in the United States (CFIUS)**, which is chaired by the Secretary of the Treasury and includes representatives from the departments of State, Defense, Commerce, and

Justice, as well as the Office of Management and Budget, the Office of the U.S. Trade Representative, and the Council of Economic Advisers. CFIUS investigates any transaction that falls under the statute and then makes a recommendation to the president, who then makes the final decision on whether to invoke the law.

The first CFIUS investigation under the Exon-Florio amendment was conducted in late 1988 and early 1989. It involved the proposed takeover of the silicon wafer division of the Monsanto Corporation by a German chemical firm, Hüls AG. While some members of the committee wanted to bar the purchase, the government negotiated an agreement with Hüls whereby the purchase would be approved if the company agreed to maintain production of wafers and continue research and development in the United States.

Between 1988 and 2005, CFIUS received 1,500 notifications of transactions, but conducted only twenty–five investigations. Thirteen proposals were withdrawn during review, including a proposed acquisition of a U.S. machine tool manufacturer by a major Japanese firm called FANUC, and twelve were sent to the President for final determination. The President ordered divestiture in only one instance.[119] A particularly contentious case was the takeover of a U.S. firm called Semi-Gas, which produced ultrapure industrial gases used in semiconductor manufacturing, by Nippon Sanso, a Japanese firm.[120] This deal was particularly sensitive because Semi-Gas had been a collaborator with U.S. semiconductor and electronics firms in an R&D consortium[121] called Sematech (short for semiconductor manufacturing technology). Sematech had been part of a U.S. effort to reestablish technological leadership in semiconductors, having lost out in some key semiconductor areas to Japan in the early 1980s. What bothered many people was that U.S. tax dollars had been spent to raise the technological capabilities of firms like Semi-Gas, and it did not seem to make sense, therefore, to allow Japanese firms to reap the benefits.

The Exon-Florio amendment was amended further in 1993 to prevent (1) foreign acquisition of U.S. firms with contracts with the U.S. Departments of Defense and Energy worth more than $500 million and (2) awarding of U.S. government contracts involving "top secret" information to firms controlled by foreign governments. The new amendment also empowered CFIUS and other government agencies to review proposals for investments in high-technology areas deemed "critical" not just for national security reasons but also for U.S. competitiveness. The open-ended nature of these provisions made it possible for the U.S. government to begin screening a much broader range of inward flows of FDI.

In June 2005, China National Offshore Oil Company (CNOOC) made an unsolicited bid of $18.5 billion for the acquisition of Unocal, an American oil company with oil properties in Central Asia. The deal was strongly opposed by members of Congress from both parties, because CNOOC was largely controlled by the government of China and because China had major restrictions on inflows of U.S. foreign investment. As a result, CNOOC chose to withdraw its bid.[122]

In February 2006, Dubai Ports World (DPW) attempted to purchase six major port facilities in the United States including the port of Newark, New Jersey. Despite the fact that CFIUS approved the deal, again it was opposed vigorously by members of Congress from both parties. This time the objections were based on the fear that DPW, a company headquartered in the United Arab Emirates, could be infiltrated by terrorists intent on smuggling weapons of mass destruction into the United States. The president personally supported the merger, but legislation proposed to block it convinced DPW to scrap the deal and sell its U.S. holdings to AIG, an American insurance company.[123]

As a result of the controversies over the CNOOC and DPW acquisition attempts, the Congress passed the Foreign Investment and National Security Act (FINSA) of 2007. Besides codifying preexisting practices, FINSA expanded the concept of national security to include mergers that involved critical infrastructure and technologies. It also mandated closer scrutiny of mergers involving **state-owned enterprises**. In addition, CFIUS was empowered to negotiate arrangements with acquiring firms that would mitigate any threat to U.S. national security arising from a merger.[124]

Motivating these recent efforts was increasing economic nationalism. There is a growing concern in the United States over excessive dependence on foreign capital to finance growth, and a vocal minority would like to see even stricter limits on foreign investment.[125] Nonetheless, the prevailing view still defends the benefits of foreign investment for the United States and would like to see a more liberal economic environment for foreign investment here and abroad. Judging by the actions of most U.S. states, one would assume that foreign investment is highly desirable. State governors are competing, intensely at times, to attract new foreign manufacturing plants. In return for the jobs and the economic stimulus of the new plants, they are willing to offer tax incentives, regulatory breaks, and other inducements. This has been taken to such a degree that a backlash has developed, in which U.S. companies argue that they are being discriminated against by their own local governments, which favor foreign companies and allow them to produce in the United States much less expensively than U.S. companies. It remains to be seen which of these two opposing points of view will prevail; but there is no doubt that the United States is facing an important new wave of protectionism and economic nationalism that is not likely to disappear in the near future.

Aside from imposing entry requirements, countries may also attempt to manage the behavior of multinational corporations once established in their state. The ability to control the multinational corporations' behavior is crucial to management, because it involves activities that affect national economic performance and national control, such as taxation, labor policy, capital movements, and competition policy. Indeed, governments in the developed countries closely regulate the operations of those firms—both national and multinational—operating within their borders. However, with some exceptions, the developed countries' governments have not sought to impose special or differential regulation on the operation of multinational corporations. Controls on intracorporate capital flows and intracompany charges, for example, would be difficult to apply, could provoke retaliation, and could act as a deterrent to foreign investment, which is viewed positively in the developed market economies. Furthermore, governments in the developed countries have the administrative and legal capacity to control the MNCs through legislation, regulation, and administrative practice, which applies to domestic as well as foreign corporations. Finally, the principle of **national treatment**—a GATT rule specifying that foreign-owned enterprises are to be treated no less favorably than are domestically owned enterprises—acts as a deterrent to discrimination against MNCs. Although national treatment is not universally accepted and is inconsistently applied, it is embodied in certain bilateral treaties such as the friendship, commerce, and navigation treaties with the United States and in the multilateral codes of the OECD and thus serves as a constraint on government policy. Exceptions to national treatment do exist in the areas of government subsidies, government purchasing, work permits and immigration policy, and participation in industry groups that set sectoral policy.

Governments have also applied informal pressure on firms to fulfill certain performance requirements in areas such as plant or export expansion and to adhere to national labor practices. They have carefully monitored foreign investors' adherence to national tax legislation and foreign exchange laws. As governments, especially in Europe, have expanded their intervention in the national economy through law and regulation, foreign investors have been increasingly obliged to adopt practices—for example, labor relations policies—consistent with those of the host country. Finally, where there has been a conflict of law or policy between the host and the home state, as in the case of the U.S. extraterritorial application of export controls, the governments of the host countries have insisted on asserting their jurisdiction over the resident MNCs. As we have already discussed, several European countries required resident companies to ignore U.S. restraints on pipeline exports to the Soviet Union.[126]

Finally, there have been increasing attempts in the major home country, the United States, to regulate home country MNCs. Concerns with balance-of-payments deficits led to capital controls; organized labor expressed concern over export of jobs and the tax "loopholes" enjoyed by multinational corporations; and the Senate Subcommittee on MNCs in the mid-1970s revealed a broad range of potential foreign policy problems posed by multinationals. In 1977, Congress enacted legislation to prohibit the use of bribery and illicit payments for political purposes by U.S. corporations operating abroad. And in the late 1970s and early 1980s, several U.S. states, in an effort to raise new revenues and to offset the ability of multinational corporations to select the state or country of lowest taxation, enacted unitary tax legislation that taxed both foreign and domestic corporations on their worldwide income instead of on income earned in that particular state. The result was an outcry from Japan and Europe, alleging violation of tax treaties that eliminated double taxation.

Because the industrialized nations have been unwilling to restrict too severely the multinational corporations, many have tried to minimize their costs in other ways. Many industrialized countries have tried to strengthen their domestic firms in order to make them more competitive with foreign MNCs. Such policies, as part of broader industrial policies, include governmental encouragement and support of industrial concentration and rationalization of national industry, research and development, maintenance of key industries or companies, and development of national capital markets and national managerial skills.

Methods include governmental financial assistance, tax preferences, government participation in industry, encouragement of mergers, financing of research and training programs, and "buy national" procurement policies. Within the European Union, many of these policies are illegal, thus discouraging the growth of national champions. Nonetheless, in certain industries, such as defense, strong domestic suppliers have been directly subsidized and/or sheltered from international competition (e.g., GEC-Marconi in the United Kingdom or Matra in France). The more usual pracice is to permit mergers among European firms to make them more internationally competitive without losing their essentially national or regional character. The Spanish government, for example, encouraged mergers of Spanish banks in order to prevent local market dominance by non-Spanish banks after 1992.[127] But the main emphasis within the European Union is on promoting competitive pan-European "sunrise" industries to fight U.S. and Japanese dominance (see section on regional governance below).

Regional Governance

Regional common markets and free-trade areas have provided new opportunities for regional governance of multinational corporations. Within the context of such agreements there is room for substantial control or liberalization of investment policies. One potentially important regional forum for the multilateral governance of multinational corporations is the EU.[128] Two approaches to regional policy have been suggested. One approach, prevalent in the 1970s, was to develop European Union regulations to limit the autonomy of MNCs in areas of frequent national conflict such as labor relations. The other approach has been the Union's encouragement of large European corporations, capable of competing globally with U.S. and Japanese corporations in high-technology sectors. The control function has not been developed as far as expected, in part because of the liberal, pro-business climate of Europe in the 1980s. Instead, the emphasis has been on the second approach in an effort to close the high-technology gap before the internal market is completed in 1992. However, it is possible that the control issues will reemerge as a priority, especially if the political left grows stronger in Europe.

European regional governance faces major obstacles.[129] In addition to political opposition on some of these issues, a more basic problem concerns the authority of the EU to impose binding regulations on its member countries. Members of the community have consistently refused to delegate to the EU any national authority for regulation of industrial policy. A French proposal in 1965 for community regulation of foreign investment was rejected by other members who opposed a restrictive policy. In 1973, the European Commission proposed a number of community regulations regarding MNCs, including the protection of employees in event of a takeover and cooperation in monitoring MNC activities. The Caborn report, adopted by the European Parliament in 1981, called for maximizing the positive effects of multinational corporations and minimizing their negative effects by "the establishment of an appropriate framework of countervailing power at the international level through legislation, guidelines, codes, and multilateral agreements, and through greater cooperation and exchange between states."[130] Specifically, it recommended binding EU regulations in the areas of information disclosure, transfer pricing, and merger controls.

Although no specific directives aimed at non–EU investment were passed until 1993 (see below), the European Union moved ahead on several directives that would shape foreign as well as EU corporations' practices and address some of the concerns mentioned in the Caborn report. The most important areas were accounting and information disclosure and antitrust policy, especially merger control. A number of directives—the EU form of legislation—in the area of company law were designed to increase the transparency of the activities of large conglomerates. The Seventh Company Law Directive, adopted in 1983, called for the consolidation of financial reporting to enable a fair review of the business as a whole. The First and Fourth Directives had already specified the type of information to be published in public companies' accounts. The draft of the Ninth Directive would oblige groups of companies to define and publish the relationships between parents and subsidiaries and increase the rights of subsidiaries against the parent. The draft of the Thirteenth Directive would lay down rules for the conduct of takeover bids, particularly with regard to information disclosure.

Another area of concern was the promotion of greater participation and consultation rights for employees. The proposed Fifth Company Law Directive, to harmonize the structure of EU public companies, includes a provision for employee participation at the board level. Another proposed directive, known as the **Vredeling proposal**, called for greater consultation between management and labor regarding company policy and plans.[131] Though interest in these proposed laws stagnated because of liberalization and deregulation in the early 1980s, they were revived after 1993.

The European Union's industrial policy was considerably strengthened in the 1980s. Industrial policy was designed initially to build EU industrial champions to counter U.S. and Japanese industrial and technological dominance. The Single European Act, signed in 1986, added a chapter to the Treaty of Rome entitled "research and technological development," which stated that "the Community's aim shall be to strengthen the scientific and technological basis of European industry and encourage it to become more competitive at [sic] international level."[132] This was to be realized through EU financial support for basic R&D, the opening up of national public sector procurement contracts, technical standardization, and the removal of fiscal and legal barriers to joint ventures and other forms of cooperation. A number of jointly funded research consortia were established in the areas of telecommunications, manufacturing technology, and information technologies and a steady increase in the number of intra-European mergers and joint ventures occurred. It soon became evident, however, that European MNCs needed to be able to construct alliances with non–European firms in certain important areas in order to be globally competitive. European laws and practices tended to reflect that reality in the 1990s.

The EU made it clear that, while it wished to maintain a liberal policy toward trade and inward investment, it did not intend to allow foreign companies to reap the greatest benefit from the unified internal market. This meant that a degree of EU preference for European firms would continue to prevail and that foreign-based multinationals would not have the same access to EU programs as local companies, unless some reciprocity was recognized in the multinationals' home countries. This policy was taken up by the United States in the late 1980s and early 1990s with the establishment of such R&D consortia as Sematech, the HDTV Grand Alliance, and the U.S. Display Consortium. Even Japan began to invite the participation of foreign MNCs in its advanced R&D efforts during this period.[133]

There was no EU policy specifically to regulate inward foreign investment, although individual EU states had their own regulations. However, Union action could be taken to disallow state financial inducements that acted as subsidies for foreign investors or to refuse to allow goods produced with less than an acceptable local content to circulate freely in the Union. This would curtail the operations of so-called "screwdriver plants," which simply assembled foreign-made components within the EU and thereby avoid external tariffs. In 1988, for example, France received permission from the EU to block the import of 300,000 television sets that were produced by Japanese companies but assembled in the EU. France claimed that these televisions did not qualify as European because of the high foreign content.

Mergers and joint ventures were permitted under European competition laws. After 1989, two separate laws governed joint ventures: Article 58 of the Treaty of Rome and the Merger Regulation of 1989. The Merger Regulation governed joint ventures that affected market structure significantly, while Article 58 covered all other joint ventures. Until the passage of the Merger Regulation, MNCs were not legally restricted in their decisions on European joint ventures. After 1989, however, all new joint ventures, including those that involved non-European MNCs, had to be approved by the European Commission.[134]

Another regional management issue in Europe was a directive of the European Commission concerning European works councils. Under this directive, all MNCs operating in Europe with 1,000 or more workers in more than one EU country were required to set up pan-European works councils to inform and consult their employees on key decisions. When the Maastricht Treaty came into effect on November 1, 1993, European legislation could no longer be vetoed by a single member state in the European Council, requiring instead three governments to be opposed. Until that time, Britain had blocked the directive by exercising its veto power. According to a study published by the European Employers' Union (UNICE), about 1,200 companies would be affected. Most foreign and some European MNCs opposed the legislation on the grounds of increased cost and reduced managerial flexibility. European unions and some MNCs supported the measure. Compagnie des Machines Bull, Thomson CSF, Grundig AG, Digital Equipment Corporation, Xerox Corporation, and IBM all set up some form of information and consultation procedure in anticipation of the new law.[135]

In addition to regional management through the EU, which is the best known and most complex regional internal market existing today, recent steps have been taken to create other regional areas for trade and investment liberalization. New Zealand and Australia have had a free-trade area for many years, and have just strengthened it through the **Closer Economic Relationship** agreement to include substantial liberalization of investment and harmonization of regulatory barriers.[136] NAFTA and the U.S.–Canada Free Trade Agreement have similar provisions, which increase cross-border competition in manufacturing by eliminating most tariffs and enable service industries, such as banks and insurance companies, to compete directly for business in the three countries. Previously, for example, U.S. financial institutions were not allowed to own more than 25 percent of federally regulated Canadian-controlled financial institutions, and Canadian companies were not allowed to offer Canadian government securities in the United States. Both of these policies have been changed under the U.S.–Canada Free Trade Agreement.

International Governance

International regulations and agreements encouraged the growth of foreign direct investment and the scope of operations of multinational corporations. Western international law enacted before World War II offered some protection for foreign investment. The traditional law of prompt, adequate, and effective compensation in the case of nationalization and various patent and copyright conventions was designed for this purpose, and the postwar agreements reinforced this general trend.[137] The IMF's provisions regarding currency convertibility allowed the repatriation of capital and earnings and thus facilitated the international flow of capital. The GATT's tariff reductions smoothed international production and transfers within the multinationals. In addition, the OECD's Codes on Liberalization of Capital Movements and of Current Invisible Operations established the norms of nondiscrimination between foreign and domestic investors within a country, freedom of establishment, and freedom of transfer of funds.

Although there were some attempts to regulate the activities of multinational corporations,[138] until the 1970s there were few attempts to create governance structures for multinational corporations at an international level, and most of those attempts failed. One such effort died with the **Havana Charter**.[139] The management of international investment had not been a part of the U.S. scheme for a new postwar economic order. Ironically, in response to strong pressure from U.S. business groups, the U.S. delegation at Geneva in 1947 proposed a draft article on foreign investment. The article, intended to codify the prevailing Western liberal attitude toward foreign investment and the rights of capital-exporting countries, provided for protection against nationalization and discrimination. Once the matter was placed on the negotiating agenda, however, its character quickly changed. The less-developed countries, led by the Latin American states, were able to redefine the proposed article to protect not capital exporters but capital importers. Provisions of the Havana Charter allowed capital-importing countries to establish national requirements for the ownership of existing and future foreign investment and to determine the conditions for further investments. The inclusion of the investment provisions was a major reason for the opposition of U.S. business to the Havana Charter and for its eventual failure. The GATT, its successor, contained no provisions for investment.

However, an agreement on trade-related investment measures (TRIMs) was part of the Uruguay Round (see Chapter 3).

Throughout the 1950s and early 1960s, a do-nothing attitude prevailed. Attempts to write international foreign investment laws, such as the United Nations' Economic and Social Council efforts in the 1950s and those of GATT in 1960 on restrictive business practices, surfaced but led nowhere.[140] In the late 1960s, as concern increased, more comprehensive proposals for a system of international control were drawn up. The most far-reaching proposals called for a body of international law under which multinational corporations would be chartered and regulated and for an international organization to administer these regulations.[141] Other proposals advocate the development of a GATT for investment.[142] This intergovernmental general agreement would consist of a few fundamental concepts of substance and procedure on which there might be a general international consensus and would establish an agency to investigate and make recommendations about the creation or infringement of rules (much as the GATT organization has done). Such an agency would not have compulsory authority, but it would have the power to publicize its findings and thus appeal to public opinion.

Although such a comprehensive, self-sufficient supranational body or even GATT-like Code for Investment seem unlikely, other options are available. These include amending existing WTO agreements, drawing up a separate agreement committing its signatories to apply WTO principles to investment, or prosecuting investment issues that are trade related through the WTO dispute resolution framework in order to set precedents covering investment. The United States participated in the Uruguay Round agreements that dealt with trade-related investment measures (TRIMS) (see Chapter 3). Although limited, the TRIMs agreement was a landmark in multilateral investment management, both because it integrated investment into the new WTO and because its emphasis was on encouraging investment flows. These included local content requirements, local equity requirements, technology transfer or export requirements, remittance restrictions, and incentives.

Governance in the OECD

The OECD has been another forum for devising a regime for international investment. In 1961, In the Codes of Liberalization of Capital Movements and of Current Invisible Operations, established in 1961, member countries agreed to "reduce or abolish obstacles to the exchange of goods and services and current payments and maintain and extend the liberalization of capital movements." Signatories of the Code of Liberalization of Capital Movements pledged themselves not to establish any new restrictions on capital movement, to notify the OECD of existing measures restricting capital movements, and to work toward reducing restrictions in a nondiscriminatory manner. The Code covered all capital movements, from daily currency trading to long-term foreign direct investments. In the Code of Liberalization of Current Invisible Operations, OECD members agreed to liberalize trade in services (also called invisibles).

At first, OECD members liberalized only long-term capital movements. It was not until the 1980s that they began to relax restrictions on short-term capital flows. The United Kingdom led the way by liberalizing all short-term capital movements in 1979. By the early 1990s, no OECD member maintained capital controls of any significance.[143]

In 1976, OECD members adopted a **Declaration on International Investment and Multinational Enterprises**. This declaration consisted of four elements:

- *Guidelines for Multinational Enterprises*: A voluntary code of conduct for multinational corporations.

- *National Treatment*: Under this principle, OECD members would "accord to foreign-controlled enterprises on their territories treatment no less favorable than that accorded in like situations to domestic enterprises."

- *Conflicting Requirements*: Members pledged themselves to cooperate to avoid the imposition of conflicting requirements on multinational corporations.

- *International Investment Incentives and Disincentives*: Members recognized the right to consider the interests of other OECD members in creating investment incentives and disincentives and pledged to make such measures "as transparent as possible."[144]

One factor leading to the Declaration was the new interest of the U.S. government and U.S. business in creating such an international code. Public revelations of corporate bribery and illegal political activity resulted in domestic pressures for regulating U.S. corporations. U.S. firms sought to deter, through an international agreement, congressional legislation and to internationalize any constraints placed on them.

The stated goal of the Declaration was to maximize international investment. It suggested guidelines for corporate behavior, such as greater disclosure of information, cooperation with the laws and policies of host governments, less anticompetitive behavior and fewer improper political activities, respect for the right of employees to unionize, and cooperation with governments in drawing up voluntary guidelines for corporate behavior. As part of the Declaration, the OECD countries further agreed on guidelines for government policy regarding multinational corporations, including nondiscrimination against foreign corporations, equitable treatment under international law, respect for contracts, and government cooperation to avoid beggar-thy-neighbor investment policies. Finally, the OECD countries agreed to establish consultative procedures to monitor and review the agreed-upon guidelines. Although the OECD code was voluntary and its guidelines were often deliberately vague, it was a step toward the development and implementation of international norms.[145]

The OECD agreed in 1979 on a Model Tax Convention, which dealt with transfer pricing. This convention attempted to establish an "arm's length principle" to prevent transfer pricing that took advantage of tax havens—geographic zones with much lower than average tax levels—by shifting profits toward the tax haven. The arm's length principle compared prices used in intrafirm transactions with those that might be used between unrelated firms. If there was a major discrepancy, then the intrafirm prices violated the arm's length principle. While this was by no means a perfect resolution of the problems posed by transfer pricing, it probably helped to prevent the most blatant abuses. In a report published in 1994, the OECD reaffirmed its commitment to the arm's length principle.[146]

In 1986, the principle of the right of establishment became part of the OECD's Code on the Liberalization of Current Invisible Operations. Under this principle, if the establishment of an office, branch, or subsidiary was a prerequisite for doing business abroad, then signatories to the Code agreed to grant the right to other signatories to establish such facilities on a nondiscriminatory basis.

The OECD convened a series of roundtables beginning in 2006 on Freedom of Investment, National Security, and "Strategic Industries." The purpose was to discuss existing practices within the membership of the OECD and to arrive at a consensus on principles that could reduce "unnecessarily restrictive policies to achieve security objectives...."[147]

Governance in the United Nations

Another limited international solution was offered by the United Nations. Largely as a result of the pressures from the Third World countries, in 1974 and 1975 two new organizations were established within the United Nations system: the **Center on Transnational Corporations (CTC)**, which gathered and generated information on multinational corporations, and also the intergovernmental **United Nations Commission on Transnational Corporations (UNCTC)**, which acted as a forum for considering issues related to multinational corporations, for conducting inquiries, and for supervising the center. The commission's activities focused on the development of an international code of conduct for multinational corporations. Because the commission was such a large, public governmental forum and because the positions of the member countries differed (thirty-three were developing countries, five were socialist, and ten were developed market economies), the bargaining process was tedious and often confrontational. After well over a decade, the negotiations on a code of conduct remained deadlocked on a number of issues. Most difficult were the definition of a transnational corporation—with the developed market countries wanting to include state-owned transnationals of the Eastern bloc and the socialist states not wanting to accept this definition—as well as the demand of the developed market economies for assurances on the treatment of MNCs by host governments in return for concessions governing the MNCs' behavior. In the 1980s, as interest shifted from controlling to encouraging foreign investment, the code negotiations languished.

The CTC attempted to remedy the dearth of information on multinationals by studying their operations and effects, offering technical advice to member countries, and making policy recommendations to the commission. In the process, the center has commissioned and compiled information on multinationals and has made available services to countries whose lack of information could place them at a negotiating disadvantage with foreign corporations.[148] When the United Nations was restructured in the early 1990s, the UNCTC was disbanded.[149]

Other steps have been taken in the United Nations toward regulating various MNC activities. The **United Nations Conference on Trade and Development (UNCTAD)** formulated a code in 1980 on restrictive business practices that establishes principles and rules for controlling anticompetitive behavior, such as abuse of market power or restraint of competition. Other agreements were reached concerning consumer protection, and transborder data flows. Negotiations took place in various parts of the United Nations system on technology transfer and international patent agreements.[150]

Bilateral and Minilateral Governance

One final form of international governance of multinational corporations involves not a unified and centralized order but, rather, a complex system of bilateral or multilateral negotiations among states, possibly leading to a series of agreements on specific matters or to methods for mediating conflicts. Conflicting national laws, in such areas as taxation, antitrust regulations, patents, export controls, and balance-of-payments controls, may be harmonized through such negotiation. In the area of taxation, for example, the OECD has written a draft convention containing proposals regarding many issues of taxation. Although never implemented, the treaty has guided subsequent bilateral negotiations and treaties among the developed market economies.[151]

Another bilateral approach might be the establishment of arbitration, adjudication, or simply consultation procedures that would accompany regulations or take the place of regulations when rules cannot be agreed upon. The World Bank set up an organization to do this called the **International Center for the Settlement of Investment Disputes (ICSID)** in 1966. By 2007, 144 countries were members.[152] As of November 2007, ICSID had 134 concluded cases and 125 pending cases.[153]

It was also possible to create bilateral or minilateral institutions or processes to which countries or companies and countries desiring a solution could turn. Such commissions existed in the socialist states to manage state-corporate disputes, and NAFTA and the U.S.–Canada Free Trade Agreement included provisions for dispute settlement panels to resolve trade disputes and to continue reviewing each country's trade remedy laws.

International Investment Agreements

International investment agreements (IIAs) are mostly bilateral agreements of three types: **bilateral investment treaties (BITs)**, double taxation treaties (DTTs), and agreements that deal with other economic activities (such as trade) but also contain investment provisions. The total number of IIAs by the end of 2006 was 5,500 (see Figure 4.9). BITs are designed to guarantee transparency in case of **expropriation** and to identify host countries who are willing to take

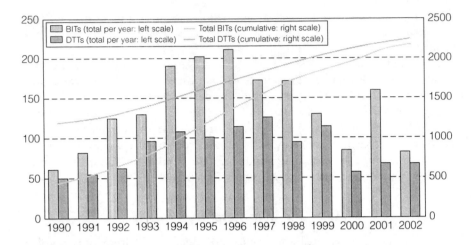

FIGURE 4.9   Number of BITs and DTTs Concluded per Year and Cumulatively, 1990–2002

SOURCE: http://www.unctad.org/.

measures to avoid expropriation. The largest number of BITs to date have been concluded between developed and developing countries, although recently there has been growth in BITs between pairs of developed and developing countries. The main purpose of BITs, from the standpoint of host countries, is to generate more inward FDI.[154] From the standpoint of home countries, the purpose is to reduce uncertainty connected with foreign investment sent abroad.[155]

The Multilateral Agreement on Investment

In 1995, the 25 members of the OECD began negotiations on new rules for international investment called the **Multilateral Agreement on Investment (MAI)**. The agreement was designed to increase investment flows by clarifying the rights of foreign investors, eliminating barriers to investment, and creating a venue for dispute settlement. The members of the OECD asked outsiders to consider joining the agreement.[156]

In February 1997, the text of the draft MAI was leaked to Public Citizen, a Washington, D.C.–based organization headed by Ralph Nader that had opposed NAFTA, the Uruguay Round, and fast-track negotiating authority. Public Citizen posted the draft on the Internet, along with many arguments against the MAI.[157] Soon a wide variety of antiglobalization groups had decided to oppose the MAI also. The reasons they gave were sometimes questionable. They claimed that the MAI would end affirmative action and other kinds of equal opportunity employment programs. They argued that the MAI would undermine environmental regulations and threaten national sovereignty, even in the United States. A diverse set of groups took anti-MAI positions including, among others, the AFL-CIO, the Sierra Club, the Western Governors Association, and the Women's Division of the United Methodist Church. In April 1998, the

OECD announced that it would suspend negotiations of the MAI for six months, effectively killing it.[158]

More important than the anti-MAI demonstrations that occurred in Paris, however, were problems in the agreement itself. So many exceptions had been written into the agreement during negotiations that it was becoming merely a "codification of existing, law, policy, and practice among the negotiating countries." In addition, some negotiators believed that measures added during the protracted negotiations actually detracted from the overall goal of promoting further liberalization of investment policies.[159]

The defeat of the MAI in 1998 was often mentioned as the first in a chain of defeats for globalizing measures that occurred in the late 1990s. As in the case of the Battle in Seattle over the WTO (see Chapter 3), there was a tendency to overestimate the impact of the antiglobalization demonstrators and to underestimate other important factors such as the lack of agreement among the major industialized countries. Nevertheless, there was clearly evidence of growing support for political movements that defined their goals in terms of stopping or at least slowing movement toward globalization of the world economy. One very important common theme in those diverse movements was suspicion of the motives of multinational corporations.

CONCLUSIONS

National, regional, and international governance of multinational corporations focused primarily on promoting rather than regulating foreign direct investment during the Bretton Woods period. Not until the 1970s were there any significant attempts to establish rules of conduct for MNCs, and even then the political impetus came largely from the developing countries. Despite some international tension and national uneasiness regarding multinational corporations during the period of interdependence, there was no dominant perception of a common interest in restricting the activities of MNCs in the industrialized countries, especially in the one country that might mobilize the system for common action—the United States. In the 1990s, during the period of globalization, resistance to institutionalizing some of the key global governance goals of MNCs—national treatment, right of establishment, guarantees against expropriation, and the creation of an international forum for the resolution of investment disputes—was effectively expressed by antiglobalization forces. The developing countries remained very suspicious of the efforts of high-technology firms to define a new regime for intellectual property protection within the WTO (again, see Chapter 3). But developing countries also were suspicious of the motives of antiglobalization NGOs, based as they were primarily in the industrialized countries. Until a change toward greater consensus on these matters was made, international governance of multinational corporations would remain limited. In the coming years, the politics of FDI would probably focus as a result on national, bilateral, and regional rather than international governance.

ENDNOTES

1. Multinational corporations (MNCs) are also referred to as **multinational enterprises (MNEs)**, **transational corporations (TNCs)**, and **transnational enterprises (TNEs)**.

2. John H. Dunning, *Multinational Enterprises and the Global Economy* (Reading, Mass.: Addison-Wesley, 1992), 3. Increasingly, a firm can come to resemble a multinational corporation by negotiating international cooperation agreements (ICAs) with firms in other countries, instead of engaging in foreign direct investment. So the most important prerequisite for calling a firm multinational is no longer the ownership of overseas assets but rather direct participation in overseas value-added activities. We are indebted to Stephen Kobrin for his comments on this point.

3. *Ibid.*

4. The 10-percent cutoff has been adopted by the Organization for Economic Cooperation and Development as a standard for measuring FDI. Unfortunately, only the United States and Japan abide by the OECD standard. See DeAnne Julius, *Global Companies and Public Policy: The Growing Challenge of Foreign Direct Investment* (London, UK: Royal Institute of International Affairs, 1990), 16.

5. Edward M. Graham and Paul R. Krugman, *Foreign Direct Investment in the United States*, 3rd ed. (Washington, D.C.: Institute for International Economics, 1995), 9–11.

6. This chapter focuses on direct foreign investment in the developed market economies; see Chapter 8 for a discussion of investment problems in North–South relations.

7. Mira Wilkins, *The Emergence of Multinational Enterprise: American Business Abroad from the Colonial Era to 1914* (Cambridge, Mass.: Harvard University Press, 1970), 201; Alfred D. Chandler Jr., *The Visible Hand: The Managerial Revolution in American Business* (Cambridge, Mass.: The Belknap Press of Harvard University Press, 1977); and Alfred D. Chandler, *Scale and Scope: The Dynamics of Industrial Capitalism* (Cambridge, Mass.: The Belknap Press of Harvard University Press, 1990).

8. UNCTAD, *World Investment Report 1994* (New York, N.Y.: United Nations, 1994); and *Transnational Corporations, Employment and the Workplace* (New York, N.Y.: United Nations, 1994), 3.

9. *World Investment Report 2007* (Geneva, Switzerland: UNCTAD, 2007), 12.

10. Alan Rugman makes this argument in *The End of Globalization: Why Global Strategy is a Myth and How to Profit from the Realities of Regional Markets* (New York, N.Y.: AMACOM, 2000).

11. We are using the World Bank's 2006 national GDP figures for comparison here: see http://siteresources.worldbank.org/DATASTATISTICS/Resources/GDP.pdf. It is not necessarily valid to compare the sales or revenues of multinational corporations to the GDPs of nation-states. Martin Wolf argues that it would be more appropriate to compare the "value added" of MNCs to GDPs and that doing so would reduce the relative size of MNCs. See Martin Wolf, "Countries Still Rule the World," *Financial Times*, February 5, 2002, http://www.ft.com; and Paul de Grauwe and Filip Camerman, *How Big Are the Multinationals?* January 2002, http://www.econ.kuleuven.be/ew/academic/intecon/Degrauwe/PDG-papers/Recently_published_articles/How%20big%20are%20the%20big%20multinational%20companies.pdf.

12. See Stephen Hymer and Robert Rowthorn, "Multinational Corporations and International Oligopoly: The Non-American Challenge," in Charles P. Kindleberger, ed., *The International Corporation* (Cambridge, Mass.: MIT Press, 1971), 57–91.

13. Raymond Vernon, *Sovereignty at Bay: The Multinational Spread of U.S. Enterprises* (New York, N.Y.: Basic Books, 1971), 11.

14. On joint ventures, see Bruce Kogut, "Joint Ventures: Theoretical and Empirical Perspectives," *Strategic Management Journal*, 9 (July/August 1988): 319–332; and Richard E. Caves, *Multinational Enterprise and Economic Analysis*, 3rd edition (Cambridge, England: Cambridge University Press, 2007), 91–100. On strategic alliances, see Gary Hamel, "Competition for Competence and Interpartner Learning within Strategic Alliances," *Strategic Management Journal*, 12 (1991): 83–103: John Child and David Faulkner, *Strategies of Cooperation: Managing Alliances, Networks, and Joint Ventures* (New York, N.Y.: Oxford University Press, 1998); Yves L. Doz and Gary Hamel, *Alliance Advantage: The Art of Creating Value Through Partnering* (Boston, Mass.: Harvard Business School Press, 1998); Michael Y. Yoshino and U. Srinivasa Rangan, *Strategic Alliances: An Entrepreneurial Approach to Globalization* (Boston, Mass.: Harvard Business School Press, 1995); Bernard M. Gilroy, *Networking in Multinational Enterprises: The Importance of Strategic Alliances* (Colombia, South Carolina: University of South Carolina Press, 1993); Peter F. Cowhey and Jonathan D. Aronson, *Managing the World Economy: The Consequences of Corporate Alliances* (New York, N.Y.: Council on Foreign Relations Press, 1993); and Lynn K. Mytelka, ed., *Strategic Partnerships: States, Firms and International Competition* (Rutherford, N.J.: Fairleigh Dickinson University Press, 1991).

15. Louis T. Wells, Jr., "The Multinational Enterprise: What Kind of International Organization?" in Robert O. Keohane and Joseph S. Nye, Jr., eds., *Transnational Relations and World Politics* (Cambridge, Mass.: Harvard University Press, 1972), 97–114; John M. Stopford and Louis T. Wells Jr., *Managing the Multinational Enterprise: Organization of the Firm and Ownership of the Subsidiaries* (New York, N.Y.: Basic Books, 1972); Yves Doz, *Strategic Management in Multinational Companies* (New York, N.Y.: Pergamon Press, 1986), 399–450; and John Dunning, *The Globalization of Business* (New York, N.Y.: Routledge, 1993);

16. Greg Linden, Kenneth L. Kraemer, and Jason Dedrick, *Who Captures Value in a Global Innovation System? The Case of the iPod*, Personal Computing Industry Center, University of California, Irvine, California, June 2007.

17. See Vernon, *Sovereignty at Bay.*

18. We are referring here to the Foreign Corrupt Practices Act of 1977.

19. Douglas E. Rosenthal and William M. Knighton, *National Laws and International Commerce: The Problem of Extraterritoriality* (London, UK: Routledge and Kegan Paul, 1982); and International Chamber of Commerce, "Extraterritoriality is Thwarting Worldwide Business," September 7, 2006, http://www.iccwbo.org/iccifgi/index.html.

20. *World Investment Report 2007.* Note that these figures are cited at book value, which means that they represent the historical value of the investments—that is, what they cost at the time of acquisition with no adjustment for inflation or changing market values since then. This means that the U.S. investments, which were generally made earlier, are undervalued. Although the increase in other countries' foreign direct investment is significant, the contrast would not be as sharp if all investments were measured at current market value.

21. Calculated by the authors from data in the *World Investment Report*. Average annual growth in exports of goods and services was only around 6 percent during the same decades.

22. Alan Rugman, *The End of Globalization*, 3–8.

23. *World Investment Report 2007*.

24. UNCTAD, *World Investment Report 2007*.

25. UNCTAD, *World Investment Report 1994*, 409.

26. UNCTAD, *World Investment Report 2001* (New York, N.Y.: UN, 2001).

27. Lars Oxelheim and Parvez Ghauri, eds., *European Union and the Race for Foreign Direct Investment in Europe* (London, UK: Pergamon, 2003); V. N. Balasubramanyam and David Greenaway, "Economic Integration and Foreign Direct Investment: Japanese Investment in the EC," *Journal of Common Market Studies*, 30 (June 1992): 175–193; Yoko Sazanami, "Determinants of Japanese Foreign Direct Investment: Locational Attractiveness of European Countries to Japanese Multinationals," *Revue Économique*. 43 (July 1992): 661–670; and Stephen Thomsen and Stephen Woolcock, *Direct Investment and European Integration* (London, UK: Royal Institute of International Affairs, 1993), 63–65.

28. *Survey of Current Business*, August 1987, tables 9 and 10. The 1992 percentage was calculated by the authors from data reported in the *World Investment Report 1994*.

29. It should be noted that these figures include holdings of real estate and government bonds, and not just flows of FDI.

30. Rugman, *The End of Globalization*, 8.

31. See, for example, Ray Barrell and Nigel Pain, "Trade Restraints and Japanese Direct Investment Flows," *European Economic Review*, 43 (1999): 29–45; and Rene A. Belderbos, "Antidumping and Tariff Jumping: Japanese Firms' DFI in the European Union and the United States," *Weltwirtschaftliches Archiv*, 133 (1997): 419–457.

32. Randall Jones, "Japan's Role in World Financial Markets," *JEI Report* no. 42A (November 14, 1986).

33. "The Top 500 Banks in the World," *American Banker* (July 26, 1988): 34; and United Nations, *Transnational Corporations in World Development: Trends and Prospects* (New York, N.Y.: United Nations, 1988), 114.

34. *Transnational Corporations in World Development: Trends and Prospects* (New York, N.Y.: United Nations, 1988), 119.

35. Martin Carnoy, "Multinationals in a Changing World Economy: Whither the Nation-State?" in Martin Carnoy, Manuel Castells, Stephen S. Cohen, and Fernando H. Cardoso, *The New Global Economy in the Information Age: Reflections on Our Changing World* (University Park, Pa.: Pennsylvania State University Press, 1993), 52.

36. Joe Peek and Eris S. Rosengren, "Japanese Banking Problems: Implications for Lending in the United States," *New England Economic Review* (January 1999): 25–36.

37. The reader should note the parallel with the rise of the mortgage-backed securities discussed in Chapter 2.

38. "Private Equity," *Wikipedia*, http://en.wikipedia.org/wiki/Private_equity.

39. On this topic, see Dennis Encarnation, *Rivals Beyond Trade: America versus Japan in Global Competition* (Ithaca, N.Y.: Cornell University Press, 1992); and Mark

Mason, *American Multinationals and Japan: The Political Economy of Japanese Capital Controls, 1899–1980* (Cambridge, Mass.: Harvard University Press, 1992).

40. For a general analysis, see Thomas L. Brewer, "Government Policies, Market Imperfections, and Foreign Direct Investment," *Journal of International Business Studies*, 24 (First Quarter 1993): 101–120. See also Alan Rugman, "Globalization and Regional International Production," in John Ravenhill, ed., *Global Political Economy* (New York, N.Y.: Oxford University Press, 2005); and United Nations Center on Transnational Corporations, *Government Policies and Foreign Direct Investment*, UNCTC current studies, series A, no. 17 (New York, N.Y.: United Nations, 1991).

41. Charles Lipson, *Standing Guard: Protecting Foreign Capital in the Nineteenth and Twentieth Centuries* (Berkeley and Los Angeles, Calif.: University of California Press, 1985), 242–248.

42. For national incentives, see Stephen E. Guisinger, *Investment Incentives and Performance Requirements* (New York, N.Y.: Praeger, 1985); Earl H. Fry, *The Politics of International Investment* (New York, N.Y.: McGraw-Hill, 1983), 127–160; and Organization for Economic Cooperation and Development, *Investment Incentives and Disincentives and the International Investment Process* (Paris, France: OECD, 1983).

43. Susan and Martin Tolchin, *Buying into America: How Foreign Money Is Changing the Face of Our Nation* (New York, N.Y.: Times Books, 1988); and James Moses, *State Investment Incentives in the USA* (London, UK: Economist Publications, 1985).

44. James R. Markusen and Keith E. Maskus, "Discriminating among Alternative Theories of the Multinational Enterprise," *Review of International Economics*, 10 (2002): 694; and Giorgio Barba Navaretti and Anthony J. Venables, *Multinational Firms in the World Economy* (Princeton, N.J.: Princeton University Press, 2004), chs. 3–4.

45. James R. Markusen, "Multinationals, Multi-Plant Economies, and the Gains from Trade," *Journal of International Economics*, 16 (1984): 205–226. See also Henrik Braconier, Pehr-Johan Nörback, and Dieter Urban, "Reconciling the Evidence on the Knowledge-Capital Model," *Review of International Economics*, 13 (2005): 770–786; and Ronald B. Davies, "Hunting High and Low for Vertical FDI," *Review of International Economics*, 16 (2008): 250–267.

46. Oliver Williamson, *Markets and Hierarchies: Analysis and Antitrust Implications* (New York, N.Y.: The Free Press, 1975).

47. Brewer, "Government Policies, Market Imperfections, and Foreign Direct Investment," 104.

48. Dunning, *Multinational Enterprises and the Global Economy*, ch. 4.

49. See, for example, Wilfred J. Ethier, "The Multinational Firm," *Quarterly Journal of Economics* 101 (November 1986): 805–833.

50. Vernon, *Sovereignty at Bay*, 65–77; and Raymond Vernon, "The Product Cycle Hypothesis in a New International Environment," *Oxford Bulletin of Economics and Statistics* 41 (1979): 255–267.

51. Raymond Vernon, *Sovereignty at Bay*; and Theodore H. Moran, *Multinational Corporations and the Politics of Dependence: Copper in Chile* (Princeton, N.J.: Princeton University Press, 1974).

52. See Stephen H. Hymer, *The International Operations of National Firms: A Study of Direct Foreign Investment* (Cambridge, Mass.: MIT Press, 1976); and Charles P. Kindleberger, *American Business Abroad: Six Lectures on Direct Investment* (New Haven, Conn.: Yale University Press, 1969), 1–36.

53. P. Nicolaides and S. Thomsen, "Can Protectionism Explain Direct Investment?" *Journal of Common Market Studies*, 29 (1991): 635–643; M. Motta, "Multinational Firms and the Tariff-Jumping Argument: A Game Theoretic Analysis with Some Uncoventional Conclusion," *European Economic Review*, 36 (1992): 1557–1571; John Lunn, "Determinants of U.S. Direct Investment in the E.E.C.," *European Economic Review*, 13 (January 1980): 93–101; Claudy G. Culem, "The Locational Determinants of Direct Investments Among the Industrialized Countries," *European Economic Review*, 32 (April 1988): 885–904; and Patrick J. O'Sullivan, "An Assessment of Ireland's Export-Led Growth Strategy via Foreign Direct Investment," *Weltwirtschaftliches Archiv*, 129 (1993): 139–158.

54. Ryuhei Wakasugi, "Is Japanese Foreign Investment a Substitute for International Trade?" *Japan and the World Economy*, 6 (1994): 45–52; and "Japan Auto Trends," at http://www.jama.org/autoTrends/detail408e.html?id=295.

55. Evidence for this convergence in the behavior of foreign MNCs in the United States can be found in Edward M. Graham and Paul R. Krugman, *Foreign Direct Investment in the United States*, 3rd ed. (Washington, D.C.: Institute for International Economics, 1995).

56. Robert Z. Lawrence, "Efficient or Exclusionist? The Import Behavior of Japanese Corporate Groups," *Brookings Papers on Economic Activity*, 1 (1991): 311–341; Richard Florida and Martin Kenney, "Transplanted Organizations: The Transfer of Japanese Industrial Organization to the United States," *American Sociological Review*, 56 (June 1991): 381–398; and Michelle Gittelman and Edward Graham, "The Performance and Structure of Japanese Affiliates in the European Community," in Mark Mason and Dennis Encarnation, eds., *Does Ownership Matter? Japanese Multinationals in Europe* (Oxford, England: Clarendon Press, 1994).

57. Alan Rugman, *The End of Globalization*, 3; Gregory W. Noble and John Ravenhill, "The Good, the Bad, and the Ugly?: Korea, Taiwan and the Asian Financial Crisis," in Gregory W. Noble and John Ravenhill, eds., *The Asian Financial Crisis and the Architecture of Global Finance* (New York, N.Y.: Cambridge University Press, 2000), 85.

58. See, for example, Lewis R. DeMello, "Foreign Direct Investment-Led Growth: Evidence form Time Series and Panel Data," *Oxford Economic Papers*, 51 (1999): 133–151; and Eduardo Borenzstein, José de Gregorio, and Jong-Wha Lee, "How Does Foreign Investment Affect Economic Growth?" *Journal of International Economics*, 45 (1998): 115–135. A more recent study suggests that FDI does not contribute directly to growth: see Maria Carkovic and Ross Levine, "Does Foreign Direct Investment Accelerate Growth?" in Theodore H. Moran, Edward M. Graham, and Magnus Blomstrom, eds., *Does Foreign Direct Investment Promote Development?* (Washington, D.C.: Peterson Institute, 2005).

59. On this point, see Dunning, *Multinational Enterprises and the Global Economy*, 281–283.

60. See Harry G. Johnson, "The Efficiency and Welfare Implications of the International Corporation," in Kindleberger, *The International Corporation*, 35–56; Kindleberger, *American Business Abroad*.

61. Graham and Krugman, *Foreign Direct Investment in the United States*, 57.

62. Encarnation, *Rivals Beyond Trade*, 28.

63. Dunning, *Multinational Enterprises and the Global Economy*, 386, 408–411. For a report on efforts to measure intrafirm trade by U.S. firms by the U.S. Department

of Commerce, see William J. Zeile, "U.S. Intrafirm Trade in Goods," *Survey of Current Business* (February 1997).

64. An example of this sort of work is Ann Harrison, "The Role of Multinationals in Economic Development: The Benefits of FDI," *Columbia Journal of World Business*, 29 (Winter 1994): 7–11. The work reported was done in developing countries but could have been done as easily in industrialized countries.

65. Graham and Krugman, *Foreign Direct Investment in the United States*, 59; and James P. Womack, Daniel T. Jones, and Daniel Roos, *The Machine That Changed the World: The Story of Lean Production* (New York, N.Y.: Rawson Associates, 1990), especially 86.

66. Borenzstein, de Gregorio, and Lee, "How Does Foreign Direct Investment Affect Economic Growth?"

67. See Stephen Hymer, "The Efficiency (Contradictions) of Multinational Corporations," *American Economic Review*, 60 (May 1970), 441–448; Graham and Krugman, *Foreign Direct Investment in the United States*, 59–66.

68. A good summary can be found in Dunning, *Multinational Enterprises and the Global Economy*, chs. 10–16.

69. (Caborn Report) European Communities, European Parliament, *Working Documents 1981–1982, Report on Enterprises and Governments in Economic Activity*, Doc. 1-169/81 (May 15, 1981), 5.

70. Giles Y. Bertin, "Foreign Investment in France," in Isaiah A. Litvak and Christopher J. Maule, eds., *Foreign Investment: The Experience of Host Countries* (New York, N.Y.: Praeger, 1970), 105–122; Dunning, *Multinational Enterprises and Nation States*, 406–408; John H. Dunning, "The Role of American Investment in the British Economy," *Political and Economic Planning*, Broadsheet No. 508 (February 1969); and Stephen Young, *Foreign Multinationals and the British Economy* (New York, N.Y.: Croom Helm, 1988).

71. See Task Force, *Foreign Ownership and the Structure of Canadian Industry*, and *Foreign Direct Investment in Canada*; United Nations, *Transnational Corporations in World Development*; Jack N. Behrman, *National Interests and the Multinational Enterprise: Tensions Among the North Atlantic Countries* (Englewood Cliffs, N.J.: Prentice-Hall, 1970), 32–84; Jean-Jacques Servan-Schreiber, *The American Challenge* (New York, N.Y.: Atheneum, 1968); and Susan and Martin Tolchin, *Buying into America*.

72. On this point, see Harry G. Johnson, "The Efficiency and Welfare Implications of the International Corporation" in Kindleberger, *The International Corporation*, 35–56.

73. Task Force, *Foreign Direct Investment in Canada*, 183–211.

74. See Eduardo Borensztein, José de Gregorio, and Jong-Wha Lee, "How Does Foreign Investment Affect Growth?" *Journal of International Economics*, 45 (1998): 115–135.

75. See Cooper, *The Economics of Interdependence*, 98–103; and Robert G. Gilpin, Jr., *U.S. Power and the Multinational Corporation: The Political Economy of Foreign Direct Investment* (New York, N.Y.: Basic Books, 1975). For an evaluation of the impact of U.S. multinationals' overseas activities on the United States, see C. Fred Bergsten, Thomas Horst, and Theodore Moran, *American Multinationals and American Interests* (Washington, D.C.: Brookings Institution, 1978); Robert Stobaugh et al., *Nine Investments Abroad and Their Impact at Home* (Boston, Mass.: Division of Research, Harvard Graduate School of Business Administration, 1976);

Richard T. Frank and Richard T. Freeman, *Distributional Consequences of Direct Foreign Investment* (New York, N.Y.: Academic Press, 1978); and AFL–CIO, 16th Constitutional Convention, *Resolution on International Trade and Investment*, October 1985. A more recent study by Martin Feldstein suggests that each dollar of outbound FDI reduces domestic investment by about a dollar and the domestic capital stock by between 20 and 38 cents. See Martin Feldstein, *The Effects of Outbound Foreign Investment on the Domestic Capital Stock*, National Bureau of Economic Research Working Paper #4668, March 1994.

76. Peninou et al., *Who's Afraid of the Multinationals?* 59–62. See also Joseph La Palombara and Stephen Blank, *Multinational Corporations in Comparative Perspective* (New York, N.Y.: The Conference Board, 1977), 6–8.

77. Peninou et al., *Who's Afraid of the Multinationals?* 69–70.

78. J. Alex Murray and Lawrence Le Duc, "Changing Attitudes Toward Foreign Investment in Canada," in John Fayerweather, *Host National Attitudes Toward Multinational Corporations* (New York, N.Y.: Praeger, 1982), 216–235.

79. John Fayerweather, "Elite Attitudes Toward Multinational Firms: A Study of Britain, Canada, and France," *International Studies Quarterly*, 16 (December 1972): 472–490.

80. For example, see the analysis of French attitudes toward sensitive industries in Allan W. Johnstone, *United States Direct Investment in France: An Investigation of the French Charges* (Cambridge, Mass.: MIT Press, 1965), 32–34.

81. See Behrman, *National Interests and the Multinational Enterprise*, 69–84.

82. Task Force, *Foreign Direct Investment in Canada*, 428.

83. Organization for Economic Cooperation and Development, *Transfer Pricing and Multinational Enterprises: Three Taxation Issues* (Paris, France: OECD, 1984); Alan M. Rugman and Lorraine Eden, eds., *Multinationals and Transfer Pricing* (New York, N.Y.: St. Martin's Press, 1985); and Roger Y. W. Tang, *Transfer Pricing in the 1990s: Tax and Management Perspectives* (Westport, Conn.: Quorum Books, 1993).

84. Dunning, *Multinational Enterprises and the Global Economy*, 509.

85. George Graham, "U.S. Tax Move Alarms Multinational Groups," *Financial Times*, August 15, 1995, 4; Jonathan Schwarz, "Survey of World Taxation," *Financial Times*, February 24, 1995, 35; and "The Unitary Tax Escape," *The Fresno Bee*, July 6, 1994. On the difficulty of administering the California unitary tax, see General Accounting Office, *Tax Policy and Administration: California Taxes on Multinational Corporations and Related Federal Issues* (Washington, D.C.: Government Printing Office, August 10, 1995).

86. Behrman, *National Interests and the Multinational Enterprise*, 73–76.

87. See Hart, *Rival Capitalists*, especially chs. 2 and 3.

88. See Wolfgang Streeck, "Lean Production in the German Automobile Industry? A Test Case," in Suzanne Berger and Ronald Dore, eds., *Convergence or Diversity? National Models of Production and Distribution in a Global Economy* (Ithaca, N.Y.: Cornell University Press, 1996).

89. See Behrman, *National Interests and the Multinational Enterprise*, 88–127.

90. See, for example, Richard Cupit, *Reluctant Champions: U.S. Presidential Policy and Strategic Export Controls* (New York, N.Y.: Routledge, 2000); Michael

Mastanduno, *Economic Containment: CoCom and the Politics of East-West Trade* (Ithaca, N.Y.: Cornell University Press, 1992); and William J. Long, *U.S. Export Control Policy: Executive Autonomy versus Congressional Reform* (New York, N.Y.: Columbia University Press, 1989).

91. Jonathan P. Stern, *The Future of Russian Gas and Gazprom* (New York, N.Y.: Oxford University Press, 2005); Bruce Jentleson, *Pipeline Politics: The Complex Political Economy of East-West Energy Trade* (Ithaca, N.Y.: Cornell University Press, 1986); Beverly Crawford, *Economic Vulnerability in International Relations: East-West Trade, Investment, and Finance* (New York, N.Y.: Columbia University Press, 1993), ch. 5; and Angela Stent, *From Embargo to Ostpolitik: The Political German-Soviet Relations Economy of West* (New York, N.Y.: Cambridge University Press, 1981).

92. Behrman, *National Interests and the Multinational Enterprise*, 104–113.

93. Mark R. Joelson, "International Antitrust: Problems and Defenses," *Law and Policy in International Business*, 2 (Summer 1970): 1121–1134.

94. John B. Goodman and Louis W. Pauly, "The Obsolescence of Capital Controls? Economic Management in an Age of Global Markets," *World Politics*, 36 (October 1993): 50–82; and John Conybeare, *U.S. Foreign Economic Policy and the International Capital Markets: The Case of Capital Export Controls, 1963–74* (New York, N.Y.: Garland, 1988).

95. A general work on the effectiveness of economic sanctions is Gary C. Hufbauer, Jeffrey J. Schott, Kimberly A. Elliott, and Barbara Oegg, *Economic Sanctions Reconsidered*, 3rd edition (Washington, D.C.: Peterson Institute, 2008).

96. See similar possibilities outlined in Task Force, *Foreign Direct Investment in Canada*, 301–306; Pat Choate, *Agents of Influence: How Japan Manipulates America's Political and Economic System* (New York, N.Y.: Simon and Schuster, 1990).

97. Task Force, *Foreign Direct Investment in Canada*, 305–307.

98. See U.S. Senate, 93rd Cong., 1st and 2nd sess., and 94th Cong., 1st and 2nd sess., *Multinational Corporations and United States Foreign Policy*, hearings before the Subcommittee on Multinational Corporations of the Committee on Foreign Relations (Washington, D.C.: U.S. Government Printing Office, 1975).

99. Dennis M. Ray, "Corporations and American Foreign Relations," *The Annals*, 403 (September 1972), 80–92.

100. For a discussion of International Telephone & Telegraph, see U.S. Senate, *Multinational Corporations and United States Foreign Policy*; see also Paul Sigmund, *The Overthrow of Allende and the Politics of Chile, 1964–1976* (Pittsburgh, Pa.: University of Pittsburgh Press, 1978); and Jerome Levinson, "The Transnational Corporations and the Home Country," in *Conference on the Regulation of Transnational Corporations*, February 26, 1976 (New York, N.Y.: Columbia Journal of Transnational Law Association, 1976): 17–22.

101. Robert W. Cox, "Labor and the Multinationals," *Foreign Affairs*, 54 (January 1976): 344–365.

102. In John Fayerweather, *Foreign Investment in Canada: Prospects for National Policy* (White Plains, N.Y.: International Arts and Sciences Press, 1973), 32.

103. See Charles Lipson, *Standing Guard: Protecting Foreign Capital in the Nineteenth and Twentieth Centuries* (Berkeley and Los Angeles, Calif.: University of California Press, 1985); Nathan M. Jensen, *Nation-States and the Multinational Corporation: A Political Economy of Foreign Direct Investment* (Princeton, N.J.: Princeton University Press,

2008); and Louis T. Wells and Rafiq Ahmed, *Making Foreign Investment Safe: Property Rights and National Sovereignty* (New York, N.Y.: Oxford University Press, 2006).

104. See Hart, *Rival Capitalists*, chs. 2 and 3.

105. For a good summary of national approaches to the management of foreign direct investment, see Linda M. Spencer, *American Assets: An Examination of Foreign Investment in the United States* (Arlington, Va.; Congressional Economic Leadership Institute, 1988), 19–27. See also Earl H. Fry, op. cit., and OECD, *Investment Incentives and Disincentives.*

106. See M. Y. Yoshino, "Japan As Host to the International Corporation," in Kindleberger, *The International Corporation*, 345–369; Lawrence B. Krause, "Evolution of Foreign Direct Investment: The United States and Japan," in Jerome B. Cohen, ed., *Pacific Partnership: United States–Japan Trade: Prospects and Recommendations for the Seventies* (Lexington, Mass.: Lexington Books for Japan Society, 1972), 149–176; Noritake Kobayashi, "Foreign Investment in Japan," in Litvak and Maule, eds., *Foreign Investment: The Experience of Host Countries*, 123–160; Mark Mason, *American Multinationals and Japan: The Political Economy of Japanese Capital Controls, 1899–1990* (Cambridge, Mass.: Harvard University Press, 1992); and Dennis J. Encarnation, *Rivals Beyond Trade: America versus Japan in Global Competition* (Ithaca, N.Y.: Cornell University Press, 1992).

107. Robert Z. Lawrence, "Japan's Low Level of Inward Investment: The Role of Inhibitions on Acquisitions," in Kenneth A. Froot, ed., *Foreign Direct Investment* (Chicago, Ill.: University of Chicago Press, 1993).

108. See Japan Economic Institute, "Recent Trends in U.S. Direct Investment in Japan," Report No. 23A (June 15, 1984), and "Foreign Direct Investment in Japan" Annual Updates for 1985 (August 16, 1985), 1986 (October 10, 1986) and 1987 (April 17, 1987), *JEI Report* (Japan Economic Institute, Washington). See also Dennis Encarnation, "American-Japanese Cross-Investment: A Second Front of Economic Rivalry" in Thomas McCraw, ed., *America versus Japan* (Boston, Mass.: Harvard Business School Press, 1986).

109. In July 1995, the United States and Japan concluded an investment agreement under which the Japanese government undertook to promote FDI inflows into Japan by giving foreign investors access to Japanese government finance and by promoting access zones and joint research facilities.

110. *World Investment Report 2001.*

111. Jon Choy, "Tokyo Gives Foreign Group First Shot at Failed Long-Term Credit Bank," *JEI Report*, no. 37 (October 1, 1999).

112. FIRA rejected only 10 percent of the proposals submitted for review between 1974 and 1985, but if one considers proposals that were withdrawn prior to review or firms that were deterred from going through the process at all, the rejection rate was probably closer to 25 percent. See Rod B. McNaughton, "U.S. Foreign Direct Investment in Canada, 1985–1989," *The Canadian Geographer*, 36 (Summer 1992): 181–189.

113. See Safarian, *Governments and Multinationals*, 14–20. For a critical review of FIRA, see Christopher C. Beckman, *The Foreign Investment Review Agency: Images and Realities* (Ottawa, ON: Canadian Conference Board, 1984).

114. On the Investment Canada Act, see Investment Canada, *Annual Report 1986–87* (Minister of Supply and Services Canada, 1987); and Thorne, Ernst and Whinney,

Canada's Investment Canada Act: An Executive Summary (Toronto, ON: Thorne, Ernst and Whinney, 1986). FIRA was renamed Investment Canada.

115. See A. E. Safarian, "The Canada–U.S. Free Trade Agreement and Foreign Direct Investment," *Trade Monitor*, no. 3, May 1988, C.D. Howe Institute, 16ff.; Earl Fry and Lee H. Radebaugh, *The Canada/U.S. Free Trade Agreement: The Impact on Service Industries* (Provo, Ut.: Brigham Young University, 1988); Jeffrey Atik, "Fairness and Managed Foreign Direct Investment," *Columbia Journal of Transnational Law*, 32 (1994): 1–42; and *The Canada–U.S. Free Trade Agreement* (Ottawa, ON: Department of External Affairs, 1987).

116. On the role of the British Monopolies and Mergers Commission in approving foreign acquisitions, see Edward Graham and Michael Ebert, "Foreign Direct Investment and U.S. National Security: Fixing Exon-Florio," *The World Economy*, 14 (September 1991): 256–261.

117. Charles Torem and William Laurence Craig, "Developments in the Control of Foreign Investment in France," *Michigan Law Review*, 70 (December 1971): 285–336; Safarian, *Governments and Multinationals*, 20–24.

118. Graham and Krugman, *Foreign Investment in the United States*, 126.

119. James K. Jackson, "The Exon-Florio National Security Test for Foreign Investment," *Congressional Research Service Report for Congress*, updated February 23, 2006.

120. Graham and Krugman, 129–130.

121. An R&D consortium is an effort, usually jointly funded by a government together with a number of private firms who are members of the consortium, to share the costs of developing a new commercial technology. Japan pioneered this form of collaborative research and was particularly successful in the semiconductor industry with its VLSI (very large scale integrated [circuits]) program between 1976 and 1979.

122. Michael Petrusic, "Recent Development: Oil and National Security: CNOOC's Failed Bid to Purchase Unocal," *North Carolina Law Review*, 84 (2006): 1388–1393.

123. Neil King Jr. and Greg Hitt, "Dubai Ports World Sells U.S. Assets," *The Wall Street Journal*, December 12, 2006.

124. Skadden Arps, "President Signs Legislation Reforming U.S. National Security Reviews of Foreign Investments in U.S. Companies," July 6, 2007, http://www.skadden.com/content/Publications/Publications1292_0.pdf.

125. See Tolchin, *Buying into America* and Robert B. Reich, "Corporation and Nation," *The Atlantic*, May 1988, 76.

126. See Cynthia Day Wallace, *Legal Control of the Multinational Enterprise* (The Hague, The Netherlands: Martinus Nijhoff, 1982); and John Robinson, *Multinationals and Political Control* (New York, N.Y.: St. Martin's Press, 1983).

127. Sofia Perez, *Banking on Privilege: The Politics of Spanish Financial Reform* (Ithaca, N.Y.: Cornell University Press, 1997).

128. See Servan-Schreiber, *The American Challenge*.

129. See J. J. Boddewyn, "Western European Policies Toward U.S. Investors," *The Bulletin* (March 1974): 45–63; Raymond Vernon, "Enterprise and Government in Western Europe," in Raymond Vernon, ed., *Big Business and the State: Changing Relations in Western Europe* (Cambridge, Mass.: Harvard University Press, 1974), 3–24; and Behrman, *National Interests and the Multinational Enterprise*, 161–172.

130. Caborn report, 7.

131. For an analysis that argues that the EC has imposed significant controls on MNCs, see Robinson, *Multinationals and Political Control*. For a survey of European Community initiatives and their status, see *Business Guide to EC Initiatives* (Brussels, Belgium: American Chamber of Commerce in Belgium, 1988). See also, R. Blancpain, F. Blanquet, F. Herman, and A. Mouty, *The Vredeling Proposal: Information and Consultation of Employees in Multinational Enterprises* (Boston, Mass.: Kluwer, 1983); and Ton DeVos, *Multinational Corporations in Democratic Host Countries: U.S. Multinationals and the Vredeling Proposal* (Aldershot, England: Dartmouth, 1989).

132. Article 130f (1), "Treaty Establishing the European Economic Community (as amended by the Single European Act, July 1, 1987)," *Treaties Establishing the European Communities* (Luxembourg: Office for Official Publications of the European Communities, 1987), 239.

133. Glenn Fong, "Follower at the Frontier: International Competition and Japanese Industrial Policy," *International Studies Quarterly*, 42 (1998): 339–366.

134. Alyssa A. Grikscheit, "Are We Compatible? Current European Community Law on the Compatibility of Joint Ventures with the Common Market and Possibilities for Future Development," *Michigan Law Review*, 92 (February 1994): 968–1033.

135. Denise Claveloux, "Pending Social Legislation Means Big Changes to How EC Does Business," *Electronics*, November 8, 1993, 13; and "Unions Love Maastricht," *The Economist*, December 4, 1993, 54.

136. For a copy of the agreement, see http://www.mfat.govt.nz/Trade-and-Economic-Relations/Trade-Agreements/Australia/index.php.

137. See Lipson, *Standing Guard*, 132–133.

138. The International Civil Aviation Organization (ICAO), the International Labor Organization (ILO), and the World Health Organization (WHO) have all witnessed attempts to do this.

139. See Clair Wilcox, *A Charter for World Trade* (New York, N.Y.: Macmillan, 1949), 145–148.

140. United Nations Economic and Social Council, *Report of the Ad Hoc Committee on Restrictive Business Practices* (New York, N.Y.: United Nations, 1953); and General Agreement on Tariffs and Trade, *Decisions of the Seventeenth Session* (Geneva, Switzerland: GATT, December 5, 1960), 17.

141. See George W. Ball, "Cosmocorp: The Importance of Being Stateless," *Columbia Journal of World Business*, 2 (November-December 1967): 25–30.

142. Paul M. Goldberg and Charles Kindleberger, "Toward a GATT for Investment: A Proposal for Supervision of the International Corporation," *Law and Policy in International Business*, 2 (Summer 1970): 195–323.

143. See http://www.oecd.org/document/6/0,3343,en_2649_34887_1838086_1_1_1_1,00.html.

144. See http://www.oecd.org/document/53/0,3343,en_2649_34887_1933109_1_1_1_1,00.html.

145. Organization for Economic Cooperation and Development, *International Investment and Multinational Enterprises* (Paris, France: OECD, 1976). Experience with the OECD guidelines to date indicates that they may indeed have some impact on the operations of multinationals within member states. See, for example, R. Blancpain, *The Badger Case and the OECD Guidelines for Multinational Enterprises* (Deventer, the Netherlands: Kluwer, 1977). For OECD reviews, see OECD, *National Treatment for*

Foreign Controlled Enterprises in OECD Member Countries (Paris, France: OECD, 1978); OECD, *International Direct Investment: Policies, Procedures and Practices in OECD Member Countries* (Paris, France: OECD, 1979); and OECD, *Controls and Impediments Affecting Inward Direct Investments in OECD Countries* (Paris, France: OECD, 1987).

146. Organization for Economic Cooperation and Development, *Transfer Pricing Guidelines for Multinational Enterprises and Tax Administrations* (Paris, France: OECD, 1994).

147. *International Investment Perspectives: Freedom of Investment in a Changing World*, 2007 Edition (Paris, France: OECD, 2007): 57.

148. For a compendium of the center's publications, see United Nations, Center on Transnational Corporations, *Bibliography on Transnational Corporations* (New York, N.Y.: United Nations, 1988). The center's periodical, *CTC Reporter*, carries summaries and announcements of the center's work.

149. The CTC, which had been based in New York, was absorbed into the United Nations Conference on Trade and Development (UNCTAD) in Geneva. Fortunately, UNCTAD has continued to publish the data on FDI and MNC activities that were previously published by the CTC.

150. Black, Blank, and Hanson, *Multinationals in Contention*, 221–225; Werner Feld, *Multinational Corporations and U.N. Politics: The Quest for Codes of Conduct* (Elmsford, N.Y.: Pergamon Press, 1980); Debra Lynn Miller, "Panacea or Problem? The Proposed International Code of Conduct for Technology Transfer," *Journal of International Affairs* (Spring-Summer 1979): 43–62.

151. See Seymour J. Rubin, "The International Firm and the National Jurisdiction," in Kindleberger, ed., *The International Corporation*, 179–204 and 475–488.

152. ICSID Annual Report 2007, accessed at http://www.worldbank.org/icsid/.

153. ICSID website at http://www.worldbank.org/icsid/.

154. Zachary Elkins, Andrew T. Guzman, and Beth A. Simmons, "Competing for Capital: The Diffusion of Bilateral Investment Treaties, 1960–2000," *International Organization*, 60 (Fall 2006): 811–846.

155. See Peter Egger and Valeria Merlo, "The Impact of Bilateral Investment Treaties on FDI Dynamics," *The World Economy*, (2007): 1536–1549 for information about the effects of BITs on FDI flows.

156. Stephen Kobrin, "The MAI and the Clash of Globalizations," *Foreign Policy*, No. 112 (Autumn 1998): 97–109; David Henderson, *The MAI Affair: A Story and Its Lessons* (London, UK: The Royal Institute of International Affairs, 1999), 1–2; and Edward M. Graham, *Fighting the Wrong Enemy: Antiglobal Activists and Multinational Enterprises* (Washington, D.C.: Institute for International Economics, 2000).

157. The OECD posted the draft on its website after the leak. See http://www1.oecd.org/daf/mai/htm/2.htm.

158. Marcus Noland, "Learning to Love the WTO," *Foreign Affairs* (September/October 1999), 87.

159. Edward Graham, *Fighting the Wrong Enemy*, 7.

5

The North–South System
and the Possibility
of Change

The governance problems of the North–South system are quite different from those of the Western system. For the system of developed market economies, the crucial issue is whether it is possible to achieve the necessary political capability at the national, regional, and global levels to ensure that international economic relations continue to result in mutually beneficial outcomes while also modernizing (although not drastically altering) the international economic institutions that have been in place since World War II. The North–South system is separate from, but also embedded in, the Western system. It is separate because the rules of the North–South system reflect the much lower income levels and resource bases of the developing countries. It is embedded because the industrialized countries of the North have veto power over important changes in the system. The main question for the North–South system is whether it is possible to change the system so that more than a small number of developing countries benefit from it.

In the Western system, control is facilitated by a perceived common interest in the system. In the North–South system, there is less perception of a common interest. The developed market economies feel that the North–South system, although not perfect, is legitimate, because it benefits them and because they have significant decision-making authority. The Southern states tend to feel that both the Western and the North–South systems are illegitimate because they have not enjoyed a large enough share of the economic rewards. From their

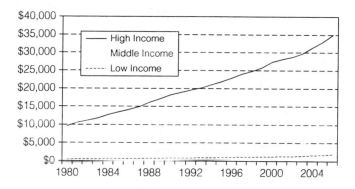

FIGURE 5.1 Gross National Income Per Capita, Purchasing Power Parity Method, 1980–2006, in Dollars, in High-, Middle-, and Low-Income Countries
SOURCE: World Bank, *World Development Indicators 2008*, online data.

viewpoint, neither system has adequately promoted their economic development. Also, they feel that their interests are not properly represented in these international economic regimes.

One of the key sources of Southern grievances with the North–South system is the inability of the South to reduce the gap in average incomes between itself and the North. Average income in 2006, as measured by gross national income (GNI) divided by the total population (GNI per capita), was $25,639 in high-income countries, $5,137 in middle-income countries, and $421 in low-income countries (see Figure 5.1). The population of the low-income countries in 2005 was 2.4 billion, of middle-income countries 3.1 billion, and of high-income countries 1 billion.[1]

Global income is distributed quite unequally, and that inequality may be increasing. Absolute gaps in per capita income between the high-income countries and others increased markedly between 1980 and 2006, continuing the postwar trend.[2] During the five years from 2001 to 2006, average growth rates were 6.1 percent in the low-income countries, 5.6 percent in the middle-income countries, and 2.2 percent in the high-income countries. Average annual growth in nominal GDP between 1991 and 2000 was 4.6 percent in the low-income countries, 3.8 percent in the middle-income countries, and 2.5 percent in the high-income countries (see Figure 5.2). While economic growth rates were higher on the average in the South than in the North during the past four decades, high population growth rates kept per capita income growth rates modest for most of the South's people, with the notable exception of a small number of very fast-growing developing countries. It is a hopeful sign, of course, that the two largest low-income countries—China and India—have experienced rapid growth in recent decade.[3]

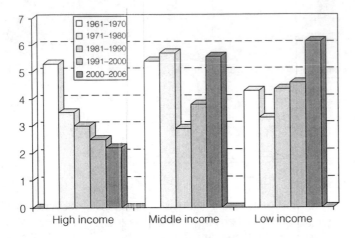

FIGURE 5.2 Average Annual Growth of Nominal GDP, 1961–2006, in Percentages
SOURCE: World Bank, *World Development Indicators 2008*, online data.

There are a variety of ways to measure the amount of inequality within and across nations. One commonly used measure is the **GINI coefficient of inequality**. The GINI coefficient measures the degree of variance from perfect equality by determining the area between the Lorenz curve of distribution and the diagonal which represents perfect equality. The **Lorenz curve** is a graphical representation of the cumulative distribution function of a probability distribution; it is a graph showing the proportion of the distribution assumed by the bottom $y\%$ of the values (see Figure 5.3). The GINI coefficient ranges from zero (perfect equality) to one (perfect inequality). Economists have attempted to measure global income inequality over relatively long periods of time. These efforts have yielded consistent findings that inequality increased steadily between 1820 and 1970, but began to decrease from 1970 on.[4] The GINI coefficient for global income inequality measured in terms of GDP per capita across countries ranges between .5 and .65 for the period between 1820 and 1998 and recently has stabilized around .6, while the GINI coefficient for domestic income inequality tends to range between .3 and .4 for most countries.[5] In short, the empirical evidence on income inequality fails to support the view of some critics that the intensification of globalization after 1989 resulted in increased global and domestic inequality. Rather, it indicates that there has been in a major decline in the number of people living on less than a dollar a day and in other indicators of "absolute poverty."[6] A large proportion of the decline in global inequality in recent years is due to high economic growth rates in China and India.[7]

Nevertheless, there are still more than a billion people on the planet who are not benefiting from globalization. Most of them live in countries which have

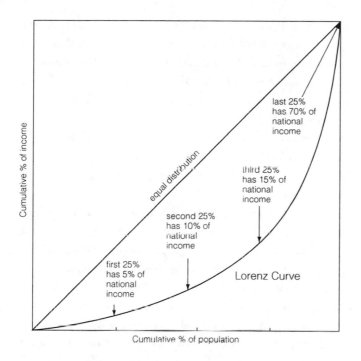

FIGURE 5.3 The GINI Coefficient: Measuring Inequality Using the Lorenz Curve

both low average per capita income and low growth rates. They are frequently victims of disease and violence, and may be trapped in a cycle of poverty by the mutually reinforcing nature of these conditions. Malaria provides an example: "Malaria keeps countries poor and because they are poor the potential market for a vaccine is not sufficiently valuable to warrant drug companies making the huge investment in research that is necessary."[8]

In 2007, three of every four poor people in developing countries lived in rural areas—2.1 billion living on less than $2 a day and 880 million on less than $1 a day—and most depended on agriculture for their livelihoods.[9] Many of those living on less than $1 a day are found in sub-Saharan Africa and South Asia. More than 1.6 billion lacked access to basic sanitation, 1.1 billion lacked access to safe water supplies, and more than 775 million were illiterate.[10] Daily caloric intake was one-third lower in the poorest fifth of the world's countries than in the richest fifth.[11] Infant mortality in the richest fifth of countries averaged 4 out of every 1,000 births; the equivalent figure of the poorest fifth of countries was 200 out of every 1,000 births. Between 170 million and 400 children in these countries were infected with intestinal parasites. About 120,000 children born each year suffered from mental retardation and paralysis caused by iodine deficiency. Vitamin A deficiency contributed to the death of around 8 million children per year. In short, global inequality has multiple, reinforcing and consistently very negative consequences for the poorest people of the world.

The impact of higher rates of economic growth on reducing poverty is positive and relatively immediate. For example, a 1-percent increase in the average income of a country translates into a 1-percent increase in the income of the poorest 20 percent of the country's population. A 10-percent increase in income results in a 6-percent reduction in infant mortality. The deaths of about half a million children in Africa in 1990 could have been averted if the region's growth rate had been 1.5 percent higher in the 1980s.[12]

While economic development should not be defined purely in terms of economic growth, the preoccupation with increasing economic growth in the South is understandable in light of what we know about its ameliorating effects. That is why there are so many arguments about the various theories of economic growth. In economics, there has been a vigorous debate in recent years about the relative importance of accumulating physical capital versus human capital and/or technological capability in generating high rates of growth.[13] In political science, especially since the end of the Cold War, the main focus has been on the policies and political institutions, that is the governance, necessary for sustained growth.[14]

The governance of North–South economic relations is quite different from that of the Western system. In the West, there is a relatively highly institutionalized system consisting of international organizations, elite networks, processes of negotiation, agreed–upon norms, and rules of the game. Although power is unequally distributed in the West, all members have access to both formal and informal management systems. North–South relations, in contrast, have no well-developed system with access for all. The South has been regularly excluded from the formal and informal processes of system management. Many Southern countries cannot afford to be full partners in international economic governance. It is too expensive for the poorest Southern countries to send representatives to the various international economic forums, and those that attend often are not adequately prepared to provide useful input to the proceedings. As a result, North–South relations are mostly controlled by the North as a subsidiary of the Western system. Understandably, the North perceives this structure as legitimate, whereas the South generally perceives it as illegitimate.

Since the end of World War II, developing countries have persistently sought to change their dependent role in international economic relations. As we shall discuss, their efforts to enhance economic growth and increase their access to global decision-making forums have varied over time and from country to country. Southern strategies have been of three main types: (1) attempts to delink themselves from some aspects of the international economic system, (2) attempts to change the economic order itself, and (3) attempts to maximize the benefits from integration into the prevailing system. These strategies have been shaped to a significant degree by the central question of whether it is possible to achieve growth and development within the prevailing international economic system. The dominant liberal philosophy argues that such development is not only possible but likely under a liberal economic regime. Two contending approaches—Marxist (and neo-Marxist) theories and **structuralism**—challenge the liberal perspective and argue that the system itself is at the root of the development problem.

LIBERAL THEORIES OF ECONOMIC DEVELOPMENT

Liberalism—especially as embodied in classical and neoclassical economics—is the dominant theory of the prevailing international economic system. Liberal theories of economic development argue that the existing international market structure provides the best framework for Southern economic development.[15] The major problems of development, in this view, are caused by the domestic economic policies of the developing countries that create or accentuate market imperfections; reduce the productivity of land, labor, and capital; and intensify social and political rigidities. The best way to remedy these weaknesses, according to liberals, is through the adoption of market-oriented domestic reforms. Given appropriate internal policies, the international system—through increased levels of trade, foreign investment, and foreign aid flows—can provide a basis for more rapid growth and economic development.

Trade, according to liberal analyses, acts as an engine of growth. Specialization that is consistent with national **comparative advantages** increases income levels in all countries engaging in free or relatively open trade. Specialization in areas where the factors of production are relatively abundant promotes more efficient resource allocation and permits economic actors to apply their technological and managerial skills more effectively. It also encourages higher levels of capital formation through the domestic financial system and increased inflows of FDI. Private financial flows from developed countries can be used to fund investment in infrastructure and productive facilities. In addition, foreign aid from developed market economies is believed to help fill gaps in resources in developing countries by, for example, providing capital, technology, and education. Finally, specialization in the presence of appropriate antitrust enforcement can stimulate domestic competition and improve international competitiveness simultaneously.

From the liberal viewpoint, the correct international Southern strategy for economic development is to foster those domestic changes necessary to promote foreign trade, inflows of foreign investment, and the international competitiveness of domestic firms. In practice, this means the reversal of policies that hinder trade and investment flows, such as high tariffs and restrictions on FDI inflows, and the adoption of policies that increase domestic levels of competition—for example through the privatization of state enterprises, deregulation of overregulated markets, and other domestic reforms.[16]

MARXIST AND NEO-MARXIST THEORIES
OF DEVELOPMENT

Marxist and neo-Marxist theories strongly criticize the liberal perspective.[17] Southern countries, it is argued, are poor and exploited not because they are illiberal but because of their history as subordinate elements in the world capitalist system. This condition will persist for as long as they remain part of that system. The international market is under the control of monopoly capitalists whose economic base is in the developed economies. The free flow of trade and investment, so much desired by liberals, enables the capitalist classes of both the developed and underdeveloped countries to extract the economic wealth of the underdeveloped countries for their own use. The result is the impoverishment of the masses of the Third World.

Trade between North and South is an unequal exchange, in which control of the international market by the monopolies/oligopolies headquartered in the developed capitalist countries leads to declining prices for the raw materials produced by the South and rising prices for the industrial products produced by the North. The **terms of trade**—export prices divided by import prices—are biased against the South.[18] In addition, international trade encourages the South to concentrate on backward forms of production that prevent development. The language of **comparative advantage** used by liberal free-traders masks their desire to maintain an **international division of labor** that is unfavorable to the South.

Foreign investment further hinders and distorts Southern development, often by controlling the most dynamic local industries and expropriating the economic surplus of these sectors through the repatriation of profits, royalty fees, and licenses. According to many Marxists, there is a net outflow of capital from the South to the North. In addition, foreign investment contributes to unemployment by establishing capital-intensive production, aggravating uneven income distribution, displacing local capital and local entrepreneurs, adding to the emphasis on production for export, and promoting undesirable consumption patterns.

Another dimension of capitalist creation and perpetuation of underdevelopment is the international financial system. Trade and investment remove capital from the South and necessitate Southern borrowing from Northern financial institutions, both public and private. But **debt service** and repayment further drain Third World wealth. Finally, foreign aid reinforces the Third World's distorted development, by promoting foreign investment and trade at the expense of true development and by extracting wealth through debt service. Reinforcing these external market structures of dependence, according to some Marxists and neo-Marxists, are clientele social classes within the underdeveloped countries. Local elites with a vested interest in the structure of dominance and a monopoly of domestic power cooperate with international capitalist elites to perpetuate the international capitalist system.

Because international market operations and the clientele elite perpetuate dependence, any development under the international capitalist system is uneven, distorted, and, at best, partial. For most Marxists and neo–Marxists, the only appropriate strategy for development is revolutionary: total destruction of the international capitalist system and its replacement with an international socialist system. Some Marxists and neo-Marxists differ on whether it is possible to achieve this revolutionary ideal on a national basis or whether it is necessary for the revolution to be global, but they agree that revolutionary change is the only way to achieve true development in the South.[19]

THE STRUCTURALISTS

Structural theory, which has had a significant influence on the international economic policy of the South, falls between liberalism and Marxism.[20] Structuralist analysis, like Marxist analysis, contends that the international market structure perpetuates backwardness and dependency in the South and encourages dominance by the North. According to this view, the market tends to favor the already well endowed and to thwart the less developed. Unregulated international trade and capital movements will accentuate, not diminish, international inequalities, unless accompanied by reforms at the national and international levels.

The structural bias of the international market, according to this school, rests in large part on the inequalities of the international trading system. Trade does not serve as an engine of growth as asserted by the liberals, but actually widens the North–South gap. The system creates declining terms of trade for the South (see Figure 5.4). Income inelasticity of demand for the primary product exports of the less-developed countries (i.e., increased income in the North does not lead to increased demand for imports from the South) and the existence of a competitive international market for those products lead to lower prices for Third World exports. At the same time, the monopoly structure of Northern markets and the rising demand for manufactured goods lead to higher prices for the industrial products of the North. Thus, under normal market conditions, international trade actually transfers income from the South to the North.[21]

Structuralists also argue that international trade creates an undesirable **dual economy**. Specialization and concentration on export industries based on comparative advantages in agriculture or the extraction of raw materials by the Southern economies do not fuel the rest of the economy as projected by the liberals. Instead, trade creates an export sector that has little or no dynamic effect on the rest of the economy and that drains resources from the rest of the economy. Thus, trade creates a developed and isolated export sector alongside an underdeveloped economy in general.

Foreign investment, the second part of the structural bias, often avoids the South, where profits and security are lower than in the developed market

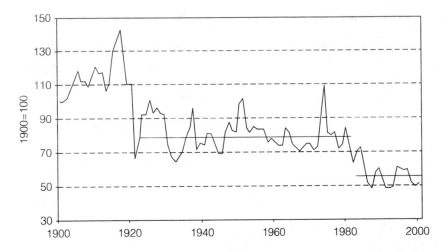

FIGURE 5.4 Terms of Trade for Developing Countries, Excluding Oil Exporters, 1900–2000

SOURCE: José Antonio Ocampo and María Angel Parra, "The Commodity Terms of Trade and Their Strategic Implications for Development," March 2004, http://129.3.20.41/econ-wp/it/papers/0403/0403001.pdf.

economies. When investment does flow to the South, it tends to concentrate in export sectors, thereby aggravating the dual economy and the negative effects of trade. Finally, foreign investment leads to a net flow of profits and interest to the developed, capital-exporting North.

The structuralist prescription for promoting economic development in the South focuses on four types of policy changes: (1) **import-substituting industrialization (ISI)**, (2) increased **South-South trade and investment**, (3) **regional integration**, and (4) **population control**. Structuralists assert that it is the specialization of Third World countries in the production and export of raw materials and agricultural commodities that hurts them in world trade because of the declining terms of trade for those products. Therefore the South needs to diversify away from agriculture and raw materials toward manufacturing and services activities. To do this, it may need to adopt high tariffs initially to encourage the establishment of domestic manufacturing facilities. This is the essence of import substitution.

Second, the South needs to reduce trade barriers among the developing countries in order to compensate for the generally small size of their domestic markets and to achieve economies of scale similar to those enjoyed by the industrialized nations of Europe, Asia, and North America. The best way to do this is to foster regional integration agreements among the developing countries, not unlike the ones that helped to bring prosperity to Western Europe after World War II. Increased South-South trade would be advantageous not just in adding to total world demand for exports from the South but also in allowing developing countries to develop technologies appropriate for the South, to counter the power of Northern MNCs, and to increase generally the competitiveness of businesses headquartered in the South.

Finally, structuralists like Raúl Prebisch and W. Arthur Lewis recognized that a key problem that had to be addressed was the depressing effect of rapid population growth on the average wages of Third World workers. If population growth could be reduced by appropriate population control policies, then it would be easier to achieve high standards of living for the impoverished masses of the South. Politically, this was the least popular part of the structuralist policy agenda, but it has received greater attention in recent years.[22]

CONTRASTING MARXIST AND STRUCTURALIST PERSPECTIVES

Although the structuralist analysis of the international market is similar to the Marxist analysis in its stress on the negative effects of the declining terms of trade of the developing countries, the two theories diverge on a critical point. Structuralist theory argues that the international system can be reformed, that the natural processes can be altered. Although the various theorists differ on preferred reforms—foreign aid, protection, access to Northern markets—they all believe that industrialization can be achieved within a reformed international economy and that industrialization will narrow the development gap.

Marxist theories, on the other hand, contend that the capitalist system is immutable, that it will defend itself, and that the only way to change it fundamentally is through revolution: destruction of the international capitalist system and its replacement with an international socialist system. Marxists explain the impossibility of reform in two ways.

One explanation is that developed capitalist economies are unable to absorb the economic surplus or profits generated by the capitalist system of production.[23] Capitalist states cannot absorb their rising surplus internally through consumption, because worker income does not grow as fast as capitalist profits. To prevent unemployment and the inevitable crisis of capitalism resulting from overproduction and underconsumption, the developed market economies invest excess capital in and export excess production to the developing countries. Another way to absorb the rising surplus and prevent the crisis of capitalism, according to some, is to invest in the military at home, which in turn leads to pressure for expansion abroad. By absorbing economic surplus, foreign expansion prevents or at least delays the collapse of the capitalist system. Thus, dominance, dependence, and imperialism are essential and inevitable consequences of capitalism.

A second explanation of the necessity of imperialism in a capitalist world economy derives from the North's need for Southern raw materials.[24] According to this argument, capitalist economies depend on imports of vital raw materials from the South, and the desire to control access to those supplies leads to Northern dominance.

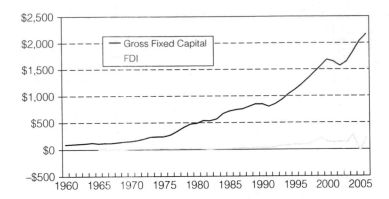

FIGURE 5.5 U.S. Gross Fixed Capital Formation and Outflows of Foreign Direct Investment in Billions of Current Dollars, 1960–2006

SOURCE: *World Investment Report 2007; Economic Report of the President 2008.*

WEAKNESSES OF THE THREE PERSPECTIVES

Empirical examination reveals important weaknesses in all three perspectives. We will start with the Marxist approach. Although some economic ties with the South are important to the developed countries, they are for the most part not crucial to the North's economic well-being. Indeed, as we shall discuss, the problem for the less-developed countries may be that they are not important enough for the North.

First, the underconsumption arguments of the Marxists are weak, because the developed market economies are mostly able to absorb their economic surpluses. While the developed economies have had difficulties maintaining aggregate demand at acceptable levels, they have managed the problem internally through modern economic policies: income redistribution, fiscal and monetary policy, and public and social expenditures—a situation that has come to be called the "welfare state." Although the developed countries have had serious economic problems—sluggish growth, surplus industrial capacity, inflation—these cannot be adequately explained by underconsumption theories.

Second, foreign investment, especially in less-developed markets, is not of vital importance to the developed market economies, as illustrated by the case of the United States, the principal foreign investor. Foreign investment is a relatively small percentage of total U.S. investment. In 1998, U.S. outward FDI was $131 billion, or 7.8 percent of total investment in fixed capital for that year (see Figure 5.5). In 2006, U.S. FDI outflows amounted to $216 billion or about 10 percent of investment in fixed capital. Furthermore, the South was not the main area of U.S. foreign investment and was, in fact, declining in importance relative to the industrialized countries. Between 1989 and 1994, the developing countries accounted for an average of 30 percent of all U.S. outward FDI stocks. By 1999, this figure had declined to 21 percent. It rose again to 28 percent in 2006 (see Figure 5.6).[25]

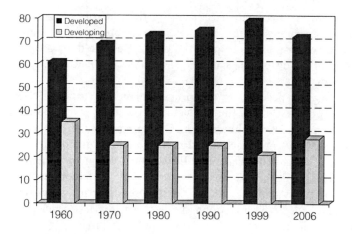

FIGURE 5.6 Percentage of U.S. Outward Stock of FDI in Developed and Developing Countries, 1960–2006

SOURCE: *Statistical Abstract of the U.S.* (various years).

Data in Chapters 3 and 4 showed that trade and investment flows are still primarily among the developed countries and that flows between developed and developing countries are still relatively smaller. There has been some change in the direction of North–South trade and investment with the rapid growth of China and India and the further globalization of production on the part of MNCs, but the overall pattern still holds.

In sum, the case for dependence on the South as a necessary outlet for capitalist surplus is not sustainable. The developing countries provide significant earnings for MNCs and the developed economies and are important investment and export outlets, but they are not crucial for the survival of the North. The available data suggest that the economic importance of the South for the North has declined in the decades since World War II, with the notable exception of dependence of the North on petroleum exports from the South (see Chapter 9).

Northern dependence on Southern raw materials is also limited. Raw materials in general are not as significant as Marxist theory suggests, and where they are significant (as with oil), raw material dependence may work to the detriment of the developing countries, not to their advantage. The United States, and to a greater extent the Europeans and Japanese, depend on the import of certain raw materials, but in only a few cases are the major suppliers of these materials Southern countries.[26] Furthermore, foreign dependence is declining as growth in overall consumption of raw materials declines due to changing growth patterns, conservation, technological improvements, and substitution.

In conclusion, the arguments that dominance and exploitation of the South are necessary for the capitalist economies as a whole do not stand the empirical test. The South is important but not vital.

There is, however, the Marxist argument that dependence, although not important to the capitalist economies as a whole, is necessary for the capitalist class that dominates the economy and polity.[27] According to these theories, capitalist groups, especially those managing the multinational corporations, seek to dominate the underdeveloped countries in their quest for profit. Because these groups control the governments of the developed states, they are able to use governmental tools for their class ends.

To evaluate this theory, it is necessary to determine whether the capitalist class as a whole has a common interest in the underdeveloped countries, even though most capitalists do not profit, as has been shown, from foreign trade and investment. Arthur MacEwan argues that the entire capitalist class has an interest in dominance and foreign expansion, including those capitalists having no relation to or profit from such expansion.[28] This is true, he explains, because there is a common interest in expansion that maintains the system as a whole. Yet the preceding analysis of the macroeconomic importance of the Third World suggests that the less-developed countries are not economically necessary to the North and that certain Northern groups, such as the petroleum industry, enjoy most of the benefits of economic ties with the South. Thus, the capitalist class as a whole does not have an interest in the South and in dominance, because only a small percentage of that class profits from dominance and because the system itself is not dependent on dominance.

A stronger argument is that some powerful capitalists, such as the managers of multinational corporations, have a crucial interest in the South and in Northern dominance. Clearly, certain firms and certain groups profit from the existing structure of the international market. The question is the role of these firms and these groups in Northern governmental policy. Certainly, those groups interested in Northern economic dominance can affect the foreign policies of developed countries.[29] But they do not inevitably dominate foreign policy in the developed market economies. In the Middle East, for example, despite the importance of oil earnings and petroleum, U.S. foreign policy has not always reflected the interests of the U.S. oil companies.[30]

On balance, then, dominance is important to the developed market economies and is especially important to certain groups within those economies. But dominance is neither necessary nor inevitable. Under the right political circumstances, change is possible. The problem is that the South has only limited ability to demand change from the North. Economically underdeveloped and politically fragmented, the South has limited leverage on the North. As we shall discuss, because the South is not vital for the North, the developed countries need not respond to Southern demands for change.

The Marxist perspective is not alone in having some difficulties in reconciling theory with evidence. The liberal perspective has trouble explaining a number of empirical anomalies as well. For example, neoclassical trade theory, as embodied in the **Heckscher-Ohlin (H-O) theory of international trade**, explains trade in terms of differences in comparative advantages across countries. Comparative advantages are determined by the relative abundance or lack of key **factors of production** (e.g., labor, land, and capital). However, "nearly half of the world's trade consists of trade between industrialized countries that are similar in their factor endowments."[31] If H-O theory were correct, then most of the world's trade would be North–South trade instead of North–North trade.

One way that neoclassical theories have tried to deal with this anomaly is by examining the effects of trade barriers on North–South trade.[32] Another is to relax the assumptions of H–O theory concerning **declining returns to scale** and the existence of competitive markets.[33] Yet another approach is to provide separate explanations of inter- and intra-industry trade.[34] Each approach has its merits, but there is still no overarching theory of trade that satisfactorily explains recent patterns in world trade.

In addition, liberals have problems explaining why countries with strongly interventionist governments, like Japan and South Korea, have done so well at promoting exports. According to the liberal orthodoxy, countries with governments that maintain a hands-off approach to promoting international competitiveness are more likely to end up with internationally competitive firms than those with interventionist governments.

Finally, despite the arguments of liberals for several decades that there should not be a long-term trend toward declining terms of trade for the developing countries, the evidence appears rather to support the contentions of both Marxists and structuralists that such a downward trend exists.[35]

The main criticism of the structuralists, besides the one just mentioned concerning the lack of solid evidence for declining terms of trade, has to do with the relative ineffectiveness and undesirability of import substitution as a development strategy. We deal with this criticism in the next section.

DEPENDENCE

Since the end of World War II, developing countries have pursued several different strategies in an effort to alter their dependence. In finance, trade, investment, and commodities, they have sought greater rewards from the greater participation in the international economic system. Over the years, those strategies have alternated between seeking to change the system and seeking to adapt to it.

During the Bretton Woods era, developing countries were dependent on the developed North and pursued national strategies designed to isolate or protect themselves from the international economic system. During the formative period of Bretton Woods, those developing states that were independent—primarily the Latin American countries—attempted to incorporate their goal of economic development and their view of appropriate international strategies for development into the North's plans for the new world economic order. The political and economic weakness of the developing world at this time doomed their efforts. At Bretton Woods, they sought, and failed, to ensure that development—meaning development for both industrial and developing countries—would have the same priority as reconstruction did in the activities of the new International Bank for Reconstruction and Development. At Havana, they argued for modification of the free-trade regime, for the right to protect their **infant industries** through trade restrictions such as import quotas, and for permission to stabilize and ensure minimum commodity prices through commodity agreements. Some LDC interests, such as the right to form commodity agreements and to establish regional preference systems to promote development, were, in fact, included in the Havana Charter. But these provisions were lost when the charter was not ratified and the GATT took its place.[36] As a result, many developing countries including Argentina, Jamaica, South Korea, Mexico, and Venezuela refused to join the GATT.[37]

In the 1950s and 1960s, developing countries abandoned these first efforts to shape the international system and turned inward. Faced with an international regime that they believed did not take their interests into account and that excluded them from management, developing countries turned to policies of diversification and industrialization via import substitution. The stress on industrialization was reinforced by the preoccupation of developing countries with decolonization and by the belief that the end of colonial political exploitation would foster economic development.

In this period, the main development strategy was import substitution. Developing countries protected local industry through tariffs, quantitative controls, and multiple exchange rates, and they favored production for local consumption over production for export. Governments became actively involved in promoting economic development, largely by channeling resources to the manufacturing sector. In many cases, those industries were owned by the state. Import substitution did not mean total isolation from the international system. Trade with the North continued to flow. Developing countries also encouraged inflows of foreign direct investment, especially in manufacturing, as a way of fostering domestic productive capacity. As a result, there was a major movement of multinational corporations into developing countries. LDCs also tried with some success to persuade developed countries to provide foreign aid for development. As decolonization swept the Third World and competition with the Soviet Union shifted to the South, aid became a useful political tool in the Cold War as well as a way for colonial powers to retain links with their former colonies. During this time, aid became a regular feature of North–South relations.

Toward the end of this period, import substitution gradually came to be seen as a failure. High tariff barriers that were supposed to be temporary became more or less permanent, thanks to the successful lobbying of domestic interests that wanted the barriers kept high. Import substitution therefore created uncompetitive industries while at the same time weakening traditional exports. The foreign investment that jumped over the high tariff barriers of the Third World came to be seen as a threat to sovereignty and development. Foreign aid and regional integration proved inadequate to ensure economic growth.

CONFRONTATION

During the era of interdependence, developing countries shifted from development strategies based on domestic change and began to argue that only changes in the international system could promote development. As independent developing countries became more numerous, they began to meet with each other and to develop plans for changing the prevailing international economic regime.

The hope was that such common action would increase the bargaining leverage of the South and enable the less-developed countries to negotiate that change with the North.

As early as 1960s, developing countries had gradually begun to work together to press for changes in the system. They created the **Group of Seventy-Seven (G-77)** to act as a permanent political bloc to represent developing country interests in U.N. forums. In Third World conferences and United Nations forums where the South commanded a majority, the G-77 pushed through declarations, recommendations, and resolutions calling for economic reforms.[38]

The developing countries achieved some largely procedural changes. They persuaded the GATT to include economic development as one of its goals. The United Nations established the United Nations Conference on Trade and Development (UNCTAD), which the South intended to be its international economic forum. UNCTAD provided the developing countries with a new economic doctrine that followed the ideas of the structuralists. As UNCTAD's first secretary general, Raúl Prebisch argued that what was needed was a redistribution of world resources to help the South: restructuring of trade, control of multinational corporations, and greater aid flows.

The strategy of seeking to change the international system reached its apex in the 1970s with the South's call for a **New International Economic Order (NIEO)**.[39] The NIEO grew out of the threat and the promise of the economic crises of the 1970s. The combination of food shortages, the rapid increase in the price of oil, and a recession in the developed countries undermined growth prospects in much of the South and made developing countries desperate for change. At the same time, the success of the oil-producing and oil-exporting countries in forcing changes in the political economy of oil held out the prospect of new leverage on the developed countries. Developing countries sought to use their own commodity power and to link their interests with OPEC and their fellow members of the G-77 to demand changes in the global economic system. The NIEO included a greater Northern commitment to the transfer of aid and new forms of aid flows; greater control of multinational corporations and greater MNC transfer of technology to developing countries; and trade reforms including reduction of developed country tariff barriers and international commodity agreements.

Success of the NIEO depended on Southern unity, the credibility of the commodity threat, and the North's perception of vulnerability. It foundered on all three. Southern unity was weakened by the differential impact of the food, energy, and recession crises; by the growing gap between the NICs and the least-developed countries; and by traditional regional and political conflicts. The credibility of the commodity threat was undermined by the inability to develop other OPECs, by OPEC's unwillingness to link the oil threat to G-77 demands in any meaningful way, and by declining demand for Southern raw materials. And, in the end, the North did not perceive any significant vulnerability to Southern threats. The North was willing to enter into a dialogue about changing the international economic system—as in the 1975 to 1977 **Conference on International Economic Cooperation (CIEC)**—but it was unwilling to make any substantive changes.

By the 1980s, developing countries had effectively abandoned the hope of reforming the international system and were once again thrown back on their own resources. The recessions and **debt restructurings** of the 1980s made the industrialized countries even less responsive to demands for systemic change and less willing to dispense foreign aid. The failure of the NIEO led developing nations to pursue different routes to development.

The G-77 survived as a bargaining group in the United Nations, but Southern unity became increasingly irrelevant to the development strategy of most Southern states. The developing countries were increasingly fragmented. A number of countries in Asia achieved rapid growth largely by integrating into the system, welcoming foreign investment, and exporting manufactured products to developed countries. Other advanced developing countries, such as Brazil and Mexico, relied on a relatively closed internal market.[40] The interests of these countries increasingly departed from those poorer countries, especially in Africa, which existed at the poverty line and relied on foreign assistance for survival. Even the NICs were divided. Those in Asia became concerned about growing protectionism in the United States; others, especially Latin American countries that had borrowed heavily from commercial banks, faced the debt crisis; and others such as Mexico and Venezuela faced the collapse of oil prices and the growing conflicts within OPEC.

GLOBALIZATION

In the 1980s and 1990s, developing countries again shifted strategy and sought to integrate into the global economic system. The debt crisis of the 1980s played an important role in the rethinking of development strategies. The need to generate new sources of exports to service the debts accumulated in the 1970s created enormous incentives to adopt export-oriented development strategies and to jettison, or at least modify significantly, the import substitution policies of the past. Indebted countries that were unable to increase exports had to adopt governmental austerity measures that generally hurt the poorest part of the population the most. The success of the Asian NICs and the failure of protectionist and statist policies led to a rethinking of effective strategies for development and to the adoption of liberal domestic and international economic policies.

In the 1990s, many developing countries that had remained outside the GATT joined that organization and its successor, the WTO. These countries participated actively in multilateral trade negotiations such as the Uruguay Round and achieved some progress on issues such as agriculture and textiles. A number of developing countries sought to form regional trade and investment arrangements among developing countries such as Mercosur in South America or ASEAN in Asia. Others entered into free trade agreements with developed countries. The United States, Canda, and Mexico created NAFTA; Japan entered into agreements with Singapore and Korea; and the European Union negotiated agreements with a number of countries in the Mediterranean basin. At home, developing countries began to reduce import barriers, promote export industries, and open capital markets—sometimes as part of international agreements and sometimes unilaterally.

While there was much movement toward liberalization of both domestic economic systems and rules restricting international trade and investments, at least some of that came from pressure and advice from the IMF, the World Bank, and the regional development banks.[41] Countries that got into trouble managing their external debt in the 1980s were often exposed to such pressure as part of negotiations for refinancing and restructuring (see Chapter 6).

One way of summarizing this new trend toward liberalization was to say that a new consensus, the **Washington Consensus**, had arisen which contained ten basic principles:

1. Fiscal displine
2. Concentration of public expenditure on public goods, including education, health and infrastructure
3. Tax reform toward broadening the tax base with moderate marginal tax rates
4. Interest rates to be market determined and positive
5. Competitive exchange rates
6. Trade liberalization
7. Openness to foreign direct investment
8. Privatization of state enterprises
9. Deregulation—abolishing regulations that impede entry into markets or restrict competition, except for those justified on safety, environmental, or consumer protection grounds and prudential oversight of financial institutions
10. Legal security for property rights.[42]

Not all liberalization in the developing world was coerced. The four original members of Mercosur (Argentina, Brazil, Chile, and Uruguay) are examples of Third World governments that decided to unilaterally reduce barriers to trade and investment flows. Chile was the earliest. In the 1970s, the Chilean government adopted a uniform tariff reduction policy as part of a larger economic reform.[43] When the other three countries joined with Chile to form Mercosur in 1991, they promised to converge toward a lower common external tariff with the rest of the world without requiring any reciprocation on the part of other countries. While they have sometimes diverged from the path of tariff reduction, the general trend in their tariff levels has been downward.[44]

The strategy of embracing globalization has worked so far for some developing countries. The first examples of the upside of embracing globalization were the four Asian Tigers—Taiwan, South Korea, Hong Kong, and Singapore. In all four of these countries, per capita income increased steadily once they successfully adopted a strategy of export-led development (see Figure 5.7). However, other developing countries remained mired in debt (see Chapter 6) and lacked

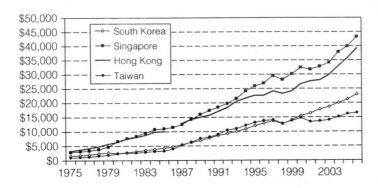

FIGURE 5.7   Per Capita Income in the Four Asian Tigers, 1975–2006

SOURCE: *World Development Indicators 2008*; and (for Taiwan only) *Taiwan Economic Statistics 6 (May 2008)*. The data for Taiwan are GNP per capita; for the others GDP per capita are at purchasing power parity.

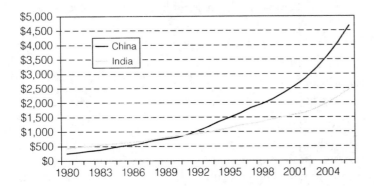

FIGURE 5.8   Per Capita Income in China and India, 1980–2006, in Dollars

SOURCE: *World Development Indicators 2008*.

attractive markets for foreign investment or products for export. These countries continued to suffer from low or even negative rates of growth.

More recently, the rise of China and India underlined the potential benefits, and also some of the challenges, for the developing world of liberalizing their interactions with the global economy. China liberalized trade and investment and took advantage of its low wage levels and undervalued currency to become a global manufacturing powerhouse. India liberalized trade and investment flows and was able to use its past investments in human capital to become a global services provider. As a result, both countries experienced rapid growth in GDP per capita (see Figure 5.8).

The issue for most developing countries at the beginning of the twenty-first century is little different than it was in 1945: whether it is possible to achieve growth and development within the prevailing system and, if so, how. While the North has not been prepared to make major changes in the system to help the South, it has been willing to transfer public funds for development, invest in some Southern markets, provide market access for some developing country exports, and offer advice and encouragement for market liberalization policies. Furthermore, the North has become increasingly interested in Southern markets, concerned about the impact of developing countries on global financial stability, and anxious about the flow of illegal immigration from developing to developed countries. Whether these new Northern preoccupations are enough to overcome the deep divisions between the two groups of countries remains to be seen.

ENDNOTES

1. World Bank Statistics, http://siteresources.worldbank.org/DATASTATISTICS/Resources/table2_1.pdf.

2. The growing gap in incomes in the last 40 years is a continuation of the growing inequality between North and South that began, according to Paul Bairoch, in the 1700s. See Paul Bairoch, "International Industrialization Levels from 1750 to 1980," *Journal of European Economic History,* 2 (1982): 268–333.

3. Branko Milanovic, *Worlds Apart: Measuring International and Global Equality* (Princeton, N.J.: Princeton University Press, 2005), see p. 2 especially.

4. François Bourguignon and Christian Morrison, "Inequality Among World Citizens: 1980–1992," *American Economic Review,* 92 (September 2002): 727–744; and Xavier Sala-i Martin, "The World Distribution of Income," NBER Working Paper 8933, May 2002. Branko Milanovic offers a somewhat skeptical view of these findings in *Worlds Apart.*

5. *World Development Report 2006* (Washington, D.C.: World Bank, 2006), 7.

6. *The Millennium Development Goals Report 2007* (New York, N.Y.: United Nations, 2007), 4.

7. Glenn Firebaugh and Brian Goesling, "Accounting for the Recent Decline in Global Income Inequality," *American Journal of Sociology,* 110 (September 2004): 283–312.

8. Paul Collier, *The Bottom Billion: Why the Poorest Countries Are Failing and What Can Be Done About It* (New York, N.Y.: Oxford University Press, 2007), 5. Collier is referring here the arguments of economist Jeffrey Sachs in *The End of Poverty: Economic Possibilities for Our Time* (New York, N.Y.: Penguin, 2005). The latter was adapted from a report to the United Nations in 2005 from the UN Millennium Project (a project directed by Sachs) which resulted in the adoption of the Millennium Development Goals (see text below).

9. *World Development Report 2008* (Washington, D.C.: World Bank, 2008), 1.

10. UNESCO, online data at http://www.uis.unesco.org.

11. William Easterly, *The Elusive Quest for Growth: Economists' Adventures and Misadventures in the Tropics* (Cambridge, Mass.: MIT Press, 2002), 11.

12. *Ibid.,* 8–14.

13. See Easterly, *The Elusive Quest for Growth;* Paul Romer, "Endogenous Technological Change," *Journal of Political Economy,* 98 (1990): S71–S102; and

Robert J. Barro, *Determinants of Economic Growth: A Cross-Country Empirical Study* (Cambridge, Mass.: MIT Press, 1997).

14. There has been a notable increase in the number of scholars attempting to deal with this question, also. See, for example, Dani Rodrik, *One Economics, Many Recipes: Globalization, Institutions and Economic Growth* (Princeton, N.J.: Princeton University Press, 2007).

15. For examples of liberal theories of economic growth and development, see Evsey Domar, *Essays in the Theory of Economic Growth* (Oxford, England: Oxford University Press, 1957); Gottfried Haberler, *International Trade and Economic Development* (Cairo, Egypt: National Bank of Egypt, 1959); Ragnar Nurkse, *Equilibrium and Growth in the World Economy* (Cambridge, Mass.: Harvard University Press, 1961); Walt W. Rostow, *The Stages of Economic Growth: A Non-Communist Manifesto* (Cambridge, England: Cambridge University Press, 1962); Walt W. Rostow, *Politics and the Stages of Growth* (Cambridge, England: Cambridge University Press, 1972); Gerald M. Meier, *International Trade and Development* (New York, N.Y.: Harper and Row, 1963); Gerald M. Meier, ed., *Pioneers in Development* (New York, N.Y.: Oxford University Press, 1984); Harry G. Johnson, *Economic Policies Toward Less Developed Countries* (New York, N.Y.: Praeger, 1967); Jagdish Bhagwati, *Essays in Development Economics: Wealth and Poverty*, vol. 1, and *Dependence and Interdependence*, vol. 2 (Cambridge, Mass.: MIT Press, 1985); Robert J. Barro and Xavier Sala-i-Martin, *Economic Growth* (New York, N.Y.: McGraw Hill, 1995); and Amartya K. Sen, *Development as Freedom* (New York, N.Y.: Random House, 1999). For eclectic overviews of the literature, see Easterly, *The Elusive Quest for Growth* and Walt W. Rostow, *Theorists of Economic Growth from David Hume to the Present* (New York, N.Y.: Oxford University Press, 1990). This tradition continues in the subfield of economics dealing with economic development, or development economics. An example of a textbook that provides an overiew is Gerald M. Meier and Jamese E. Rouch, *Leading Issues in Economic Development*, 8th edition (New York, N.Y.: Oxford University Press, 2005).

16. For a very clear exposition of the types of policies recommended by liberal theorists, see John Williamson, "What Should the World Bank Think About the Washington Consensus," *The World Bank Research Observer*, 15 (August 2000): 251–254.

17. For examples of Marxist and neo-Marxist perspectives, see Samir Amin, *Accumulation on a World Scale* (New York, N.Y.: Monthly Review Press, 1974); Samir Amin, *Unequal Development: An Essay on the Social Formations of Peripheral Capitalism* (New York, N.Y.: Monthly Review Press, 1976); Paul A. Baran, *The Political Economy of Growth* (New York, N.Y.: Monthly Review Press, 1968); Fernando Henrique Cardoso and Enzo Faletto, *Dependency and Development in Latin America*, transl. Marjory Mattingly Urquidi (Berkeley and Los Angeles, Calif.: University of California Press, 1979); Arghiri Emmanuel, *Unequal Exchange: A Study of the Imperialism of Trade* (New York, N.Y.: Monthly Review Press, 1972); Andre Gunder Frank, *Capitalism and Underdevelopment in Latin America*, rev. ed. (New York, N.Y.: Monthly Review Press, 1969); Harry Magdoff, *Imperialism: From the Colonial Age to the Present* (New York, N.Y.: Monthly Review Press, 1978); Dan W. Nabudere, *The Political Economy of Imperialism* (London, UK: Zed Press, 1977); Theotonio Dos Santos, "The Structure of Dependence," in K. T. Fann and Donald C. Hodges, eds., *Readings in U.S. Imperialism* (Boston, Mass.: Porter Sargent, 1971); and Immanuel Wallerstein, *The Capitalist World Economy* (Cambridge, England: Cambridge University Press, 1979). See also "Facing the 1980s: New Directions in the

Theory of Imperialism," a special issue of the *Review of Radical Political Economics*, 11 (Winter 1979). For more recent works in this traditions, see David Gordon, "The Global Economy: New Edifice or Crumbling Foundations?", *New Left Review*, 168 (1988): 24–64; Giovanni Arrighi, *The Long Twentieth Century: Money, Power, and the Origins of Our Times* (London, UK: Verso Books, 1994); David L. Blaney, "Reconceptualizing Autonomy: The Difference Dependency Theory Makes," *Review of International Political Economy*, 3 (1996): 459–97; and Samir Amin, *Capitalism in the Age of Globalization: The Management of Contemporary Society*, various translators, (London, UK: Zed, 1997). A more recent effort to revive this tradition is Michael Hardt and Antonio Negri, *Empire* (Cambridge, Mass.: Harvard University Press, 2001).

18. This is a view shared by non-Marxist theorists as well. See the section below on structuralist approaches.

19. This brief summary does considerable violence to the richness and diversity of views within the Marxist and neo-Marxist schools. For more nuanced summaries, see Fernando Henrique Cardoso, "The Consumption of Dependency Theory in the United States," *Latin American Research Review*, 7 (Fall 1977): 7–24; Raymond Duvall, "Dependence and Dependencia Theory," *International Organization*, 32 (Winter 1978): 51–78; Ronald Chilcote, "Dependence: A Critical Synthesis of the Literature," *Latin American Perspectives*, 1 (Spring 1974): 4–29; Gabriel Palma, "Dependency: A Formal Theory of Underdevelopment or a Methodology for the Analysis of Concrete Situations of Underdevelopment," *World Development*, 6 (1978): 881–924; and David Blaney, "Reconceptualizing Autonomy."

20. For examples of structuralist theory, see Gunnar Myrdal, *Rich Lands and Poor: The Road to World Prosperity* (New York, N.Y.: Harper and Row, 1957); Raúl Prebisch, "Commercial Policy in the Underdeveloped Countries," *American Economic Review*, 49 (May 1959): 251–273; Raúl Prebisch, *The Economic Development of Latin America and Its Principal Problems* (New York, N.Y.: United Nations, 1950); W. Arthur Lewis, *The Evolution of the International Economic Order* (Princeton, N.J.: Princeton University Press, 1978); and Johan Galtung, "A Structural Theory of Imperialism," *Journal of Peace Research*, 8 (1971): 81–117. See also Bill Gibson, "An Essay on Late Structuralism," in Amitava K. Dutt and Jaime Ros, eds., *Economic Development and Structuralist Macroeconomics* (Northampton, Mass.: Edward Elgar, 2002). This volume is a tribute to the work of Lance Taylor who was a major advocate of structuralism in economics. Taylor summarized his thinking on this topic in *Reconstructing Macroeconomics: Structuralist Proposals and Critiques of the Mainstream* (Cambridge, Mass.: Harvard University Press, 2004). The structuralist school of thought has recently transitioned into a subfield of globalization studies, where the key question is how developing countries are constrained in responding positively to the opportunities and challenges of globalization. One early example is Dani Rodrik, *Has Globalization Gone Too Far?* (Washington, D.C.: Institute for International Economics, 1997).

21. This is the essence of the argument put forward by Raúl Prebisch, one of the most influential advocates of the structuralist perspective. See Joseph L. Love, "Raúl Prebisch and the Origins of the Doctrine of Unequal Exchange," *Latin American Research Review*, 15 (1980): 45–72.

22. For an interesting counterargument to the idea that population growth negatively affects economic growth in the South, see William Easterly, *The Elusive Quest for Growth*, ch. 5.

23. Paul A. Baran and Paul M. Sweezy, *Monopoly Capital: An Essay on the American Economic and Social Order* (New York, N.Y.: Monthly Review Press, 1966). These authors define economic surplus as "the difference between what a society produces and the costs of producing it" (p. 9). For a critical analysis of the concept, see Benjamin J. Cohen, *The Question of Imperialism: The Political Economy of Dominance and Dependence* (New York, N.Y.: Basic Books, 1973): 104–121. The latest effort to revive imperialism theory can be found in Hardt and Negri, *Empire*.

24. See, for example, Pierre Jalée, *Imperialism in the Seventies*, trans. R. and M. Sokolov (New York, N.Y.: Third World Press, 1972).

25. UNCTAD, *World Investment Report 2001* (New York, N.Y.: United Nations, 2001).

26. United State Geological Survey, *Mineral Commodity Summaries* (Washington, D.C.: USGPO, 2007).

27. See Arthur MacEwan, "Capitalist Expansion, Ideology and Intervention," *Review of Radical Political Economics*, 4 (spring 1972), 36–58; and Thomas Weisskopf, "Theories of American Imperialism: A Critical Evaluation," *Review of Radical Political Economics*, 6 (fall 1974), 41–60.

28. MacEwan, "Capitalist Expansion."

29. See U.S. Senate, *Multinational Corporations and United States Foreign Policy*, hearings before the Subcommittee on Multinational Corporations of the Committee on Foreign Relations, 93rd Cong., 2nd sess. (Washington, D.C.: U.S. Government Printing Office, 1975).

30. On this question, see Stephen Krasner, *Defending the National Interest* (Princeton, N.J.: Princeton University Press, 1978); G. John Ikenberry, *Reasons of State: Oil Politics and the Capacities of American Government* (Ithaca, N.Y.: Cornell University Press, 1988); and Daniel Yergin, *The Prize: The Epic Quest for Oil, Money, and Power* (New York, N.Y.: Simon and Schuster, 1991). Some critics of the U.S. intervention in Iraq argue that the main purpose was to secure access to Iraqi oil fields. There is some evidence for this argument, given U.S. troop deployments in Iraq immediately following the invasion in 2003 and the 2008 bidding by oil MNCs for service contracts. See, for example, Dilip Hero, *Blood of the Earth: The Battle for the World's Vanishing Oil Resources* (New York, N.Y.: Nation Books, 2006); and Michael Klare, *Blood & Oil: The Dangers and Consequences of America's Growing Dependency on Imported Petroleum* (New York, N.Y.: Metropolitan Books, 2005).

31. Elhanan Helpman and Paul Krugman, *Increasing Returns, Imperfect Markets, and International Trade* (Cambridge, Mass.: MIT Press, 1985), 2.

32. See, for example, James R. Markusen and Randall M. Wigle, "Explaining the Volume of North–South Trade," *Economic Journal*, 100 (December 1990): 1206–1215.

33. This is the approach suggested by the work of Helpman and Krugman and other strategic trade theorists.

34. See Edward E. Leamer, *Sources of International Comparative Advantage: Theory and Evidence* (Cambridge, Mass.: MIT Press, 1984).

35. See, for example, Harry Bloch and David Sapsford, "Whither the Terms of Trade? An Elaboration of the Prebisch-Singer Hypothesis," *Cambridge Journal of Economics*, 24 (2000): 461–481; James M. Cypher and James L. Dietz, "Static and Dynamic Comparative Advantage: A Multi-Period Analysis with Declining Terms of

Trade," *Journal of Economic Issues*, 32 (June 1998): 305–314; and E. R. Grilli and M. C. Yang, "Primary Commodity Prices, Manufactured Good Prices, and Terms of Trade of Developing Countries," *World Bank Economic Review*, 2 (1988): 1–48. A more recent review of the literature is José Antonio Ocampo and María Angel Parra, "The Commodity Terms of Trade and Their Strategic Implications for Development," March 2004, http://129.3.20.41/eps/it/papers/0403/0403001. pdf. The literature seems to indicate that price shocks like the oil price increases of the 1970s and perhaps the current rise in oil and food prices can temporaily interrupt the downward trend.

36. See Richard Gardner, *Sterling Dollar Diplomacy* (Oxford, England: Clarendon Press, 1956); Robert Hudec, *The GATT Legal System and World Trade Diplomacy* (New York, N.Y.: Praeger, 1975); and Janette Mark and Ann Weston, "The Havana Charter Experience: Lessons for Developing Countries," in John Whalley, ed., *Developing Countries and the Global Trading System*, vol. 1, Thematic Studies for a Ford Foundation Project (Ann Arbor, Mich.: University of Michigan Press, 1989).

37. For a list of GATT members and their dates of membership, see http://www.wto. org/english/thewto_e/gattmem_e.htm.

38. Branislav Gosovic and John G. Ruggie, "On the Creation of the New International Economic Order," *International Organization*, 30 (spring 1976): 309–346; Robert A. Mortimer, *The Third World Coalition in International Politics*, 2nd ed. (Boulder, Colo.: Westview, 1984), ch. 3; and Marc Williams, *Third World Cooperation: The Group of 77 in UNCTAD* (New York, N.Y.: St. Martin's Press, 1991), 78.

39. Robert Rothstein, *Global Bargaining: UNCTAD and the Quest for a New International Economic Order* (Princeton, N.J.: Princeton University Press, 1979); Jeffrey Hart, *The New International Economic Order: Conflict and Co-operation in North–South Economic Relations 1974–77* (New York, N.Y.: St. Martin's Press, 1983); Craig Murphy, *The Emergence of the NIEO Ideology* (Boulder, Colo.: Westview, 1984); and Stephen D. Krasner, *Structural Conflict: The Third World Against Global Liberalism* (Berkeley and Los Angeles, Calif.: University of California Press, 1985).

40. Stephan Haggard, *Pathways from the Periphery* (Ithaca, N.Y.: Cornell University Press, 1990); Alice H. Amsden, *Asia's Next Giant: South Korea and Late Industrialization* (New York, N.Y.: Oxford, 1989); and Robert Wade, *Governing the Market: Economic Theory and the Role of Government in East Asian Industrialization* (Princeton, N.J.: Princeton University Press, 1990).

41. See, especially, Beth A. Simmons, Frank Dobbin, and Geoffrey Garrett, "Introduction: The International Diffusion of Liberalism," *International Organization*, 60 (Fall 2006): 781–810.

42. John G. Williamson, "What Washington Means by Policy Reform," in John G. Williamson, ed., *Latin American Readjustment: How Much Has Happened* (Washington, D.C.: Institute for International Economics, 1989).

43. WTO Press Release for the September 1997 Trade Policy Review for Chile, PRESS/TRPB/60, 10 September 1997, at http://www.wto.org/english/tratop_ e/tpr_e/tp60_e.htm.

44. See WTO Press Releases for Argentina's Trade Policy Review, PRESS/TPRB/ 100, 13 January 1998 and Brazil's, PRESS/TPRB/140, 1 November 2000.

6

Financial Flows to Developing Countries

The effort of the South to obtain financial capital for development is a central theme in North-South relations. Developing countries, short of their own funds, traditionally turned to capital surplus countries for private funds in the form of bank loans and the purchase of bonds to finance infrastructure and productive facilities. In the nineteenth century, for example, British capital helped build U.S. railroads and industry; and in the first half of the twentieth century, foreign capital flowed to Latin America to finance industrialization. During the Bretton Woods era, public funds for development were more important than private lending in North-South financial relations. Foreign aid, virtually nonexistent before World War II, came to account for a large portion of financial transfers to developing countries. Then, during the period of interdependence, private financial flows reemerged as commercial banks in the developed countries financed public works and private industry in a number of developing countries. This was followed by a global debt crisis that temporarily stemmed the flow of new private bank loans to the Third World. Public flows resumed their growth during the debt crisis, partly to compensate for the interruption of private flows. During the period of globalization, private investments (both FDI and more short-term forms of capital) began to flow again to the most creditworthy developing countries. Private bank loans did not play as large a role during this period as they had in the 1970s. Instead, much of the increased flow of private capital to the South came from the foreign direct investments of multinational corporations and from new private sources such as international mutual funds, private equity funds, and sovereign wealth funds. The developing countries with low credit ratings continued to depend heavily on public flows. In this chapter, we examine the evolution of financial flows, both public and private, in North-South relations.

BRETTON WOODS AND FOREIGN AID

The Original Bretton Woods

Although foreign aid was one of the most innovative developments in North-South relations in the Bretton Woods era, it was not part of the original postwar vision of the developed countries. The World Bank was established along with the IMF as one of the two international institutions of the Bretton Woods system. However, its original purpose was not to help developing countries but to finance the rebuilding of war-torn economies and the development of members of the bank. With capital provided by member states, the World Bank was to borrow in private capital markets and make loans at market rates to cover the foreign exchange needs of borrowing countries.

After the war, the less-developed countries sought to ensure that development would have the same priority as reconstruction and that they would have access to World Bank financing. However, the developed countries that dominated the World Bank unanimously agreed that European postwar reconstruction would be the first priority for the bank and rejected the developing country argument that public capital was needed for economic development. In the view of the North, a combination of domestic capital and new funds from trade expansion was the appropriate route to growth. External capital, where necessary, would have to be private. In those rare cases where public external financing might be appropriate, financing was to be limited in amount and offered on market or hard, not concessional or soft, terms.[1] Thus, in its first five years, one-half of World Bank lending went to European reconstruction and development; the other half was extended to developing countries on hard terms.[2]

Northern policy on bilateral aid closely resembled that in international forums. Emphasis was on self-help; where external capital was needed, it was to be primarily private; and where private capital was unavailable, external financing was to come primarily from the World Bank. The United States was the only country able to transfer resources to developing countries and its economic aid was very limited. Between 1950 and 1955, bilateral overseas development aid (that is, public transfers of funds directly from one country to another) from all of the developed market countries averaged $1.8 billion a year, and multilateral flows amounted to $100 million a year.[3]

The Link Between Aid and Foreign Policy

In the mid-1950s, Northern policies shifted. One reason was the emergence of the less-developed countries as increasingly active, albeit weak, actors in international relations. In the two decades following World War II, much of Africa and Asia achieved political independence. By 1965, 85 out of 118 members of the United

Nations were developing countries. As the less-developed countries became more numerous, they also became more outspoken and somewhat more united and specific in their demands for international economic reform, including more financial aid. Gradually, the newly independent countries began to coordinate policies within the UN system and to meet together in international conferences of developing countries where they formulated common demands on the North.

The new Third World became significant when the United States and the Soviet Union decided to make the developing world an arena of competition in the Cold War. Following the communist takeover of China in 1949 and the Korean conflict of 1950, the United States began a program of military assistance to developing countries bordering the Soviet Union and the People's Republic of China and to certain Middle Eastern countries.[4] After Stalin's death in 1953, the Soviet Union for the first time contributed to United Nations technical assistance programs, entered into trade agreements with Southern countries, and provided financial assistance to Egypt, India, Syria, Indonesia, and Afghanistan. Then, in 1956, Soviet Premier Nikita Khrushchev announced that competition with the West would be expanded to the less-developed countries.[5]

The Soviet Union's threat to the West's position of dominance in the developing world led the United States for the first time to conclude that economic assistance to the South could be a powerful tool in the Cold War.[6] According to economic analysis at the time, the growth of the less-developed countries was constrained primarily by insufficient investment in physical capital, which was in turn limited by insufficient savings and/or foreign exchange. External financial assistance, it was argued, would fill this resource gap. Capital flows plus technical assistance to improve the use of both domestic and external capital would create the conditions for self-sustaining economic growth. Economic growth, in turn, would provide a constructive outlet for nationalism, foster social progress, develop political leadership, and encourage confidence in the democratic process.[7] Aid would serve U.S. foreign policy by "help[ing] the societies of the world develop in ways that will not menace our security—either as a result of their own internal dynamics or because they are weak enough to be used as tools by others."[8] This focus on foreign aid as part of U.S. political and security policy has been a central theme in U.S. aid policy throughout the postwar era.

France and the United Kingdom, motivated both by security concerns and by the desire to maintain political and economic relationships with their former colonies, adopted similar policies.[9] As a result, bilateral foreign aid programs expanded dramatically. Annual U.S. aid increased from $2.0 billion in 1956 to $3.7 billion in 1963.[10] British aid doubled from $205 million in 1956 to $414 million in 1963, and French aid rose from $648 million in 1956 to $863 million in 1963.[11] Between 1960 and 1962, new development aid authorities were created in Canada, Japan, the United Kingdom, Denmark, Sweden, and Norway.

Multilateral aid also increased. As Europe recovered from the war, World Bank lending shifted to developing countries, and the Bank's capital was increased to allow greater lending. In 1956, World Bank members created the subsidiary **International Finance Corporation (IFC)** to promote private investment in developing countries. In 1960, the **International Development Agency (IDA)** was established as a sepa-

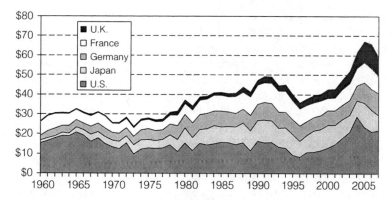

FIGURE 6.1 Annual Bilateral ODA by the G-5 Countries,
1960–2007, in Billions of Constant 2006 Dollars
SOURCE: *OECD Statistics online.*

rate institution closely integrated with the World Bank with a mandate to make soft or
highly **concessional loans**. In 1958, the United States, reversing its long-standing
opposition, agreed to the establishment of the **Inter-American Development
Bank** and provided $350 million of the bank's initial capital of $1 billion.[12] African
and Asian development banks followed in 1964 and 1966, respectively.

Thus aid emerged in the 1950s and 1960s as a new form of international
economic interaction. Never before in history had states voluntarily transferred
funds on concessional terms to other countries; never before had multilateral
institutions played such a role in economic relations. While aid thus ushered in
a new form of international relations, it did not, as we shall examine, change the
balance of economic power between North and South.

Stagnation of Aid

Although aid became a regular feature of North–South economic relations,
Northern political support for public financial assistance to developing countries
was uneven and the flow of aid proved to be somewhat erratic. Between 1960
and 1980, total aid flows from all the industrialized countries remained roughly
constant in real terms (see Figure 6.1).[13] Most European countries regularly
increased their aid as their economies strengthened. Germany and Japan became
major donors in the late 1950s and 1960s, in part because of reparation payments
after the war and partially as a reflection of their high domestic growth rates. The
Nordic countries and the Netherlands, motivated by a sense of moral responsibility, provided dramatic increases in aid flows throughout the 1960s and 1970s.

At the same time, however, official development assistance from the United
States, the United Kingdom, and France declined. United States aid, for example, declined from $3.5 billion in 1967 to $3.0 billion in 1973, but in constant
1967 dollars it fell to $2.0 billion.[14] In 1973, U.S. overseas development aid fell
to a postwar record low in current dollars of $2.97 billion.[15]

One reason for the shift in U.S. aid policy was disillusionment after a period of high expectations about the link between aid and foreign policy. The heavy emphasis of the U.S. aid program on the foreign policy benefits of foreign assistance led to disappointment when the political and security goals of economic assistance were not realized. The long and frustrating war in Vietnam played an important role in this dissatisfaction. Aid did not generally lead, as predicted, to economic development, democratic government, and political stability. Growth was uneven, instability seemed to increase with development, and aid did not necessarily win friends and influence people.[16] Meanwhile, the cost of aid grew, and willingness to assume such costs decreased in the face of growing U.S. external payments and budget deficits and the rising cost of prosecuting the war in Vietnam.[17]

The South's political and military significance to the United States also diminished. As the strategic relationship between the United States and the Soviet Union stabilized and superpower conflict moderated, "winning" or "losing" Third World allegiances was still important to each side, but both discovered that it was difficult to win friendship through economic assistance. The South also began to look less suitable as a testing ground for rival forms of political and economic organization. The South was insufficiently democratic for the West to use it as a site for proving the general viability of democracy; it was insufficiently socialist for the East to use it as a showcase for **socialism**. Proportionally greater amounts of shrinking United States aid were devoted to a few militarily strategic countries: for example, India, South Vietnam, and Indonesia in the early 1970s; Egypt, Israel, and Central America in the 1980s; Afghanistan after September 11, 2001; and Iraq after the invasion in 2003. At the same time, a shrinking share of development aid went to needy but less strategically important countries.

The link between foreign aid and foreign policy also became less important for France and the United Kingdom.[18] Although sub-Saharan Africa remained important for French prestige and economic benefit, its significance for French security disappeared, and its role in French foreign policy generally declined. Similarly, as Britain cut its military commitments east of the Suez Canal and moved toward a more Atlantic-oriented foreign policy, its political and security motivations for aid to the Commonwealth faded.

Overall aid flows stagnated in the 1960s as increases in European Community and Japanese aid flows were offset by decreases in aid from the United States, the United Kingdom, and France. Furthermore, after 1960 the South was increasingly burdened with debt service on earlier public financial flows. From 1965 to 1969, the rise in debt service payments on the official and officially guaranteed loans to 80 less-developed countries exceeded the rise in gross flows of new capital aid. As a result, the net transfer of resources fell slightly during this period.[19]

The stagnation, and in some cases decline, in aid flows also disillusioned Southern governments. A few developing countries, such as Myanmar (then called Burma), rejected aid and turned to other self-help policies.[20] Most developing countries tried to increase the amount and improve the conditions of aid by acting together to negotiate with the developed countries. In the early 1960s, they expanded their earlier coordination by forming the **Group of Seventy-Seven (G-77)**, a united Southern bloc, to improve their bargaining position and to confront the North with common demands for changes in the international economic system (see Chapters 5 and 7).[21] Acting primarily in the United Nations, they sought to increase aid flows by pressing the Northern countries to transfer first 1.0 percent and then 0.7 percent of their respective GNPs to developing countries. They also proposed improvements in the terms of aid: more soft loans and grants, longer duration of loans, easing the debt burden, and ending the policy of tying aid to purchases in the donor country.[22] Finally, the Group of Seventy-Seven sought to limit Northern control by increasing the multilateral component of aid and by making aid transfers more automatic. One such proposal was to allocate newly created Special Drawing Rights (SDRs) to underdeveloped countries, the IDA, or regional development banks.[23]

The strategy of Southern unity was largely unsuccessful. Although the North (with the exception of the United States) eventually agreed to transfer 0.7 percent of its GNP to developing countries, with the exception of a few small but wealthy European donors this goal has not been met. Unfortunately for the South, none of the largest donors of aid came close to the 0.7 percent goal (see Figure 6.1). The developed countries also rejected other reform proposals including the SDR-aid link.

FINANCIAL FLOWS IN THE ERA
OF INTERDEPENDENCE

Confrontation and the New International Economic Order

In the 1970s, the issue of aid flows became highly politicized as Southern countries confronted developed countries with demands for a New International Economic Order (NIEO). The setting for the political confrontation was the rapid increases in the price of food and oil in the early 1970s. These posed a major threat to Southern economies but weakened the South's ability to address the threat, because they affected the South in different ways and thereby accentuated the divisions among the developing countries.

The food crisis had its roots in postwar industrialization strategies. Development funds were channeled to industry and agricultural prices kept low to feed the growing urban population. As a result, Southern food production did not keep up with a rapidly expanding population.[24] Many developing countries became dependent on agricultural imports that strained their balance of payments.

Until the 1970s, major increases in Northern production and international food aid helped fill the supply and foreign exchange gap. But in the early seventies, a decline in Northern food production led to a sharp rise in world food prices, severe food shortages, a decline in Northern food aid, and balance-of-payments crises for many Southern states. In much of the South, improvements in agricultural production and food aid were offset by population increases.

The second crisis for the South in the 1970s was that of oil and energy. Price increases that took the cost of a barrel of oil from $1.80 in 1971 to over $35 in 1981 threatened development in countries without oil resources and caused new divisions within the South between oil exporters and importers, and between oil importers able to obtain commercial loans and those dependent on aid. The rising price of oil and oil-related products, such as petrochemical fertilizers, combined with a recession in the North caused the current account deficit of LDC oil importers to increase from $11.3 billion in 1973 to $46.3 billion in 1975, and to $89.0 billion in 1980.[25] Middle-income oil importers financed current account deficits and maintained their growth by borrowing from private commercial banks. For the low-income countries, higher oil costs combined with recession drained foreign exchange and forced a curtailment of imports necessary for development and survival.

In the face of these crises, the South sought to increase public financial flows to the developing countries and to make those flows more automatic. The major strategy of the 1970s was Southern unity and confrontation. In the 1960s, the developing countries had tried with little success to increase their bargaining strength and to obtain greater concessions from the North by acting as a bloc in negotiating with the developed countries. With the onset of the oil crisis of the 1970s, the South felt that it had obtained new leverage in negotiating with the North and tried to use that leverage to obtain a variety of structural changes, including more aid on better terms.

Ironically, the actions of the oil-producing states—which posed a severe threat to the South—also served as a force for Southern unity and cooperation. One effect was psychological. The ability of a unified **Organization of Petroleum Exporting Countries (OPEC)** to attain significant rewards from the North demonstrated the potential effectiveness of Southern unity in bargaining with the North. It also created, at least temporarily, a sense of Southern solidarity.

The oil crisis, too, held out the hope of a new bargaining chip for the South. The oil-producing countries could hurt the North by withholding petroleum or raising prices, or they could offer the North inducements such as energy agreements or an energy dialogue. If the oil-producing states remained part of the Southern bloc, then the oil stick or the oil carrot could be linked to demands for systemic reform, and the balance of power could be altered. Some oil-producing states, especially Venezuela and Algeria, encouraged the linkage of Southern development demands with raw materials threats or inducements. However, others, in particular the Persian Gulf states, played little or no role in the Southern group and had no interest in using their oil weapon for broader purposes.

In the heady days following OPEC's initial success, the South boldly tried to force systemic reform on the North. In the spring of 1974, the Group of Seventy-Seven issued a call for a new international economic order that included changing the system of financial flows (see Chapters 5 and 7). The Declaration and Action Programme on a New International Economic Order called for a link between SDR allocation and development finance, the implementation of the 0.7-percent-of-GNP goal for industrial country foreign aid established by the United Nations, and greater participation by the less-developed countries in World Bank and IMF decision making.[26] Throughout the 1970s, the developing countries consistently urged the realization of the new international economic order in their multilateral negotiations with the developed countries.

The North, itself a victim of the energy and recession crises, firmly resisted the South's efforts to create the NIEO. Southern stridency and Northern resistance increased the contentiousness of relations in this period. The South was able to force the North to discuss the concept of reform at the United Nations and other multilateral forums, but it was not able to make the North actually negotiate for systemic change, nor was the South able to play its oil card to force the North to respond. The OPEC countries, in the end, were not willing to link the price and availability of oil to the NIEO.

Because of Southern pressure and the Northern desire to alleviate the crises of the 1970s, however, there was some improvement in financial flows, especially multilateral flows, to the South. Food aid increased. Several temporary mechanisms were created within the IMF: an oil facility was created in 1974 to finance the payments deficits caused by the increase in petroleum prices; a trust fund was financed by the sale of IMF gold; the **Supplementary Finance Facility** was created in 1979 to help alleviate serious payments imbalances; and an enlarged access policy allowed countries with protracted and structural balance-of-payments problems to borrow larger percentages of their quotas. There were also permanent changes in the IMF that benefited the developing countries: the **Extended Fund Facility** was created in 1974 to make money available for longer periods and in larger amounts than the usual IMF drawings, and the **Compensatory Finance Facility**, which helps countries suffering from severe drops in primary commodity prices, was enlarged and extended to cover cereal imports.[27]

As the United States and other developed countries gave increasing emphasis to multilateral aid, the World Bank also expanded in the 1970s. In addition to its traditional support for infrastructure projects, the bank began to make loans for basic human needs projects, including the development of subsistence farming, minimally adequate housing, and rudimentary health care.[28] In the late 1970s, the bank increased its lending for energy development. In response to the second oil crisis, it launched **structural adjustment lending**, a form of medium-term balance-of-payments support to enable countries to adapt the structure of production to prevailing world conditions, especially to changes in the cost of energy and food.[29] Finally, the bank sought to promote commercial lending to developing countries through cofinancing: mixed projects combining private and World Bank funding.[30]

Another success of the 1970s was the attempt to obtain aid from the oil exporters. Because major oil producers were unable to absorb their new wealth, they found it relatively easy to assist in development finance. New IMF facilities and the **International Fund for Agricultural Development (IFAD)**, for example, were based in part on financing by OPEC members.[31] Although the South was unable to achieve its vision of a new international economic order based in part on increased aid flows and significant changes in decision making, there were important changes in financial flows during the 1970s: greater concessional flows to the low-income developing countries; more multilateral aid; and a new source of aid from OPEC.

Privatization of Financial Flows

In the 1970s, another important trend emerged which would more closely link some developing countries to the Northern system of interdependence. Certain developing countries were able to borrow from the private commercial banks of

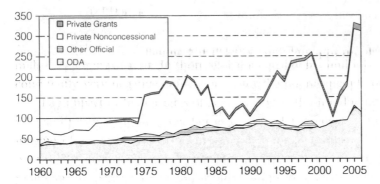

FIGURE 6.2 Total Official and Private Flows from DAC Countries to Developing Countries, 1960–2006, in Billions of Constant 2006 Dollars
SOURCE: *OECD Statistics online.*

developed countries. The result was a massive surge in private financial flows to the South and a decline in the share of aid in total flows from North to South (see Figure 6.2).

The new borrowing of developing countries was made possible by changing policies of commercial banks. Until the late 1960s, less-developed countries, with their slow growth and bad credit records, appeared as undesirable markets for Northern banks. Thus, bank lending to the developing countries was limited primarily to short-term trade finance. In the late 1960s and early 1970s, however, many banks from the OECD countries became attracted to the profits in international markets. With rapid growth and rising exports, many developing countries appeared capable of servicing increased debt. As a result, banks were willing to expand from short-term trade finance to longer-term project lending. Interest in lending to developing countries was reinforced by the inflow of petrodollar deposits following 1973 that left banks with vast amounts of funds available for lending and only limited markets for such lending in the slowly growing developed countries. Finally, bank lending was actively encouraged by the governments of developed countries, which saw it as a mechanism for petrodollar recycling (see Chapter 2).

With an ample supply of petrodollars on deposit, massive demand from the LDCs, and official encouragement from the OECD governments, bank flows to LDCs surged. Large loans were made at floating interest rates calculated at a percentage over the interbank lending rate and were syndicated or divided up among many banks. From 1973 to 1981, oil-importing developing countries' annual borrowing from private financial institutions went from $6.5 billion to $293 billion.[32]

In the 1970s, the rapid growth of bank lending did not pose a problem for developing country borrowers. Lending helped expand productive capacity and maintained growth, even after the first oil shock. From 1973 to 1980, middle-income oil importers achieved an average annual GDP growth of 5.7 percent, whereas the industrial countries' GDP grew at only 2.8 percent per year.[33] Furthermore, because developing countries' exports increased, their ability to service debt remained strong. Finally, debt service was eased by inflation, which meant that real interest rates were low or negative.

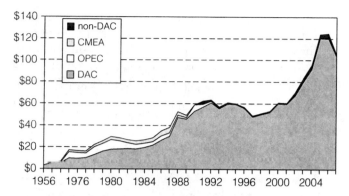

FIGURE 6.3 ODA from DAC Countries, OPEC, CMEA, and non-DAC Countries, 1956–2007, in Billions of Current Dollars
SOURCE: *OECD Statistics online.*

Not all countries, however, had access to private financial markets. Low-income developing countries, unable to borrow from banks, remained dependent on concessional flows. Fortunately, although overall aid flows did not rise by much after the first oil shock (see Figure 6.3), flows to the low-income countries—especially from multilateral agencies and OPEC—did increase and helped offset the effects of the oil price rise.

The Decline of Aid in the 1980s

While the promise of public and private financial flows was great at the end of the 1970s, that promise had turned sour by the mid-1980s. The combination of recession and new conservative governments in the North in the early 1980s increased the focus on nonconcessional flows and private market solutions and decreased the flow of aid. Two additional external shocks hit the developing countries between 1979 and 1981. First, the second oil crisis of 1978–1979 caused a surge in the price of oil to a high of $35 in 1981 (see Chapter 9). Second, anti-inflationary policies in the developed countries and a steep recession (see Chapter 2) caused a precipitous drop in commodity prices and an adverse shift in the LDCs' terms of trade (see Chapters 5 and 7). A related problem for indebted countries was the rapid rise in international interest rates that resulted from the efforts of the U.S. Federal Reserve after 1979 to reduce inflation in the United States. Higher interest rates meant that indebted countries had to work harder to repay the interest on their loans. In short, a series of changes in the world economic situation turned private bank flows into the debt crisis. As a result, total financial flows to developing countries (concessional and commercial) declined in the early 1980s.

Although a handful of developing countries were able to increase their exports of manufactured products to the North, demand for most of the South's products stagnated. The industrial recession also intensified protectionist pressures that further limited the export of manufactured goods. At the same time, the rise in the value of the dollar reduced commodity prices and increased the cost of many LDC imports denominated in dollars. Anti-inflationary policies combined with fiscal deficits in the developed countries led to unprecedented high interest rates and a resultant rise in the burden of debt servicing. Finally, these international shocks were aggravated by expansionary domestic economic policies in many of the LDCs: increased government spending to maintain growth rates exacerbated both fiscal and trade deficits.

The result of these shocks was an increase in the trade deficits of developing countries from $22.2 billion in 1979 to $91.6 billion in 1981; increases in interest payments from $24.3 billion in 1979 to $41.8 billion in 1981; and current account deficits that rose from $31.3 billion in 1979 to $118.6 in 1981. By 1981, interest payments almost offset new private lending. By 1982, when the debt crisis struck, interest payments exceeded new lending by $3.5 billion.[34]

With the recession of the early 1980s, domestic political opposition to foreign aid expenditures grew in the North. At a time of domestic unemployment and—at least in the United States—a cutback in domestic welfare programs, increased or even constant expenditures on foreign aid were politically impossible. Opposition to foreign aid was reinforced by an ideological challenge to economic aid as a route to development and a tool of foreign policy. Conservative governments elected to power in the 1980s in the United States and the United Kingdom argued that foreign aid had only a limited role to play in the development process. According to the view of the Reagan and Thatcher governments, economic recovery and development in both the developed and the developing countries had to be based on a return to free-market principles. The developing countries above all had to provide incentives and commercial opportunities for private enterprise, both domestic and foreign. Economic aid would be limited in amount, would not compete with private efforts, and would have as its main purpose the support of private enterprise and free markets. According to this view, much foreign aid—especially aid from multilateral institutions—did not meet these criteria.

In the 1980s, foreign economic aid also lost much of its political rationale, at least for the United States. With a strong East-West defense orientation, the Reagan administration was more interested in increasing its defense budget, in offering military assistance instead of foreign aid for development, and in granting bilateral rather than multilateral aid.

From 1980 to 1983, these economic and political changes led to another decline in multilateral aid, although levels still remained higher than in the late 1970s. The United States reduced its contributions to the International Development Agency, cut back on its commitment to IFAD, resisted capital increases in the World Bank, and dragged its heels on increasing IMF quotas. The United States also pushed for changes in the use of multilateral aid. It vetoed projects such as government funding of alternative energy sources which, it contended, could be privately financed. It argued that countries like India and China should not benefit from concessional funds because they could go to private markets for capital. Finally, the United States sought to attach conditions to aid flows so that they would promote private enterprise and investment capital. In the United Kingdom, the Thatcher government also decreased its official development assistance by almost 38 percent during this period, both bilaterally and multilaterally.

As a result of the recession's pressures, aid from the OECD countries actually fell from $27.3 billion in 1980 to $25.6 billion in 1981, before rebounding in 1982 to $27.9 billion. From 1980 to 1981, U.S. aid fell from $7.1 billion to $5.8 billion, then rose in 1982 to $8.3 billion. In constant prices, however, OECD and U.S. aid continued to decline.[35]

While overall aid stagnated, bilateral aid became increasingly defense oriented instead of development oriented. In 1973, 22 percent of U.S. bilateral aid was for political/strategic purposes, and 78 percent was for development. By 1985, 67 percent of the total was for political/strategic purposes, and 33 percent was for development assistance.[36] The changing political economy of oil (see Chapter 9) also undermined OPEC's interest in aid transfers. Beginning in 1980, OPEC aid decreased in absolute amounts, as a percentage of GNP, and as a percentage of total official development assistance. From 1980 to 1985, total OPEC aid fell by more than 50 percent, from $8.7 billion to $3.0 billion (see again Figure 6.3).

By the mid- to late-1980s, however, some concessional aid was restored. New surplus countries, such as Japan, began extending more aid to the developing countries. As Japan's trade and financial surplus soared, it came under pressure from the United States to recycle those surpluses in part to developing countries. The United States saw this as a way to alleviate pressures on the United States for aid flows. At the same time, Japanese leaders sought to define a greater world role for Japan. They perceived that leadership in the Third World was a role that Japan could assume without threatening the United States and without taking on military responsibilities forbidden under Japan's constitution and unacceptable to the Japanese public. Thus, Japanese aid increased significantly, from $3.1 billion in 1981 to $11.3 billion in 1993, terms were eased, and the scope of recipients broadened.[37]

In 1987, Japan announced a program to recycle a part of its current account surpluses to the developing countries through bilateral loan programs and multilateral institutions. A total of $67.2 billion was disbursed under the program, which ended in June 1992. A new program called the Funds for Development Initiative was proposed to succeed it in June 1993. The goal for the new program was to provide between $120 and $125 billion in official flows to the South over five years. Both plans channeled the funds through the Exim Bank of Japan, OECD yen loans, and multilateral development banks.[38]

Despite budgetary problems, the United States became more receptive to the need for some concessional flows in particularly hard-hit areas such as sub-Saharan Africa and also as a means of promoting "growth with adjustment" as a way out of the debt crisis under the **Baker Plan**. Following the announcement of the Baker Plan in 1985, the United States approved a $75 billion increase in the World Bank's authorized capital; agreed to fund a new World Bank agency, the **Multilateral Investment Guarantee Agency (MIGA)**, to insure foreign direct investment in developing countries; and provided new funds for the concessional lending arm of the World Bank, the International Development Agency (IDA). However, the lopsided distribution of U.S. aid to strategic countries was not changed.

Total net resources flowing to the developing countries reached a postwar peak of $344 billion in 1996 (see Figure 6.2). After a tremendous decline in the early 2000s, they almost hit that level again by 2006. ODA reached a plateau,

TABLE 6.1   Bilateral Aid to Former Colonies, 1970–1994

Donor	Former Colony Share of Total Aid (in percentages)
Portugal	99.6
United Kingdom	78.0
France	57.0
Belgium	53.7
Netherlands	17.1

SOURCE: Alberto Alesina and David Dollar, "Who Gives Foreign Aid and Why? *Journal of Economic Growth*, 5 (March 2000), p. 37.

hovering between $50 and $60 billion per year between 1987 and 1999, resuming its earlier upward trend in 2000. Private nonconcessional resource flows declined in absolute and real terms during the 1980s, but by the end of the 1980s they had begun to grow again. Between 1996 and 2002, private nonconcessional flows plummeted from $273 billion to $7 billion before again reversing course.

One significant change in the periods of interdependence and globalization was the growing importance of aid from Western Europe and Japan. In 1988, Japan overtook the United States as the largest donor of aid. In 2000, Japanese ODA was $13.1 billion while U.S. ODA was $9.6 billion. The distribution of recipients across the major donor countries reflected a specialization of donors in aid to particular regions. The Europeans tended to provide aid to former colonies. The Europeans specialized in aid to African countries and the formerly communist countries, the United States was the main aid donor to the Middle East (mainly Egypt and Israel) and Latin America, while Japan focused most of its aid efforts in Asia (see Table 6.1).

In 2007, the United States, as in most of the period since the end of World War II, was the largest single donor of ODA (see Figure 6.4). The total ODA originating from Western European countries was much larger than that coming from the US. ODA from Japan was somewhat lower than it had been in the 1990s but remained substantial. OPEC was no longer a major donor. In the aftermath of the September 11 attacks, the developed countries had increased their aid donations and refocused them somewhat in the direction of poverty alleviation (more on this below). However, a substantial proportion of developed country aid was still motivated by political and strategic rather than economic concerns, and many of the old practices of tying aid and using it as a tool of diplomacy remained unchanged.

The Debt Crisis of the 1980s

One of the major developments in the 1980s was the dramatic change in private flows caused by the debt crisis. The rise in the price of oil (see Chapter 9), combined with restrictive monetary policies in the major industrial countries, led to

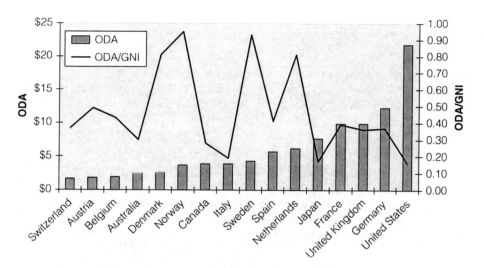

FIGURE 6.4 Net ODA by Donor Country in Billions of Current Dollars and ODA/GNI in Percentages in 2007

SOURCE: *OECD Statistics online.*

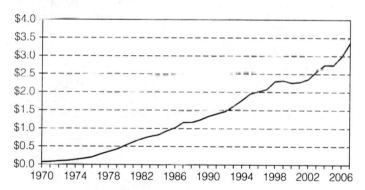

FIGURE 6.5 Long-Term Debt Outstanding, Low- and Middle-Income Countries, 1970–2006, in Trillions of Current Dollars

SOURCE: World Bank, *World Development Indicators.*

record-high real interest rates and world recession. As a result, the LDC debtor nations faced declining terms of trade—plunging commodity prices and a three-fold increase in the price of oil—and falling export volumes.

By 1982, external LDC debt was 264 percent above 1975 levels. The highly indebted countries, consisting of (in order of exposure), Brazil, Mexico, Argentina, Venezuela, Nigeria, Philippines, Yugoslavia, Morocco, Chile, Peru, Colombia, Ivory Coast, Ecuador, Bolivia, Costa Rica, Jamaica, and Uruguay, by 1982 had outstanding debt 305 percent higher than in 1975.[39] Borrowing from private commercial sources accounted for an ever greater portion of total debt (see Figure 6.5), rising from 60 percent of the highly indebted countries' debt in 1975 to 76 percent by 1982.

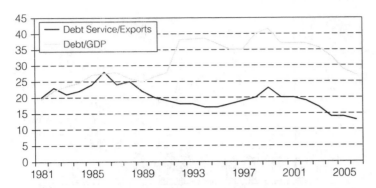

F I G U R E 6.6 Debt/GDP and Debt Service/Exports of Goods and Services in Percentages, 1981–2006, Emerging and Developing Countries

SOURCE: World Bank, *World Development Indicators;* International Monetary Fund, *World Economic Outlook Database*, April 2008. Debt service data are for low- and middle-income countries.

Because of rising interest rates, developing countries also faced sharp increases in the cost of servicing their greatly increased debt. By 1982, the **debt service ratio**, measured by the dollar value of interest and principal amortization payments as a percentage of the dollar value of exports, rose to 21 percent for all debtors (see Figure 6.6) and to 38.8 percent for the highly indebted countries.[40]

Before 1979 borrowing had been for relatively long terms of three to five years. But as lenders became cautious in 1979 to 1981, they turned increasingly to **short-term credits**, which made the borrowers much more vulnerable to a change in the lenders' willingness to continue the flows. Significantly, in many, although not all, cases, this new lending was used for consumption, not for increases in productive capacity. In some countries, including Argentina, Venezuela, and Mexico, some lending was dissipated in capital flight.

The first signs of the increasingly fragile structure of international debt came with Argentina's decision to suspend payments on its $37 billion in external debt following its defeat by Britain in the 1982 Falklands war lowered confidence in the capital markets. Then in August 1992, the Mexican government announced that it would be unable to service its foreign debt. Mexico's ambitious growth policies had resulted in an overheated and increasingly inflationary economy and surging budgetary and balance of payments deficits (see Figures 6.6 and 6.7). The weakening world oil market (see Chapter 9) reduced the value of Mexico's oil exports, which comprised three-fourths of its total export earnings; higher interest rates and growing debt drove up the annual cost of debt service; the greatly overvalued peso led to a surge in Mexico's imports; and the situation was aggravated by **capital flight**.[41] An upcoming presidential election made the government particularly unwilling to take far-reaching measures to avert a crisis. One month after the July 1982 election, a financial panic erupted.

The Mexican debt crisis of 1982 posed a major challenge to the world's financial system. Until then, external debt problems like Mexico's had been rare and had generally involved relatively small amounts of commercial bank borrowings. By contrast, Mexico's external debt totaled more than $85 billion and included loans

FIGURE 6.7 Balance on Current Account, Brazil and Mexico, 1980–2007, in Billions of Current Dollars

SOURCE: International Monetary Fund, *World Economic Outlook Database*, April 2008.

that accounted for a significant percentage of the capital of the largest U.S. banks in 1982. Moreover, Mexico was just the tip of the iceberg. At the end of 1982, loans to Argentina, Brazil, Mexico, Venezuela, and Chile alone amounted to over $260 billion. Brazil by itself had borrowed $91 billion.[42] The world's major private banks, especially U.S. banks, had significant exposure in these countries.[43]

In the developed countries, the LDC debt crisis was treated primarily as a threat to the international financial system. Defaults by debtor nations could have led to a collapse of confidence in the international banking system, possible illiquidity or insolvency of the banks, dangerous disruption of the financial markets, and, in a worst-case scenario, world recession or depression.[44]

The United States forwarded $2 billion to Mexico, helped arrange a $1 billion bridging loan from a group of central banks, and pressed Mexico and the IMF to begin negotiations for a longer-term arrangement. Thus the immediate crisis was averted.

In November 1982, Mexico and the IMF reached an accord. In exchange for $3.84 billion in IMF credits between 1983 and 1985, Mexican authorities agreed to carry out a strict **austerity program** that included reducing the budget deficit, limiting public sector external borrowing, and reducing or eliminating subsidies and public works projects. Significantly, the IMF refused to conclude its agreement until the commercial banks agreed to lend an additional $5 billion to Mexico. This was the first time that the IMF insisted on large complementary financing from banks as an essential element of an IMF lending agreement. At the same time, the Mexican government, acting on behalf of all Mexican borrowers and its private creditors, agreed to begin negotiations to postpone debt repayments and lengthen repayment timetables.[45]

As bank lending to developing countries abruptly halted after August 1982, the debt crisis spread rapidly through Latin America and the rest of the developing world. By December 1982, Brazil, with $91 billion in foreign debt, was in trouble. By the end of 1983, Brazil, almost all the other Latin American countries, and a number of African countries had rescheduled their debts.[46] By the end of 1983, more than twenty-five countries around the world, with a combined outstanding bank debt of more than $200 billion, had gone into arrears.

Debt Crisis Management

Mexico became the model for managing these debt crises. Although the process varied from country to country, a pattern of crisis management emerged. The central focus was an agreement with the IMF on a new loan from the IMF that was conditional upon the adoption of a **structural adjustment program**—a program of government reforms, often including reduced public spending. Although its loans were small compared with total indebtedness, IMF **conditionality** provided a vehicle for imposing and surveying national economic policies deemed necessary for debt repayment. In order to facilitate IMF lending to debtor developing countries, IMF members agreed in 1983 to increase the Fund's quotas by almost 50 percent and the Group of Ten agreed in February 1983 to increase the **General Arrangements to Borrow (GAB)** from 6 billion to 17 billion SDRs and to allow nonmembers access to the that facility.[47]

An IMF agreement was followed by negotiations between creditor banks and the debtor government. Under debtor-creditor agreements, repayment schedules were extended, grace periods given on principal repayment, and rates adjusted. But debtors were always expected to service debts fully, and no debt relief such as reduction of interest or principal was provided. In addition, the central banks and the IMF virtually required private creditor banks to commit additional funds to debtor countries.[48] Finally, creditor governments, whose various credit-granting institutions, such as export credit agencies, had outstanding loans to debtor countries, also rescheduled their debts through the Paris Club of government creditors, which negotiated as a group with debtor countries.[49]

From 1982 to 1984, the strategy of debt management through austerity, rescheduling, and new lending seemed to work. Cooperation among key parties in developing a system of crisis management averted the feared world financial crisis and enabled borrowers to service their debts. Despite these successes, the strategy actually undermined the long-term ability of the indebted countries to service their debts. Austerity policies, which dramatically reduced domestic demand and imports, also brought growth to a halt. Cutbacks in investment and imports removed catalysts for growth. Devaluations designed to improve balance-of-payments adjustment made it more costly in local currency to service external debt and aggravated the fiscal problems of the government, which had to purchase foreign exchange for debt service.

A few debtor countries—particularly Korea and Turkey—made quick structural adjustments and resumed growth. Most, however, fell into recession. Most seriously affected were the highly indebted countries. Real GDP growth for the highly indebted group fell by 0.4 percent in 1982 and by 2.9 percent in 1983 before rising by 1.9 percent in 1984—half the rates of the 1960s and 1970s, and barely faster than population growth.[50]

Because GDP and exports grew slowly or not at all, the debt service capacity of the major countries did not improve. Furthermore, because of new private sector lending and increased loans from the IMF and World Bank, long-term debt outstanding increased further from $791 billion in 1982 to $924 billion in 1985 (see again Figure 6.5). From 1982 to 1985, the ratio of debt to GNP for the highly indebted countries rose from 32.4 percent to 49.5 percent. It became clear that the debt crisis was more than a temporary liquidity problem.

In September 1985, United States Treasury Secretary James Baker proposed a three-part plan to restore growth in 15 of the most heavily indebted countries and to complement the ongoing country-by-country debt restructuring efforts. First, debtor governments would implement market-oriented structural changes including reducing tariffs and quotas; financial liberalization such as improved access for foreign direct investment; deregulation, including reducing subsidies, interest rate controls and exchange rate regulations; and privatization of state-owned industry. Second, the Baker Plan called on commercial banks to provide $20 billion in new loans over three years and on multilateral development banks, particularly the World Bank, to increase disbursements by $3 billion per year and to promote economic reform in debtor countries. The combination of economic reforms and new financial flows was expected to lead to a growth in output and exports and, eventually, to a return to solvency and access to credit markets.

The Baker Plan, however, did not lead to a resurgence of growth. While countries such as Mexico, Chile, and Uruguay pursued reforms, most debtors found it politically difficult to implement sigificant economic changes. Economic reality also left little room for maneuvering. Governments remained burdened by inadequate tax systems and large public sector deficits, which were heavily driven by their huge debt burdens.

Growth in the developed countries slowed; there was a persistent weakness in nonoil commodity prices; and turmoil in OPEC led to a sharp drop in oil prices after 1985. As a result, the overall terms of trade moved sharply against the major debtors from 1985 to 1987, falling at an average annual rate of 6.7 percent.[51] Lower inflation and lower interest rates in the industrial countries were not enough to offset the decline in the terms of trade.

Finally, the financial inflows prescribed by the Baker Plan were not forthcoming. By 1988, commercial banks had largely met the $20 billion target of new loans set by the Baker Plan. However, due to debt servicing by LDCs to banks, net commercial bank flows to debtor countries were actually negative. World Bank commitments to the highly indebted countries increased significantly, but net transfers fell short of the Baker Plan goals and in 1987 were actually negative.

IMF net flows to the heavily indebted countries declined as debtors repaid loans from the fund. While some improvements were made after 1985, the Baker Plan did not fulfill its goal of achieving sustained growth in major debtor countries. Real GDP growth for the group rose only 2.4 percent per year for the period 1985 to 1988. Per capita growth was lower, averaging 1 percent per year. Per capita consumption levels fell and poverty levels increased.

Some modifications were made in an effort to improve the working of the Baker Plan. An increase in World Bank capital authorized in 1988 was intended to enable bank flows to continue and possibly increase. A variety of financial techniques were developed. **Secondary debt markets** enable creditors to exchange debt with each other as a way of balancing exposure to certain countries or of balancing debt maturities. Sale of debt on a secondary market at a discount is a way for banks to dispose of a nonperforming loan without having to write off the total amount of the loan. **Debt–equity swaps** involve the exchange of discounted bank debt for equity investments in debtor countries. Through such swaps, a commercial bank can reduce its debt exposure by selling it or turning it into a real asset; the debtor country lowers its debt and promotes new investment; and the investor obtains favorable financing for investment. Other financial techniques include **exit bonds**, which give creditors a lower rate of interest but exempt them from providing new money as part of a **debt restructuring**. Overall, these financial techniques were helpful in reducing the debt service burden, but only at the margins. Despite the Baker Plan and the menu modification, debtor economies stagnated and the system continued to lurch from crisis to crisis.

Debt Fatigue

By the mid-1980s, the debt crisis had entered a new phase characterized by debt fatigue and disintegrating cooperation among the participants. As slow or no growth persisted and the debt burden grew, social and political tensions within debtor countries rose, and dissatisfaction with the system emerged. With access to credit markets an elusive goal, economically painful and politically difficult policies designed to satisfy creditors became less acceptable. In 1984, the newly elected government of Argentina resisted a proposed IMF austerity program and refused to pay interest on its debt. Some smaller debtors suspended payments and Brazil tried unsuccessfully to impose a moratorium on its debt service. The creditor countries and banks resisted efforts by debtors to coordinate their policies vis-à-vis the creditors.

There was restiveness among creditor banks as well. While debtors had been divided, creditors had been united from the beginning through the advisory committees, which were a form of creditor cartel. Now, creditor unity had begun to weaken. Small and regional banks and even some larger banks, which did not see long-term future business in the debtor countries, sought to limit or reduce their lending to LDC debtors. It became increasingly difficult for the lead creditor banks and governments to persuade these banks to provide new money as part of the restructuring packages. Pressure on big banks increased, not only from reluctant creditors and from the secondary market where loan values were significantly discounted, but also from the stock markets where values of the major banks with exposure in developing countries were depressed because of the LDC debt overhang. More banks became interested in reducing lending to LDC debtors, and many major lenders sold debt in the secondary market.

Finally, banks from different countries took different positions in the restructuring negotiations. For example, differences in regulatory and tax treatment between countries led banks to have different positions on setting up reserves against potential losses on LDC loans, and this led to opposing views on concessions to debtor countries. Debt-restructuring packages became harder to negotiate because of the divisions among banks and raised concern that overall new flows would decline.

Despite growing pressures, the United States continued to insist on the viability of the Baker Plan and to oppose any form of debt relief. Other industrial countries also began wavering in their support of the U.S. government. Britain, France, and Germany supported debt relief for the poorest debtors in Africa, whose debt was largely to governments. In 1987, with U.S. acquiescence, they approved the creation of an **Expanded Structural Adjustment Fund** in the IMF to provide greater funds for the least-developed countries to adjust to market changes. Despite U.S. resistance, the heads of state at the 1988 Toronto Summit agreed on a plan to alleviate the debt-service burden for the poorer sub-Saharan African countries. The plan gave these debtors various options for lowering interest rates, stretching out repayments, and actual forgiveness of debt to developed country governments. This was the first recognition of a need for debt relief.

One of the first initiatives of the new administration of President George H. W. Bush was to face up to these new realities. In December 1988, President-elect Bush proposed "a whole new look" on U.S. policy toward the world's debtor countries.[52] As the Bush administration worked to develop a new approach, the new Mexican president called for debt reduction in his inaugural address in January and, then, in March rioting and hundreds of deaths followed the imposition of austerity measures by the newly elected Venezuelan government, which demonstrated dramatically the political threat.[53]

In March 1989, Treasury Secretary Nicholas Brady announced a new LDC debt strategy.[54] This strategy called for a shift in emphasis from new lending to debt reduction by banks and stated that World Bank and IMF resources should be available to debtor countries with sound economic reform policies for use in encouraging debt reduction. The United States proposed mostly voluntary exchanges of old debt for new bonds (later called **Brady bonds**). These bonds were either bonds paying market rates but exchanged for bank loans at a discount, or bonds paying sharply reduced interest but exchanged at par value. It was envisaged that the principal and at least one year of interest on the new bonds would be secured by a country's existing reserves or funds from IMF or World Bank loans. The Treasury proposal also envisioned lending by international financial institutions to countries to buy back debt at secondary market prices.

Implementation of the **Brady initiative** was left to negotiations between banks and specific debtor countries. Negotiations over Mexican debt provided the first test case. After months of stalled talks between Mexico and bank representatives, a new debt reduction agreement was reached in late July 1989 under pressure from Secretary Brady and with the assistance of U.S. officials. The agreement followed the main points for debt resolution set out by Brady earlier in the year. It covered $54 billion of the $69 billion owed by Mexico to private banks. The Mexican plan specified three options for the banks: (1) swapping old loans in return for 30-year bonds paying interest at the same rate as the old loans but valued at 35 percent less than the old loans; (2) swapping old loans for 30-year bonds with the same value, but with a lower, fixed interest rate; or (3) agreeing to lend new money (or recycle interest received from Mexico) for four years, at levels equal in amount to 25 percent of the bank's exposure. In return, the agreement called for a guarantee of the interest payments on the bonds for 18 months, to be financed by funds from the IMF, the World Bank, Mexico, and Japan.[55]

The Mexican agreement was seen by many as a new departure, for it represented the first time that private banks accepted **debt forgiveness** and voluntarily reduced debt levels. Following the Mexican experience, numerous other debtor countries restructured their commercial bank debt and issued Brady bonds. Restructuring of bank debt was linked with macroeconomic stabilization and broad structural reform in debtor countries. The IMF and World Bank, strongly supported by the United States and other bilateral lenders, conditioned their lending on adoption of sound macroeconomic policies such as deficit reduction and on economic restructuring programs including domestic deregulation, privatization, trade liberalization, and more open investment policies.[56]

Total long-term debt rose steadily from $924 billion in 1985 to $3.36 trillion in 2007 (see Figure 6.5). The proportion of debt to gross national product rose from 19 percent in 1981 to a high of 27.8 percent in 1990 before declining. Debt service as a percentage of exports peaked at 41.6 percent in 1999 before declining (see Figure 6.6). The goal of reducing the overall debt burden for developing countries was finally accomplished by the first decade of the twenty-first century, but the low-income developing countries still faced a heavy debt burden. Concern over the negative impact of debt on the poorest countries resulted in the formation of a political movement to support debt relief during the period of globalization.

GLOBALIZATION

Emerging Markets

In the 1990s, a number of developing countries became participants in a new, global financial system that changed them from debtors to **emerging markets**.[57] The successful implementation of macroeconomic and structural adjustment policies plus debt restructuring enabled a number of these countries to return to a state of creditworthiness. Large-population countries like Argentina, Brazil, and Mexico in Latin America and China, India, and Indonesia in Asia were included in the list of emerging markets.[58] At the same time, securities markets were growing rapidly and becoming more global as an increasing number of countries experimented with setting up their own stock exchanges and bond markets (see Chapter 2).

Whereas, in the period of interdependence, only banks lent to developing countries, in the period of globalization, portfolio investors also invested in emerging markets. Starting in the 1990s, professional managers of mutual funds, insurance companies, pension funds, and proprietary equity funds in the industrialized nations became increasingly willing to invest abroad to increase their yields and diversify their portfolios. The rapidly growing and newly creditworthy emerging market countries became attractive locations for investments. These countries were in the process of privatizing state enterprises, creating or expanding domestic equity markets, and liberalizing controls on inward flows of investment. Stocks and bonds of emerging markets in Asia and Latin America were issued, sold, and traded in global financial markets. For example, in 1987, only 0.5 percent of foreign portfolio investment from industrial countries went to emerging markets; by 1993, that figure was 16 percent. In 1990, net portfolio investment in all developing countries was only $6.2 billion;[59] between 1992 and 2000, net portfolio investment in emerging markets and developing countries averaged $61.2 billion per year. After 2000, net flows were mostly negative. In 2006, for example, the net outflow of portfolio investment from the emerging and developing countries was $19 billion.[60]

Financial Crises of the 1990s

Net private financial flows to emerging markets in the 1990s were primarily in two categories: FDI and portfolio investments. Net lending went from somewhat positive in the early part of the decade to strongly negative by the end of the decade. This was due primarily to a series of debt-related financial crises, and to a slowdown in new loans to emerging markets.

A series of major financial crises occurred in the developing world between 1994 and 1999, mostly in the emerging markets. The globalization of financial markets had made it easier for many developing countries to gain access to foreign investment flows. A good portion of those flows were short term investments—either in currencies or in stocks, bonds, or mutual funds—that were highly responsive to small fluctuations in macroeconomic conditions. While many developing countries liberalized their domestic capital markets during this period, they did not always quickly increase their capability to regulate domestic financial markets, thus leaving an opening for incompetent and corrupt behavior on the part of the managers of financial firms and institutions. Even in countries with robust regulatory systems, the rapidity of change caught the government off guard and sometimes defenseless in the face of highly volatile markets. International financial institutions like the World Bank and the IMF confronted crises that were different from those of previous periods. They were subjected to increasing criticism for inappropriate or inflexible responses to the new crises.[61]

The following sections focus on what happened in the 1990s in four countries: Mexico, Indonesia, South Korea, and Argentina.[62] These countries all had with large populations and economies that were growing rapidly prior to their crises. In each country, questions about the stability of the exchange rate arose. International financial institutions played an important role in resolving each crisis, although there was controversy over whether the policies of these institutions enhanced or impeded resolution.

Mexico   The premier emerging market in Latin America was Mexico. Between 1982 and 1988, the Mexican economy suffered from stagflation: virtually zero growth, and high inflation. Between 1988 and 1992, however, the Mexican economy grew at an annual average rate of 3.5 percent, inflation was reduced to 15 percent by 1992, and the government succeeded in reducing spending and raising revenues by privatizing state enterprises. Mexico had joined the GATT in 1986 and subsequently reduced both tariff and nontariff barriers to imports as part of a shift toward an export-oriented development strategy. The peso was pegged against the dollar at a fixed rate to signal the government's intent to rein in inflation and to reduce uncertainty about exchange rates with North America. The announcement of the signing and ratification of NAFTA helped to cement the confidence of both domestic and foreign investors in the overall health of the Mexican economy. From 1990 to 1993, Mexico received $94 billion in net capital inflows, about one-fifth of all such flows to developing countries.[63] These investment inflows enabled Mexico to increase its foreign exchange reserves and created a boom on the Mexican stock market. The foreign inflows also enabled the government to maintain a fixed exchange rate between the dollar and the peso, which was both a way of fighting inflation and a sign of the overall strength of the Mexican economy.

In 1994, a combination of economic and political events ended the ability of the Mexican government to maintain a fixed peso/dollar exchange rate. Confidence in Mexico was undermined by signs of political instability. A rebellion broke out in the southern state of Chiapas in January and flared off and on over the year. In March, just five months before the presidential elections, the candidate of the ruling PRI party was assassinated. In September, one month after the election of the new PRI candidate, Ernesto Zedillo, just as the political situation seemed to be stabilizing, the secretary general of the PRI was assassinated.

At the same time, the situation in world capital markets was changing. U.S. investments became more attractive as the Federal Reserve raised interest rates to prevent inflation. In 1994, net inflows of portfolio investment into Mexico fell to $4.5 billion, down from $14.3 billion the year before. As a result, it became more costly and more difficult for the Mexican government to finance its fiscal and trade deficits. No longer able to finance its deficits in pesos and unwilling to change its economic policies before a critical election, Mexico began to issue **tesobonos**, short-term debt securities denominated in pesos but indexed to the dollar. Instead of devaluing the peso, the government gradually depleted its foreign exchange reserves in a futile effort to maintain what it saw as the symbol of its economic and political strength.

By the end of the year, the situation had become untenable. Portfolio investors once enamored of Mexico as an emerging market left in droves. Interest rates rose dramatically, stock prices plummeted, and the peso-dollar exchange rate came under considerable downward pressure. On December 20, 1994, the Mexican government devalued the peso and on December 22 allowed it to float against the dollar. The peso crisis immediately affected the equity markets of other Latin American countries, notably those of Argentina and Brazil, and created speculative pressures on their currencies as well.

The U.S. government quickly recognized the threat that the peso crisis posed not only to international financial markets and the international monetary system, but also to the economy and political system of its southern neighbor. It led in the mobilization of an international rescue package to stabilize the Mexican economy and, thereby, the international financial system. The first step was an $18 billion international credit package including $9 billion from the United States, which was accompanied by the announcement of a stabilization plan by Mexico. Markets continued to deteriorate, however. The Clinton administration then proposed a loan guarantee program but was forced to withdraw this proposal when it met with opposition from the newly elected, Republican-controlled Congress. Finally, the United States led in the development of a loan package of $50 billion, including up to $20 billion of loans and guarantees from the United States and $18 billion from the IMF.

The announcement of this loan package was accompanied by development of a new economic plan by the Mexican government, which included substantial increases in government revenues, spending cuts, and curbs on wage increases. As in the 1980s, Mexico found itself once again obliged to pursue a domestic austerity program which, while promoting confidence in financial markets, caused a severe recession at home. By the end of 1995, the financial situation had almost returned to normal. The success of the Mexican stabilization program plus new loans from the World Bank and IMF helped to stabilize the financial turmoil in Argentina and Brazil.[64]

Following the Mexican crisis, the G-7 countries led by the United States worked to devise ways to prevent and manage future crises of this dimension. Learning from the Mexican experience that the best way to prevent crises is for borrowing countries to follow appropriate national policies, the G-7 agreed that the IMF should develop an early warning system by enhancing its surveillance, that is, its review and critique of national policies. They agreed that it should find ways to make more information public in a timely manner to help financial markets operate effectively. They also agreed to create an emergency lending facility in the IMF and to expand the resources available in the GAB in the event of a crisis. Finally, unlike the debt crisis of the 1980s, when the IMF and the creditor governments worked with the lending banks and the debtor governments to restructure loans, the international financial institutions and creditor government realized that they had no mechanisms for restructuring debt held by millions of investors who owned securities issued by debtor countries and companies. Thus, they agreed to explore how it might be possible to restructure or otherwise work out such debt in the future.

Following U.S.-led support for Mexico at the Halifax economic summit in the summer of 1995, markets remained stable but cautious. Mexico used the money borrowed from the United States to pay off its maturing tesobonos. Eventually, the tide was stemmed and Mexico was able to borrow again on international capital markets, albeit at higher interest rates. The Mexican crisis illustrated both the promise and the dangers for countries availing themselves of the new financial resources made possible by the rapid increases in capital flows to emerging markets. Countries that borrowed heavily but did not simultaneously pursue appropriate domestic policies were at grave risk because of the potential for rapid outward movements of capital.

Argentina, Part I   Following Mexico's devaluation of the peso in December 1994, the Argentine peso became the object of a **speculative attack**. A speculative attack occurs when there is massive selling of a country's currency assets by both domestic and foreign investors. This usually occurs when there is speculation that the currency is on the verge of being devalued.[65] In 1995, bank deposits fell by approximately 18 percent, GDP declined by 8 percent, and unemployment rose from 12 percent in December 1994 to 18.6 percent in May 1995. Despite these pressures, the Argentine authories kept the peso at parity against the dollar and President Carlos Menem was re-elected for a second term in May 1995. This was considered at the time to be evidence that the Argentine approach to currency stability could be a model for the rest of the developing world.

That approach came out of an earlier debt crisis. When President Menem was elected for his first term in 1989, the external debt of Argentina was $61 billion and the country was in the middle of a period of hyperinflation. Menem appointed Domingo Cavallo, a Harvard trained PhD economist, as his Economy Minister in April 1991. Cavallo devised a Convertibility Plan to end Argentina's economic doldrums. In January 1992, the previous Argentine currency, the austral, was retired and replaced with the peso at a rate of 10,000 australs to the peso. The government committed itself to maintaining parity between the peso and the U.S. dollar at a rate of one peso per dollar. It would henceforth back all pesos in circulation with dollars held in reserves. The legislature authorized commercial banks to issue dollar-denominated deposits to individuals as well as corporations. The government privatized a number of major state enterprises in order to raise money for government operations. Debt restructuring agreements under the Brady Plan were negotiated in 1993 calling for a modest write-down in loans in exchange for U.S. guarantees backed by special Treasury bonds (Brady bonds) that were denominated in dollars.

The combination of the dollar–peso parity and dollar-denominated bank deposits in Argentina was later called **dollarization**. In essence, dollarization meant that Argentina had relinquished national control over its currency and now relied on the U.S. Federal Reserve to set monetary policy. This was something like having a **currency board** without actually having one.[66] By the end of 1995, about half of all commercial bank deposits in Argentina were denominated in dollars. Foreign investment began to flow into Argentina at historically unprecedented rates. The ability of the Argentine government to maintain a stable currency in the wake of the Mexican crisis was considered a victory for dollarization.

Indonesia   Prior to Indonesia's financial crisis in 1997, the country was growing at impressive rates, partly on the basis of its oil revenues, but also because of its ability as an oil exporter to borrow extensively on international capital markets. The Indonesian financial crisis was part of the larger Asian financial crisis (see Chapter 2), but it was also to some extent a result of specific domestic problems. Indonesia's economy suffered from high levels of corruption in government and what some came to call "crony capitalism"—a tendency of government-owned or -controlled banks to make loans to politically powerful friends of politicians in office. A sudden devaluation of the Indonesian currency, the rupiah, occurred in August 1997, in the wake of the devaluation of the Thai baht. In October 1997, the government announced that 16 commercial banks were to be closed in exchange for an IMF bailout package of $23 billion. The IMF recommended that there should be an increase in interest rates to stem inflation and to stabilized the exchange rate. These standard policies unfortunately did not have the desired effect.[67]

In November, President Suharto reneged on his promises to reform the banking sector and permitted one of the sixteen banks to be reopened under the management of his son. Rumors about Suharto's ill health and rampant corruption in the regime encouraged speculators to hedge against a major devaluation. On January 8, 1998, the rupiah began a free fall that resulted in a general economic panic, a run on the banks, and widespread hoarding of food. Things got progressively worse in the first few months of 1998. Despite two more increases in IMF allocations, rioting broke out over increases in gasoline prices and bus fares. The riotingspread after the military killed a number of students at a demonstration at Trisakti University. Rioters targetted ethnic Chinese Indonesians for violence in Jakarta and elsewhere. On March 6, 1998, the IMF suspended disbursement of $3 billion of bailout loans. The World Bank and the Asian Development Bank followed suit.

Suharto resigned on May 21, 1998, announcing that he would be replaced by his protégé, Vice President B. J. Habibie. After taking office, Habibie announced that elections would be held in June 1999, but protests continued and more killings occurred. On March 13, 1999, the government announced the closing of 38 banks and the taking over of seven others by a new government agency called the Indonesian Bank Restructuring Agency (IBRA). Unfortunately, the IBRA did not impose the required regulatory discipline on the private banks. Too little was being done too late.

Real GDP declined in 1998 by 13.7 percent, inflation increased to an annual rate of 60 percent, domestic interest rates rose rapidly, and companies began to default on their debts. The result was a large increase in the number of nonperforming loans in the portfolios of Indonesian banks. Rather than acknowledging this by writing off the value of bad loans and accepting bank failures where necessary, the IBRA (with the full backing of the Suharto regime) engaged in costly bailouts. The underlying problem was that the banks were part of a larger political patronage system controlled by Suharto and his family. In his effort to preserve political power, bailouts looked like a better bet than prudent banking policies. The result was to postpone but possibly prolong and deepen the pain associated with resolving the banking crisis.

In general elections in June 1999, an opposition party led by Megawati Sukarnoputri won a plurality of the vote. In October 1999, a new Parliament convened but the government continued to be controlled by Suharto's cronies. Presidential elections held later in the month resulted in the election of Abdurrahman Wahid as President and Megawati Sukarnoputri as Vice President. The crisis and its aftermath had resulted in the end of Suharto's long political reign.[68]

South Korea   As in Indonesia, the financial crisis in South Korea was part of the larger Asian crisis. South Korea did not immediately experience problems with its exchange rate after the collapse of the Thai baht in July 1997. The South Korean equities market suffered a sudden drop, but the Korean currency, the won, remained strong for several months after the crisis began. In November 1997, however, after the Bank of Korea gave up defending the won, its value on foreign exchange markets fell rapidly. A team of IMF economists was invited to come to South Korea to propose remedies. They recommended a series of measures to stabilize the currency and to reestablish economic stability, including the usual raising of interest rates and reductions in government spending. They went considerably further than that in recommending a reorganization of the Korean banking system and a relaxation of restrictions on inward foreign invest-ment in the financial sector. Their recommendations were officially accepted by the Governor of Korea's central bank and the Korean finance minister on December 3, 1997. The IMF approved a standby loan arrangement the next day and the World Bank announced a bailout package of approximately $56 bil-lion conditional upon changes in financial governance, including an opening of Korea's financial markets to foreign investment. Korea was in the midst of a pre-sidental election campaign. Presidential candidate Kim Dae Jung, who emerged victorious on December 18, declared his support for the IMF agreement and pledged that he would "...open the market...so that foreign investors will invest with confidence...."[69]

The Koreans recovered relatively quickly from the crisis. Although many companies were closed or restructured and a large number of Koreans lost their jobs, the willingness of the Korean government to make the necessary reforms, including opening up Korea for more inflows of foreign investment, helped to reduce the length of the recession that followed the devaluation of the won. The won itself recovered some of its losses as did the value of shares on the Korean stock market.

Argentina, Part II   In the wake of the Asian crisis of 1997, currency traders and investors believed that Brazil was more likely than Argentina to devalue its currency because of Argentina's dollarization policy. When Brazil finally floated its currency in January 1999, the Argentine peso remained stable. As a result, Argentina's exports to Brazil declined and Brazilian exports to Argentina rose rapidly. The Argentine government persisted in its dollarization policy even though growth slowed, the balance-of-payments deficit widened, and foreign direct investment stopped flowing into Argentina for a while. The country began to experience severe difficulties in servicing its external debt.

In December 1999, Fernando de la Rua was inaugurated president of Argentina. He immediately confronted a projected budgetary deficit of about a half billion dollars. De la Rua's first Economy Minister resigned on March 2, 2001, after being criticized for not adequately addressing government deficits. His successor, who announced an austerity program with deep cuts in spending for education, resigned three days later after other government officials protested his recommended policies. On March 20, 2001, de la Rua appointed Domingo Cavallo, the Economy Minister of the previous government, to run the Ministry. Cavallo was granted special powers by the Argentine Congress to deal with the crisis and began to assemble a set of policies that he hoped would make it possible for the country to service its public external debt of approximately $132 billion.

On December 1, 2001, Cavallo told the citizens of Argentina that he was restricting the amount of money that could be withdrawn from their banking accounts in an effort to stop a run on the banks. The International Monetary Fund had previously approved of a variety of Cavallo's austerity measures, but now announced that they were not sufficient and withheld a loan of $1.3 billion to underline its disapproval. By mid-November, unemployment had reached 18.3 percent. The Argentine unions called for a general strike and violent protests occurred in a number of cities. The Argentine government declared a state of emergency to deal with the violence on December 19, 2001. Then the Argentine Congress repealed the special powers they had previously granted to Cavallo. On December 20, 2001, both de la Rua and Cavallo resigned their positions. A caretaker government under the presidency of Eduardo Duhalde took power on January 2, 2002. On February 11, 2002, the peso was permitted to float against the dollar.

Common Causes, Distinct Consequences

The crises in Argentina, Indonesia, Mexico, and South Korea in the 1990s shared a number of common characteristics. They all involved a period of speculation about the value of the currency followed by devaluations and large outflows of mostly short-term foreign investments. In this respect, the crises reflected the change in North-South investment flows toward more short-term investments. In every country, the crisis resulted in reduced growth rates and increased unemployment. Each crisis was either preceded by or resulted in a change of government. Thus, the crises demonstrated the increased volatility of international investment flows and the increased economic and political dependence of recipients on those flows.

These similarities masked important differences, however. For example, Mexico and South Korea recovered within a year or two, while Argentina and Indonesia suffered from prolonged difficulties. Whereas the first three countries quickly adopted austerity programs and embraced the need for economic reforms, the latter did not. Some observers criticized the IMF and World Bank for imposing too much austerity on the Asian countries during their crisis, pointing in particular to Malaysia as an example of a country that emerged from its crisis without following their advice and without suffering as great a decline in economic growth as the others. Others argued that the IMF went beyond its usual calls for macroeconomic austerity to require changes in financial and political institutions that were not necessarily connected with the crisis itself.[70]

In spite of the differences and difficulties experienced during the 1990s crises, the overall system was never really in danger of collapsing. International economic institutions like the IMF and the World Bank, though criticized for their performance during this period, emerged more or less intact and with new mandates for monitoring the economies of fast-growing developing nations in order to predict and head off future crises.[71] The main casualty of the period was a

brief flirtation with the idea of dollarization—that is, replacing domestic currencies with hard foreign currencies (like the dollar) as a permanent solution to the
problem of encouraging inflows of foreign investment. The collapse of the
Argentine peso, following hard on the similar Mexican and Russian crises,
sounded the death knell for that idea.[72]

Financial Flows to the Poorest Developing Countries

By the end of the twentieth century, uneven growth rates in the developing
world had created ever greater differentiation in wealth and income among
developing countries. Among the emerging market countries, one group, the
newly industrializing countries (NICs), experienced phenomenal growth
and became important players on the world economic stage. A number of factors
led to self-sustaining growth in the **four Asian tigers**—South Korea, Taiwan,
Hong Kong, and Singapore—and also (to a lesser extent) in Mexico and Brazil.
By the 1970s, these countries had "graduated" from concessional flows and were
able to tap private capital markets.Other rapidly developing countries including
Argentina, Chile, Indonesia, and Malaysia had joined the **emerging markets**
group of countries that no longer relied on concessional flows and were able to
access private capital markets. Smaller oil–exporting countries also bridged the
development gap in terms of per capita income. China and India, accounting for
two–thirds of the population of the developing world, had undertaken significant
economic reforms, achieved important successes in both economic growth and
indicators of public welfare, and attracted significant inward financial flows.[73]

Other developing countries, however, including many sub-Saharan African
nations and others such as Myanmar, Bangladesh, and Haiti, experienced negligible growth or even found themselves worse off. The low-income developing
countries were the hardest hit by price increases in food and energy in the 1970s,
the debt crises in the 1980s, the trend toward trade in advanced technology
goods in the 1990s, and the oil and commodity inflation of the early twenty–
first century. Furthermore, they had virtually no access to commercial credit,
which made them almost completely dependent on aid.

In the 1990s, while the emerging market countries confronted the volatility
of private financial flows, the poorest developing countries also struggled with
their own growing debt burden. Most of the debt of the poorest countries was
owed to foreign governments and multilateral financial institutions and not to
private lenders. As we have seen, the Paris Club had been devised to restructure
debt owed by developing countries to foreign governments, but debt owed to the
World Bank, the International Monetary Fund, and the regional development
banks had never been restructured. In the 1990s, members of the international
system finally addressed the problem of indebtedness of the poorest developing
countries to multilateral financial institutions.

In 1996, the International Monetary Fund and the World Bank launched an
initiative for debt relief for the **Heavily Indebted Poor Countries (HIPC)**.
The goals of the program were to both reduce debt and make more money
available for poverty reduction in participating countries. To be eligible, a coun-

try had to be officially classified as an IDA-only borrower by the World Bank, it had to have an IMF structural adjustment program in place, and it had to have previously rescheduled debts on concessional terms with the Paris Club. After qualifying for eligibility, participants in the program moved into the first stage of participation in which they established a three-year record of good performance on IMF and World Bank programs, prepared a **Poverty Reduction Strategy Paper (PRSP)**, and submitted to a debt sustainability analysis carried out by the World Bank. During the second stage, the country would attempt to establish a track record of actually reducing poverty by using the funds freed up by debt relief measures, at which point additional aid would be forthcoming from both multilateral and bilateral creditors.

Over the years, the IMF expanded and enhanced the HIPC program. At their 2005 Summit, G-8 leaders proposed that the IMF and World Bank expand the HIPC program by adopting the **Multilateral Debt Relief Initiative**, which made it possible for eligible countries to receive complete forgiveness of their debt to the Bank and the Fund and to use those funds for development goals. This approach to debt relief, which began in the 1990s, was part of a larger pattern of making aid conditional on the adoption of good policies on the part of aid recipients. Eventually, over 30 countries were able to reduce their debt to the Bank and the Fund and to use funds that would have gone to debt service for poverty alleviation and development.[74]

In the late 1990s, the broader public awareness of the plight of the poorest countries led to the involvement of civil society groups in aid and debt issues. One example was Jubilee 2000, an international political movement in favor of debt cancellation, which was formed in Britain in 1997. The goal of the group was to reduce the $90 billion in debt owed by the poorest developing countries to $37 billion by the year 2000. Its initial core supporters consisted of evangelical Christians, the Vatican, British trade unions, the British Medical Association, as well as numerous celebrities. By 2000, there were groups from 166 countries in the supporting coalition.

At G-8 meetings in Birmingham (1998), Cologne (1999), Okinawa (2000), and Genoa (2001), Jubilee 2000 members demonstrated (along with many other political groups) while G-8 delegates discussed various debt relief measures.[75] The formation of new civil society organizations such as Jubilee 2000 helped to give the leaders of G-8 countries a domestic political reason to push forward in the twenty-first century with new programs to address the problems of the poorest countries.

Financial Flows in the Twenty-First Century

At the beginning of the twenty-first century, new forces were emerging that affected both aid and private capital flows. Leaders in the South responded to pressure from bilateral donors and multilateral institutions as well as their own recognition that no single type of financial flow could solve the problems of global poverty and inequality. Many began to focus on strategies that combined domestic economic reforms with increased emphasis on exports and on reducing

T A B L E 6.2   U.S. Foreign Aid Programs, 2004

Department	Name of Program	$Millions
Department of State	Refugee	756
	International Organizations and Programs	320
	ESF (policy)	3,263
	NIS (distribution)	584
	SEED (distribution)	442
	HIV/AIDS (distribution)	488
	Andean Counter-Drug	727
Treasury Department	Contributions to Intl. Financial Institutions	1,383
	Debt Relief	94
Dept. of Agriculture	PL-480 II (budget)	1,185
USAID	DA, child survival, disaster	4,511
MCA		994
Iraq Reconstruction		18,439
Other		1,000–1,500

SOURCE: Carol Lancaster and Ann Van Dusen, *Organizing U.S. Foreign Aid* (Washington, D.C.: Brookings Institution, 2005), p. 14.

their dependence on both aid and loans (see Chapter 7). Countries such as India and China, for example, carried out domestic economic reforms that privatized government-owned businesses, liberalized capital markets, and opened up trade.

As developing countries liberalized their economies and financial markets, private capital flows of both financial and direct investment increased dramatically, but only to fast-growing countries. At the same time, aid budgets in most of the developed countries came under pressure. Aid decreased overall in real terms (see again Figure 6.1). Furthermore, the preponderance of concessional aid still went to countries that were strategically important to donors. For example, Table 6.2 shows the budgetary allocation of U.S. aid in 2004. Over $18.4 billion was allocated to reconstruction in Iraq (the actual amount spent was much lower). This type of aid was usually not subject to any form of conditionality, and therefore had little impact on reducing poverty or inequality. Elsewhere, however, donors made aid increasingly conditional on domestic reforms (see below for specific examples).

Despite budgetary and political constraints, there was also a growing consciousness in the North about the desperate plight of large numbers of poor people in the least-developed countries. The ability of Al Qaeda and other extremist groups to easily recruit militants from such populations in Afghanistan and Pakistan was a particularly poignant object lesson for the North. The spread of AIDS/HIV in the impoverished countries of sub-Saharan Africa reached crisis proportions in the

1990s. Three million people died of AIDS in 2000, 2.4 million of whom lived in sub-Saharan Africa. Twelve million children were orphaned by the disease in Africa; and if more effective measures were not taken against the spread of the disease that number was projected to increase to 40 million by 2010.[76] Since the AIDS pandemic affected every country in the world, it was impossible to ignore the danger to global public health that would result from ignoring the plight of Africans. Finally, the increasing Northward movement of impoverished people in the South—thanks in part to the very transportation networks that made economic globalization possible—was a constant reminder of the need to reduce inequalities in economic opportunities between North and South.

The increased awareness in both the North and the South of the need to better manage global resources and the global environment was another hopeful aspect of North-South relations at the turn of the millennium. Resource scarcities as well as higher energy, commodity, and food prices affected both the North and the South in the early years of the twenty-first century. Increased global concerns about protecting the environment and addressing the threat of climate change and global warming resulted in calls for improving North-South cooperation and for increasing aid that was designed to encourage better environmental and energy practices in the South. New aid programs were created by the World Bank and under NAFTA, for example, to address Southern environmental problems. Negotiations on a new climate change regime also addressed possible support for the South to acquire new green technologies. Over time, the South might benefit eventually from the growing recognition that the North cannot solve many of its environmental and climate problems without cooperation from the South. However, increased assistance will be forthcoming only when the South shows it is willing to adopt more environmentally sound practices.

Millennium Development Goals

The new thinking about development, poverty, and global issues was reflected in the Millenium Development Goals of the United Nations. In September 2000, the United Nations held a Millennium Summit attended by 150 world leaders, including 100 heads of state, 47 heads of government, and over 8,000 other delegates. One of the major results of this meeting was an agreement to adopt the Millennium Declaration which contained eight Millennium Development Goals (MDGs) and 21 "targets" or subgoals (see Table 6.3). The MDGs reflected a new and fuller approach to poverty alleviation including improvement of education, gender equality, and environmental sustainability. Three of the MDGs focused on health.

The adoption of the Millennium Development Goals was the result of an effective campaign by UN Secretary General Kofi Annan to persuade the members of the UN to focus development efforts on targets that reflected the new realities of the global economy. Annan created the Millenium Development Project, a new entity within the UN, to oversee progress toward the MDGs. It assembled data in support of more specific subgoals, created a mechanism for

T A B L E 6.3   Millennium Development Goals

1   *Eradicate extreme poverty and hunger*

2   *Achieve universal primary education*

3   *Promote gender equality and empower women*

4   *Reduce child mortality*

5   *Improve maternal health*

6   *Combat HIV/AIDS, malaria, and other diseases*

7   *Ensure environmental sustainability*

8   *Develop a global partnership for development*

SOURCE: http://www.unmillenniumproject.org/goals/index.htm.

monitoring progress using quantitative indicators, and published reports including a highly influential report in 2005.[77]

The ambitious Millennium Development Goals did not lead to a major resurgence in foreign assistance, but they did, over the years, influence the agenda for aid programs. At a follow-up meeting to the Millennium Summit, the 2005 World Summit also held at the United Nations in New York, leaders from 191 members of the UN came to discuss implementation of the Millennium Development Goals, among other agenda items. The Secretary General of the UN presented the first of what was to become an annual report on progress toward achievement of the Millenium Development Goals.[78]

Prime Minister Tony Blair made the Millennium Development Goals and aid to Africa a major centerpiece of the 2005 G-8 Summit in Gleneagles, Scotland. At that meeting, the G-8 agreed to double aid to Africa by 2010. President George Bush also stated his commitment to increasing aid to the poorest countries and especially those in Africa in his 2007 State of the Union address. While foreign aid policies of the developed countries did not change overnight as a result of these decisions, there was a decided trend toward directing aid increasingly to disease prevention and poverty alleviation in the poorest countries.

One example of the shift in U.S. policy was the President's Emergency Program For AIDs Relief (PEPFAR). Under PEPFAR the United States committed to spend $15 billion for five years, from 2003 to 2008, to combat the HIV pandemic in poor countries. The goal of the program was to provide anti-retroviral treatments to 2 million HIV-infected patients, to prevent 7 million new infections, and to support care for 10 million individuals (the "2-7-10 goals"). The program was reauthorized and extended for five years in 2008. The goals were expanded to treat 3 million patients, to prevent 12 million new infections, and to support care for 12 million individuals.[79]

In 2002, the U.S. government announced the creation of a new bilateral development fund, the Millennium Challenge Account (MCA), to be run by the

Millennium Challenge Corporation (MCC), to promote entreneurship in the developing countries. The MCC began operation in 2004. Congress was asked to authorize approximately $3 billion annually for the MCA, but actual funding was closer to $2 billion. In order to qualify for funds from the MCC, potential recipients were required to meet a set of criteria involving human rights, investments in education and poverty alleviation, and economic freedom. Additional criteria involving environmental policies and gender politics were added in 2006. Most of the recipients of MCA funds were sub-Saharan African countries.

Another example of changing development policies was the Global Fund to Fight AIDS, Tuberculosis, and Malaria in which multilateral institutions, governments, and private foundations are partners and funders. The fund was established in 2002 as a consequence of decisions made at the 2001 G8 summit in Genoa. While the United States contributed only $700 million to the fund, the European Union pledged over $2.4 billion at the 2005 G-8 summit in Gleneagles. The Bill and Melinda Gates Foundation contributed $500 million to the Fund in 2006, and proceeds from the Product Red campaign, launched by the rock star Bono that same year, went to the fund. The Global Fund established a secretariat in Geneva to review applications for funding. Over $7 billion was spent between 2002 and 2008 in over 130 countries.[80]

The Impact of Financial Flows

Numerous attempts have been made to assess the impact of financial flows to the developing world.[81] The reviews are generally positive, but with important caveats and qualifications. Even with the volatility described above, the generally upward trend in financial flows has resulted in more rapid economic growth in the recipients.[82] Because of the concentration of private flows in a small (but important) number of mostly middle-income countries until the 1990s, they did not have much effect on reducing global poverty and inequality.[83] Public flows, especially after the 1990s, were increasingly focused on the poorest countries, but either the amounts were too low or other factors militated against their having a major impact on poverty. Most scholars believe that trade and private investment flows are more effective than public flows in promoting economic development, but again only where governments of developing countries have been able to abandon failed policies of the past and adopt policies and practices that generally liberalize economies.

There was still a tremendous income gap between rich and poor countries at the beginning of the twenty-first century (see Figure 5.1). Nonetheless, standards of living had improved in the South. Importantly, life expectancy increased and infant mortality decreased significantly. The percentage of undernourished children declined from 20 percent in 1990–1992 to 17 percent in 2001–2003. Rates of education and literacy also increased. The percentage of school-age children enrolled in school increased from 80.2 percent in 1991 to 87.9 percent in 2005. Moreover, the percentage of the population with an income of less than a dollar a day declined from 31.6 percent in 1990 to 19.2 percent in 2004.[84] While there was plentiful evidence that a considerable proportion of the recent successes in global poverty alleviation were due to the adoption of export-oriented development strategies, particularly in large countries like China and India, it was more difficult to attribute success to increased levels of foreign aid.

There was considerable controversy over the impact of aid on economic growth. Some empirical studies indicated that aid could add significantly to growth in individual countries, particularly when accompanied by other sensible policies. One study estimated, for example, that significant amounts of aid used reasonably efficiently can add 0.6 percent to 1.5 percent to the annual growth rate of a developing country.[85] Some scholars argued, in contrast, that aid can have perverse effects. For example, aid can allow governments to postpone key reforms that are necessary for development. Corrupt, authoritarian governments, in particular, may misallocate aid funds or divert them to other uses that have no positive benefits for the poor. One economist argued that there was a principal/agent problem associated with aid:

> ...aid bureaucrats have incentives to satisfy the rich countries doing the funding....Internal bureaucratic incentives...favor grand global schemes over getting the little guy what he wants.[86]

A number of empirical studies showed that the effectiveness of aid depended on good governance, the abandonment of import substitution policies, and the absence of civil strife and corruption.[87] These conditions are not present in many countries in the developing world. Nevertheless, there is evidence that aid has contributed positively to economic growth and poverty alleviation in certain parts of the world.

For example, aid contributed in important ways to growth in countries such as South Korea and Taiwan, which received massive aid inflows during the Cold War. Even in these cases, however, aid had a positive impact because of other factors such as effective private initiatives.[88] In the past several decades, aid that was focused on solving specific problems occasionally succeeded. For example, U.S. aid to Nigeria wiped out rinderpest, a disease that attacks cattle. Aid to Peru helped Peruvian fishermen catch fish more efficiently. U.S. efforts to eradicate smallpox were successful, saving as many as 45 million lives. On the other hand, in some countries, such as China, Mexico, and Thailand, growth took place without significant aid.[89] Finally, there were cases of countries such as Egypt, Pakistan, and Bangladesh that received significant amounts of foreign aid but whose growth rates were still far below average. A more recent example of this was U.S. aid to Iraq after the invasion in 2003.[90]

Quality of life, including health, would certainly have been worse in most developing countries had it not been for substantial medical and poverty-alleviation aid. In many cases, aid has been responsible for real increases in health and welfare. Unfortunately, in some cases aid has merely prevented bad situations from becoming worse. In general, aid strategies have improved as practitioners have learned more about development. Many disappointing episodes in the early days resulted in later, more sophisticated, realistic, and carefully planned strategies. For example, the early efforts at rapid industrialization were replaced by greater recognition of the role of agriculture in development. Early emphasis on aggregate growth was tempered by concern for poverty alleviation, meeting basic human needs, and equity. At the same time, individual project lending was supplemented with comprehensive structural lending, and greater emphasis on free-market solutions. Most recently, planners have recognized the importance of analyzing the environmental impact of new projects.[91]

Finally, aid had a political as well as an economic impact. The aid policies of most Northern states reinforced their economic links with recipient countries and occasionally gave them extra leverage in their relations with the South. The United States, for example, used aid to discourage the expropriation of existing investment. An amendment to the Foreign Assistance Act of 1962 stipulated that U.S. aid must be withheld in the event of nationalization or expropriation without prompt, adequate, and effective compensation.[92] Many donor countries also encouraged new foreign investment by providing information, sharing the costs of investment surveys, and guaranteeing such investment against risk. Aid also supported trade links by encouraging the use of donor goods, especially through tied aid.[93]

Aid is frequently used to influence economic policies in recipient countries.[94] The United States, for example, places economic conditions on aid that shapes monetary and fiscal policy, investment policy, and international economic policy, such as exchange rate and nationalization policy. Through the supervision of aid projects, the aid bureaucracies in all countries have become involved in decision making in recipient countries. Such economic influence occurs in multilateral aid programs as well. The World Bank, for example, has used its aid to promote market-oriented reforms in developing countries.[95]

Aid can also be used to support the preferred internal and external policies of the recipient governments. The United States, for example, has given emergency support in economic crises to the Philippines in 1987 and to Mexico in 1982, 1988, and 1995. Also, the withdrawal or threatened withdrawal of aid has been used to express disapproval of or opposition to internal and external policies. The United States withheld aid from Haiti in 1987, from Panama in 1988, and from Nigeria in 1994. And, reflecting the political/security focus of the U.S. foreign aid program, assistance has been used to promote foreign policies, such as granting basic rights and supporting countries in conflict with the Soviet Union (e.g., in Pakistan), supporting the Middle East peace process (e.g., in Egypt), reducing international trafficking in narcotics (e.g., in Colombia), and, more recently, supporting the fight against terrorism (e.g., in Afghanistan).[96]

Aid has not always enhanced the North's bargaining power. The degree of Northern dominance through aid varied not only in some "objective" measurement of Northern influence but also in the eye of the beholder. Scholars in the North have argued about whether aid was given for altruistic reasons and without political strings; or whether it was given primarily for political or strategic reasons. There is evidence for both perspectives. Others have argued that the effects of aid on the recipients were nil or even counterproductive. The recipients, on the other hand, often felt that aid constituted not influence but unwanted intervention in national policy.[97]

Conclusion: The Future of Financial Flows

Financial flows to the developing countries have changed significantly since the end of World War II. During the Bretton Woods period, private capital flows to developing countries were relatively minor and aid flows were initially modest. Aid flows grew rapidly in the 1960s because of the pursuit of Cold War objectives by the superpowers. During the period of interdependence, private capital flows to the Third World increased, particularly in the form of bank loans, while aggregate aid levels levelled off and donors became more diverse. In the period of globalization, private financial flows in the form of portfolio and direct investment increased dramatically as many developing countries liberalized and as Northern investors sought to profit from the rapid growth of emerging markets. At the same time, concessional flows to the poorest countries from the Northern governments and multilateral institutions remained limited.

The South became increasingly differentiated between groups of fast-growing and slow-growing economies. Countries that were growing rapidly and opening their markets were in a better position than the rest to gain access to private capital flows. Thus, private flows reinforced the growing differentiation of the South. Some Third World countries—China, Brazil, Mexico, Taiwan, and South Korea, for example—appeared much more likely than before to be able to bridge the economic gap between themselves and the North and graduate to full status as industrialized countries. Korea and Mexico actually became members of the OECD. China began to invest in the developed world both directly through its sovereign wealth funds and indirectly through its large multinationals and state-owned enterprises. China purchased U.S. treasury securities, just as Japan had done earlier, as a way of balancing its large bilateral current account surpluses with the United States. But a large group of developing countries continued to fall behind.

One of the more important consequences of differential growth rates among developing countries was the emergence of a **Fourth World**—a disparate group of poorer and slower-growing countries—that remained dependent on concessional flows and whose populations were often burdened by disease, hunger, and other attributes of extreme poverty. Aid flows from the developed world to these Fourth World countries increased after 2000 and increasingly focused on reaching the neediest people in the poorest countries. There was also a new emphasis on pursuing concrete and measurable results of these resource flows and on supporting governments that pursued appropriate development policies. Increased political support for alleviating global poverty as expressed in the United Nations' Millennium Development Goals became one of the more important changes in the domestic politics and policies of developed countries as well as in the policies of multilateral institutions. Whether increased aid and capital flows and the new focus on poverty alleviation and the Millennium Development Goals would have the desired effect, however, remained to be seen.

ENDNOTES

1. On early financing priorities for the World Bank, see Henry J. Bitterman, "Negotiation of the Articles of Agreement of the International Bank for Reconstruction and Development," *The International Lawyer*, 5 (January 1971): 59–88; and Edward S. Mason and Robert E. Asher, *The World Bank Since Bretton Woods* (Washington, D.C.: Brookings Institution, 1973), 1–35.

2. Mason and Asher, *World Bank Since Bretton Woods*, 178–179.

3. Goran Ohlin, *Foreign Aid Policies Reconsidered* (Paris, France: Organization for Economic Cooperation and Development, 1966), 66.

4. See Military Assistance and the Security of the United States, 1947–1956: a study prepared by the Institute of War and Peace Studies of Columbia University, in U.S. Senate, *Foreign Aid Program, a compilation of studies and surveys under the direction of the Special Committee to Study the Foreign Aid Program*, 85th Cong., 1st sess. (Washington, D.C.: U.S. Government Printing Office, 1957), 903–969.

5. See Marshall I. Goldman, *Soviet Foreign Aid* (New York, N.Y.: Praeger, 1967), 60–167; and Robert S. Walters, *American and Soviet Aid: A Comparative Analysis* (Pittsburgh, Pa.: University of Pittsburgh Press 1970), 26–48.

6. Several official and unofficial reports at this time showed that there was a link between U.S. security and Southern economic development. See *Report to the President on Foreign Economic Policies* (Washington, D.C.: Government Printing Office, 1950); International Development Advisory Board, *Partners in Progress: A Report to the President* (March 1951); U.S. Mutual Security Agency, Advisory Committee on Underdeveloped Areas, *Economic Strength for the Free World: Principles of a U.S. Foreign Development Program, a report to the director for mutual security* (Washington, D.C.: Government Printing Office, 1953).

7. See Max F. Millikan and Walt W. Rostow, *A Proposal: Key to an Effective Foreign Policy* (New York, N.Y.: Harper, 1957), 34–38.

8. *Ibid.*, 39. For an analysis of the role of aid in political development, see Robert A. Packenham, *Liberal America and the Third World: Political Development Ideas in Foreign Aid and Social Science* (Princeton, N.J.: Princeton University Press, 1973).

9. See Ohlin, *Foreign Aid Policies Reconsidered*, 27–36. See also Teresa Hayter, *French Aid* (London, UK: Overseas Development Institute, 1966); and Overseas Development Institute, *British Aid—A Factual Survey* (London, UK: Overseas Development Institute, 1963–1964).

10. Organization for Economic Cooperation and Development, *Flow of Financial Resources to Less-Developed Countries, 1956–1963* (Paris, France: OECD, 1964), 19.

11. *Ibid.*

12. David A. Baldwin, *Economic Development and American Foreign Policy* (Chicago, Ill.: University of Chicago Press, 1966), 204.

13. See Walt W. Rostow, *Eisenhower, Kennedy, and Foreign Aid* (Austin, Tex.: University of Texas Press, 1985), 88–89.

14. Organization for Economic Cooperation and Development, *Development Cooperation 1974 Review* (Paris, France: OECD, 1974).

15. *Ibid.*, 133.

16. Samuel P. Huntington, *Political Order in Changing Societies* (New Haven, Conn.: Yale University Press, 1968), 1–92. Many subsequent analyses have shown a

positive relationship between aid levels and economic growth rates when the re-cipient country adopts the proper fiscal, monetary, and trade policies. One fre-quently reported finding is that aid given for political or strategic reasons tends to have less desirable economic effects than other types of aid, partly because it is not made conditional on good policies. This type of aid tends to result in increased gov-ernment expenditure but not in increased investment, thus reducing its potential effect on growth. See Craig Burnside and David Dollar, "Aid, Policies, and Growth," *American Economic Review*, 90 (September 2000): 847–868.

17. See Samuel P. Huntington, "Foreign Aid for What and for Whom," *Foreign Policy*, 1 (Winter 1970–1971): 161–189; and Samuel P. Huntington, "Does Foreign Aid Have a Future?" *Foreign Policy*, 2 (Spring 1971): 114–134.

18. On French and British aid during this period, see Teresa Hayter, *French Aid* (London, UK: Overseas Development Institute, 1966), and Bruce Dinwiddy, ed., *European Development Policies: The United Kingdom, Sweden, France, EEC and Multilateral Organizations* (London, UK: Praeger Publishers for the Overseas Development Institute, 1973).

19. United Nations Conference on Trade and Development, *Debt Problems of Developing Countries* (New York, N.Y.: United Nations, 1972), 1.

20. See "The Policy of Self-Reliance: Excerpts from Part III of the Arusha Declaration of February 5, 1967," *Africa Report*, 12 (March 1967): 11–13; and Henry Bienen, "An Ideology for Africa," *Foreign Affairs*, 47 (April 1969): 545–559. On Burma, see Mya Maung, *Burma and Pakistan: A Comparative Study of Development* (New York, N.Y.: Praeger Publishers, 1971); and David I. Steinberg, *Burma: A Socialist Nation in Southeast Asia* (Boulder, Colo.: Westview Press, 1982).

21. On the Group of 77, see Karl P. Sauvant, *Group of 77: Evolution, Structure, Organization* (New York, N.Y.: Oceana, 1980); and Marc Williams, *Third World Cooperation: The Group of 77 in UNCTAD* (London, UK: Pinter, 1991).

22. United Nations Conference on Trade and Development, *Towards a New Trade Policy for Development* (New York, N.Y.: United Nations, 1964), 79–89; and United Nations Conference on Trade and Development, *Towards a Global Strategy of Development* (New York, N.Y.: United Nations, 1968), 32–44.

23. See Y. S. Park, *The Link Between Special Drawing Rights and Development Finance* (Princeton, N.J.: Princeton University, Department of Economics, International Finance Section, September 1973).

24. On the food crisis, see Raymond Hopkins and Donald Puchala, eds. "The Global Political Economy of Food," *International Organization*, 32 (summer 1978), entire issue; and World Bank, *World Development Report 1986*, ch. 4.

25. International Monetary Fund, *Annual Report, 1983* (Washington, D.C.: IMF, 1983), 33.

26. "Declaration and Action Programme on the Establishment of a New International Economic Order," in Guy F. Erb and Valeriana Kallab, eds., *Beyond Dependency: The Developing World Speaks Out* (New York, N.Y.: Praeger, 1975), 193–194.

27. See James M. Boughton, *Silent Revolution: International Monetary Fund, 1979–1989* (Washington, D.C.: IMF, 2001); John Williamson, *The Lending Policies of the International Monetary Fund* (Washington, D.C.: Institute for International Economics, 1982); and Stephan Haggard, "The Politics of Adjustment: Lessons from the IMF's Extended Fund Facility," in Miles Kahler, ed., *The Politics of International Debt* (Ithaca, N.Y.: Cornell University Press, 1986).

28. See Robert L. Ayres, *Banking on the Poor* (Washington, D.C.: Overseas Development Council, 1983). For a highly critical study of the World Bank, see Teresa Hayter, *Aid as Imperialism* (Harmondsworth, England: Penguin Books, 1971).

29. See G. K. Helleiner, "Policy-Based Program Lending: A Look at the Bank's New Role," in Richard E. Feinberg and Valeriana Kallab, eds., *Between Two Worlds: The World Bank's Next Decade* (New Bruswick, N.J.: Transaction Books, 1986); and Ed Brown, *Structural Adjustment: Theory, Practice, and Impacts* (New York, N.Y.: Routledge, 2000).

30. Richard E. Feinberg, "Bridging the Crisis: The World Bank and U.S. Interests in the 1980s," in Lewis and Kallab, eds., *U.S. Foreign Policy and the Third World. Agenda 1983*, 141–149.

31. See Shireen Hunter, *OPEC and the Third World: Politics of Aid* (Bloomington, Ind.: Indiana University Press, 1984).

32. World Bank, *World Debt Tables: External Debt of Developing Countries* (Washington, D.C.: World Bank, 1983), xiii.

33. World Bank, *World Development Report 1988* (New York, N.Y.: Oxford University Press, 1988), 37.

34. World Bank, *World Development Report 1983*, 182; OECD, *Development Cooperation: 1983 Review*, 52.

35. John W. Sewell and Christine E. Contee, "U.S. Foreign Aid in the 1980s: Reordering Priorities" in John W. Sewell, Richard E. Feinberg, and Valeriana Kallab, eds., *U.S. Foreign Policy and the Third World: Agenda 1985–1986*, 99.

36. Organization for Economic Cooperation and Development, *Development Cooperation: 1987 Review* (Paris, France: OECD, 1987), 327.

37. On increased Japanese lending and aid, see Toshihiko Kinoshita, *Japan's Current "Recycling Measures": Its Background, Performance, and Prospects*, Export-Import Bank of Japan, 1988 (mimeo); Margee M. Ensign, *Doing Good or Doing Well? Japan's Foreign Aid Program* (New York, N.Y.: Columbia University Press, 1992); Alan Rix, *Japan's Foreign Aid Challenge: Policy Reform and Aid Leadership* (New York, N.Y.: Routledge, 1993); Robert M. Orr Jr., *The Emergence of Japan's Foreign Aid Power* (New York, N.Y.: Columbia University Press, 1990); and Shafiqul Islam, ed., *Yen for Development: Japanese Foreign Aid and the Politics of Burden-Sharing* (New York, N.Y.: Council on Foreign Relations, 1991). For an update on Japanese aid, see Carol Lancaster, *Foreign Aid: Diplomacy, Development, Domestic Politics* (Chicago, Ill: University of Chicago Press, 2007), ch. 4.

38. World Bank, *World Debt Tables 1993–94: External Finance for Developing Countries*, vol. 1 (Washington, D.C.: World Bank, 1993), 16.

39. World Bank, *World Debt Tables* (Washington, D.C.: World Bank, 1988), 5, 30.

40. World Bank, *World Development Report* (New York, N.Y.: Oxford University Press, 1988), 31.

41. William R. Cline, "Mexico's Crisis, the World's Peril," *Foreign Policy* no. 49 (winter 1982–1983): 107–120; Jeffry Frieden, *Debt, Development and Democracy: Modern Political Economy and Latin America, 1965–1985* (Princeton, N.J.: Princeton University Press, 1991), ch. 6; and Robert R. Kaufman, Carlos Bazdresch, and Blanca Heredia, "Mexico: Radical Reform in a Dominant Party System," in Stephan Haggard and Steven B. Webb, eds., *Voting for Reform: Democracy, Political Liberalization, and Economic Adjustment* (New York, N.Y.: Oxford University Press for the World Bank, 1994).

42. World Bank, *World Debt Tables 1985–1986* (Washington, D.C.: World Bank, 1985), 254, 274, 278, 326, 358.

43. For statistical evidence about bank exposure, see data from an IBCA Banking Analysis as cited in the *Financial Times*, January 5, 1989, 15.

44. On systemic problems, see Jack M. Guttentag and Richard Herring, *The Lender of Last Resort Function in an International Context*, Essays in International Finance (Princeton, N.J.: International Finance Section, Princeton University, 1983).

45. "Mexico under the IMF," *The Economist*, August 20, 1983, 19–20. See also Karin Lissakers, "Dateline Wall Street: Faustian Finance," *Foreign Policy* no. 51 (Summer 1983): 160–175; and M. S. Mendelsohn, *Commercial Banks and the Restructuring of Cross-Border Debt* (New York, N.Y.: Group of Thirty, 1983).

46. R. C. Williams, Eduard H. Brau, Peter Keller, and M. Nowak, *Recent Multilateral Debt Restructuring with Official and Bank Creditors* (Washington, D.C.: International Monetary Fund, December 1983).

47. International Monetary Fund, *The General Arrangements to Borrow (GAB); The New Arrangements to Borrow (NAB): A Factsheet*, August 2001 at http://www.imf.org/external/np/exr/facts/gabnab.htm.

48. See Jack Guttentag and Richard Herring, *The Current Crisis in International Banking* (Philadelphia, Pa.: University of Pennsylvania, Wharton Program in International Banking and Finance, October 1983); Charles Lipson, "Bankers' Dilemma: Private Cooperation in Rescheduling Sovereign Debts," in Kenneth A. Oye, ed., *Cooperation Under Anarchy* (Princeton, N.J.: Princeton University Press, 1986); and Charles Lipson, "International Debt and International Institutions," in Miles Kahler, ed., *The Politics of International Debt* (Ithaca, N.Y.: Cornell University Press, 1986).

49. The Paris Club has its own website at http://www.clubdeparis.org. See also David Sevigny, *The Paris Club: An Inside View* (Ottawa, ON: North-South Institute, 1990); and Alexis Riefel, *The Role of the Paris Club in Managing Debt Problems* (Princeton, N.J.: International Finance Section, Department of Economics, Princeton University, 1985).

50. World Bank, *World Debt Tables* (Washington, D.C.: World Bank, 1988), xvii.

51. *Ibid.*, 192.

52. "Bush Backs U.S. Shift on World Debt," *New York Times*, December 20, 1989, B10.

53. The demonstrations were followed two years later by an unsuccessful coup d'état. See Andrés Serbin, Andrés Stambouli, Jennifer McCoy, and William Smith, eds., *Venezuela: La democracia bajo presión* (Caracas, Venezuela: Editorial Nueva Sociedad, 1993).

54. "Statement of the Honorable Nicholas F. Brady to the Brookings Institution and the Bretton Woods Committee Conference on Third World Debt," *Treasury News* (Washington, D.C., March 10, 1989).

55. "Relief from Washington as Brady Plan Passes Its Test," *Financial Times*, July 25, 1989, p. 3. See also "Brady's Mexican Hat-Trick," *The Economist*, July 29, 1989, 61–62.

56. For more on the Baker and Brady Plans, see James M. Boughton, *Silent Revolution: The International Monetary Fund 1979-1989* (Washington, D.C.: International Monetary Fund, 2001), chapters 9-11.

57. It should be noted that the definition of this term remains a bit vague. The International Monetary Fund uses the term to refer to the set of all developing countries and transition economies. Others use the term to refer only the the faster-growing and more creditworthy countries in this group. See Chapter 7 for more discussion of this topic.

58. More recently, analysts have focused on the **BRICs**, an acronym standing for Brazil, Russia, India, and China, because of the high growth rates experienced by those four large emerging economies. Again, see Chapter 7 for more discussion.

59. *Ibid.*, 4.

60. International Monetary Fund, *International Capital Markets Developments: Prospects and Key Policy Issues* (Washington, D.C.: May 8, 1995), 5–6; and International Monetary Fund, *World Economic Outlook 2005*, Table 1.2.

61. The most prominent example is Joseph E. Stiglitz, *Globalization and Its Discontents* (New York, N.Y.: Norton, 2003).

62. We will discuss the Russian debt crisis in Chapter 10.

63. World Bank, *Global Development Finance 2001*, 380.

64. Riordan Roett, ed., *The Mexican Peso Crisis: International Perspectives* (Boulder, Colo.: Lynne Rienner, 1996); Nora Lustig, *Mexico: The Remaking of an Economy*, 2nd edition (Washington, D.C.: Brookings Institution, 1998); and Gary C. Hufbauer and Jeffrey Schott, *NAFTA Revisited: Achievements and Challenges* (Washington, D.C.: Institute for International Economics, 2005). See also interviews with Robert Rubin, Laura d'Andrea Tyson, and Bill Clinton in the video series "The Commanding Heights" at http://www.pbs.org/wgbh/commandingheights/.

65. Barry Eichengreen, Andrew K. Rose, Charles Wyplosz, Bernard Dumas, and Axel Weber, "Exchange Market Mayhem: The Antecedents and Aftermath of Speculative Attacks," *Economic Policy*, 21 (October 1995): 249–312; and Maurice Obstfeld, "Models of Currency Crises with Self-Fulfilling Features," *European Economic Review*, 40 (April 1996):1037–1047.

66. For a detailed discussion of currency boards and dollarization see J. Benjamin Cohen, *The Geography of Money* (Ithaca, N.Y.: Cornell University Press, 1998). A currency board determines the growth of domestic money supply the same way a central bank does. However, unlike the central bank, the currency board is a "monetary authority that issues notes and coins convertible into a foreign anchor currency or commodity (also called the reserve currency) at a truly fixed rate and on demand." An orthodox currency board, unlike a central bank, typically does not accept deposits.

67. The bailout package later grew to around $37 billion.

68. Kimberly J. Niles, "Indonesia: Cronyism, Economic Meltdown and Political Stalemate," in Shale Horowitz and Uk Heo, eds., *The Political Economy of International Financial Crisis: Interest Groups, Ideologies, and Institutions* (Lanham, Md.: Rowman & Littlefield, 2001; Andrew MacIntyre, "Political Institutions and the Economic Crisis in Thailand and Indonesia," in T. J. Pempel, ed., *The Politics of the Asian Economic Crisis* (Ithaca, N.Y.: Cornell University Press, 1999); Stephan Haggard, *The Political Economy of the Asian Financial Crisis* (Washington, D.C.: Institute for International Economics, 2000), 65–70; and Natasha Hamilton-Hart, "Indonesia: Reforming the Institutions of Financial Governance?" in Gregory W.

Noble and John Ravenhill, eds., *The Asian Financial Crisis and the Architecture of Global Finance* (New York, N.Y.: Cambridge University Press, 2000).

69. Michel Chossudovsky, "The IMF Korea Bailout," http://www.kimsoft.com/1997/sk-imfc.hjtm.

70. See especially Joseph Stiglitz, *Globalization and Its Discontents*; and Martin Feldstein, "Refocusing the IMF," *Foreign Affairs*, March–April 1998, 20–33.

71. International Monetary Fund, "Early Warning System Models: The Next Step Forward," *Global Financial Stability Report*, March 2002; and Andrew Berg, Eduardo Borensztein, and Catherine Pattillo, "Assessing Early Warning Systems: How Have They Worked in Practice?" *IMF Working Paper*, WP 04/52, 2004.

72. See, especially, Nouriel Roubini, "The Case Against Currency Boards," http://www.geocities.com/Eureka/Concourse/8751/jurus/vs-cbs.htm.

73. On China, see David Shambaugh, *Power Shift: China and Asia's New Dynamics* (Berkeley and Los Angeles, Calif.: University of California Press, 2006); on India, see Arvind Panagariya, *India: The Emerging Giant* (New York, N.Y.: Oxford University Press, 2008).

74. International Development Association and International Monetary Fund, *Heavily Indebted Poor Countries (HIPC) Initiative and Multilateral Debt Relief Initiative (MDRI —Status of Implementation* (Washington, D.C.: September 27, 2007).

75. Even though Jubilee 2000 was disbanded after the Genoa summit, the movement continued with a new organization called the Jubilee Debt Campaign. For a history of Jubilee 2000, see Ann Pettifor, "The Jubilee 2000 Campaign: A Brief Overview," in Chris Jochnick and Fraser A. Preston, eds., *Sovereign Debt at the Crossroads: Challenges and Proposals for Resolving the Third World Debt Crisis* (New York, N.Y.: Oxford University Press, 2006). See also *Unfinished Business: Ten Years of Dropping the Debt* (London, UK: Jubilee Debt Campaign, 2008). The British website for Make Poverty History is http://www.makepovertyhistory.org/. The U.S. partner's website is at http://www.one.org.

76. *Macroeconomics and Health: Investing in Health for Economic Development*, Report of the Commission on Macronomics and Health, Chaired by Jeffrey D. Sachs (Geneva, Switzerland: World Health Organization, 2001), 47.

77. Millennium Project, Report to the UN Secretary-General, *Investing in Development: A Practical Plan to Achieve the Millennium Development Goals* (Sterling, Virgina: EarthScan, 2005).

78. The reports and other information about progress toward achieving the Millennium Development Goals can be found at http://www.un.org/millenniumgoals/.

79. The PEPFAR website is http://www.pepfar.gov. See also Board on Global Health, *PEPFAR Implementation: Progress and Promise* (Washington, D.C.: National Academies Press, 2007).

80. The website for the Global Fund is http://www.theglobalfund.org. See also Chelsea Clinton, *The Global Fund to Fight AIDS, TB, and Malaria*, M. Phil Thesis, University of Oxford, 2003.

81. See Robert Cassen and Associates, *Does Aid Work? Report to an Intergovernmental Task Force* (Oxford, England: Clarendon Press, 1986); John P. Lewis and Valeriana Kallab, eds., *Development Strategies Reconsidered* (New Brunswick, N.J.: Transaction Books, 1986); Sarah J. Tisch and Michael B. Wallace, *Dilemmas of Development Assistance: The*

What, Why, and Who of Foreign Aid (Boulder, Colo.: Westview, 1994); Joan M. Nelson, *Global Goals, Contentious Means: Issues of Multiple Aid Conditionality* (Washington, D.C.: Overseas Development Council, 1992); Joan M. Nelson and Stephanie J. Eglinton, *Encouraging Democracy: What Role for Conditional Aid?* (Washington, D.C.: Overseas Development Council, 1992); Tony Killick, *Aid and the Political Economy of Policy Change* (London, UK: Routledge, 1998); and Stephen Browne, *Foreign Aid in Practice* (New York, N.Y.: New York University Press, 1990). For a critical view of the role of aid, see Peter Bauer, *Equality, the Third World, and Economic Illusion* (Cambridge, Mass.: Harvard University Press, 1981) and William Easterly, *The White Man's Burden: Why the West's Efforts to Aid the Rest Have Done So Much Ill and So Little Good* (New York, N.Y.: Penguin, 2006).

82. Eduardo Borenzstein, José de Gregorio, and Jon-Wha Lee, "How Does Foreign Investment Affect Economic Growth?" *Journal of International Economics*, 45 (1998): 115–135; Bichaka Fayissa and Mahammed I. El-Kaissy, "Foreign Aid and the Economic Growth of Developing Countries (LDCs): Further Evidence," *Studies in Comparative International* Development, (Fall 1999): 37–50; Craig Burnside and David Dollar, "Aid, Policies, and Growth," *American Economic Review*, 90 (September 2000): 847–868; and Henrik Hansen and Finn Tarp, "Aid and Growth Regressions," *Journal of Development Economics*, 64 (2001): 547–570.

83. Robert Lensink and Howard White, "Does the Revival of International Private Capital Flows Mean the End of Aid?: An Analysis of Developing Countries' Access to Private Capital," *World Development*, 26 (1998): 1221–1234.

84. United Nations, *Millennium Development Goals Report 2007*.

85. Cassen, *Does Aid Work*, 24–25.

86. Willam Easterly, *The White Man's Burden*, 167.

87. William R. Cline and John Williamson, "Fostering Development," in Fred Bergsten, ed., *The United States and the World Economy: Foreign Economic Policy for the Next Decade* (Washington, D.C.: Institute for International Eocnomics, 2005), pp. 419–413. See also David Roodman, *The Anarchy of Numbers: Aid, Development, and Cross-Country Empirics*, Center for Global Development Working Paper 32 (Washington, D.C.: Center for Global Development, 2003); William Easterly, "Can Foreign Aid Buy Growth?" *Journal of Economic Perspectives*, 17 (2003): 23–48; Michael Clemens, Steven Radelet, and Rikhil Bhavnani, *Counting Chickens When They Hatch: The Short-Term Effects of Aid on Growth*, Center for Global Development Working Paper 44 (Washington, D.C.: Center for Global Development, 2004); and Raghuram G. Rajan and Arvind Subramanian, *What Undermines Aid's Impact on Growth?* IMF Working Paper 126 (Washington, D.C.: International Monetary Fund, 2005).

88. Irving Brecher and S. A. Abbas, *Foreign Aid and Industrial Development in Pakistan* (Cambridge, Mass.: Harvard University Press, 1972); Gustav F. Papenek, *Pakistan and Development: Social Goals and Private Incentive* (Cambridge, Mass.: Harvard University Press, 1967); Irma Adelman, ed., *Practical Approaches to Development Planning: Korea's Second Five-Year Plan* (Baltimore, Md.: Johns Hopkins University Press, 1969); and Neil H. Jacoby, *U.S. Aid to Taiwan* (New York, N.Y.: Praeger, 1966).

89. Roger D. Hansen, *Mexican Economic Development: The Roots of Rapid Growth* (Washington, D.C.: National Planning Association, 1971).

90. For official information about U.S. aid to Iraq see http://www.usaid.gov/iraq/.

91. John P. Lewis, "Overview: Development Promotion: A Time for Regrouping," in Lewis and Kallab, *Development Strategies Reconsidered*, 3–46.

92. This amendment is called the Hickenlooper Amendment. See Paul Sigmund, *Multinationals in Latin America: The Politics of Nationalization* (Madison, Wis.: University of Wisconsin Press, 1980), 8–10.

93. See Joan M. Nelson, *Aid, Influence, and Foreign Policy* (New York, N.Y.: Macmillan, 1968), 69–90. On aid tying, see Organization for Economic Cooperation and Development, "Aid Tying and Mixed Credits," in *Twenty-five Years of Development Cooperation* (Paris, France: OECD, 1985), 241–250.

94. For an early discussion of this subject, see Klaus Knorr, *The Power of Nations* (New York, N.Y.: Basic Books, 1975), ch. 16.

95. See Gerald K. Helleiner, "Policy-Based Program Lending," and Joan M. Nelson, "The Diplomacy of Policy-Based Lending," in Feinberg and Kallab, *Between Two Worlds*; and Miles Kahler, "External Influence, Conditionality, and the Politics of Adjustment," in Stephan Haggard and Robert R. Kaufman, eds., *The Politics of Economic Adjustment: International Constraints, Distributive Conflicts, and the State* (Princeton, N.J.: Princeton University Press, 1992).

96. Howard Wriggins, "Political Outcomes of Foreign Assistance: Influence, Involvement, or Intervention?" *Journal of International Affairs*, 22 (1968): 217–230; and Joan M. Nelson and Stephanie J. Eglinton, *Encouraging Democracy: What Role for Conditional Aid?* (Washington, D.C.: Overseas Development Council, 1992).

97. Carol Lancaster, *Foreign Aid*; International Monetary Fund, *World Economic Outlook* (Washington, D.C.: IMF, April 1984), 205; David H. Lumsdaine, *Moral Vision in International Politics: The Foreign Aid Regime 1949–1989* (Princeton, N.J.: Princeton University Press, 1993); Brian Smith, *More Than Altruism: The Politics of Private Foreign Aid* (Princeton, N.J.: Princeton University Press, 1990); and Sarah J. Tisch and Michael B. Wallace, *Dilemmas of Development Assistance: The What, Why, and Who of Foreign Aid* (Boulder, Colo.: Westview, 1994), ch. 3.

7

Trade and Development Strategies

Most Southern economies are highly dependent on trade with the North. Export earnings constitute a large share of their GNP, and imported goods are crucial to their development. Many people in developing countries believe that their participation in the world economy has not promoted their development and that they are excluded from the trade governance system established by the North. This chapter examines the strategies that developing countries have pursued to achieve development and to gain access to the trade governance system.

BRETTON WOODS: ISOLATION FROM THE TRADING ORDER

Import Substitution

In the early Bretton Woods period, most independent developing countries were isolated from trade decision making and from many aspects of international trade itself. Many of these Southern states pursued a strategy of **import substitution**, which was based on promoting domestic industrial development behind protective (high tariff) walls. The economic rationale for this development policy was the structuralist approach outlined in Chapter 5. The structuralist approach recommended the combination of import substitution with regional integration, with the goal of diversifying production away from agriculture and raw materials and toward manufacturing and services.

Thus, in the negotiations leading up to the Havana Charter, the Southern countries sought exemptions from the new rules, including the ability to use import quotas and tariffs to protect infant industries, to establish new preferential trading systems, and to enter into commodity agreements to stabilize and ensure minimum commodity prices.[1] Because the North wanted approval by the developing countries for the new trade charter, the South was able to achieve some limited modifications in the Havana Charter, most notably a new chapter that recognized the special needs of developing countries.[2]

However, the General Agreement on Tariffs and Trade (GATT), which replaced the Havana Charter as the constitution of the new trading order, was dominated by the developed North. GATT was designed as an interim measure and included none of the provisions for development that the South had fought to include in the Havana Charter. All that was left was a GATT article that authorized a country under certain restricted conditions to use tariffs and quantitative restrictions to assist economic development or deal with payments imbalances.[3]

While virtually all the developed countries joined the GATT, many developing countries did not. GATT's negotiating process excluded the developing countries from the international governance of trade. The GATT's reciprocity rule stated that all trade concessions had to be mutual. But the South, with its small markets, had little to exchange for concessions in its favor. Under the GATT, trade concessions were negotiated among the importing countries and principal suppliers of any particular item. Because there were no principal suppliers, many products of interest to the developing countries, such as raw materials, were left out of the GATT negotiations. Even when the developing countries were the principal suppliers, they were unable to put products or issues of interest to them on the agenda, because the South represented only a minority of the GATT membership and power. The developing countries were also hampered by the lack of staff and resources to sustain difficult and sophisticated trade negotiations with the powerful developed countries.

Isolated from the international trading regime, developing countries attempted to develop an internal market for domestic production through high rates of protection for domestic industry: tariffs that were sometimes several hundred percent or more, exchange controls, multiple exchange rates for different products, import licensing, and outright bans on the importation of goods produced domestically.[4] Protection provided powerful incentives for the development of local production to replace imports by providing an assured market and by channeling domestic savings into industry through increased industrial profits.[5]

Import substitution fostered some industrialization, but often at a high price. The new industries were often inefficient and their output costly and uncompetitive. Faced with small domestic markets, unsuccessful efforts at regional integration, and strong competition abroad, most developing countries could not achieve adequate scales of production to build efficient industries. Furthermore, policies that encouraged the importation of capital-intensive production technologies discouraged the growth of demand for labor and thus had only a minor effect on employment levels.

Import substitution also often created a balance-of-payments deficit. Production of high-cost domestic manufactures came at the expense of both export-oriented manufacturing and traditional agricultural exports. Furthermore, high tariff barriers for manufactured imports did not necessarily decrease total imports but, rather, changed the composition of imports. Instead of importing finished products, Southern countries now imported raw materials, parts, and capital goods.[6] New systems of licensing and currency exchange controls created new rigidities in Southern economies that discouraged competition and promoted inefficiency.[7] Foreign multinationals tried to jump over the high tariff barriers for assembled products by establishing assembly plants, which tended to increase imports of components without expanding exports.

Industrialization through import substitution also damaged agriculture. New investment in agriculture was limited; real earnings declined as industrial profits rose; and income inequalities between agriculture and industry were exacerbated. As a result, people began to leave the countryside for the town, but the new industry in the cities could not absorb the burgeoning urban population. Thus unemployment and income inequalities worsened.[8]

Trade Expansion and Declining Terms of Trade

By the end of the 1950s, many Southern states came to believe that export growth combined with protection of domestic markets could maximize efficiency of production and increase earnings and foreign exchange available for development, much as the liberals had always argued. According to a number of influential spokespersons for the developing countries, most notably Raúl Prebisch, such benefits could not occur without a restructuring of the international trading system, because the existing system was biased against Southern exports, because of their dependence on exporting agricultural commodities and raw materials.

First, there was, Prebisch claimed, a long-term deterioration in the South's terms of trade.[9] The prices of raw materials exported by the developing countries were declining in relation to the prices of manufactured products imported from the developed countries. Because of trade unions and monopoly markets in the developed market economies, it was argued, increased productivity in manufacturing in the North was absorbed by higher wages and profits and did not lead to a fall in the price of manufactures. On the other hand, because of unemployment and the absence of labor organization in the developing countries plus the existence of a competitive international market for Southern raw materials, increased productivity in **primary products** led not to increased wages or profits but to a decline in prices.

The terms of trade also turned against the South because demand in the North for primary products from the South was inelastic with respect to income and consequently an increase in the production of raw materials led to a decline

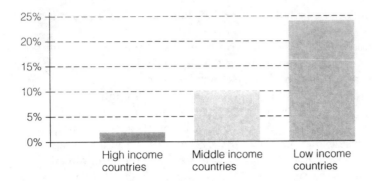

FIGURE 7.1 Dependence on Agriculture, as Percentage of GDP, by Income Level, 2000

SOURCE: World Business Council for Sustainable Development, http://www.wbcsd.org/web/doingbiz.htm.

in prices rather than to an increase in consumption. Finally, the prices of Southern products tended to fall because of the increased production of synthetics and substitutes—for example, polyester fabrics replacing cotton cloth—in the North. The structural decline in terms of trade for primary producers was aggravated by Northern protectionist policies and by the inherent instability of commodity prices. In the view of the developing countries, fluctuations in prices and thus in export earnings hindered investment and disrupted development planning.

The empirical evidence on the declining terms of trade thesis is mixed. The original research by Prebisch and his associates was strongly challenged in the 1950s and 1960s for using inappropriate measures of the terms of trade and being dependent on time periods that were most likely to yield the expected results. Subsequent research on the relative prices of primary commodities (including fuels) versus those of traded manufactures indicate a long-term decline of about 36 percent between 1900 and 1986, or about 0.5 percent per year.[10] Just for the purposes of illustration, Figure 5.6 displays the average terms of trade for non-oil-exporting developing countries between 1900 and 2000. There is a slight downward trend in the long term punctuated by short-term upward spikes.

Despite problems in the evidence for declining terms of trade theories, there is little question that countries that remain largely dependent on agriculture and raw materials production generally are less able to grow their way out of poverty than countries that have diversified into manufacturing and services (see Figure 7.1). We will see below that there is generally a positive relationship between this sort of economic diversification and the ability of developing countries to benefit from globalization.

Finally, the South felt that its real potential to export manufactured products was constrained by Northern dominance of international markets. Developed countries benefited from established positions, while Northern protection prevented the expansion of Southern manufactured exports. **Escalated tariffs** favored the import of raw materials from the developing countries, discouraged the import of processed or semiprocessed products, and thus discouraged the development of Southern industry. Unusually high tariffs or import quotas were imposed on many Southern manufactures, such as textiles, footwear, and leather goods, that competed effectively with Northern industries. Where there were no tariff or quantitative restrictions, the North often forced voluntary export restraint agreements (VERs) on Southern states.[11] Such nontariff barriers as health standards, labeling requirements, and customs procedures posed difficult hurdles for the Southern states with their lack of marketing expertise and experience.[12]

These constraints on developing country exports were reflected in the South's diminished role in international trade. The Southern share of world exports dropped from 31.6 percent in 1950 to 21.4 percent in 1960. In the same period, the trade of the developed market economies grew from 60.4 percent of total world exports to 66.8 percent, and the socialist states went from 8.0 percent of total world exports to 11.8 percent. Between 1950 and 1960, exports from the developed countries grew 8.7 percent, whereas those of the developing countries grew only 3.5 percent.[13]

As the South turned from isolation to trade expansion, Southern political pressure for a change in the GATT system increased. At Third World conferences and at the United Nations and within the GATT itself, developing states pushed for greater consideration of their trade problems. Southern pressure was reinforced by the independence of many colonial states and by the expansion of the Cold War to the developing world. As part of its new initiatives in the South, the Soviet Union proposed an international conference on trade and the creation of a world trade organization outside the GATT. The North persuaded the South to reject the Soviet proposal in favor of reform within the GATT.

For the developed countries, reforming the GATT meant little more than studying the problems of developing countries. A panel of experts appointed by GATT members recommended establishing a GATT committee to consider problems of Southern exports of primary products and manufactured goods. Developing countries used this new committee and the ongoing trade rounds to push for better access to Northern markets through unilateral concessions from developing countries, including a standstill on tariff and nontariff barriers for exports of Southern states, elimination of quantitative restrictions inconsistent with the GATT rules, duty-free entry for tropical products, elimination of customs duties on primary products important to the trade of developing countries, reduction and elimination of customs tariffs on semiprocessed and processed Southern exports, and reduction by the North of internal taxes and revenue duties on products produced primarily or wholly in Southern states. The Northern countries, however, were prepared to agree only to a set of goals, not a policy commitment.[14] The developing countries, frustrated with the realities of trade and with the structure of governance, turned to a new strategy: changing the GATT not from within but through an assault from without.

Unity and Confrontation

Beginning in 1961, the South developed a united front to press the North for changes in trade governance and in the operation of the international trading system. In Third World conferences and in the United Nations General Assembly, where the South commanded a majority, the developing countries pushed through their demands for trade and other economic reforms. A key plank in the Southern platform was a call for an international conference on trade and development. Confronted with the South's persistence and growing unity plus its increasing numerical control of the General Assembly, the North agreed to convene a United Nations Conference on Trade and Development (UNCTAD), which was held in 1964.[15]

The Southern countries then focused on achieving trade reform through UNCTAD. They formed the Group of Seventy-Seven (G-77), named for the cosponsors of the Joint Declaration of the Developing Countries made to the General Assembly in 1963.[16] The declaration spelled out for the first time its common goals for trade reform:

> The existing principles and patterns of world trade still mainly favor
> the advanced parts of the world. Instead of helping the developing
> countries to promote the development and diversification of their
> economies, the present tendencies in world trade frustrate their efforts
> to attain more rapid growth. These trends must be reversed.[17]

In order to make international trade "a more powerful instrument and vehicle of economic development,"[18] the G-77 offered a series of goals for UNCTAD, ranging from the improvement of institutional arrangements to the progressive reduction and early elimination of all barriers and restrictions impeding Southern exports (without reciprocal concessions on their part), to increased exports of primary products to the developed countries, and the stabilization and establishment of fair prices.[19] The G-77, which retained its original name but which came to include 130 states by 2008,[20] became a permanent political group representing Southern interests within the UN system.

UNCTAD also became a permanent United Nations organization in 1964.[21] Its doctrine, which served as a basis for united G-77 action, was developed by UNCTAD's first secretary-general, Raúl Prebisch.[22] In UNCTAD's structuralist analysis of North–South relations, the world is divided into a center (the developed countries) and a periphery (the developing countries). The market works against the developing countries because of the long-term structural decline in Southern terms of trade and because of Northern protectionist policies that discriminate against Southern exports. As a result, the South has "a persistent tendency toward external imbalance"— what Prebisch called the "trade gap." Unless measures are taken to counteract the structural bias against the South and to fill the trade gap, argued UNCTAD, the underdeveloped countries will not be able to meet reasonable growth targets.

The united Southern front did not greatly alter the governance of trade or the operation of the international market. The South was divided by politics, ideology, differing levels of development, and different relations with Northern states. Despite agreement on common general goals, these differences made it difficult to reach agreement on specific, short-term policies. The cleavages also prevented the group from establishing priorities and contributed to the accumulation and escalation of demands, which politicized conflict and confrontation with the North and prevented serious bargaining.[23] The South was also weakened by a united front of Northern opposition to the creation of a powerful UNCTAD and the North's insistence on dealing with trade issues in the GATT. The South's marginal economic importance, its declining importance as an area of superpower competition, and its own internal divisions enabled the North to defeat, weaken, or ignore the South's proposed resolutions.

Nevertheless, UNCTAD became a permanent United Nations organization, albeit one with no negotiating authority. The North also agreed to add to the GATT agreement a new section on trade and development. Part IV, which came into operation in 1965 and which is nonbinding,[24] called on states to refrain from increasing trade barriers against products of special concern to the developing countries, to give priority to the reduction and elimination of such barriers, and to implement a standstill on internal taxes on tropical products. More important, Part IV provided for exceptions to the free-trade rules for the developing countries: It eliminated the rule of reciprocity in trade negotiations and accepted commodity agreements to stabilize and ensure more equitable prices. Finally, the new section called for joint action to promote trade and development, which was the basis for establishing a Trade and Development Committee in the GATT to work on the elimination and reduction of trade barriers.

The continued weakness of the developing countries in the GATT was evidenced during the Kennedy Round negotiations of 1964 to 1967 (the first trade negotiation that followed the implementation of Part IV). Although developing countries participated actively for the first time, the results of the round for the South were slim. Restrictions against Southern manufactures, such as textile products and clothing, remained higher than the norm; agricultural protectionism, including that on tropical products, remained intact; and quantitative restrictions and nontariff barriers continued to limit Southern exports generally.[25]

The South had one minor success: preferential access to developed country markets for industrial exports from developing countries. Preferences, argued the South, would help Southern industries overcome the problem of high initial costs of infant industries and, by opening larger markets, would enable them to achieve economies of scale, lower their costs, and eventually compete in world markets without preferences.[26]

Following years of conflict over the concept of a **generalized system of preferences (GSP)**, agreement was reached in 1968 on the principle of establishing a preferential scheme, and in 1971, the GATT authorized the preference scheme. However, there were important limits on GSP schemes implemented by the Northern states.[27] Because the North was unable to agree on a common general system, individual states adopted similar but different schemes. These individual preference schemes have been temporary, subject to ceiling limitations on the quantity or value imports and exclude many import-sensitive goods for which the South enjoys a comparative advantage.[28] Furthermore, evidence suggests that only

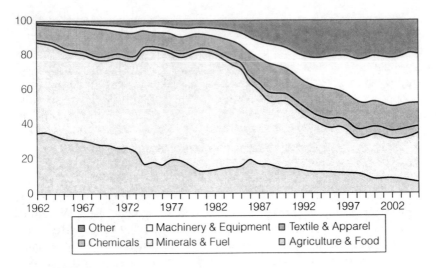

FIGURE 7.2 Share of Developing Country Exports by Broad Commodity Categories, 1962–2005, in Percentages

SOURCE: World Bank World Integrated Trade Solution (WITS).

a few countries, including South Korea and Hong Kong, have benefited from GSP and that these countries could have competed in international markets without any preferences.[29]

The story of commodity schemes, the third Southern demand, was shorter and even less successful.[30] Commodities and raw materials used to represent a huge share of Southern exports and foreign exchange earnings. In 1962, for example, over 80 percent of the South's export earnings came from raw materials and commodities; by 2005, only 40 percent of exports were in this category (see Figure 7.2). Developing countries were still highly dependent on exports of raw materials and commodities, but exports of manufactures and services grew more rapidly in value than primary exports, especially because of the rapid growth in exports from Asian countries.

The problems of commodity trade are numerous: price fluctuations that affect foreign exchange earnings; Northern protectionism and discriminatory tax policies; and competition from synthetics and substitutes.[31] Southern proposals to UNCTAD were equally numerous: commodity agreements to stabilize prices and to establish remunerative and equitable prices; compensatory finance schemes to ease earnings fluctuations; the liberalization of Northern protection against Southern commodities; and aid for products facing competition from substitutes and synthetics. The North successfully resisted all such proposals.[32]

In sum, Southern unity and confrontation without further leverage proved to be weak bargaining tools. The UNCTAD "victories" led to only minor revisions in Southern dependence. The result was more frustration in and hostility from the developing world.

INTERDEPENDENCE: STRATEGIES TO INCREASE SOUTHERN POWER

Commodity Power and the New International Economic Order

In the 1970s, the South discovered a tool to use in its bargaining with the North: commodity power. The North was becoming increasingly dependent on a variety of raw material imports from the South. While overall consumption was rising, high-grade Northern supplies of many materials were being depleted, and extraction in the North was becoming increasingly expensive. Because supplies in the developing countries were plentiful and production costs were low, demand for raw material imports from the developing countries was increasing.[33]

An economic boom in the developed countries at the end of the 1960s and the beginning of the 1970s led to a surge in Northern demand for raw materials from the developing countries. Inflation and the uncertainties of floating exchange rates led to a shift of speculative funds into commodities, further increasing demand and creating price increases and supply shortages. Furthermore, as the oil crisis demonstrated, the North's ability to ensure access to supplies through political and military action was weakened by the end of colonialism and the waning influence of the West on Third World governments. Suddenly, in the early 1970s, OPEC's ability to seize control of the international oil system suggested that Southern producers could pose a serious threat to the North by withholding or threatening to withhold supplies of raw materials (see Chapter 9). Not surprisingly, many developing countries concluded that the North was now vulnerable to commodity threats.

The credibility of the threat was enhanced by a growing Southern ability to control access to their raw materials. New, skilled cadres in many Southern states had acquired expertise in the raw materials industry and in world commodity market conditions and operations (see Chapter 8). Greater national control over raw material production facilitated the control of supplies. Moreover, as frustration with the North grew, the South's political leaders become more willing to use these new skills to manipulate raw material supplies.

Southern states united to use aggressively the commodity weapon and other economic and political resources at their disposal to persuade the North to restructure the international economic system (for commodity cartels, see Chapter 9). At Third World Conferences in 1974, 1975, and 1976, the G-77 drew up a coordinated program for a new international economic order (NIEO). The South proclaimed that

> [t]he developing world has become a powerful factor that makes its
> influence felt in all fields of international activity. These irreversible
> changes in the relationship of forces in the world necessitate the active,
> full and equal participation of the developing countries in the formulation and application of all decisions that concern the international
> community.[34]

While the Southern program for the new international economic order touched all areas of international economic interaction, the South placed special emphasis on trade reform. It called for a reduction in Northern tariff barriers on a nonreciprocal basis, improvement in the preference schemes implemented by the developed countries, and international commodity agreements, and an Integrated Programme for Commodities that was to consist of an international agency and a common fund of $6 billion to support the prices of ten commodities.[35]

The ability of the developing countries to change the old economic order depended in part on Southern unity. The South stood a much better chance of forcing the North to make concessions if it could link its various potential commodity threats and if it could link the oil threat, the inducement of an international agreement on oil prices, or OPEC's considerable financial power to other Third World demands. However, unifying this heterogeneous group of states continued to be a difficult task. The impact of rising oil prices on the oil-importing developing countries and the growing economic divergence between the newly industrialized countries (NICs) and the other developing countries were particularly divisive.

Initially, the South demonstrated a surprising degree of cohesion. Over a decade of common action gave the group an understanding of how to conduct international negotiations. Some oil producers, Algeria and Venezuela in particular, played a leadership role in mobilizing a common Southern front and linking the oil issue to other Third World demands. The credibility of the South's threat to the North was enhanced by the projections of most resource economists at this time that demand for developing country raw materials would rise due to the rapid growth in consumption of durable goods and the depletion of known mineral resources.[36] Because of the perceived seriousness of the commodity threat, coupled with Northern concerns about growing financial linkages with the developing countries, the tremendous financial power of the capital-surplus oil exporters, and a growing interest in Southern markets, the developed countries agreed to several special sessions of the United Nations General Assembly to discuss the NIEO and they supported special producer-consumer negotiations.

European countries that were more vulnerable to supply interruption were the most receptive to the NIEO demands. The EC, for example, agreed to the first **Lomé Convention** between the Community and forty-six associated **African, Caribbean, and Pacific (ACP) states**.[37] The agreement increased aid to the ACP states and gave them a greater voice in aid governance; provided for preferential access for ACP products to EC markets without reciprocal advantages for EC products; and created a compensatory finance scheme, **STABEX**, to stabilize the export earnings of the associated states from twelve key commodities.[38]

The United States—more self-sufficient and, thus, less vulnerable to external supply control—felt that the developed market economies should not make impetuous bargains with the South based on what it saw as a temporarily unfavorable situation. In the view of U.S. policymakers, the only threat came from the oil-producing states. When the Southern oil consumers recognized that OPEC was damaging their economies, the United States believed they would turn on the oil producers. The cyclical factors that led to temporary Northern vulnerability would eventually disappear and commodity prices would fall.

As the 1970s wore on, the North did come to feel less vulnerable. The oil countries, in particular the Gulf states, were not willing to use their leverage on behalf of other developing countries. Furthermore, as raw material prices began to decline, it became clear that the rise in commodity prices in the 1970s was a cyclical and not a structural phenomenon. Finally, developing countries were unable to unite to create cartels similar to OPEC.

The various efforts to establish a new international economic order (held in the 1970s) revealed the limits of Southern power. The results of the **Conference on International Economic Cooperation (CIEC)**, which met from 1975 to 1977 were meager: an agreement in principle to establish a common fund for commodity-price stabilization, a promise by the North to redouble its efforts to reach the 0.7-percent-of-GNP aid target, and a pledge by the North to give $1 billion to the least-developed countries. The common fund was eventually adopted by UNCTAD in 1980 but never implemented because of an inadequate number of ratifications. The 0.7-percent target was not reached. And the $1 billion for the least-developed countries had, by and large, already been committed.[39]

UNCTAD efforts to create an Integrated Programme on Commodities were also unsuccessful. UNCTAD called for the negotiation of **international commodity agreements (ICAs)** for raw materials exports important to developing countries and the establishment of a common fund to stabilize the prices of developing country commodities.

ICAs are accords among producers and consumers designed to stabilize or increase the price of particular products. They may be of three types or combinations thereof: (1) **buffer-stock** schemes, such as that of the International Tin Agreement, whereby price is managed by purchases or sales from a central fund at times of excessive fluctuation; (2) export quotas, such as those used by the International Coffee Agreement, whereby price is managed by assigning production quotas to participating countries in order to control supply; and (3) multilateral contracts, whereby the importing countries contract to buy certain quantities at a specified low price when the world market falls below that price and the exporting countries agree to sell certain quantities at a fixed price when the world market price exceeds the maximum.

UNCTAD's efforts to implement international commodity agreements foundered on the traditional problems of ICAs. Producers who would like to use ICAs to raise prices and consumers who want only to stabilize prices often have difficulty agreeing on objectives. When they have been able to reach agreement, ICAs have been plagued by such problems as temptations to cheat when prices rise, variations of price and supply among different qualities of the same commodity, encouragement of using substitutes, the difficulty of imposing drastic production or export reductions, the high cost of financing buffer stocks, and the political and financial difficulty of managing an ICA when there is a long-term downward trend in commodity prices. Moreover, most Northern governments oppose ICAs as inefficient, encouraging waste and the misallocation of resources, helpful to only a few developing countries, and actually damaging to others faced with higher prices due to ICAs.[40] Despite UNCTAD efforts, few ICAs—tin, sugar, coffee, cocoa, natural rubber, and tropical timber—have been negotiated. Most of these date back to the 1960s and are not a result of UNCTAD's efforts. Only the rubber and tropical timber agreements were formally concluded under UNCTAD, and the latter provides only for cooperation and consultation on product and market development, conservation and reforestation, not on price stabilization.[41]

UNCTAD's common fund never saw the light of day.[42] Although the Southern vision of the new international economic order was never implemented, there were some limited achievements in the 1970s. Both the IMF and the EEC established compensatory financing facilities that attempted to stabilize or increase the export earnings of developing countries by lending money to them when the fall in the price of a commodity leads to a decline in export earnings.[43]

During the GATT's Tokyo Round of multilateral trade negotiations that took place from 1975 to 1979, the developing countries obtained "special and differential treatment" which exempted developing countries from the GATT's rules on reciprocity and most-favored-nation obligations, gave permanent legal authorization for GSP preferences and preferences in trade between developing countries and authorized special favorable treatment for the least-developed developing countries.[44]

In return, the developed countries insisted on the inclusion of a "graduation clause" in the GATT articles. This clause set forth the principle that as Southern countries reached higher levels of development, preferential treatment would be withdrawn and countries would be expected to assume the full rights and obligations of the GATT.[45] One problem with the graduation provision was that it included no criteria or standards for graduation.

By the close of the 1970s, the South's strategy based on unity, commodity power, and the NIEO had reached a dead end. While the G-77 continued to call for its vision of a new international economic order in the United Nations and UNCTAD, developments in the international market were changing the South's bargaining power and creating a very different economic order.

Export-Led Growth

By the 1980s, commodity power had proved an illusion. Despite the predictions of experts that the world faced a future of ever-diminishing raw materials, the soaring commodity prices of the mid-1970s turned out to be a cyclical phenomenon. If anything, the long-term trend seemed to be a decline and not an increase in the growth of world demand for raw materials. In the 1970s and 1980s, rates of growth of GNP in the developed countries fell from the rapid rates of the 1960s, thus slowing demand for commodities. Demand also declined as output in the Northern states shifted away from manufacturing to services, which use far fewer raw materials (see Chapter 3). The dramatic rise in prices in the 1970s encouraged conservation, greater recycling, and the substitution of traditional materials by synthetics or by technology and energy-intensive materials. This decline in demand growth combined with a new capacity created by investment during the commodity shortages of the 1970s led to excess capacity, oversupply, and weakening of prices.[46]

TABLE 7.1   Share of Non-Oil Commodities in Total Exports of Low-Income Countries, 2003–2005

Country	Share (%)	Which Focus Commodities are Important?
Burundi	93.76	Coffee
Mali	89.32	Cotton
United Rep. of Tanzania	85.18	(gold), cotton, coffee, tobacco
Malawi	85.00	Tobacco
Burkina Faso	84.24	Cotton
Ghana	83.22	(gold), cocoa
Rwanda	82.01	Coffee
Benin	81.40	Cotton
Nicaragua	74.54	Coffee
Zimbabwe	73.71	tobacco, cotton
Ethiopia	73.61	Coffee
Uganda	72.07	Coffee
Honduras	63.35	Coffee
Côte d'Ivoire	59.15	cocoa, coffee, cotton
Togo	58.47	cocoa, coffee, cotton
Kenya	51.40	tea

SOURCE: Colin Poulton, "Bulk Export Commodities: Trends and Challenges," Background Paper for the *World Development Report 2008*, p. 7.

Prices of non-oil commodities of developing countries fell by 24 percent between 1980 and 1986. They recovered somewhat, rising 14 percent between 1986 and 1988, but then fell again by 16.6 percent between 1989 and 1993.[47] From 1985 to 1992, the terms of trade fell by 10 percent for the low-income developing countries, by 4, 2, and 0 percent, respectively, for the lower-middle, middle, and upper-middle income developing economies.[48] From 1982 to 1991, the industrial countries' terms of trade improved by an average rate of .9 percent per year. It increased by only .1 percent per year between 1992 and 2001.[49]

The decline in commodity prices seriously affected the poorest of the developing countries, who still relied heavily on commodity exports. For example, the value of Zambia's exports, over 90 percent of which are copper, declined by over one-half between 1980 and 1985. In the same period, Liberia's export earnings, largely from iron ore and rubber, and Bolivia's earnings, largely from tin, declined by nearly 40 percent.[50] Table 7.1 shows the dependency of various low-income countries on exports of specific non-oil commodities, such as coffee, tea, cocoa, cotton, tobacco, and gold. Table 7.2 illustrates how the prices of commodities

TABLE 7.2   Trade in Selected Commodities Ranked by Unit Price Change, 1993/95–2003/05

Commodity	Change in volume 93/5 to 03/05 (%)	Change in value 93/5 to 03/05 (%)	Unit.price change 93/5 to 03/05 (%)	Av. value of trade 1993-95 ($ bill.)	Av. value of trade 2003-05 ($ bill.)
Fresh & chilled Veg	69.7	106.8	17.5	3.2	6.7
Soybeans	99.9	118.9	9.5	7.1	15.5
Bananas	39.7	43.4	3.1	3.5	5
Tea	54	65.4	3	1.8	3
Cotton	48.3	51.1	1.9	5.4	8.1
Beef	21.5	23.4	1.6	14.9	18.4
Corn/Maize	25.6	21.5	-0.3	9.3	11.3
Cocoa	44.3	38.3	-4.2	2.5	3.5
Cut flowers	72.9	48.7	-4.4	3.4	5.1
Natural Rubber	45.2	38.6	-4.5	5.4	7.5
Tropical Logs	-12.6	-20.8	-9.3	2.3	1.8
Trop. S/wood	-5.1	-15.9	-11.5	2.9	2.4
Sugar	38.8	14.6	-17.7	9.2	10.5
Chicken	97.8	61.3	-18.4	6.9	11.1
Rice	67.5	41.7	-18.4	5.2	7.4
Coffee	16.9	-32	-41.9	8.6	5.9
Seafood	n/a	47.8	n/a	31.1	46

SOURCE: Colin Poulton, "Bulk Export Commodities: Trends and Challenges," Background Paper for the *World Development Report 2008*, p. 4.

like coffee and cocoa have declined in the last decade. While some commodities like tea went up somewhat in price, the increase was modest.

While many of the poorest developing countries were caught in the collapse of commodity prices, others were developing strong manufacturing capabilities and increasing their exports of manufactured products. In the 1970s, export-oriented industrialization policies of a number of developing countries began to bear fruit. Lower labor costs in labor-intensive industries, such as textiles and shoes, and production innovations often acquired or adapted from the North, as in the case of steel, consumer electronics, and semiconductors, enabled certain developing countries to compete successfully in Northern markets. **Big-box retailers** like Kmart and Wal-Mart began to use manufacturers in export-oriented developing countries as suppliers of low-cost consumer items.[51]

From 1970 to 1990, the share of manufactured goods in exports from the developing countries doubled, reaching 57.5 percent of the total value of their exports in 1990, up from 23.7 percent in 1970. By 1993, Southern manufactured

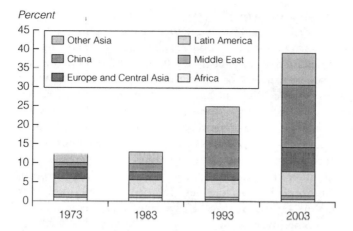

FIGURE 7.3 Developed Countries' Imports of Manufactures from Developing Countries, 1973–2003

SOURCE: World Trade Organization.

exports accounted for 27 percent of world manufactured exports; by 2003, it was almost 45 percent.[52] Southern manufactures also came to represent a large share of Northern imports. Between 1963 and 1987, Southern manufactures increased from 4 to 13 percent of their share of industrial country manufactured imports.[53] By 1990, 32 percent of U.S. imports of manufactured products came from developing countries, up from 15 percent in 1972. In 1990, Japan obtained 11 percent of its manufactured imports from the South, up from 18 percent in 1972.[54] Imports, by the developed countries, of manufactures from the developing countries continued to increase rapidly (see Figure 7.3).

The principal beneficiaries of this change in the structure of trade initially were the NICs, especially the four Asian tigers—South Korea, Taiwan, Singapore, and Hong Kong.[55] In the 1950s and early 1960s, the East Asian NICs, with the exception of Hong Kong, had followed successful import substitution policies. Domestic production of consumer nondurables replaced imports, resulting in a period of rapid growth. However, in the 1960s and 1970s, import substitution reached its limits. Expansion into machinery and consumer durables would have required extending protection and investment into more capital-intensive sectors; the costs of deepening import substitution would have been high given the small domestic markets in these countries; and domestic industries would not have been able to take advantage of economies of scale without expanding into foreign markets via exports.

The four tigers also realized they needed the foreign exchange earnings to import essential goods including raw materials. For South Korea and Taiwan, which were receiving extensive foreign assistance, export earnings would eventually have to replace foreign aid as a source of financing. However, import substitution discriminated against export sectors. Protection raised the cost of imported inputs essential for many export industries and thus decreased export competitiveness. In addition, import substitution was often accompanied by overvalued currencies that increased the price of exports.

The switch to **export-led growth policies** did not mean eliminating all protection. All the tigers except Hong Kong retained many import tariffs and quantitative restrictions. Outward-oriented policies did mean eliminating the bias against exports: maintaining realistic exchange rates that did not discriminate against exports, reducing import barriers for inputs to the export sector, as well as removing any other export disincentives such as export taxes. In South Korea, Taiwan, and Singapore, outward-oriented policies also involved government promotion of exports through favorable credit terms for exporters, tax incentives, undervalued exchange rates that decreased export prices, encouragement of foreign investment in export industries, and direct subsidies for targeted sectors. Tiger governments were criticized for targeting certain sectors, such as the heavy and chemical industries in South Korea, that were relatively less successful than industries that were "chosen" by the markets. However, general export incentives clearly aided the competitiveness of the NICs. Exports also increased through "offshore assembly" or "sourcing" arrangements, whereby multinational companies were encouraged to invest for export (see Chapter 8).[56]

These strategies led to a dramatic increase in exports. The four tigers' share of world trade increased from around 2 percent in 1960 to 10.5 percent in 2006.[57] The four tigers accounted for around a quarter of the manufactured exports from developing countries in 2000. With the addition of several other middle-income countries such as Brazil, Mexico, and Argentina, the share of the NICs of manufactured exports from developing countries reached almost 70 percent in 1998.[58] The four tigers' share in OECD imports of manufactured goods increased from 1.3 percent in 1964 to 5.6 percent in 2000.[59] More importantly, outward-oriented strategies resulted in higher growth rates than inward-oriented policies.[60]

Theoretical Controversies over Export-Led Growth

There was controversy among specialists in development economics about the reasons for the success of the Asian tigers. Some stressed the importance of the market liberalization policies, while others stressed the importance of government intervention via industrial polices. The former included key analysts at the World Bank and the International Monetary Fund;[61] the latter consisted mainly of academic economists and political scientists.[62] The views of the former were consistent with the Washington Consensus (see Chapter 6) and of what came increasingly to be called **neo-liberalism**. The latter came to be seen as advocates of a school of thought that advocated a **developmental state**—a state that actively and successfully promoted economic development. This was an important debate because it would help to shape the policies of both governments and international organizations during the period of globalization.

Many economists were skeptical about the claims of the developmental state school of thought that industrial policies could account for the rapid growth of the Asian tigers.[63] They were trying to make as strong a case as possible for the need to reduce artificial restraints on the market in the developing world and the desirability of opening the economy to both trade and investment flows. Their research focused on the strong correlation between openness and economic growth and downplayed the role of governmental policies or governmental institutions in ensuring that economic openness would have desirable effects. Their general perspective on the role of the state was that it was part of the problem and therefore could not be part of the solution.

Political economists from various disciplines—including political science, sociology, and economics—argued, in contrast, that it was precisely the existence of appropriate governmental policies and institutions that enabled the Asian tigers to make the difficult transition from import substitution to export-led growth. Openness without these policies and institutions could and would lead to bad results.

After the World Bank and the International Monetary Fund used structural adjustment programs to impose openness policies on developing countries, which had adopted import substitution policies, the consequences were sometimes quite negative, at least in the short run. In Jamaica, for example, agriculture and food processing industries had grown in the 1970s under high tariffs on imports as part of an import substitution strategy. When those tariffs were eliminated, many farmers and food processors went out of business. Urban Jamaicans benefited from lower prices of food in the shops, but rural Jamaicans suffered greatly as a result. When barriers to foreign investment were eliminated, some MNCs invested in manufacturing of products requiring low-skilled labor in export processing zones. As soon as wages rose, they moved their investments to countries with lower wages. Opponents of globalization fastened upon these kinds of displacements in their arguments against further liberalization of trade and investment flows.[64]

New Pressures for Protection in North–South Trade

The success of the four tigers, however, created strong pressures for protection in the North. In the 1980s, the United States removed GSP privileges from these countries, limited imports of textiles, footwear, and steel and other items, and put pressure on the Asian NICs to allow their currencies to appreciate vis-à-vis the dollar.[65] The United States also put pressure on South Korea and Taiwan to remove domestic protection and open their markets to U.S. goods and services. In the 1990s, this pressure was directed toward other Asian countries also experiencing rapid export growth, including the People's Republic of China.

The trade problems of the Asian NICs were characteristic of North–South trade relations generally. Southern manufactured imports posed a significant threat to important industrial sectors with high concentrations of employment in the North and thus provoked powerful political pressures for protection. As a result, North–South trade in manufactures was increasingly subjected to trade barriers, especially voluntary export restraints.

The classic example was textiles.[66] The South has a comparative advantage in significant portions of the textile industry, which are labor-intensive and require simple technology. Those same segments of the textile industry, however, represent an important share of the GDP and employment of the developed countries. Furthermore, the textile industry tends to be geographically concentrated and well organized politically, making it a powerful force in domestic trade politics in all the developed countries.

In 1962, as some LDCs became competitive in Northern textile markets, the members of the GATT negotiated the Long-Term Arrangement (LTA) regarding international trade in cotton textiles that allowed for such departures from the GATT as quotas on textile imports and regulation of market share. Restrictive bilateral agreements were then negotiated within the framework of the LTA.[67] In 1974, when LDCs had become competitive in artificial fibers and wool, the GATT contracting parties concluded the Arrangement Regarding International Trade in Textiles, known as the Multi-Fiber Arrangement (MFA). It created a multilateral framework for restricting trade in textiles, under which specific bilateral controls are negotiated. Over the years, MFA agreements were regularly extended and made more restrictive by broadening the coverage and lowering the growth in market share of the LDCs. By 1986, 61 percent of Southern exports of textile yarn and fabrics and 78 percent of Southern exports of clothing were subjected to import restrictions.[68] Originally intended as temporary safeguard measures, the textile agreements became firmly entrenched institutionally, and significantly limited textile exports of the LDCs.[69]

The case of textiles was repeated, in less comprehensive but equally pernicious ways, in many other sectors. Voluntary export restraints (VERs) increasingly restricted Southern access to Northern markets. Forty-seven percent of all export restraint arrangements in place in 1987 applied to exports from developing countries.[70]

As a result of the new importance of manufactures and new forms of protectionism, the trade policy of the LDCs focused more and more on access to the markets of the developed countries in general and on controlling VERs in particular. A new safeguards agreement in the GATT became a high priority concern for the South in the Uruguay Round. The increasing importance of manufactured exports also raised the graduation issue. As the NICs became more competitive in a variety of manufactured products, the Northern governments claimed that they no longer deserved special privileges such as GSP or special and differential treatment in the GATT. In several forums, the North began to demand that the NICs graduate and assume the same commitments and responsibilities in the international trading system as the developed countries.

In the 1970s, the South became not only an important exporter of manufactured products to the North, but it also became a more important market for the developed countries. From 1973 to 2000, the developing countries' share of the merchandise exports from the developed countries rose from 17 to 28 percent.[71] In 2006, 48.2 percent of U.S. exports went to developing countries, up from 37 percent in 1980 and 29 percent in 1973.[72]

The LDC debt crisis demonstrated the significance of Southern trade for the North. In an effort to generate foreign exchange to service their debt, developing countries reduced imports through austerity policies, rationing of foreign exchange, and import restrictions. Imports by the highly indebted countries grew at an average of 5.5 percent from 1973 to 1980 and fell by 6.3 percent per year on average between 1980 and 1987.[73] From 1980 to 1987, total U.S. exports increased 8 percent, but exports to Latin America dropped 19 percent; worldwide U.S. exports of manufactured goods fell 23 percent, but manufactured exports to Latin America fell 32 percent.[74] At the same time, in order to increase foreign exchange earnings, debtor countries tried to export more to the North, thus aggravating protectionist pressures. United States imports from the heavily indebted countries increased by 18 percent between 1980 and 1987.[75]

The New Pragmatism

The new realities of the 1980s altered the trade strategy of the developing countries. The South's demand for a new international economic order was undermined by the collapse of commodity power, including the OPEC threat; by deep cracks in the G-77's solidarity, as several advanced developing countries were integrated into the existing international economic order; and by the weakened economic position of the South, especially the debt crisis. Meanwhile, the North was becoming both more protectionist at home and more insistent on market-oriented policies abroad. As we have seen, one of the main elements of Northern policies for developing country debtors was the implementation of domestic market-oriented reforms and international liberalization (see Chapter 6). The South's main bargaining chip in such a situation was to persuade the North that maintenance of world economic stability and prosperity depended on improving the lot of the developing countries.

The new forces of the 1980s also called into question the effectiveness of the South's preferred forums for governance, especially UNCTAD and the United Nations. Although the South continued to use these forums to call for a new international economic order, the North–South dialogue in the United Nations system increasingly became a dialogue of the deaf.

As the strategy of confrontation and the NIEO collapsed, developing countries shifted their focus to the GATT. One reason for the shift was the pressure of the developed countries, especially the United States, for a new round of multilateral negotiations. (see Chapter 3). Developed countries wanted a new multilateral trade round to bring agriculture and the so-called "new" areas of trade (services, intellectual property rights, and investment) under GATT discipline. There was also a growing sense of alarm at the proliferation of protectionist measures both outside of and in violation of the WTO rules. The United States, in particular, became convinced that without significant reform of the GATT rules and procedures, the GATT system would become increasingly divorced from economic reality and would ultimately collapse.

The dramatic export success of the newly industrialized countries was another motivation behind the drive for a new multilateral trade round. As concern mounted over the NICs' deepening penetration of U.S. and European markets, the industrialized countries accused the NICs of "free riding" on the international system by continuing to take advantage of the special treatment accorded developing countries by the GATT and by GSP programs despite overwhelming evidence that they had now become internationally competitive exporters. The industrialized countries insisted that the time had come for the NICs to "graduate" from developing country status (and the attendant benefits) and to be fully integrated into the GATT system, thereby becoming subject to obligations consonant with their new economic stature. As part of this push for "graduation," in January 1989 the United States removed the four tigers of Asia from the list of nations eligible for GSP privileges.

The industrialized countries also complained that the NICs engaged in unfair trade practices, ranging from export subsidies and dumping to restrictions on foreign imports and direct investment. The developed countries, especially the United States, also criticized the NICs for maintaining undervalued currencies that served to promote exports. Consequently, the number of bilateral trade disputes and unilateral trade actions initiated against these countries by the United States and by EC member states rose dramatically.

While most concern focused on the NICs, developed countries also increased pressure on the non-NIC developing countries to liberalize their domestic trade and economic regimes, arguing that protectionist policies and demands for "special and differential" treatment made little economic sense. This change in approach was most evident in the growing emphasis of the World Bank and the IMF on the need for developing countries to undertake "structural" market-oriented economic reforms. A parallel approach was evident in the U.S. determination to use a new trade round to circumscribe the definition and application of "special and differential" treatment, to reform the GATT provision permitting developing countries to institute trade restrictions for "balance of payments" reasons, and to persuade developing countries to bind—and perhaps reduce tariffs for—a substantial portion of their tariff schedules.

At the same time, the developing countries had become increasingly dissatisfied with what they regarded as the meager gains of previous trade rounds. Although, as discussed previously, some developing countries had participated in the GATT negotiations, most had chosen to take a passive role, largely out of the conviction that the GATT—as a "rich man's club"—had little to offer poor countries with no substantial political or economic leverage. Since tariff reductions agreed to in the GATT were applied on a most-favored-nation (MFN) basis, developing countries felt they could reap the benefits of the GATT negotiations without necessarily participating. Furthermore, since most developing countries played a very small role in international trade, they had little incentive to engage in pragmatic bargaining and preferred to take an ideological stance marked by North–South confrontation, as discussed earlier in this chapter.

By the late 1980s, however, developing countries had become more dependent than ever on trade, and their stake in the maintenance of a liberal international trading regime had risen proportionately. In 1970 the average ratio of exports to gross domestic product in the developing countries was 10 percent. By 2006, that ratio had grown to 35 percent.[76] A handful of countries—the NICs—had become highly successful exporters in a relatively short time, and other developing countries were eager to follow in their footsteps. Given the failure of the inward-looking economic policies of the past, the example of successful export-led growth of the NICs, and the continuing commodity and debt crises, the developing countries were forced to reevaluate their development strategies. Slowly but surely, a number of developing countries began reforming their domestic economic policies, liberalizing their trade regimes, and shifting toward a more export-oriented growth strategy.[77]

The importance of actively participating in the GATT was underlined by rising protectionism against developing country exports. Between 1981 and 1986, the EC, Japan, and the United States collectively increased the application of "hard-core" nontariff barriers from 19 to 21 percent of their imports from developing countries, compared to an increase from 13 to 16 percent for imports from other industrialized countries. The figures are even more telling for individual export sectors. Nontariff barriers were applied by the industrial market economies to 55 percent of iron and steel imports and 31 percent of manufactures imports (nonchemicals) from developing countries, including 80 percent of clothing imports and 27 percent of footwear imports.[78]

Market access thus became a priority trade issue for the developing countries in the 1980s and 1990s. Despite market access problems in Japan and Europe, the primary focus of this fear was the United States, which for many developing countries was by far their largest export market. As the United States continued to toughen its trade laws and as nontariff barriers continued to multiply, many developing countries came to view the GATT as their only chance of imposing discipline on U.S. trade policy and ensuring continued access to U.S. markets. This view was reinforced by the negotiation of NAFTA, which some countries saw as an indication that the United States was turning away from multilateralism. The European Community's renewed efforts after 1985 to achieve full economic integration similarly provoked fear that the GATT system was on the verge of disintegrating into protectionist regional and bilateral trading blocs. Developing countries also hoped that the Uruguay Round would force Japan to offer greater access to its markets.

Finally, by the mid-1980s there was greater recognition of the diversity of interests among developing countries and the problems that posed for the traditional bloc approach to relations with the North. At one extreme were the NICs, some of which seemed on the verge of joining the exclusive club of industrialized nations. At the other extreme were the poorest developing countries, clinging to the frayed margins of the international trading system. In the middle lay a wide range of countries at different levels of economic development, each differing in its degree of export dependence, in comparative advantage, and in its political and social objectives. In the face of such diversity, many developing countries came to believe that their interests would best be served by a pragmatic rather than ideological or bloc approach to negotiations in the GATT.

GLOBALIZATION: JOINING THE TRADE REGIME

The Uruguay Round

Initially, the developing countries resisted the call by the developed countries for a new trade round and argued that instead of discussing new issues, the GATT talks should focus on old, unresolved issues. For example, Brazil proposed addressing the elimination of nontariff barriers and the Multi-Fiber Arrangement, liberalization in trade of tropical products, restraint in the use of antidumping and subsidy actions, and an improved dispute settlement mechanism.[79] Using the threat of nonparticipation in the round to bargain for greater attention to Southern concerns, the LDCs achieved some concessions such as a special negotiating group and a commitment to an early agreement on tropical products. With these concessions in hand, they concurred in the 1986 agreement to launch the Uruguay Round and entered the negotiations determined to be active participants in the GATT process. While only 17 developing countries had joined the GATT in the 20 years up to 1987, between 1987 and 1994, 29 additional developing countries joined the organization. As of 2008, approximately 100 developing countries were members of the WTO.[80]

The most active developing country participants in the negotiations were those that believed they had a great deal at stake: the middle-income developing countries plus the so-called emerging low-income economies like China and India. A handful of countries chose to pursue a hard line, making traditional G-77 demands, for example, for unqualified "special and differential" treatment. The hard-line countries were led by Brazil and India, which had large domestic markets and felt they would lose from overly rapid liberalization of their economies.

Although many developing countries were reluctant to mar the appearance of Southern unity in international forums, they frequently chose to pursue a more pragmatic strategy in domestic, bilateral, and regional policies. Believing that only those who played the game had any chance of winning concessions, they worked with developing and industrialized countries alike in an effort to reach agreements on issues of importance to them. As a result, despite clear differences in priorities between the industrialized and developing countries, the Uruguay Round negotiations did not split along North–South lines. Instead, coalitions developed along issue lines which, in contrast to early rounds, often included both industrialized and developing countries. One pivotal coalition was the so-called "Cairns group" of fourteen agricultural exporting nations— nine of them developing countries—organized in 1986 to pressure the United States and the EC to find a solution to the problem of excess production and subsidization of agricultural products.[81] Many other North–South informal groupings developed in the course of the negotiations on issues as varied as non-tariff barriers, dispute settlement procedures, trade in services, tariffs, and tropical products.

Since the most important goal of the developing countries was increased access to industrialized country markets, they tended to focus their efforts in the Uruguay Round negotiations on such issues as enforcing the standstill and rollback of protectionist measures agreed to at the beginning of the trade round; bringing agriculture and textiles under GATT discipline; strengthening safeguards and discipline over "gray area" measures; eliminating nontariff barriers to trade; tightening GATT rules (e.g., the antidumping code) to limit the ability of developed countries to invoke their trade laws against alleged offending nations; and reforming the dispute settlement mechanism and other GATT procedures in order to improve surveillance and enforcement. The developing countries continued to insist on special treatment in recognition of their development needs, although a number of them indicated a willingness to be flexible on the precise form taken by such special treatment.

The strategy of pragmatic engagement led to important achievements for developing countries in the Uruguay Round (see Chapter 3).[82] Ninety-one developing countries participated in the negotiations, far more than in previous rounds, and their participation was more active and wide-ranging than ever before. As a result, they made important progress toward their goal of market access. For example, the Uruguay Round agreement provided for elimination over a ten-year period of quotas on textiles negotiated under the Multi-Fiber Arrangement, thus ending over 30 years of managed trade in textiles. The new regime for agricultural products that brought agriculture into the system of trade liberalization reflected the efforts of the developing country members of the Cairns group. And tariff cuts on a variety of tropical- and natural resource–based industrial products benefited developing countries.[83]

Developing countries also benefited from the development of new trading rules. The elimination of voluntary export restraints and import surveillance measures through the safeguards code was a significant achievement. In 1992, approximately 10 percent of all LDC exports to developed countries were covered by such gray area measures.[84] In addition, the new rules on antidumping stood to benefit developing countries who were often the subjects of such actions. Finally, developing countries were able to gain special treatment that enabled them to continue to use subsidies for development.

There was also some progress in the Uruguay Round Agreement on Agriculture. The industrialized countries' agreement to reduce agricultural subsidies by 20 percent by the year 2000 was a major victory for the South. In addition, the Agreement on Agriculture called for applying the same disciplines to agriculture as were applied to trade in manufactures, largely through the "tariffication" of nontariff barriers (see Chapter 3). Unfortunately, both developed and developing countries bound tariffs at levels far higher than actual or applied tariffs in many cases.

Concerning the so-called "new" issues under negotiation (services, intellectual property, and investment), the majority of developing countries were either lukewarm or hostile. They saw services, intellectual property, and investment negotiations as efforts aimed at changing developing country policies in areas not appropriately covered by the GATT. Only a handful of countries (e.g., the Asian tigers) expressed a qualified willingness to consider entering into agreements on these topics—and that was primarily because they suspected that they would be better off entering into multilateral agreements than being subjected to bilateral pressure from the developed countries, especially the United States.

Those developing countries that participated in the agreements on new issues were able to avoid having to give in to a number of developed countries' demands. For example, they insisted on and achieved long phase-in periods for implementation of intellectual property rules and resisted pressure to significantly open their financial services markets. All the developing countries insisted that any concessions on the "new" issues would be linked to progress made on the more traditional issues of importance to them.

In sum, while developing countries made important gains in the Uruguay Round, the task remained unfinished, both in gaining greater access to the markets of the developed countries and in reforming their own economies to meet the challenges of international markets. Despite these limitations, the Uruguay Round negotiations were a landmark in expanding the role of developing countries in the international trading system. Having concluded that the traditional strategies of import substitution and North–South confrontation had yielded few concrete benefits, the developing countries pursued more pragmatic policies and sought greater engagement in international trade. Forums traditionally preferred by the South such as UNCTAD became increasingly irrelevant as a locus for bargaining with the North; and the South shifted its attention to the new World Trade Organization (WTO). Previous nonmembers of the GATT, including China, Taiwan, and Vietnam, entered into negotiations for membership in the WTO. As a result of their achievements in the Uruguay round, developing countries now had a greater stake in the successful implementation of the round. In particular, developing countries became strong advocates of using the WTO's new rules and dispute settlement mechanisms as tools to defend themselves against Northern protectionism.

After the signing of the Marrakesh Treaty, the developing countries began calling for the completion of "unfinished business" from both the Tokyo and Uruguay Rounds. For example, the Secretary General of UNCTAD called for more access to markets for developing country goods and services, more access to **greenfield investments,**[85] an end to escalated tariffs in the shoe, apparel, and textile industries, restrictions on the abuse of antidumping laws by the industrialized nations, help for developing countries in developing the technical skills needed to take advantage of the dispute settlement machinery in the WTO, more finance for development needs, and a more sympathetic and flexible attitude on the part of the North toward the efforts of developing countries to pursue their own paths to development.[86] Overall, developing countries sought improved access to developed country markets for their manufactured products and agricultural exports. Specifically, they pressed the industrialized countries to honor their Uruguay Round commitments to reduce agricultural subsidies.

The Rise of the BRICs

In the late 1990s, a number of countries began to rival the Asian tigers in rapid economic growth. The four largest of these were Brazil, Russia, India, and China—the **BRIC** countries.[87] BRIC was a subset of a new category of countries called emerging markets that included both fast-growing developing countries and formerly communist countries (also called **transition economies**).[88] What made the BRICs distinctive was that they were considerably larger in population than the Asian tigers and hence had the possibility to eclipse the latter as major destinations/origins for both trade and investment flows.

The case of China was particularly important (see Chapter 10 for further details). China's exports increased from $184 billion in 1998 to $1.2 trillion in 2007 (see Figure 7.4). China's trade surplus increased from $44 billion in 1998 to $262 billion in 2007, leading to increasing pressure on China from both the United States and the European Union to upwardly revalue its currency, the yuan.

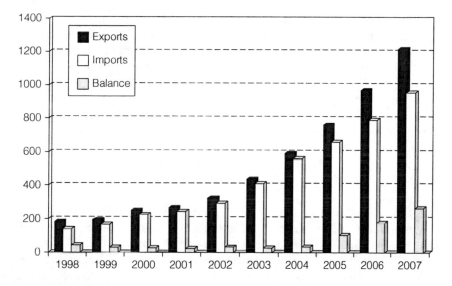

FIGURE 7.4   China's Imports, Exports, and Trade Balance, 1998–2007, in Billions of Dollars

SOURCE: U.S. International Trade Commission; U.S. Department of Commerce; and U.S. Census.

By the late 1990s, Brazil and India were abandoning the last vestiges of their import substitution strategies and began to focus, like the Asian tigers, on greater access to industrialized markets for their exports. In the mid-1990s, Brazil moved rapidly to reduce its chronic high inflation. The government adopted a stabilization plan for the real (Brazilian currency), in 1994 that reduced inflation and permitted a reduction in the country's external debt. Growth between 2003 and 2007 averaged around 2.3 percent, down from the previous average of around 5 percent as a result of efforts to eliminate deficits in government spending. The country continued to experience problems associated with low rates of savings and investment, low investment in public education, and high levels of crime and corruption. The government maintained trade and investment barriers in some industries that had been erected in earlier decades. Brazilian national champion firms, like Petrobras and Embraer (see Chapter 8), continued to receive preferential treatment. Nevertheless, public policy changed in a direction more favorable to integrating the Brazilian economy into the world economy. The stability of the Brazilian democratic system, responsible macroeconomic policies, the large potential size of the domestic market, and the country's success in increasing exports to other Latin American countries made Brazil an attractive site for new investments.[89]

In India, reforms adopted in 1991 reduced average tariff barriers from as high as 200 percent to below 15 percent. The financial sector was reformed so that Indian banks could operate under fewer restrictions. As in Brazil, the Indian government adopted macroeconomic policies that reduced inflation and began to reduce deficits in government spending. Unlike Brazil, India had not been able to accumulate a high level of external debt, so it did not face major debt servicing problems. After 2000, India undertook major investments in infrastructure, especially a new national highway network and efforts to improve access to the Internet. People began to move from impoverished rural areas to the major cities, where there was now a greater chance of supporting a family.

India still faced major problems quite similar to those in Brazil: an inadequate educational system, too much bureaucratic red tape (a leftover from the so-called "license Raj"), and low levels of savings and investment. Nevertheless, India experienced average growth rates of around 8 percent.[90] Major improvements in the living standards have occurred in the past two decades. Overall poverty levels declined, school enrollments increased, and urban–rural and gender gaps were reduced.[91]

The first international summit of foreign ministers of the BRICs was held in Yekaterinburg, Russia, on March 16, 2008, a sign that the leaders of the four countries were beginning to recognize their potential power in the world economy and were thinking about how to define and pursue their common interests.[92] All of the BRICs were members of the G-20 and three of them played key roles in the Doha Round.

The Doha Round

At the conclusion of the Uruguay Round in Marrakesh, the members of the WTO agreed to pursue future negotiations in what they called the built-in agenda. The built-in agenda items included agriculture, trade in services, anti-dumping, customs valuation, dispute settlement, import licensing, rules of origin, sanitary and phyto-sanitary measures, safeguards, subsidies and countervailing measures, technical barriers to trade, textiles and clothing, TRIPs, TRIMs, and theTrade Policy Review Mechanism. Some of these negotiations, such as the General Agreement on Trade in Services (GATS), resumed immediately after the conclusion of the Uruguay Round. Negotiations on trade in telecommunications and financial services were successfully concluded in 1997.

However, the South and some industrialized countries resisted efforts by the United States to start a new round of multilateral trade negotiations in the late 1990s. In Seattle in 1999 and Doha in 2001 (see Chapter 3) the developing countries argued that they had achieved little in the Uruguay Round, had made important and costly concessions to the developed countries in services and intellectual property, and were looking for the next round to make up for lost time. The South was strongly opposed to including four "new issues"—trade and investment, competition policy, transparency in government procurement, and trade facilitation—in the next Round until the old issues were satisfactorily resolved.

At the First Ministerial Meeting of the WTO in Singapore in 1996, attempts by industrialized countries to put these issues on the table were firmly rebuffed by the key countries in the South. Nevertheless, the trade ministers at Singapore agreed to establish four working groups to discuss the new issues. At the Second Ministerial Meeting in Geneva in May 1998, the United States put forward the issue of making the WTO responsible for electronic commerce. Again, the South resisted adding this new issue until the old issues were properly addressed.

At the Fourth Ministerial Conference in Doha in December 2001, the trade ministers agreed to continue the negotiations on agriculture and services that had already begun in 2000 and to begin negotiations on 19 other issues, including the built-in agenda issues, e-commerce, and the so-called new issues. They set January 1, 2005 as the date for completing all but two of the negotiations.[93] That goal, as discussed in Chapter 3, was not met. The negotiations collapsed in July 2006, in June 2007, and once again in July 2008. They were not likely to resume until after the inauguration of a new U.S. president in 2009.

The Asian tigers and the BRICs played a prominent role in the Doha Round. The BRICs and the tigers were under major pressure from the developed countries to open their economies to foreign trade and investment in exchange for maintaining access for their manufactured goods in developing-country markets. They wanted to make sure that any concessions they made on nonagricultural market access (NAMA) would be balanced with concessions on the other side.

On the question of agriculture, the BRICs were divided. India and China were concerned about the impact on their farmers of liberalizing trade in agriculture. Brazil, in contrast, saw large potential gains for domestic agricultural exporters in reduced subsidies to farmers in developed countries, particularly in cotton and biofuels. As a result, Brazil supported the deal proposed by the U.S. government in August 2008, but the insistence of India and China on the need for a "special safeguard mechanism" made it impossible to conclude the Round successfully.

The importance of the Doha Round from the standpoint of developing countries is that, this time, it was not possible for the developed countries to force their agenda on the rest of the world. The talks collapsed in 2008, not so much because the developed countries disagreed among themselves, but because they could not convince some of the increasingly powerful fast-growing developing countries that the concessions offered in agricultural trade were worth the concessions demanded in exchange. China and India led the rest of the developing world in saying "no" to a deal.[94]

Regionalism Redux   In the absence of a new multilateral trade agreement, the South would be forced to secure its trade interests through bilateral and regional agreements. In the 1990s, Southern governments began to experiment with new forms of regional integration as a way to promote exports and increase the international competitiveness of regionally based MNCs. Until the 1990s, regional integration in the South had not, for the most part, resulted in much growth in intraregional trade largely because of import substitution policies (see Table 7.3 and Figure 7.5). Figure 7.5 shows that North–North regional agreements produced higher levels of intraregional trade than South–South agreements, with North–South agreements like NAFTA somewhere in between. However, in the 1990s, regional strategies for South–South trade become more promising as developing countries began to reduce tariffs, sometimes unilaterally, in an effort to expand exports.

TABLE 7.3   Important Regional Trade Agreements

Region	Name	Acronym
Europe	European Union	EU
	European Free Trade Association	EFTA
North America	North American Free Trade Agreement	NAFTA
Latin America and the *Caribbean*	Latin American Integration Association	LAIA
	Andean Common Market	ANCOM
	Central American Common Market	CACM
	Southern Cone Common Market	Mercosur
	Caribbean Community	CARICOM
Africa	Arab Maghreb Union	UMA
	Economic Community of Central African States	ECCAS
	Central African Customs and Economic Union	CACEU
	Economic Community of West African States	ECOWAS
	West African Economic Community	CEAO
	Southern African Development Community	SADC
Asia	Association of South-East Asian Nations	ASEAN
	Asia Pacific Economic Cooperation	APEC
	Economic Cooperation Organization	ECO
	South Asian Association for Regional Cooperation	SAARC
Middle East	Gulf Cooperation Council	GCC

One example of that new regional trade strategy was the customs union formed by Argentina, Brazil, Paraguay, and Uruguay called Mercosur (Mercosul in Portuguese) in 1991. Chile joined Mercosur in 1996; Venezuela joined in 2006. The combined population of the Mercosur countries in 2007 was 250 million with a combined GDP around $1.1 trillion. The central elements of the custom union were reduced internal tariffs and a common external tariff. Mercosur built upon a set of unilateral commitments to lower tariffs on the part of both Argentina and Brazil. These commitments arose because of a new consensus that import substitution was not working and that Chile's government had succeeded in making the Chilean economy more internationally competitive by unilaterally reducing tariffs.

The formation of Mercosur resulted in a rapid increase in intraregional trade. In 1984–1986, only 6.7 percent of regional trade was accounted for by intraregional trade. By 1994, this figure had risen to around 20 percent but declined to about 17 percent in 2003 (again see Figure 7.5).[95] Exports among the Mercosur countries rose from $4 billion in 1991 to $26 billion in 2006.[96]

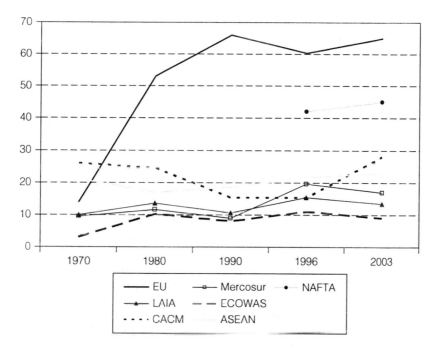

FIGURE 7.5 Intra-Regional Trade as a Percentage of Total Trade of Members of Regional Economic Organizations, 1970–2003

SOURCE: United Nations Conference on Trade and Development, *Handbook of International Trade and Development Statistics 1993, 1997* (Geneva, Switzerland: UNCTAD, 1993, 1997), WTO *International Trade Statistics 2007*.

The **Andean Common Market (ANCOM)**[97] was another example of a regional trade strategy in South America. ANCOM had five member countries: Bolivia, Colombia, Ecuador, Peru, and Venezuela. The combined population of the five countries was 113 million in 2000; combined GDP was around $270 billion. While the common market has been in existence only since 2000, the Andean Community that preceded it was formed in 1969 with the signing of the Cartagena Agreement. A free-trade zone was created in 1993, a common external tariff in 1995, and a framework for talks between the Andean Community and Mercosur in 1998.[98] Intraregional trade increased from $553 million in 1990 to $5 billion in 2006.[99]

At the summit of the Americas in Miami in 1994, the countries of the Americas including the United States and Canada agreed to begin discussions intended to lead to a Free Trade Area of the Americas (FTAA) by the year 2005. The FTAA negotiations were formally launched in April 1998 at the Second Summit of the Americas in Santiago, Chile. A draft of the FTAA agreement was made public in July 2001.[100] It included separate chapters on agriculture, government procurement, investment, market access, subsidies, antidumping, and countervailing duties, dispute settlement, services, intellectual property rights, and competition policy. The draft repeatedly stated a desire of the negotiating parties

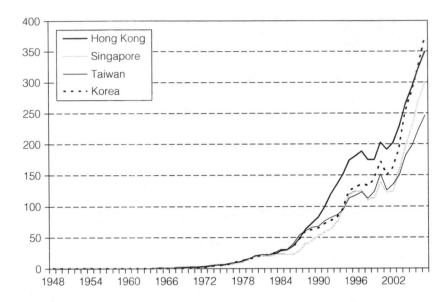

FIGURE 7.6 Merchandise Exports from the Asian Tigers, 1948–2007, in Billions of Current Dollars

SOURCE: World Trade Organization, *International Trade Statistics 2007*.

to act within the rules established by the WTO, but also to use the FTAA as an alternative forum for promoting free trade and resolving disputes.[101]

From the U.S. perspective, pursuing the FTAA was important as a means to ensure that regional initiatives like Mercosur and ANCOM remained consistent with the principles of NAFTA and the WTO and did not become small fortresses with high external tariffs. Some Latin American leaders, like Presidents Fernando Henrique Cardoso of Brazil and Vicente Fox of Mexico, considered the FTAA to be useless without a firm commitment on the part of the United States to lower its barriers to imports from the region. These leaders did not believe such a commitment would be forthcoming, so they remained skeptical about the desirability of the FTAA.[102] As a consequence, at the final summit for FTAA held in Argentina in 2005, there was no agreement and further discussions were not likely to occur.

Efforts to form new regional trade agreements also intensified in the Pacific region. The members of the Association of South-East Asian Nations (ASEAN) agreed in 1992 to form the **ASEAN Free Trade Area (AFTA)**, with the goal of eliminating barriers and achieving free trade by the year 2008.[103] The **Common Effective Preferential Tariff (CEPT)** agreement for AFTA called for reductions in tariffs for certain products traded within the region to be reduced to between 0 and 5 percent. Quantitative restrictions on these products were to be eliminated. After the Asia Crisis of 1997, the timetable for completion of AFTA was accelerated so that it would be completed by 2002 instead of 2008. Average tariffs were reduced from 12.76 percent in 1993 to 3.87 percent in 2000. Intraregional exports increased from $29 billion in 1990 to $193 billion in 2006, or about 25 percent of ASEAN's total exports to the world.[104]

In November 2001, the leaders of ASEAN and China agreed to begin negotiations for an ASEAN-China Free Trade Area. This was a natural extension of AFTA and a recognition of the heightened importance of China in the Asian regional economy. One of the consequences of the ASEAN-China negotiations was renewed efforts on the part of Japan to strengthen its ties with the ASEAN economies.[105]

In 1994, the leaders of Asia-Pacific Economic Cooperation (APEC), whose members included both developing and developed countries,[106] agreed in Bogor, Indonesia, to achieve free trade and investment in the region, with developed countries achieving that goal by 2010 and developing countries by 2020 (see Chapter 3).[107] APEC is organized into a variety of forums and working groups, many of which deal with trade. The **Market Access Group (MAG)**, for example, was established to handle the Committee on Trade and Investment's work on tariffs and nontariff measures.[108]

The EU and ACP countries renegotiated their regional trade agreement in the late 1990s. An adverse decision by a WTO dispute resolution panel ruling regarding EU-ACP banana **trade preferences** in 1997 forced the EU and the ACP to renegotiate their earlier agreements. In any case, the fourth Lomé Convention was due to expire in February 2000, so the two groups of countries began negotiations in September 1998 for a post-Lomé partnership. On June 23, 2000, the EU and the ACP countries signed a new agreement in Cotonou, Benin, later referred to as the Cotonou agreement. This new agreement recognized explicitly the failure of the Lomé Agreements to reduce poverty in the ACP countries by improving access to EU markets. The Cotonou agreement set new goals for poverty reduction, focusing on increasing aid levels in exchange for domestic political and economic reforms.[109] It was revised in 2005 to include specific references to the Millennium Development Goals and to provide new measures for poverty alleviation, to promote information and communications technologies (ICTs) in the ACP countries, to incorporate nonstate actors in related programs, and to strengthen special provisions for island countries.[110]

Despite the likely positive impact of bilateral and regional trade agreements on North–South and South-South trade, they were no substitute for multilateral agreements. There was a potential for the multiple- and overlapping bilateral and regional agreement to produce a confusing "spaghetti bowl" of rules and regulations and thereby to undermine efforts to alleviate poverty in the poorest developing countries.[111]

North–South Trade in the Twenty-First Century

The South's search for bargaining leverage in all of these forums will continue to be tested as it attempts to persuade the North that it is in the self-interest of the industrialized countries to make changes that will help the developing countries export, earn more, service their debts, and provide markets for Northern products. Strong protectionist pressures in both traditional manufacturing sectors and agriculture will make it difficult, although not impossible, for Northern governments to respond credibly to the South's demands. This task is made somewhat easier for the South by the growing importance to Northern multinational corporations of their operations in the South for serving global markets (see Chapter 8).

As developing countries pursued engagement and trade liberalization, the disparity between the Third and Fourth Worlds became more apparent. Some developing countries were able to grow rapidly enough to approach the per capita income levels of the North. Singapore, Taiwan, and Korea, for example, experienced steady growth in their per capita income between the 1960s and the beginning of the new milennium. Other developing countries, like China and India, starting from a lower level of per capita income, also began to grow rapidly in the 1990s. Some of these high-growth developing countries joined organizations like the OECD and the WTO in recognition of their new status.[112] As the number of middle-income developing countries grew, however, many other developing countries remained mired in debt, dependent on exports of agricultural commodities and raw materials, and trapped in poverty. One major question for the period beyond the Uruguay Round, therefore, was what could be done to help these countries escape the vicious circle of poverty. In the first decade of the new millennium, the connection between trade and development would continue to be at the heart of North–South economic relations. Success or failure in making this connection work to reduce global inequalities would profoundly affect the future of the international system.

ENDNOTES

1. Clair Wilcox, *A Charter for World Trade* (New York, N.Y.: Macmillan, 1949); and Williams Adams Brown, Jr., *The United States and the Restoration of World Trade* (Washington, D.C.: Brookings Institution, 1950), 97–104, 152–158.

2. Wilcox, *A Charter for World Trade*, 140–167; and Brown, *The United States*, 178–180, 203–211, 217–222.

3. Only four less-developed countries—Ceylon (Sri Lanka), Cuba, Haiti, and India—sought and obtained permission to impose quantitative restrictions under Article 18. The limitations imposed by the contracting parties, however, destroyed much of the benefit of their use. Article 18 was revised in 1955 to provide a greater possibility for withdrawal or modification of concessions previously made and to enable the use of quantitative restrictions for balance-of-payments reasons. But once again, the many safeguards included rendered it of little use to the South. Sidney Wells, "The Developing Countries, GATT and UNCTAD," *International Affairs,* 45 (January 1969): 65–67; and Karin Kock, *International Trade Policy and the GATT, 1947–1967* (Stockholm, Sweden: Almqvist and Wiksell, 1969), 227–232.

4. Although it was not permitted under GATT, the South was able to follow protectionist policies under IMF rules, which allowed quantitative restriction for balance-of-payments reasons, or under GATT waivers, or because they were not members of GATT.

5. Little et al., *Industry and Trade in Some Developing Countries*, 1–29. For the Latin American experience with protection, see Economic Commission for Latin

America, *The Process of Industrial Development in Latin America* (New York, N.Y.: United Nations, 1966), 21–35.

6. For the limits of import substitution, see Little et al., *Industry and Trade*, 1–29; and United Nations Conference on Trade and Development, *Toward a New Trade Policy for Development, Report by the Secretary-General* (New York, N.Y.: United Nations, 1964), 21–22.

7. Anne O. Krueger and Constantine Michalopoulos, "Developing-Country Trade Policies and the International Economic System," in Ernest H. Preeg, ed., *Hard Bargaining Ahead: U.S. Trade Policy and Developing Countries* (New Brunswick, N.J.: Transaction Books, 1985), 40–45.

8. World Bank, *World Development Report, 1986* (New York, N.Y.: Oxford University Press, 1986), ch. 4.

9. See United Nations Conference on Trade and Development, *Toward a New Trade Policy for Development*. For a summary of Prebisch's argument and the arguments of the critics of the theory of declining terms of trade, see Alfred S. Friedeberg, *The United Nations Conference on Trade and Development of 1964: The Theory of the Peripheral Economy at the Centre of International Political Discussions* (Rotterdam, the Netherlands: Rotterdam University Press, 1969), 33–67.

10. David Sapsford, Prabirjit Sarkar, and Hans W. Singer, "The Prebisch-Singer Terms of Trade Controversy Revisited," *Journal of International Development*, 4 (May-June 1992): 318. See also Chapter 5, f. 35.

11. One of the most flagrant examples of restrictive export agreements was the Long-Term Arrangement Regarding International Trade in Cotton Textiles, which was negotiated in the GATT. The North, in particular the United States, forced the less developed exporters (as well as Japan) to agree to "voluntarily" limit their cotton textile exports with the threat that the alternative—national import quotas imposed by national legislatures—would be worse. Later, the cotton agreement was expanded to a Multi-Fiber Arrangement.

12. For the Southern view of trade barriers, see United Nations Conference on Trade and Development, *Toward a New Trade Policy for Development*; and United Nations Conference on Trade and Development, *Toward a Global Strategy of Development* (New York, N.Y.: United Nations, 1968). For other analyses, see Harry G. Johnson, *Economic Policies Toward Less Developed Countries* (New York, N.Y.: Praeger, 1967), 78–110; and Alexander J. Yeats, *Trade Barriers Facing Developing Countries* (London, UK: Macmillan, 1979).

13. Economic Commission for Latin America, *Economic Survey 1969* (New York, N.Y.: United Nations, 1969), 61–62.

14. Kock, *International Trade Policy*, 235–244; and Hudec, *Developing Countries*, 39–46.

15. For a history of events leading up to UNCTAD I, see Diego Cordovez, "The Making of UNCTAD"; Friedeberg, *The United Nations Conference on Trade and Development of 1964*; and Charles L. Robertson, "The Creation of UNCTAD," in Robert W. Cox, ed., *International Organization: World Politics* (London, UK: Macmillan, 1969), 258–274. UNCTAD's website is http://www.unctad.org.

16. For an analysis of the Group of Seventy-Seven, see Branislav Gosovic, *UNCTAD, Conflict and Compromise: The Third World's Quest for an Equitable World Economic Order Through the United Nations* (Leiden, the Netherlands: A. W. Sijthoff, 1972), 271–292. For a discussion of Southern unity, both in the Group of Seventy-Seven

and UNCTAD, see Robert L. Rothstein, *Global Bargaining: UNCTAD and the Quest for a New International Economic Order* (Princeton, N.J.: Princeton University Press, 1979), 118–122; and Jeffrey A. Hart, *The New International Economic Order* (New York, N.Y.: St. Martin's Press, 1983), 145–146.

17. United Nations General Assembly, *Official Records: Eighteenth Session, Supplement No. 7 (A 5507)*, 24.

18. *Ibid.*

19. *Ibid.*, 25.

20. For a list of current members see http://www.g77.org/doc/members.html.

21. Gosovic, *UNCTAD, Conflict and Compromise*, 271. On UNCTAD see Joseph S. Nye, "UNCTAD: Poor Nations' Pressure Group," in Robert W. Cox and Harold K. Jacobson, *The Anatomy of Influence: Decision Making in International Organization* (New Haven, Conn.: Yale University Press, 1973), 348–349.

22. For a statement of the UNCTAD doctrine, see United Nations Conference on Trade and Development, *Toward a New Trade Policy for Development and Toward a Global Strategy of Development*.

23. See Gosovic, UNCTAD, *Conflict and Compromise*, 279–286, on Southern cleavages and 293–301, for the Northern bloc within UNCTAD. There is also a group composed of the socialist states of Eastern Europe, known as Group D. For an analysis of bargaining within the Northern bloc over commodity issues, see Rothstein, *Global Bargaining*, 123–125.

24. On the addition of Part IV generally, see Kenneth W. Dam, *The GATT: Law and International Economic Organization* (Chicago, Ill.: University of Chicago Press, 1970), 236–244; and Hudec, *Developing Countries in the GATT Legal System*, 56–60.

25. United Nations Conference on Trade and Development, *The Kennedy Round, Estimated Effects on Tariff Barriers: Report by the Secretary General of UNCTAD, Parts I and II* (New York, N.Y.: United Nations, 1968); and International Bank for Reconstruction and Development and International Development Agency, *Annual Report 1968* (New York, N.Y.: IBRD and IDA, 1968), 33–34.

26. United Nations Conference on Trade and Development, *Toward a New Trade Policy for Development*, 65–75.

27. For the details of the various preference schemes, see United Nations Conference on Trade and Development, *Operations and Effects of the Generalized System of Preferences: Fourth Review* (New York, N.Y.: United Nations, 1979).

28. United Nations Conference on Trade and Development, *Proceedings of the United Nations Conference on Trade and Development, Third Session* (April 13 to May 21, 1972), vol. 2, Merchandise Trade (New York, N.Y.: United Nations, 1973), 104–140; Tracy Murray, "How Helpful Is the Generalized System of Preferences to Developing Countries?" *Economic Journal*, 83 (June 1973): 449–455; U.S. Code, *Congressional and Administrative News*, 93rd Cong., 2nd sess., 1974, vol. 2, (St. Paul, Minn.: West Publishing, 1975), 2398–2399; U.S. House of Representatives, Committee on Ways and Means, 98th Cong., 2nd sess., *Summary of Provisions of H.R. 3398, Trade and Tariff Act of 1984* (Washington, D.C.: Government Printing Office, 1984); U.S. Congress, House, Committee on Ways and Means, *Report to the Congress on the First Five Years' Operation of the U.S. Generalized System of Preferences (GSP)*, 96th Cong., 2nd sess. (Washington, D.C.: Government Printing Office, 1980). See also, Pitou van Dijck, "Toward a Global System of Trade

Preferences among Developing Countries," in Hans Linnemann, ed., *South-South Trade Preferences: The GSTP and Trade in Manufactures* (London, UK: Sage, 1992), 53–60; and John Madeley, *Trade and the Poor: The Impact of International Trade on the Developing Countries* (New York, N.Y.: St. Martin's Press, 1993), 61–63. The GSTP is the Global System of Trade Preferences.

29. Rolf J. Langhammer and André Sapir, *Economic Impact of Generalized Tariff Preferences* (London, UK: Trade Policy Research Centre, 1987). For an analysis of the effects of tariff reductions on GSP, see Thomas B. Birnberg, "Trade Reform Options: Economic Effects on Developing and Developed Countries," in William R. Cline, ed., *Policy Alternatives for a New International Economic Order: An Economic Analysis* (New York, N.Y.: Praeger, 1979), 234–239.

30. For histories of the commodity issue, see Gosovic, *UNCTAD, Conflict and Compromise*, 93–114; Carmine Nappi, *Commodity Market Controls: A Historical Analysis* (Lexington, Mass.: Heath, 1979); F. Gerard Adams and Jere R. Behrman, *Commodity Exports and Economic Development* (Lexington, Mass.: Lexington Books, 1982); and Alfred Maizels, *Commodities in Crisis: The Commodity Crisis of the 1980s and the Political Economy of International Commodity Policies* (Oxford, England: Clarendon Press, 1992).

31. For background on the problems the commodity market poses for developing countries, see Paul Collier and Jan W. Gunning and Associates, *Trade Shocks in Developing Countries* (New York, N.Y.: Oxford University Press, 1999); David L. McNicol, *Commodity Agreements and Price Stabilization* (Lexington, Mass.: Heath, 1978), 15–24; and Alton D. Law, *International Commodity Agreements* (Lexington, Mass.: Heath, 1975), ch. 1.

32. Gosovic, *UNCTAD, Conflict and Compromise*, 99–101.

33. World Bank, *Commodity Trade and Price Index 1986* (New York, N.Y.: Oxford University Press, 1986), tables 5 and 16.

34. "Declaration and Action Programme on the Establishment of a New International Economic Order," in Guy F. Erb and Valeriana Kallab, *Beyond Dependency: The Developing World Speaks Out* (Washington, D.C.: Overseas Development Council, 1975), 186. For another summary of NIEO proposals, see Branislav Gosovic and John G. Ruggie, "On the Creation of a New International Economic Order," *International Organization*, 30 (Spring 1976): 309–345.

35. The mechanisms for increasing and stabilizing prices were to include buffer stocks, a common fund for financing such stocks, multilateral purchase and supply agreements for particular commodities, and compensatory finance. For details on the Integrated Programme for Commodities, see United Nations Conference on Trade and Development, "An Integrated Programme for Commodities and Indexation of Prices," in Karl P. Sauvant and Hajo Hasenpflug, eds., *The New International Economic Order: Confrontation or Cooperation Between North and South?* (Boulder, Colo.: Westview, 1977), 85–102. For an analysis of the negotiations surrounding the program, see Rothstein, *Global Bargaining*, part I; and Hart, *The New International Economic Order*, 36–40.

36. See, for example, C. Fred Bergsten, "The Threat from the Third World," *Foreign Policy*, 11 (Summer 1973): 102–124; C. Fred Bergsten, "The New Era in World Commodity Markets," *Challenge*, 17 (September-October 1974): 34–42; and Donella H. Meadows et al., *The Limits to Growth: A Report for the Club of Rome's Project on the Predicament of Mankind* (New York, N.Y.: Universe Books, 1972).

37. As of 2000, there were 15 member states of the EU and 71 ACP countries signatory to the Lomé Agreements. See Richard Gibb, "Post-Lomé: The European Union and the South," *Third World Quarterly*, 21 (2000): 457–481.

38. This first Lomé Convention was renewed and revised in 1979 and 1984. Negotiations on Lomé IV began in 1990. See Isebill V. Gruhn, "The Lomé Convention: Inching Toward Interdependence," *International Organization*, 30 (Spring 1976): 240–262; and John Ravenhill, "What Is to Be Done for the Third World Commodity Exporters? An Evaluation of the STABEX Scheme," *International Organization*, 38 (Summer 1984): 537–574. For background on Lomé II, see Carol C. Twitchett, "Lomé II Signed," *Atlantic Community Quarterly*, 18 (Spring 1980): 85–89; and Jonathan Fryer, "The New Lomé Convention: Marriage on the Rocks but No Separation," *International Development Review*, 1 (1980): 53–54.

39. For details of this analysis, see Jahangir Amuzegar, "Requiem for the North–South Conference," *Foreign Affairs*, 56 (October 1977): 136–159.

40. Johnson, *Economic Policies Toward Less Developed Countries*, 137–149. For a more recent work on international commodity agreements, see Christopher L. Gilbert, "International Commodity Agreements," in William A. Kerr and James D. Gaisford, eds., *Handbook on International Trade Policy* (Northampton, Mass.: Edward Elgar, 2008).

41. In 1985, one of the most effective and long-lasting ICAs, the International Tin Agreement, collapsed when the tin buffer stock ran out of funds. For background on the various ICAs, see Gilbert, "International Commodity Agreements;" and Nappi, *Commodity Market Controls*, 61–83. On the International Rubber Agreement, see Ursula Wassermann, "UNCTAD: International Rubber Agreement, 1979," *Journal of World Trade Law*, 14 (May-June 1980): 246–248; and *UN Report* (January 20, 1984), 5–6.

42. For background on the common fund, see Nappi, *Commodity Market Controls*, ch. 6; Paul D. Reynolds, *International Commodity Agreements and the Common Fund* (Lexington, Mass.: Heath, 1978); Jock A. Finlayson and Mark W. Zacher, *Managing International Markets: Developing Countries and the Commodity Trade Regime* (New York, N.Y.: Columbia University Press, 1988), ch. 2; and Gamani Corea, *Taming Commodity Markets: The Integrated Program and the Common Fund in UNCTAD* (New York, N.Y.: St. Martin's Press for Manchester University Press, 1992).

43. John Ravenhill, *Collective Clientelism: The Lomé Convention and North–South Relations* (New York, N.Y.: Columbia University Press, 1985).

44. For background on the Southern countries and the Tokyo Round, see Bela Belassa, "The Developing Countries and the Tokyo Round," *Journal of World Trade Law*, 14 (March-April 1980): 93–118; Thomas R. Graham, "Revolution in Trade Politics," *Foreign Policy*, 36 (Fall 1979): 49–63; Stephen D. Krasner, "The Tokyo Round: Particularistic Interests and Prospects for Stability in the Global Trading System," *International Studies Quarterly*, 23 (December 1979): 491–531; Robert Hudec, *Developing Countries in the GATT Legal System*, 71–102; General Agreement on Tariffs and Trade, *The Tokyo Round: Report by the Director-General of GATT* (Geneva, Switzerland: GATT, 1979); and Robert Hudec, *Developing Countries in the GATT Legal System* (London, UK: Trade Policy Research Center, 1987), 85.

45. On the graduation issue, see Isaiah Frank, "The Graduation Issue for the Less Developed Countries," *Journal of World Trade Law*, 13 (July-August 1979): 289–302.

46. Raymond F. Mikesell, "The Changing Demand for Industrial Raw Materials," in John W. Sewell, Stuart K. Tucker, and contributors, *Growth, Exports, and Jobs in a Changing World Economy: Agenda 1988* (New Brunswick, N.J.: Transaction Books, 1988), 139–166.

47. International Monetary Fund, *World Economic Outlook 1988* (Washington, D.C.: International Monetary Fund, 1988), 141; and United Nations, *World Economic and Social Survey 1994* (New York, N.Y.: United Nations, 1974), 72–73.

48. World Bank, *World Development Report 1994* (Washington, D.C.: World Bank, 1994), 186–187.

49. International Monetary Fund, *World Economic Outlook 2000* (Washington, D.C.: IMF, 2000).

50. Mikesell, "The Changing Demand for Industrial Raw Materials," 140, 155; and Finlayson and Zacher, *Managing International Markets*, 4–5.

51. On this point, see Gary Gereffi and Miguel Korzeniewicz, *Commodity Chains and Global Capitalism* (Westport, Conn.: Praeger, 1994).

52. *World Development Report 1993*, 14; and World Bank, *World Integrated Trade Solution* database.

53. General Agreement on Trade and Tariffs, *International Trade 1987–1988* (Geneva, Switzerland: GATT, 1988), table AC3.

54. GATT, *International Trade*, various issues.

55. See Organization for Economic Cooperation and Development, *The Newly Industrializing Countries: Challenge and Opportunity for OECD Countries* (Paris, France: OECD, 1988); Lawrence B. Krause, *Introduction to Foreign Trade and Investment: Economic Growth in the Newly Industrializing Asian Countries* (Madison, Wis.: University of Wisconsin Press, 1985), 22; Neil McMullen and Louis Turner, with Colin L. Bradford, *The Newly Industrializing Countries: Trade and Adjustment* (London, UK: Allen and Unwin, 1982); and David Yoffie, *Power and Protectionism: Strategies of the Newly Industrializing Countries* (New York, N.Y.: Columbia University Press, 1983).

56. The key works are cited in Chapter 5, note 30.

57. World Trade Organization, *International Trade Statistics 2007*.

58. IMF, *World Economic Outlook 1988*, 80; and calculated by the authors from IMF, *Direction of Trade Statistics 2001*.

59. OECD, *The Newly Industrializing Countries*, 19; and World Bank, *World Development Report 1995*, 193.

60. Other factors have been crucial to the East Asian NICs' success. The four tigers all have a highly educated and skilled workforce that is highly disciplined and motivated. The four also have high savings rates, which has provided the credit for investment and enabled them to avoid heavy external borrowing. To the extent that they relied on foreign borrowing, it was usually channeled into export sectors that provided the foreign exchange necessary to service the debt. In addition, during the early stages of their industrialization, authoritarian regimes in South Korea, Singapore, and Taiwan allowed the political elites greater freedom to determine economic policies, resulting in greater continuity of economic policies. These countries had either undergone land reform or never had a landed class, and so they did not have political pressure from an entrenched privileged class. In addition, the political legitimacy of these governments rested heavily on their economic success. Economic growth has led to a decrease in absolute poverty, a more

equitable income distribution, and an improvement in living conditions that has eased political pressures and promoted important democratization in both South Korea and Taiwan. These governments also felt insecure surrounded by Communist countries and believed that economic strength would increase their independence and security. In addition, under authoritarian governments, trade unions had limited bargaining authority and minimum wages were discouraged, which kept wages from increasing significantly. See Stephan Haggard, *Pathways from the Periphery* (Ithaca, N.Y.: Cornell University Press, 1990).

61. World Bank, *The East Asian Economic Miracle: Economic Growth and Public Policy* (Washington, D.C.: The World Bank, 1993); Deepak Lal, *The Poverty of Development Economics* (London, UK: The Institute of Economic Affairs, 1983); and Ian Little, *Economic Development* (New York, N.Y.: Basic Books, 1982).

62. See, for example, Dani Rodrik, *One Economics Many Recipes: Globalization, Institutions, and Economic Growth* (Princeton, N.J.: Princeton University Press, 2007), especially ch. 4; Peter Evans, *Embedded Autonomy: States and Industrial Transformation* (Princeton, N.J.: Princeton University Press, 1995); Alice H. Amsden, *Asia's Next Giant: South Korea and Late Industrialization* (New York, N.Y.: Oxford University Press, 1989); Stephan Haggard, *Pathways from the Periphery*; and Robert Wade, *Governing the Market* (Princeton, N.J.: Princeton University Press, 1997).

63. See, for example, Paul Krugman, "The Myth of Asia's Miracle: A Cautionary Fable," *Foreign Affairs*, 73 (November/December 1994): 62–78; and Marcus Noland and Howard Pack, *Industrial Policy in an Era of Globalization: Lessons from Asia* (Washington, D.C.: Institute for International Economics, 2003).

64. This particular case is illustrated in a documentary film, *Life and Debt*, by Stephanie Black, available for viewing on the Internet at http://www.lifeanddebt.org/.

65. GATT, *International Trade 1987–1988*, tables A14–A17.

66. Martin Wolf, "Managed Trade in Practice: Implications of the Textile Arrangements," in William R. Cline, ed., *Trade Policy in the 1980s* (Washington, D.C.: Institute for International Economics, 1983), 455–482.

67. Niels Blokker, *International Regulation of World Trade in Textiles* (Berlin, Germany: Springer, 1989).

68. World Bank, *World Development Report 1987* (New York, N.Y.: Oxford University Press, 1987), 142.

69. Wolf, "Managed Trade in Practice," 468–469. The MFA ended in 2004 with the creation of the World Trade Organization and was replaced with the Agreement on Textiles and Clothing.

70. United Nations, *World Economic Survey 1988* (New York, N.Y.: United Nations, 1988), 34.

71. GATT, *International Trade 1987–1988*, table AA10; and International Trade 1990–1991, table A2; and IMF, *Direction of Trade Statistics 2001*.

72. *Economic Report of the President 1988* (Washington, D.C.: Government Printing Office, 1988), 367; and WTO, *International Trade Statistics 2007*.

73. World Bank, *World Development Report 1988*, 197.

74. U.S. Department of Commerce, *Highlights of U.S. Export and Import Trade* (Washington, D.C.: Government Printing Office, various issues).

75. GATT, *International Trade 1987–1988*, table AA-7.

76. World Bank, *World Development Indicators 2007*.

77. The shift was incremental rather than dramatic, however, since the domestic political influence of the export sector—although growing throughout the decade —remained minimal in most countries. As one analyst put it, the political balance between trade-liberalizing and trade-protectionist forces is the critical "knife's edge" on which national trade policy turns.

78. UNCTAD Database on Trade Control Measures, http://r0.unctad.org/ trains_new/database.shtm..

79. Carlos Luiz Marone and Carlos Alberto Primo Braga, "Brazil and the Uruguay Round" (paper presented at the Conference on the Multilateral Trade Negotiations and Developing Countries, Washington, September 15–18, 1988).

80. See http://www.wto.org/english/thewto_e/gattmem_e.htm for a list of GATT members as of 1994 and http://www.wto.org/english/thewto_e/whatis_e/tif_e/ org6_e.htm for a current list of WTO members. Countries in the WTO decide whether they want to be considered developing countries, but can be challenged by others if the latter think a particular country does not qualify for the special privileges accorded to developing countries.

81. Diana Tussie, "Holding the Balance: The Cairns Group in the Uruguay Round," in Diana Tussie and David Glover, eds., *The Developing Countries in World Trade* (Boulder, Colo.: Lynne Rienner, 1993).

82. See also International Monetary Fund, *The Uruguay Round: Economic Implications* (Washington, D.C.: IMF, July 15, 1994).

83. IMF, *The Uruguay Round*, 6, 9.

84. *Ibid.*, 10.

85. A **greenfield investment** is an investment in completely new physical plant, usually in a location that was not previously used for any productive purpose. A **brownfield investment**, in contrast, is used to modernize or upgrade a previously existing facility or to convert if for another use. The reader should note that "brownfield" also refers to an environmentally degraded facility.

86. Chakarvarthi Ragavan, "New Round Should Adresss 'Unfinished Business,'" Third World Network, at http://www.twnside.org.sg/title/unfin-cn.htm.

87. The acronym BRIC was first coined by Jim O'Neill of Goldman Sachs in "Building Better Global Economic BRICs," *Global Economics Paper* (New York, N.Y.: Goldman Sachs, November 30, 2001).

88. Goldman Sachs analysts argued that the main emerging countries to watch were the BRICs and the N-11 (Next Eleven) countries: Bangladesh, Egypt, Indonesia, Mexico, Nigeria, Pakistan, the Philippines, South Korea, Turkey, and Vietnam.

89. Goldman Sachs Global Economics Group, *BRICs and Beyond* (New York, N.Y.: Goldman Sachs Group, 2007), ch. 5.

90. *Ibid.*, ch. 1; and Arvind Panagariya, *India: The Emerging Giant* (New York, N.Y.: Oxford University Press, 2008), chs. 4–5. Panagariya argues that "liberalization by stealth" occurred in the 1981–1988 period, laying the groundwork for the explicit liberalization policies of the 1990s.

91. Panagariya, *India*, ch. 7. For detailed discussion of Russia and China, see Chapter 10.

92. Carl Mortished, "Russia Shows Its Political Clout by Hosting BRIC Summit," *The Times*, May 16, 2008.

93. http://www.wto.org/english/tratop_e/dda_e/dda_e.htm#dohadeclaration.

94. China became a member of the WTO in 2001. Brazil split from China and India and supported a deal in July 2008 after being guaranteed better access to developed markets for its biofuels; Russia had not yet acceded to the WTO.

95. Alexander J. Yeats, "Does Mercosur's Trade Performance Raise Concerns about the Effects of Regional Trade Agreements?" *The World Bank Economic Review*, 12 (1998): 1–28.

96. WTO *International Trade Statistics 2007.* See also Riordan Roett, ed., *Mercosur: Regional Integration World Markets* (Boulder, Colo.: Lynne Rienner, 1999); Rafael A. Porrata-Doria, Jr., *Mercosur: The Common Market of the Southern Cone* (Durham, N.C.: Carolina Academic Press, 2005); and Francisco Duina, *The Social Construction of Free Trade* (Princeton, N.J.: Princeton University Press, 2006).

97. The Spanish name of the organization is *La Comunidad Andina de Naciones* (CAN).

98. http://www.comunidadandina.org/.

99. WTO *International Trade Statistics 2007.*

100. http://www.ftaa-alca.org.

101. FTAA.TNC/w/133/Rev. 1, July 3, 2001, http://www.ftaa-alca.org/ftaadraft/eng/draft_e.doc.

102. Henry Kissinger, "Brazil's 'Destiny:' An Obstacle to Free Trade," *Los Angeles Times*, May 15, 2001, p. A17; and Robin Wright, "Bush Says Free Trade is Key in Meeting the Needs of the Poor," *Los Angeles Times*, April 22, 2001, p. A6.

103. The original six members of ASEAN were Brunei, Indonesia, Malaysia, the Philipines, Singapore, and Thailand. Vietnam joined in 1996; Lao PDR and Myanmar in 1997; Cambodia in 1999.

104. Megawati Soekarnoputri, keynote address at the AFTA 2002 Conference, Jakarat, Indonesia, January 31, 2002; and WTO *International Trade Statistics 2007.*

105. George Yeo, "Building an ASEAN Economic Community," keynote address at the AFTA 2002 Conference in Jakarta, Indonesia, January 31, 2002; and Jingdong Yuan, *China-ASEAN Relations: Perspectives, Prospects, and Implications for U.S. Interests* (Carlisle, Pa.: Strategic Studies Institute of the U.S. Army War College, October 2006).

106. The members of APEC are Australia, Brunei, Canada, Chile, China, Hong Kong, Indonesia, Japan, South Korea, Malaysia, Mexico, New Zealand, Papua New Guinea, Peru, Philippines, Russia, Singapore, Taiwan, Thailand, the United States, and Vietnam.

107. *APEC Economic Leaders' Declaration of Common Resolve*, November 15, 1994, http://www.apecsec.org.sg/.

108. http://www.apecsec.org.sg/. See also Richard E. Feinberg, ed., *APEC as an Institution: Multilateral Governance in the Asia-Pacific* (Singapore: Institute of Southeast Asian Studies, 2003); and Charles Morrison and Eduardo Pedrosa, eds., *An APEC Trade Agenda? The Political Economy of a Free Trade Area of the Asia-Pacific* (Singapore: Institute of Southeast Asian Studies, 2007).

109. http://europa.eu.int/comm/development/cotonou/lome_history_en.htm. See also Clara Mira Salama and Stephen J. H. Dearden, "The Cotonou Agreement," DSA European Development Policy Study Group, Discussion Paper No. 20, February 2001 at http://www.edpsg.org/index.pl.

110. European Commission, Development and Relations with the African, Caribbean, and Pacific States, "Revision of the Agreement 2005," http://ec.europa.eu/development/geographical/cotonou/cotonou2005_en.cfm.

111. Kimberly Ann Elliott as cited in Robert McMahon and Lee Hudson Teslik, "The Doha Trade Talks," Council on Foreign Relations Backgrounder, http://www.cfr.org/publication/10555/. See also Jagdish Bhagwati, *Termites in the Trading System: How Preferential Agreements Undermine Free Trade* (New York, N.Y.: Oxford University Press, 2008).

112. Mexico joined the OECD in 1994 and Korea in 1996.

8

Multinational Corporations in the Third World

The nature of multinational corporations and foreign direct investment in developing countries has changed significantly over the three postwar periods, as have government policies and public attitudes to MNCs. During the **Bretton Woods** period, most flows of foreign direct investment to the Third World were for the purpose of funding the extraction of raw materials or the growing and processing of agricultural commodities. Many of these foreign investments were based on colonial relationships as with the British and French in Africa and Asia or on political and economic spheres of influence as with the United States and Latin America. In the 1950s and 1960s, the United States, as the dominant world economic power, led the way in foreign direct investment in developing countries, which by and large welcomed that investment as a route to economic development.

By the period of interdependence, FDI flows to the South began to reflect the spacial diffusion of manufacturing activities made possible by cheaper transportation and communications costs and reduced barriers to trade and investment. Using the terms introduced in Chapter 4, vertical FDI began to be more important than it had been previously and multinational corporations were beginning to look for lower cost inputs, especially lower-cost labor for simple manufacturing tasks, in the developing world. The sources of FDI flows became more diverse. No longer were FDI flows coming mainly from U.S. MNCs: West European and Japanese MNCs were also making major investments in the Third World.

In the 1970s, as foreign investment grew and the South sought to redress the international economic imbalance, criticism of multinational corporations began in Latin American and spread throughout the South. As we shall see, critics contended that multinational corporations distorted development and perpetuated the South's economic dependence on the North. Governments responded to this criticism by nationalizing or expropriating many foreign operations on their territories, imposing a variety of regulations on foreign investment, and seeking to develop international rules to control multinational corporations.

By the 1980s, however, attitudes changed once again and developing countries had begun to accept the possibility that FDI flows and MNC activities could have a positive effect on economic growth and that the negative effects of MNCs could be reduced by adopting appropriate regulatory strategies. Number of developing countries sought to implement public policies that shifted the perceived imbalance of power between host government and foreign corporations and to regulate multinational corporations in order to capture more of the benefits of foreign direct investment.

The greater receptivity of developing countries to foreign direct investment set the stage for the growing **globalization** of the 1990s and beyond. Many Third World countries, including China, welcomed multinational corporations but sought to do so in ways that would maximize their benefits and minimize their costs. Nationalizations and expropriations of foreign-owned raw materials MNCs in the 1970s had resulted in the creation of large state-owned or state-regulated private firms in the Third World. By the beginning of the era of globalization, some fast-growing, middle-income developing countries had manufacturing MNCs almost as large and powerful as those found in the developed world. These Third World MNCs were beginning to behave like the MNCs of the North.

As many developing countries became more receptive to foreign investment, criticisms of the MNCs shifted to the North. Unions and nongovernmental organizations (NGOs) in the North criticized MNCs for exporting jobs and for engaging in dubious labor and environmental practices. These Northern critics of MNCs constituted an important wing of the anti-globalization movement of the late 1990s and early twenty-first century.

THE ROLE OF MNCS AND FDI IN THE SOUTH

The importance of foreign direct investment (FDI) in the South varies from country to country. In some states, it is relatively insignificant, whereas in others it plays a key role. Multinational corporations have tended to concentrate their investments in a small number of developing countries. The top 20 developing country recipients of FDI accounted for 67 percent of all private foreign

**T A B L E 8.1   Top 20 Developing Country Recipients of FDI, 2006
Stocks, in Billions of Dollars**

Hong Kong, China	769
China	293
Mexico	228
Brazil	222
Singapore	210
Chile	81
South Africa	77
Korea, Republic of	71
Thailand	68
Argentina	59
Malaysia	54
India	50
Taiwan Province of China	50
Venezuela	45
Colombia	45
Nigeria	40
Egypt	39
Vietnam	33
Morocco	30
Tunisia	22

SOURCE: *World Investment Report 2007.*

investment flows to the South in 2004 and 66 percent of all FDI stocks.
Although less concentrated than in previous decades, FDI still tended to go
mostly to a limited number of countries (see Table 8.1).[1]

FDI inflows into the developing world have tended to go disproportionately
to Asia and Latin America (see Figure 8.1). The inflows into Asia accelerated in
the late 1980s and early 1990s. They went primarily to Malaysia, Singapore, and
China (see Figure 8.2). China was the largest single recipient of inward FDI in
the developing world from 1992 on. In Latin America, the primary destinations
for FDI inflows were Argentina, Brazil, and Mexico, the three largest economies
in the region (see Figure 8.3). During the Argentine economic crisis at the end
of the 1990s, flows dropped sharply. Although inflows have increased rapidly in
recent years, FDI flows to two Asian tigers, Taiwan and South Korea, have
been historically lower than those to China and the big three Latin American
recipients. This is because both countries have strongly favored domestically
owned enterprises over MNCs in their development policies (see Table 8.1 and
Figure 8.4).

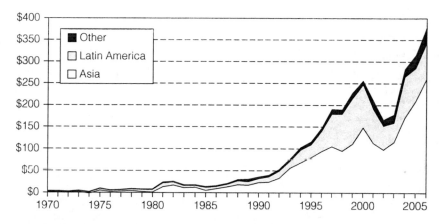

FIGURE 8.1 FDI Inflows into the Developing Countries by Region, 1970–2006, in Billions of Current Dollars

SOURCE: UNCTAD, *World Investment Report 2007.*

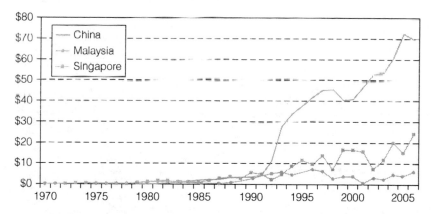

FIGURE 8.2 Inflows of FDI into China, Malaysia, and Singapore, 1970–2006, in Billions of Current Dollars

SOURCE: UNCTAD, *World Investment Report 2007.*

The power of multinational corporations grows out of their structural position within the relatively small and underdeveloped economies of many Southern states. Because agriculture still accounts for much of the gross national product of the poorer developing countries (see Figure 7.1), the multinational corporations may account for only a relatively small part in their total GNP. But foreign investment often accounts for a large share of the extractive, manufacturing, and services activity in those countries.

Historically, Northern firms controlled the South's extractive sector, long the key to development. Multinationals, for example, controlled oil in the Middle

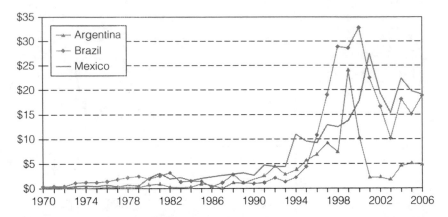

FIGURE 8.3 Net Inflows of FDI into Argentina, Brazil, and Mexico, 1970–2006, in Billions of Current Dollars

SOURCE: UNCTAD, *World Investment Report 2007.*

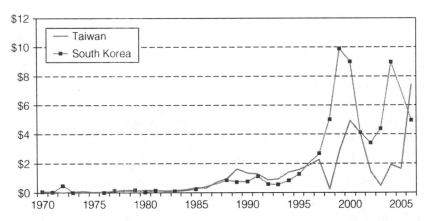

FIGURE 8.4 FDI Inflows into Taiwan and South Korea, 1970–2006, in Billions of Current Dollars

SOURCE: UNCTAD, *World Investment Report 2007.*

East, copper in Chile and Zambia, and bauxite in Jamaica and Guyana. In many cases, even when the ownership and control of production was transferred from multinational corporations to state-owned companies, the developing countries often remained dependent on the multinationals for processing, shipping, marketing, and distributing their raw materials. For example, in 1980, despite widespread nationalization of the petroleum industry in the developing countries, 43 percent of all crude oil produced outside North America and the socialist countries was either produced or purchased by the seven major international oil companies, and 24 percent was produced or purchased by smaller international oil companies or trading companies.[2] In 1982, 46 percent of the world's bauxite capacity, 50 percent of its alumina capacity, and 45 percent of its aluminum capacity were owned by six large multinational corporations.[3]

Since World War II, the developing countries have sought to expand their industrial sector as a primary means of development and have offered incentives for investment in manufacturing. The multinational corporations have often taken the lead in these new growth sectors. Foreign investment is growing most rapidly in manufacturing and is thus moving to dominate certain sectors of the new Southern industry. In 1988, for example, foreign affiliates controlled 32 percent of production, 32 percent of exports, and 23 percent of the employment of Brazil's manufacturing sector. In Singapore, foreign affiliates controlled 63 percent of production, 90 percent of exports, and 55 percent of employment in manufacturing.[4] By 1996, foreign affiliates controlled 72 percent of the value-added in the motor vehicles industry in Brazil, 65 percent in pharmaceuticals, and 54 percent in electronics and telecommunications. By 1999, foreign affiliates controlled 81 percent of total sales in Singapore.[5]

Foreign firms also represent a significant percentage of the largest and most powerful firms in Southern economies. Foreign investment in the Third World generally is found in industries dominated by a small number of large firms. For example, U.S. foreign investment is often found in such highly concentrated industries as petroleum, chemicals, pharmaceuticals, transportation, insurance, food products, electronics, and machinery. The large firms that dominate such industries have more power to control supply and price than do firms in more competitive industries. Thus the **oligopolistic structure** of many MNC markets means that significant economic power is concentrated in the hands of a few large foreign firms.[6]

Bargaining for Greater Control

Such a situation of economic dominance, however, need not mean the removal of decision making from national control. In principle, Southern governments could assert the control necessary to retain decision making at home. Host state laws could be passed to regulate multinational corporations, and host governments could impose restrictions on multinational corporations when investment agreements are negotiated. To impose such controls, Southern governments could use the one important bargaining advantage they possess: control over access to their territories and markets.[7] Control over access to resources that the multinational wants—local raw materials, labor, and markets—could be used by developing countries to impose controls on foreign investors.

In practice, however, the bargaining advantage of control over access is offset by the bargaining tools of the multinational corporation. The foreign investor often controls resources such as capital, technology and know-how, and access to foreign markets that the developing countries need for development. The South's desire for the benefits of foreign direct investment—for example, the ability to exploit a valuable raw material deposit or the possibility of expanding industrialization through new factories—poses a dilemma to policymakers in those countries. On the one hand, officials want to regulate the multinationals so as to maximize national benefits and minimize national costs. But on the other hand, officials do not want to make regulation so restrictive that it will deter potential investors.

Related to the desire to regulate and the fear of overregulating is the problem of uncertainty.[8] Before a foreign investment is actually made, potential investors are uncertain about the operation's eventual success and final cost. For example, a corporation proposing to explore for and develop oil in a developing country cannot be certain of the ultimate success of the project until it has prospected and built up an extracting capability—that is, until it has determined whether oil will be discovered and at what cost. Similarly, a corporation proposing to manufacture personal computers for a local foreign market may not be able to determine the potential of that market and the final costs of production. Another risk faced by the corporation is the political instability in Third World host states and the uncertainty of the effect of political change and possible turmoil on investment. For foreign investors, such uncertainties serve to reduce the attractiveness of the local factors of production and the local market and thus weaken the hand of the host country (see the discussion of the obsolescing bargain in Chapter 4).

Another factor weakening the bargaining power of the developing countries is the absence of competition for investment opportunities. The availability of alternative sources of raw materials and cheap labor elsewhere can diminish the bargaining power of any one Southern state. At times, the oligopolistic nature of multinational corporations—the fact that few companies dominate the industry and that those companies may collude with one another to decrease competition—can also weaken the hand of the developing countries.[9]

Furthermore, even if a country resolves the dilemma in favor of regulation, there remain constraints on the country's ability to carry out regulatory policies. The ability of Southern governments to control MNCs is shaped by the availability of the skilled persons necessary to draft and enforce laws and to negotiate agreements to regulate foreign investment. Without skilled lawyers, financial experts, and specialists in the particular businesses that the state seeks to regulate, many Third World governments are no match for the multinational corporation.

Another governmental problem has been the ability of multinationals to intervene in the host state's domestic political process to advance their corporate interests. Multinational corporations are able to use their resources in legal or even illegal political activities in host countries. Tactics such as public relations activities, campaign contributions, bribery, and economic boycotts are available to the corporation. In their ability to intervene in domestic politics, MNCs are, in one sense, no different from national corporations; the problem they pose is not in the area of foreign investment but in their ability as private institutions to influence the government.

There are, however, several characteristics of multinational corporations that distinguish them from national corporations and that make their participation in host politics a problem for the Southern states. Because MNCs are foreign-owned, they are not considered legitimate participants in the national political process. Their interests may not necessarily be compatible with those of the host state; their policies may, in varying degrees, reflect their own corporate interests or the interests of their home state. For these reasons, numerous countries have barred foreign firms from political activities. Political participation by multinational firms carries the connotation and, at times, the reality of a challenge to national sovereignty. In addition, MNCs bring many resources to their political activities. Their financial resources and international structure can be powerful political tools.

Multinational corporations also can derive great power from their relationship with the **home government**, the government of the country in which their parent firm has its headquarters. Investment in Southern states tends to be highly concentrated according to the home country. United States investment, for example, is predominant in Latin America, whereas French investment is dominant in the former French colonies in sub-Saharan Africa.[10] In the home country, these giant corporations often play a powerful political role. The ability of a multinational to pressure its home government to take certain actions and follow specific foreign policies to influence host governments adds to the imbalance between southern governments and MNCs.[11]

In sum, because of their powerful position within the Third World's economies and vis-à-vis the Third World's governments, multinational corporations can influence politics in Southern host countries. The crucial question then, is, when and how have these corporations used their power?

Political Factors that Influence the Location of Foreign Direct Investment

Investments by MNCs in the developing world are subject to the same variables identified as important to investments in the developed world (see Chapter 4). The **gravity equation** is often the beginning point for economic analyses of bilateral investment patterns.[12] Under the gravity equation, a key determinant of the level of investment is the size of both the source and destination economies. Thus, two large economies are most likely to exchange investments and two small economies least likely to do so—everything else is in between. Another key determinant is geography: the distance between the two countries is a major factor because distance creates not only costs of communication and transportation, but also coordination. A simple gravity model includes only these variables and often explains a large percentage of the variance in regression equations.

To test the impact of variables, scholars often add other variables to the gravity model to see if they are statistically significant. After several decades of research on this topic, a consensus has developed on the impact of the following economic variables: (1) the rate of economic growth of the destination country, (2) past level of FDI flows, (3) GDP per capita, and (4) past level of trade.[13] Cultural variables also seem to provide additional explanatory power. For example, both trade and investment levels tend to be higher between countries that share the same dominant language than between those that do not. In effect, the cultural differences between countries produce a form of distance similar to that created by geographic distances.[14]

Political variables can also be important. Because foreign investment is usually a long-term relationship between a multinational and its host, the multinational is generally concerned about the risks involved in that relationship. Risk increases when there are political upheavals such as those associated with war and domestic turmoil. It also increases when governments are able to act aggressively and in an unchecked manner against the interests of the firm through, among other things, increased taxes, arbitrary uses of licensing and trade barriers, capital restrictions, rapid changes in exchange rates, and (the ultimate threat) expropriation without compensation. MNCs are still willing to invest in risky locations, but the return on investment has to be higher to justify the additional risk. Given uncertainty about returns, MNCs will generally choose less risky locations.

There are a number of studies that indicate that MNCs prefer politically stable host countries, countries with federalist democratic systems, and countries that have adopted policies favorable to multinational corporations. One surprise is that MNCs do not necessarily prefer countries with low tax rates and low government spending, since these countries also tend to have low levels of investment in health, infrastructure, and human capital.[15]

Arguments about the Positive Impact of MNCs on Economic Development

Proponents argued that foreign investment had a positive effect on Southern economic development.[16] Such investment filled resource gaps in developing countries and improved the quality of factors of production. One of the most important contributions was capital. Multinational corporations brought otherwise unavailable financial resources to the South through the firm's own capital and its access to international capital markets. An increasingly important share of the flow of private capital to developing countries came from foreign investment. In the 1960s and 1970s, foreign direct investment accounted for approximately 15 percent of total flows, averaging $7 billion a year. These flows declined in the early 1980s due in part to the inflow of other forms of foreign investment (see Chapter 6). Nonetheless, in the late 1990s and the first decade of the twenty-first century, net inflows of foreign direct investment to developing countries averaged over $200 billion annually and were the main source of capital inflows (see Figures 4.3 and 6.2).[17]

Fourth, inflows of foreign direct investment generally increased the level of overall domestic investment. A cross-national study of 69 developing countries found that in the 1990s foreign investment increases of a dollar resulted in increases in total investment of between $1.50 and $2.30.[18] FDI inflows accounted for 26.7 percent of gross capital formation in the developing countries in 2006.[19] As in the developed countries, domestic savings and investment was the main source of overall capital formation, particularly in the larger countries.[20] A high proportion of FDI flows to the developing world (as well as to developed countries) took the form of acquisitions of existing firms (see Figure 8.5).[21]

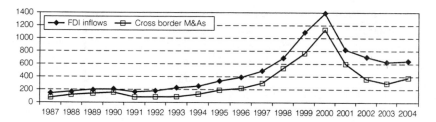

FIGURE 8.5 Mergers and Acquisitions vs. Total FDI Inflows, 1987–2004, in Billions of Current Dollars

SOURCE: UNCTAD, FDI/TNC database and cross-border M&A database 2005, (www.unctad.org/fdistatistics).

Multinational corporations also contributed crucial foreign exchange earnings to the developing world through their trade effect. First, proponents argued, the marketing skills and knowledge of foreign markets of the MNCs and their competitive products generated exports and thus increased the foreign exchange earnings of the host countries. Foreign affiliates of multinational corporations contributed to the growing role of developing countries in world trade (see Chapter 7). For example, foreign affiliates of U.S. firms in developing countries more than doubled their share of world trade between 1966 and 1983. In Latin America, U.S. affiliates outperformed domestic firms as exporters.[22] In China, exports of foreign affiliates in 2005 were $444 billion or 58 percent of total Chinese exports.[23] There was abundant evidence that MNCs used FDI as part of their overall strategy for selling goods and services abroad. In the absence of FDI flows, exports would have been considerably lower. Furthermore, the manufacture for the local market of products that otherwise would have been imported also saved precious foreign exchange for the host country. The increasing number of MNCs that were headquartered in developing countries were an important new source of export revenues for home countries. See Table 8.2 near the end of this chapter for examples.

A second crucial resource gap filled by the multinational, according to proponents of foreign investment, was technology. The desire to obtain modern technology was perhaps the most important attraction of foreign investment for developing countries. Multinational corporations allowed Southern states to profit from the sophisticated research and development carried out by the multinational and to obtain technology that would otherwise have been out of the reach of developing countries. Foreign firms trained local staff, stimulated local technological activities, and transferred technology throughout the local economy. Technology transfers and demonstration effects of new technology improved the total factor productivity of developing countries and enhanced their international economic competitiveness.

Third, said proponents, foreign investment raised the level of labor skills in the South. It provided needed exposure to world-class managerial techniques, and it created well-paying jobs for trained workers. Multinationals became less dependent on expatriate labor over time, especially in developing countries that already had a good educational system in place, and provided more opportunities for local professionals to manage and operate their facilities. The rapidly growing service sector, in particular, promoted the development of high-level skills in the local workforce.

Supporters contended, finally, that MNCs had a positive impact on welfare. The creation of new better paying jobs, the provision of new and better products and services, competitive prices, and programs to improve health, housing, and education for employees and local communities improved the standard of living in the Third World.[24]

Criticisms of the Role of MNCs in Economic Development in the 1970s

This positive view of the role of multinational corporations in growth, efficiency, and welfare was challenged by critics of the multinationals in the 1970s. A new body of analysis of multinational corporations emerged at that time. It argued that, policies encouraging inflows of FDI were not necessarily good for the population of the host states and that the multinationals exploited the developing countries and perpetuated their dependence on the North.[25]

Multinational corporations, argued the critics of this period, did not bring in as much foreign capital as their proponents suggested. The financing of foreign investment was done largely with host-country, not foreign, capital.[26] For example, between 1958 and 1968, U.S. manufacturing subsidiaries in Latin America obtained 80 percent of all their financing locally, through either borrowing or subsidiary earnings.[27] Furthermore, according to the critics, MNCs, because of their strength, often have preferred access to local capital sources and are able to compete successfully with and thus stifle local entrepreneurs. Critics contend that such local financing is often used to acquire existing nationally owned firms. One study of the Mexican economy revealed that 43 percent of U.S. multinational corporations entered Mexico by acquiring existing firms and that 81 percent of these firms were formerly owned by Mexicans.[28] And in Brazil, 33 percent of U.S. multinational corporations began operations in Brazil by acquiring local firms. In the late 1960s and early 1970s, acquisitions accounted for 50 percent of the new multinational affiliates in Brazil, 63 percent of which were formerly owned by Brazilians.[29]

Critics argued that foreign investment in developing countries actually led to a net outflow of capital. Capital flows from South to North occurred through repatriation of profits, debt service, payment of royalties and fees, and illicit manipulation of import and export prices. Such reverse flows were, in themselves, not unusual or improper. Indeed, the reason for investment was to make money for the firm. What critics argued, however, was that such return flows are unjustifiably high. They pointed to the fact that, in the 1970s, profits in developing countries were substantially higher than profits in developed market economies. The average return on book value of U.S. foreign direct investment in the developed market economies between 1975 and 1978 was 12.1 percent, whereas the average return in developing countries was 25.8 percent.[30]

Furthermore, contended the critics, profits represented only a small part of the effective return to the parent. A large part of the real return came from the licensing fees and royalties paid by the subsidiary to the parent for the use of technology controlled by the parent. In 1972, the payment by foreign affiliates for the use of technology accounted for 30 percent of total dividend income and 60 percent of all income from manufacturing received by U.S. parent corporations.[31] Critics did not argue that subsidiaries should not pay the parent for research and development costs incurred by the parent that eventually benefit the subsidiary. Rather, they contended that the subsidiaries in developing countries paid an unjustifiably high price for technology and bore an unjustifiably high share of the research and development costs. The monopoly control of technology by the multinational corporation enabled the parent to exact a monopoly rent from its subsidiaries.[32] And the parent chose to use that power and to charge inordinately high fees and royalties to disguise high profits and avoid local taxes on those profits, according to the critics.

Critics identified trade as yet another mechanism of capital outflow in which MNCs disguised profits and evaded taxes. Much of the trade by multinational subsidiaries in developing countries was intracompany trade. Often, subsidiaries located in developing countries were obliged by agreements with the parent to purchase supplies from and to make sales to the parent.[33] The parent thus was able to manipulate the price of such intracompany imports and exports—the transfer price—to benefit the firm (see the discussion of this topic in Chapter 4). Critics of MNCs argued that firms used transfer prices to underprice exports and overprice imports, thereby invisibly shifting profits from the South to the North.[34] In one study of an extreme case, it was argued that the overpricing of pharmaceutical imports into Columbia amounted to $3 billion.[35]

The negative effects of such decapitalization would have been limited if, in the process of removing capital, the MNCs had made a significant contribution to local development. Critics contended that the contribution of multinational corporations was limited or negative. Technology, they felt, was not the great boon for the South that the proponents of multinational corporations suggested. The high cost of technology was frequently mentioned. Another criticism was that the importation of technology stunted the development of local technological capabilities.[36] Yet another problem was the **appropriateness of technology**. Although some foreign investment entered the South to take advantage of abundant Southern labor and thus contributed to employment, some MNCs brought with them advanced, capital-intensive technology developed in and for developed countries that did not contribute to solving the problem of unemployment in developing states.[37] Energy-intensive technology imported from the North might have contributed to balance of payments problems for Third World energy-importing countries and accentuated existing problems of pollution and resource depletion.

Critics also argued that MNCs did not benefit Southern labor. They made only a small contribution to employment, and they discouraged local entrepreneurs by competing successfully with them in local capital markets by acquiring existing firms, by using expatriate managers instead of training local citizens, and by hiring away local skilled workers.[38] Finally, the trade benefits from the MNCs, according to the critics, were limited by restrictive business practices. Written agreements between parent and subsidiary might have included clauses confining exports and requiring subsidiaries to produce only for the local market. Management policy, similarly, could have held down subsidiary production and marketing.[39]

In sum, said the critics, MNCs created a distorted and undesirable form of growth. They often created highly developed enclaves that did not contribute to the expansion of the larger economy. These enclaves used capital-intensive and energy-intensive technology that employed few local citizens; acquired supplies from abroad, not locally; used transfer prices and technology agreements to avoid taxes; and sent most of their earnings back home. In welfare terms, the benefits of the enclave accrued to the home country and to a small part of the host population allied with the corporation.

Not only did the enclave not contribute to local development, said the critics, but it often hindered it.[40] In other words, the MNC-dependent economy developed at the expense of the local economy and thus of local welfare. It absorbed local capital, removed capital from the country, destroyed local entrepreneurs, and created inappropriate consumer demands that turned production away from economically and socially desirable patterns.

The Economic Impact of MNCs in the Developing World:
Empirical Evidence

Empirical studies examining the economic impact of MNCs on the developing countries appear to indicate that while inflows of FDI have a generally positive effect on economic growth, the extent of the impact depends on other variables. The impact of foreign investment varies from country to country, from sector to sector, from firm to firm, and from project to project. One important country-level variable that influences the aggregate impact of FDI flows is the level of human capital development in the host country. FDI flows have a more strongly positive effect on economic growth in countries that have made significant investments in education and worker training than in countries that have not done this.[41] Finally, there is empirical evidence to suggest that genuine technology transfer is limited, except in the cases where the MNC has been able to maintain at least majority control over its subsidiaries and has organized its subsidiaries in different countries to trade with one another. This last finding suggests that it is not wise for the governments of developing countries to require MNCs to give up majority control of their subsidiaries to domestic joint venture partners if they want to receive the benefits of technology transfer.[42]

In recent years, scholars have attempted to systematically study the ability of MNCs to foster backward and forward linkages and to generate spillovers in host countries. A **backward or upstream linkage** is a relationship between an MNC and a local supplier firm; a **forward or downstream linkage** is a relationship between an MNC and a local customer. The more backward and forward linkages between a multinational and local firms, the more likely that the FDI associated with it will have a positive impact on development.

A **spillover** is the spread of something valuable from the MNC to the local economy. Spillovers are of three main types: wage, technology, and productivity.

A wage spillover may occur if the higher wages paid by a multinational resulted in higher wages for workers of competing local firms. A technology spillover occurs if a technology employed by the MNC is adopted or copied by local firms. A productivity spillover occurs when the presence of a multinational not only raises the productivity of the workers and capital associated with that firm but also raises productivity of local firms.

The empirical evidence on linkages indicates that they are most extensive when the host country has already achieved a certain level of technological sophistication and when the multinational has adopted a strategy of making its foreign subsidiaries part of an international intrafirm network designed to produce competitive products and services for the world market. If the MNC is simply trying to service the local market and the local market is protected by high tariff barriers, as is generally the case in countries adopting and import substitution strategy, these linkages will tend to be minimal.

The evidence on spillovers is mixed. Wage spillovers occur in many countries but are largest in developing countries that have invested domestically in improving the skill levels of the workforce. Also, rather predictably, wage spillovers tend to be greater for skilled than for unskilled workers. Technology spillovers are most common in developing countries that have already reached a certain level of technological sophistication. Productivity spillovers are particularly difficult to study empirically, but again the evidence indicates that they are more likely to occur in countries that have adopted export-led growth strategies and have invested both in education and in research and development.[43]

Interference by MNCs in National Politics: Empirical Evidence

The evidence suggests that multinational corporations have at times intervened in political processes in their host states in the Third World. While most foreign investors do not become actively involved in host country politics, some MNCs have taken both legal and illegal actions within host states to favor friendly governments and oppose unfriendly governments, to obtain favorable treatment for the corporation, and to block efforts to restrict corporate activity. MNCs have engaged in such legal activities as contributing to political parties, lobbying with local elites, and carrying out public relations campaigns.[44] They have also engaged in illegal activities (illegal contributions to political parties),[45] bribes to local officials,[46] and refusals to comply with host laws and regulations.[47] MNCs have even used such extralegal methods as international boycotts to pressure an unfriendly government.[48]

Multinational corporations have also used their power in the politics of the home state to obtain foreign policies favorable to corporate interests. They have helped shape the liberal world vision that the U.S. government has sought to implement since World War II and that has favored foreign direct investment. MNCs have worked for specific legislation, such as the **Hickenlooper amendment**, which empowered the U.S. government to cut off aid to any country nationalizing U.S. investments without compensation; the **Gonzalez amendment**, which required the United States to vote against any multilateral bank loan to a nationalizing country; the Overseas Private Investment Corporation (OPIC), which insured foreign investment in many Southern countries; and the trade legislation which with-drew generalized system of preferences (GSP) tariff benefits from any country that expropriated U.S. companies without compensation.[49] At times, corporations have gone beyond influencing legislation to seek governmental support for their opposition to unfavorable regimes in specific host countries.[50]

Not only have corporations sought to shape home government policy, but they have also served as tools of that policy. For example, in 1988 the United States used multinationals to put pressure on the Panamanian government of General Manuel Noriega by forbidding subsidiaries and branches of U.S. compa-nies to issue any direct or indirect payments to the Noriega government. In the 1980s, it encouraged foreign investment to move to Jamaica following the change from a restrictive to a more open regime under Prime Minister Edward Seaga. However, multinational corporations do not necessarily advance the for-eign policy of their home government. For example, foreign oil companies op-erating in Angola actively opposed U.S. sanctions on the Angolan government because the sanctions conflicted with their own interests.

One of the most notorious examples of interference in host country politics was the intervention of the International Telephone & Telegraph Company (ITT) in Chile in the early 1970s in an effort to prevent its profitable Chilean subsidiary from being nationalized.[51] From 1970 to 1972, ITT actively sought, first, to pre-vent the election of Salvador Allende as the president of Chile and, once Allende was elected, to engineer his overthrow. In the process, ITT not only resorted on its own to a variety of illegal or extralegal activities but also tried to involve the U.S. government in both open and clandestine activities against Allende and was solicited by the U.S. government to serve as an agent of its policy.

The intervention of ITT into Chilean politics is not an example of typical behavior on the part of MNCs in developing world; most MNCs do not pursue such ruthless politics of intervention. The historical record shows that MNCS have rarely posed threats to the autonomy of Southern political processes.

INTERDEPENDENCE

Regulation of Inflows of Foreign Investment by Developing Countries in the 1970s

In the 1950s and 1960s, most developing country governments encouraged for-eign investment and placed few restrictions on the operation of foreign investors in their states. By and large, developing countries accepted the prevailing interna-tional liberal regime based on national treatment; prompt, adequate, and effective compensation in the event of expropriation; and the right of foreign investors to appeal to their home country governments for assistance. Latin America was the exception. Since the beginning of the twentieth century, Latin American countries have adhered to the **Calvo doctrine**, which asserts the right of host nations to na-tionalize foreign investments and make their own determination of what constitutes fair compensation; thus these countries reject the right of foreign investors to appeal to their home governments for help. Even in periods when FDI has been actively encouraged in Latin America, the Calvo doctrine has been maintained.[52]

In the 1970s, attitudes and policies toward MNCs shifted dramatically. The criticism of MNCs discussed above spread from Latin America throughout the Third World and many Southern governments altered their open-door policies. The principal effect of this criticism was to alter, at least for a time, the political reality of foreign investment in the developing countries. After the 1970s, most Third World governments no longer assumed that foreign investment would automatically promote development. As a result, they tried to regulate that investment to maximize the rewards and minimize the costs to the host economy.[53]

A shift in public attitudes toward foreign investment was an important factor behind this change. As nationalist sentiment developed in the late 1950s and 1960s, the multinational corporation came to be seen as a threat to economic and political independence.[54] Furthermore, the development process increased demands for improved economic welfare, housing, transportation, and jobs.[55] To satisfy these new pressures and to preserve their own political power, some Southern elites turned against the multinational corporation.[56] Opposition to MNCs became a politically useful and powerful platform for those elites.

In the 1970s, exposés of political intervention by MNCs in Southern politics outraged Southern publics and led to a new spurt of antimultinational opinion. The ITT scandal played an important catalytic role in public mobilization against MNCs. The initial revelations led to a U.S. Senate inquiry into multinationals in general, which revealed other instances of their intervention in politics.[57] Publicity regarding ITT and Chile also led to a unified Southern outcry against MNCs and to a United Nations investigation of them.[58]

The new critical economic analysis that pointed out the detrimental effects of foreign investment also contributed to changing public attitudes toward multinational corporations. As one critic of multinational corporations observed:

> Serious and competent economists can make a strong case against a
> permissive attitude toward private foreign investment and thus bring
> respectability even to attitudes originally based upon an unthinking,
> emotional reaction.[59]

A second factor behind the new policies toward MNCs was a shift in power from the multinational to the host government. One reason for the change in the power relationship was what one analyst called the **learning curve**.[60] Over the years, host governments developed significant expertise in monitoring and regulating foreign investment. They trained cadres in the legal, financial, and business skills necessary to regulate foreign subsidiaries. This movement up the learning curve made it possible for host governments to develop the laws and bureaucratic structures for managing multinational corporations.[61]

By the same token, the MNCs themselves began to learn how to deal with Third World hosts in order to counter the loss of initial bargaining advantages. They created joint ventures with local entrepreneurs, started new projects that appealed to local preferences, financed new investments with local capital, learned more about the local political system, and so forth, in order to counter the maneuvers of local nationalist forces. These countermeasures, while useful in many cases, were often insufficient to stop or slow down the growth of the political power of nationalist coalitions.

Decreasing uncertainty also contributed to the shift in power. Analysts have pointed out that a distinction must be made between the bargaining position of a host country vis-à-vis a potential investor and its bargaining position vis-à-vis an investor who has already made a significant and successful investment in its country.[62] When a country is seeking investment, it is in a weak bargaining position. Foreign investors are uncertain about the success of the proposed operation and its final cost. To overcome these uncertainties and to attract investment, host countries must follow permissive policies regarding investment. But once a foreign investment is made and is successful, the bargaining relationship changes, and the power of the host country increases. The host country now has jurisdiction over a valuable multinational asset. As uncertainty decreases, the host government comes to regret and resent earlier permissive policies and agreements. The operation's success leads the host government to seek revision of agreements with foreign investors, whereas the company's financial commitment and interest weaken its bargaining position and ability to resist new terms for operation.

A third factor contributing to the power shift was the increasing competition for investment opportunities in the South. The greater numbers of countries with major MNCs meant that Southern states had more alternatives in choosing foreign investors. These alternatives are important at the level of individual investments, allowing greater competition and thus better terms for the host countries. Alternatives are also important in that they allow the Southern states to diversify investment away from one traditionally dominant Northern home state. Thus, for example, Japanese multinationals emerged as an alternative to U.S. firms in Latin America, and U.S. companies in turn emerged as an alternative to French firms in Africa.[63]

This shift in power from foreign investor to host government has clearly been the case in raw materials, such as copper and oil, where host-government policy has evolved from permissive policies to attract investment, to more strict application of local laws in such areas as taxation and labor policy once the foreign investment has been successful, and to eventual ownership of equity or direct involvement in business decision making on such matters as price or supply.[64] It is less clear whether the shift in power applies to manufacturing. Some analysts argue that it is more difficult for developing countries to control global manufacturing firms with worldwide production and worldwide marketing, because local subsidiaries remain dependent on the parent for supplies, capital, technology, and markets.[65]

In the 1970s, these various forces of change led to new Southern attempts to regulate MNCs. As discussed, one such abortive effort was launched in the United Nations (see Chapter 4). Part of the Southern plan for the **New International Economic Order (NIEO)** was an attempt to bring MNCs under international control. In 1974, the United Nations made two major statements on the NIEO: the Declaration of the Establishment of the New International Economic

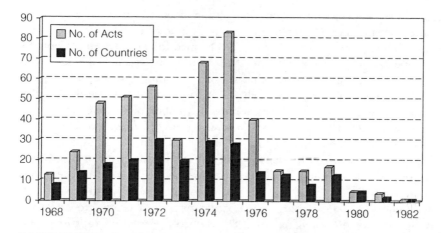

FIGURE 8.6   Expropriation Acts by Year, 1968–1982

SOURCE: *UNCTC Reporter*, No. 25, as cited in John Madeley, *Trade and the Poor* (New York: St. Martin's Press, 1993), p. 91.

Order and the Charter of Economic Rights and Duties of States. Both documents asserted the full sovereignty of each nation over its natural resources and all economic activities including the right of nationalization. The Declaration of the Establishment of the NIEO made no reference to any compensation, and the Charter simply said that any compensation should be "appropriate." Although the United Nations did establish a Center on Transnational Corporations, the attempt to draw up an international code of conduct proved impossible. The real effort to control multinational corporations came at the national level and, in the case of the Andean Common Market (ANCOM), whose original members were Bolivia, Chile, Colombia, Ecuador, Peru, and Venezuela, at the regional level.[66]

The most publicized Southern policies to manage multinational corporations have been nationalizations and expropriations of foreign subsidiaries. Peru's government, for example, nationalized the International Petroleum Corporation, various banks, and the fishmeal and fish oil industry.[67] Chile and Zambia have taken over their copper industries,[68] and many oil-producing states have nationalized their oil industries.[69] Expropriation, although highly visible, is not the main method of Southern management or the prevailing trend of Southern attempts at control. In fact, after reaching a peak in 1975, nationalization declined dramatically (see Figure 8.6).[70]

More important than well-publicized nationalizations were new tax laws, regulations, and bureaucratic structures designed to strengthen governmental control and to increase the host country's share of the economic rewards from foreign investment.[71] Attempts to manage the multinational corporation through such laws and policies varied from country to country and within countries from industry to industry. Nevertheless, certain trends emerged.

Governments often put strict limits on the entry of new investment. Many countries enacted investment laws limiting the sectors in which foreign investment is permitted. Banking, communications, transportation, and public utilities were commonly reserved for national ownership. Restrictions were also placed on the amount of equity that foreigners may hold in local companies. For example, Mexico's foreign investment law of 1973 banned foreign investment entirely in sectors mentioned above and confined foreign equity and management control to 49 percent or less in many other sectors, including mineral exploitation, automobile manufacturing, and petrochemical by-products. One-hundred percent ownership was only allowed in a limited number of sectors: nonelectric equipment and machinery, electronics, machine tools, electronic machines and appliances, biotechnology, transportation equipment, chemicals, and hotels.[72] Several states also controlled the takeover of nationally owned firms by MNCs. Mexico, for example, required prior authorization before allowing a foreign investor to acquire 25 percent of the capital stock or 49 percent of the fixed assets of a nationally owned firm and gave Mexican investors a chance to make the purchase in place of the foreigner. In 1989 Mexico's restrictions on foreign investment were relaxed.[73]

Some countries sought with varying degrees of success to reduce the level of existing foreign investment. In the ANCOM Uniform Code on Foreign Investment, reserved sectors were to be closed not only to new but also to existing foreign investment. Foreign firms operating in reserved sectors were to offer at least 80 percent of their shares for sale to national investors.[74] ANCOM's effort foundered due to the conflicts among its member states and the difficulty of implementing such strict divestiture procedures. India was more successful in its divestitive efforts. Between 1977 and 1980, India reduced foreign ownership in almost 400 companies by requiring the issue of shares to the Indian public.[75]

Through these sectoral and equity restrictions and reinforced by new domestic abilities to enforce these restrictions, governments sought to encourage new forms of foreign participation—joint ventures, licensing agreements, management contracts, and turnkey arrangements—to replace total or majority ownership. The goal was to unbundle the foreign investment package: to separate technology, managerial skills, and market access from equity and control.[76] As a result, joint ventures, production sharing, and technical assistance agreements became more common, and many MNCs accepted less than majority ownership of affiliates in developing countries.[77] By the early 1970s, 38 percent of the affiliates of U.S.-based corporations in developing countries were co-owned or minority-owned. Multinationals based in other countries have shown even more flexibility: by the late 1960s, the proportion of minority-owned affiliates of corporations based in Europe was 49 percent, and that of other (primarily Japanese) corporations was 82 percent.[78]

Developing countries also sought to regulate behavior by the multinationals after entry. Restrictions on **profit and capital repatriation** were widely implemented throughout the developing world. The Andean Group, for example, limited remittances of profits and capital to 20 percent of registered investments. A number of countries, such as Mexico, supervised technology and licensing agreements.[79] Some countries required registration and greater disclosure of such information as capital structure, the technology used and restrictions on its use, and reinvestment policies.[80]

An additional control technique relies not on restrictions but on positive incentives. Inducements, such as tax advantages or exemptions from import restrictions, have been used to encourage companies to invest in new fields or to use new technologies, to invest in export industries and in developing regions of the country, and to increase sectoral competition. Brazil has relied on such positive tools of public policy to manage multinational corporations. In the 1970s the Brazilian Industrial Development Council distributed incentives to foreign investors to regulate them and direct their investments into desirable sectors of the economy.[81]

Another technique is the support of state-owned firms. In many industries with high barriers to entry, **state-owned enterprise** is the only viable national alternative to foreign investment. In both Mexico and Brazil, for example, state-owned corporations have been formed in such basic industries as petroleum, steel, finance, utilities, and transportation.[82] Significantly, the emphasis on state-owned industry as a strategy for balancing foreign investment contributed to greater borrowing from foreign commercial banks in order to invest in national industry.[83]

A final method of control was the **producer cartel** (see Chapter 9). Various exporters of raw materials—particularly oil, copper, and bauxite—tried to manage MNCs by cooperating to increase prices as well as the national share of profits and national ownership. Until now, only OPEC, the oil producers' cartel, has used this technique successfully. Even OPEC has not always been successful in controlling output and prices.

The New Pragmatism

In the 1980s, the Southern strategy of control and confrontation shifted again, this time toward more pragmatic policies concerning multinational corporations. Although developing countries continued to closely monitor and control the activities of foreign investors, MNCs gradually came to be seen less as a threat and more as a potential opportunity for promoting growth and development.[84]

The new pragmatism was the result of several converging forces. The decline in foreign direct investment flows to developing countries in Latin America during the debt crisis played an important role. Restrictive policies enacted in the 1960s and 1970s deterred some direct investment and led foreign investors to turn to nonequity arrangements as a way of gaining access to LDC markets.[85] Particularly troublesome for potential investors were controls on remittances of earnings. Depressed economic conditions and low rates of return in most developing countries during the 1980s were an important factor in the decline in investment flows. For example, rates of return on U.S. foreign direct investment in Latin America fell from 18.8 percent in 1980 to 2.4 percent in 1983 before rising to 10.8 percent in 1985. Rates of return on U.S investment in other developing countries fell from 41.3 percent in 1980 to 22.5 percent in 1983 and to 18.6 percent in 1985.[86] The debt crisis further discouraged investment by making capital repatriation from many developing countries difficult or impossible. These unfavorable conditions in developing countries contrasted

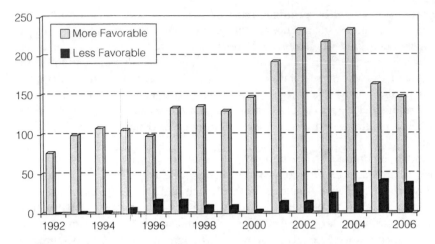

FIGURE 8.7 Regulatory Changes Favorable and Unfavorable to FDI, 1992–2006
SOURCE: UNCTAD *World Investment Report 2007*, p. 14.

with rapid growth, rising rates of return, and few restrictions on foreign investment in many developed countries.

As a result, multinational corporations shifted their investment toward the developed countries and away from developing countries. Between 1982 and 1989, the share of FDI flowing to developing countries fell from around 30 percent to around 14 percent. The share of the South in FDI flows rose rapidly during the 1990s to a peak of around 40 percent before dropping off once again in the wake of the Peso and Asian Crises (see Figure 4.3).[87]

Latin America's share of the South's inflows of FDI fell from around 85 percent in 1980 to around 20 percent in 1993 before expanding once again to over 45 percent in 1999 in the wake of the Asia Crisis. The Latin American share declined once again to 22 percent by 2006 (see Figure 8.1).[88]

In the 1980s, Asia became a central focus of FDI. Foreign investors were attracted by the large domestic markets in countries such as China, Indonesia, and Thailand; skilled, low-cost labor and well-developed infrastructure for export-oriented manufacturing, as in Hong Kong, Malaysia, Singapore, and Taiwan; petroleum and other natural resources, as in Indonesia and Malaysia; and generally more favorable policies regarding foreign investment (see Figure 8.7).[89]

The ready availability of loan capital in the 1970s had enabled developing countries to adopt the restrictive policies that contributed to the fall in direct investment flows in the 1980s. Commercial bank loans replaced both direct investment and foreign aid as the major source of development finance for many middle-income developing countries in the 1970s. In the 1980s, however, the debt crisis increased the relative attractiveness of FDI as a source of capital for growth. While foreign banks continued to lend to debtor countries, usually under pressure from their governments and the IMF, new lending was devoted overwhelmingly to debt service and not investment. Although they were important borrowers from the World Bank, the middle-income debtors were no longer major recipients of foreign aid. Investment levels and growth rates in the highly indebted countries were greatly depressed. Rates of return on foreign investment were related to the long-term success of a project and were not as subject as debt repayments to short-term fluctuations in international interest and currency exchange rates. Direct foreign investors were more likely to have a long time-horizon in making investments in the South than foreign lenders or portfolio investors. Increasingly, foreign direct investment emerged as the most desirable source of needed foreign capital flows.

More receptive policies toward foreign investment were also part of the prescription of developed countries and multilateral institutions for resolving the debt crisis. Improved access for FDI was one of the pillars of the Baker Plan. A more positive approach to foreign investment was also fostered by the World Bank. The Bank's structural adjustment lending encouraged the easing of restrictions on foreign investment, and the Bank established a Multilateral Investment Guaranty Agency (MIGA) to insure and, thereby, promote direct investment in developing countries. In Pakistan and other nations, the World Bank encouraged governments to allow private foreign investors to build and operate major infrastructural facilities, such as power plants and highways. These projects were occasionally even owned by the foreign investors, but eventually ownership and operation of the facilities was transferred back to the government or to local private enterprises. Furthermore, debt-equity swaps that were part of the menu for reducing commercial bank debt involved exchanging financial debt for foreign equity investment.

At the same time, developed countries generally took a more aggressive role on the issue of access for foreign investment to the markets of developing countries. The U.S. Trade and Tariff Act of 1984, for example, broadened the definition of barriers to market access to include investment as well as trade barriers, and the United States used the trade approach to push for access to markets for U.S. firms. In addition, the developed countries pushed for new investment provisions as part of the Uruguay Round (see Chapters 3 and 7).

This encouragement to open their policies and be more receptive to foreign investment fit well with the change in development strategies of many Southern countries. In the 1980s, many developing countries shifted from import substitution policies combined with support of state enterprises in basic industries like steel and telecommunications to emphasizing the advantages of private ownership and investment and greater openness to the world economy. The clearest manifestations of this new approach in Latin America were the policies of developing countries like Chile, Mexico, and Argentina. In an effort to promote more efficient and competitive industries and to reduce the financial burden on government budgets, many developing countries sold state-owned companies to private investors. Sometimes these investors were domestic firms, but often they were foreign-owned MNCs.

Privatization policies complemented the new emphasis on export-led growth. As discussed in Chapter 7, in this period many developing countries turned to the export-led development strategy that had been successful in the Asian NICs. In several of the NICs, promotion of foreign investment in the export sector was part of the export-led growth strategy. These countries attracted foreign direct investment through the establishment of **export processing zones (EPZs)** or by contractually requiring foreign firms to export in return for the right to invest (see below). Also related to the new emphasis on export-led growth was the growing interest of developing countries in obtaining access to new technologies. Increased global demand for products and services that required advanced technology raised LDC receptivity to MNCs, the major holders of such technology.

These various forces converged in more liberal policies toward foreign direct investment. The new pragmatism did not reverse established restrictive policies. Countries continued to control the entry and operations of foreign investors; most laws, regulations, and institutions put in place to control foreign investment remained. While countries opened up some sectors, such as those that exported or involved high technology, they maintained tightly closed policies in others (e.g., the service sector). The liberalizing trend applied more to Asia and Africa than to Latin America where long-held concerns about the technological dependency associated with foreign investment inhibited change. Nevertheless, there was a clear trend toward encouraging FDI by reducing restrictions placed on the entry and operations of multinational corporations and by streamlining procedures and offering incentives to foreign investors (again see Figure 8.7).

New investment laws and policies adopted in the 1980s removed a variety of restrictions placed on foreign investors. A number of developing countries, including Korea, Mexico, and the ANCOM members, increased the number of sectors open to foreign investment. The opening tended to be in high-technology or export-oriented industries. In some countries, existing laws were implemented more flexibly. For example, IBM was given an exemption from Mexico's stringent limitation on foreign control of the informatics sector in order to set up a wholly owned subsidiary to produce microprocessors in Mexico. In return, IBM accepted a number of obligations regarding, for example, location of research and development in Mexico and exports from Mexico.[90] Similarly, in Brazil, the government's informatics policy, which excluded foreign firms from the small computer market, was attacked and greatly weakened in the late 1980s.[91] Privatization actions also involved foreign investors and not infrequently involved debt-equity swaps. Argentina allowed foreign private participation in petroleum extraction and telecommunications. In the case of telecommunications, foreign participation was financed in part with a debt-equity swap. Brazil sold part of its steel industry to foreign interests. Chile allowed foreign investors to use debt-equity swaps to buy stock in a state holding company. And the Philippines permitted foreign banks to convert their loan exposures into equity in its National Steel Company.[92]

Controls on operations were also eased in many developing countries. For example, Algeria eliminated requirements that the local partner exercise control, and ANCOM removed restrictions on profit remittances. Policies requiring gradual divestiture, in Mexico and ANCOM for example, were relaxed. Restrictions on operations were relaxed in certain preferred sectors. Venezuela and others, for example, exempted foreign investment in electronics, informatics, and biotechnology from limitations on reinvestment of profits, remittances, repatriation of capital, and divestiture requirements.[93] A number of developing countries, such as Algeria, India, Indonesia, Korea, Mexico, and the Philippines, also simplified administrative procedures for approving FDI. Finally, certain socialist countries, such as Ethiopia, Mozambique, North Korea, and China, passed new laws making foreign investment possible, primarily through joint ventures. China's liberalization policy was the most dramatic. Starting from scratch in 1979, China developed a foreign investment regime and implemented a policy that attracted a significant number of foreign corporations.[94]

A number of other developing countries have set up EPZs, which encourage investment for production of goods for export by making imports and exports free from tariffs or other trade restraints as well as through such techniques as providing infrastructure facilities for manufacturing and offering streamlined regulatory and administrative procedures. Their use has grown dramatically in recent years. While only ten developing countries had EPZs in 1970, at least 130 Southern countries had them by 2006.[95] Although EPZs are designed for both foreign and domestic producers, many foreign firms have invested in EPZs as a way of gaining access to low-cost labor for the production of such labor-intensive goods as electronics and textiles. Export processing zones have clearly helped promote the export of manufactured products from the South, although sometimes at the expense of poor working conditions and environmental degradation.[96]

As national policies became more accommodating, international efforts to control multinationals also shifted from hostility to greater cooperation. One important contributing factor was the rise of FDI outflows from the NICs, especially in Asia.[97] By the early 1990s, some developing countries had a growing stake in ensuring the access of their MNCs to other markets. A growing number of Southern countries, primarily in Africa and Southeast Asia, signed bilateral investment treaties (BITs) with developed countries. These treaties are designed to promote foreign investment by providing certain protections and a predictable foreign investment regime. They generally establish terms for entry of foreign investment; basic standards of treatment, such as national treatment or most-favored-nation treatment; conditions for nationalization and forms of compensation; rules for transfer of profits and capital repatriation; and dispute settlement mechanisms.[98] MIGA was set up under the World Bank to guarantee private investment in developing countries against noncommercial risks, such as currency transfer, expropriation, breach of contract, war, and civil disturbance (see Chapter 4). Guarantees are contingent upon MIGA's judgment about the economic soundness and development validity of the investment as well as the approval of the host government.[99]

Meanwhile, negotiations for a **United Nations Code on Transnational Corporations**, originally conceived at the time of the NIEO, languished and seemed increasingly irrelevant. As attitudes toward foreign investment changed, Southern interest in the code declined. Developed countries remained adamantly opposed to the code and pushed instead for negotiations on investment under GATT (see Chapters 3 and 7). However, developing countries still wanted to maintain national sovereignty and to control entry and operations of foreign investors and thus strongly resisted negotiating investment issues, even the so-called trade-related investment measures (TRIMs) in the Uruguay Round. In the end, they accepted TRIMs grudgingly because they were part of a package deal that included concessions from the industrialized countries on agriculture, textiles, and safeguards. In the Doha Round, the developing countries asked for exemptions or delays in the implementation of TRIMs rules.

GLOBALIZATION

Foreign direct investment in South grew rapidly in the era of globalization, although that investment remained highly concentrated in a few of the more advanced developing countries. Total FDI flows to the South rose from $36 billion in 1990 to $379 billion by 2006 (see Figure 4.3). As explained above, there was growing investment in and receptivity of developing countries to the presence of MNCs. New regional trade organizations like NAFTA, AFTA, APEC, and Mercosur were designed to encourage MNCs to locate new facilities in the South. NAFTA, for example, provided investors assurances that they would be accorded national treatment and that disputes would be settled rapidly.[100] The financial crises of the 1990s led to greater receptivity to FDI in places like South Korea, partly because the interruption of short-term investment flows from the North (see Chapter 7), but also because of increased demands from the industrialized nations that Korea open itself up to the participation of foreign MNCs in a variety of sectors such as electronics and financial services. As incomes and wages rose in the Asian tigers, many locally owned firms contracted out labor-intensive work to countries in Asia with lower wage levels, including China.

Continuing the trend begun in the 1980s, FDI outflows were directed heavily toward Asia and China, reflecting investor perceptions that, even after the Asia crisis of the late 1990s, the prospects for growth in that area of the world were better than in other Third World regions. There was a marked increase in FDI flows to China and South Korea (see Figures 8.2 and 8.4). Although FDI flows to these countries also increased, they did not increase as rapidly as they did for China and South Korea (see Chapter 10).

Some important emerging countries in Latin America such as Venezuela and Bolivia remained highly skeptical and politically divided about MNCs. When Hugo Chávez was elected president of Venezuela in 1999, he focused immediately on the activities of MNCs in the oil industry with an eye toward reversing the privatization and pro-FDI policies of his predecessors. He halted the planned privatizations of both the aluminum and petroleum industries and began to attack the leadership of Venezuela's state-owned oil company, Petróleos de Venezuela SA (PDVSA), for spending too much money abroad in acquiring downstream distribution channels through its Citgo subsidiary. In 2007, Chávez announced that he would be nationalizing oil projects in the Orinoco region. When Exxon Mobil decided to challenge this by requesting and receiving injunctions from courts in the United States, the United Kingdom, the Netherlands, and the Dutch Antilles to freeze Venezuelan assets abroad, Chávez threatened to halt oil exports to the United States.[101]

When Evo Morales became the president of Bolivia in 2006, one of his first acts was to nationalize the natural gas reserves of the country. Instructing the Bolivian military and engineers of the state-owned petroleum company, Yacimientos Petrolíferos Fiscales Bolivianos (YPFB), to occupy the natural gas facilities of foreign companies, he gave those companies six months to renegotiate contracts with the Bolivian government or face expulsion. One of the companies affected by this move was the Brazilian oil multinational, Petrobras. Also affected were Exxon Mobil, Total of France, and several other European companies.[102]

Chavez and Morales were exceptions to the rule in Latin America and the rest of the developing world. Most leaders of developing countries had come to accept the potentially positive role of MNCs and, instead of engaging in nationalizations and blackmail tactics, bargained for the best possible deals for their citizens.

The Rise of International Production Networks

During the period of globalization, a major shift occurred in the organization of production by multinationals as competition among the developed countries intensified and as the rest of the world became more open to trade and investment flows. Firms began to reorganize their entire **value chains**—from research and development, product definition and design, manufacturing, to final marketing—on an international basis in order to take advantage of lower cost inputs wherever they could be found in the world. Because of lower transportation and communication costs, it became economically viable to organize and manage cross-border production networks where value chain activities were very widely dispersed.[103]

A good example of value chain reorganization is the manufacturing of disk drives for computers. Hard disk drives were originally developed in the 1980s and manufactured by independent companies in the United States and Japan and then sold to computer assemblers. When Singapore developed the necessary expertise to assemble disk drives, the assembly process was moved to Singapore, even though research and development remained primarily in the United States and Japan. United States and Japanese companies established subsidiaries in Singapore to maintain control over the technology but also worked with local contractors. As Singaporeans acquired expertise in disk-drive engineering, some of the components that had previously been made only in Japan and the United States began to be fabricated there. As wages rose in Singapore, some of the labor-intensive operations were moved to lower-wage countries in the regions, such as Malaysia, the Philippines, and later China.[104]

The globalization of production coincided with a major change in the retailing sector in developed countries that favored the creation of large stores, called big-box retailers.[105] Big-box discount stores such as Kmart, Target, and Wal-Mart and electronics stores like Circuit City and Best Buy in the United States were growing rapidly and were constantly searching for cheaper goods to provide to their customers. They took advantage of their ability to purchase in large quantities and to offer preferred shelf space in their stores to bargain effectively with manufacturers of consumer goods who were eager and sometimes desperate to be their suppliers. Many of the goods they sold initially were brand-name products manufactured in developed countries. Over time, the retailers encouraged manufacturers to relocate labor-intensive activities to lower-wage countries while holding the manufacturers accountable for maintaining high quality. This forced the manufacturers to look for low-cost production sites outside the developed countries and then to make sure that overseas factories and contractors used the same quality-control techniques used at home.

The change in retailing coincided with the shift toward export-led development strategies first in the Asian tigers and later in emerging countries, including Mexico, China, and India. Soon clothing and shoes from developed countries were hard to find in retail stores; the same was true for color TVs, VCRs, refrigerators, and other low-end consumer items. By the first decade of the twenty-first century, firms in the fastest-growing developing countries were beginning to move into higher-end consumer markets, such as laptop computers, flat-panel televisions, third-generation mobile phones, and high-definition video cameras.[106]

As a result of the new global production networks, the concern in the early 1990s about low-wage jobs leaving the United States for Mexico in the wake of NAFTA became a more generalized fear of losing not only manufacturing but also service sector jobs to the developing world, especially from **offshoring** and **outsourcing**. Offshoring refers to the relocation of some business activities overseas while outsourcing refers to the use of domestic or foreign contractors to do work that had originally been done within the firm.[107] Clearly, manufacturing jobs had been moving offshore for decades. However, in the 1990s and the beginning of the twenty-first century, computing and information technologies made it possible to send service sector jobs offshore as well. The new technologies enabled firms from developed countries to access highly skilled but lowerwage workers in developing countries. For example, Indian programmers and engineers provided services for the software industry; English speaking workers staffed call centers and help desks in India, Jamaica, and the Phillipines; and Japanese speakers in China staffed Japanese call centers. Business process outsourcing firms based in the South, such as the Indian companies Infosys and Wipro, offered services that competed effectively with mid- and high-wage workers in the developed countries. Gradually, routine architectural, audit, and even medical services such as reading X-rays, could be be handled offshore. Thus, a broader array of jobs in developed countries were exposed to international competition.

Third World MNCs

By the 1990s, there were significant numbers of large MNCs headquartered in developing countries. Some of these companies were formed to manage the raw materials firms nationalized or expropriated in the 1970s; others were manufacturing firms and banks set up in mostly middle-income developing countries as part of their policies either of deepening industrialization after experiencing the limits of import substitution or of turning away from import substitution to export-led development. Still others—for example, consumer electronics, computer, and business process outsourcing—represented the increasing sophistication of Southern MNCs in the high technology industries.

An example of increasing sophistication of MNCs from the developing world is a Chinese company, Lenovo. Lenovo partnered with IBM in producing inexpensive laptop and personal computers and eventually became the primary location for IBM's computer assembly operations. When IBM decided to exit the personal computer business, it sold some of its proprietary technologies to Lenovo enabling the latter to become a globally competitive PC company.

Another example is Dubai Ports World (DPW). DPW is a state-owned enterprise headquartered in the United Arab Emirates that owned and operated 45 port facilities in 29 countries. DPW specializes in handling container-ship cargo but also has expertise in general and bulk cargo operations. In Chapter 4, we discussed the controversy over DPW's attempt to take over the operations of several ports in the United States.

ArcelorMittal steel, a multinational company controlled by an Indian family, became the world's largest steel firm with the merger of Arcelor, a European firm, with Mittal in June 2006. Despite a controversy over this merger in the European Union, the deal went through.

Table 8.2 provides a list of major Third World MNCs with information about where they are headquartered and in what industry they participate. The list includes only relatively large firms and does not include the many smaller firms that, in countries like Taiwan, Hong Kong, India, Costa Rica, and Mauritius, participated in less concentrated global industries like the apparel and shoe industries.

The experiences of Third World countries in managing their own multinationals contributed to the general acceptance of MNCs. State-owned companies tended to be managed much like private firms. Countries like South Korea, Taiwan, and India were able to participate in high-technology industries like electronics and software because of their investments in education and the creation of supporting institutions like technology incubators, venture capital markets, and science parks.

MNCs and the Antiglobalization Movement

As the issue of foreign direct investment became less politicized in the South, the activities of MNCs came under increasing scrutiny in the North. Unions in the industrialized countries expressed concerns about the movement of jobs from industrialized to developing countries and about the unfairness of losing jobs to countries that did not have or did not enforce laws to protect the environment or workers, especially children. For example, trade union opposition to NAFTA focused heavily on the accusation that the agreement would export jobs from the United States to Mexico, which had not only lower cost labor but also less restrictive labor and environmental regulations.

Beginning in the 1990s, a variety of large, Northern-based MNCs came under the critical scrutiny not only of labor but also of students and environmental groups because of their operations in developing countries. Private organizations of citizens of the industrialized nations criticized the labor and environmental operations of MNCs in the Third World and joined the movement to resist

T A B L E 8.2   Third World Multinationals

Industry	Firm	Headquarters
Oil	Petróleos de Venezuela SA	Venezuela
	Aramco	Saudi Arabia
	Yacimientos Petrolíferos (YPF)	Argentina
	Petrobras	Brazil
	Pemex	Mexico
	National Iranian Oil	Iran
	Chinese Petroleum	Taiwan
	Kuwait National Petroleum	Kuwait
	Philippine National Oil	Philippines
	Pakistan State Oil	Pakistan
	Empresa Colombiana de Petroleos	Colombia
	Petroleum Authority of Thailand	Thailand
	Petronas	Malaysia
	Pertamina	Indonesia
Shipbuilding	Hyundai	South Korea
	China Shipbuilding	China
Engineering	Tata Engineering	India
	Nan Ya Plastics	Taiwan
	Hyundai	South Korea
Iron and Steel	Tata Steel	India
	ArcelorMittal	India
	Imsa Acero	Mexico
	Posco	South Korea
	ISCOR	South Africa
	Baosteel	China
	CSN Group	Brazil
Automobiles	Hyundai	South Korea
	Kia	South Korea
	Daewoo	South Korea
	Mahindra & Mahindra	India
	Tata Motors	India
	Chery	China
Electronics	Flextronics	Singapore
	Hyundai	South Korea
	LG	South Korea

T A B L E   8.2   (Continued)

Industry	Firm	Headquarters
	Samsung	South Korea
	Acer	Taiwan
	Tatung	Taiwan
	Lenovo	China
	Hisense	China
Business Process Outsourcing	Infosys Technologies	India
	Wipro	India
	Tata Consultancy Services	India
White Goods	Haier	China
	Hisense	China
Aerospace	Embraer	Brazil
	AIDC	Taiwan
Cement	Cemex	Mexico
Pharmaceuticals	Dr. Reddy's Laboratories	India

SOURCES: Leslie Sklair and Peter T. Robbins, "Global Capitalism and Major Corporations from the Third World," *Third World Quarterly*, 23 (2002): 81–100; and "Emerging Market Multinationals: The Challengers," *The Economist* (January 10, 2008).

globalization. These groups used protests, boycotts, and public relations campaigns to criticize and pressure multinational companies such as McDonalds, Coca-Cola, Nike, Starbucks, Wal-Mart, and Levi Strauss. These consumer companies depended on the reputation of their brands and wanted to be seen as socially responsible in the eyes of consumers. Thus, concerted attacks on their brands and reputations could be especially damaging. Branding itself became a target of some critics of globalization, mainly because of its association with the power of the multinationals, but also because of allegations that MNC advertising and other branding activities were penetrating and corrupting local cultures.[108]

For example, an organization called Students Against Sweatshops, one of the groups represented in the protests in Seattle in 1998, organized expressly to protest the use of sweatshop labor to produce clothing with college and university logos in Third World countries. Another organization called Vietnam Labor Watch formed to investigate reports about Nike shoe operations in Vietnam.[109] It published a report in 1997 after a visit to the Vietnamese plants uncovered evidence of violations of labor laws, bad working conditions, and sexual harassment. Nike was forced to respond and promised to correct the situation. The company began to fund an organization called the Global Alliance for Workers and Communities[110] and joined the Fair Labor Association, along with other shoe and apparel producers, as a sign of its good faith in avoiding sweatshop labor practices.

A similar campaign was mounted by a group called the Rainforest Alliance against firms like Sam's Club (a subsidiary of Wal–Mart) and Starbucks for purchasing coffee from farmers who damaged the environment. The Rainforest Alliance urged consumers to purchase only those coffee products that displayed the Rainforest Alliance Certified Seal of Approval. A company could display the seal only if it purchased a certain percentage of coffee grown in a socially responsible manner using sustainable agricultural techniques and integrated pest management.[111] Environmentalist critics argued that it was too easy to win a seal of approval, while defenders like *Consumer Reports* praised the organization for its pioneering efforts in organizing consumers on behalf of coffee workers and the environment.

The Future: Cooperation or Conflict?

By the 1990s, there was clearly a shift in Southern attitudes toward multinational corporations. Developing countries became less confrontational and more concerned about promoting desired forms of investment. By the end of the twentieth century, most developing countries had made their peace with foreign investment and were soliciting greater flows as part of their new, more outward-looking development strategies. Nevertheless, for many developing countries, particularly those in Latin America and South Asia, deeply held concerns about the economic and political consequences of foreign investment remained.[112]

Northern investment continued to flow to a number of developing countries. However, for many investors in the industrialized countries, the climate for investment in many developing countries, especially the poorer countries, continued to appear inhospitable, overly risky, or otherwise economically unattractive. Despite liberalization of policies toward inward FDI, access and operations in some countries remained overly constrained from their point of view. Increasingly, the developing countries had to compete with the formerly communist countries for available FDI. In some cases, as in India versus China, the communist country was better able than the noncommunist one to convince potential foreign investors that there would be fewer restrictions. The risk of economic downturns brought on by debt and currency crises reduced the flow of FDI to certain recipients. While interest in investment in the rapidly growing countries of Asia and Latin America remained high, the depressed economic conditions in most of the rest of the Third World remained a deterrent to investment.

Ironically, just as the Third World seemed to accept the spread of MNCs, offshoring began to emerge as a political issue in the North and some private groups in the industrialized nations began to express dissatisfaction with the activities of MNCs in the Third World. In the twenty-first century, labor and environmental issues seemed to be joining questions of sovereignty and development as part of the politics of foreign direct investment.

ENDNOTES

1. Theodore H. Moran, *Harnessing Foreign Direct Investment for Development: Policies for Developed and Developing Countries* (Washington, D.C.: Center for Global Development, 2006), 47–48. For comparisons with 1994, see United Nations Conference on Trade and Development, *World Investment Report 1994: Transnational Corporations, Employment and the Workplace* (New York: United Nations, 1994), 14.

2. United Nations Commission on Transnational Corporations, *Transnational Corporations in World Development: Third Survey* (New York: United Nations, 1983), 197.

3. *Ibid.*, 210.

4. United Nations Commission on Transnational Corporations, *Transnational Corporations in World Development: Trends and Prospects*, (New York: United Nations, 1988), 159.

5. Eliane Franco and Ruy de Quadros Carvalho, "Technological Strategies of Transnational Corporations Affiliates in Brazil," *Brazilian Administrative Review*, 1 (July/December 2004): 16–33; and UNCTAD, *Transnational Corporations and Foreign Affiliates* (Geneva, Switzerland: UNCTAD, 2004), 45, http://www.unctad. org/en/docs/gdscsir20041c3_en.pdf.

6. Gary Gereffi and Richard S. Newfarmer, "International Oligopoly and Uneven Development: Some Lessons from Industrial Case Studies," in Richard S. Newfarmer, ed., *Profits, Progress and Poverty: Case Studies of International Industries in Latin America* (Notre Dame, Ind.: University of Notre Dame Press, 1985), 385–442. The expansion of FDI flows in the last three decades and the rise in the number of MNCs hosted outside the United States means that multinational firms are now more likely to be participants in competitive industries. The thesis that MNCs tend to be in oligopolistic industries was originally put forward by Stephen Hymer. For a discussion of Hymer and subsequent questions about his approach, see Mohammad Yamin, "A Critical Re-Evaluation of Hymer's Contribution to the Theory of the Transnational Corporation," in Christo N. Pitelis and Roger Sugden, eds., *The Nature of the Transnational Firm*, 2nd edition (New York: Routledge, 2000). More recent theories suggest that MNCs tend to be "in industries in which intangible, firm-specific assets are important." See James R. Markusen, *Multinational Firms and the Theory of International Trade* (Cambridge, Mass.: MIT Press, 2002), ch. 1.

7. For an analysis of control over access, see Samuel Huntington, "Transnational Organizations in World Politics," *World Politics*, 25 (April 1973): 333–368. Theodore Moran argues that developing host countries can control some types of access better than others. See Theodore H. Moran, "How Does FDI Affect Host Country Development? Using Industry Case Studies to Make Reliable Generalizations," in Theodore H. Moran, Edward M. Graham, and Magnus Blomström, eds., *Does Foreign Direct Investment Promote Development?* (Washington, D.C.: Institute for International Economics, 2005).

8. See Raymond Vernon, "Long-Run Trends in Concession Contracts," *Proceedings of the American Society for International Law*, sixty-first annual meeting (Washington: American Society for International Law, 1967), 81–90; Theodore H. Moran, *Multinational Corporations and the Politics of Dependence: Copper in Chile* (Princeton, N.J.:

Princeton University Press, 1974), 157–162; and Theodore H. Moran, "How Does FDI Affect Host Country Development?".

9. This applies particularly to collusion by the major international oil companies; see Chapter 9.

10. UNCTC, *Transnational Corporations in World Development: Third Survey*, 336–342.

11. See Dennis M. Ray, "Corporations and American Foreign Relations," in David H. Blake, ed., *The Annals of the American Academy of Political and Social Science: The MNC* (Philadelphia: 1972), 80–92.

12. Robert Feenstra, "Gravity Equation," in Steven M. Durlauf and Lawrence E. Blume, eds., *The New Palgrave Dictionary of Ecnomics* (New York: Palgrave Macmillan, 2008).

13. Nathan M. Jensen, *Nation-States and the Multinational Corporation* (Princeton, N.J.: Princeton University Press, 2006), p. 45.

14. Jean-François Hennart and Jorma Larimo, "The Impact of Culture on the Strategy of Multinational Enterprises: Does National Origin Affect Ownership Decisions?" *Journal of International Business Studies*, 29 (1998): 515–538.

15. Nathan Jensen, *Nation-States and the Multinational Corporation*, chs. 4–6.

16. See, for example, Harry G. Johnson, "The Efficiency and Welfare Implications of the International Corporation," in Charles P. Kindleberger, ed., *The International Corporation: A Symposium* (Cambridge, Mass.: MIT Press, 1970), 35–56; Lester B. Pearson, *Partners in Development: Report of the Commission on International Development* (New York: Praeger, 1969), 99–123; United Nations Conference on Trade and Development, *The Role of Private Enterprise in Investment and Promotion of Exports in Developing Countries*, report prepared by Dirk U. Stikker (New York: United Nations, 1968); and Herbert K. May, *The Effects of United States and Other Foreign Investment in Latin America* (New York: Council for Latin America, 1970).

17. Organization for Economic Cooperation and Development, *Development Cooperation 1993: Efforts and Policies of the Members of the Development Assistance Committee* (Paris: OECD, 1993), 65. Please note that the UNCTAD estimates for FDI inflows to the developing countries in 1992 were considerably higher: $51.5 billion. See UNCTAD, *World Investment Report 1994* (New York: United Nations, 1994), 409.

18. Eduardo Borenzstein, José de Gregorio, and Jong-Wha Lee, "How Does Foreign Investment Affect Economic Growth?" *Journal of International Economics*, 45 (1998): 115–135.

19. UNCTAD, *World Investment Report 2007*, annex tables.

20. Peter Nunnenkamp, "To What Extent Can Foreign Direct Investment Help Achieve International Development Goals?" *World Economy*, 27 (May 2004), 660.

21. For data on this issue see UNCTAD, *World Investment Report 2007*, annex tables.

22. UNCTC, *Transnational Corporations in World Development: Third Survey*, 161–162. For a careful review of this subject, see Sheila Page, *How Developing Countries Trade* (New York: Routledge, 1994), ch. 6.

23. UNCTAD, *World Investment Report 2007*, annex tables.

24. On wages paid to developing country employees, see Theodore Moran, *Harnessing Foreign Direct Investment*, pp. 61-65.

25. Leading critics include Celso Furtado, *Obstacles to Development in Latin America* (Garden City, N.Y.: Doubleday, 1970); Stephen Hymer, "The Multinational Corporation and the Law of Uneven Development," in Jagdish N. Bhagwati, ed., *Economics and World Order: From the 1970s to the 1990s* (New York: Macmillan, 1972), 113–140; Ronald Muller and Richard J. Barnet, *Global Reach: The Power of the Multinational Corporations* (New York: Simon and Schuster, 1974); Constantine V. Vaitsos, *Intercountry Income Distribution and Transnational Enterprises* (Oxford, England: Clarendon Press, 1974); and Fernando Henrique Cardoso and Enzo Faletto, *Dependencia and Development in Latin America* (Berkeley and Los Angeles: University of California Press, 1979). An excellent summary of both critical and "neoconventional" perspectives on multinational corporations, as well as a case study of the Nigerian experience, is Thomas Biersteker, *Distortion or Development? Contending Perspectives on the Multinational Corporation* (Cambridge, Mass.: MIT Press, 1978). See also Theodore H. Moran, "Multinational Corporations and Dependency: A Dialogue for Dependistas and Non-Dependentistas," *International Organization*, 32 (Winter 1978): 79–100.

26. Sidney M. Robbins and Robert Stobaugh, *Money in the Multinational Enterprise: A Study of Financial Policy* (New York: Basic Books, 1972), 63–71; R. David Belli, "Sources and Uses of Funds of Foreign Affiliates of U.S. Firms, 1967–68," *Survey of Current Business* (November 1970): 14–19; Grant L. Reuber, *Private Foreign Investment in Development* (Oxford, England: Clarendon Press, 1973), 67; Sanjaya Lall and Paul Streeten, *Foreign Investment, Transnationals and Developing Countries* (London: Macmillan, 1977); and L. E. Westphal, Y. W. Ree, and G. Pursell, "Foreign Influences on Korean Industrial Development," *Oxford Bulletin of Economics and Statistics*, 41 (November 1979): 359–388.

27. Ronald J. Muller, "Poverty Is the Product," *Foreign Policy*, 13 (Winter 1973–1974): 85–88.

28. Newfarmer and Mueller, *Multinational Corporations in Brazil and Mexico*, 67–72.

29. *Ibid.*, 121–125.

30. *Survey of Current Business*, 57 (August 1977): 39; *Survey of Current Business*, 59 (August 1979): 22.

31. Newfarmer and Mueller, *Multinational Corporations in Brazil and Mexico*, 17.

32. See Johnson, "The Efficiency and Welfare Implications of the International Corporation"; Walter A. Chudson, *The International Transfer of Commercial Technology to Developing Countries* (New York: United Nations Institute for Training and Research, 1971); and Lynn K. Mytelka, "Technological Dependence in the Andean Group," *International Organization*, 32 (Winter 1978): 101–139.

33. Vaitsos, *Intercountry Income Distribution and Transnational Enterprises*, 42–43.

34. *Ibid.*, 44–54.

35. For a general discussion of transfer pricing, see the sources cited in note 76 in Chapter 4.

36. Constantine V. Vaitsos, "Foreign Investment Policies and Economic Development in Latin America," *Journal of World Trade Law*, 7 (November-December 1973): 639; and Albert O. Hirschman, *How to Divest in Latin America and Why*, Essays in International Finance (Princeton, N.J.: International Finance Section, Department of Economics, Princeton University, November 1969), 5–6.

37. For a Mexican case study, see Fernando Fajnzylber and Trinidad Martínez Tarragó, *Las empresas transnacionales: expansión a nivel mundial y proyección en la industria mexicana* (Mexico City: Fondo de Cultura Económica, 1976).

38. The International Labor Organization has commissioned a number of studies on the employment impact of foreign direct investment in host developing countries. See, for example, Norman Girvan, *The Impact of Multinational Enterprises on Employment and Income in Jamaica* (Geneva, Switzerland: International Labor Office, 1976); Juan Sourrouille, *The Impact of Transnational Enterprises on Employment and Income: The Case of Argentina* (Geneva, Switzerland: International Labor Office, 1976); Sung-Hwan Jo, *The Impact of Multinational Firms on Employment and Income: The Case Study of South Korea* (Geneva, Switzerland: International Labor Office, 1976); and *Technology Choice and Employment Generation by Multinational Enterprises in Developing Countries* (Geneva, Switzerland: International Labor Office, 1984).

39. United Nations, *Multinational Corporations in World Development: Third Survey*, 195; Vaitsos, *Intercountry Income Distribution and Transnational Enterprises*, 54–59; and United Nations Conference on Trade and Development, *Restrictive Business Practices* (New York: United Nations, December 1969), 4–6.

40. For statistical evidence to this effect, see Michael B. Dolan and Brian W. Tomlin, "First World–Third World Linkages: External Relations and Economic Development," *International Organization,* 34 (Winter 1980): 41–64.

41. Borensztein, De Gregorio, and Lee, "How Does Foreign Direct Investment Affect Economic Growth?," 12.

42. Gerald K. Helleiner, "The Role of Multinational Corporations in the Less Developed Countries' Trade in Technology," in Edward K. Y. Chen, ed., *Technology Transfer to Developing Countries* (New York: Routledge for UNCTAD, 1994), 52; and Ann Harrison, "The Role of Multinationals in Economic Development," *Columbia Journal of World Business*, 29 (Winter 1994): 7–11. According to Theodore Moran, *Harnessing Foreign Investment*, pp. 12–15, wholly owned subsidiaries are much more likely to transfer technologies and train employees than partially owned ones.

43. We are summarizing here the arguments of the authors of Chapters 2–7 and 11 in Theodore H. Moran, Edward M. Graham, and Magnus Blomström, eds., *Does Foreign Direct Investment Promote Development?*.

44. For interesting case studies, see Adalberto J. Piñelo, *The Multinational Corporation As a Force in Latin American Politics: A Case Study of the International Petroleum Company in Peru* (New York: Praeger, 1973); Franklin Tugwell, *The Politics of Oil in Venezuela* (Stanford: Stanford University Press, 1975); Paul E. Sigmund, *Multinationals in Latin America: The Politics of Nationalization* (Madison: University of Wisconsin Press, 1980); and Benjamin F. Bobo, *Rich Country, Poor Country: The Multinational as Change Agent* (Westport, Conn.: Praeger, 2005).

45. Gulf Oil, for example, contributed $4 million illegally in South Korea. See *New York Times*, May 17, 1975, p. 1.

46. Bribes have been made, for example, by United Brands in Honduras for favorable tax treatment, and in arms and airplane sales, such as those of the Northrop Corporation in Saudi Arabia and Brazil. See Yerachmiel Kugel and Gladys Gruenberg, *International Payoffs: Dilemma for Business* (Lexington, Mass.: Heath, 1977).

47. See, for example, Piñelo, *The Multinational Corporation*, 17–25; and Neil H. Jacoby, Peter Nehemkis, and Richard Eells, *Bribery and Extortion in World Business* (New York: Macmillan, 1977).

48. The control of international markets, for example, made possible the boycott by the major international oil companies of Iranian oil in 1951–1953 that contributed to the overthrow of Premier Muhammed Mossadegh.

49. The Hickenlooper amendment was passed in October 1964 (*Public Law 88-633*, 78 Stat. 1009, Sec. 301). The Gonzalez amendment was passed as part of a general appropriations bill for multilateral banks in January 1974. See Anthony Sampson, *The Sovereign State of ITT* (New York: Stein and Day, 1973). On the Overseas Private Investment Corporation, see U.S. Senate, 93rd Cong., 1st sess., *The Overseas Private Investment Corporation: A Report to the Committee on Foreign Relations*, United States Subcommittee on Multinational Corporations, October 17, 1973 (Washington, D.C.: U.S. Government Printing Office, 1973).

50. See, for example, accounts of the role of the United Fruit Company in the United States in the overthrow of President Jacobo Arbenz of Guatemala, in Richard J. Barnet, *Intervention and Revolution: The United States in the Third World* (New York: World Publishing, 1968), 229–232; David Wise and Thomas B. Ross, *The Invisible Government* (New York: Random House, 1964), 165–183; U.S. Senate, Committee on Foreign Relations, Subcommittee on Multinational Corporations, 93rd Cong., 1st sess., *The Overseas Private Investment Corporation, A Report with Additional Views* (Washington, D.C.: Government Printing Office, 1974); and the careful analysis of the role of U.S. multinationals in the ouster of President Salvador Allende of Chile in Paul E. Sigmund, *Multinationals in Latin America: The Politics of Nationalization*, ch. 5.

51. Sigmund, *Multinationals in Latin America*, ch. 5.

52. Sigmund, *Multinationals in Latin America*, 20–23.

53. For analyses of recent empirical studies see UNCTC, *Transnational Corporations in World Development*, 132–237; and Theodore H. Moran, ed., *Multinational Corporations: The Political Economy of Foreign Direct Investment* (Lexington, Mass.: Lexington Books, 1985).

54. For an analysis of economic nationalism, see Harry G. Johnson, "A Theoretical Model of Economic Nationalism in New and Developing States," *Political Science Quarterly* 80 (June 1965): 169–185. See criticism by Vaitsos, "Foreign Investment Policies," 632. For evidence of this rising nationalism, see Jorge Domínguez, "National and Multinational Business and the State in Latin America" (paper presented at the annual meeting of the American Political Science Association, Washington, D.C. 1979). See also Richard L. Sklar, *Corporate Power in an African State: The Political Impact of Multinational Mining Companies in Zambia* (Berkeley and Los Angeles: University of California Press, 1975).

55. Samuel P. Huntington, *Political Order in Changing Societies* (New Haven, Conn.: Yale University Press, 1968).

56. Moran, *Multinational Corporations and the Politics of Dependence: Copper in Chile*, 164–166.

57. See U.S. Senate, *Multinational Corporations and United States Foreign Policy*.

58. See United Nations, *Multinational Corporations in World Development and Report of the Group of Eminent Persons to Study the Impact of Multinational Corporations on Development and on International Relations* (New York: United Nations, 1974).

59. Edith Penrose, "The State and the Multinational Enterprise in Less-Developed Countries," in John Dunning, ed., *The Multinational Enterprise* (London: Allen and

Unwin, 1971), 230. For the role of the new economic analysis in Chile, see Moran, *Multinational Corporations and the Politics of Dependence: Copper in Chile*, 57–88.

60. Moran, *Multinational Corporations and the Politics of Dependence: Copper in Chile*, 164.

61. *Ibid.*; and Alfred Stepan, *The State and Society: Peru in Comparative Perspective* (Princeton, N.J.: Princeton University Press, 1978), 235.

62. Vernon, "Long-Run Trends in Concession Contracts"; and Moran, *Multinational Corporations and the Politics of Dependence: Copper in Chile*, 157–162.

63. UNCTC, *Transnational Corporations in World Development: Third Survey*, 18–19.

64. Vernon, "Long-Run Trends in Concession Contracts."

65. See Gary Gereffi and Richard S. Newfarmer, "International Oligopoly and Uneven Development: Some Lessons from Industrial Case Studies," in Newfarmer, *Progress, Profits, and Poverty*, 432. See also Newfarmer and Mueller on Mexico, in their *Multinational Corporations in Brazil and Mexico*, 59. In addition, once established in the host economy, multinational corporations form alliances with domestic groups and thereby actually improve their bargaining position vis-à-vis the local government.

66. Even ANCOM resolutions must be enacted nationally. See further discussion of ANCOM in Chapter 7.

67. On International Petroleum Corporation, see Piñelo, *The Multinational Corporation*.

68. Moran, *Multinational Corporations*; and Sklar, *Corporate Power in an African State*.

69. For oil and other minerals, see Raymond F. Mikesell, ed., *Foreign Investment in the Petroleum and Mineral Industries: Case Studies of Investor-Host Country Relations* (Baltimore, Md.: Johns Hopkins University Press, 1971). Two interesting studies of nationalizations in developing countries are by Stephen J. Kobrin, "Foreign Enterprise and Forced Divestment in LDCs," *International Organization*, 34 (Winter 1980): 65–88; and David A. Jodice, "Sources of Change in Third World Regimes for Foreign Direct Investment, 1968–1976," *International Organization*, 34 (Spring 1980): 177–206.

70. UNCTC, *Transnational Corporations in World Development: Trends and Prospects*, 315.

71. For a summary of the policies of various developing host countries toward foreign investment, see UNCTC, *Transnational Corporations in World Development: Trends and Prospects*, 261–298. A good summary of the problems that developing countries face in controlling foreign enterprises and a case study of Peru is in Stepan, *The State and Society: Peru in Comparative Perspective*, 230–289.

72. Rosemary R. Williams, "Has Mexico Kept the Promise of 1984? A Look at Foreign Investment Under Mexico's Recent Guidelines," *Texas International Law Journal*, 23 (1988): 417–441. See also Sandra F. Maviglia, "Mexico's Guidelines for Foreign Investment: The Selective Promotion of Necessary Industries," *The American Journal of International Law*, 80 (1986): 281–304. For a review of Venezuelan foreign investment regulations, see Robert J. Radway and Franklin T. Hoet-Linares, "Venezuela Revisited: Foreign Investment, Technology and Related Issues," *Vanderbilt Journal of Transnational Law*, 15 (Winter 1982): 1–45.

73. Ana María Pérez Gabriel, "Mexican Legislation Affecting the Maquiladora Industry," in Khosrow Fatemi, ed., *The Maquiladora Industry: Economic Solution or Problem?* (New York: Praeger, 1990), 214–216; and Patricia A. Wilson, *Exports and Local Development: Mexico's New Maquiladoras* (Austin: University of Texas Press, 1990), ch. 1.

74. Chile withdrew from ANCOM in 1976 rather than impose restrictions on foreign investment. See Dale B. Furnish, "The Andean Common Market's Common Regime for Foreign Investments," *Vanderbilt Journal of Transnational Law*, 5 (Spring 1972): 313–339; Robert Black, Stephen Blank, and Elizabeth C. Hanson, *Multinationals in Contention: Responses at Governmental and International Levels* (New York: Conference Board, 1978): 174–184; and Roger Fontaine, "The Andean Pact: A Political Analysis," *The Washington Papers* 5, no. 45 (Beverly Hills, Calif.: Sage, 1977).

75. United Nations, *Transnational Corporations: Third Survey*, 60–61.

76. Charles Oman, *New Forms of International Investment in Developing Countries* (Paris: OECD, 1983).

77. United Nations, *Transnational Corporations: Third Survey*, 102–122.

78. *Ibid.*, 229.

79. Lacey and Garza, "Mexico—Are the Rules Really Changing?" 572–573.

80. *Ibid.*

81. See, for example, Business International Corporation, *Investment, Licensing and Trading Conditions Abroad: Brazil* (New York: Business International, 1973).

82. Newfarmer and Mueller, *Multinational Corporations in Brazil and Mexico*, 55, 112, 150; Peter Evans, *Dependent Development: The Alliance of Multinational, State, and Local Capital in Brazil* (Princeton, N.J.: Princeton University Press, 1979); and Peter Evans, *Embedded Autonomy: States and Industrial Transformation* (Princeton, N.J.: Princeton University Press, 1995).

83. Jeffry Frieden, "Third World Indebted Industrialization: International Finance and State Capitalism in Mexico, Brazil, Algeria and South Korea," *International Organization*, 35 (Summer 1981): 407–431.

84. UNCTAD, *World Investment Report 1994*, pp. xxviii–xxxiv. For a skeptical view on this, see Alvin G. Wint, "Liberalizing Foreign Direct Investment Regimes: The Vestigial Screen," *World Development*, 20 (October 1992): 1515–1529.

85. UNCTC, Transnational Corporations in World Development: Trends and Prospects, 67–71.

86. *Ibid.*, 82.

87. The South's share increased again in the first decade of the twenty-first century to over 30 percent on average.

88. These numbers are based on data presented in Figure 8.1.

89. *Ibid.*, 82–83.

90. Theodore Moran, *Harnessing Foreign Direct Investment*, p. 39; and Van R. Whiting, Jr., *The Political Economy of Foreign Investment in Mexico: Nationalism, Liberalism, and Constraints on Choice* (Baltimore, Md.: Johns Hopkins University Press, 1992), ch. 8.

91. Jorg Meyer-Stamer, "The End of Brazil's Informatics Policy," *Science and Public Policy*, 19 (April 1992): 99–110; Emanuel Adler, *The Power of Ideology: The Quest for Technological Autonomy in Argentina and Brazil* (Berkeley and Los Angeles: University of California Press, 1987), ch. 10; and Evans, *Embedded Autonomy*.

92. UNCTC, *Transnational Corporations in World Development: Trends and Prospects*, 264–265.

93. *Ibid.*, 269.

94. Jean-Pierre Singa Boyenge, *ILO Database on Export Processing Zones (Revised)*, Working Paper 251 (Geneva, Switzerland: International Labor Office, April 2007). It should be noted that EPZs do not lead to long-term development in countries that continue import substitution policies and that do not attempt to upgrade the skills of their manufacturing workforce. On this question, see Moran, p. 55.

95. John Madeley, *Trade and the Poor: The Impact of International Trade on Developing Countries* (New York: St. Martin's Press, 1993), p. 68; and Ana T. Romero, *Export Processing Zones: Addressing the Social and Labor Issues* (Geneva, Switzerland: International Labor Office, 1995).

96. Moran, pp. 40–41 and 53–56; Madeley, *Trade and the Poor*, p. 68; and Jeffrey A. Hart, "Maquiladorization as a Global Process," in Steve Chan, ed., *Foreign Direct Investment in a Changing Global Economy* (New York: Macmillan, 1995).

97. Hans Jansson, *Transnational Corporations in Southeast Asia: An Institutional Approach to Industrial Organization* (Brookfield, Vt.: Edward Elgar, 1994); and Sanjaya Lall, ed., *New Multinationals: The Spread of Third World Enterprises* (London: Wiley, 1983).

98. UNCTC, *Transnational Corporations in World Development: Trends and Prospects*, 332–337.

99. *Ibid.*, 348.

100. T. Leigh Anenson, "Defining State Responsibility Under NAFTA Chapter Eleven: Measures 'Relating To" Foreign Investors," *Virginia Journal of International Law* 45 (2005): 675-735.

101. "Exxon's Wrathful Tiger Takes On Hugo Chavez," *The Economist*, February 14, 2008.

102. "Bolivia Gas Under State Control," *BBC News*, May 2, 2006.

103. For an overview of the literature, see Michael Borrus, Dieter Ernst, and Stephan Haggard, "Cross-Border Production Networks and the Industrial Integration of the Asia-Pacific Region," in Michael Borrus, Dieter Ernst, and Stephan Haggard, eds., *International Production Networks in Asia: Rivalry or Riches?* (New York: Routledge, 2000). See also Dieter Ernst, "The New Mobility of Knowledge: Digital Information Systems and Global Production Networks," in Robert Latham and Saskia Sassen, eds., *Digital Formations: IT and New Architectures in the Global Realm* (Princeton, N.J.: Princeton University Press, 2005).

104. Peter Gourevitch, Roger E. Bohn, and D. McKendrick, *Who is Us? The Nationality of Production in the Hard Disk Drive Industry*, Information Storage Industry Center Paper No. 97-01, University of California at San Diego, March 1997; and Greg Linden, "China Standard Time: A Study in Strategic Industrial Policy," *Business and Politics*, 6 (2004).

105. See Robert C. Feenstra and Gary Hamilton, *Emergent Economies, Divergent Paths: Economy Organization and International Trade in South Korea and Taiwan* (New York: Cambridge University Press, 2006), pp. 218–238.

106. See chapters by Dieter Ernst on Taiwan, Yougsoo Kim on Korea, and Pokkam Wong on Singapore in Michael Borrus, et al., *International Production Networks in Asia*; Thomas P. Murtha, Stefanie Ann Lenway, and Jeffrey A. Hart, *Managing New Industry Creation: Global Knowledge Formation and Entrepreneurship in High Technology* (Stanford, Calif.: Stanford University Press, 2002); and Jeffrey Macher and David Mowery, eds., *Running Faster To Keep Up: Globalization of Innovation in U.S. High-Technology Industries* (Washington, D.C.: National Academy Press, 2008).

107. Catherine Mann, "Offshore Outsourcing and the Globalization of US Services: Why Now, How Important and What Policy Implications," in C. Fred Bergsten, ed., *The United States and the World Economy* (Washington, D.C.: Institute for International Economics, 2005); Ron Hira and Anil Hira, *Outsourcing America: What's Behind Our National Crisis and How Can We Reclaim American Jobs* (New York: AMACOM, 2005); and Ashok Deo Bardham, Dwight M. Jaffee, and Cynthia Kroll, *Globalization and a High Tech Economy: California, the United States, and Beyond* (Berlin: Springer, 2004).

108. The best example of this is Naomi Klein, *No Space No Choice No Jobs No Logo* (New York: Picador, 2002).

109. See http://www.saigon.com/~nike/report.html.

110. See http://www.theglobalalliance.org.

111. See http://www.rainforest-alliance.org/.

112. On Indian attitudes toward FDI, see Peter Evans, *Embedded Autonomy*; and Joseph M. Grieco, *Between Dependency and Autonomy: India's Experience with the International Computer Industry* (Berkeley and Los Angeles: University of California Press, 1984). Indian attitudes toward FDI changed dramatically in the 1980s. See Arvind Panagariya, *India: The Emerging Giant* (New York: Oxford University Press, 2008).

9

Oil and Politics

Because of its importance as a fuel for modern industrial economies and for military forces, petroleum has long been the subject of domestic and international politics. Over the years, countries have sought to gain control of petroleum resources and to manage the use of those resources for their own political, military, and economic benefit. From the nineteenth-century battles over the Caspian Sea to the War in Iraq in 2003, oil has been the prize in numerous military conflicts. Since 1900, when oil became central to modern industry, multinational companies and both exporting and importing countries sought in vain to create international economic governance systems that would allow them to manage the supply and demand for petroleum, to no avail.

During the Bretton Woods period, the oil industry was dominated by a small group of multinational companies, most of which were headquartered in the United States. The U.S. government, perhaps unwisely, imposed quotas on imports of petroleum to protect the interests of domestic oil producers. This artificial restriction of supply in the United States produced dramatic pressures for increased prices in the early 1970s.

During the period of interdependence, a group of developing countries that produced and exported oil managed to seize control over the international oil system and to restrict supply in order to reap the benefits of much higher prices. For a time, it seemed that their model of unity and control could not only change the oil regime but also serve as a model and as leverage to alter the international economic system as a whole. But this was an illusion. The oil exporting countries did not have the necessary leverage to change the world. In fact, they did not even have the wherewithal to change their own economies. By the 1990s, a combination of low domestic economic growth rates and stable or declining world oil prices made it impossible for even the richest oil exporters to consider reducing production to raise prices.[1]

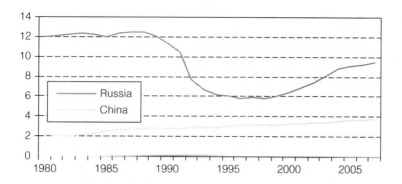

F I G U R E   9.1   Oil Production in the Soviet Union/Russia and China, 1980–2007, in Millions of Barrels per Day

SOURCE: Department of Energy, Energy Information Agency, *International Energy Annual* (various years).

The period of globalization witnessed important changes in the politics of oil. First, a new set of countries—the formerly communist countries—entered the world market for petroleum as buyers and sellers. The Soviet Union had been a major producer of oil for the Soviet bloc. After the breakup of the Soviet Union and about a decade of difficulties in making the transition to capitalism, Russia became a key player in world oil markets (see Chapter 10 and Figure 9.1).

The newly independent countries of the Caspian region—Azerbaijan, Kazakhstan, Turkmenistan, and Uzbekistan—began to develop their petroleum and natural gas deposits. However, to do this they needed to build pipelines, so they looked for partners to help finance them. There were a variety of routes. Some went through Russia, others through Iran, still others through China and Pakistan (via Afghanistan). As a result, Central Eurasia became a new area of interest for students and practitioners of geopolitics.

Supply from the 1990s on fluctuated somewhat with wars and other conflicts, resulting in temporary price fluctuations, not as great as those experienced during the period of interdependence (see Figure 9.2), but still worrisome. U.S. participation in the Gulf War in 1991, its invasion of Iraq in 2003, and the subsequent occupation of Iraq were motivated at least in part by concerns about control over oil in the Middle East.

The first decade of the twenty-first century witnessed rapid growth in consumption in large, fast-growing countries like China and India resulting in major increases in global demand. Global supply could not keep up, leading to a major increase in the price of oil between 2005 and 2008.

In short, the politics of oil was a major concern for participants in the global economy in all three periods. While there were attempts to establish international regimes from time to time, no real global governance existed in this area.

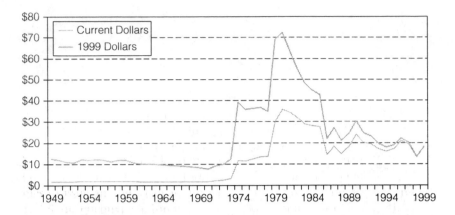

FIGURE 9.2 Posted Prices of Arabian Light Oil (Ras Tanura), 1949–1999, in Current and Constant 1999 Dollars per Barrel

SOURCE: Department of Energy, Energy Information Agency, *International Energy Annual* (various years).

CORPORATE OLIGOPOLY

Seven Sisters

For much of the twentieth century, the international oil system was controlled by an oligopoly of international oil companies headquartered in the United States, the United Kingdom, and the Netherlands. Known as the **Seven Sisters**,[2] these companies dominated their home markets through **vertical integration**, that is, controlling supply, transportation, refining, and marketing as well as exploration and refining technologies. They also worked together to control international supplies of petroleum by keeping out competitors; entering into a series of cooperative ventures such as joint production and refining arrangements and long-term supply agreements; and by refraining from price competition.

In the late nineteenth century, the oil companies began to move abroad and obtain control of foreign supplies on extremely favorable terms.[3] After World War I, the seven formed joint ventures to explore foreign oil fields, and eventually in the 1920s they began to divide up sources of supply by explicit agreements. They were thus able to divide markets, fix world prices, and discriminate against outsiders.[4] Northern political dominance of the oil-producing regions— the Middle East, Indonesia, and Latin America—facilitated the activities of the oil companies. Governments provided a favorable political and military environment and actively supported the oil companies owned by their nationals.

In bargaining with the oil companies, the oil exporting countries faced an oil oligopoly supported by powerful Northern governments as well as uncertainty about the success of oil exploration and the availability of alternative sources of supply. It is not surprising that the seven sisters obtained concession agreements that gave them control over the production and sale of much of the world's oil in return for the payment of a small fixed royalty to the seven sisters' host governments.[5]

Beginning in the late 1920s and continuing through the Great Depression, oil prices tumbled despite the efforts of the seven sisters to stabilize markets. At that time, the United States was the largest producer in the world and exported oil to Europe and elsewhere. Government efforts (including not only the U.S. federal government but more significantly the largest producer state, Texas) succeeded where the seven sisters could not in regulating production in order to create a price floor. Thus, the Texas Railroad Commission emerged as the single most significant political force in the international oil industry.[6]

Changes in this system began to emerge after World War II. In the 1950s, relatively inexpensive imported oil became the primary source of energy for the developed world. Western Europe and Japan, with no oil supplies of their own, became significant importers of oil. In 1950, U.S. oil consumption outdistanced its vast domestic production, and the United States became a net importer of oil. In the host countries, growing nationalism combined with the great success of oil exploration led to dissatisfaction with concession agreements and to more aggressive policies. In these years, the host governments succeeded in revising concession agreements negotiated before the war. They redefined the basis for royalty payments, instituted an income tax on foreign oil operations, and established the principle that the new royalties and taxes combined would yield a fifty-fifty division of profits between the companies and their respective host governments.[7] As a result, profits accruing to host governments increased significantly.

Nonetheless, the seven sisters, also known as the majors, continued to dominate the system by controlling almost all the world's oil production outside the communist world from wellhead to refining, transportation, and marketing. They blocked other companies from entering upstream operations such as crude oil exploration and production by locking in concession agreements with many oil-rich areas and by the long lead times required for finding and developing oil in territory unclaimed by the majors. The majors deterred competition downstream—that is, in refining, transportation, and marketing operations—by charging a high price for crude oil, which limited profits for downstream operations.

The management of the price of oil was facilitated by the highly **inelastic demand** for oil. Because there are no readily available substitutes and because it is difficult to decrease consumption, an increase in the price does not greatly decrease the demand for oil in the short run. Thus, if companies can maintain a higher price for oil, they will not lose sales volumes and so will reap high profits.

Price management by the majors was designed to keep the price of oil economically attractive but also low enough to discourage competing forms of energy. Developed country governments did not resist this price management. Europeans added a tax on petroleum in order to protect the politically powerful domestic coal industry. The United States supported higher oil prices to protect the domestic oil industry from lower international prices.[8]

Finally, the dominance of the seven sisters was backed by political intervention. One extreme example occurred in the early 1950s when the government of Iran sought a new agreement with the Anglo-Iranian Oil Company, a predecessor of British Petroleum, and nationalized the company's assets in Iran. The British government became actively involved in the negotiations, imposed an economic embargo on Iran, and threatened military intervention. After trying unsuccessfully to mediate between Britain and Iran, the United States worked with opposition parties and the shah to overthrow the Iranian government. A new concession was soon negotiated under which the U.S. companies replaced Anglo-Iranian.[9]

Decline of the Oligopoly

However, over time, changes in the international oil industry, the oil-producing states, and the oil-consuming developed countries undermined the dominance of the seven sisters.[10] Competition increased upstream, as new players obtained concessions to explore for and produce crude oil in existing and new oil-producing regions such as Algeria, Libya, and Nigeria. Downstream, more refineries were built and competition grew in markets for refined oil. In 1952, the seven majors produced 90 percent of crude oil outside North America and the communist countries; by 1968 they produced 75 percent.[11]

As a result, the seven sisters were no longer able to restrict supply and maintain the price of oil. U.S. quotas on the import of foreign oil cut off the U.S. market and aggravated the problem. Quotas were instituted in 1958 ostensibly for national security reasons: to protect the U.S. market from lower-priced foreign oil in order to ensure domestic production and national self-sufficiency. In fact, quotas also helped domestic U.S. producers that could not have survived without protection.[12] In 1959 and 1960, the international oil companies were forced to lower the **posted price** of oil, the official price used to calculate taxes. This act was to be a key catalyst for producer–government action against the oil companies.

Changes in the oil-producing states also weakened the power of the oil company cartel. Changing elite attitudes, improved skills, less uncertainty, and the emergence of new competitors increased the bargaining power of the host governments. In negotiations with the oil companies, producer states obtained larger percentages of earnings and provisions for relinquishing unexploited parts of concessions.[13] As a result, the oil-producing governments, especially large producers such as Libya and Saudi Arabia, increased their earnings and began to accumulate significant foreign exchange reserves. Monetary reserves further strengthened the hand of the oil producers by enabling them to absorb any short-term loss of earnings from an embargo or production reduction designed to increase the price of oil or to obtain other concessions.

At the same time, producer governments began to cooperate with each other. Infuriated by the price cuts of 1959 and 1960 that reduced their earnings, five of the major petroleum-exporting countries—Iran, Iraq, Kuwait, Saudi Arabia, and Venezuela—met in 1960 to form an Organization of Petroleum Exporting Countries (OPEC) to protect the price of oil and their government revenues.[14] In its first decade, OPEC expanded from five to thirteen members (see Table 9.1), accounting for 85 percent of the world's oil exports.[15] Initially, the new organization had little success. OPEC was unable to agree on production reduction schemes. Nevertheless, the individual oil-producing states succeeded in increasing their revenues, and the posted price of oil was never again lowered.[16]

T A B L E   9.1   Members of OPEC

Country	Membership
Algeria	1969
Angola	2007
Ecuador	1973–1992, Rejoined 2007
Indonesia	1962
Iran	1960
Iraq	1960
Kuwait	1960
Libya	1962
Nigeria	1971
Qatar	1961
Saudi Arabia	1960
United Arab Emirates	1967
Venezuela	1960

Finally, the Western consuming countries became vulnerable to the threat of supply interruption or reduction. As oil became the primary source of energy and as U.S. supplies diminished, the developed market economies became increasingly dependent on foreign oil, especially from the Middle East and North Africa. By 1972, Western Europe derived almost 60 percent of its energy from oil, almost all of which was imported. Oil from abroad supplied 73 percent of Japan's energy needs. And 46 percent of U.S. energy came from oil, almost one-third of which was imported. By 1972, 80 percent of Western European and Japanese oil imports came from the Middle East and North Africa. By 1972, even the United States relied on the Middle East and North Africa for 15 percent of its oil imports.[17] This economic vulnerability was accentuated by declining political influence in the oil-producing regions and by the absence of individual or joint energy policies to counter any manipulation of supply.

THE OPEC SYSTEM

Negotiation

In the 1970s, these changes enabled OPEC to take control of oil prices and assume ownership of oil investments. The OPEC revolution was triggered by Libya.[18] Libya supplied 25 percent of Western Europe's oil imports; independent oil companies relied heavily on Libyan oil; and the country had large official foreign exchange reserves. After seizing power in 1969, Colonel Muammar al-Qaddafi demanded an increase in the posted price of and the tax on Libyan oil.

When talks with the companies stalled in 1970, the government threatened nationalization and a cut in oil production. It targeted the vulnerable Occidental Petroleum, which relied totally on Libya to supply its European markets. Shortly after production cuts were imposed, Occidental, having failed to gain the support of the majors and of Western governments, capitulated, and the other companies were forced to follow.

In December 1970, OPEC followed the Libyan example and called for an increase in the posted price of and income taxes on oil. The companies, with the backing of oil consuming governments, agreed to negotiate with all oil-producing countries for a long-term agreement on price and tax increases.[19] In February 1971, following threats to enact changes unilaterally and to cut off oil to the companies, the companies signed a five-year agreement that provided for an increase in the posted price of Persian Gulf oil from $1.80 to $2.29 per barrel, an annual increase in the price to offset inflation, and an increase in government royalties and taxes. In return, the companies received a five-year commitment on price and government revenues. After the devaluation of the dollar in 1971 and 1972 and thus of the real price of oil, the producers demanded and received a new agreement that provided for an increase in the posted price of oil and continuing adjustment to account for exchange rate changes. The price of Persian Gulf oil rose to $2.48.

No sooner had the issue of price and revenue been settled than OPEC requested a new conference to discuss nationalization of production facilities. A December 1972 agreement among Saudi Arabia, Qatar, Abu Dhabi, and the companies provided a framework: government ownership would start at 25 percent and rise gradually to 51 percent by 1982. Individual states then entered into negotiations with the oil concessionaires.

Despite their successes, the oil producers were dissatisfied. Although surging demand for oil drove up the market price, the posted price remained fixed by the five-year agreements. Thus, the oil companies, not the oil producers, benefited. Furthermore, the companies were bidding for new government-owned oil at prices above those of the five-year agreements. Finally, increasing inflation in the West and continuing devaluation of the dollar lowered the real value of earnings from oil production.

Because of rapidly rising demand and shortages of supply, the developed market economies were vulnerable to supply interruption. Negotiations between OPEC and the oil companies began on October 8, 1973. The oil producers demanded substantial increases in the price of oil; the companies stalled; and on October 12 the companies requested a two-week adjournment of talks to consult with their home governments. The adjournment was not for two weeks but forever.

The First Oil Crisis: Unilateral Power

Political as well as economic conditions now enhanced the bargaining position and escalated the demands of the most powerful oil producers: the Arab states. The fourth Arab-Israeli war, called in Israel the Yom Kippur War, had begun on October 6, two days before the oil talks began. A common interest in supporting the Arab cause vis-á-vis Israel and its supporters unified the Arab members of OPEC in their confrontation with the companies and the consumers. On October 16, the **Organization of Arab Petroleum Exporting Countries (OAPEC)** unilaterally increased the price of their crude oil to $5.12.[20] Other oil producers followed. On December 23, OPEC unilaterally raised the price of Persian Gulf oil to $11.65.

After the autumn of 1973, oil prices were controlled by OPEC. Operating in a market where supplies were limited and demand high, the producers negotiated among themselves to determine the posted price of oil and the production reductions needed to limit supply and maintain price. The key to reducing supply was the role of the major reserve countries and large producers. Saudi Arabia and Kuwait were willing to support the cartel by themselves, absorbing a large part of the production reductions necessary to maintain the price. Tight oil markets meant that price could be managed when necessary by only limited production reductions. Power over price was quickly translated into equity control. All the major oil-producing states signed agreements with the oil companies for immediate majority or total national ownership of subsidiaries located in those states.

The monopoly control of oil by OPEC, the unity of the producers, and tight market conditions undermined the position of the oil companies. Furthermore, the companies had little incentive to resist. They were able in most cases to pass the price increases along to consumers and thus did not suffer financially from the loss of control over price. Although no longer either the arbiters of supply and price or the owners of oil concessions, the seven sisters and their many smaller relatives still played a vital role in international oil markets. As owners of vital technology, global distribution networks, and significant refining capacity, they were needed by the newly powerful producer governments. As their holdings in OPEC countries were nationalized, the companies became vital service contractors to the producer states. Still, it was a far cry from the days when the companies divided up the producing regions among themselves and obtained control of the world's oil for almost nothing.

With the decline of the companies, the Northern consumer governments tried but failed to agree on a common policy toward the producers. The United States urged Western Europe and Japan to form a countercartel that would undermine producer solidarity by presenting a united front and by threatening economic or military retaliation. The Europeans and Japanese—more dependent on foreign sources of oil, less interested in support for Israel, and somewhat fearful of U.S. dominance—instead advised cooperation with the producers. A consumer conference in early 1974 failed to reconcile these opposing views. The only agreement was to establish an **International Energy Agency (IEA)** to develop an emergency oil-sharing scheme and a long-term program for the development of alternative forms of energy. France, the strongest opponent of the U.S. approach, refused to join the IEA and urged instead a producer–consumer dialogue.[21]

After the conference, consumer governments went their own ways. The United States tried to destroy producer unity by continuing to press for consumer unity and the development of the IEA. The Europeans sought special bilateral political and economic arrangements with the oil producers and resisted consumer bloc strategies. In late 1974, a compromise was reached between the United States

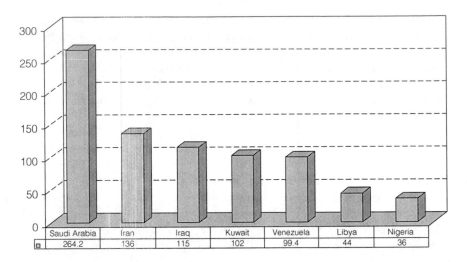

F I G U R E 9.3 World Proven Crude Oil Reserves by Country of the Top Eight Countries, 2007, in Billions of Barrels

SOURCE: *Annual Statistical Bulletin* (Vienna, Austria: OPEC, 2007).

and France. The United States obtained France's grudging acceptance of the IEA, although France still refused to join, and France obtained the grudging support of the United States for a producer–consumer dialogue. The CIEC and the effort to achieve a forum for a producer–consumer dialogue began in 1975 and ended in failure in 1977 (see Chapter 7).

Stable OPEC Management

For five years OPEC under the leadership of Saudi Arabia managed the international oil system. Saudi Arabia accounted for close to one-third of OPEC's production and exports, controlled the largest productive capacity and the world's largest reserves of petroleum, and possessed vast financial reserves (see Figure 9.3).

In periods of excess supply, Saudi Arabia maintained the OPEC price by absorbing a large share of the necessary production reductions. The burden of such reductions was minimal because of the country's huge financial reserves and because even its ambitious economic development and military needs could be more than satisfied at a lower level of oil exports. In periods of tight supply, Saudi Arabia increased its production to prevent excessive price rises. With a small population, limited possibilities of industrial development, and the world's largest oil reserves, Saudi Arabia's future was dependent on oil. Furthermore, with its financial reserves invested largely in the developed countries, it had a stake in the stability of the international economic system.

Thus, Saudi Arabia and the other Gulf states did not want a price high enough to jeopardize the future of an oil-based energy system and the viability of the world economy. The Saudis were willing and able to threaten or actually to raise production to prevent the price increases desired by other more

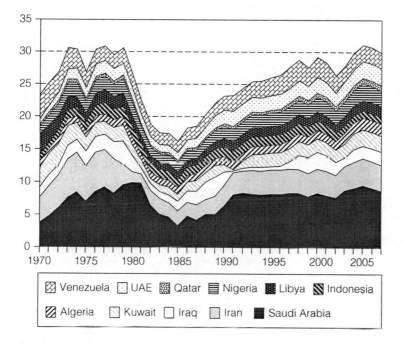

FIGURE 9.4 Production of Crude Petroleum by OPEC Countries, 1970–2007, in Millions of Barrels per Day

SOURCE: U.S. Department of Energy, Energy Information Agency, *International Energy Annual* (various years).

hawkish OPEC members. These countries, including Iran, Iraq, Venezuela, and Nigeria, had large populations, ambitious development plans, and smaller reserves and, therefore, they sought to maximize their oil revenues in the short term. For example, in 1975, Saudi Arabia and the United Arab Emirates forced the rest of OPEC to limit a proposed price increase, and in 1978, when oil markets eased, the Saudis maintained the price by absorbing the majority of reductions of production, exports, and earnings. In 1979 and 1980, when supplies became tight, the Saudis increased production to prevent a price explosion (see Figure 9.4).

A propitious environment also contributed to stability. In the mid-1970s, recession in the OECD countries, combined with conservation efforts arising from price increases, led to a stabilization of demand (see Figure 9.5). At the same time, the supply of oil was steady and even growing as new sources of oil—from the North Sea, Alaska, Mexico—came on line (see Figure 9.6).

Political factors also enhanced stability. OPEC states, pursuing ambitious economic development programs, were spending their earnings at a rapid rate and, therefore, had an interest in maintaining production, and therefore earnings, at a high level. Key OPEC states friendly to the West, in particular Saudi Arabia and Iran, were responsive to Western concerns about the dangers of economic disruption from irresponsible management of the price and supply of oil.

The Western countries remained divided, acquiescent and, as time went on, increasingly complacent. Although they were unable to restructure

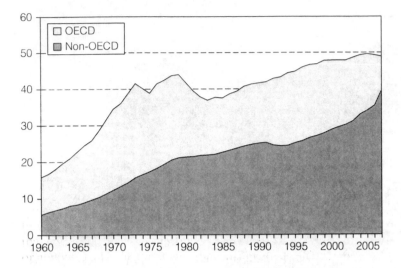

FIGURE 9.5 World Consumption of Petroleum, 1960–2007, in Millions of Barrels per Day

SOURCE: U.S. Department of Energy, Energy Information Agency, *International Energy Annual* (various years).

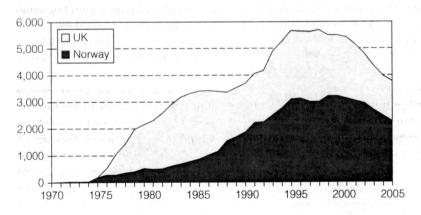

FIGURE 9.6 Oil Production in Norway and the United Kingdom, 1970–2007, in Thousands of Barrels per Day

SOURCE: Department of Energy, Energy Information Agency, *International Energy Annual* (various years).

energy consumption significantly and rapidly, the system stabilized at an acceptable level of price and supply. Furthermore, Western foreign policies—the U.S. policy of developing and relying on special relations with Saudi Arabia and Iran, and the European and Japanese policies of general political support for the oil producers—seemed to promise security of supply and stability of price. Indeed, after the beginning of 1974, the price of oil in real terms actually dropped, as the periodic price increases by OPEC were offset by inflation (see Figure 9.2).

The Second Oil Crisis: A System Out of Control

By 1978, however, the political and economic environment had become highly unstable, and the ability and willingness of the Saudis to manage the price and to ensure the supply of oil had diminished. The demand for oil imports increased as Western economies moved out of the 1974–1975 recession, as the initial shock effect of the price rise wore off, and as the real price of oil declined. Because world oil supplies were only barely adequate, any slight decrease in supply or increase in demand would precipitate a world shortage and put serious upward pressure on prices. If a supply reduction or demand increase was small, Saudi Arabia might be able to fill the gap and stabilize the system. But if the shifts were large, even the Saudis might not be able to control the system.

The event that created a world shortage of oil and disorder in world oil markets was the 1978 revolution in Iran. At the beginning of 1978, Iran exported 5.4 million barrels of oil a day, about 17 percent of total OPEC exports. At the end of 1978, as part of a successful effort to depose the shah, oil workers cut off all oil exports from that country. By the spring of 1979, the loss of Iranian oil had been to a great extent offset by increased production in the other oil-producing states including Saudi Arabia.[22] However, the crisis led to greater demand for oil, as consumers tried to augment stocks to protect against anticipated future shortfalls in supply. The result was escalating prices and turbulence in the world oil markets.

In December 1978, OPEC agreed to increase prices above the expected Western inflation rates—the first real increase in the price of oil in five years. The new price, however, did not hold. The Iranian revolution set off panic in the spot market for oil, which spilled over into the long-term contract markets. Most crude oil was then sold by long-term contract between the oil-producing countries and the oil companies at a price determined by OPEC. Oil not under long-term contract was sold in spot markets where the price fluctuates according to market conditions. In 1978 and 1979, those conditions were very tight, creating severe upward pressure on the spot market prices. In early 1979, spot prices rose as much as $8.00 above the OPEC price of $13.34 for Saudi Arabian light crude, their chief traded oil. The differential between the OPEC price under long-term contract and the higher spot price benefited the oil companies, which were able to purchase contract oil at relatively low prices. Many OPEC members, unwilling to allow the companies to benefit from such a situation, put surcharges above the agreed OPEC price on long-term contract oil and even broke long-term contracts in order to sell their oil on the spot markets. Despite its production increases and its refusal to add surcharges, Saudi Arabia was unable by itself to restore order to the world oil markets.

In March 1979, OPEC announced an immediate 14.5-percent price increase and let members impose surcharges on their oil, demonstrating that even OPEC and the Saudis were unable to control the price of oil. In July 1979, OPEC raised the price again. As the oil minister of Saudi Arabia explained, the world was on the verge of a free-for-all in the international oil system.[23]

By the middle of 1980, the free-for-all appeared to be at an end. High levels of Saudi production and stable world consumption led to an easing of markets.

In this climate, Saudi Arabia and other OPEC moderates sought to regain control over prices, reunify price levels, and develop a long-term OPEC strategy for gradual, steady price increases geared to inflation, exchange rate changes, and growth in the developed countries.

But the plan was destroyed by the outbreak of war between Iraq and Iran. In September 1980, Iraq launched an attack on Iran's oil-producing region, and Iran's air force attacked Iraq's oil facilities. Oil exports from these two countries stopped, world supplies fell by 3.5 million barrels per day—roughly 10 percent of world oil exports—and pressure grew in the spot market. In December 1980, OPEC members set a new ceiling price of $33 a barrel and spot prices reached $41 a barrel. As the hostilities continued, spot-market prices rose, putting further pressure on long-term prices. Furthermore, damage to the oil production and export facilities in both countries raised questions about oil supplies even after the cessation of hostilities.

As the market conditions disintegrated, the foreign policies of the West, particularly that of the United States, were substantially weakened. The special relationship of the United States with Iran under the shah became one of hostility under the new Islamic government. Even the relationship of the United States with Saudi Arabia seemed threatened. The Camp David agreement between Israel and Egypt had led to a cooling of Saudi–U.S. relations. For the Saudis, the overthrow of the shah and the inability of the United States to keep him in power or even to prevent the holding of U.S. hostages raised doubts about the value and reliability of U.S. support. The events in Iran and an internal insurrection in Mecca in 1980 also raised the specter of internal political instability for both Saudi Arabia and the United States, which Tehran was seeking to foster.

Unstable market conditions and political uncertainty gave rise to widespread pessimistic predictions of chronic shortages and periodic interruptions in the supply of oil.[24] Few observers foresaw the profound changes that would undermine the OPEC system of management.

OTHER OPECS?

The success of the oil producers in the 1970s led to a revolution in the thinking of Southern raw material producers. Suddenly it seemed that producer cartels could bring the end of dependence. Producer organizations in copper, bauxite, iron ore, bananas, and coffee were either formed or took on new life after October 1973. In a variety of U.N. resolutions, the Third World supported the right of Southern exporters to form producer associations and urged the North to "respect that right by refraining from applying economic and political measures that would limit it."[25]

Yet by the late 1970s these new producer cartels had failed. None had succeeded in maintaining higher commodity prices in the face of depressed market conditions, most were fraught with internal dissension, and a few never even got off the ground. In contrast with OPEC, the failed cartels lacked several essential characteristics.

Several market factors set the stage for OPEC's success in the 1970s. The demand for oil imports was high. Oil imports played an important and growing role as a source of energy in the North. Europe and Japan were dependent on foreign sources for oil. Even the once self-sufficient United States had become increasingly dependent on oil imports. In the medium term, the demand for oil and oil imports is also inelastic with respect to prices. No substitutes exist for petroleum as a transportation fuel in modern industrial economies, and there is no way to decrease consumption significantly except at much higher prices. Thus, an increase in the price of oil does not immediately lead to a noticeable decrease in demand.

Supply factors also favored OPEC in the medium term. The supply of oil is price inelastic; that is, an increase in its price does not lead to the rapid entrance of new producers into the market. Large amounts of capital and many years are required to develop new sources of oil. In addition, **supply inelasticity** was not relieved by the stockpiles of oil. In 1973, the developed countries did not have oil reserves to use even in the short run to increase supply and alleviate the effect of supply reductions.

Finally, at the time of the OPEC price increases, an extremely tight supply of oil existed in the international market. Rapidly rising demand in the consuming countries was not matched by rising production. As a result, a few important producers, or even one major producer, could be in a position to influence price by merely threatening to limit supply.

This economic vulnerability of consumers set the stage for OPEC's action. Several political factors, however, determined whether such action would take place, and an understanding of the behavior of interest groups helps explain the ability of the oil producers to take joint action to raise the price of oil.[26]

First, there is a relatively small number of oil-exporting countries. Common political action is more likely when the number of participants is so limited, as the small number maximizes all the members' perception of their shared interest and the benefits to be derived from joint action.

The oil producers were also helped by the experience of more than a decade of cooperation. OPEC encouraged what one analyst described as "solidarity and a sense of community."[27] It also led to experience in common action. Between 1971 and 1973, the oil producers tested their power, saw tangible results from common action, and acquired the confidence to pursue such action. This confidence was reinforced by the large monetary reserves of the major producers. The reserves minimized the economic risks of attempting some joint action such as reducing production or instituting an embargo. The reserves were money in the bank that could be used to finance needed imports if the joint effort to raise the price of petroleum was not immediately successful. According to one analyst, it enabled the oil producers to take a "long-term perspective," to adopt common policies in the first place, and to avoid the later temptation of taking advantage of short-term gains by cheating.[28]

The common political interest of the Arab oil producers in backing their cause in the conflict with Israel reinforced their common economic interest in increasing the price of oil. The outbreak of the 1973 war greatly enhanced Arab cohesiveness and facilitated the OPEC decision of October 16 to raise oil prices unilaterally.

Group theory suggests, however, that the perception of a common interest is often insufficient for common action. A leader or leaders are needed to mobilize the group and to bear the main burden of group action. Leadership was crucial to common oil-producer action. In 1973, the initiative by Arab producers in unilaterally raising prices made it possible for other producers to increase their prices. After 1973 the willingness and ability of Saudi Arabia to bear the major burden of production reductions determined the ability of producers to maintain higher prices.

Producer action was facilitated by the nature of the problem. Manipulating the price was relatively easy because it was a **seller's market**. Given the tight market, it was not necessary to reduce the supply significantly to maintain a higher price. Ironically, the international oil companies also helped joint-producer action. Producing nations were able to increase their price by taxing the oil companies. The companies acquiesced because they were able to pass on the tax to their customers.[29] Producing nations were also able to reduce the supply simply by ordering the companies to limit production. Increasing governmental control of the companies helped implement these reductions.

Finally, the success of the producers was assured by the absence of countervailing consumer power. The weakness of the corporations and the consumer governments was demonstrated by the Libyan success in 1970 and by subsequent negotiations. The disarray and acquiescence of the oil companies and the oil-consuming governments in 1973 sealed the success of the producing nations. Particularly important was the inability of the developed market economies to take joint action—in contrast with the group action of the producers—to counter the cartel.

In the aftermath of OPEC's success, several factors seemed to suggest that in the short term, and perhaps in the medium term, some producer cartels might succeed. In the near term, economic conditions were propitious for many commodities, particularly for those on which consuming states are highly dependent. The United States, for example, relies on imports of bauxite, tin, bananas, and coffee. Western Europe and Japan, less endowed with raw materials, depend also on imports of copper, iron ore, and phosphates. Disrupting the supply of many of these commodities, particularly critical minerals, would have a devastating effect on the developed market economies.

In addition, over the short and medium terms, the demand for and supply of these commodities are price inelastic. As discussed earlier, with few exceptions, a price increase for these materials would not be offset by a decrease in consumption, which would lead to an increase in total producer revenues. Similarly, when supply is price inelastic, a rise in price will not immediately lead to the emergence of new supplies, because it takes time and money to grow new crops and exploit new mineral sources. It should be noted that for some critical raw materials, an inelasticity of supply can be cushioned by stockpiles, and developed countries have accumulated such supplies for strategic reasons. Nevertheless, although stockpiles can serve to resist cartel action over the short term, not all commodities can be stockpiled, and stockpiles in many commodities are generally insufficient to outlast supply interruptions that persist for more than a few months.

Tight market conditions favor producers in the short term. As demonstrated by the oil action, a seller's market facilitates cartel action by enabling one or a small number of producers to raise prices, as occurred in 1973–1974. At that time, the simultaneous economic boom in the North and uncertain currency markets that encouraged speculation in commodities led to commodity shortages and sharp price increases. The developed countries were particularly vulnerable to threats of supply manipulation, and the producer countries were in a particularly strong position to make such threats. For example, Morocco (phosphates) and Jamaica (bauxite) took advantage of this situation to raise prices.

In addition to these economic factors, several political conditions also favored producer action, again primarily over the short run. For many commodities—for example, bauxite, copper, phosphates, bananas, cocoa, coffee, natural rubber, and tea—relatively few Southern producers dominate the export market, and some of these producers have formed associations with the goal of price management. Several political developments made producer cooperation more likely in the mid-1970s. One was a new sense of self-confidence. The OPEC experience suggested to other producers that through their control of commodities vital to the North, they might possess the threat they had long sought. Thus, many Third World states felt that they could risk more aggressive policies toward the North.

Another new development stemmed not from confidence but from desperation. The simultaneous energy, food, recession, and inflation crises left most Southern states with severe balance-of-payments problems. Some states may have felt that they had no alternative to instituting risky measures that might offer short-term economic benefits but that would probably prove unsuccessful or even damaging in the long run.

Reinforcing economic desperation was political concern. Political leaders, especially those in the Third World, tend to have short-run perspectives, as the maintenance of their power may depend on achieving short-term gains despite inevitable long-run losses.[30] However, this argument is directly opposite to the OPEC model for a successful producer cartel, wherein monetary reserves enabled the producing nations to take a long-term perspective, to risk short-term losses for long-term gains. In other cases, producers with huge balance-of-payments deficits may be moved to risk long-term losses for short-term gains. And as has been argued, the short-term maximization of revenues may in fact be rational action for the long-term view; that is, if producers feel that their short-term profits will be sufficient to achieve economic diversification and development, they may rationally pursue short-term gains.[31]

The emergence of leaders in some producer groups was yet another new development. Jamaica's unilateral action in raising taxes and royalties on bauxite production and Morocco's unilateral action to raise the price of phosphate altered the conditions for other bauxite and phosphate producers.

Finally, cooperation was sometimes made easier by the nature of the task of managing price and supply. In commodities such as bauxite and bananas, vertically integrated oligopolistic multinational corporations could be taxed according to the OPEC formula. In these and other commodities, production control was facilitated by increasing governmental regulation or ownership of production facilities.

With all of these factors working in favor of cartel success, why then were the raw–material producer associations so unsuccessful after 1974? Some of the reasons for the problems of cartels can be traced to the depressed economic conditions of the late 1970s and 1980s, whereas others are of a more general nature.

Although, as we have noted, the demand and supply of many commodities are price inelastic over the short and medium terms, in the long run the demand and supply are more elastic and thus less conducive to successful cartel action, as is illustrated by the OPEC experience of the 1980s. A rise in price above a certain level will generally lead to a shift in demand to substitutes. Aluminum will be substituted for copper; coffee will be replaced by tea. With time, it is also possible to develop new sources of supply for most commodities. New coffee trees can be planted; new mineral resources, including resources in the seabed, can be exploited. Of course, some of these new supplies may be relatively more expensive, as new production will often have to rely on costly technologies and lower-quality ores. Thus, it should be noted, new production may undermine a cartel, but it may have little effect on price.

Because of the long-term elasticity of demand and supply, the successful survival of a cartel generally depends on two complex factors. First, producers have to manage price so that it does not rise above a level that would encourage the use of substitutes. Such management requires sophisticated market knowledge and predictive ability. Because the threshold price may be lower than the preferred price for many producers, agreement on joint action may be quite difficult to achieve. Second, and equally difficult, the supply response from other producers must be managed. Currently existing cartels have been generally unable to manage successfully either prices or supply: price cutting among fellow cartel members has been common, and few producers have agreed to supply controls.

Despite some incentive for cooperation, there have been major problems in joint action. Although many commodities are supplied by a few producers, these producers often find they have more in conflict than in common. The copper producers, for example, are divided by political as well as economic differences. Moreover, although the foreign exchange crisis may encourage cooperation, it also may facilitate consumer resistance. Producing nations that have no reserves and that rely on the export of one commodity for the bulk of their foreign exchange earnings are not in a position to endure long-concerted corporate or consumer-government resistance. Furthermore, the temptation to take short-term profits from concerted action at the expense of longer-term gains is greater during a balance-of-payments crisis. And although the task of price management may be easy in some cases, as when there is a leader and multinational corporations are present, there are no such advantages for many commodity-producing nations.

One of the greatest barriers to producer cartels has been the task of managing supply. Few countries have a large enough share of production and large enough reserves to assume the kind of leadership role played by Saudi Arabia. No one country or small group of countries is able to bear the burden of supply reduction for the entire commodity group.

Without tight markets, then, supply can be controlled only through buffer stocks or export or production reductions—methods that are politically complex and economically costly. Many commodities are perishable and hence cannot be stored in a buffer stock, whereas other commodities require enormous buffer stocks and financing to maintain prices. Export and production reductions are equally difficult to accomplish. Export reduction without production controls poses the same problems of storing and financing as buffer stocks do. And agreements to reduce production are difficult to achieve, as OPEC's experience illustrates, and may be costly in terms of employment.

Perhaps the most devastating blow to the producer associations was dealt by the stagnant or declining demand for their commodities. In 1974 and 1975, as economic activity in the industrialized countries declined, the demand for industrial raw materials fell precipitously. Faced with reductions or slow growth in the demand for their commodities, the only hope for the producer associations was to reduce production and supply in order to maintain prices at desired levels. Yet, as we have indicated, most producing nations found it politically or economically difficult to cut back production, and many cartel members cut prices in order to increase their international competitiveness. The result was a general oversupply of many raw materials and a drop in their prices that the cartels were unable to counteract.

OPEC IN DECLINE

In the 1980s, OPEC began to face many of the problems encountered by other producer cartels. OPEC's difficulties stemmed from its success. Because of the cartel's ability to increase the price of oil, the demand for oil fell, non-OPEC production grew, prices fell, and it became increasingly difficult for OPEC to manage prices. According to one expert,

> The oil price is high and unstable because the competitive thermostat has been disconnected. Producers no longer set output independently of each other, with higher-cost output disappearing by individual operator's choices. Instead, a cartel of low-cost producer nations restrains their output to support prices. Since cooperation is usually difficult, reluctant, and slow, members' output overshoots or undershoots the demand. Prices are volatile not because of methods of production or consumption, but because of the clumsy cartel.[32]

The Impact of Higher Oil Prices

Oil consumption in the industrial countries fell significantly in the 1980s after rising almost continuously for decades.[33] Slow growth rates in consuming countries contributed significantly to the decline in demand. Oil price increases also played a critical role. Higher prices led to substitution of other fuels such as coal, natural gas, and nuclear energy for oil. They also stimulated conservation and more efficient use of energy. Government policy was also a factor. In Europe and Japan and to a lesser degree in the United States, government policy encouraged conservation. In the United States, the removal of price controls, which had cushioned the United States from the effects of the price increases, promoted energy conservation.[34]

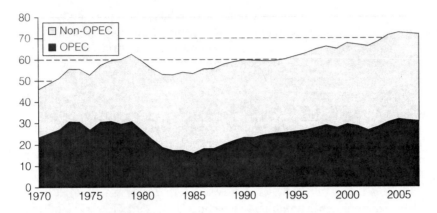

FIGURE 9.7 OPEC and Non-OPEC Oil Production, 1970–2007, in Millions of Barrels per Day

SOURCE: Department of Energy, Energy Information Agency, *International Energy Annual* (various years).

Supplies also increased. Higher oil prices attracted new suppliers to the international market. OPEC's management task became considerably more difficult, as the cartel lost a substantial portion of its share of world production to non–OPEC producers. OPEC's share of the world oil market fell from 63 percent in 1973 to around 30 percent in 1983 but then rose again to 43 percent in 2007 (see Figure 9.7).[35] Non-OPEC production rose steadily, from 22.5 million barrels per day in 1970 to 38.3 million barrels per day in 1988, but then it flattened out at around 40 million barrels per day in the first decade of the twenty-first century.

Several large reservoirs of new oil in the developed countries came into full operation in the 1990s. The North Sea made Norway and Britain players in the international oil game (see Figure 9.6). Higher prices and price decontrol in the United States promoted greater investment in the petroleum sector and encouraged new oil companies to enter the market, exploring for new crude sources as well as developing new purchase and distribution lines. Even though U.S. production did not increase during this period, it might have declined sharply without these new investments (see Figure 9.8).[36] In addition, the Soviet Union increased its exports to noncommunist countries in order to boost its foreign exchange earnings.[37]

As a result of conservation, adjustment, and increased domestic production, the noncommunist developed countries reduced their total demand for imported oil by 40 percent, decreasing their reliance on foreign oil from two-thirds of total consumption in 1979 to less than half in 1983.[38]

Trends in the developing countries were different from those in the developed countries. Oil consumption in the developing countries expanded by approximately 7 percent a year from 1973 to 1979, attributable to relatively high rates of economic growth, generally low domestic oil prices, a lack of substitutes for fossil fuels, and a limited capacity for conservation. After the second oil shock, however, oil consumption in the developing world rose much more slowly, with most of the increase in consumption attributable to the net oil-exporting coun-

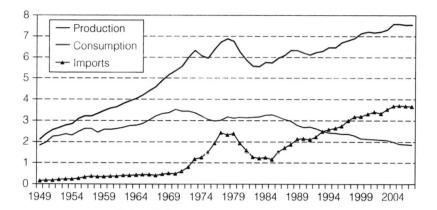

FIGURE 9.8 U.S. Production, Consumption, and Imports of Crude Petroleum, 1949–2007, in Millions of Barrels per Day

SOURCE: Department of Energy, Energy Information Agency, *International Energy Annual* (various years).

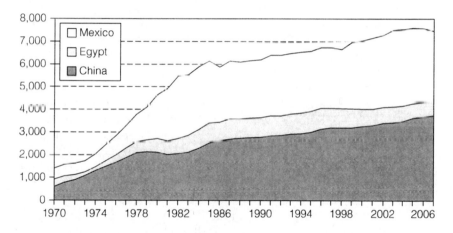

FIGURE 9.9 Oil Production in Mexico, China, and Egypt, 1970–2000, in Thousands of Barrels per Day

SOURCE: Department of Energy, Energy Information Agency, *International Energy Annual* (various years).

tries.[39] A few oil-importing developing countries were able to expand their domestic oil production. Brazil increased its production by 50 percent between 1973 and 1983, and India raised its output fivefold. China and Mexico also increased their production of oil (see Figure 9.9).

Downward pressure on oil prices from the sharp drop in demand and the rise in non-OPEC production was exacerbated by an unprecedented drawdown of oil inventories by the international oil companies. Companies had built up their reserve stocks to their highest levels ever during the uncertainties of the 1979–1980 oil shock. Lower oil prices, high interest rates that raised the cost of holding inventories, and, most important, the growing realization that the sluggish world demand for oil was the result of qualitative changes in demand and not merely a cyclical phenomenon led to a massive reduction in inventories.[40]

Shifting supply and demand depressed oil prices. On the spot market, prices fell from $40 per barrel in 1980 to $30 per barrel at the end of 1982, further lowering long-term contract prices.[41] As a result, the GNP of the OPEC countries as a whole also fell. Although Saudi Arabia and some of the high-income OPEC countries maintained positive trade balances, the current-account surpluses of many OPEC members disappeared, constraining their development plans, imports, and, for heavily indebted countries like Nigeria and Venezuela, payment of debt-service obligations.[42] The fall in demand imposed a particularly heavy burden on Saudi Arabia, which, in its informal role as OPEC's market manager, was forced to reduce its production drastically, from a peak of 9.9 million barrels per day in 1980 to less than 3.4 million barrels per day by 1985, in order to defend OPEC's prices (see Figure 9.4). Saudi oil revenues fell from a peak of $102 billion in 1981 to $37 billion in 1983. The Gulf countries suffered similar production and revenue reductions.[43]

The changing pattern of oil production and consumption increased OPEC's management problems and undermined the cartel's cohesion. Whereas the demand for oil had been inelastic in the 1970s, conservation and interfuel substitution increased elasticity by the 1980s. Whereas the oil supply seemed inelastic in the 1970s, by the 1980s, new sources had diminished much of the cartel's original advantage as the main source of the world's oil. New non-OPEC suppliers also made the cartel's management more difficult. Finally, as the tight supply eased and prices fell, political differences within the cartel further undermined OPEC's capacity for joint action. Excess supply gave rise to enormous strains within OPEC, and the hardship exacerbated traditional conflicts between those OPEC members who sought to maximize their short-term revenues in order to boost imports and hasten development plans and those like Saudi Arabia and the Gulf states who wanted to maintain foreign dependence on OPEC oil for as long as possible by limiting the price increases.

Eventually, OPEC became a victim of the classic cartel problem: cheating. In the 1980s, a number of OPEC members—in particular Algeria, Iran, Libya, Venezuela, and Nigeria—undercut the cartel's price-management system by producing over their prescribed ceiling, offering price discounts, and indirectly cutting prices through extended credit terms, barter deals, and the absorption of freight costs by the seller. As long as Saudi Arabia was willing to shore up prices by restraining its own production, these countries were able to violate OPEC's rules without creating a collapse of prices. The Saudis, however, became more and more unwilling to make that sacrifice in the face of rampant cheating by their fellow cartel members.

The expanded volume of oil traded on the spot market made it more difficult for OPEC to monitor its members' oil transactions and thus aggravated OPEC's price-management problem. With new non-OPEC sources of supply, greater availability of cheaper oil from OPEC cheaters, slackened demand, and less fear of rising prices, the oil companies saw less need for long-term contracts and more often met their supply needs through the spot market. Whereas in 1973 over 95 percent of all oil was traded on long-term contracts, by 1983 at least 20 percent of the world's oil was traded on the spot market.[44] The situation improved somewhat for OPEC members in the second half of the 1980s, as demand recovered and everyone was able to increase production, including the Saudis (see Figure 9.4). But oil prices declined gradually (when controlling for inflation) so oil revenues did not increase as rapidly as they had in the economic recoveries of the 1970s (see Figure 9.2).

Oil Price Wars

Beginning in the early 1980s, OPEC fought a losing battle to maintain control over the declining price of oil. In 1983, OPEC was forced to reduce the price of oil for the first time in its history. Algeria, Libya, Iran, and Nigeria were selling oil as much as $4 below the $34 OPEC price. Saudi Arabia and its Gulf allies threatened to lower their prices to undercut the cheaters. Spot market prices fell, oil companies began depleting their inventories, and producers came under increasing pressure to reduce their long-term contract prices. Thus, in March 1983, OPEC reduced the price of oil, from $34 per barrel to $29 per barrel. To maintain this price, the members agreed for the first time to a concerted production reduction scheme that limited OPEC output and allocated production among the members. Saudi Arabia formally accepted the role of "swing producer" and committed to adjust its output to support the newly agreed-upon price.[45]

The new production reduction scheme slowed but did not stop the decline in OPEC's power as a price-setting cartel. Sluggish demand and increasing production by countries outside OPEC continued to put downward pressure on oil prices. Domestic economic problems and financial shortages tempted members to break ranks by reducing prices and expanding production to obtain more revenues. As non-OPEC production grew and as non-OPEC producers such as Norway and the United Kingdom lowered prices below that of OPEC, it became more and more difficult for the cartel to reach agreement on production ceilings and quotas among members. In 1984, OPEC lowered the price to $28 per barrel, reduced its production ceiling, and lowered individual production quotas. Despite OPEC's production allocation scheme, virtually all of the decline in output was absorbed by Saudi Arabia. By August 1985, Saudi output had fallen to 2.5 million barrels per day, less than one-fourth of its production in 1980–1981.[46] Saudi foreign exchange earnings suffered a steep decline.

In the second half of 1985, Saudi Arabia refused to play the role of swing producer. In order to increase its production and restore its market share, Saudi Arabia abandoned selling crude oil on the basis of official OPEC prices and instituted "netback" sales contracts—a market-responsive price formula based on the value of products into which its oil was refined. Once this happened, OPEC was no longer able to manage the price of oil. In December 1985, OPEC abandoned the system of fixed official selling prices and concerted production reductions. For the first time since the seven sisters agreed to set prices, the oil cartel agreed to allow prices to be determined by the market.

Largely due to the dramatic increase in Saudi production, OPEC output soared and the price of oil in the spot market prices fell from between $27 and $31 per barrel in November 1985 to between $8 and $10 per barrel in July

1986.[47] Pressure to restore concerted production reductions and higher prices built both within and outside OPEC. In 1986, OPEC agreed on new production reductions and quotas and on a new fixed export price of $18 per barrel. Once again, the cartel pulled back from a price war and reestablished market discipline and prices, albeit at a lower level.

Nonetheless, economic and political conflicts continued to threaten OPEC's ability to implement concerted production reductions. The traditional split remained between hawks like Iran and Iraq, which sought to maximize oil earnings in the short term, and moderates like Saudi Arabia and the Gulf countries, which sought to maximize oil earnings over the long-term. This conflict was complicated by an internal conflict over quota allocations. Although a number of OPEC members felt their quota allocations were unfair, the cartel was hopelessly divided and unable to revise the existing agreement. As concerted supply restraint weakened, prices of oil slipped downward.

The Iran–Iraq war signaled a change in oil markets. Iraqi air attacks on Iranian oil fields put them out of commission until the end of the war. Iranian attacks on Iraqi oil fields in Basra seriously reduced Iraqi production.[48] Despite the bombing of oil fields, tankers, and shipping facilities in the Persian Gulf, there was no run-up in oil prices during the 1980s. The spare capacity of the other OPEC and non-OPEC oil producers, public stocks in consuming countries, as well as the oil-sharing arrangement of the International Energy Agency cushioned any potential threat.

The end of the Iran-Iraq war in 1988 posed a threat to oil prices. Iraq was in the process of significantly expanding its production capacity. Both countries faced higher revenue needs for rebuilding and resuming economic development after the lengthy war, and both felt justified in producing more because of post-war needs and because of their reduced production during the war. However, because of the mutual distrust and antagonism arising from the war, OPEC was initially unable to negotiate a new allocation scheme. In an effort to force other OPEC members to resume discipline, Saudi Arabia increased production, creating a glut of Saudi oil and leading to a fall in oil prices to $13 to $14 per barrel by late 1988. In real terms, oil prices were below the 1974 level (see Figure 9.2). The decline in prices hurt the finances of all oil exporters; put severe pressure on indebted oil exporters such as Nigeria, Mexico, and Venezuela; and contributed to political instability in Algeria. By November, action by Saudi Arabia and Kuwait had forced OPEC to agree on a new production agreement to limit production and raise prices to $18 per barrel. Iran received its old share allocation and agreed to allow Iraq to return to the OPEC system with a quota equal to its own. Iraq's increase came at the expense of other cartel members, especially Saudi Arabia, whose quotas were decreased.

In the absence of OPEC discipline, some cartel members sought to protect themselves from price competition by buying refining and marketing operations in the major oil-consuming countries. During the 1980s, a number of OPEC members— Venezuela, Libya, Kuwait, Saudi Arabia, and the United Arab Emirates— acquired downstream operations in the United States and Western Europe. Petróleos de Venezuela, S.A. (PDVSA), for example, acquired 50 percent of CITGO in 1985 and the rest in 1990. CITGO owned and operated refineries and service stations primarily in North America. Moving downstream was intended to protect crude oil exporters when prices fall, because it guaranteed an outlet for oil and because prices for refined products fell less than prices for crude oil. As these OPEC members developed refining and marketing capacity, their oil operations came to resemble the large, integrated oil companies that once dominated the oil system. These members found themselves in even greater conflict with other OPEC members that remained dependent on crude oil exports for revenues and sought therefore to maximize oil earnings in the short term. The downstream diversification strategy, therefore, further weakened OPEC.

The events of the 1980s thus led to a major change in OPEC's power as a price-setting cartel. Sluggish demand, sustained oversupply, competition from outsiders, economic temptations to break ranks by reducing prices and increasing production, and internal political conflicts undermined the role of the oil-producing cartel. Saudi Arabia could offset some cheating by other members but was no longer willing or able to single-handedly manage the cartel by playing the role of the swing producer.

ERA OF GLOBALIZATION

In the 1990s and beyond, oil remained central to the international economy and to international relations. However, unlike earlier periods, no one—not OPEC, the oil companies, or the consumers—was able to manage the international oil system. As we have seen, OPEC was severely weakened by new non-OPEC sources of oil and by internal conflicts. The fragmented oil industry was unable to control prices by limiting or increasing supply. Developed country governments, complacent because of the oil glut and the low prices of the 1980s, actually reduced their influence over energy markets through deregulation and the failure to formulate comprehensive, long-term national energy strategies.

Cooperation among the developed countries on oil issues remained weak and ad hoc. The International Energy Agency had never been strong and remained limited to facilitating cooperation on reserves in the event of an emergency. Nevertheless, oil played an important role in Northern foreign policy. France used diplomatic initiatives to forge ties with Iran and Iraq. The United States protected its oil interests by playing an active role in the Middle East and by maintaining a close relationship with Saudi Arabia. In the following sections, we discuss two important examples of the role of oil in global politics: the 1991 Gulf War when developed countries sought to protect Persian Gulf oil supplies and the effort to assure access to oil in the Caspian region.

The Gulf War

The Gulf War of 1991 dramatically demonstrated both the inability of OPEC to manage the international oil system and the critical importance of Middle Eastern oil for the North. Differences among OPEC members over the price of oil and production quotas were a major factor in Iraq's invasion of Kuwait in August 1990. Concern about the consequences of the Iraqi invasion for world oil markets was a central reason for the strong reaction of the United States, Saudi Arabia, and their allies.

In 1989 and 1990, Iraq and Kuwait were on opposite sides of a significant conflict within OPEC. Iraq emerged from its war with Iran, which lasted from 1980 to 1988, facing severe limits on its ability to produce and export oil. Huge debts made it impossible for Iraq to borrow funds to rebuild its oil production and export facilities. These constraints combined with its desperate financial situation led Iraq to advocate a policy of maintaining high prices within OPEC through greater member discipline. Kuwait took the opposite position. With a large production capacity of 2.5 million barrels per day and large reserves of 100 billion barrels, Kuwait, like Saudi Arabia, advocated lower prices as a way of discouraging production by alternative suppliers of petroleum and investment in alternative energy sources.

Because Kuwait was not as influential within OPEC as Saudi Arabia, it did not feel responsible for maintaining the organization's effectiveness. Thus, Kuwait refused to go along with the production quota assigned to it by OPEC in the late 1980s. Although OPEC increased Kuwait's quota in November 1989, the new agreement did not hold, and oil prices continued to fall to under $17 per barrel. Iraq claimed with increasing vehemence that Kuwait was deliberately undermining the Iraqi economy by overproducing, and that it was, in addition, siphoning oil from a disputed field on the border of the two countries. President Saddam Hussein began massing troops along the Iraqi-Kuwaiti border. A last ditch effort by OPEC to resolve the dispute collapsed in July, and on August 2, 1990, Iraq invaded Kuwait.[49]

The Iraqi invasion led to a spike in the price of oil to nearly $40 per barrel by October 1990. The invasion also led to a swift reaction by both producers and consumers of oil. The United States formed a broad international coalition that included Saudi Arabia, numerous Middle Eastern countries, France, and the United Kingdom. In October 1990, the coalition supported a U.N. resolution authorizing an embargo that would close all world oil markets to Iraqi exports. This embargo affected a flow of 4.3 million barrels per day of oil to world markets, about 7 percent of the world total. U.N. action combined with increased production by both OPEC and non-OPEC producers helped to reduce the impact of this very effective embargo on the rest of the world. In addition, the oil-consuming members of the IEA released their strategic oil reserves in order to cushion the impact of U.N. embargo on world oil markets.[50] The coalition then sent military forces to the region and, on January 16, 1991, launched a military action that liberated Kuwait and led to a record short-term drop in oil prices from $33 to less than $18 per barrel.[51] The allies did not succeed in toppling Saddam Hussein, however.

While numerous factors motivated the United States and its allies in reacting strongly to the invasion of Kuwait, concern about oil was one of the most important. Control over Kuwait's petroleum reserves would have given Iraq control over a total of 205 billion barrels, about one-fifth of the world's known oil reserves, and would have put Iraq in a position to dominate the weakened OPEC.[52] Combined

Iraqi and Kuwaiti daily production capacity would have been around 5.5 million barrels per day, still below that of Saudi Arabia (8.5 million barrels per day) but large enough to give the Iraqi government significant market power. Furthermore, with control of strategic military positions in Kuwait and with its large army, Iraq would have been able to threaten other key oil producers in the region, including Saudi Arabia. Such dominance of world oil markets by a single country was unacceptable to both consumers and producers of petroleum and helped to explain the unique alliance that formed against Saddam Hussein.

Following the war, due to Iraq's continuing attempts to manufacture weapons of mass destruction and its refusal to agree to effective monitoring of its activities, the United Nations maintained sanctions on all exports to Iraq except for food and medical supplies and other humanitarian needs. The United Nations also maintained its embargo on exports of Iraqi oil. In 1995, the United Nations established an Oil-for-Food Program under Security Council Resolution 986 that was intended to permit Iraq to sell oil on the world market in exchange for food, medicine, and other humanitarian needs. The Clinton administration introduced the program as a response to the criticism that Saddam Hussein was shifting the burden of economic sanctions onto the backs of ordinary Iraqi citizens. The program suffered from corruption and abuse. It ended in 2003 when the United States and its allies invaded Iraq.[53]

Oil in the Caspian Region

The end of communism and the breakup of the Soviet Union unleashed a variety of political forces, including a new scramble to control oil resources in the former Soviet Union. In Russia itself, the Yeltsin government relinquished control over the oil and natural gas industries as a result of its privatization efforts (see Chapter 10 for details). The new private owners did not have sufficient resources to invest in exploration and exploitation of existing oil and gas deposits. Investment and production in Russia declined markedly in the 1990s (see again Figure 9.1). The political excesses of the Yeltsin-era oligarchs, many of whom owned controlling shares in the newly privatized oil and gas enterprises and openly opposed Putin's rise to power, combined with their attempts to negotiate partnerships with foreign energy companies, gave Putin the opportunity he needed to wrest control of Russian energy resources from private owners. Putin then used renewed state control over oil and gas firms and pipelines to influence the politics of bordering countries that were formerly members of the Soviet Union (Belarus, the Ukraine, Kazakhstan, and Georgia) and more generally to reassert Russia's role as a great power.

In the 1990s, new oil and natural gas deposits were discovered in the former states of the Soviet Union located in the Caspian region: Azerbaijan, Kazakhstan, and Turkmenistan. Russia and Iran also bordered the landlocked Caspian Sea and all five countries laid claim to seabed oil and gas deposits there. Caspian oil reserves were estimated to be approximately 47 billion barrels at the end of 2005—about 3 percent of world reserves—less than 20 percent of Saudi reserves but more than Libyan reserves. Natural gas reserves were estimated to be 6.6 trillion cubic meters. The largest deposits were in Kazakhstan.[54]

Caspian Region Oil Pipelines (U)

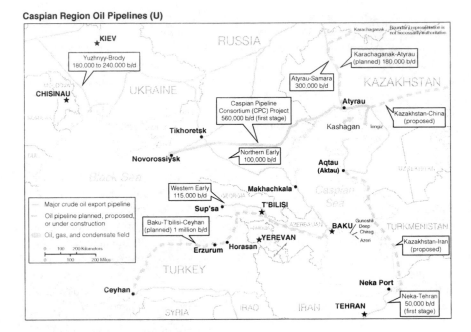

F I G U R E 9.10   Pipelines in the Caspian Region

SOURCE: http://www.eia.doe.gov/cabs/Caspian/Full.html

Development of the Caspian oil fields began in earnest following the breakup of the Soviet Union in 1991. In April 1993, Chevron concluded a historic $20-billion deal with Kazakhstan to create the Tengizchevroil joint venture[55] to develop the Tengiz and Korolev oil fields. Tengizchevroil produced over 500,000 barrels per day of oil in mid 2008.[56]

Development of the oil and gas industies in the Caspian region was hindered by the difficulty of transporting Caspian oil to world markets. Prior to 1997, exporters of Caspian oil had only one major pipeline option available to them, the Atyrau-Samara pipeline from Kazakhstan to Russia. In addition, smaller amounts of oil were shipped by rail and barge through Russia, and by a second, small pipeline from Kazakhstan to Russia. The Caspian region's relative isolation from world markets, as well as the lack of export options, stifled exports outside of the former Soviet republics.

Thus, for the newly developed Caspian oil to reach world markets, it was necessary to build pipelines to transport the oil from the landlocked Caspian region to new foreign markets. The main alternatives were: (1) the Baku–Tbilisi–Ceyhan (BTC) pipeline, (2) the Baku–Tbilisi–Supsa (BTS) pipeline, and (3) the Baku–Novorosiisk (BN) pipeline (see Figure 9.10).

The BTC pipeline was built and operated by the Caspian Pipeline Consortium and was completed in May 2005. The Caspian Pipeline Consortium consists of BP, ConocoPhilips, ChevronTexaco, and ExxonMobil. The BTC pipeline goes from Baku in Azerbaijan to Tbilisi in Georgia to Ceyhan, a Turkish port on the Bosphorus, thus completely bypassing Russia.

The BTS pipeline goes from Baku to Supsa, a Georgian port on the Black Sea. Negotiations between the governments of Azerbaijan and Georgia for building it began in 1994. The contract was awarded to a Norwegian firm, Kraemer, and the pipeline was completed in 1998 at a cost of approximately $0.5 billion. It is essentially a refurbished Soviet-era pipeline with some newly built sections. The BTS pipeline was closed for repairs between October 2006 and August 2008. When Russia invaded Georgia in August 2008 some Russian bombs fell near the pipeline, and it was again shut down for a short time.

The BN pipeline goes from Baku to Novorosiisk, a Russian port on the Black Sea. It was built originally during the Soviet era and then expanded after the Caspian deposits were discovered. It travels through Azerbaijan and Russia only, and thus is the route preferred by the Russian government for Caspian energy flows. The Azeri portion of the BN pipeline is operated by the State Oil Company of the Azerbaijan Republic (SOCAR), and the Russian portion is operated by Transneft, a Russian state-owned pipeline firm.

The main goal of the Western countries was to assure that there were multiple routes for the export of Caspian oil and gas so that no one country had the capability to block the region's exports or to use control of transportation routes for political leverage. Thus, plans were developed to build additional pipelines connecting oil and fields in the Caspian region to Pakistan (via Afghanistan), Iran, and China. Natural gas deposits in the Caspian region were as large or larger than petroleum deposits so natural gas pipeline projects were planned in addition to the oil pipelines already noted.

Some observers compared this recent period of oil and gas development in the Caspian with an earlier period of great power competition sometimes called "the Great Game." The Great Game was a competition between the British and Russian governments for supremacy in Central Asia that occurred between 1813 and 1907. The Anglo-Afghan war inspired Rudyard Kipling's short story, "The Man Who Would Be King," and George MacDonald Fraser's novel, *Flashman*. Some scholars argue that the current competition between Russia and the United States over the Caspian is a new Great Game.[57] And although the old Great Game was about control over territory, the new Great Game is all about control over energy.

CHANGING ECONOMICS OF OIL AT THE END
OF THE TWENTIETH CENTURY

By the end of the twentieth century, the economic and political dynamics of oil had shifted. The Gulf War demonstrated that OPEC was no longer able to manage the international oil system. The divergent interests of OPEC members made price and production management increasingly difficult despite the powerful position of Saudi Arabia. As we shall see, even that dominant country began to face financial problems as the price of oil declined and the Saudi budget grew faster than the growth in oil revenues.

Furthermore, because OPEC's share of the world oil market was smaller, price management increasingly required the cooperation of non–OPEC producers. Such cooperation could not be guaranteed, however, since many non-OPEC producers, like the United Kingdom, Norway, and Mexico, continued to pursue independent strategies. In Mexico, the NAFTA treaty, which opened up sectors of the oil industry to foreign investment, combined with the aftermath of the 1994 peso crisis to make it difficult for the Mexican government to think of cooperating with OPEC to bolster oil prices. OPEC's weakness and the success of the coalition against Iraq set the stage for turmoil in international oil markets.

By the end of the twentieth century, oil markets had come to resemble those of other commodities: highly volatile and subject to swings in supply and demand, but still subject at times to the actions of a small number of oil producers. The problem was not a shortage of petroleum in the world, as new fields were discovered and older fields made more productive through technology. For example, advances were made in secondary and tertiary recovery. Secondary recovery involves maintaining or enhancing reservoir pressure by injecting water, gas or other substances into the formation. Tertiary recovery involves technologies that, for example, heat the petroleum reservoir in order to reduce viscosity. While secondary and tertiary recovery are more expensive than primary recovery, improvements in technology can reduce the differences in cost.[58]

Advances in offshore drilling technology greatly reduced the per barrel cost of exploiting offshore petroleum deposits. North Sea oil costs were reduced as much as 80 percent in the 1990s, and per barrel costs descended to around $3 per barrel, making North Sea crude oil almost as inexpensive as oil from the Middle East.[59]

Despite advances in technology, however, worldwide capacity to extract, refine, and distribute petroleum was constrained for a number of reasons. Above all, falling real prices for oil in the 1980s and early 1990s reduced the incentive to make the massive investments in extraction, transportation, and refining capacity needed to exploit new sources of petroleum.

Investment was also complicated by environmental regulation. Environmental regulations, put in place to address concerns about oil spills and destruction of wildlife habitat, raised the costs of exploration and exploitation for energy companies in the United States and other industrialized countries. Energy companies were also burdened with expenses connected with cleaning up older or abandoned sites where environmental damage was extensive. In the United States, the so-called Superfund Program was of particular concern to the oil industry.[60]

While investment stagnated, global demand for petroleum increased steadily in the 1990s (see Figure 9.5). Because of the oil glut of the 1980s and their success in the Gulf War, the North became increasingly complacent about the need to implement national energy policies and to manage the international oil system. Although Europe and Japan encouraged conservation by imposing taxes on oil consumption, the United States rejected such taxes, maintaining relatively low prices of oil and encouraging a return to gas guzzling vehicles and high consumption of petroleum.

Meanwhile, developing countries consumed ever-greater quantities of petroleum to fuel development. Between 1960 and 1999, average annual growth in oil consumption the OECD countries was around 3 percent; in the developing countries it was 4.2 percent. Between 2000 and 2007, growth in OECD oil consumption was 0.3 percent;

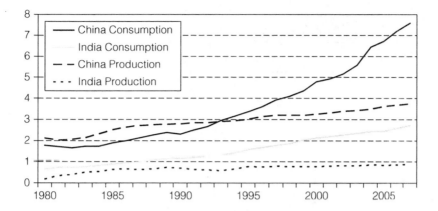

FIGURE 9.11 Oil Consumption and Production in China and India, 1980–2007, in Millions of Barrels per Day

SOURCE: Energy Information Agency, U.S. Department of Energy, http://www.eia.doe.gov/emeu/international/oilconsumption.html.

in the rest of the world it was 4.7 percent.[61] China, which was short of hydrocarbon resources, posed a particular threat. Because of China's high rate of economic growth, the demand for fossil fuels increased rapidly. China became the third largest oil consumer after the United States and Japan and in 1993 China became a net importer of oil. After that date, the gap between domestic production and consumption increased dramatically (see Figure 9.11). Rising energy demands combined with supply constraints created unstable conditions in oil markets. In such markets, OPEC was able to act only at the margins and only when oil exporters were desperate. One of the key factors affecting OPEC in this new era was the changed role of Saudi Arabia. Remember, the ability and willingness of Saudi Arabia to play the role of swing producer was weakened in the 1980s by growing non-OPEC production and by OPEC internal conflicts. In the 1990s, a new factor intervened: Saudi finances.

In the 1970s and 1980s, Saudi Arabia used its massive oil earnings to support its economy, social services, and foreign policy as well as to accumulate large financial reserves. The Saudis built an economy based on government ownership of industry and a social and political system built on extensive government services and assured employment. Saudi leaders also used oil earnings to support a costly foreign policy, which included significant financial support for Iraq—estimated at $26 billion—during the Iran–Iraq war, and for the coalition against Iraq during the Gulf War—estimated at $60 billion.[62] The government also made significant purchases of foreign military equipment, largely from the United States. For many years, Saudi Arabia had been able support these expenditures without draining its vast financial reserves.

By the 1990s, lower oil prices, rising costs of inefficient domestic industries and of services for a rapidly growing population, and the burden of foreign and military expenditures had taken their toll. Saudi budgets were in chronic deficit, financial reserves declined dramatically (see Figure 9.12), and the country was obliged to borrow from both domestic and foreign sources to cover its expenses. In an effort to limit the financial drain, Saudi leaders implemented limited

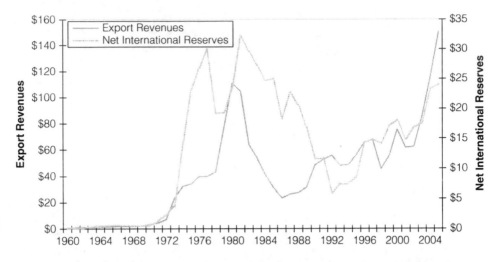

FIGURE 9.12 Saudi Export Revenues and Foreign Currency Reserves, 1960–2005, in Billions of Current Dollars

SOURCE: *World Development Indicators 2007*; and Saudi Arabian Monetary Agency, *Annual Report*, Monetary and Banking Statistics.

economic reforms. However, they were unwilling to undertake significant economic and budgetary reforms that would lead to unemployment and a loss of government control over the economy that, in turn, would weaken their domestic political support. As a result, the Saudis became increasingly concerned about maintaining the price of oil, their market share, and their oil earnings.[63]

The Saudi dilemma became clear in 1998, when the price of oil collapsed. In 1997, despite the Asian economic crisis, OPEC increased production, driving oil prices down to $12 per barrel. Saudi Arabia now faced what other oil exporters had confronted: a dearth of government revenues, an inability to fulfill social and political demands, and the threat of political instability. In desperation, Saudi Arabia along with other OPEC and non-OPEC producers including Mexico, Norway, and Oman agreed on production reductions. Nevertheless, in December 1998, oil prices fell to below $10 per barrel. Saudi Arabia then led negotiations among OPEC and non-OPEC members to further reduce production. On March 23, 1999, OPEC announced that its members had agreed to reduce oil production quotas by a total of 1.7 million barrels per day.[64] These reductions, combined with a more rapid than expected Asian recovery, helped to stabilize oil prices.

OIL IN THE TWENTY-FIRST CENTURY

Rising Price of Oil

At the dawn of the twenty-first century, the stage was set for a massive rise in the price of oil with its attendant political consequences. Global demand grew dramatically because of continued growth in the industrialized countries, the low cost of oil during the 1980s and 1990s (which encouraged consumption and a shift toward less energy-efficient vehicles in the United States), and rapid economic growth in emerging markets, particularly large developing countries like China and India.

Supply could not keep up with demand because (1) low investments in refining capacity created a bottleneck in the supply chain; (2) new environmental regulations in industrialized countries made it more expensive to invest in refineries; (3) wars in the Middle East (especially the Gulf War and the war in Iraq) and the Iraqi insurgency reduced production in the Persian Gulf; (4) production in OPEC members Nigeria, Venezuela, and Mexico was declining; and (5) major non-OPEC sources like the North Sea were experiencing a major decline in production (see Figure 9.6).[65]

As a result, there was less of a cushion in the form of excess production and refining capacity that could handle both real and threatened disruptions in supply. Events such as hurricanes in the Gulf of Mexico, political unrest in Nigeria, efforts by the Chávez government in Venezuela to nationalize foreign investment in the oil sector, attacks on oil facilities in Iraq, threats by Iran to interrupt flows of oil through the Straits of Hormuz, and breakdowns in refineries led to huge spikes in the price of oil. These major changes were reinforced by growing speculation on oil prices in financial markets during the commodity boom of the early twenty-first century.

OPEC remained weak and was unsuccessful in its efforts to manage the price of oil by allocating production quotas. Saudi Arabia was no longer in a position to impose discipline on the other members of OPEC. The Saudis did not control refining capacity, a key to maintaining control over prices. Oil markets became vulnerable to even limited disruptions in supply.

In 2003, oil prices began to climb once again. Oil prices rose again in 2005 and then accelerated at the end of 2007 (see Figure 9.13). Per barrel prices went above $100 for the first time in March 2008. By late summer prices had risen to over $140 per barrel before dropping back to around $80 in October. Again, steady supply and growing demand were the main reasons for price increases. Saudi Arabia increased production by about 0.5 million barrels per day in June. The Saudis were happy to receive the windfall revenues from higher oil prices, but were concerned about the possibility of a global slowdown. The price decreases in the autumn of 2008 were driven primaily by reduced consumption in the industrialized world resulting in growing fears of a global recession. Within OPEC, the price hawks—especially Iran and Venezuela—pushed for a reduction in production, while Saudi Arabia maintained the existing level of production (above its OPEC quota) as prices declined.

Gasoline prices in the United States quickly adjusted upward as crude oil prices increased (see Figure 9.14) and became an important issue in domestic politics including the 2008 election campaign. Republicans began to push for more offshore drilling and exploitation of Alaskan reserves. Democrats countered with demands for releasing oil from the Strategic Petroleum Reserve and new proposals for conserving fossil fuels. Others argued for greater use of nuclear power, solar power, wind power, biofuels, and other alternative energy sources.

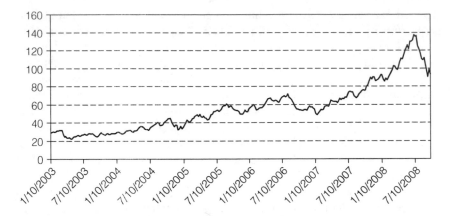

FIGURE 9.13   Weekly All Countries Spot Price of Oil per Barrel FOB Weighted by Estimated Export Volume in Current Dollars

SOURCE: Department of Energy, Energy Information Agency.

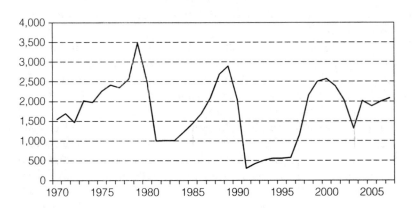

FIGURE 9.14   Crude Oil Production in Iraq, 1970-2007, in Thousands of Barrels per Day

SOURCE: Energy Information Agency, U.S. Department of Energy, http://www.eia.doe.gov/ipm/supply.html.

Consumers reacted to higher gasoline prices by reducing their driving mileage and by trading in their gas-guzzling SUVs for hybrids and other more fuel-efficient vehicles.

The impact of higher oil prices on world politics was significant. Russia emerged as the world's largest energy producer and increased global oil prices enabled Russia to become much more assertive on the world stage (see Chapter 10). Another major oil exporter, Iran, was able to shrug off international pressures to cease its nuclear weapons development program. Iran continued to fund Shi'ite insurgents in Iraq, Hezbollah in Lebanon, and Hamas in the Gaza Strip, and periodically threatened to disrupt world oil supplies from the Gulf, which flowed through the Straits of Hormuz controlled by Iran. Venezuela challenged Brazil for regional hegemony in Latin America.

Because of their increasing dependence on imported oil and natural gas, the Western economies were more vulnerable to threats of disruption in oil supply. This was demonstrated in 2005 and 2006 when Russia disrupted oil and natural gas flows to Western Europe through pipelines in the Ukraine and Belarus.

In March 2005, the Russian natural gas company, Gazprom, demanded increased prices for natural gas exports to the Ukraine. In addition, the Russians wanted to pay lower fees for the transmission of gas to Western Europe through the pipelines. The Ukrainians traditionally demanded 15 percent of the gas flowing through the pipeline as payment for transit rights. Negotiations between the two governments to settle the dispute were unsuccessful. On January 1, 2006, Gazprom stopped the flow of natural gas to the Ukraine. The flow was restored three days later, with both sides claiming that a satisfactory agreement had been reached. Observers in Europe and the United States speculated that the dispute was motivated by Russia's displeasure over the success of the Orange Revolution and the 2004 defeat of their favored candidate for the presidency, Viktor Yanukovych, by Viktor Yuschenko, who favored closer ties to Europe. Both the Russians and the Ukrainians later denied that this was a major factor in the dispute.

In Belarus, the dispute began in 2006 when Gazprom demanded increased prices for natural gas exports. The president of Belarus, Alexander Lukashenko, refused to pay, so Gazprom threatened to cut off gas supplies. Lukashenko backed down but then retaliated by upping the transit fees that Belarus charged Russia for the Druzhba pipeline, an oil pipeline operated by the Russian state enterprise, Transneft. When Transneft refused to pay the fees, the Belarus government began siphoning oil from the pipeline. In retaliation, Transneft shut down the pipeline entirely. Because most of the oil flowing through the Druzhba pipeline was destined for Western Europe, the European Union objected strenuously. Three days later, negotiations between Russia and Belarus resulted in the reopening of the pipeline.

Emerging countries like China and India became anxious to secure access to foreign sources of oil. China launched a diplomatic initiative, negotiating a series of agreements with oil-producing countries like Sudan, Somalia, Ethiopia, Kenya, and Sri Lanka. The Chinese National Overseas Oil Company (CNOOC) was one of the bidders in 2007 and 2008 for service contracts with the Iraqi national oil company. CNOOC and Taiwan's state-run oil refiner, CPC Corporation, agreed to cooperate in developing offshore deposits in the East China Sea.

China's need for oil also drove other Chinese diplomatic positions. For example, the Chinese blocked U.N. action on the humanitarian crisis in Darfur so as not to offend their new Sudanese partners.

India was competing with China in some places to secure access to foreign oil. The Oil and Natural Gas Corporation (ONGC) of India held talks in October 2008 with the Iranian government for exploring an oil block in Northern Iran, in competition with the Chinese company, Sinopec.[66] Similar talks were going on with the Colombian government.[67]

The War in Iraq

In addition to shaping a variety of political and diplomatic relations, access to oil again became a factor in issues of war and peace. Oil did not cause the United States and its allies to invade Iraq in 2003, but oil did become an important element in bringing peace and stability to that country and had ramifications for the oil market well beyond the Middle East.

After the 1991 Gulf War, as noted above, the regime of Saddam Hussein in Iraq had been subjected to severe sanctions by the United Nations and its member nations with the purpose of ending the Iraqi nuclear weapons development program. U.S. strategy during the 1990s had been to keep Saddam in check through these sanctions by imposing military no fly zones in Northern Iraq. However, following the election of George W. Bush and the terrorist attacks of 9/11, concern grew (particularly in the United States and within the Bush Administration) about Iraq's nuclear weapons program and its possible possession of other weapons of mass destruction as well as about Saddam's alleged link to Al-Qaeda. Intelligence information—later proven to be false—suggested that sanctions had not stopped Saddam's nuclear program and that the 9/11 terrorists had consulted with Iraqi officials.

Despite concern over Iraq's possession of weapons of mass destruction (including Hussein's refusal to permit U.N. inspection of Iraqi weapons facilities) and despite strong pressure from the United States, the United Nations did not authorize the use of force against Saddam. Instead, the Bush Administration convinced the U.S. Congress to authorize the use of force against Iraq in 2003. Although the U.S. government was not able to assemble a broad international supporting coalition as it had in 1991—a number of NATO allies including France and Germany refused to participate—the United Kingdom, Australia, and Poland did participate alongside the United States in the 2003 invasion in the so-called Coalition of the Willing.[68]

The major military battles were quickly concluded, and Saddam Hussein was eventually captured and executed. The U.S. intervention then turned into a difficult and lengthy occupation dealing with resistance from Sunni and Shi'ite militias and extremist Islamist groups sympathetic to Al-Qaeda. Sectarian violence between Shi'ites and Sunnis added to the deadly mix.

Oil rapidly became a factor in the Iraqi equation. The United States had anticipated that oil revenues would finance the Iraqi government operations and that new investment in the oil sector would fuel the economic recovery and political renaissance of Iraq. Instead, Iraqi oil fields and pipelines became a major target of terrorists. The Iraqi military, which had been disbanded after the invasion, and the weak and ineffective Iraqi police force were unable to protect Iraqi oil fields and pipelines; therefore, protecting those facilities fell to U.S. military forces in the aftermath of the invasion.

Despite U.S. military protection, Iraqi oil production declined (see Figure 9.14). U.S. efforts to promote new investment in the oil sector faltered. The inability of the Iraqi government to negotiate an agreement among the major political factions also delayed the recovery in production levels. As a result, the decline in Iraqi oil production after 2003 caused dislocations in the global supply of oil and contributed to the increase in world oil prices.

Looking Ahead

The future of oil politics will be shaped by a variety of factors. Supply and demand will continue to determine the price of oil. Future demand will depend on rates of economic growth in the oil-consuming countries. Because of their rapid growth, the newly emerging economies, particularly China and India, will increasingly shape the global demand for and price of oil.

Demand in the new century will also depend on whether developed and developing countries decide to address climate change by investing in energy-conserving technologies and other efforts to reduce consumption of fossil fuels including oil. The burning of fossil fuels (e.g., oil, coal) contributes significantly to the accumulation of greenhouse gases that cause global warming. Thus, in order to reduce greenhouse gases, both developed and developing countries will have to reduce the per capita consumption of fossil fuels by creating and deploying more efficient technologies or by switching to other sources of energy. One example of such an effort was the Kyoto Protocol, signed in December 1997, which called for international cooperation to create and enforce an upper ceiling for global CO_2 levels.[69] The ability of developed and developing countries to adopt national policies to reduce energy consumption and to reach future international agreements to reduce greenhouse gases will be an important factor in the future political economy of oil.

Geopolitical forces such as political instability, war, and terrorism will also affect the political economy of oil in this century. High prices of oil will enable major oil producers such as Russia and Iran to attempt to wield the oil weapon to achieve foreign policy goals. The ability of terrorists to continue to threaten disruption of supply will be enhanced if oil is in short supply and if the price is high. A war in the Persian Gulf or the Caspian region could threaten economic and political stability. Thus, the politics of oil, a key element of international politics in the twentieth century, is likely to remain so in the twenty-first century.

ENDNOTES

1. Edward L. Morse, "A New Political Economy of Oil?" *Journal of International Affairs*, 53 (Fall 1999): 1–29; Terry Lynn Karl, "The Perils of the Petro-State: Reflections on the Paradox of Plenty," *Journal of International Affairs*, 53 (Fall 1999): 31–48; and Jahangir Amuzegar, "OPEC as Omen: A Warning to the Caspian," *Foreign Affairs*, 77 (November/December 1998): 95–112.

2. The Seven Sisters were Exxon, Mobil, Gulf, Socal, Texaco, Shell, and British Petroleum (BP). See Anthony Sampson, *The Seven Sisters: The Great Oil Companies and the World They Made* (London, UK: Hodder and Stoughton, 1975).

3. See Zuhayr Mikdashi, *A Financial Analysis of Middle Eastern Oil Concessions: 1901–1965* (New York, N.Y.: Praeger, 1966); Charles Issawi and Mohammed Yeganeh, *The Economics of Middle Eastern Oil* (New York, N.Y.: Praeger, 1962), 24–40; and Daniel Yergin, *The Prize: The Epic Quest for Oil, Money, and Power* (New York, N.Y.: Simon and Schuster, 1991), chs. 1–6.

4. In 1928, for example, Shell, Standard Oil, and Anglo-Persian (the predecessor of BP) in order to bring order out of soft and volatile markets concluded the "As Is," or "Achnacarry," agreement to divide world markets and stabilize or determine world prices. In that same year a group of British, Dutch, United States and French companies agreed to divide up much of the old Ottoman Empire in the Red Line agreement. Also important was the basing-point pricing system that established a common price at several locations, or basing points, and standard, not actual, freight charges from the basing point to the destination. This system prevented low-cost producers from expanding their market share by reducing prices. See Penrose, *The Large International Firm*, 180–183. Apparently, there is some controversy about the success of the Achnacarry Agreement: see Yergin, *The Prize*, 264–265.

5. See Mikdashi, *A Financial Analysis*; Issawi and Yeganeh, *The Economics of Middle Eastern Oil*; Gertrude G. Edwards, "Foreign Petroleum Companies and the State in Venezuela," in Raymond F. Mikesell et al., eds., *Foreign Investment in the Petroleum and Mineral Industries* (Baltimore, Md.: Johns Hopkins University Press, 1971), 101–128; Franklin Tugwell, *The Politics of Oil in Venezuela* (Stanford, Calif.: Stanford University Press, 1975); and Donald A. Wells, "Aramco: The Evolution of an Oil Concession," in Mikesell et al., *Foreign Investment in the Petroleum and Mineral Industries*, 216–236.

6. David Prindle, *Petroleum Politics and the Texas Railroad Commission* (Austin, Tex.: University of Texas Press, 1984).

7. Wells, "Aramco: The Evolution of an Oil Concession." See also Anthony Cave Brown, *Oil, God and Gold: The Story of Aramco and the Saudi Kings* (New York, N.Y.: Houghton Mifflin, 1999).

8. See, for example, Robert Engler, *The Politics of Oil: Private Power and Democratic Directions* (Chicago, Ill.: University of Chicago Press, 1961).

9. Stephen Kinzer, *All the Shah's Men: An American Coup and the Roots of Middle East Terror* (New York, N.Y.: Wiley, 2007); Benjamin Shwadran, *The Middle East, Oil and the Great Powers* (New York, N.Y.: Council for Middle Eastern Affairs, 1955), 103–152; J. C. Hurewitz, *Middle East Politics: The Military Dimension* (New York, N.Y.: Praeger, 1969), 281–282; and Yergin, The Prize, ch. 23.

10. See Penrose, *The Large International Firm*, 248–263; Adelman, *The World Petroleum Market*, 196–204; and Yergin, The Prize, chs. 35–36.

11. Mira Wilkins, *The Maturing of Multinational Enterprise: American Business Abroad from 1914 to 1970* (Cambridge, Mass.: Harvard University Press, 1974), 386–387.

12. See, for example, Engler, *The Politics of Oil*.

13. See note 3.

14. For a history of OPEC, see Zuhayr Mikdashi, *The Community of Oil Exporting Countries: A Study in Governmental Cooperation* (Ithaca, N.Y.: Cornell University Press, 1972). See also Mohammed E. Ahrari, *OPEC: The Failing Giant* (Louisville, Ky.: University of Kentucky Press, 1986); Wilfrid L. Kohl, *After the Oil Price Collapse* (Baltimore, Md.: Johns Hopkins University Press, 1991); and Nathan Citino, *From Arab Nationalism to OPEC* (Bloomington, Ind.: Indiana University Press, 2002).

15. Zuhayr Mikdashi, "The OPEC Process," *Daedalus*, 104 (Fall 1975): 203. The new members were Algeria, Libya, Qatar, the United Arab Emirates, Nigeria, Ecuador, Indonesia, and Gabon.

16. Mikdashi, *The Community of Oil Exporting Countries*, 196–207.

17. Joel Darmstadter and Hans Landsberg, "The Economic Background," *Daedalus*, 104 (Fall 1975): 21.

18. On the evolution of events in Libya, see U.S. Senate Committee on Foreign Relations, *Multinational Corporations and United States Foreign Policy: Multinational Petroleum Companies and Foreign Policy*, hearings before the Subcommittee on Multinational Corporations, 93rd Cong., 1st and 2nd sess., Part 5 (Washington, D.C.: Government Printing Office, 1974). See also Dirk Vandewalle, *A History of Modern Libya* (New York, N.Y.: Cambridge University Press, 2006), ch. 4.

19. There was some consultation by the developed market states. The U.S. Department of Justice issued a waiver to oil companies under antitrust law, enabling them to cooperate in bargaining to resist unreasonable demands for higher prices. See U.S. Senate, *Multinational Corporations and United States Foreign Policy*, Part 5, 145–173. President Nixon then sent Undersecretary of State John N. Irwin to the Middle East to encourage governments to enter into joint negotiations with the companies. Secretary Irwin, however, capitulated to the demand of the shah of Iran for separate negotiations.

20. The Organization of Arab Petroleum Exporting Countries was formed by three Arab states—Kuwait, Libya, and Saudi Arabia—in 1968. It was expanded in 1970 to include Algeria, Abu Dhabi, Bahrain, Dubai, and Qatar. The website for OAPEC is http://www.oapecorg.org/.

21. The International Energy Agency's website is http://www.iea.org/. See also Richard Scott and Craig S. Bamberger, *IEA, the First Twenty Years: The History of the International Energy Agency, 1974–1994* (Paris, France: OECD/IEA, 2004).

22. National Foreign Assessment Center, *International Energy Statistical Review* (Washington, D.C.: Central Intelligence Agency, November 28, 1979), 2.

23. Anthony J. Paris, "OPEC Lifts Price 9%: At Least Five Members to Add Surcharges," *New York Times*, March 28, 1979, p. 1.

24. Edward L. Morse, "An Overview: Gains, Costs and Dilemmas," in Joan Pearce, ed., *The Third Oil Shock: The Effects of Lower Oil Prices* (London, UK: Royal Institute of International Affairs, 1983), 3.

25. Guy F. Erb and Valeriana Kallab, eds., *Beyond Dependency: The Developing World Speaks Out* (New York, N.Y.: Praeger, 1975), 206.

26. The following analysis is to a great extent influenced by the theory of collective action developed by Mancur Olson, *The Logic of Collective Action: Public Goods and the Theory of Groups* (Cambridge, Mass.: Harvard University Press, 1965 and 1971).

27. Mikdashi, *The Community of Oil Exporting Countries*, 196–207.

28. Stephen D. Krasner, "Oil Is the Exception," *Foreign Policy*, 14 (Spring 1974): 78–79.

29. See Raymond F. Mikesell, "More Third World Cartels Ahead?" *Challenge*, 17 (November-December 1974): 24–26, on the OPEC method of taxing multinational corporations.

30. John E. Tilton, "Cartels in Metal Industries," *Earth and Mineral Sciences*, 44 (March 1975): 41–44. See also John Hillman, "Bolivia and the International Tin Cartel, 1893–1941." *Journal of Latin American Studies*, 20 (1987): 83–110; John Hillman, "Malaya and the International Tin Cartel," *Modern Asian Studies*, 22 (May 1988): 237–261; Stephen K. Holloway, The *Aluminum Multinationals and the Bauxite Cartel* (New York, N.Y.: St. Martin's Press, 1988); Helge Hveem, *The Political Economy of Third World Producer Associations* (New York, N.Y.: Columbia University Press, 1978);

and Debora L. Spar, *The Cooperative Edge: The International Politics of International Cartels* (Ithaca, N.Y.: Cornell University Press, 1994).

31. Harry G. Johnson, *Economic Policies Toward Less Developed Countries* (New York, N.Y.: Praeger, 1967), 136–162.

32. Morris A. Adelman, "World Oil Production and Prices, 1947–2000," *The Quarterly Review of Economics and Finance*, 42 (2002): 171.

33. International Monetary Fund, *World Economic Outlook 1984: A Survey by the Staff of the International Monetary Fund* (Washington, D.C.: IMF, April 1984), 128.

34. Morse, "An Overview," 8.

35. IMF, *World Economic Outlook 1984*, 133.

36. Morse, "An Overview," 4.

37. IMF, *World Economic Outlook 1984*, 130–133.

38. IMF, *World Economic Outlook 1984*, 128.

39. *Ibid.*, 129–131.

40. *Ibid.*, 134.

41. *Ibid.*, 135.

42. Morse, "An Overview," 14–15.

43. IMF, *International Financial Statistics 1984* (Washington, D.C.: IMF, August 1984).

44. Louis Turner, "OPEC," in Pearce, *The Third Oil Shock*, 85.

45. *Ibid.*

46. International Monetary Fund, *World Economic Outlook 1986* (Washington, D.C.: IMF, April 1986), 151.

47. International Monetary Fund, *World Economic Outlook 1987* (Washington, D.C.: IMF, April 1987), 98.

48. Efraim Karsh, *The Iran–Iraq War 1980–1988* (Westminster, Md.: Osprey Publishing, 2002).

49. *The First Oil War: Implications of the Gulf Crisis for the Oil Market* (Oxford, England: Oxford Institute for Energy Studies, August 1990). See also Alistair Finlan, *The Gulf War* (Oxford, England: Osprey, 2003); and John Bulloch and Harvey Morris, *The Gulf War: Its Origins, History, and Consequences* (London, UK: Methuen, 1989).

50. U.S. Department of Energy, Energy Information Agency, *The U.S. Petroleum Industry: Past as Prologue, 1970–1992* (Washington, D.C.: Government Printing Office, October 1, 1993), 57. See also Bruce A. Beauboeuf, *The Strategic Petroleum Reserve: U.S. Energy Security and Oil Politics, 1975–2005* (College Station, Tex.: Texas A&M Press, 2007), ch. 5.

51. http://www.eia.doe.gov/emeu/cabs/chron.html.

52. Morse, "A New Political Economy of Oil?", 23.

53. "Oil for Food Programme," *Wikipedia*, http://en.wikipedia.org/wiki/Oil_for_Food_program.

54. Bernard A. Gelb, *Caspian Oil and Gas: Production and Prospects* (Washington, D.C.: Congressional Research Service Report for Congress, updated September 8, 2006), p. 3.

55. The four firms that formed the joint venture were Chevron (25 percent); ExxonMobil (25 percent); LukArco (5 percent), a Russian firm; and KazMunayGas (20 percent), a Kazakh state enterprise.

56. Eric Watkins, "Tengizchevroil Raises Production, Seeks Outlets," *Oil and Gas Journal*, September 25, 2008.

57. Zbigniew Brzezinski, *The Grand Chessboard: American Primacy and Its Geostrategic Imperatives* (New York, N.Y.: Perseus Books, 1997); see also Lutz Kleveman, *The New Great Game: Blood and Oil in Central Asia* (New York, N.Y.: Grove Press, 2004).

58. Office of Natural Gas and Petroleum Technology, U.S. Department of Energy, *Reservoir Life Extension Program* (Washington, D.C.: 1999), http://www.fossil. energy.gov/programs/oilgas/publications/programplans/1999/4life.pdf.

59. Morse, "A New Political Economy of Oil?", 22.

60. The Comprehensive Environmental Response, Compensation and Liability Act (CERCLA) of 1980 is the formal name of the Superfund legislation. See http:// www.epa.gov/superfund/policy/cercla.htm.

61. Calculated by the authors from data used in Figure 9.5.

62. F. Gregory Gause III, "Saudi Arabia Over a Barrel," *Foreign Affairs*, 79 (May/June 2000): 82; and Rick Atkinson, "Murky Ending Clouds Desert Storm Legacy," http://www.washingtonpost.com/wp-srv/inatl/longterm/fogofwar/intro.htm.

63. Energy Information Administration, Department of Energy, "Saudi Arabia," January 2002, http://www.eia.doe.gov/emeu/cabs/saudi.html.

64. Energy Information Administration, Department of Energy, "OPEC Revenues Fact Sheet," December 2001, http://www.eia.doe.gov/emeu/cabs/ OPEC Revenues/Factsheet.html

65. Daniel Yergin, "Oil at the Break Point," testimony at a hearing entitled "Oil Bubble or New Reality: How Will Skyrocketing Prices Affect the U.S. Economy," U.S. Congress, Joint Economic Committee, Washington, D.C., June 25, 2008.

66. "OVL in Talks with Iran for Oil Block," *Tehran Times*, October 9, 2008.

67. "India and Colombia Sign Agreement for Cooperation in the Energy Sector," ONGC press release, September 5, 2008.

68. Other countries supported the invasion but did not participate. For details, see "Coaltion of the Willing," Perspectives on World History and Current Events, http://pwhce.org/willing.html.

69. http://www.unfccc.int/resource/docs/convkp/kpeng.html.

10

East–West Economic Relations: From Isolation to Integration

One of the major characteristics of globalization was the geographic expansion of the capitalist international economic system to include the former communist countries of Europe and Asia. During the era of the Cold War from 1947 to 1991, which spanned both the Bretton Woods era and the age of interdependence, the **Union of Soviet Socialist Republics (USSR)** and its communist allies in Eastern Europe and China were isolated from the Western system. They created a separate, communist international economic system with its own institutions and rules based on **centrally planned economies** with state ownership of the means of production. Eastern Europe and the Soviet Union formed a closed economic bloc consisting of managed international trade complemented by technical assistance and joint planning. The bloc was dominated by the Soviet Union. China was linked to this economic bloc through trade, investment, and finance.

The end of the Cold War marked the beginning of the age of globalization and the collapse of the communist international economic system. In 1989, communist governments were replaced in Poland, Czechoslovakia, Bulgaria, and Romania; Germany was unified under a Western capitalist government; and Soviet troops withdrew from many parts of Eastern Europe. In 1991, the communist regime in the Soviet Union collapsed and the USSR itself broke apart.

The end of the Cold War brought about major changes in the Eastern economic system. Russia, the **newly independent states (NIS)**[1] that formed after the breakup of the Soviet Union, and the former communist states of Central and Eastern Europe sought to make the transition from communism to capitalism and to more democratic forms of government. **Central planning** was replaced with greater emphasis on market mechanisms and many state enterprises were privatized. Multiparty parliamentary systems with elected governments were established in most countries. Making a successful transition to democracy and capitalism simultaneously proved a major challenge.

Communist countries in Asia followed a different path, maintaining their communist regimes while attempting to transform themselves into market economies. The Communist Party remained dominant in China and Vietnam, but these countries implemented major changes in their domestic economies and their interaction with the world economy.

This chapter examines the communist international economic system, why it was formed, how it operated, and why it collapsed. This chapter then explores the efforts of the former communist states to make the transition from communist to capitalist economies and the efforts of both East and West to create one global international economic system.

THE COLD WAR

The Creation of an Eastern Economic Bloc

The British and American planners constructing the new international economic order between 1943 and 1947 (see Chapter 2) expected that the East would be part of the postwar system. Between World War I and World War II, the Soviet Union had been separated from the international economic system by the West's opposition to the communist regime and by Stalin's autarchic development policy. But the USSR continued to trade with the developed countries and Soviet imports of Western raw materials and technology made an important contribution to Soviet growth.[2] The countries of Eastern Europe had been closely integrated with the West, especially Western Europe, in the interwar period, and Western European countries assumed "a substantial and ready resumption" of trade of principal goods with the East after the war.[3]

However, the outbreak of the Cold War led to an effort on both sides to separate the economies of East and West and to use that separation as a tool of political confrontation. The creation of a separate Eastern economic system was part of the Soviet Union's postwar policy of dominance in Eastern Europe and of its international political strategy.[4] Marxist ideology and concerns about postwar security provided the justification for Soviet control. According to Marxist theory, the formation of a separate Eastern economic bloc would deepen the crisis of world capitalism and speed its inevitable demise. Stalin stated that denying the Eastern markets to the West would decrease Western exports, create idle industrial capacity, and lead to the inevitable internal economic and political collapse of capitalism.[5] The formation of a separate socialist bloc would insulate the East from the coming economic chaos in the West and enhance socialist economic development.[6]

The primary motivation, however, was political. A separate Eastern economic bloc, in the Soviet Union's view, would provide a buffer zone of friendly, that is, communist, states on its borders and would prevent Germany or other "hostile" Western powers from posing a threat of military invasion. Furthermore, the Soviet Union would obtain access on favorable terms to raw materials and capital equipment that could be used to rebuild the Soviet Union after the war and to advance its economic development.

Through wartime diplomacy, military occupation, and coups d'état, the Soviet Union established communist satellite regimes in all the states of Eastern Europe.[7] The Soviet Union, in cooperation with national communist leaders, restructured the economies of Eastern Europe, introducing state ownership of the means of production, central planning, and the Soviet model of economic growth based on self-sufficiency and all-around industrialization.[8] The Soviet Union also built a socialist international economic system centered on the Soviet Union, which had limited interaction with the West.

The Soviet Union refused to join the new international economic institutions created by the West and prevented eligible satellites from participating in Western institutions. Although the Soviet Union participated in the Bretton Woods conference, it refused to ratify the Bretton Woods agreements and become a member of the International Monetary Fund (IMF) or the World Bank.[9] Czechoslovakia and Poland, which initially joined the IMF and the World Bank, withdrew in 1950 and 1954, respectively, under strong Soviet pressure.[10]

Although invited, the Soviet Union refused to attend the preparatory meetings and international negotiations that led to the Havana Charter. Czechoslovakia and Poland participated in the Havana negotiations, but did not ratify the charter. No Eastern states were contracting parties of the GATT.[11] The Soviet Union rejected the U.S. offer of aid under the Marshall Plan and refused to allow Poland and Czechoslovakia, the two Eastern states offered Marshall Plan aid, to accept U.S. aid and join the Organization for European Economic Cooperation (OEEC), the European organization established to coordinate European use of Marshall Plan funds.[12]

In 1949, in response to the Marshall Plan, Soviet Union and the states of Eastern Europe (except Yugoslavia) created the **Council for Mutual Economic Assistance (CMEA** or **Comecon)**.[13] This international economic organization pursued technical cooperation and joint planning, but its main function was to reorient trade eastward and to buttress the new political relationship between the Soviet Union and Eastern Europe.

Through Comecon and a series of bilateral trade agreements between the Soviet Union and the satellite countries, Eastern European trade was redirected from West to East. In 1938, 10 percent of Eastern exports went to Eastern countries including the Soviet Union, 68 percent to Western Europe, 4 percent to the United States and Canada, and 5 percent to Latin America. By 1953, 64 percent of Eastern exports went to Eastern countries, 14 percent to Western Europe, and less than 1 percent to the United States, Canada, and Latin America.[14] In the first postwar decade, trade tended to benefit the Soviet Union, which was able to negotiate extremely favorable prices for its imports and exports.[15]

The Soviet Union's system of state ownership and central planning was imposed on Eastern Europe. In a **centrally planned economy**, decisions about the allocation of resources—decisions about what to produce, how to produce it, and to whom to distribute it—are made by a central state planning organiza-tion.[16] Eastern Europe's economic plans were prepared with the assistance of Soviet economic advisers by handpicked economists trained in the Soviet Union.[17] Because trade was controlled centrally, economic planners could use administrative decisions to shift trade from West to East. Under their plans, Eastern European states produced and exported those products desired by the Soviet Union.

Reparations imposed on the former Axis countries were an important element in the relationship between Eastern Europe and the Soviet Union. In East Germany, Hungary, Romania, and Bulgaria (former allies of Germany), the Soviet Union uni-laterally dismantled factories and claimed goods from current production for the Soviet army and the Soviet economy.[18] The Soviet Union acquired numerous German industrial enterprises operating in Hungary, Romania, and Bulgaria. These enterprises operated primarily as joint companies with the local national gov-ernment. They enjoyed preferential taxes and access to foreign exchange and raw materials and often offered favorable prices to the Soviet Union. Because of their powerful and preferential position, these companies became a source of intrabloc conflict and were liquidated after 1954.[19]

Financial ties were also redirected from West to East. Eastern European cur-rencies were made inconvertible (on inconvertibility, see below). The nationali-zation of foreign investment disrupted private capital flows. The Soviet Union and most of the satellites were not eligible for IMF or World Bank assistance, and they rejected Marshall Plan aid. The principal source of external financing for Eastern Europe was credit from the Soviet Union for the purchase of raw materials and equipment from the Soviet Union.[20]

Western Economic Warfare

Western economic warfare increased the East's self-imposed isolation. The Cold War erupted following the establishment of communist regimes in the Soviet-occupied states of Eastern Europe, Soviet pressure on Iran and Turkey, the out-break of civil war in Greece, and political instability in Western Europe. These events plus the East's rejection of Marshall Plan assistance, the coup in Czechoslovakia, and the Berlin blockade of 1948 confirmed the U.S. view that the Soviet Union was a political and military threat to the West.

In addition to building a united and prosperous Western economy and cre-ating a powerful Western military alliance, the aim of United States and Western policy was to deny the Soviet Union and its allies economic resources that would enhance their military capability and political power. The Western strategic embargo began in full force with the passage of the **U.S. Export Control Act of 1949**. This act, which remained in force for 20 years, authorized the president to "prohibit or curtail" all commercial exports and to establish a licensing system to regulate exports to communist countries. Any product that had military appli-cability or that would contribute to the military or economic potential of a com-munist state was placed on the restricted list.[21]

The United States sought, with mixed success, to persuade other Western states to impose similar embargoes. In 1949 under U.S. pressure, the **Coordinating Committee (CoCom)** was set up to discuss and coordinate Western strategic embargo lists. Although it had no binding authority, CoCom succeeded in drawing up an international list of restricted items for its 15 members.[22] However, the difference in views between the United States and its allies over the goals and content of the economic embargo became a source of tension throughout the postwar era. For the United States, the strategic embargo was intended to impair not only the East's military strength but also its political and economic power. The U.S. embargo therefore was directed not only at military goods but also at nonmilitary goods that would enhance economic performance and development. The Europeans and Japanese, who had a greater economic stake in trade with the East than the United States did, felt that a broad embargo would encourage greater Eastern solidarity without hindering military and political capability. Thus, they advocated a more limited definition of strategic goods—namely, those with direct military implications.[23] As a result of allied resistance, the international list was less comprehensive than the U.S. control list.

Another form of economic warfare was to deny the East access to Western markets. In 1951 at the height of tensions in Korea, the U.S. Congress passed the Trade Agreements Extension Act, which withdrew all trade concessions negotiated with the Soviet Union and any communist country (except Yugoslavia). As a result, products from Eastern countries remained subject to the onerous Smoot-Hawley tariffs. Many European states also adopted restrictions on imports from communist countries.[24] Finally, the United States also used legislation to prohibit private persons or institutions from extending credit to the Soviet Union and most Eastern European governments.[25] Other **North Atlantic Treaty Organization (NATO)** countries did not restrict Eastern access to credit, and an effort by the United States to impose restrictions through international agreement failed.[26]

Thus the East and the West established separate international economic systems with separate institutions, rules, and patterns of interaction, mainly for political reasons. At the height of economic separation during the Korean War, East–West trade was actually lower in absolute terms than it had been in 1937.[27] The policy of economic warfare continued throughout the Cold War.

Throughout the Cold War era, economic relations between East and West ebbed and flowed with political and military relations. When tensions eased, the United States and its allies sought to use promises of increased trade or investment flows in exchange for changes in the behavior of the Soviet Union and the rest of the Eastern bloc. When tensions increased, the West imposed new sanctions. Thus, following the end of the Korean conflict and the death of Stalin in 1953, the East–West political-security conflict relaxed somewhat and Western countries eased some trade restrictions. The West's control list was shortened; Western Europe, Canada, and Japan negotiated most-favored-nation agreements with Eastern Europe and the Soviet Union and reduced trade restrictions; and East–West trade increased.[28]

In the mid-1960s, the Johnson administration tried to expand East–West trade in order to encourage greater pluralism in Eastern Europe and greater stability in relations between the United States and the Soviet Union.[29] Congress, however, refused to pass legislation permitting trade agreements with communist countries because of concern about Soviet involvement in the war in Vietnam. After the Soviet invasion of Czechoslovakia in 1968, President Johnson abandoned the policy.

During the period of U.S.-Soviet détente—the lessening of tensions—in the 1970s there were efforts for change in both East and West. By the early 1970s, the Soviet Union had achieved effective equality with the United States in strategic weapons. Nuclear parity enabled Soviet leaders to view the West with more confidence, to modify the fear of military invasion, and to entertain the idea of limiting expenditures on strategic weapons. The combination of Soviet nuclear parity and greater Soviet flexibility in foreign policy led the United States and its Western allies to look more favorably on easing conflict with the Soviet Union.[30] The interest of the West in opening economic relations with the communist countries varied. Western Europeans, for both economic and political reasons, were more anxious to trade with the Soviet Union and its allies than the United States was. Japan was constrained by ongoing political disputes over the Soviet occupation of several Japanese islands. U.S. policymakers were caught between their desire to expand trade for economic and political reasons and their feeling that Western trade concessions should be linked to Eastern political concessions or to an easing in political and security relations.

In 1972, at the same time as the signing of the SALT I agreement, President Nixon and Chairman Brezhnev established a high-level, joint commercial commission that then negotiated a series of agreements designed to normalize U.S.-Soviet commercial relations and to open the way for increased trade and financial flows. Congress, however, sought to use expanded trade and access to financing as a lever to force the Soviet Union to change its internal policies on emigration.[31] The Soviet Union refused to give any assurances regarding emigration and charged the United States with interfering in its internal affairs. In January 1975 the United States and the Soviet Union agreed to nullify the 1972 commercial agreement.

The Carter administration policy followed a similar pattern, urging Congress to repeal trade restrictions on trade and credits. The Soviet Union's invasion of Afghanistan in 1979 ended the Carter effort to expand economic relations and terminated the 1970s era of détente. President Carter saw the invasion of Afghanistan as an indication of growing Soviet expansionism and particularly of Soviet designs on the nearby Persian Gulf oil fields. He withdrew the SALT II arms control treaty from consideration by the Senate and, in January 1980, announced new economic sanctions against the Soviet Union: an embargo on sales of wheat and other grains; an embargo on sales of high-technology goods; tightened restrictions on the sale of oil and gas exploration and production equipment; the suspension of service by the Soviet purchasing commission office in New York; and a more restrictive regime of access to U.S. ports for Soviet ships.[32]

President Reagan adopted an even harder line with the Soviet Union, increasing military expenditures, downplaying arms control negotiations, and providing military support to anticommunist forces such as the Contras in Nicaragua.[33] The Reagan administration pursued a policy of economically isolating the Soviet Union. The administration maintained embargoes on the export of oil and gas exploration equipment and high-technology goods to the Soviet Union, tightened the enforcement of export controls generally, and favored more stringent export control legislation. The administration adopted a broad definition of the strategic goods that were to be denied to the Soviet Union, including not only defense or defense-related equipment but also many items that had either a limited or indirect impact on the East's military capability. The Reagan administration also tried to use CoCom and NATO to impose this view of strategic exports on the West European allies. One such effort involved an unsuccessful U.S. attempt to stop its Western European allies from helping to build a pipeline from Siberian gas fields to customers in Western Europe.[34]

THE COLLAPSE OF THE COMMUNIST SYSTEM

Forces of Change in the East

While the state of political-security relations was central to Western policy toward the East, internal economic problems were the major motivation of the communist countries for opening economic relations with the West. Serious economic difficulties in agriculture and the industrial sector emerged in the 1960s and reached near-crisis proportions by the 1980s, particularly in the Soviet Union.

Low agricultural productivity, a longstanding problem, had several causes: collectivization that gravely injured the peasantry; excessive interference in local farm management by the large and unwieldy Soviet agricultural bureaucracy; inadequate infrastructure in many areas ranging from roads to storage facilities; a lack of incentives given the weak links between effort and reward; and poor inputs from the industrial sector.[35] Periodic efforts to improve agricultural productivity had been undermined by the Soviet agricultural bureaucrats for whom any change in the prevailing system was a threat to their power. Despite significant capital investment in the years after 1960, productivity of the Soviet agricultural sector in the 1980s stood at 20 to 25 percent of U.S. productivity according to Soviet statistics and at 10 percent of U.S. productivity according to Western measures.[36] In the 1960s, the Soviet Union, once a food exporter, became a net importer of food especially grain from the West (see Figure 10.1).

Industrial growth was another problem for the Eastern system. In the 1950s and 1960s, the Soviet Union and Eastern Europe achieved high rates of industrial growth by a significant expansion in the labor force—the employment of women, the transfer of labor from agriculture to industry, and long working hours—and by the rapid increase in capital formation at the expense of agriculture and of improvement in the standard of living.[37] By 1960, however, this type of expansion, known as **extensive growth**, had reached its limits. Economic growth in the Soviet Union and Eastern Europe communist bloc

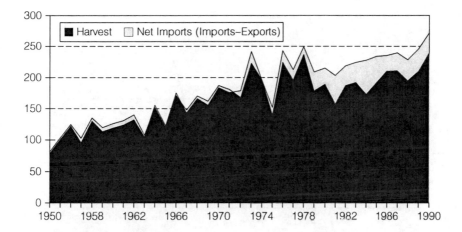

FIGURE 10.1 Soviet Grain Harvests and Net Imports in Millions of Metric Tons, 1950–1990

SOURCE: Marshall I. Goldman, *Gorbachev's Challenge* (New York, N.Y.: Norton, 1987), p. 33; Marshall I. Goldman, *What Went Wrong with Perestroika?* (New York, N.Y.: Norton, 1991), p. 79.

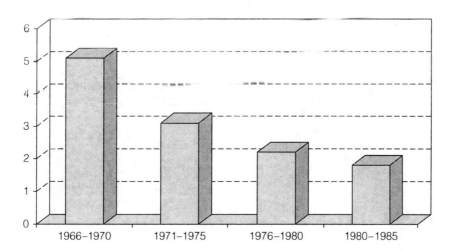

FIGURE 10.2 Average Annual Growth in Real GNP in the Soviet Union and Eastern Europe, 1961–1985

SOURCE: Central Intelligence Agency, *Handbook of Economic Statistics 1988* (Washington, D.C.: U.S. Government Printing Office, 1988), p. 33.

fell and, at the end of the 1980s, the Soviet economy actually began to contract (see Figures 10.2, 10.3, and 10.4).

Growth slowed for a number of reasons. The Eastern states needed to shift to **intensive growth**, which is achieved by improving productivity. Intensive growth relies primarily on the application of technology: advanced machinery and production processes, modern computer and communications technology,

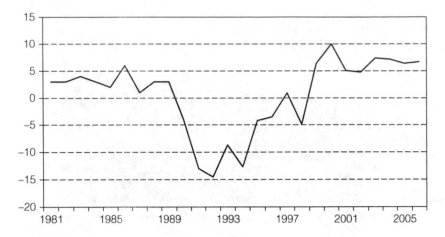

FIGURE 10.3 Annual Growth in GDP in the Russian Federation, 1981–2006, in Percentages

SOURCE: World Bank, *World Data '95 CD-ROM* (Washington, D.C.: World Bank, 1995); World Bank, *World Development Indicators 2008*.

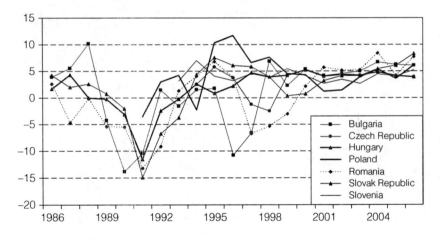

FIGURE 10.4 Annual Growth in GNP in Eastern Europe, 1986–2006, in Percentages

SOURCE: World Bank, *World Development Indicators 2008*.

sophisticated management techniques, and energy. The Eastern system encountered severe difficulties in improving productivity, largely because of the central planning system that discouraged innovation, productivity improvements, and quality. Rewards for plant managers were based on fulfillment or overfulfillment of quantitative goals and not on improving the quality of the product or the production process. Indeed, there were disincentives to experiment with new methods because experiments threatened to interrupt production at least temporarily and thus to jeopardize fulfillment of the quantitative goals. Furthermore, the absence of competition and the existence of guaranteed markets eliminated incentives for managers to cut costs or improve quality. Above all, prices did not provide a guide to help managers determine what goods consumers wanted and how to improve productivity by lowering costs.[38]

Despite great emphasis on scientific research, there was little relationship between research and actual production. Unlike the West, where most industrial research is carried out by private enterprise, research in the East was generally carried on in research institutes that had few links with production facilities. Scientists and engineers were thus not positioned to respond directly to the needs of industry or to make industry responsive to scientific development.[39] As a result of these systemic biases, the East fell far behind the West in the development of technology.

In the 1960s and 1970s, the Eastern countries tried to solve the problem of technology and productivity through limited national economic reforms, intra-Comecon trade, and greater trade with the West. In the mid-1960s, managers were given greater freedom to decide what to produce and how, incentives were based on profit as well as quantitative goals, and prices were made more "rational." But the reforms did not go far enough. The reforms were strongly opposed by party conservatives and government bureaucrats who saw their power threatened by the potential new power of the plant managers and who eventually reasserted centralized control.[40] Thus the Eastern economies continued to stagnate.[41]

The East also attempted to solve the problem of growth through Comecon. An effort began in the late 1950s to revitalize Comecon and change it from a tool of Soviet dominance to a tool of development. Attempts were made to increase trade within the bloc, as Eastern leaders hoped that trade would lead to economies of scale, force competitiveness, and thus encourage modernization. An agreement on methods for establishing trade prices, a clearing institution (the International Bank for Economic Cooperation), and programs for national specialization in production were designed to encourage trade. Technological cooperation was also promoted.[42] However, Comecon trade remained hampered by internal biases against multilateral trade, lack of complementarity with the Eastern economies, the poor quality of goods, unsatisfactory currency arrangements, and political unwillingness to delegate power to a supranational body—especially one in which the Soviet Union had a powerful voice. Trade within Comecon remained largely bilateral trade between the Soviet Union and Eastern European countries rather than multilateral integration among all Comecon nations.[43]

Finally, the East sought to bridge the technology gap by acquiring foreign technology. Industrial cooperation agreements between Western firms and Eastern European enterprises became increasingly important in the early 1970s. For the East, they were intended to provide access to Western technology, improve competitiveness in the West, and reduce foreign exchange needs. The West sought greater access to Eastern markets and the opportunity to reduce costs. West Germany, which was by far the most active in seeking such agreements, entered into more than 200 agreements with Comecon nations in the 1970s.[44]

Western technology, however, had little impact on Soviet and Eastern European productivity and growth. Despite the easing of CoCom controls, the

West was not willing to sell sophisticated technologies such as computer and telecommunications technologies that could contribute to the East's military strength. Financial constraints hampered the East's ability to purchase Western technology. Most important, foreign technology imports had little impact as long as there was no reform in the domestic economic system that would permit their effective use.

By the 1980s, the Eastern economic system was in need of drastic economic reform. Growth rates declined steadily, and investment and productivity remained low. From 1981 to 1985, growth in the Soviet Union averaged only 1.8 percent and total factor productivity declined to 0.9 percent compared with 1.9 percent from 1975 to 1980.[45] Soviet agricultural problems were so great that some products were rationed and lines for goods became long in major Soviet cities. Between 1983 and 1985 the growth rate of agricultural production per capita actually fell 2 percent.[46] Shortages of all consumer products caused public dissatisfaction, creating a potential political challenge to the regime. At the same time, the Soviet Union faced a number of political reversals. The war in Afghanistan had become a costly economic drain that was unpopular at home and damaged Soviet relations abroad. Eastern Europe was also restless. In Poland, for example, labor unrest arising in part from economic problems challenged the legitimacy of the communist regime in that important Soviet ally.

Gorbachev's Economic and Political Reforms

In March 1985, Mikhail Gorbachev became General Secretary of the Communist Party and began a program to address these economic, political, and foreign policy problems.[47] Gorbachev argued that the possibility of nuclear holocaust and the nature of contemporary world problems such as the environment made the world interdependent and called for a more cooperative foreign policy.[48] Gorbachev adopted several key foreign policy initiatives: a defensive military strategy; an agreement with the United States on intermediate-range nuclear weapons and negotiations on strategic and short-range nuclear weapons; a unilateral reduction of conventional forces in Europe; greater autonomy in Eastern Europe and withdrawal of Soviet troops from Afghanistan; and improved relations with the People's Republic of China.

These foreign policy initiatives not only eased political and military confrontations but also enabled the Soviet Union to focus more attention and resources on domestic economic reform. Under his domestic political policy known as **glasnost**, or openness, Gorbachev improved the Soviet government's human rights policy allowing greater emigration, more freedom in public discussion and the arts, and greater democratization of the political process. In 1989, for example, he implemented a reform of the political system, creating a presidency and more open elections. Political reform was also designed to facilitate economic reform, in particular, by providing a popular check on the powerful, conservative bureaucracy.[49]

In the economic arena, Gorbachev announced a policy known as **perestroika**, or restructuring of the Soviet economy.[50] According to Gorbachev's plan for the industrial sector, decision making—with a number of exceptions— was to be decentralized from central planners to individual firms. Under the Law on State Enterprise adopted in June 1987, the central planning system was to be phased out by 1991 and replaced by annual plans drafted by individual firms. Central planners would develop voluntary guidelines for individual enterprises, establish long-term economic objectives, issue state orders for products of critical importance to the economy and national defense, and negotiate with firms to obtain those products. Instead of responding to obligatory targets set by central planners, firms would pursue revenue and profit. Individual enterprises would be responsible for production, sales, and investment. They would have more freedom to hire and fire workers and to set wages. Under the new law, they would also face the possibility of bankruptcy.

New markets responsive to these more autonomous enterprises were to be developed. Decisions on capital flows once made by state planners were to be made instead by newly liberalized financial markets. The existing system of centralized supply would be replaced by a wholesale distribution system that was to be responsive to the decisions of individual enterprises.

Reform of the agricultural system was also on the agenda. Gorbachev's "new agrarian policy" in 1989 called for decentralization and a greater role for the private sector. The state bureaucracy was to be dismantled; decision making would be delegated to regional and local levels; agricultural enterprises, like industrial enterprises, were to pursue profits and to be self-financing; prices were to become more flexible; there was to be greater scope for private farming through lifetime leases of farms with the possibility of passing leases on to children.

Perestroika also had an international dimension. Part of Gorbachev's plan, albeit a minor one, was to improve trade and financial interaction with the West in order to speed the restructuring process. In 1986, the Soviet Union announced a plan to decentralize the trade system and end the monopoly of the Ministry of Foreign Trade over trade transactions. A number of ministries, authorities, and enterprises were authorized to conduct foreign trade directly through foreign trade organizations under their control. In 1986, the Soviet Union also requested observer status in the GATT, arguing that domestic economic reforms would remove impediments to its participation in a market-oriented organization. The Western countries, fearful that Soviet involvement would politicize the GATT, suspicious of Soviet motives, and wanting to see if reform really did move the Soviet Union toward a market-oriented economy, denied the request.[51]

The Soviet government also pursued economic cooperation with Western firms in order to promote exports and to obtain Western technology. In a major departure from previous policy, the government issued new guidelines that allowed foreign equity and management participation in joint ventures. Some Western firms responded. Western Europeans were quicker to initiate joint ventures than U.S. and Japanese firms. To finance new ventures, the Soviet Union increased its borrowing from Western financial institutions (see below on Eastern borrowing from the West). Finally, Soviet policymakers considered various schemes for making the ruble convertible, including the possibility of introducing a convertible or "hard" ruble for international transactions that could be backed by gold, foreign exchange, or exports (see below on ruble inconvertibility).[52]

Gorbachev's foreign policy initiatives led to a thaw in East–West political-security relations. U.S.-Soviet summits were revived. Arms control talks led to agreements on medium-range nuclear weapons in Europe and conventional forces in Europe. Some U.S. officials came to believe that trade and finance could be used to support Gorbachev and his allies who favored the new thinking in foreign policy, *glasnost* and *perestroika*.[53] U.S. allies in Western Europe, less fearful of Gorbachev's Soviet Union and as usual interested in greater trade, urged a more moderate policy on the United States and specifically pressed for an easing of CoCom controls. Finally, the need to reduce the huge U.S. budget deficit led to pressure for reducing military expenditures, which could be justified in a more friendly East–West environment.

The Reagan administration's steps on the economic front were cautious: reestablishment of the U.S.-USSR Joint Commercial Commission at the ministerial level to discuss improving economic relations and encouragement of "commercially viable joint ventures complying with the laws and regulations of both countries."[54] After the Soviet withdrawal from Afghanistan, the Bush administration eased export controls somewhat. Following the political revolution in Eastern Europe in the fall of 1989, U.S. policy shifted toward using trade and investment to promote change in the East. President Bush called for opening markets to the Soviet Union and endorsed observer status for the USSR in the GATT after the completion of the Uruguay Round.

Western European countries moved further and faster than the United States to increase economic flows with the East. For all the economic and political reasons discussed above, many countries of Western Europe were more interested than the United States in economic and political rapprochement with the East. Furthermore, Gorbachev deliberately courted Western Europe, publicly advocating the concept of a "common European home."[55]

As the leading trade partner of the Soviet Union and Eastern Europe and in continuing pursuit of its **Ostpolitik**, West Germany took a strong interest in increasing economic relations with the East, especially since it wanted to keep alive the possibility of reuniting with East Germany. West Germany responded positively to the interest of the East in increased political ties with the European Union; and German firms, with the support of their government, aggressively pursued trade and joint-venture opportunities and signed numerous trade and joint-venture agreements with the East.

The Failure of *Perestroika*

The policies actually implemented by the Gorbachev government differed from the plans announced in 1987. Decision-making power was transferred from the economics ministries of the government to the managers of individual enterprises, and the ministries lost their power to appoint managers of enterprises. However, many prices were still controlled centrally, and the ministries were theoretically still in control of allocating inputs to enterprises. In addition, the ministries still controlled the research institutes, other vital sources of economic and business information, and international trade (via their power to grant export licenses). Some prices were freed selectively so that there would be room for profit-making ventures on the part of the managers, but this was done purely at the discretion of the bureaucracy.

The result was an economic crisis. The ministries could not guarantee the allocation of inputs because they could no longer insist upon fulfillment of production quotas. The managers therefore turned to a self-help system combining personal connections, barter, and bribery to obtain the necessary inputs to keep their enterprises going.[56] The outcome was a major decline in production and general failure of the system. Real GNP declined by 4 percent in 1990 and 13 percent in 1991 (see again Figure 10.3). Since privatization efforts were still quite modest at this point, price increases for consumer goods led not to increased productive capacity but rather to inflationary pressures, massive shortages, supply bottlenecks, and higher monopoly rents for state enterprises.

Senior economic bureaucrats in the Soviet government responded to this crisis by insisting on rapid privatization of state enterprises. These ministers preferred continued state ownership, but under *perestroika*, privatization was the only way to retain control over their own sources of revenues, which depended mainly on the cash flows generated by the firms. The privatization the economic ministers advocated involved extensive cross-holdings of shares in firms that were already linked by vertical ties—firms that were "upstream" and "downstream" from the major producers in any given industry—in order to maintain the intra-industry relationships that had existed under the pre *perestroika* system. In addition, the ministers favored transfer of ownership to the existing managers of firms rather than the sale of assets on the open market. Such an approach would enable them to preserve their own power and privileges in the new system.

In 1988, workers were given the right to strike, a right denied since the time of Stalin. As a result, wages rapidly increased. Workers in some state enterprises were also given some control over management, resulting in a low incidence of layoffs, even in severely overmanned firms. The more productive workers had to be bribed to stay on the job so as not to go to work for the "cooperatives" that sprang up everywhere between 1988 and 1991. The cooperatives were thinly disguised private operations that lived off the supposedly "redundant" but actually quite valuable assets purchased on very favorable terms from the state enterprises. Managers of the state enterprises pursued profit-making opportunities in the cooperatives rather than in their own firms, because the cooperatives were not as heavily burdened with obsolete production equipment and unproductive workers as the state enterprises.

The collapse of the central government's control over its own revenues and its power to allocate resources made the future of state enterprises look bleak indeed. Thus, increasingly, the ministries, the managers, the more productive workers in state enterprises, and many local government officials supported a form of privatization called **spontaneous privatization**, which amounted to the expropriation of state-owned assets for the private benefit of those individuals.

There was renewed debate about economic reforms in 1990, with a number of new proposals for speeding up the privatization process and further liberalizing the economy. However, Gorbachev, worried about opposition to quickening the pace of reform from conservative forces in the Communist Party, opposed further reforms at this time.[57] That he was right to worry became evident in August 1991 when those forces attempted a coup d'état. When the coup failed, the conservatives were neutralized politically and pro-reform elements of the newly elected Russian government of Boris Yeltsin were able to dominate the scene. Gorbachev was forced to resign after his halfhearted attempts to salvage the leading role of the Communist Party failed, the Russian government replaced the Soviet government in Moscow, and the Soviet Union fell apart.

FROM COMMUNISM TO CAPITALISM

Problems of Transition from Communism

The transition from Communism had both political and economic dimensions. The political dimension generally involved the creation of a multiparty electoral system, the dismantling of authoritarian institutions like the secret police, and the institutionalization of the political rights and freedoms that go along with a more democratic political system. The economic dimension involved the replacement of central planning with a market system. Economic changes usually included the elimination of price controls, the privatization of state enterprises, and the creation of new economic instruments and institutions that allowed the government to extract resources from and stabilize the private economy.

The timing of these measures was critical. If one allowed prices to be determined by market forces without rapidly privatizing state enterprises, then the state enterprises, which were usually monopoly suppliers, could simply charge higher prices without increasing production. If one freed controlled prices and privatized state enterprises without creating the appropriate state and market institutions to prevent irresponsible or criminal behavior by market actors, then the country could end up with a system unable to rein in corruption. If the government failed to create market-stabilizing mechanisms, then the country might suffer from excessive inflation, rapid currency devaluations, low rates of private investment, and high rates of unemployment for prolonged periods of time.

The government of an economy in transition takes on a variety of new roles, many of them unfamiliar. It must police the marketplace to prevent gross malfeasance. The government must guarantee the property rights of private firms and individuals and adjudicate economic disputes among them. It has to ensure transparency of prices for both producers and consumers so that they can respond correctly to market signals. The central bank must concern itself with monitoring and controlling the rate of growth of the money supply in order to prevent excessive inflation. Finally, the government has to adopt and promulgate new accounting procedures so that it can collect taxes from private businesses to replace the revenues previously obtained from state enterprises.

It cannot be assumed that government officials will have the knowledge or the will to do all of the above in a timely and effective manner. Officials are sure to meet resistance from a variety of public and private actors. Some countries will have more difficulty than others in achieving the efficiency gains that are connected with the end of central planning because of differences in their resource endowments, accumulated investments in human and physical capital, and abilities to make the required institutional changes. Therefore, the speed and consequences of economic transition will vary significantly from country to country.

In Russia and Eastern Europe, the transition to capitalism occurred at the same time as the form of government was changing. The general desire to cast off communism resulted in both political and economic reforms. Political reforms were mainly in the direction of establishing genuine representative democracies. One key question was whether to permit former communists and communist parties to participate in electoral politics. Another was how much power to grant the head of state, the legislature, and the judiciary. An area where the political and the economic overlapped was the question of how best to structure the government so that it could effectively regulate the market. A related question was whether to allow the central bank to be autonomous from political forces so that it could focus on maintaining stability in the growth of the money supply, which was necessary for stemming inflation and maintaining the value of the national currency.

Yeltsin: Crisis and Reform

Boris Yeltsin faced three major domestic economic challenges when he came to power in 1991. The first task was to stabilize the Russian economy in the face of hyperinflation. The drop in government revenues, but not in government spending, led to a major budget deficit in 1991 equivalent to 20 percent of GDP. The annual inflation rate for 1992 was almost 1,500 percent (see Figure 10.5).[58]

The Russian central bank dealt with the deficit in the worst possible manner from the standpoint of limiting inflation: it simply issued more currency. The governor of the central bank, appointed by the Parliament not the president, issued vast amounts of cheap credits to the state enterprises.[59] As a result, the money supply increased by more than 700 percent in 1992. Confidence in the ruble plummeted, and many Russian enterprises insisted on payment in hard currencies instead of rubles, even for domestic transactions. Not until the late spring of 1993 did the Ministry of Finance agreed to limit state subsidies in order to reduce the budget deficit and the inflationary pressures it was causing. The rate of inflation remained between 15 and 20 percent per month through the end of 1994, finally dropping to less than 5 percent per month starting in mid-1995. During the financial crisis of 1998 (see below), the annual inflation rate soared upward again to 84.5 percent. By 1999, however, inflation was reduced to 36.7 percent. By 2000, it had declined to 20 percent.[60]

The second challenge was to restart the process of creating a market economy, a process that had been aborted under Gorbachev. Yeltsin first sought to privatize state enterprises through mandatory **commercialization**. Under commercialization, the state enterprises were to be converted into joint stock companies with shares that were to be publicly traded on stock exchanges, with boards of directors

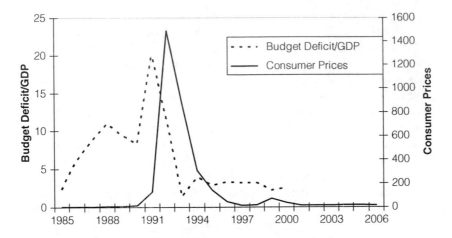

FIGURE 10.5 Budget Deficit/GDP and Growth in Consumer Prices in the Former Soviet Union and Russia, 1985–2006, in Percentages

SOURCE: Stanley Fischer, "Russia and the Soviet Union Then and Now," in Oliver J. Blanchard, Kenneth A. Froot, and Jeffrey D. Sachs, eds., *The Transition in Europe: Country Studies* (Volume 1) (Chicago, Ill.: University of Chicago Press, 1994), p. 234; and Keith Bush, *The Russian Economy in March 2002* (Washington, D.C.: Center for Strategic and International Studies, 2002).

representing the interests of shareholders. This approach, already tried in Poland, was designed to speed the process of privatization and reduce incentives for corruption.

Under the new privatization scheme, all the state enterprises were divided into three main categories according to their locus of control: federal, provincial (*oblast*), or municipal. The governmental responsibility for privatization was then divided according to this scheme. This approach gave the provincial and local governments—which had previously opposed privatization on the principle that it would lead to shutting down of factories in their locality—a stake in privatization. It also made it more difficult for the coalitions of managers, workers, and local governments discussed above to appropriate government assets.

Russia launched its privatization program in 1992. Tens of thousands of small- and medium-sized enterprises under the control of local authorities were sold through auctions and tender offers. The mass privatization program, directed at medium- and large-scale enterprises, utilized employee buyouts and voucher auctions to transfer ownership. Enterprises selected one of three privatization options, all of which gave enterprise insiders—workers and management—an opportunity to hold a majority of enterprise shares. To achieve fairness, the Government distributed **privatization vouchers** free to every Russian to enable them to acquire shares in enterprises through voucher auctions. Remaining blocks of shares were reserved for the government. While some Russians traded their vouchers for cash or participated in the auctions, many more sold their vouchers to investment funds. During the first year of the program, however, investment funds were limited legally to acquiring no more that 10 percent ownership in any single enterprise.

Voucher privatization was successful in a large number of state enterprises and created a new class of property owners with a stake in the reform process. Between 1992 and mid-1994 when voucher privatization was completed, over 15,000 medium- and large-scale enterprises employing 80 percent of Russia's industrial workforce were privatized. Over 75 percent of small enterprises were privatized by June 1994.[61] The transfer of ownership, however, did not result in enterprise restructuring. Indeed, the prevalence of insider ownership, lack of capital, and continuing responsibility to provide social services for employees obstructed enterprise reform.

In July 1994, President Yeltsin initiated a second phase of privatization based on sale of enterprise shares for cash. The objective was to complete the privatization of larger state-owned enterprises, raise funds for federal and local government budgets, and generate investment funds for privatized firms. The government also hoped to attract investors, including foreigners, who would intensify enterprise restructuring. The program entailed sales of government-owned shares of already privatized companies as well as blocks of shares in enterprises not yet privatized. While cash privatization proceeded relatively well at the municipal and regional levels, the federal program suffered from delays due to policy struggles and the ruble crash of October 1994, which shook confidence and diverted the attention of policy makers. Ultimately, only 136 firms were put up for sale under the program, and bidding was sluggish. The Government had expected to raise some $2 billion in revenues for the budget; in the end, less than $1 billion was raised.[62]

In September 1995, the government announced a new **loans-for-shares program** in an effort to raise substantial sums from the sale of shares of more than 20 of Russia's crown jewel companies. These included the oil, metals, timber, and shipping companies.[63] Under the program, the government would auction share-backed securities to Russian banks and other institutions. In return for these loans, the banks were to receive an immediate voice in management and a commitment to receive equity shares of the companies three years down the road when the value of the shares was expected to have increased dramatically. The program was widely criticized as nontransparent and dominated by insider deals, and was terminated after the initial transactions.

Yeltsin's third domestic challenge was countering political resistance to economic reform. As privatization and efforts at macroeconomic stabilization proceeded, resistance to reform mounted, especially from the Duma (Parliament) that had been elected under the prior regime and was dominated by the communists. In an effort to offset continued Duma opposition to his program, Yeltsin called for a referendum on economic reform in April 1993. With 64 percent of the electorate voting, 59 percent expressed confidence in the leadership of Boris Yeltsin and 53 percent approved of the policies pursued by the government after 1992.[64]

In October 1993, Yeltsin faced his most serious political challenge by breaking the resistance of a group of dissident members of the Russian Parliament in a quickly suppressed but bloody rebellion. The Parliament had voted to impeach Yeltsin, and he retaliated by dissolving Parliament and calling for new elections. The opposition occupied the Parliament building (the Russian "White House").

The Russian Army backed Yeltsin against the rebels in the fighting that ensued, sending a volley of cannon fire into the Parliament building and capturing the opposition leaders.

Parliamentary elections held in December 1993 resulted in a major defeat for the reformist political party. A rapid drop in industrial production in 1992 and 1993—together with continued high inflation rates—had made economic reform very unpopular, despite progress made toward reducing hyperinflation.[65] The liberal reformers suffered further losses in the parliamentary elections of December 1995.

Yeltsin himself had to mass a major campaign in 1996 to win a second term as Russia's president. He decided to stand for reelection as President, despite severe health problems, the growing unpopularity of the military intervention in Chechnya, growing unrest over the failure of the Russian government to pay salaries of workers in state enterprises, and complaints about the erosion of pension benefits caused by high inflation. During the election campaign, Yeltsin promised to seek compensation for those who lost their savings due to high rates of inflation and to continue efforts to reduce inflation. He also called on the Russian legislature to pass a bill to allow the buying and selling of land and promised other agricultural reforms. Yeltsin won the July election with 53.7 percent of the vote. His closest rival, Gennady Zyuganov, a former communist, received only 40.4 percent of the vote.[66]

Russian Foreign Economic Policies under Yeltsin and the West's Response

Pursuing an aggressive foreign economic policy of integration with the Western international economy was, of necessity, part of managing the severe domestic crises that the Yeltsin government faced at the end of 1991. The ruble was not yet fully convertible and remained the main currency of most of the countries that had split off from the Soviet Union. The former Soviet republics competed with Russia to issue rubles, making the problem of reducing inflationary pressures more difficult to solve. To address this problem, in 1993 the Central Bank of Russia moved to issue a new Russian ruble to replace the Soviet ruble, asserted its right to have a monopoly over controlling the supply of rubles, and established a foreign-currency auction system making the ruble convertible inside Russia.[67] Then, in 1994, the Central Bank of Russia severed its connections with the central banks of former Soviet republics.[68] Although the rapid decline in the value of the ruble after 1991 contributed to inflation by raising the prices of imports, it also made Russian exports more competitive internationally. The various efforts to stabilize the Russian economy after 1992, especially efforts to reduce the budget deficit and control inflation, eventually helped to reduce the downward pressures on the ruble.

Russia also continued to face difficulties servicing its heavy burden of foreign debt. The Russian government assumed the debt of the Soviet Union in 1993, which at the time amount to around $105 billion.[69] Faced with economic crisis and the huge challenge of a transition to a market economy, Yeltsin turned for help to the West and to major international economic bodies like the G-7, the World Bank, and the IMF.

In May 1990, the developed countries set up a new multilateral bank, the **European Bank for Reconstruction and Development (EBRD)**, to channel aid into Russia, the other former Soviet Republics, and Eastern Europe.[70] Both aid and FDI flows to Russia were constrained, however, by worries about the commitment of the Russian government to economic reforms. In a historic development, the G-7 leaders invited President Yeltsin to the London economic summit of the G-7 in the summer of 1991. At that meeting, President Yeltsin requested increased economic assistance and political support for Russian membership in the IMF and World Bank.

Pleased by Yeltsin's economic policies, including his efforts to privatize Russian state enterprises, the G-7 countries strongly supported Russian membership in the IMF and World Bank. Because they remained concerned about Yeltsin's commitment to sustained reform, however, they held back on making major new commitments for economic aid. Most of the aid to Russia at this time came from Germany, as part of German payments to speed the removal of Russian troops from the former East Germany. The G-7 took a major step toward supporting economic reform in Russia in 1993, just prior to the referendum on reform called by President Yeltsin. The G-7 assistance package included approximately $34 billion in new financial flows: $13 billion in loans from the IMF, $1.5 billion in loans from the World Bank, a new G-7 Privatization Fund, an additional $10 billion in export credits from G-7 countries, and $6.5 billion in U.S. aid (which included aid to other former Soviet Republics). About $2.5 billion in loans were made available immediately.[71] The new flows, plus the IMF and World Bank conditions requiring stabilization and privatization, proved to be a major economic and political boost to Russia's reform program.

Following the 1993 program, the IMF and World Bank engaged in intensive and regular dialogue with Russia on its macroeconomic policy and structural reform program. Support and pressure from these two institutions contributed to the stabilization and reform efforts described above. In 1996, for example, the Fund and Russia concluded a new lending arrangement of $10 billion to support stabilization, which was monitored and disbursed on a monthly basis. At the same time, the developed countries supported Russian reform in other ways: ending CoCom controls on trade with Russia and the former Communist countries, beginning negotiations for Russian membership in the WTO, and rescheduling Russian debt. As a symbol of growing Russian integration into the institutions of the West, Russia became a regular participant in the discussion of political, though not economic, issues at the G-7 summits.

The Crisis of 1998

The budget deficit problem continued to plague the Russian government. Although the government stopped financing government deficits by printing money, and sought to increase revenues and reduce spending, the budget deficit remained very large. After 1992, tax revenues had declined dramatically due primarily to tax evasion in the form of officially sanctioned "tax arrears." Economically marginal business enterprises in Russia were allowed to stay in business by not paying their taxes (they also did not pay their workers or the workers' pensions).[72]

Part of the government deficit was caused by the continued need to make payments on the debt accumulated by the former Soviet Union. Between 1993 and 1996, four rescheduling agreements were signed with the Paris Club. The fourth of these, concluded in April 1996, allowed $38.5 billion of Russian debt to be repaid over 25 years with a grace period of six years. The debt owed to the 600 London Club banks was rescheduled in October 1997, greatly reducing the overall debt servicing burden. Russia became a member of the Paris Club in 1997 and, as a result, became eligible for repayment of debts to the former Soviet Union amounting to over $85 billion.[73] Nevertheless, Russia was still unable to meet its obligations.

The Russian government tried to solve the deficit problem by attracting foreign investors. Starting in 1993, the government issued short-term bonds called GKOs[74] denominated in dollars and deutsche marks at high interest rates. The revenues from sales of these bonds were used to finance the deficit. By mid-1998, the value of outstanding GKOs totaled around $40 billion. However, as tax collection problems persisted, speculation grew concerning the future devaluation of the ruble. The Central Bank of Russia had to raise interest rates several times in 1997 and 1998 in order to keep investment funds flowing into GKOs and to reduce downward pressures on the ruble. Speculators believed, rightly, that the Russian government would be unable to honor its commitments to pay interest on GKOs. In addition, the Asian financial crisis of 1997 had made the global investment community unusually nervous. As a result, in the summer of 1998 foreign investors rapidly began to withdraw their funds from Russia.

Russian Prime Minister Sergei Kiriyenko announced on August 17, 1998, that the Russian government had decided to float the ruble and default on $40 billion of the bonds. The government also announced a unilateral and legally dubious 90-day moratorium on payments by Russian entities on their foreign obligations. President Boris Yeltsin fired Kiriyenko on August 23 and replaced him with former Prime Minister Victor Chernomyrdin in a move intended to calm the country and to reassure international investors. The head of the Russian Central Bank resigned three weeks later. The ruble had fallen from around 6 rubles to the dollar on August 17 to about 22 rubles to the dollar on September 20.[75]

The 1998 crisis had an important impact on the internal distribution of power within Russia. About one-third of the assets of the Russian banking system had been put into GKOs by mid-1998. The total amount of GKO assets was over 12 percent of GDP. The floating of the ruble and the default on GKO payments resulted not only in the flight of foreign investors but also in the ruination of many of Russia's fledging private banks.[76] Prior to 1998, an alliance among the private banks, the larger enterprises, and Russian underworld figures had dominated both the economy and the political system. After 1998, the power of the private banks was severely diminished.

Domestic Economic Policies of the Putin Regime

The Russian financial crisis of August 1998 resulted in a major drop in Yeltsin's political popularity. Because of the political stalemate, very little reform occurred in the Russian economic system between 1996 and 1998. The Russian debt ratio (debt/GDP) increased dramatically, mainly because of declining GDP but also because the government financed growing budget deficits by borrowing from abroad. Yeltsin selected Vladimir Putin to be prime minister of Russia in August 1999 after firing his predecessor, Sergei Stepashin.

Yeltsin resigned on December 31, 1999, and appointed Prime Minister Putin acting president. In the presidential elections held on March 26, 2000, Putin received 52.94 percent of the vote.[77] Although he was a former KGB officer and the hand-picked successor of Yeltsin for the presidency, Putin showed soon after his election that he was committed to economic reform. Putin moved immediately to cut the budget deficit by enforcing tax laws and decreasing public spending. He reduced taxes on business activity and instituted a flat income tax for individuals. Between 1999 and 2001, Putin proposed and the Russian Duma passed a new and badly needed bankruptcy law, along with new laws regarding the hiring and firing of workers, the sale of land, pensions, and anticompetitive behavior.

One of Putin's most important policy initiatives was to reverse some of the devolution of power from the central to the provincial governments of Russia.[78] Devolution was used by Yeltsin to secure support from provincial politicians who could not otherwise be counted upon to support the changes taking place in Moscow. One of the results of devolution was loss of control over the levying and collection of taxes in the provinces and an inability to enforce decisions made by both the president and the Duma. By the end of the Yeltsin administration, there was broad consensus that devolution had gone too far and that there was a need for some recentralization of authority and control. The recentralization undertaken by Putin was later seen as excessive and undemocratic.

Another Putin policy objective was to take control of Russia's fossil fuels and minerals industries out of the hands of private owners and to put it back under the control of the state. Yeltsin had permitted the so-called oligarchs to gain control over the large natural gas (Gazprom and Rosneft), petroleum (Yukos, Sibneft, Lukoil, and Tyumen Oil), and nickel (Norilsk) state-owned enterprises during the loans for shares period. Putin believed that Russia could not afford to allow these firms to be controlled by the private sector and he particularly opposed ownership by foreigners. Putin made sure that Gazprom, the world's largest natural gas producer, became a state enterprise under the direct control of the Russian government. Only private firms that were willing to follow the directions of the Kremlin were permitted to operate unhindered.[79]

The recovery of oil prices after 1998 helped to produce a large and sustained increase in GDP growth rates (see Figure 10.3). Higher economic growth had a direct and positive impact on poverty alleviation.[80] The Russian public responded by giving Putin consistently high ratings in opinion polls. His party, United Russia, came to dominate the political system. The reduction in the value of the ruble after 1998 made Russian exports more competitive worldwide while also increasing the prices of imports. The Russian economy, however, remained highly dependent on the exploitation of raw materials and agriculture, and the manufacturing sector outside the energy complex had not yet benefited from Russian integration into the world economy. One of the strategies that Putin adopted to diversify the economy and to reduce the economic and political power of the large (and often monopolistic) privatized state enterprises was to seek early entry into the WTO.[81] More importantly, he reduced the red tape associated with the establishment of new enterprises, simplified the tax code, and reduced the level of business taxes after the successful introduction of a **value-added tax (VAT)**.

International Economic Relations in the Putin Era

By the end of the Yeltsin era, Russia was on the road to becoming fully integrated into the Western system. It had obtained membership in the IMF and the World Bank in 1992 and had requested membership in the OECD in 1996. Russia applied for accession to the GATT in 1993. Its application was taken up by the WTO in 1995. Russia first attended a G-7 meeting in 1994 and was included in the G-8 in 1997.

Putin made accession to the WTO a high priority when he took office in 1999. He pushed for an agreement prior to the G-8 summit in St. Petersburg in 2006. However, bilateral negotiations between Russia and the United States at the summit were unsuccessful, so accession was delayed. The delay was due to U.S. refusal to give in to a Russian demand for the right to audit the facilities of U.S. beef and pork exporters. The Russian government (like the Chinese and Indian governments, see Chapter 7) was concerned about the impact of the WTO's agricultural liberalization agreements on Russian farmers.[82] Nevertheless, after the failure of the Doha Round in the summer of 2008, the Russian government expressed hopes that the talks would resume in the near future.

Russian trade grew rapidly during the Putin era from $89 billion in 2000 to $300 billion in 2007. Exports exceeded imports by $130 billion in 2007.[83] Russia's largest trade partner was the European Union. Over 50 percent of Russian exports went to the EU and over 50 percent of Russian imports came from the EU. Over 65 percent of EU imports from Russia consisted of energy products.[84] Russian exports to Asia were roughly one-third exports to the EU— about 60 percent higher than exports to the Americas.[85]

After the invasion of Georgia, there was speculation about further delays in Russia's accession to the WTO, along with not-so-veiled threats about speeding up the expansion of NATO and expelling Russia from the G-8. Putin began to argue that Russia did not need the WTO and that the government would "abandon some of the deals it has reached to join the organization....We see virtually no advantages ...."[86]

Foreign investment inflows into Russia increased rapidly during the Putin era. During the Yeltsin presidency, the highest annual inflow of FDI was $5 billion in 1997; by 2007, inflows had increased to over $52 billion. The main sources of FDI inflows into Russia were the Western European countries and the United States. Receiving the largest inflows were the food and drink, retail, mining, timber, and automotive industries. Restrictions on foreign ownership in the energy sector remained in place, but bureaucratic administration of these restrictions was made more predictable and less arbitrary by a new law on strategic sectors that entered into force in May 2008.[87]

Russia achieved many but not all of its economic policy goals by the beginning of the twenty-first century. After two major crises in the 1990s, the Russian economy was stable and growing. Increases in world oil and natural gas prices helped spur an economic recovery after 1999. The decline in the value of the ruble in 1998 encouraged exports and removed a source of instability in the economy. Economic recovery helped the government of Vladimir Putin establish its legitimacy in the wake of Yeltsin's resignation. Russia was a member of the G-8, the IMF, and the World Bank, although it had not yet become a member of the WTO or the OECD.

The primary challenges that remained were to diversify and modernize Russian manufacturing and create a firmer foundation for democracy and economic development. The Russian economy was now capitalist, but still overly dependent on oil and natural gas exports. The Russian political system was increasingly autocratic and Russian foreign policy appeared to be headed in a dangerous direction.

Economic Reform in Eastern Europe

In the wake of dramatic political changes in 1989, Eastern Europe also moved toward economic reform. The pace there was sometimes quicker, sometimes slower than in Russia. Even before 1989 and the end of the Cold War, some Eastern European states had adopted extensive economic reforms. Before 1989, Hungary went furthest by allowing more competitive pricing, reducing subsidies, introducing personal income and value-added taxes, liberalizing the financial sector and foreign trade sector, and introducing a bankruptcy law.[88] The impetus for Hungary's economic reform, which had come from some sectors within the Communist Party, was poor economic performance in the 1980s and the need to service the country's foreign debt. Political reform, aimed at allowing greater pluralism and the right of association, had gone hand in hand with economic reform and even outpaced it. Thanks to economic reforms implemented prior to 1989, liberalization of the Hungarian economy was somewhat easier than in other countries. In addition, as in Russia, a significant amount of spontaneous privatization took place in Hungary after 1989. The Hungarians were not as successful as the Russians in moving away from spontaneous privatization to a more genuine form of privatization. The electoral success of a reconstituted version of the Hungarian Communist Party in 1994 slowed the pace of reform considerably.

Things went better for the Hungarians in the first decade of the twenty-first century. Hungary joined the European Union in 2004. It had shifted most of its trade away from the former Soviet bloc countries to Western Europe after 1989. Hungary received a large share of the FDI flowing to Eastern Europe, much of it from the United States. It paid off its outstanding debts to the IMF. A new government was elected in 2006 that promised "reform without austerity," but high deficit spending by the previous government had resulted in a need to reduce government deficits (and therefore some austerity) as part of reform.[89]

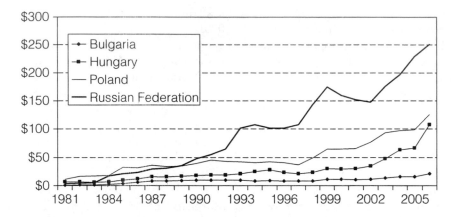

FIGURE 10.6 Long-Term Debt Outstanding in Russia and Three Countries in Eastern Europe in Billions of Current Dollars, 1981–2006

SOURCE: World Bank, *World Development Indicators 2008.*

Poland had gone furthest in political reform before 1989 by legalizing Solidarity and other trade unions, introducing free elections, granting opposition parties seats in Parliament, and easing censorship of the press.[90] When the coalition government with Solidarity participation took over in Poland in September 1989, it had to deal with hyperinflation, chronic shortages of goods, a large trade deficit, and a debt crisis. Tadeusz Mazowiecki, the new prime minister, implemented a rapid stabilization program that included the freeing of prices and the liberalization of domestic and international trade. This program of rapid transition to capitalism was later to be called "the big bang." The new government supported a policy of reducing real wages to compensate for overly generous wage increases of the 1988–1989 period. Subsidies to state enterprises were cut back drastically, as were plans for new state investments. The government stabilized the zloty, Poland's currency, and made it fully convertible into foreign currencies. Finally, in early 1990, official creditors agreed to a generous rescheduling of Poland's official debt and in 1991 to a 50-percent reduction in that debt (see Figure 10.6).

The Polish stabilization program reduced annual inflation from 600 percent in 1990 to 42 percent in 1992. The cost of stabilization, however, was quite high. In 1990, GDP decreased by 12 percent, and real wages fell by 33 percent. Many government expenditures, even in basic areas like health and education, were cut to reduce the budgetary deficit.[91]

The new Polish government embarked on a privatization program in July 1990. State enterprises were converted into joint stock companies (this was called "commercialization") and the government was empowered to sell its interest in the firms after a two-year transition period or close them down. However, two years after the big bang, only 11 percent of Polish state enterprises had been privatized. The top-down approach to privatization—which had worked well in the case of East Germany because the West Germans controlled the privatization board (the *Treuhandanstalt*)—did not work well in Poland.[92]

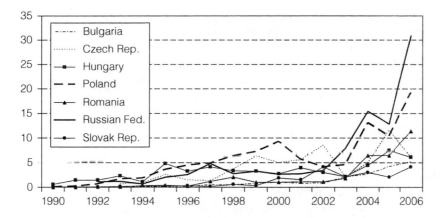

FIGURE 10.7   FDI Inflows in Billions of Current Dollars, 1990–2006

SOURCE: World Bank, *World Development Indicators 2008*.

In early 2002, the government announced a new set of economic reforms, designed in many ways to complete the process launched in 1990. The package acknowledged the need to improve Poland's investment climate, particularly the conditions for small- and medium-sized enterprises, and better prepare the economy to compete as a member of the European Union.[93] Poland became a member of the EU in 2004. Foreign investment inflows were second only to those of Russia between 2000 and 2006 (see Figure 10.7). Foreign firms that had a major presence in Poland included Fiat, Volkswagen, Daewoo, and General Motors.[94] The government also aimed to improve Poland's public finances to prepare for adoption of the Euro (planned for 2012).

Czechoslovakia split into the Czech Republic and the Slovak Republic on January 1, 1993. Like Poland, the Czech Republic pursued privatization vigorously for small enterprises but more slowly for larger state enterprises. Economic results were good until 1996 when growth slowed dramatically. Part of the problem, as in Russia later, was dealing with the various stakeholders, and particularly with the managers of state enterprises and organized labor.

One could argue that the Czech and Slovak republics combined features of the Hungarian and Polish approaches to economic reform. The Czech Republic's democratic political system functioned well in the early 1990s under the leadership of the Civic Forum, a conservative party that had few successful rivals for power. Limited party competition made it possible for the Czech government to implement economic reforms rapidly after 1993, but may have contributed to the low growth rates the country experienced in the mid 1990s.[95] Whatever the reason, growth resumed in the late 1990s and continued on through the next decade.[96]

No formerly communist country in Eastern Europe approached East Germany in the rapidity and depth of its transition to a market economy. East Germany had the benefit of being integrated into a larger industrialized capitalist nation in 1990, inheriting all the legal institutions (with a few notable exceptions) of West Germany, and receiving major subsidies from the German federal government, which were designed to bring its infrastructure and capital stock quickly up to the West German standards. The communists in East Germany were completely delegitimized by the acts of the regime prior to 1989, and the West German political parties quickly established a dominant role in East German politics after 1990. The transition in former East Germany was not accomplished without dislocations, however, as high levels of unemployment accompanied a general decline in living standards, especially for those on fixed incomes. As Germany recovered from the shock of unification, however, these problems began to abate.

As in Russia, the immediate impact of economic reforms in Eastern Europe was a drop in production and increased unemployment. In some cases, hyperinflation was deeply embedded and hard to eliminate. People who were used to steady jobs and stable incomes, even if low by Western standards, began to vote against the governments who had implemented economic reforms. Some voters, especially in the former Soviet Union, wanted to return to central planning. Partly to head off this opposition, governments increased social spending in the mid-1990s, with much of the new spending allocated for early-retirement plans designed to increase overall labor productivity.[97] There were signs of a turnaround in the Eastern European economies in the mid 1990s (see again Figure 10.4), and prosperity under capitalism began to appear more and more likely, especially for those countries able to join the European Union.

One of the goals of the East European countries was to join the European Union. EU members were of two minds on expanding to the East. Some, especially Germany, felt it was essential for political as well as economic reasons to bring the Eastern Europeans into the union. Others felt Europe needed to be "deepened," that is, the Maastricht agreements needed to be implemented, before it could be "widened." Thus, the EU negotiated association agreements providing for gradual movement toward free trade with the expectation of eventual membership (see Table 10.1).

The timing of accession of each country to the EU depended on the progress it made in preparing for membership, according to the criteria laid down by the European Council in Copenhagen in 1993. The Copenhagen criteria required (1) stability of institutions guaranteeing democracy, the rule of law, human rights, and respect for and protection of minorities; (2) the existence of a functioning market economy as well as the capacity to cope with competitive pressure and market forces within the Union; and (3) the ability to take on the obligations of membership, including adherence to the aims of political, economic, and monetary union.[98] The Czech Republic, Hungary, Poland, Slovakia, and Slovenia became EU member-states in 2004. Bulgaria and Romania became members in 2007. The integration of these countries into the EU meant that they were effectively integrated into the world economy and that their political systems would probably not revert to authoritarianism.

T A B L E   10.1   **EU Association Agreements and Partnership and Cooperation Agreements with Russia, and Central European and CIS Countries**

Country	Date of EU Association Agreement	Date of EU Partnership and Cooperation Agreement	Date of EU Membership
Russia		June 1994, extended in 1997	
Poland	March 1992		2004
Czech Republic	March 1992		2004
Slovakia	March 1992		2004
Slovenia	February 1999		2004
Hungary	March 1992		2004
Romania	March 1993		2007
Bulgaria	January 1994		2007
Estonia	June 1995		2004
Latvia	June 1995		2004
Lithuania	June 1995		2004
Belarus		June 1994, currently in negotiation	
Ukraine		June 1995, extended in 1998	
Moldova		November 1994, extended in 1998	
Armenia		April 1996, extended in 1999	
Azerbaijan		April 1996, extended in 1999	
Georgia		April 1996, extended in 1999	
Kazakhstan		January 1995, extended in 1999	
Kyrgyzstan		February 1995, extended in 1999	
Tajikistan		February 1995, currently in negotiation	
Turkmenistan		November 1997, currently in negotiation	
Uzbekistan		June 1996, extended in 1999	

SOURCE: Anders Åslund, *Building Capitalism: The Transformation of the Former Soviet Bloc* (New York, N.Y.: Cambridge University Press, 2002), 174; and "European Union Association Agreement," *Wikipedia*, http://www.en.wikipedia.org/wiki/European_Union_Association_Agreement.

CHINA

Cold War and Isolation

For most of the postwar period, China, like the Soviet Union and Eastern Europe, was isolated from the Western trading and financial system. China pursued a policy of independent economic development that was based not only on Marxist-Leninist theory but also on China's historical experience with foreign occupation and exploitation beginning with the Opium Wars and unequal treaties of the nineteenth century and ending with the Japanese occupation in the twentieth century.

Following the victory of the Communists in 1949, Mao Zedong declared that China would "lean to one side," that is, emphasize its relationship with the Soviet Union. A treaty of friendship, alliance, and mutual assistance against aggression by Japan or "any other state" (a veiled reference to the United States) was signed in February 1950. During the 1950s, China relied exclusively on the Soviet Union for technology transfers, capital equipment, and financial support. Originally, joint-stock companies in mining and other natural resources, like those in Eastern Europe after the war, were the preferred form of aid; these were liquidated after Stalin's death. In addition, the Soviet Union lent China $60 million a year from 1950 to 1955 and another $26 million a year from 1954 to 1959.[99] Thousands of Chinese went to Moscow for technical training, while thousands of Soviet technicians worked in China on over 330 industrial projects.[100] Domestically, Mao followed the Soviet model of urban-led industrialization based on the Marxist-Leninist tenets of collectivization, state ownership of the means of production, and central planning. China's strategy of independence was reinforced by its isolation by the West. The United States refused to recognize the People's Republic of China and maintained diplomatic relations with Taiwan.

China's relations with the West became particularly strained when the Korean War erupted. Following China's attack on U.S. troops in Korea in 1950, the United States imposed a complete embargo on China. The United Nations, which continued to recognize Taiwan until 1971, also imposed an embargo on the export of strategic materials to China in 1951 in response to its "aggression" in Korea.[101] As a result, trade with the West was minimal. China's total trade with all noncommunist countries amounted to only $550 million in 1952.[102]

As the fifties progressed, the Sino-Soviet alliance deteriorated. A history of border disputes and mistrust between the Soviet Union and China under girded their differences, which were exacerbated in the 1950s by ideological disputes. When Khrushchev began his de-Stalinization campaign and his policy of peaceful coexistence with the West, Mao accused him of revisionism. A struggle ensued over doctrinal purity and whether the Chinese or the Soviet Communist Party would be the rightful leader of the international communist movement. Eventually the Soviet Union retracted its offer to help China develop nuclear weapons, and in 1960 all of the Soviet Union's technical and economic advisors were ordered to return to Moscow.

Beginning in the late 1950s, China adopted a policy of self-sufficiency and turned inward. In 1958 it embarked on the **Great Leap Forward**, a plan to modernize its industry and increase output by way of structural changes and greater ideological purity. Agriculture had already been collectivized, but grain production had stagnated during the 1950s. Further concentration of collectives was promoted to produce a mass mobilization of the energies of the rural laborers. The collectives were encouraged to place a priority on small-scale local industry to provide for the needs of the farmers. Economic management was decentralized and more responsibility was given to the local communist parties.

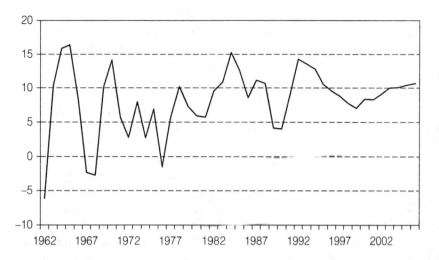

F I G U R E 10.8 GDP Growth in China, 1961–2006, in Percentages

SOURCE: World Bank, *World Development Indicators 2008*.

Although Mao believed that ideological incentives could unlock the potential of the workers, productivity declined as collectivization continued. This decline in productivity, combined with the withdrawal of Soviet advisors, the decentralization of the economy, and bad weather conditions, led to disaster for the Chinese economy. China's GNP decreased by one-third in 1960 (see Figure 10.8). The poor harvest resulted in large-scale starvation and malnutrition. The decentralization of the economy led to the breakdown of industry and transportation, and eventually to wide-scale demoralization. The crisis reached such proportions that Mao was forced to step down from the chairmanship of China in April 1959 (although he remained chairman of the Communist Party). The communes were broken down, some private plots were restored, and control was returned to nonparty managers.

Although China's domestic economy began to recover in the early 1960s, it suffered another major economic setback during the **Cultural Revolution**, from 1966 to 1976. In his search for ideological purity, Mao incited the public to rebel against the party, which Mao felt had lost its revolutionary fervor. Major party leaders, educators, and factory managers were purged and parts of the country fell into anarchy. The economy was crippled as basic institutions fell apart and as China deepened its isolation from world contact. Eventually the army was forced to intervene to restore order. Throughout the 1960s, China decreased its trade in real terms and repaid all of its outstanding loans in order to achieve complete self-sufficiency.[103] It had no diplomatic and few economic ties with the United States and continued to be subject to export controls and other U.S. restrictions on trade.

As the 1960s drew to a close, pressures for change began to force China away from its isolationism. The Great Leap Forward and the Cultural Revolution left China technologically backward and politically isolated. Population growth continued to strain China's ability to feed its people. The most important impetus for change at the time, however, was political. Relations with the Soviet Union had continued to deteriorate, and in 1969 the two countries came close to war on the Sino-Soviet border. In 1969, China, motivated by its desire to form a tactical alliance against the Soviet Union, began sending diplomatic signals indicating its willingness to open relations with the West.

Improving relations with Beijing was an important component of President Nixon's policy of détente. For the Nixon administration, China offered a counterbalance in the U.S. relations with the Soviet Union. Accordingly, the United States responded to China's signals and indicated its interest in improving relations. Some of the U.S. unilateral trade barriers were removed, and the United States voted to support the entry of the PRC into the United Nations, although it voted against expelling Taiwan. In 1972, at the time of President Nixon's dramatic visit to China, the U.S. and Chinese governments issued the Shanghai Communiqué—the first of three joint U.S.-PRC Communiqués—in which the United States established its "one China" policy by acknowledging that "all Chinese on either side of the Taiwan Strait maintain there is but one China and that Taiwan is a part of China." At the same time, the United States and China signed a bilateral trade agreement and trade resumed after a 26-year interruption. Through the 1970s, bilateral trade grew steadily to reach $4.0 billion in 1979. However, it remained a small fraction of the overall trade of both nations.

The second joint communiqué between the U.S. and the PRC was signed in 1979 during the Carter presidency. It formally changed U.S. diplomatic recognition from Taipei to Beijing. At the same time, the U.S. and China negotiated a third joint communiqué, which resolved a number of political questions regarding U.S. unofficial relations with Taiwan, particularly U.S. arms sales.

During the 1970s Japanese-Chinese relations also improved. China's trade with Japan grew rapidly once diplomatic relations were reestablished in 1972. Total bilateral trade between Japan and China reached $1 billion in 1972[104] and $4.3 billion by 1979. Growth of trade continued into the 1980s, increasing 15 times in value in 15 years. China's main export to Japan was crude oil; Japan won contracts to build various chemical and steel plants in China.[105] On the political side, tension remained between China and Japan due to continuing Chinese resentment over Japan's wartime occupation.

Deng Xiaoping's Economic Reforms

One of the most important events in recent Chinese history occurred in 1978, when Deng Xiaoping consolidated his power and initiated a profound reform of the Chinese economy. China's need to embark on economic reform can be traced to many of the same inherent weaknesses of the communist system that the Soviet Union experienced. Under the socialist economic model, China's economy suffered from inefficient allocation of resources and lack of incentives for workers, resulting in poor agricultural and industrial performance. Flexibility and technological change were discouraged, resulting in an increasing technological gap between China and the West, which adversely affected its economic and military capabilities.

Deng's reforms affected both the domestic economy and China's external relations, and they focused on four areas: agriculture, industry, science and technology, and defense.[106] Beginning in the agricultural sector, China implemented a **household responsibility system**, which contracted work to individuals and families and gave them more power to manage their own production decisions and more latitude to engage in economic activities outside the central state economy. Peasants were allowed to lease their own farm plots from their collectives and, after producing a certain quota for the state, to sell the rest of their production on an open market. China's 1982 constitution declared that the existence of an individual economy would complement, not threaten, the socialist economy.

Agricultural production was also encouraged through price reform. The government allowed prices for agricultural products to increase across the board and stimulated production of certain products, such as vegetables and meat, by increasing their prices even further. In 1984 farmers were allowed to contract land from the communes for 15-year periods and transfer the rights to their farmland to other people, although the state still owned the means of production. In 1988, farmers were actually allowed to buy and sell **land use rights**, the closest a socialist economy had come to allowing private ownership of land. The household responsibility system was extended into other sectors of the rural economy, such as light industry, fishing, and restaurants. After 1985, purchase quotas for agricultural production were replaced by open market transactions.[107]

Reforms in the industrial sector focused on the development of light industry, to correct for previous overemphasis on heavy industry. In 1981, for the first time, production in light industries equaled that of heavy industries. The largest growth was in **township and village enterprises (TVEs)**. Firms began to be responsible for locating their own raw materials and customers. Their profits, although taxed by the state, were theirs to keep.[108]

The initial results of reform were strong. Agriculture improved from 4.2 percent average annual growth between 1953 and 1977 to 12.3 percent growth from 1978 to 1983. Industrial growth slowed from 10.8 percent to 6.8 percent in the respective periods, but overall national income increased from 6.1 percent average annual growth before the reforms to 8 percent growth from 1978 to 1983.[109] Between 1978 and 2006, GDP expanded at an average annual rate of 9.5 percent (see Figure 10.8).[110] China's per capita income was around $4,600 in 2006 (see Figure 10.8).[111] The steady increase in per capita income improved the general well-being of the Chinese population, even though there continued to be major regional and urban–rural differences.[112]

As Chinese economic reforms progressed and the government relinquished some of its central planning functions, it became evident that further price reform would also be necessary to allow the market to work. Goods, labor, and land markets were also decontrolled, although some residual controls remained on land sales and prices. The state retained control over the financial sector through continued state ownership of banks and bureaucratic allocation of credit through the banking system. After 1986, innovations occurred in the development of interbank markets in some cities and the opening of equity markets in Beijing, Shenyang, and Shanghai.[113] New forms of financial intermediaries, such

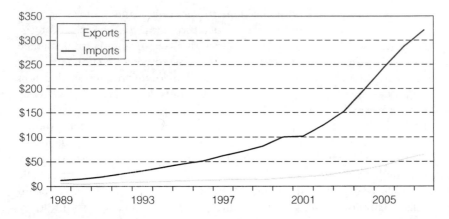

FIGURE 10.9 U.S. Exports to and Imports from China, 1989–2007, in Billions of Current Dollars

SOURCE: U.S. Census Bureau, *Foreign Trade Statistics.*
Note: The trade balance is the difference between exports and imports.

as insurance companies and leasing operations, began to function. However, the financial system was still dominated by state-owned banks.[114]

In its external affairs, China adopted a new open-door policy that placed emphasis on diplomatic relations with the West and the role of international trade, finance, and foreign investment in China's economic development. China's trade increased rapidly after 1978, after stagnating in the 1960s (see Figure 7.4). The government's strategy was to earn enough hard currency through its exports of textiles, petroleum, and other goods to support necessary capital and technology imports. China also depended on receipts from tourism, foreign investments, and transfers from overseas Chinese to bolster its foreign exchange reserves. The most important imports were heavy capital goods, iron and steel, oil- and gas-exploring and processing equipment, and, to a lesser extent, grain. After 1984, regulations on imports of consumer goods were relaxed, which led to occasional trade deficits.

China's largest trading partner in the 1980s and early 1990s was Japan. Hong Kong was China's second largest trading partner and the main source of FDI inflows, because of substantial indirect trade relations between China and other East Asian countries such as Taiwan and South Korea. Since no trade officially existed between these countries and China, the goods and money passed through Hong Kong. The EU as a whole was China's third largest trading partner, although the United States had more trade with China than any single member state of the EU. Both Europe and the United States experienced deficits in their trade with China in the early 1990s, in marked contrast with Japan's growing trade surplus with that country. In 2007, the U.S. trade deficit with China was approximately $266 billion, up from around $10 billion in 1990 (see Figure 10.9).

U.S.–Chinese trade relations were cemented on July 7, 1979, when the two countries signed a trade agreement that granted China most-favored-nation trading status. However, because China remained a nonmarket economy, MFN treatment was limited by a provision of the 1974 Trade Act, requiring the

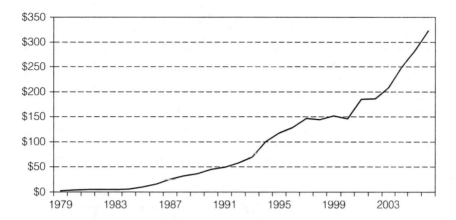

FIGURE 10.10 Long Term Debt Outstanding in China in Billions of Current Dollars, 1979–2006

SOURCE: World Bank, *World Development Indicators 2008.*

U.S. President to certify each year that China permitted citizens to leave the country. The agreement reduced U.S. tariffs on Chinese imports and made China eligible for Export-Import Bank financing. The pact also provided for the establishment of commercial trade offices in the two countries. In addition, President Reagan played the China card by encouraging trade with that country. Export controls were relaxed, allowing approximately one-third of U.S. exports to China in recent years to consist of high-technology equipment.[115] Under the Reagan administration, trade with China grew, so that by 1988, U.S. exports to China amounted to $6.6 billion, compared with $1.7 billion in 1979.[116]

To pursue a more active trade policy, China restructured its system of foreign trade. Beginning in 1988, the system was decentralized so that state-owned trade corporations and manufacturers could make their own export and import plans. In addition, factories were allowed to retain up to 80 percent of the export earnings that exceeded their export targets. On the other hand, factories were increasingly asked to become responsible for their own losses. For foreign traders, the system was more difficult. Instead of negotiating with one central trade authority, as before, they now had to court three organizations: the central trade authority, the provincial trading firms, and the manufacturers themselves. China's desire to increase its trade also led it to apply in July 1986 to become a contracting party to the GATT. Bringing a partially reformed, nonmarket economy with a thriving export sector into the GATT and WTO with rules designed for market economies proved difficult (see discussion below of China's accession to the WTO).

In the financial realm, China signaled the end of its isolationism by joining the IMF and World Bank in 1980. China increased its borrowing from Western financial markets and international organizations, although it was wary of incurring an excessive debt burden. By 2006, China's total long-term debt out-standing was $323 billion (see Figure 10.10) or about 10 percent of GDP.[117]

Another major change for China was its interest in encouraging foreign direct investment and joint ventures with the West. Like many developing countries, China hoped to benefit from technology transfers embodied in these investments and also to take advantage of revenues generated from the exports created by these companies. China took a number of steps to encourage foreign investment. In 1979, it established four **special economic zones (SEZs)**[118] to encourage inflows of foreign investment and production for export by offering favorable tax treatment, special profit repatriation agreements, and other induce-ments to foreign investors. In 1984, 14 other coastal cities offer similar incentives. In 1991, the entire Chinese economy was opened to foreign investment on the same terms offered in the SEZs. By 2000, there were 124 SEZs in China, employing around 18 million people.[119] A joint-venture law was passed in April 1988, to provide a legal framework for foreigners doing business in China. Modifications were made in labor regulations to allow foreign companies to hire and fire employees freely; in general, Chinese companies had to have permission to hire and fire workers. Although thousands of joint and cooperative ventures were created, many barriers remained.[120] Primary among these was the limited convertibility of the renminbi (China's currency). China maintained re-strictive foreign exchange regulations that hindered foreign investment and profit repatriation. In addition, infrastructure problems, excessive bureaucracy, worker attitudes, and differences in management attitudes were cited as barriers to more joint ventures.

Overcoming Opposition to Further Domestic Reforms   Despite China's economic successes, there remained many barriers to continued change. Although the basic premise of reform was well accepted in the Communist hier-archy, there was strong conservative opposition to the speed and extent of eco-nomic reforms. High inflation rates in 1987 and 1988 resulted in fears of an overheated economy, which strengthened the position of the conservatives and allowed them to occasionally stop and even roll back the process of reform. Ongoing concerns about unemployment with its potential economic and politi-cal consequences constituted an important barrier to reform of the state enterprises.

Chinese conservatives resisted pressures for greater political reform. Indeed, thus far, China's reform process has been notable by the absence of political reform. Student demonstrations for more democratic politics became common in the 1980s before erupting into widespread demonstrations for more political liberalization in 1989. The confrontation between the students and the army in Tiananmen Square in June 1989 demonstrated the strength of the desire for political participation and freedom to choose where to live and work— but it just as clearly demonstrated the government's determination not to allow it.

China's reform policy has thus proceeded unevenly. For example, in mid-1989, in the wake of the Tiananmen revolt, China took a major step backward from its market-based reforms when Prime Minister Li Peng announced a return to central planning in many sectors of its economy. The new policy was presented as a temporary austerity measure to regain control of the economy, but it is a reminder that China's road to reform will continue to be unpredictable. The main concerns of the government were the decentralization of power to the separate provinces, especially the wealthy SEZs, and the social unrest that was symptomatic of the inequalities caused by the half-reformed economy. This step backward was accompanied by the apparent victory of the more conservative element of the Chinese government. In the 1990s, as the aging Deng Xiaoping ceded control of government policy, reform momentum was again slowed by the absence of a powerful, reformist leader.

In June 1989, Deng Xiaoping selected Jiang Zemin to be leader of the Communist Party and eventually Deng's successor as leader of the Chinese Communist hierarchy. Although Jiang became President of China in 1993, Deng remained the unquestioned leader of China until his death in 1997 at the age of 93. Zhu Rongji joined the Politburo in 1993 and in 1997 was appointed Prime Minister. Zhu was responsible for reining in inflation during the 1990s.[121] While Jiang and Zhu were firmly committed to continuing Deng's policies of economic reform, they, too, faced the prospect of substantial internal opposition, for example, to China's entry into the WTO and the changes that were likely to result. In 2003, a new administration took power. Hu Jintao became the Paramount Leader of the Chinese government (he was already General Secretary of the Communist Party) and Wen Jiabao succeeded Zhu Rongji as premier. Hu and Wen made a greater commitment than previous governments to reducing the urban-rural divide and more generally to improving the lot of those who had not yet benefited from rapid economic growth.[122]

In addition to political opposition, structural and ideological problems existed with the reform process. The riskiest part of that process, price reform, was not fully implemented. Prices of daily necessities, basic urban services, and key commodities remain controlled in an effort to curb inflation. The half-adjusted system placed strains on the economy in severe shortages in some areas. The uneven development of different regions was also unsettling, resulting in regional discontent and internal migration problems. Official corruption was a growing problem, but also a necessary way of rewarding Communist Party loyalists. Finally, reform efforts were slowed by bottlenecks in the energy and transportation sectors and by underinvestment in general infrastructure.

Despite the economic reforms, China remained a highly centralized, authoritarian system. Nevertheless, China's reforms produced greater aggregate economic growth than those undertaken in Russia and Eastern Europe. China grew faster primarily because the Chinese prereform economy was much less developed, more heavily dependent on agriculture and, thus, benefited greatly from agricultural reforms and the movement of rural workers to the cities.[123] Prices for state enterprises were rationalized prior to decontrol, making the transition somewhat easier for them. Much less privatization of state enterprises took place in China than in Russia or Eastern Europe. Jiang and Zhu had adopted policies after 1993 that rapidly diminished the size and importance of the state-controlled sector of the economy, with the notable exception of the financial sector.[124] In addition, China was more careful than Russia to pursue its reforms in a context of macroeconomic stability. There were no major devaluations of the Chinese currency until 2007 and inflation remained moderate.[125] Finally, China benefited greatly from a major influx of foreign direct investment in the 1990s, whereas in Russia and Eastern Europe inflows of FDI were relatively modest.

The main questions in China were whether the very rapid growth of the past three decades would continue and whether the political system would be able to survive a future period of low growth. The growing importance of private entre-preneurs was not reflected in the Chinese political system except in growing levels of official corruption. Chinese workers had no right to bargain collectively and were not protected against exploitative labor practices. Organizations not con-trolled by the government or the Communist Party were not tolerated. Independent consumer rights and environmental groups did not exist. The Chinese government was intolerant of religious and ethnic minorities, especially in the case of the Tibetans but also in other parts of the country. In bad economic times, these underlying tensions would come to the fore. The Chinese leadership had to ensure high rates of economic growth to maintain the legitimacy of their autocratic regime.[126]

China's International Economic Relations in the Era of Globalization   China entered the WTO on December 11, 2001, after 15 years of bilateral and multi-lateral negotiations. Accession to the WTO obligated China to conduct a num-ber of major reforms that would prove difficult to implement. For example, China was required to provide full trading and distribution rights to foreign firms, which would mean taking away the monopoly rights of certain state-owned enterprises to import specific products. The Chinese government would have to reduce tariffs and phase out quantitative restrictions on imports, make safety and health restrictions on imports consistent with WTO standards, and stop protecting domestic farmers from international competition by subsidizing agricultural production.[127]

Despite these difficulties, Chinese authorities went ahead with the reforms they were obligated to undertake. Exports continued to expand at a rapid pace and even accelerated as FDI inflows increased. Every large MNC had to have a China strategy to gain access to the growing domestic markets of Asia and rela-tively low wage rates of Chinese workers and engineers.

The rapid growth of the Chinese economy served as a major inducement for the growth of inward flows of foreign direct investment. China received over $78 billion in FDI in 2006, up from less than $4.4 billion in 1991 (see Figure 10.11). Much of this investment came from overseas Chinese investors in Hong Kong, Taiwan, and Singapore, but many U.S., European, and Japanese multina-tional firms also increased their presence in China during this period. Much of this investment went into export-oriented production enclaves in the southern and eastern coastal areas, Beijing, and the northeast and thus had only a limited effect on other parts of the country.[128] Foreign investment played a major role in

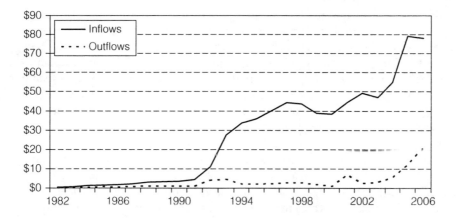

FIGURE 10.11 Inflows and Outflows of Foreign Direct Investment into and from China, 1982–2006, in Billions of Current Dollars

SOURCE: World Bank, *World Development Indicators 2008*.

expanding China's exports. One estimate is that nearly 60 percent of Chinese exports came from foreign-invested enterprises and about half from wholly foreign-owned factories.[129]

China: Regional Power or Global Economic Superpower?

With a population of 1.3 billion people, a GDP of $3 trillion in 2007, and foreign currency reserves of over $1.5 trillion, China is a major regional power with a potential for becoming a global economic superpower. Military spending is increasing rapidly.[130] China is a permanent member of the UN Security Council and contributes troops to numerous UN peacekeeping missions. China engages in a wide variety of infrastructure projects in Africa, with a particular focus on developing raw material and fossil fuels extraction capabilities. China played a key role in the Doha Development Round. It seeks a greater role in the IMF and the World Bank,[131] and it wants to be the ninth member of the G-8.[132]

China's emergence as an economic superpower depends on its ability to maintain a high level of economic growth while simultaneously dealing with major political problems, such as high levels of official corruption, growing inequality, severe environmental degradation, and a repressive authoritarian government unable to tolerate genuinely independent private interest groups. China has come a long way, but its future is still uncertain.[133]

CONCLUSION

The end of the Cold War presented the world economy and its system of management with an unprecedented set of challenges. The most difficult was that faced by the new governments: how to manage the transition from planned to market economies and from authoritarian to democratic political systems. Such a transition was without historical precedent and, thus, there were few principles or theories let alone practical experience to guide the process. The transformation of national economies varied from country to country depending on the existing level of development and the characteristics of the local economy. Thus, Eastern European countries and China benefited from a shorter experience with communism while Russia's economy suffered from the legacy of over 60 years of state management.

Political reform, the transition from authoritarian to more democratic regimes, accompanied economic reform and also varied from country to country. China, still governed by a communist party, followed a more restricted path to political liberalization while the countries of the former Soviet bloc moved more rapidly toward democracy. Scholars debated the optimum sequencing of reform—whether, for example, the Asian model of Korea and Taiwan where economic reforms preceded and led to political reforms, or the Eastern Europe and Russian model of simultaneous reforms was preferable.[134] In the real world, however, each country followed its own path.

A second major challenge raised by the end of the Cold War was the integration of the new market economies into the international economic governance institutions developed by the West. The former communist countries sought to integrate themselves into the capitalist world economy not only to benefit from trade and investment but also as part of a larger effort to make their political and economic transitions irreversible. The rest of the world, especially the industrialized capitalist world, had to decide how and on what terms to allow the formerly communist countries to join their economic regimes. The transition economies, for their part, had to decide whether they could accept the discipline and play by the long-established rules of the multilateral system.

Another goal of the formerly communist countries was to join the existing multilateral institutions. As we have seen, the members of the former Soviet bloc joined the IMF and the World Bank and benefited from financial support from those institutions. A new multilateral bank, the **European Bank for Reconstruction and Development (EBRD)**, was created in 1991 to assist Eastern Europe and the Confederation of Independent States (CIS) countries in their reform.[135] China and many of the new market economies of Eastern Europe joined the World Trade Organization while others including Russia applied for membership in the WTO. The applications of Russia and China to join the world trading regime raised important questions about their ability to achieve the domestic economic reforms which would enable them to accept the rules and disciplines of the prevailing regime.[136]

During the Bretton Woods and interdependence periods, economic relations between the Soviet Union and its allies and the rest of the world were a function of perceptions about the degree of enmity between the Soviet bloc and the West. After the end of the Cold War and the adoption of economic reforms in China, the formerly communist countries were absorbed into the globalizing world economy at various speeds but increasingly in a way that was irreversible.

Even the largest remaining communist country, China, behaved more and more like a capitalist country with an authoritarian political system. Considerable variance existed among these countries in the degree to which the government was successful in pursuing macroeconomic stability, state enterprises were privatized, and the market was permitted to become a competitive one. These differences may have accounted for some of the variance in post-1989 economic performance.[137] Nevertheless, one similarity is more striking than the differences. China and the formally communist countries, like the rest of the world, were all subject to the forces of globalization and were dealing with them in their own way. Whether they would be able to do so without making further and possibly radical changes in their domestic systems remained to be seen.

ENDNOTES

1. These countries are now usually referred to as the Confederation of Independent States (CIS). They include Belarus, Ukraine, Moldova, Armenia, Azerbaijan, Georgia, Kazakhstan, Kyrgyzstan, Tajikistan, Turkmenistan, and Uzbekistan. Russia is also a member of the CIS.

2. Marshall I. Goldman, *Détente and Dollars: Doing Business with the Soviets* (New York, N.Y.: Basic Books, 1975), 4–20; Anthony C. Sutton, *Western Technology and Soviet Economic Development, 1917 to 1930* (Stanford, Calif.: Hoover Institution on War, Revolution and Peace, 1968); and Anthony C. Sutton, *Western Technology and Soviet Economic Development, 1930 to 1945* (Stanford, Calif.: Hoover Institution on War, Revolution and Peace, 1971).

3. William Diebold, Jr., "East–West Trade and the Marshall Plan," *Foreign Affairs*, 26 (July 1948): 715.

4. For a discussion of motives and policies, see Zbigniew K. Brzezinski, *The Soviet Bloc: Unity and Conflict*, rev. ed. (Cambridge, Mass.: Harvard University Press, 1967), 3–151.

5. Joseph Stalin, *Economic Problems of Socialism in the USSR* (New York, N.Y.: International Publishers, 1952), 26–30. Stalin was not alone in his predictions of postwar economic problems in the West. Many Western economists and policy-makers were also concerned. See John Lewis Gaddis, *The United States and the Origins of the Cold War, 1941–1947* (New York, N.Y.: Columbia University Press, 1972).

6. On Marxist justification, see Zygmunt Nagorski, Jr., *The Psychology of East–West Trade* (New York, N.Y.: Mason and Lipscomb, 1974), 58–59.

7. See, for example, Gaddis, *The United States and the Origins of the Cold War*; and Adam B. Ulam, *Expansion and Coexistence: The History of Soviet Foreign Policy, 1917–1967* (New York, N.Y.: Praeger, 1968), 314–455.

8. See Nicholas Spulber, *The Economics of Communist Eastern Europe* (New York, N.Y.: Technology Press of MIT, John Wiley, 1957).

9. See Charles Prince, "The USSR's Role in International Finance," *Harvard Business Review*, 25 (autumn 1946): 111–128.

10. See J. Keith Horsfield, ed., *The International Monetary Fund, 1945–1965*, vol. 1, Chronicle (Washington, D.C.: International Monetary Fund, 1969), 263, 359–364.

11. Clair Wilcox, *A Charter for World Trade* (New York, N.Y.: Macmillan, 1949), 164–167. Czechoslovakia was a contracting party to the GATT, but the United States suspended its application of GATT provisions to that country in 1948 after a communist government came to power.

12. See Ulam, *Expansion and Coexistence*, 432–440. It is debated whether or not the U.S. offer of aid to the Soviet Union was serious. In any case the Soviet rejection was clear. For a critical analysis of U.S. policy, see Joyce Kolko and Gabriel Kolko, *The Limits of Power: The World and United States Foreign Policy, 1945–1954* (New York, N.Y.: Harper and Row, 1972), 359–383. For a more recent analysis of Stalin's reaction to the Marshall Plan, see Michael J. Hogan, "American Marshall Planners and the Search for a European Neocapitalism," *American Historical Review*, 90 (February 1985): 44–72.

13. Michael Kaser, *Comecon: Integration Problems of the Planned Economies* (London, UK: Oxford University Press, 1965), 1–12; and Michael Marrese, "CMEA: Effective but Cumbersome Political Economy," in Ellen Comisso and Laura D'Andrea Tyson, eds., *Power, Purpose, and Collective Choice: Economic Strategy in Socialist States* (Ithaca, N.Y.: Cornell University Press, 1986).

14. Nicholas Spulber, "East–West Trade and the Paradoxes of the Strategic Embargo," in Alan A. Brown and Egon Neuberger, eds., *International Trade and Central Planning: An Analysis of Economic Interactions* (Berkeley and Los Angeles, Calif.: University of California Press, 1968), 114.

15. Paul Marer, "The Political Economy of Soviet Relations with Eastern Europe," in Steven J. Rosen and James R. Kurth, eds., *Testing Theories of Economic Imperialism* (Lexington, Mass.: Lexington Books, 1974), 244–245.

16. Alec Nove, "Planned Economy," *The New Palgrave: A Dictionary of Economics*, v. 3 (New York, N.Y.: Palgrave Macmillan, 1987), 879–885.

17. See Brzezinski, *The Soviet Bloc*, 101.

18. Marer, "The Political Economy," 233–235.

19. Spulber, *The Economics of Communist Eastern Europe*, 166–223.

20. Spulber, *The Economics of Communist Eastern Europe*.

21. For a discussion of earlier actions, see Gunnar Adler-Karlsson, *Western Economic Warfare, 1947–1967: A Case Study in Foreign Economic Policy* (Stockholm, Sweden: Almqvist and Wiksell, 1968), 5 and, for the text of the Export Control Act, see 217–219. For an excellent discussion of the Export Control Act and its consequences, see Michael Mastanduno, *Economic Containment: CoCom and the Politics of East–West Trade* (Ithaca, N.Y.: Cornell University Press, 1992). See also John P. Hardt and George Holliday, *U.S.-Soviet Commercial Relations: The Interplay of Economics, Technology Transfer, and Diplomacy*, for the Subcommittee on National Security Policy and Scientific Developments of the Committee on Foreign Affairs (Washington, D.C.: Government Printing Office, June 19, 1973), 48–49.

22. Members were the United States, Canada, Japan, Belgium, Denmark, France, Greece, Italy, Luxembourg, the Netherlands, Norway, Portugal, Turkey, the United Kingdom, and West Germany (i.e., all the NATO members except Iceland, plus Japan). Spain joined in 1985 after becoming a member of NATO; Australia joined in 1989.

23. Adler-Karlsson, *Western Economic Warfare*, 1–6, 31–45; and Mastanduno, *Economic Containment*, chs. 3–4. For a summary of Western European and Japanese views on CoCom, see Angela Stent, "East–West Technology Transfer: European Perspectives," *The Washington Papers*, vol. 8, no. 75 (Beverly Hills, Calif.: Sage Publications, 1980); and Stephen Sternheimer, "East–West Technology Transfer: Japan and the Communist Bloc," *The Washington Papers*, vol. 8, no. 76 (Beverly Hills, Calif.: Sage Publications, 1980), 12–23.

24. Samuel Pisar, *Coexistence and Commerce Guidelines for Transactions Between East and West* (New York, N.Y.: McGraw-Hill, 1970), 102–107. For other U.S. restrictions on imports, see Goldman, *Détente and Dollars*, 98–102.

25. Romania, Hungary, and Poland became eligible when they joined the IMF and the World Bank in 1972, 1981, and 1986, respectively.

26. See Goldman, *Détente and Dollars*, 52; and Pisar, *Coexistence and Commerce*, 111–114. The Berne Union, a group of governmental and private credit insurance organizations in the developed market economies, agreed to limit commercial credits to the East to five years and to require an initial cash payment of at least 20 percent of the purchase price. The agreement was nonbinding, however, and proved ineffective.

27. Spulber, "East–West Trade and the Paradoxes of the Strategic Embargo," 114.

28. Adler-Karlsson, *Western Economic Warfare, 1947–1967*, 83–99; and Franklyn D. Holzman, *International Trade Under Communism— Politics and Economics* (New York, N.Y.: Basic Books, 1976), 138–143.

29. U.S. Senate, 89th Cong., 2nd session, Bill 5-3363.

30. John Lewis Gaddis, *The Long Peace: Inquiries into the History of the Cold War* (New York, N.Y.: Oxford University Press, 1987). It has to be noted, however, that the period of rule of Leonid Brezhnev was not one of good U.S.-Soviet relations, but rather of temporary détente, ending around 1974, followed by increasing tension and escalation of hostilities, especially with the invasion of Afghanistan in 1978 and the coming to office of Ronald Reagan in 1981.

31. P.L. 93-618, the Trade Act of 1974. Senator Henry Jackson and Representative Charles Vanik developed a proposal to link most-favored-nation treatment and **Eximbank** loans for the Soviet Union and Eastern Europe to freer policies of emigration in these countries. And they offered that proposal as an amendment to the U.S. trade bill that the administration needed to launch the Tokyo Round. After resisting the **Jackson-Vanik amendment** for two years, the Nixon administration capitulated on the assumption that the Soviet Union would change its policies in return for the inducements of credits and trade.

32. See Zbigniew Brzezinski, *Power and Principle: Memoirs of the National Security Advisor, 1977–1981* (New York, N.Y.: Farrar, Straus, Giroux, 1983), especially ch. 12; and Fred Halliday, *The Making of the Cold War* (London, UK: Verso, 1983), for accounts of the development of President Carter's foreign policy. See also Raymond Garthoff, *Détente and Confrontation: American-Soviet Relations from Nixon to Reagan* (Washington, D.C.: Brookings Institution, 1985).

33. Strobe Talbott and Michael Mandelbaum, *Reagan and Gorbachev* (New York, N.Y.: Vintage Books, 1987). For a more specific discussion of changes in U.S. East–West trade with the Soviet Union, see Bruce Parrott, ed., *Trade, Technology and Soviet American Relations* (Bloomington, Ind.: Indiana University Press, 1985). Ironically, one

of the first steps taken by the Reagan administration in early 1981 was to lift the grain embargo and to announce that the administration would not use grain as a foreign policy tool. The reason for this departure from President Reagan's hard-line policy was one of domestic politics. The highly controversial grain embargo had become an issue in the 1980 campaign, with President Carter defending the embargo and candidate Reagan insisting that it was both ineffective and economically inequitable and that, if elected, he would end it. Despite the removal of the embargo, the Soviet Union, citing U.S. unreliability, refused to increase its purchases of U.S. grain and limited its imports to the amount it was committed to purchase under the terms of the grain agreement.

34. Bruce Jentleson, *Pipeline Politics: The Complex Political Economy of East–West Energy Trade* (Ithaca, N.Y.: Cornell University Press, 1986).

35. See Ann Goodman, Margaret Hughes, and Gertrude Schroeder, "Raising the Efficiency of Soviet Farm Labor: Problems and Prospects," in U.S. Congress, Joint Economic Committee, *Gorbachev's Economic Plans*, vol. 2, 100–125.

36. Goodman et al., 102.

37. Joseph Wilczynski, *Socialist Economic Development and Reforms: From Extensive to Intensive Growth Under Central Planning in the USSR, Eastern Europe, and Yugoslavia* (New York, N.Y.: Praeger, 1972), 26–33.

38. See, for example, Alec Nove, *The Soviet Economic System*, 3rd ed. (London, UK: Routledge, 1986).

39. See Wilczynski, *Socialist Economic Development and Reforms*, 234–237; Bruce Parrott, *Politics and Technology in the Soviet Union* (Cambridge, Mass.: MIT Press, 1983); Goldman, *Détente and Dollars*, 32–33; and Franklyn D. Holzman and Robert Legvold, "The Economics and Politics of East–West Relations," *International Organization*, 29 (Winter 1975): 278. The problems of technology did not apply to the space and military sectors; rather, advances in these fields were made possible by the close relationship of research with end users, competition among research units and with the West, and preferences on supplies.

40. Wilczynski, *Socialist Economic Development and Reforms*; and Nagorski, *The Psychology of East–West Trade*, 104–156.

41. Holzman and Legvold, "The Economics and Politics of East–West Relations," 288.

42. See Wilczynski, *Socialist Economic Development and Reforms*, 218–220, 252.

43. Josef Van Brabant, "CMEA Institutions and Policies versus Structural Adjustment: Comments on Chapter 5," in Josef C. Brada, Ed A. Hewett, and Thomas A. Wolf, eds., *Economic Adjustment and Reform in Eastern Europe and the Soviet Union* (Durham, N.C.: Duke University Press, 1988), 170–184.

44. Klaus Bolz, "Industrial Cooperation," in Reinhard Rode and Hanns D. Jacobsen, eds., *Economic Warfare or Détente: An Assessment of East–West Economic Relations in the 1980s* (Boulder, Colo.: Westview Press, 1985), 63–73.

45. Joint Economic Committee Report, ix.

46. UNCTAD, *Handbook of International Trade and Development Statistics 1988* (New York, N.Y.: United Nations, 1988), 452.

47. See Mikhail Gorbachev, *Perestroika: New Thinking for Our Country and the World* (New York, N.Y.: Harper and Row, 1987); Zbigniew Brzezinski, *The Grand Failure: The Birth and Death of Communism in the Twentieth Century* (New York, N.Y.: Scribner's,

1989); Anders Åslund, *Gorbachev's Struggle for Economic Reform*, 2nd ed. (Ithaca, N.Y.: Cornell University Press, 1991); and Brendan Kiernan, *The End of Soviet Politics: Elections, Legislatures, and the Demise of the Communist Party* (Boulder, Colo.: Westview Press, 1993).

48. See David Holloway, "Gorbachev's New Thinking," *Foreign Affairs* 68 (Winter 1989): 66–81; and Robert Legvold, "Soviet Foreign Policy," *Foreign Affairs* op. cit., 82–98.

49. See Seweryn Bialer, "Gorbachev's Move," *Foreign Policy* (Fall 1987): 59–87; and Brendan Kiernan, *The End of Soviet Politics*.

50. Gorbachev, *Perestroika*; Padma Desai, *Perestroika in Perspective: The Design and Dilemmas of Soviet Reform* (Princeton, N.J.: Princeton University Press, 1989); Marshall I. Goldman, *What Went Wrong with Perestroika?* (New York, N.Y.: Norton, 1992); Ed A. Hewett, *Reforming the Soviet Economy: Equality versus Efficiency* (Washington, D.C.: The Brookings Institution, 1988); and Jerry F. Hough, *Opening Up the Soviet Economy* (Washington, D.C.: Brookings Institution, 1988).

51. Joan F. McIntyre, "Soviet Efforts to Revamp the Foreign Trade Sector," in U.S. Congress, Joint Economic Committee, *Gorbachev's Economic Plans*, vol. 2 (Washington, D.C.: Government Printing Office, 1987), 501–503.

52. *Financial Times*, April 4, 1989, p. 2.

53. See Marshall D. Shulman, "The Superpowers: Dance of the Dinosaurs," *Foreign Affairs*, 66 (Spring 1988): 494–550.

54. Department of State, "Joint Summit Statement," *Bulletin*, December 10, 1987, p. 16.

55. Gorbachev, *Perestroika*, 190–209.

56. They had always used these methods but they applied them with greater urgency after the Gorbachev reforms.

57. See Anders Åslund, *How Russia Became a Market Economy* (Washington, D.C.: Brookings Institution, 1995), 36–40.

58. Richard E. Ericson, "The Russian Economy since Independence," in Gail W. Lapidus, ed., *The New Russia: Troubled Transformation* (Boulder, Colo.: Westview Press, 1995), 46; and Brigitte Granville, *The Success of Russian Economic Reforms* (London, UK: Royal Institute of International Affairs, 1995), 107.

59. Maxim Boycko, Andrei Shleifer, and Robert Vishny, *Privatizing Russia* (Cambridge, Mass.: MIT Press, 1995), 5.

60. UNCTAD, *Trade and Development Report* (Geneva, Switzerland: UNCTAD, 2000); European Bank for Reconstruction and Development, *Transition Report* (London, UK: EBRD, 2000).

61. OECD Economic Surveys, *The Russian Federation 1995* (Paris, France: Organization for Economic Cooperation and Development, 1995), 77.

62. Russian Government Statistics.

63. "Russia Sees Budget Boost in Shares-for-Loans Plan," *Reuters*, downloaded from the Internet newsgroup *clari.world.europe.russia*, Article #9066, September 25, 1995.

64. Åslund, *How Russia Became a Market Economy*, 55.

65. Daniel Yergin and Thane Gustafson, *Russia 2010 and What It Means for the World* (New York, N.Y.: Random House, 1994), 89–92.

66. "Yeltsin Has Triumphant Re-Election Victory," *CNN Interactive World News*, July 4, 1996, http://www.cnn.com/WORLD/9607/03/russia.runoff/.

67. The Moscow Currency Exchange (MICEX) was established in November 1989. See Paul Hare, Saul Estrin, Mikhail Lugachyov, and Lina Takla, "Russia's Foreign Trade: New Directions and Western Policies," *The World Economy,* 21 (January 1998): 95–119.

68. Thane Gustafson, *Capitalism Russian-Style* (New York, N.Y.: Cambridge University Press, 1999), 97; and Benjamin J. Cohen, *The Geography of Money* (Ithaca, N.Y.: Cornell University Press, 1998), 78–80.

69. External debt remained roughly constant until 1996 when the government stopped financing budget deficits by printing money and began borrowing on short-term bond markets (see Figure 10.6). For a discussion of Russian debt issues, see Ognian N. Hishow, "Russia's External Debt: Infinite Rescheduling," *Communist and Post-Communist Studies*, 34 (2001): 113–128; and Vladimir Tikhomirov, "Russian Debt Problems in the 1990s," *Post-Soviet Affairs*, 17 (2001): 262–284.

70. Enzo R. Grilli, *The European Community and the Developing Countries* (New York, N.Y.: Cambridge University Press, 1993), 315–316, 327–328.

71. Susan B. Garland and Owen Ullman, with Bill Javetski, "A Sticky Summit: It Won't Be the Triumph Clinton Envisioned," *Business Week*, January 10, 1994, 38.

72. Gustafson, *Capitalism Russian-Style*, 193–196.

73. Hishow, "Russia's External Debt." Unfortunately, most of these debts were held by countries like Cuba, Mongolia, and Iraq that were not in a position to repay them.

74. GKO stands for *Gossudarstvennye kratkasrochnye obligatsii*, or short-term state treasury notes. Along with GKOs, the Russian Central Bank issued long-term securities called OFZs (short for *Obligatsii federal'nogo zaima*). Gustafson, *Capitalism Russian-Style*, 92.

75. Niko Gobbin and Bruno Merlevede, "The Russian Crisis: A Debt Perspective," *Post-Communist Economics*, 12 (June 2000): 142–163.

76. Gobbin and Merlevede, "The Russian Crisis."

77. "Vladimir Putin: His Career," http://www.geocities.com/CapitolHill/Parliament/5160/Putin/career.html.

78. Anders Åslund, *Russia's Capitalist Revolution: Why Market Reform Succeeded and Democracy Failed* (Washington, D.C.: Peterson Institute, 2007), 211–214.

79. Ibid., ch. 7; and Marshall I. Goldman, *Petrostate: Putin, Power, and the New Russia* (New York, N.Y.: Oxford, 2008), ch. 5.

80. John M. Letiche, *Russia Moves into the Global Economy* (New York, N.Y.: Routledge, 2007), 8–9.

81. John Odling-Smee and Poul M. Thomsen, "Putin at Mid-Term: Where Should Economic Reforms Go from Here?" *Vedomosti*, April 15, 2002, http://www.imf.org/external/np/vc/2002/041502.htm.

82. William H. Cooper, "Russia's Accession to the WTO," Congressional Research Service (CRS) Report for Congress, Washington, D.C., July 17, 2006.

83. Foreign Trade of Russia, http://www.users.globalnet.co.uk/~chegeo/index2.htm.

84. Eurostat data reported in European Union, Directorate General for Trade, *Russia: EU Bilateral Trade and Trade with the World*, September 10, 2008, http://www. trade.ec.europa.eu/doclib/docs/2006/september/tradoc_113440.pdf.

85. IMG Consulting, http://www.users.globalnet.co.uk/~chegeo/.

86. "Doubts Grow on Russia's WTO Plans," *BBC News*, August 26, 2008, http:// www.news.bbc.co.uk/go/pr/fr/-/2/hi/business/7582079.stm.

87. *OECD Investment Policy Review: Russian Federation: Strengthening the Policy Framework for Investment* (Paris, France: OECD, 2008).

88. On reforms in Hungary and East Germany, see Marshall Goldman, *Gorbachev's Challenge*, 148–173.

89. Anna Seleny, *The Political Economy of State-Society Relations in Hungary and Poland: From Communism to the European Union* (New York, N.Y.: Cambridge University Press, 2006), chs. 5–7.

90. On reforms in Poland, see Anna Seleny, *The Political Economy of State-Society Relations in Hungary and Poland*, ch. 4; Urszula Plowiec, "Economic Reform and Foreign Trade in Poland," in Brada, Hewitt, and Wolf, *Economic Adjustment and Reform in Eastern Europe and the Soviet Union*, 340–369.

91. Alain de Combrugghe and David Lipton, "The Government Budget and the Economic Transformation of Poland," in Oliver Blanchard, Kenneth Froot, and Jeffrey Sachs, eds., *The Transition in Eastern Europe* (Chicago, Ill.: University of Chicago Press, 1994), 114; and Tadeusz Kowalik, "The Great Transformation and Privatization: Three Years of Polish Experience," in Christopher G. A. Bryant and Edmund Mokrzycki, eds., *The New Great Transformation? Change and Continuity in East–Central Europe* (New York, N.Y.: Routledge, 1994).

92. Andrew Berg, "The Logistics of Privatization in Poland," in Blanchard et al., *The Transition in Eastern Europe*, vol. 2; and Wendy Carlin and Colin Mayer, "The Treuhandanstalt: Privatization by State and Market," also in the Blanchard volume.

93. See John Edgar Jackson, Jacek Klich, and Krystyna Poznanska, *The Political Economy of Poland's Transition: New Firms and Reform Governments* (New York, N.Y.: Cambridge University Press, 2005).

94. Magdalena Wdowicka, "Foreign Investment Capital in Poland since 1990," in Miroslawa Czerny, ed., *Poland in the Geographic Center of Europe* (New York, N.Y.: Nova Publishers, 2006).

95. Vick Duke and Keith Grime, "Privatization in East–Central Europe: Similarities and Contrasts in Its Application," in Bryant and Mokrzycki, *The New Great Transformation?*; Karen Henderson, "Transformation in the Czech and Slovak Republics: Elite Receptions and Responses," in Herman W. Hoen, ed., *Good Governance in Central and Eastern Europe: The Puzzle of Capitalism by Design* (Northampton, Mass.: Edward Elgar, 2001); and Anders Åslund, *Building Capitalism: The Transformation of the Former Soviet Bloc* (New York, N.Y.: Cambridge University Press, 2002), 390–391.

96. For details, see Frank Bönker, *The Political Economy of Fiscal Reform in Central-Eastern Europe* (Northampton, Mass.: Edward Elgar, 2006).

97. "Eastern Europe: Paradox Explained," *The Economist*, July 22, 1995, 52.

98. http://www.europa.eu/scadplus/glossary/accession_criteria_copenhague_en.htm.

99. John King Fairbank, *The United States and China*, 3rd ed. (Cambridge, Mass.: Harvard University Press, 1971), 351–354.

100. *Ibid*.

101. Donald P. Whitaker and Rinn-Sup Shinn, *Area Handbook for the People's Republic of China* (Washington, D.C.: Government Printing Office, 1972), 309.

102. U.S. Commerce Department statistics, cited in Congressional Quarterly, *China and U.S. Foreign Policy*, 2nd ed. (Washington, D.C.: Congressional Quarterly, 1973), 60.

103. Nicholas R. Lardy, *China's Entry into the World Economy: Implications for Northeast Asia and the United States* (New York, N.Y.: University Press of America for the Asia Society 1987), 3.

104. Selzo Maysamuora, "Japan-China Trade in Retrospect—The 15th Anniversary of Normalizing Relations," in JETRO, *China Newsletter*, no. 72 (January-February 1988): 19.

105. *Ibid*.

106. For a summary of China's reforms, see Loren Brandt and Thomas G. Rawski, "China's Great Economic Transformation," in Loren Brandt and Thomas G. Rawski, eds., *China's Great Economic Transformation* (New York, N.Y.: Cambridge University Press, 2008); Barry Naughton, *The Chinese Economy: Transitions and Growth* (Cambridge, Mass.: MIT Press, 2007); A. Doak Barnett and Ralph N. Clough, eds., *Modernizing China: Post Mao Reform and Development* (Boulder, Colo.: Westview Press, 1986); and Harry Harding, *China's Second Revolution: Reform after Mao* (Washington, D.C.: Brookings Institution, 1987).

107. Jikun Huang, Keijiro Otsuka, and Scott Rozelle, "Agriculture in China's Development: Past Disappointments, Recent Successes, and Future Challenges," in Loren Brandt and Thomas G. Rawski, eds., *China's Great Economic Transformation*; and Nicholas R. Lardy, *Agriculture in China's Modern Economic Development* (New York, N.Y.: Cambridge University Press, 2008).

108. Barry Naughton, *The Chinese Economy*, 51–52 and 272–282.

109. Joint Economic Committee, *China's Economy Looks Toward the Year 2000*, 44–47.

110. Nicholas R. Lardy, *China in the World Economy* (Washington, D.C.: Institute for International Economics, 1994), 3.

111. *Ibid*., 25.

112. Martin Ravallion and Shaohua Chen, "China's (Uneven) Progress Against Poverty," Policy Research Working Paper #3408, World Bank, September 2004; and Barry Naughton, *The Chinese Economy*, ch. 5.

113. See Franklin Allen, Jun Qian, and Meijun Qian, "China's Financial System: Past, Present, and Future," in Loren Brandt and Thomas G. Rawski, eds., *China's Great Economic Transformation*; Phillip Grub and Bryan L. Sudweeks, "Securities Markets and the People's Republic of China," in *JETRO, China Newsletter*, no. 74, (May-June 1988): 11–16.

114. Lardy, *China in the World Economy*, 13–14.

115. Central Intelligence Agency, *China: Economic Performance in 1987 and Outlook for 1988* (Washington, D.C.: CIA, May 1988), 8.

116. On U.S.-China trade in general, see Eugene K. Lawson, ed., *U.S.-China Trade: Problems and Prospects* (New York, N.Y.: Praeger, 1988).

117. World Bank, *World Tables 1987* (Washington, D.C.: World Bank, 1988), 99.

118. The four initial SEZs were in Shenzhen in Zhuhai province, Shantou in Guangdong province, Xiamen in Fujian province, and the entire island province of Hainan.

119. Charles Oman, *Policy Competition for Foreign Direct Investment: A Study of Competition among Governments to Attract FDI* (Paris, France: Development Center of the OECD, 2000), 99; and Ernest H. Preeg, *India and China: An Advanced Technology Race and How the United States Should Respond* (Washington, D.C.: Center for Strategic and International Studies, 2008), 5.

120. "China Data," *The China Business Review*, 57, published by the National Council for U.S.-China Trade, May-June 1988.

121. Jasper Becker, *The Chinese. An Insider's Look at the Issues which Affect and Shape China Today* (New York, N.Y.: Oxford University Press, 2000), 389 and 393.

122. See Barry Naughton, *The Chinese Economy*: 108 for his summary of the differences between the new and old administrations.

123. Wing Thye Woo, "The Art of Reforming Centrally Planned Economies: Comparing China, Poland, and Russia," *Journal of Comparative Economics*, 18 (June 1994): 276–308; Jingjie Li, "The Characteristics of Russian and Economic Reform," *Journal of Comparative Economics*, 18 (June 1994): 309–313; and Minxin Pei, *From Reform to Revolution: The Demise of Communism in China and the Soviet Union* (Cambridge, Mass.: Harvard University Press, 1994).

124. Barry Naughton, *The Chinese Economy*: 105–108.

125. Ronald I. McKinnon, "Financial Growth and Macroeconomic Stability in China, 1978–1992: Implications for Russia and Other Transitional Economies," *Journal of Comparative Economics*, 18 (June 1994): 428–469; and Barry Naughton, "What Is Distinctive about China's Economic Transition? State Enterprise Reform and Overall System Transformation," *Journal of Comparative Economics*, 18 (June 1994): 470–490.

126. Barry Naughton, "A Political Economy of China's Economic Transition," in Loren Brandt and Thomas G. Rawski, eds., *China's Great Economic Transformation*.

127. Nicholas R. Lardy, "Problems on the Road to Liberalization," *Financial Times*, March 15, 2002, http://www.brook.edu/views/op-ed/lardy/20020315.htm.

128. John Henley, Colin Kirkpatrick, and Georgina Wilde, "Foreign Direct Investment in China: Recent Trends and Current Policy Issues," *The World Economy*, 22 (March 1999): 223–243; Yizheng Shi, "Technological Capabilities and International Production Strategies of Firms: The Case of Foreign Direct Investment in China," *Journal of World Business*, 36 (Summer 2001): 184–204; Barry Naughton, *The Chinese Economy*, ch. 17; and Kevin Honglin Zhang, "What Attracts Foreign Multinational Corporations to China?" *Contemporary Economic Policy*, 19 (July 2001): 336–346.

129. George Koo, "China's Economy is Not a Zero Sum," *Chinese American Forum*, 23 (April 2008), 6.

130. Susan Shirk, *China: Fragile Superpower*, 9.

131. China's IMF quota was raised from 2.98 percent to 3.72 percent in September 2006.

132. Andrew F. Cooper and Gregory Chin, "China's Knocking on the G8 Door," *Far Eastern Economic Review* (July 2008).

133. See Susan Shirk, *Fragile Superpower*; and Elizabeth C. Economy, *The River Runs Black: The Environmental Challenge to China's Future* (New York, N.Y.: Council on Foreign Relations, 2004).

134. See, for example, Stephan Haggard and Yasheng Huang, "The Political Economy of Private-Sector Development in China," in Loren Brandt and Thomas G. Rawski, eds., *China's Great Economic* Transformation; Anders Åslund, *Building Capitalism: The Transformation of the Former Soviet Bloc* (New York, N.Y.: Cambridge University Press, 2002); Joachim Ahrens, "Governance, Conditionality, and Transformation in Post-Socialist Countries," in Herman W. Hoen, ed., *Good Governance in Central and Eastern Europe* (Northampton, Mass.: Edward Elgar, 2001); Marc Suhrcke, *Economic Growth in the Transition Economies of Central and Eastern Europe* (Baden-Baden, Germany: Nomos Verlagsgesellschaft, 2001); and Werner Baer and Joseph L. Love, eds., *Liberalization and Its Consequences: A Comparative Perspective on Latin America and Eastern Europe* (Northampton, Mass.: Edward Elgar, 2000).

135. http://www.ebrd.org.

136. Nicholas Lardy, *Integrating China into the Global Economy*.

137. Anders Åslund, *Building Capitalism*, 161; Marc Suhrcke, *Economic Growth in the Transition Economies of Central and Eastern Europe* (Baden-Baden, Germany: Nomos Verlagsgesellschaft, 2001); and Stanley Fischer and Ratna Sahay, "The Transition Economies after Ten Years," IMF Working Paper, WP//00/30, February 2000.

11

Conclusion: Globalization and Governance

This book has focused on two interrelated themes: the influence of politics on international economic relations and the governance of the world economy in the years since World War II. The examination of international economic relations in those six decades has revealed the many ways in which political factors have shaped economic outcomes. We have seen that the postwar security system significantly affected the postwar economic system. The creation of a bipolar diplomatic-security system following the outbreak of the Cold War between the United States and the Soviet Union led to the separation of the Eastern and Western economic systems and provided a base for the dominant role of the United States in the Western system and of the Soviet Union in the Eastern system. The end of the Cold War led in turn to the end of the East-West economic divide and integration of the formerly communist countries and China into a global capitalist economy.

We have also seen the influence of domestic policymaking on international economic relations. Political concerns often outweighed economic considerations in policy outcomes. The Marshall Plan, for example, was a security policy as well as an economic program. Similarly, aid by the West to the formerly communist countries after the end of the Cold War was motivated strongly by security concerns, such as the desire to prevent nuclear proliferation and to make a return to communism as unattractive as possible.

In addition, monetary, trade, and investment policy debates have been influenced by the mobilization of interest groups. For example, organized labor and environmental groups opposed the ratification of the North American Free Trade Agreement in 1993, despite strong support from U.S. manufacturing interests and the executive branch of the government, because the groups thought the agreement would create downward pressure on wages and environmental standards in the United States. The same groups opposed further globalization of the world economy in the late 1990s. In formerly communist countries, some government officials and the managers of state enterprises organized politically to oppose economic reforms, while others supported them. Private business interests organized effectively to influence electoral outcomes in the fledgling democracies of Russia and Eastern Europe.

Finally, and most important, international economic relations has itself become a political arena where both governments and nonstate actors (like multinational corporations and transnational environmental groups) try to manage conflict and seek cooperative outcomes. These actors are searching for new ways to govern the global economy. As the world economy becomes more globalized, MNCs and NGOs are increasingly playing a role in both domestic and international politics. Economic globalization has raised the issue of global governance and with it the question of how to make global governance as democratic as possible. Thus, economic globalization has led to an internationalization of domestic politics.

THE EVOLUTION OF INTERNATIONAL ECONOMIC GOVERNANCE

Our review of international economic relations in the years since World War II traced the system of political control established immediately after World War II, during the Bretton Woods period (1945–1971) to the age of interdependence (1971–1989) and finally to the era of globalization (1989 to the present). Each chapter has offered some conclusions about the future of economic governance in particular areas—money, trade, investment—and in particular subsystems—North-North, North-South, East-West. Some of these subsystems have changed in major ways since 1945. The South is an increasingly diversified group with a major divide between the fast-growing and slow-growing countries. Since the breakup of the Soviet Union and the economic reforms in China, the East-West system no longer possesses the Cold War ideological overtones that it once had. Instead, capitalism is everywhere. In this chapter, we will summarize the arguments in previous chapters and then look to the future of the system as a whole to suggest some answers to the question of how it might be possible to deal with the key problem of our time: the governance of globalization.

The international regimes governing monetary affairs, trade, and investment flows evolved quite differently. The development of the regimes over time reflected the distinctive challenges of the three periods in the three different subsystems (see Table 11.1). After World War II, most international economic

TABLE 11.1 **Characteristics of Management and Governance in the Three Subsystems**

Subsystem	Bretton Woods (1945–1971)	Interdependence (1971–1989)	Globalization (1989 to present)
North-North	U.S. hegemony, Europe and Japan recover from WW2	Relative decline of the U.S., rise of Europe and Japan	U.S. dominance restored, formation of EMU, Japanese economic recession
	Creation of multilateral institutions and rules: IMF, World Bank, GATT	Evolution of international economic regimes: IMF reform, Group of Ten, economic summits, trade rounds	Evolution of international economic regimes: creation of WTO
	Numerous barriers to international economic flows gradually reduced: currency convertibility, tariff reductions	Liberalization of trade and finance, economic growth	Liberalization domestically and internationally
		Rising international economic flows	Rapidly increasing international economic flows
North-South	End of colonialism	Efforts to unite and confront the North to achieve greater equity, OPEC model	Spread of policies of deregulation, liberalization, privatization
	Superpower competition for influence in the Third World	Rapid growth of newly industrializing countries, flows of trade, investment, capital to NICs	Greater integration into global economy: investment and financial flows, trade
	Southern underdevelopment and dependence on the developed market economies	Continuing stagnation of Fourth World	Instability arising from volatile capital flows, inadequate domestic policies and regulations
	Isolation from the international economic institutions, import substitution strategies		Rise of China and India
			Continuing stagnation of Fourth World
East-West	Creation of separate international economic systems for East and West	Limited reconnection with the West via *ostpolitik*, détente, and Chinese economic reforms	End of the Cold War, breakup of the Soviet Union
	State-led domestic and international economies	Limits on economic growth inherent in central planning	Russia joins the G-7
	Recovery from WW II and growth		In Russia and Eastern Europe: transition from communism to capitalism and from autocracy to democracy
			In China: successful economic reforms but continued political dominance of the Communist Party

SOURCE: Chapters 2–10.

regimes were created by the United States acting either alone or jointly with Britain with the consent of the other industrialized capitalist countries. The U.S. and British governments focused on money and trade after World War II because of their shared belief that instability in monetary affairs and protectionism had played a critical role in the rise of the dictatorships after World War I. The leaders of the United States and the United Kingdom believed that a fixed currency exchange-rate regime backed by gold and a liberal trading order were the best guarantees against both fascism and communism. The exchange rate regime they established after 1945 grew weaker over time, while the trade regime grew stronger. Fixed exchange rates proved unsustainable and were replaced with floating rates in 1973. The original GATT system expanded through trade liberalization and new rule making and was eventually replaced with the more ambitious WTO in 1995. No formal regime governed investment flows during the three periods. Trade-related investment measures were added to the WTO in 1995 (see Table 11.2) but the attempt to establish a Multilateral Agreement on Investment failed in 1998. In all three areas, there was movement away from management by the hegemonic power (the United States) toward genuine multilateral governance. However, the legitimacy of that evolution was increasingly challenged by antiglobalization forces.

Despite the uneven institutionalization of international economic regimes, the world economy grew rapidly as money, goods, and services flowed more easily across national boundaries.[1] Trade grew faster than GDP, and FDI grew faster than trade, but the volume of financial flows and currency transactions grew faster than either trade or FDI, especially during the third period.

Increasing international economic interaction was driven, in part, by technological change. Transportation and communication costs declined dramatically after World War II. The combination of new computing and telecommunications technologies decreased the cost, increased the speed, and altered the possibilities of international economic production and exchange.[2] New transportation technologies increased the volume and speed of trade and the movement of people. Average ocean freight and port charges fell from $95 per short ton of U.S. import and export cargo in 1920 to less than $20 in 2000. Small, lightweight products were increasingly shipped via wide-body jet aircraft at rates that were highly competitive with ocean freight prices. The cost of a three-minute telephone call from New York to London fell from $317 in 1930 to $.30 in 1996 (in constant 1990 dollars). Satellite television and later the Internet and the World Wide Web made the communication of text, audio, and video images about world events instantaneous. The reduction in communication and transportation costs enhanced the ability and willingness of actors to cooperate across national boundaries.[3]

Political choices also drove growing international economic interaction. The creation of the Bretton Woods regime was a critical political decision. At the time of the establishment of the Bretton Woods system, trade barriers, investment restrictions, and capital controls separated the industrialized economies. The common goal of the founders of Bretton Woods was to promote economic prosperity and political stability by reducing barriers to trade and financial flows

T A B L E 11.2   Summary of Regime Changes in the Three Periods in Monetary Affairs, Trade, and Investment Flows

Regime	Bretton Woods (1945–1971)	Interdependence (1971–1989)	Globalization (1989 to present)
Monetary Affairs	Dominant role of dollar Exchange rates fixed relative to the dollar with adjustable pegs Movement to currency convertibility Periodic currency crises and stress on fixed exchange rates IMF and United States are managers of fixed exchange rate regime	Floating exchange rates with central bank interventions Efforts to fix exchange rates among Europeans Increased volatility with rising international financial flows: petrodollar recycling, Third World debt crises Increased IMF involvement in developing countries G-7 finance ministers and central banks manage exchange rate system and financial crises	Increase in worldwide financial flows, major financial crises become global Creation of EU and rise of the Euro G-7 finance ministers and central banks joined by IMF and World Bank as crisis managers
Trade	Gradual reductions in tariffs among developed market economies through GATT negotiating rounds Many areas excluded from GATT: defense, agriculture, services	Tokyo Round; major reductions in tariffs and increases in nontariff barriers Increased conflict over North-North trade	Uruguay Round: expansion of regime to cover services, investment, and intellectual property; creation of the WTO and extension of the trade regime's scope and authority Formerly communist countries and China join the WTO Doha Round not completed
Investment Flows	No regime other than preexisting international laws governing foreign investments	Latin American and OPEC nationalizations and other challenges to MNCs	MNCs increasingly accepted as developed, developing, and formerly communist countries seek inflows of foreign investment direct investment TRIMs added to WTO Failure of the MAI

SOURCE: Chapters 2–8.

through institutions, rules, and processes of liberalization. This liberalization combined with national policies of domestic compensation via the welfare state, deregulation, and privatization eventually led to greater openness to trade, financial flows, and direct investment in the world economy.[4] By the beginning of the twenty-first century, the industrialized nations were linked by a "dense network" of international flows of goods, services, capital, information, ideas, and people. This network was known as globalization.[5]

Developing countries made different political choices. In the period after World War II, the developing countries found themselves in dependent relationships with the powerful, developed North. Many Southern states chose not to participate in the Bretton Woods system and pursued economic development through import-substituting industrialization policies. In the 1970s, they sought to improve their bargaining position and to gain economic benefits by uniting and using their control of raw materials such as oil. By the 1980s and 1990s, many developing countries found that isolationism and confrontation were dead ends and shifted their strategies toward deregulation, privatization, and international liberalization. They sought to benefit from integration into the global economy by increasing their share of growing trade, foreign investment, and other international capital flows. Large and faster-growing developing countries such as Mexico, Brazil, China, India, Taiwan, and South Korea became important regional players who also sought a seat at the table of global decision making.

Political decisions also shaped the interaction of the USSR, China, and the communist states of Eastern Europe with the world economy. After World War II, with the onset of the Cold War, the East isolated itself from the Western international economic system by establishing state-managed economies and creating a separate, independent international economic system. Politically motivated barriers created by Western states accentuated their isolation. At the end of the twentieth century, interaction between East and West increased significantly when the communist regimes in the USSR and Eastern Europe collapsed, China and Vietnam adopted market-oriented economic policies, and the West eliminated its economic sanctions. Integration of the formerly communist countries into the international economic system became a key political challenge for the West. Its efforts in Eastern Europe and Russia focused on supporting the consolidation of their new democratic systems. In China, which had successfully integrated itself into the world economy without abandoning authoritarianism and communism, the challenge was figuring out how to accommodate growing Chinese economic power while encouraging and supporting political liberalization.

CHALLENGES FOR GLOBAL GOVERNANCE

Globalization has significantly altered the conditions for achieving cooperation and managing conflict in international economic relations. It has changed the nature of the state, the major player in international relations. National sovereignty, national decision making, and national boundaries have not disappeared and states remain the principal actors in international economic relations. However, states are increasingly open and subject to external influences. For example, the Mexican peso and Asian financial crises reverberated around the globe, disrupting national financial markets and national economies in both developed and developing countries. The slowing of growth in the United States in 2001 profoundly affected economic performance in Asia, Europe, and the Americas. The financial crisis in the United States in 2008 quickly spread to other nations before it could be contained. As a result, states are restructuring to reduce their vulnerability to international economic changes and to adapt quickly to those changes to which they remain exposed.[6]

Another challenge centers on the continuing need for leadership within the system. Throughout the second half of the twentieth century, the United States acted in concert with other developed market economies to lead the global economic system. In the twentieth century, the United States was the principal beneficiary of globalization and emerged as the world's superpower both after World War II and after 1989. United States leadership in the twenty-first century is still essential but also problematic.

Part of the problem with U.S. leadership lay in resistance to globalization. Debate and conflict over globalization and the U.S. role in international economic management intensified at the dawn of the twenty-first century. American advocates of globalization, much like policymakers at Bretton Woods, pointed to the economic and political benefits of greater trade and financial flows and supported the continued liberalization of national economies and the removal of barriers to international economic flows. These advocates recognized that globalization undermines the ability of national governments to manage their economies and supported the creation of multilateral regimes to govern global economic interaction.[7]

American critics of globalization included labor unions fearing the loss of jobs to foreign competition, environmentalists concerned that globalization would undermine national environmental laws and policies, and isolationists and neo-imperialists who opposed foreign influence and multilateral decision making. Critics on the left pointed to the instabilities and inequities of globalization. Much like the structuralists and Marxists of an earlier era, they argued that international trade, investment, and finance favored the developed countries and harmed developing countries who suffered from financial crises and from the harsh policies of international financial institutions, especially the IMF. Critics on the right focused on the impact of globalization on national sovereignty and independence. They wanted to erect new barriers to trade, capital, and labor flows, claiming that existing flows threatened national security. Opponents of globalization on both the left and the right mobilized politically against U.S. leadership in liberalizing the international economy and expanding multilateral economic institutions and rules.[8]

In Europe and Japan, traditional allies in strengthening international economic governance, the debate over globalization mirrored that in the United States and was reinforced by the fear that globalization was a vehicle for U.S. dominance. European, Latin American, African, and Asian governments formed regional economic regimes, which also played a role in global governance. Some of those regional organizations, especially the European Union and Mercosur, were formed in part to offset U.S. predominance and enhance the role of their member–states in international economic decision making.

Furthermore, states are no longer the only actors in international economic relations. A variety of nonstate players that are working across national boundaries emerged. Besides MNCs, labor unions, NGOs, and other nongovernmental transnational actors are playing a growing role in global governance. These actors argue that they are similar to interest groups in domestic polities by asserting their independence from governments and their ability better to represent the interests of citizens in specific policy areas. Unlike domestic interest groups, however, they attempt to influence decision making at both the domestic and international levels. They seek to reform international regimes to make them more responsive to nongovernmental actors. To do this effectively, they have to communicate and coordinate policies transnationally and to form alliances with other nongovernmental actors.[9]

While national political systems have devised a wide variety of ways to provide access for domestic interest groups, international institutions have been largely closed to such groups. Decision processes of most international economic institutions are based on the idea of **intergovernmentalism**, participation by government officials only, and are not always transparent. Thus, another challenge for global governance is whether and how to provide access for nonstate actors. In the long term, the ability of the system to provide the right amount of access and transparency will be critical to enhancing the legitimacy and effectiveness of the global governance.[10]

Because of globalization, interaction must also be managed in many arenas that traditionally have been in the purview of states and that are deeply imbedded in national policies and practices. A level playing field in international trade is shaped by national competition policies. The stability of the international financial system has become dependent on the safety and soundness of national financial systems. The effective transition from communism to capitalism in Russia and Eastern Europe is an international as well as a national concern.

In addition, social goals are becoming linked to global governance. Environmentalists would like the WTO to incorporate rules to protect the environment while also promoting the liberalization of trade. The NAFTA agreement included separate codicils on labor standards and environmental protection. The G–8 has considered methods to deal with the global problems created by the AIDS pandemic, including the problem of getting expensive AIDS medicines to low-income individuals at reasonable prices while maintaining incentives for drug companies to develop new treatments and possible cures. Policies to deal with the threat of climate change have been discussed in the United Nations, the G–8, and other global forums.

These linkages between the global economy and traditionally national areas of decision making have led to significant tension between state and international decision-making. The WTO, for example, found in several rulings that national social policies designed to control use of alcohol or gambling violated international trade agreements. Similarly, as financial markets grow exponentially in the era of globalization, national bank supervisory and regulatory structures have become increasingly inadequate to assure safety and soundness of the global markets. However, national authorities were not ready or able to create a global financial regulatory structure. The challenge is to develop an economic order that preserves the sovereignty of nation-states while also addressing the need for global governance.

CHARACTERISTICS OF A NEW SYSTEM
OF GOVERNANCE

The future order will continue to rely on political management by a core of powerful, developed countries. The developed economies and especially the "big five"—the United States, Japan, Germany, France, and the United Kingdom—will remain key actors in the system. The size and vitality of their economies will ensure their continuing leadership. Their growing interdependence will be a force for cooperation. Nevertheless, power relationships among the big five and between them and the rest of the world are changing, and this will affect governance arrangements.

Japan, as the second-largest developed market economy after the United States, will seek over time to play a more important role. Japan has already staked out a greater role in a wide variety of global economic regimes, including the World Bank and the IMF. Japan is one of the leading users of the dispute settlement machinery of the WTO.[11] The Japanese played a key role in pushing for the Doha Development Round. The ability of Japan to restructure and revitalize its economy will shape its ability to increase its influence. At the same time, the big three countries of Western Europe—France, Germany, and the United Kingdom—continue to enhance their global economic power primarily through European integration and expansion of the EU. The ability of the EU to achieve its goal of a common economic system with a free flow of goods, services, money, and people will shape the role of its member states in the new systems of global governance.

Governance institutions will have to be broadened in some cases and in some areas to reflect the rise of new centers of power. In particular, China's new economic power will have to be taken into account in overall governance mechanisms, including the economic summits. As a major factor in international trade as well as a financial power due to its large financial surpluses, China must increasingly take on responsibility in its domestic and international economic policies for the entire system.

Members of OPEC and other major oil and natural gas exporters such as Russia, for example, will continue to have a major say regarding energy issues. In the area of trade and foreign investment, the fast-growing developing countries will play a greater role. Brazil, China, India, Mexico, and South Korea, whose trade and investment flows are of great importance to the world economy, will be in a position to demand and receive greater access to global governance institutions. Their views will have to be taken into account, especially in future negotiations about the trade and investment regimes.

Whereas the governments of some developing countries will be involved to a greater extent than they are now in global governance, the role of other governments in the South is unlikely to change. The poorer and slower-growing developing countries are not likely to play a significant role in global governance institutions beyond the United Nations system, but they can expect to receive greater attention from the powers-that-be in the years to come. The Fourth World will be helped by allies in the South and by nongovernmental organizations in the North that have mobilized against the inequities of the international economic system. The rich countries of the North are paying more attention to the Fourth World because they see that as part of a necessary response to the challenges posed by global terrorism, the AIDS pandemic, and global warming.

Finally, the new system of governance will need to continue to promote the economic and political restructuring of Russia and Eastern Europe to integrate these countries into the system of global governance. Russia has joined the IMF, the World Bank, and the economic summits, and should eventually become a member of the WTO. Eastern European countries have been brought into the system through the EU, the OECD, the WTO, World Bank, and IMF as well as through membership in NATO.

Among the powerful core, a recognized cluster of common interests will remain. Despite conflicts raised by economic change and in particular by globalization, the developed market economies continued to support a liberal, capitalist global economy. The postwar experience has reinforced their belief in the need to cooperate to achieve a stable and prosperous economic system. The persistence of the shared goal of cooperation was demonstrated by the behavior of the industrialized nations during the crises of the 1990s as well as the successful conclusion of the Uruguay Round and the formation of the World Trade Organization. In the early twenty-first century, the ability of the powerful core to continue to support a liberal, capitalist global economy will be tested again, particularly by the new challenges of trade (completing the Doha Round) and finance (addressing the global financial crisis of 2008).

There are signs that the second tier of states—some members of OPEC, the Asian tigers, and the BRICs, among others—share at least some of the norms of cooperation currently held by the industrialized countries. Adoption by many developing countries of more pragmatic policies toward trade and foreign investment in the 1980s and beyond represent significant movement toward greater global consensus. The Asian tigers and the BRICs are more receptive to supporting effective global economic governance than the rest of the South because they have a greater stake in the system. They seek to preserve liberal trade and investment regimes because these regimes are vital to the continued success of their export-led development strategies.

Still, it seems quite likely that North-South tensions will persist. Despite the growing differentiation between the more-advanced and the least-developed countries, the wealthier Southern states continue to support greater emphasis on poverty alleviation and the reduction of global inequality. They now have important political allies in the form of NGOs based in the developed world. Although the industrial core does not reject the Millennium Development Goals, they are still not seen as a primary goal of global economic governance or as a responsibility of the developed market economies. Even though the NGOs and the South have succeeded in putting reducing global poverty and inequity on the agenda and the developed countries are willing to support some aid programs (especially in the case of humanitarian emergencies), the North so far has been unwilling to alter noticeably the established system's operation in the direction of redistribution.

Furthermore, many Northern critics have questioned whether equity, as demanded by the less-developed countries, is a legitimate goal. Some charge that redistribution as now conceived will benefit only a few or only a small stratum of the population of the less-developed countries and not the poorest in the poor countries. Without extensive internal political, social, and economic reform in the less-developed countries, international efforts at redistribution and development will be useless, according to many in both the North and the South. Conflict over equity and redistribution therefore is likely to continue to be a political dynamic in the new international system.

Finally, the new international economic regime will be a system of multilateral governance. In the past, a single leader to a great extent carried out the management of conflict and cooperation. In the nineteenth century, Great Britain was this leader, and in the postwar era, the United States took the part. The more even distribution of power in the future, however, will require the active participation of a coalition of powerful states—that is, it will require collective governance.

Collective governance is difficult. Throughout history, agreement among sovereign powers in the absence of world government has proved to be a difficult and often an impossible task. Several factors, however, enhance the possible success of collective governance. The basic consensus among the powerful will be an important factor; so, too, will be the experience in cooperation since World War II. Collective governance will be facilitated by a variety of formal and informal methods developed over the last four decades. A relatively sophisticated and complex structure of cooperative mechanisms has unfolded in the postwar era, and experience in using these mechanisms has grown. Yet, as evidenced by the financial and economic crisis of 2008, those mechanisms may prove inadequate to the demands of a global economy.

Even within a collective governance system, however, leadership will be important. Existing institutions are insufficiently developed to govern the system without supplementary action on the part of leading nation-states. Most often, that leadership will have to come from the United States. Unless and until the European Union becomes politically unified, and the EU or Japan assumes a more assertive posture in world affairs, the United States, by the very size of its economy, will continue to be the most important international economic actor. Although the United States will be unable to govern the system by itself, management and reform will be impossible without U.S. approval, and U.S. initiatives and support for reforming global governance will be crucial to success.

Because of the political setting and the nature of the task, the process of international economic reform will be piecemeal and evolutionary. Reform will result, in part, from international negotiations such as multilateral trade negotiations. It will arise from the evolution by negotiation of international institutions such as the IMF, the World Bank, and the WTO. Reform will also grow out of common law, the establishment of rules and procedures through trial and error, and through ad hoc responses to problems and crises. International monetary management through consultations among central bankers and finance ministers of the G-7 will most likely evolve through such a process. Reform will come not only from such international agreement and managed change but also from sporadic crises. The currency crises of the 1960s and 1970s, not international agreement, led to the floating exchange rate system. The debt crises in Venezuela and Mexico led to a new approach to the debt problem; the Mexican peso crisis of 1994–1995, the Asian financial crisis of 1997–1998, and the Russian crisis of 1998 led to IMF reform. In the absence of agreed-upon rules, structures, and processes, such disturbances may multiply.

Finally, there is no assurance that multilateral cooperation among the major industrialized countries will continue or that it will be successful. The evolutionary process of reform is in many ways precarious, for it relies on mutual restraint and cooperation by the major powers until reform is achieved. Without agreed-upon rules, institutions, and procedures, a major economic shock could undermine cooperation and lead to economic warfare, as occurred in the 1930s. Without strong multilateral institutions such as the G-8, the WTO, the IMF, and the World Bank, the world could gradually evolve into a series of economic blocs: a Western hemisphere block centered on the United States, Canada, and Mexico; a European-African block based on the EU; and a Pacific block built around Japan. If the multilateral system is weakened, regional management could become a hedge against the possibility of a breakdown in global multilateralism. Nevertheless, recent experience suggests that the will and ability to find mutual solutions persists and that cooperation among the powerful will continue.

ENDNOTES

1. Robert O. Keohane and Joseph S. Nye, "Introduction," in Joseph S. Nye and John D. Donahue, eds., *Governance in a Globalizing World* (Washington, D.C.: Brookings Institution Press, 2000).

2. Jeffry A. Frieden and Ronald Rogowski, "The Impact of the International Economy on National Policies," in Robert O. Keohane and Helen V. Milner, eds., *Internationalization and Domestic Politics* (New York, N.Y.: Cambridge University Press, 1996), 30.

3. Taken from a presentation on globalization prepared by the staff of the World Bank. See also Matthias Busse, "Tariffs, Transport Costs, and the WTO Doha Round: The Case of Developing Countries," *The Estey Center Journal of International Law and Trade Policy*, 4 (Winter 2003): 15–31; Jeffrey Frankel, "Globalization of the Economy," in Keohane and Milner, eds., *Internationalization*

and Domestic Politics; and Jonathan Aronson, "Global Networks and Their Impact," in James N. Rosenau and J. P. Singh, eds., *Information Technologies and Global Politics: The Changing Scope of Power and Governance* (Albany State University of New York Press, 2002).

4. John G. Ruggie, "International Regimes, Transactions, and Change: Embedded Liberalism in the Postwar Economic Order," *International Organization*, 36 (Spring 1982): 379–415.

5. Robert Keohane and Joseph Nye, "Introduction."

6. Jeffrey A. Hart and Aseem Prakash, "Globalization, Governance, and Strategic Trade and Investment Policies," in Aseem Prakash and Jeffrey A. Hart, eds., *Globalization and Governance* (New York, N.Y.: Routledge, 1999).

7. See, for example, Jagdish Bhagwati, *Free Trade Today* (Princeton, N.J.: Princeton University Press, 2002); Sylvia Ostry, "Convergence and Sovereignty: Policy Scope for Compromise?", in Aseem Prakash and Jeffrey A. Hart (eds.), *Coping with Globalization*, (New York, N.Y, 2000); and Douglas Irwin, *Free Trade Under Fire* (Princeton, N.J.: Princeton University Press, 2002).

8. Kevin Philips, *Bad Money: Reckless Finance, Failed Politics, and the Global Crisis of American Capitalism* (New York, N.Y.: Viking, 2008); Evan Osborne, *The Rise of the Anti-Corporate Movement: Corporations and the People Who Hate Them* (Westport, Conn.: Praeger, 2007); Sidney Tarrow, *The New Transnational Activism* (New York, N.Y.: Cambridge University Press, 2005); and Dani Rodrik, *Has Globalization Gone Too Far?* (Washington, D.C.: Institute for International Economics, 1997).

9. See Ann Florini, *The Coming Democracy: New Rules for Running a New World* (Washington, D.C.: Brookings Institution, 2005); and Ann Florini, *The Third Force: The Rise of Transnational Civil Society* (Washington, D.C.: Carnegie Endowment for International Peace, 2000).

10. Keohane and Nye, "Introduction."

11. Saadia Pekkanen, *Japan's Aggressive Legalism: Law and Foreign Trade Politics Beyond the WTO* (Stanford, Calif.: Stanford University Press, 2008).

Glossary

adjustment Macroeconomic policies aimed at enabling a country to adapt its structure of production to prevailing world conditions by ending imbalances in its economy and changing its structure. These policies usually involve cutting governmental expenditures to reduce imbalances in the external accounts (balance of payments) and the domestic budget; expanding the supply of tradeables to improve the balance of trade; and privatizing companies owned by the public sector.

affiliate See *subsidiary*.

African, Carribean, and Pacific (ACP) states African, Caribbean and Pacific countries are the countries that are signatories of the Lomé Convention.

Agreement on Safeguards One of the treaties negotiated during the Uruguay Round that permits countries to restrict imports if those imports cause injury. Restrictions must be for a limited time and nondiscriminatory.

Andean Common Market See *Andean Community*.

Andean Community (ANCOM) An organization of five Andean countries—Bolivia, Colombia, Ecuador, Peru, and Venezuela—formed in 1997 out of the Andean Pact. ANCOM provides for economic and social integration, including regional trade liberalization and a common external tariff, as well as harmonization of other policies.

antidumping petition A complaint by a domestic producer that imports are being dumped, and the resulting investigation and, if dumping and injury are found, the imposition of an antidumping duty.

Apartheid the official name of the South African system of racial segregation which existed after 1948.

appropriateness of technology One concern of critics of multinational corporations is that they tend to employ technologies appropriate for capital-rich and labor-poor industrialized countries in developing countries when they should be employing technologies appropriate for the relative abundance of labor and the scarcity of capital in those countries.

ASEAN Free Trade Area (AFTA) A free trade area announced in 1992 among the ASEAN countries. The goal was to eliminate lists of tariffs among the original six ASEAN members by 2002.

Asian tigers Four fast-growing developing countries of East Asia: South Korea, Taiwan, Hong Kong, and Singapore.

Asia-Pacific Economic Cooperation (APEC) An organization, formed by countries in the Asia-Pacific region in 1989, devoted to promoting open trade and practical economic cooperation.

Association of Southeast Asian Nations (ASEAN) An organization of countries in southeast Asia that promotes economic, social, and cultural development as well as peace and stability in the region. Formed with five member countries in 1967, ASEAN had expanded to ten members as of July 2000.

austerity programs Sets of policies designed to restrict domestic demand, government spending, and economic growth in order to reduce budget and balance-of-payments deficits. These programs often were prescribed as part of structural adjustment programs for countries experiencing financial crises.

authoritarian A political system in which the administration of government is centralized. The ruler's personality may play an important role in maintaining the system and advancing the notion and practice of extreme authority as a political virtue. This type of system is characterized by the curtailment of individual freedoms; excessive reliance on violence and punishment, and on the threat of violence and punishment; virtual unaccountability of government officials; and the aversion of the decision-making process to consultation, persuasion, and the necessity of forging a policy consensus.

backward linkage A relationship between a firm and a supplier that benefits the supplier.

Baker Plan A plan introduced in September 1985 by U.S. Treasury Secretary James Baker to restore growth in the most heavily indebted countries. The proposed plan consisted of three parts: (1) the implementation of market-oriented structural changes to remove economic inefficiencies; (2) the provision of $20 billion in new loans over three years by commercial banks; and (3) an increase in the amount disbursed by multilateral development banks, particularly the World Bank. A host of factors prevented the Baker Plan from achieving a resurgence of growth. Efforts to carry out structural reforms were limited by political constraints. Inadequate tax systems and demands on the banking system for debt financing undermined the success of the proposed economic reforms. Finally, slow growth in the developed countries constrained their ability to provide the financial inflows prescribed by the plan.

balance of payments An annual accounting of all economic transactions between one nation and the rest of the world. The balance of payments on current accounts includes the trade balance, which measures the movement of goods and some services, and the short-term capital account, which measures the flow of short-term investments and payments.

Bank for International Settlements (BIS) An international organization, headquartered in Basel, Switzerland, that fosters cooperation among central banks and other agencies in pursuit of monetary and financial stability.

Battle in Seattle Protests staged by antiglobalization forces at a WTO Ministerial Meeting in Seattle in 1999.

Big Bang Reforms centering on the stock exchange in Britain that were put into effect in 1986.

big-box retailer A large store that provides discounted prices to consumers because of its focus on high-volume merchandise.

bilateral investment treaty (BIT) An agreement between two countries regarding how to settle disputes over foreign direct investments.

Brady bonds Bonds collateralized by U.S. Treasury zero coupon bonds (and other high-grade bonds) that are used to replace private bank loans in developing countries, thereby converting sovereign debt into liquid debt instruments. Brady bonds are used to accomplish the debt reduction and restructuring called for in the Brady initiative.

Brady initiative A strategy for dealing with LDC debt introduced in March 1989 by U.S. Treasury Secretary Nicholas Brady in the wake of the failure of the Baker Plan to achieve its objectives. The strategy called for a shift in emphasis from new lending to debt reduction by banks and called for making available the resources of multilateral development banks, such as the World Bank and the IMF, to debtor countries that adopt sound economic reform policies. In terms of debt reduction, the initiative proposed a menu of options that included voluntary exchanges of old debt for new bonds.

Bretton Woods system The set of rules, institutions, and procedures developed to regulate international monetary interactions in the post–World War II period. It derived its name from the agreement forged in Bretton Woods, New Hampshire, in July 1944. This regime, which shaped the postwar international monetary relations until the United States suspended the convertibility of the dollar into gold in 1972, was founded on three political bases: the concentration of power in a small number of states, the existence of a cluster of important interests shared by those states, and the presence of a dominant power willing and able to assume a leading role. Bretton Woods participants set up the International Monetary Fund (IMF) and the International Bank for Reconstruction and Development (IBRD, also known as the World Bank), to manage exchange rates, ensure international liquidity, and deter balance-of-payments crises.

BRIC an acronym that refers to the fast growing developing economies of Brazil, Russia, India, and China.

brownfield investment An investment in the improvement or upgrading of an existing facility. This is the opposite of a *greenfield investment*.

buffer stock The storage of non-perishable commodities for the purpose of regulating fluctuations of price. Commodities are purchased for the buffer stock in order to reduce supply and thereby to increase the price; they are sold in order to increase supply and reduce the price.

built-in agenda A negotiating agenda for the WTO that included mandates to complete negotiations on liberalizing agricultural and services trade and to develop rules on government procurement and subsidies by 1999.

Calvo doctrine An economic policy approach named after Carlos Calvo (1824–1906), an Argentine diplomat. The doctrine asserts the right of host countries to nationalize foreign investments and make their own determination of what constitutes fair compensation. As such, the doctrine rejects the right of foreign investors to lay claim to diplomatic protection or to appeal to their home governments for help since this could ultimately result in violating the territorial sovereignty and judicial independence of the host nations. By the turn of the twentieth century, the Calvo doctrine became the main guiding principle for the policies of Latin American countries toward multinational investment. With the shift in Southern public attitudes against multinational corporations in the 1970s, many Southern governments adopted this Latin American position, thus altering their open-door policies.

Cairns group A trade interest group of 19 agricultural exporting countries, composed of Argentina, Australia, Bolivia, Brazil, Canada, Chile, Colombia, Costa Rica, Guatemala, Indonesia, Malaysia, New Zealand, Pakistan, Paraguay, Peru, the Philippines, South Africa, Thailand, and Uruguay.

capital flight When investment capital leaves a country in a hurry because investors are worried about the risks associated with keeping their capital in that country.

capital formation The process that occurs when a nation's capital stock increases as a result of new investments in physical capital (plant and equipment). Unlike gross capital formation, net capital formation makes allowances for depreciation and repairs of the existing capital stock. See also *human capital formation*.

capital goods Manufactured products that are used to produce other goods.

capitalism A socioeconomic system characterized by private initiative and the private ownership of factors of production. In such a system, individuals have the right to own and use wealth to earn income and to sell and purchase labor for wages. Furthermore, capitalism is predicated on a relative absence of governmental control of the economy. The function of regulating the economy is achieved largely through the operation of market forces, whereby the price mechanism acts as a signaling system that determines the allocation of resources and their uses.

capital markets Financial institutions such as banks, insurance companies, and stock exchanges that channel long-term investment funds to commercial and industrial borrowers. Unlike the money market, on which lending is ordinarily short term, the capital market typically finances fixed investments like those in buildings and machinery.

cartel An organization of producers seeking to limit or eliminate competition among its members, most often by agreeing to restrict output to keep prices higher than would occur under competitive conditions. Cartels are inherently unstable because of the potential for producers to defect from the agreement and capture larger markets by selling at lower prices.

Center on Transnational Corporations (CTC) A United Nations organization created in 1984 as a result of pressures from Third World countries to study the global impact of multinational corporations.

central bank The bank that issues national currency, acts as banker to both government and private banks, and oversees the financial system. Central banks also administer national monetary policy, using their influence over the money supply and interest rates to implement macroeconomic policies.

central planning The economic system adopted by socialist countries. In this system, the processes of allocating resources, establishing production targets, and setting product prices are determined by government planners rather than the operation of market forces. Such a system discourages innovation, productivity, and quality. It provides little incentive for plant managers to experiment with new technology. The stress of fulfilling quantitative goals set by the state inhibits improving the quality of the product or the production process. The absence of competition and the existence of guaranteed markets eliminates incentives for managers to cut cost or improve quality. Above all, prices do not provide a guide to help managers determine what goods are needed by consumers and how to improve productivity by lowering costs.

Centrally planned economies Economies in which central economic planning by the government is so extensive that it controls all major sectors of the economy and formulates all decisions about their use and about the distribution of income.

Closer Economic Relationship A free trade agreement formed in 1983 between Australia and New Zealand. One of the most comprehensive bilateral free trade agreements in the world, it was also the first to include trade in services.

Cold War A period of high tension between the United States and its allies and the Soviet Union and its allies that began after World War II and did not end until the breakup of the Soviet Union in 1991.

Commercialization the process of introducing a new product into the market.

Committee of Twenty Established within the IMF in 1972 to reform the international monetary system, it was composed of the Group of Ten plus ten representatives of the developing countries and charged with devising ways to manage world monetary reserves, establishing a commonly accepted currency, and creating new adjustment mechanisms.

Committee on Foreign Investment in the United States (CFIUS) An inter-agency committee, authorized by the Exon-Florio provision of the Omnibus Trade Act of 1988 and chaired by the Secretary of Treasury, that reviews foreign takeovers of U.S. firms. It aims to protect national security while maintaining the credibility of U.S. open investment policy and preserving foreign investors' confidence that they will not be subject to retaliatory discrimination.

Common Agricultural Policy (CAP) The regulations of the European Union that seek to merge their individual agricultural programs, primarily by stabilizing and elevating the prices of agricultural commodities.

Common Effective Preferential Tariff (CEPT) An agreement within AFTA that called for reductions in tariffs for certain products traded within ASEAN to be reduced to between 0 and 5 percent. Quantitative restrictions on these products were to be eliminated.

common external tariff The single tariff rate agreed to by all members of a customs union on imports of a product from outside the union.

common internal market One of the tasks assigned to the European Union under various treaties including the Single European Act was to create an internal market free of barriers to the movement of money, goods, and people.

Commonwealth of Independent States (CIS) a regional organization whose partici-pating countries are former Soviet Republics.

comparative advantage This doctrine, which was formulated by the English economist David Ricardo (1772–1823), refers to the ability of a country to produce a certain product or service in ways that employ the factors of production differ-ently than in other trading countries. Comparative advantage is determined by the relative abundance of key factors of production (e.g., labor, land, and capital) in different countries. It explains why a country that could afford to produce a wide range of products and services at a cheaper cost than any other country should still concentrate on producing and trading only those products or services for which it had comparative advantages, leaving the production of other products and services to others and obtaining those other products and services through trade. The concept of comparative advantage provides rationales for both specialization on the part of countries and freedom of trade. Under a pure free trade system, each country would specialize only in those goods and services for which it had comparative advantages and exchange its surplus production for imports of goods and services for which it lacked compar-ative advantages in an unimpeded manner. According to the theory, all would be better off as a result.

Compensatory financing facility An entity that attempts to reduce the impact of export instability on national economies.

competition policy Policies intended to prevent collusion among firms and to prevent individual firms from having excessive market power. Major forms include oversight of mergers and prevention of price fixing and market sharing. Called antitrust policy in the United States.

competitiveness The ability of an entity to operate efficiently and productively in relation to other similar entities. Competitiveness has been used most recently to describe the overall economic performance of a nation, particularly its level of productivity, its ability to export its goods and services, and its maintenance of a high standard of living for its citizens.

concessional loans Loans that are made at lower than market interest rates and therefore have a subsidy element.

Conditionality the use of conditions attached to a loan, debt relief, bilateral aid or membership of international organizations, typically by the international financial institutions, regional organizations or donor countries.

Conference on International Economic Cooperation (CIEC) A conference held in Paris in 1975 as part of the negotiations for a New International Economic Order (see New International Economic Order).

confidence A perception on the part of savers and investors that the financial system is sound overall and not in danger of collapse.

convertibility An attribute of a currency that enables its holders to freely exchange it into another currency, or into gold. Under the pressure of certain international monetary crises, nations might resort to suspending the convertibility of their currencies in order to ensure that holders of their currency will spend it in the country that issued it.

Coordinating Committee (CoCom) An organization set up within NATO in 1950 to discuss and coordinate strategic embargoes. It was dissolved in 1994.

copyright The legal right to the proceeds from and control over the use of a created product, such as a written work, audio, video, film, or software. This right generally extends over the life of the author plus fifty years. Copyright is one form of intellectual property that is a subject of the *trade-related aspects of intellectual property rights (TRIPs) agreement.*

Cotonou agreement A partnership agreement between the EU and the ACP countries signed in June 2000 in Cotonou, Benin, replacing the Lomé Convention. Its main objective was poverty reduction.

Council for Mutual Economic Assistance (CMEA or Comecon) An international economic organization of communist countries, created in 1949 in response to the Marshall Plan, that pursued technical cooperation and joint planning. Its main functions were to reorient trade eastward and to buttress the new political relationship between the Soviet Union and Eastern Europe.

crony capitalism A form of capitalism in which there are close links between banks, governments, and private corporations.

Cultural Revolution A difficult period in China, beginning in 1966 and ending in 1976, in which the Chinese government attempted to repress counterrevolutionary tendencies in the population by forcing intellectuals, professionals, and party officials to spend time working in factories and rural collectives. Students were organized into "Red Guards" and charged with renewing the revolutionary spirit of the population, which in practice meant simply terrorizing them.

currency board An extreme form of pegged exchange rate in which management of both the exchange rate and the money supply are taken away from the central bank and given to an agency with instructions to back every unit of circulating domestic currency with a specified amount of foreign currency.

customs union A union formed when two or more countries agree to remove all barriers to free trade with each other, while establishing a common external tariff against other nations. A free trade area exists when nations remove trade barriers with each other while retaining individual tariffs against nonmembers.

debt crisis The heavy borrowing of many newly industrializing countries, particularly those in Latin America, that resulted in a prolonged financial crisis as evidence mounted indicating that some debtor nations might not be able to continue making payments on their loans. The crisis was triggered in the summer of 1982 when a number of highly indebted nations, including Mexico, Brazil, Argentina, and Poland, announced that they did not have the cash liquidity necessary to pay their creditors and, hence, raised the specter of defaulting on their loans. The debt crisis posed a threat not only to the development and political stability of the indebted nations but also to the international financial system itself.

debt-equity swap An exchange of debt for equity, in which a lender is given a share of ownership to replace a loan. This is used as a method of resolving debt crises.

debt forgiveness A policy option that involved the cancellation of debts. This option was considered by the G-7 for dealing with the official debt of very poor countries.

debt rescheduling (or debt restructuring) A process that occurs when a borrower and a lender renegotiate the original terms of a loan, altering the payment schedule or debt-service charges. This usually occurs when debtor nations cannot meet the payments due on loans from creditors.

debt service The total amount of principal and interest due on a loan in a given period.

Debt service ratio the ratio of debt service payments of a country to that country's export earnings.

Declaration on International Investment and Multinational Enterprises A document adopted by the members of the OECD in 1976 that defined the principle of national treatment, called for transparency in investment incentives, asked OECD countries to avoid conflicting requirements for MNCs, and spelled out a voluntary code of conduct for MNCs.

Declining returns to scale The decline in marginal productivity that occurs as the volume of production increases beyond a certain threshold.

declining terms of trade See *terms of trade*.

deficit A national *budget deficit* occurs when a country's public spending exceeds government revenues. A *current-account deficit* exists when exports and financial inflows from private and official transfers are worth less than the value of imports and transfer outflows. A *trade deficit* occurs when imports of goods and services exceed exports.

democracy Literally, the term means power of the people (combining the Greek words *demos*, meaning "the people," and *kratien*, meaning "to rule"). It is usually used to describe a political system in which the legitimacy of exercising power stems from the consent of the people. Accordingly, a democratic polity is often identified by the existence of constitutional government, in which the power of the leaders is checked and restrained; representative institutions based on free elections, which provide a procedural framework for the delegation of power by the people; competitive parties, in which the ruling majority respects and guarantees the rights of minorities; and civil liberties, such as freedoms of speech, press, association, and religion.

demonstration effect A copying of behavior that results from observation of that behavior in others. An example of a demonstration effect in consumer behavior is when consumers are more likely to purchase SUVs when a certain percentage of their neighbors purchase SUVs. Another example is when domestic firms copy the practices of the local subsidiaries of foreign firms in order to increase productivity.

dependency theory A theory arguing that the exploitative nature of the relationship between advanced capitalist societies and the Third World has resulted in the development of the former and the underdevelopment of the latter. Because of its reliance on external sources of demand and investment opportunities, Western capitalism penetrated virtually all parts of the Third World and eventually laid down the foundations of dominance-dependence relationship structures between North and South, which tended to engender and perpetuate underdevelopment in the Third World. According to this theory, exchanges between the North and the South, such as trade, foreign investment, and aid, are asymmetric and tend to stifle the development of the latter and to reinforce their dependence. The theory also contends that local elites with vested interest in the structure of dominance and in monopolizing domestic power cooperate with international capitalist elites to perpetuate the international capitalist system.

depression A prolonged and severe decline in national business activity, ordinarily occurring over several fiscal years. Depressions are characterized by sharply falling rates of production and capital investment; by the rapid contraction of credit; and by mass unemployment and high rates of business failure.

derivative A contract, the value of which depends on the price of some underlying asset or a particular reference rate or stock-market index.

détente The relaxation of tensions between two or more countries previously engaged in a conflictual relationship. It refers in this book mainly to the relaxation of tensions between the United States and the Soviet Union that occurred in the 1970s.

Developmental state Refers to states that were late to industrialize where the state itself led the industrialization drive, that is, it took on developmental functions.

dispute settlement mechanism The method of settling trade disputes under the GATT and the WTO. See also *Dispute Settlement Understandings*.

Dispute Settlement Understandings (DSU) The treaty negotiated during the Uruguay Round that established the procedure by which the WTO settles disputes among members, primarily by means of a three-person panel that hears the case and issues a report, subject to review by the appellate body.

Doha Round The round of multilateral trade negotiations begun in January 2002 as a result of agreement at the Doha Ministerial.

dollarization Dollarization occurs when residents of a country extensively use U.S. dollars alongside or instead of the domestic currency. Dollarization can occur unofficially, without formal legal approval, or it can be official, as when a country ceases to issue a domestic currency and uses only dollars.

downstream A firm is downstream from another when the latter provides inputs to the former.

Dual economy the existence of two separate economic systems within one country, sometimes referring to the gap between the urban industrial and rural agricultural sectors of that economy.

dumping The practice of selling goods abroad below their normal market value or below the price charged for the same goods in the domestic market of the exporting country. Dumping can be a predatory trade practice whereby the international market or a certain national market is flooded with dumped goods in order to force competitors out of the market and establish a monopoly position. Often, government subsidies are used to help absorb temporarily the losses caused by predation, leading to friction among trade partners. Dumping and predation are considered to be unfair trade practices and, as such, are prohibited under many national trade laws. The most common antidumping measure is an added import duty calculated to offset the "dumping margin"—that is, the discrepancy between home price or cost and the export price.

Economic and Monetary Union (EMU) A currency area formed in 1999 as a result of the Maastricht Treaty. Members of the EMU share the common currency, the euro.

economic development The process of raising the level of prosperity and material living in a society through an increase in the productivity and efficiency of its economy. In less industrialized regions, this process is believed to be achieved by an increase in industrial production and a relative decline in the importance of agricultural production.

economic efficiency Production that is organized to minimize the ratio of inputs to outputs and to produce goods at minimum cost in money and resources. This typically occurs where input prices are used to find the least expensive production process.

economic nationalism The set of practices that dominated international economic interactions during the interwar years and eventually brought about the collapse of the international monetary system in the 1930s. Foremost among these practices are instituting competitive exchange rate devaluations, formation of competing monetary blocs, adoption of beggar-thy-neighbor trade policies, and aversion to the norms of international cooperation.

electronic commerce The conduct of business via electronic means, including the Internet.

electronic trading system An online system that gives investors direct access to markets, thereby eliminating or reducing the role of intermediaries such as stock brokers.

emerging markets The combined set of developing countries and economies in transition from communism. Sometimes the term refers only to the faster-growing countries in that group.

Enhanced Initiative Talks begun in 1998 between the United States and Japan concerning a framework for deregulation and harmonization of competition policies.

environmental and labor policies Policies regarding the protection of the environment or the rights of working people. This was an issue in the negotiations for NAFTA and for PNTR for China.

environmental dumping The relocation of economic activity to countries where the regulations regarding the protection of the environment are more lax than in the original location. An example of a *race to the bottom*.

Escalated tariffs a taxation system in which tariffs vary according to the degree of processing of the final product, from no tariffs or low tariffs on raw materials to the highest tariffs on finished goods.

equity Stocks or shares in a company. The ownership of equity capital often conveys voting rights, whereas the ownership of loans or bonds does not. An equity market is also called a stock exchange.

Euro A currency that replaced the national currencies of the twelve members of the EMU in 1999. Euro coins and bills actually replaced national currencies on January 1, 2002, but prior to that time noncash transactions could be denominated in euros and all prices had to be marked in both euros and national currencies.

eurocurrencies Currencies held outside their country of issue, such as dollars (eurodollars) deposited in banks outside the United States, mostly in Europe. Eurocurrency markets are generally free from most national controls, so they are a flexible outlet for deposits and a source of loans for major international corporations and for national governments. This is also true of eurobonds, or securities issued on loosely controlled international markets.

European Bank for Reconstruction and Development (EBRD) A multilateral bank set up in Europe in 1990 to channel aid into Russia, the other former Soviet republics, and Eastern Europe.

European Central Bank (ECB) The central bank of the euro zone—the group of countries using the euro as their currency.

European Currency Unit (ECU) A basket of European currencies created in December 1978 serving as a basis for fixing exchange rates, a means of settlement, and a potential future reserve asset.

European Economic Community (EEC) An economic bloc that was established in 1957 by the signing of the Treaty of Rome agreed to by Belgium, France, Italy, Luxemburg, the Netherlands, and West Germany. The organization is now called the European Union, its current membership now fifteen. The signatories of the Treaty of Rome agreed to work for the gradual formation of a full customs union; the elimination of all barriers to the free movement of capital, labor, and services; and the harmonization of agricultural, industrial, trade, and transportation policies.

European Monetary System (EMS) An ambitious effort at international monetary cooperation within Europe that was launched in 1979 and ended in 1992 during a financial crisis.

European System of Central Banks (ESCB) An organization that comprises the central banks of the fifteen EU member states and the European Central Bank and that decides on monetary policies for Europe.

exchange rate The price of a currency expressed in terms of other currencies or gold. Fixed exchange rates prevail when governments agree to maintain the value of their currencies at preestablished levels. This is also known as maintaining parity. Floating exchange rates allow the market to determine the relative value of currencies.

Exchange Rate Mechanism (ERM) A system of limiting fluctuations among the currency exchange rates established by the members of the European Monetary System in 1979 that was supposed to maintain exchange rates within 2.25-percent fluctuation margins. Some countries were permitted larger margins of fluctuation. The ERM ended with the collapse of the EMS in 1992.

Eximbank The Export-Import Bank of the United States.

exit bonds Banks not wishing to participate in new loans to insolvent debtors may exit by replacing their old loans with bonds issued by debtors at a concessional discount. This allows them to write down the nonperforming loans without writing off the entire amount.

Exon-Florio amendment An amendment to the Omnibus Trade Bill of 1988 named after its sponsors Senator J. James Exon and Representative James J. Florio. It extends the scope of the International Investment and Trade in Services Act (IITSA) of 1976, which established a mechanism to monitor foreign investment in the United States and to prohibit mergers, acquisitions, or takeovers of American firms by foreign interests when such actions are deemed injurious to the national security of the United States.

Expanded structural adjustment fund A special fund created by the World Bank and the International Monetary Fund to finance structural adjustment programs.

export controls Law and regulations regarding the exportation of specific products or technologies to specific countries. Export controls were used by the United States and its allies to prevent the exportation of weapons and advanced technologies to the Soviet Union and its allies. They are now used to limit the spread of weapons of mass destruction to countries like Iraq.

export-led growth A development strategy designed to expand the overseas markets for a country's manufactured products by improving their competitiveness abroad—that is, by developing and enhancing domestic export industries. The mainstay of export-oriented development does not lie in eliminating all protection. Rather, it is based on eliminating the bias against exports: maintaining realistic exchange rates that do not discriminate against exports; reducing import barriers for inputs to the export sector; and removing any other export disincentives such as export taxes. In many countries, export-led growth involves government promotion of exports through favorable credit terms for exporters, tax incentives, undervalued exchange rates that decrease export prices, encouragement of foreign investment in export industries, and direct subsidies for targeted sectors.

Export-led growth policies See *export-led growth*.

export processing zone (EPZ) Geographic area set aside from the rest of the country for the purpose of encouraging exports by offering better infrastructure, reduced rates of taxation, and other inducements to firms engaged primarily in production for export.

expropriation The taking of private property by a government for public purposes. See also *nationalization*.

Extended Fund Facility A financing facility under which the IMF supports economic programs that generally run for three years and are aimed at overcoming balance-of-payments difficulties resulting from macroeconomic and structural problems.

Extensive growth based on the expansion of the quantity of inputs in order to increase the quantity of outputs, the opposite of intensive growth.

external economy or externality A situation in which the private costs or benefits to the producers or purchasers of a good or service differ from the total social costs or benefits entailed in its production and consumption.

external indebtedness The total amount of money owed by a government to lenders outside the country.

Extraterritoriality the extension of the power of a nation's laws to its citizens abroad, which sometimes impinges upon the national sovereignty of other nations.

factor endowment The original share of the inputs needed to produce other commodities. These inputs or factors of production are broadly classified into land, labor, capital, and entrepreneurship. The availability of these factors of production helps set the price for and determine the supply of commodities produced for domestic use and for international trade.

factors of production Economic resources or inputs that are employed in the process of production. These are usually divided into two main categories: human resources and nonhuman resources. Human resources include two main composites: labor, which includes all human physical and mental talents and efforts employed in producing goods, such as manual labor, managerial and professional skills, etc.; and entrepreneurship or entrepreneurial organization, which encompasses everything that facilitates the organization of the other composite factors for productive purposes, such as innovation, risk taking, and applications analysis. Nonhuman resources include two other composites: land, which includes the entire stock of a nation's natural resources such as territory, mineral deposits, forests, airspace, territorial waters, water power, wind power, and the like; and capital, which includes all man-made aids to production, such as buildings, machinery, and transportation facilities.

fast track authority The congressional delegation of negotiating authority to the president of the United States in the area of reducing tariffs by specific amounts without subsequent congressional approval. The practice, which was begun in 1934 to avoid the pressure of special interest groups for protection, was used during the Tokyo and Uruguay Rounds of the multilateral trade negotiations under the GATT and during the negotiations for NAFTA. The current term is *trade promotion authority*.

Fast-track negotiating authority (also called Trade Promotion Authority, TPA) for trade agreements is the authority of the President of the United States to negotiate agreements that the Congress can approve or disapprove but cannot amend or filibuster.

Federal Reserve The central bank of the United States.

fiscal policies An outgrowth of Keynesian economics, fiscal policies refer to the use of government tax and spending policies to achieve desired macroeconomic goals. Accordingly, they involve discretionary efforts to adjust governmental tax and spending to induce changes in economic incentives and, hence, to stabilize fluctuations in aggregate demand. These discretionary adjustments in the government tax and spending levels are believed to effect desired changes in aggregate demand; to manipulate subsequent levels of employment, disposable income, consumption and economic activity; and to smooth fluctuations in nominal gross national product (GNP). Fiscal policies could be stimulative and expansionary, or contractionary and restrictive. As such, a budget deficit or a tax cut is considered to be stimulative (i.e., providing a fiscal stimulus) because it is believed to generate a rise in national wealth and investment. In contrast, a budget surplus achieved by raising taxes is considered to be contractionary because it is believed to reduce aggregate demand.

fixed exchange rate Fixed exchange rates prevail when governments agree to maintain the value of their currencies at preestablished levels relative to others. This is also known as maintaining *parity*.

floating exchange rate Exchange rates that allow the market to determine the relative value of currencies.

foreign direct investment (FDI) Financial transfers by a multinational corporation from the country of the parent firm to the country of the host firm to finance a portion of its overseas operations. Foreign direct investment occurs when a corporation headquartered in one nation invests in a corporation located in another nation, either by purchasing an existing enterprise or by providing capital to start a new one. In *portfolio investment*, foreign investors purchase the stock or bonds of national corporations but do not control those corporations directly.

Foreign Investment Review Agency (FIRA) An agency established in Canada in 1972 that screened inflows of FDI. It was replaced in 1984 with an agency that promoted inflows of FDI.

fortress Europe The tendency of the European Union to replace national barriers to trade and investment with regional ones. Most Europeans deny that this is the intent of their actions, and the bulk of the evidence favors their viewpoint.

forward linkage A relationship between a firm and a customer of the firm that benefits the customer.

Fourth World The poorer and slower-growing developing countries that became the primary focus of global poverty alleviation efforts. Despite increased growth in the rest of the world, these countries remained dependent on concessional aid flows. Their populations were often burdened by disease, hunger, and other attributes of extreme poverty.

Framework for a New Economic Partnership Negotiations begun in 1993 between the United States and Japan to address macroeconomic, sectoral, and structural measures for reducing the U.S. trade and payments deficits with Japan.

free trade A situation that exists when the international exchange of goods is neither restricted nor encouraged by government-imposed trade barriers. Subsequently, the determination of the distribution and level of international trade is left to the operation of market forces.

Free Trade Area of the Americas (FTAA) A proposed agreement to eliminate or reduce trade barriers among all the countries in the Western Hemisphere.

functioning of the GATT system (FOGS) Negotiations during the Uruguay Round concerning reforms that were intended to strengthen the role of the GATT as an institution.

General Agreement on Tariffs and Trade (GATT) A multilateral treaty entered into in 1948 by the intended members of the International Trade Organization, the purpose of which was to implement many of the rules and negotiated tariff reductions that would be overseen by the ITO. With the failure of the ITO to be approved, the GATT became the principal institution regulating trade policy until it was subsumed within the World Trade Organization in 1995.

General Agreement on Trade in Services (GATS) The agreement negotiated in the Uruguay Round that brings international trade in services into the WTO. It provides for countries to provide national treatment to foreign service providers and for them to select and negotiate the service sectors to be covered under GATS.

General Arrangements to Borrow (GAB) A large fund established in 1961 by the Group of Ten to help manage changes in exchange rates.

Generalized system of preferences (GSP) An arrangement that was introduced and negotiated under the auspices of UNCTAD. According to this agreement, a preferential tariff treatment is granted by industrialized countries to manufactured and semimanufactured products imported from developing countries. This system was designed to increase the export earnings and to promote the economic growth and industrialization of developing countries.

GINI coefficient of inequality a measure of statistical dispersion most prominently used as a measure of inequality of income distribution or inequality of wealth distribution.

glasnost **(openness)** A domestic initiative of political reform introduced by Soviet president Mikhail Gorbachev in the mid-1980s to allow more freedom in public discussion and the arts, and to foster the process of the democratization of the political process.

Glass-Steagall Act of 1933 Legislation enacted by the U.S. Congress in 1933 in response to abuses that allegedly contributed to the Great Depression. It forbade interstate banking and created barriers among different sectors of the financial system—commercial banks, investment banks, and insurance companies.

globalization A dense network of international flows of goods, services, capital, information, ideas, and people that linked most of the world after 1989.

gold standard An international monetary system in which the value of a currency is fixed in terms of gold. A government whose currency is on the gold standard agrees to convert it to gold at a preestablished price. This creates a self-regulating mechanism for adjusting the balance of payments, since disequilibria can be remedied by inflows and outflows of gold.

Gonzalez amendment An amendment to a general appropriations bill for multilateral banks in January 1974 that required the U.S. government to vote against any multilateral bank loan to a nationalizing country.

governance The resolution of collective action problems through the establishment and maintenance of regimes and institutions. Governance can include the actions of both governments and private actors, and it can occur at various levels, from small groups to nation-states to the world system.

Gravity equation An equation that represents a frequently tested hypothesis about the role of the size of economies and distance in determining the level of bilateral trade and investment flows.

Great Depression During the 1930s, a prolonged period of negative or low growth, competitive exchange rate devaluations, competing monetary blocs, and the absence of international cooperation that contributed greatly to the rise of fascism and that eventually led to World War II.

Great Leap Forward A set of policies pursued by the Chinese government under the leadership of Mao Zedong between 1958 and 1960 aimed at accomplishing the economic and technical development of the country at a vastly faster pace and with greater results. It was a colossal failure.

greenfield investment An investment made in a geographic location where there had been no previous facility. This is the opposite of a *brownfield investment*.

gross domestic product (GDP) An estimate of the total money value of all the final goods and services produced in a given one-year period using the factors of production located within a particular country's borders.

gross national product (GNP) The monetary value of a nation's total output of goods and services during a one-year period. Gross national product at factor cost is based on the total earnings of all national factors of production (wages, rent, interest, and profits). Gross national product at market cost is computed by adding total national expenditures on consumption, foreign and domestic investment, and government spending on goods and services.

Group of Three (G-3) The United States, Japan, and Germany.

Group of Five (G-5) The five largest industrial countries: Britain, France, Germany, Japan, and the United States.

Group of Seven (G-7) The seven countries who participate in annual international economic summits: Britain, Canada, France, Germany, Italy, Japan, and the United States. The European Union also sends a representative.

Group of Eight (G-8) The Group of Seven plus Russia. The G-7 became the G-8 in 2002.

Group of Ten (G-10) The ten countries that met in 1961 to create the General Agreements to Borrow (Belgium, Canada, France, Germany, Italy, Japan, the Netherlands, Sweden, the United Kingdom, and the United States).

Group of Seventy-Seven (G-77) A coalition of developing countries within the United Nations, established in 1964 at the end of the first session of UNCTAD, intended to articulate and promote the collective economic interests of its members and enhance their negotiating capacity. Originally with 77 members, as of 2002 it had 133.

hard currencies Freely convertible currencies that can be used to finance international trade, such as those held in national foreign exchange reserves. *Soft currencies* are not freely convertible and are not held as reserve currencies.

Havana Charter The charter for the never-implemented International Trade Organization. The draft was completed at a conference in Havana, Cuba, in 1948.

Heavily Indebted Poor Countries (HIPC) initiative This initiative, adopted in 1996, provides exceptional assistance to eligible countries to reduce their external debt burdens to sustainable levels, thereby enabling them to service their external debt without the need for further debt relief and without compromising growth. It is a comprehensive approach to debt relief that involves multilateral, Paris Club, and other official and bilateral creditors.

Heckscher-Ohlin (H-O) theory of international trade A theory of international trade in which comparative advantage derives from differences in relative factor endowments across countries and differences in relative factor intensities across industries.

hedge fund A fund in which investors hope to benefit financially from investments that "hedge" against downturns in the market by the flexible use of options, puts and calls, futures markets, derivatives, and other, mostly short-term financial instruments.

hegemonial stability theory The theory that international economic regimes and institutions are created by hegemonies (militarily or economically dominant countries) and are weakened when hegemony erodes.

Hickenlooper amendment Legislation passed by the U.S. Congress in 1962 that empowered the government to cut off aid to any country nationalizing U.S. investments without compensation.

home government The government of a country that serves as the headquarters for a multinational corporation.

horizontal FDI Investment that replicates home country activities of a multinational corporation in host countries in order to gain access to overseas markets.

Host firm

household responsibility system A system implemented in China in the late 1970s that contracted work to individuals and families in the agricultural sector and gave them more power to manage their own production and sales. This marked the beginning of major economic reforms in post-Mao China.

human capital formation Investment in education and research that results in an improvement in human skills and knowledge.

hyperinflation A rapidly accelerating rate of inflation that is perilous to a country's economy because it undermines the ability of its currency to perform its traditional functions (i.e., standard of value, store of value, and reliable medium of exchange) and occasions a shift in the utilization of the nation's resources from productive efforts toward speculation. Hyperinflation could cause a high exponential rise in prices in as short a period as a single month.

import-substituting industrialization (ISI) An inward-looking development strategy designed to reduce imports by setting up domestic industries behind protective walls to produce previously imported products. The strategy involves the adoption of protectionist trade policies (import tariffs, quantitative controls, multiple exchange rates, and so forth) to allow "infant" industries to develop and grow, and the encouragement of the inward flow of foreign direct investment, especially in manufacturing. Once the infant stage is completed, protection can be removed and free trade resumed. Typically, ISI starts with the production of consumer goods in the hope of moving to intermediate goods and then to capital goods in the future. In most cases, the strategy fails to generate capital savings sufficient to finance the transition from producing one type of goods to another. The reason is that substitution in the area of consumer durables usually leads to the expansion of imports in the areas of intermediate and capital goods needed for the production of the consumer goods. ISI also tends to create industries that are not internationally competitive while at the same time weakening traditional exports.

import substitution See *import-substituting industrialization.*

industrial policies Policies designed to promote the development of new or existing industries. They are sometimes referred to as supply-side policies to differentiate them from demand-side policies such as those included in the category of fiscal policies.

inelastic demand Demand that does not vary with changes in price. Often used in connection with the short-term demand for key resources like petroleum.

infant industry An industry in its early stages of development, unable to withstand competition from overseas competitors. To guarantee the success and growth of such an industry, most analysts argue that tariffs, import quotas, and other barriers to international trade need to be imposed to provide the industry with protection from international competition and to allow it to achieve cost competitiveness by exploiting economies of scale and employing new, productivity-enhancing technologies. The industry is believed to grow out of the infantile stage when it is able to compete with foreign competitors in a system of free trade.

inflation A persistent upward movement in the general price of goods and services that ordinarily results in a decline of the purchasing power of a nation's currency. Inflation resulting from government action to stimulate the economy is known as *reflation*. *Disinflation* is a downward movement of wages and prices that erases the effects of a previous round of price increases. Price inflation is most likely to set in under one (or a combination) of the following conditions: (1) an increase in demand at a time when supply of labor is tight and industrial capacity is fully utilized; (2) a lack of congruence between increases in wage rates and increases in productivity; (3) a sharp decline in the sources of supply; or (4) a rise in the money supply that is faster than increases in output.

infrastructure The communication networks, transportation systems, and public services needed to conduct business. These are often considered to be public or collective goods because individuals and firms will not supply them in adequate quantities and because they are, as a result, at least partly financed with public funds

and therefore are often subject to government regulation. Social infrastructure refers to human services such as education and health care that affect the quality of the workforce.

intellectual property Property rights granted to creators of inventions or ideas embodied in products or production technologies for the purpose of promoting creativity in the arts and innovation in the economy. Legally sanctioned intellectual property rights include patents, copyrights, trademarks, and semiconductor chip designs. These property rights generally grant their holders a temporary monopoly for the sale of the right to use the item in question, allowing them to fix whatever price they deem adequate compensation for their creative efforts.

Intensive growth the adoption of new production techniques that result in increased output without necessarily requiring increased inputs, the opposite of extensive growth.

Inter-American Development Bank A regional development bank for Latin America.

Inter-industry trade Trade that occurs across industries, generally involving different types of goods.

Intra-industry trade Trade that occurs within industries, involving similar types of goods (e.g. the exchange of different brands of automobiles).

interdependence A relationship of mutual dependence characterized by mutual sensitivity and mutual vulnerability on the part of all the parties involved. As such, managing interdependence requires the coordination of national economic policies and the observance of some international discipline in the formulation of policies that have always been the prerogative of national governments. Economic interdependence has led to the growing convergence of the economies of developed countries. The rapid accumulation of physical and human capital, the transfer of technology, and the growing similarities of wages have narrowed the differences in factor endowments, which are the basis for comparative advantage and trade.

interest rate The cost of money that fluctuates (rises and falls) in correspondence with changes in the demand for and supply of money. Moreover, the interest rate varies over the length of a loan or deposit as well as the type of financial instrument.

intergovernmental organization An organization whose members are national governments and whose participants and decision makers are official representatives of those governments.

intermediate inputs Goods, like steel, that are used to produce finished products or final goods, like automobiles. The value of intermediate inputs is not counted directly in calculating gross national product (GNP). Demand for these inputs (derived demand) is related to demand for the final goods they help to produce.

internalization theory A theory explaining why firms may prefer foreign direct investment to alternative ways of doing business, like exporting and licensing. The ownership location and internalization theory (OLI) contends that firms expand abroad in order to internalize activities in the presence of transaction costs arising from market imperfections just as they expand domestically for similar reasons. Since it is generally less expensive for local firms to conduct business activities in their home markets than for foreign firms, the extra costs connected with doing business abroad must be offset by advantages that a particular foreign firm may have (such as managerial or marketing techniques or new production processes). Because knowledge is a public good, a firm's profits from developing that knowledge cannot be optimized if the firm resorts to such open market practices as exporting or licensing. Consequently, the firm internalizes the market by setting up a foreign subsidiary that can ensure maximum control over the use of that knowledge.

International Bank for Reconstruction and Development (IBRD) A public international organization created by the Bretton Woods agreement to facilitate the postwar economic recovery. With capital provided by member states, the IBRD sought to achieve its objectives by extending loans at market rates to cover foreign exchange needs of borrowing countries, thus making possible a speedy postwar recovery and promoting economic development. Currently, the IBRD is the world's foremost intergovernmental organization involved in the external financing of projects aimed at fostering the economic growth of developing countries. The IBRD is better known as the World Bank.

International Center for the Settlement of Investment Disputes (ICSID) One of the five institutions that comprise the World Bank group, the ICSID provides facilities for the settlement—by conciliation or arbitration—of investment disputes between foreign investors and their host countries.

international commodity agreements (ICAs) Accords between producers and consumers aimed at stabilizing or increasing the price of particular products. ICAs may be of three types or combinations thereof: buffer-stock schemes, whereby price is managed by purchases or sales from a central fund at times of excessive fluctuation; export quotas, whereby price is managed by assigning production quotas to participating countries in order to control supply; and multilateral contracts, whereby the importing countries sign contracts committing them to buy certain quantities at a specified low price when the world market falls below that price and the exporting countries agree to sell certain quantities at a fixed price when the world market price exceeds the maximum.

International Development Association (IDA) One of the five institutions that comprise the World Bank group, the IDA provides interest-free loans and other services to the poorest countries.

international division of labor The international distribution of production that results from specialization.
See also *comparative advantage*.

international economic regime Rules, norms, procedures, and institutions that are intended to achieve common economic goals by constraining the behavior of governments.

International Energy Agency (IEA) a Paris-based intergovernmental organization founded by the Organisation for Economic Co-operation and Development (OECD) in 1974 in the wake of the oil crisis.

International Finance Corporation (IFC) One of the five institutions that comprise the World Bank group, the IFC promotes growth in the developing world by financing private-sector investments and providing technical assistance and advice to governments and businesses.

International Fund for Agricultural Development (IFAD) A fund for the poorest developing countries set up in 1977 mainly by OECD and OPEC countries in the wake of the oil price increases of the 1970s.

International Monetary Fund (IMF) A public international organization created by the Bretton Woods agreement in 1944 as the main instrument of international monetary management. The IMF helps countries with payments deficits by advancing credits to them. Originally, its approval was made necessary for any change in exchange rates. It advises countries on policies affecting the monetary system. The IMF is provided with a fund composed of member countries' contributions in gold and in their own currencies. The system of weighted voting allows the United States to exert a preponderant influence in this body.

International Trade Commission A quasi-judicial system established by the U.S. Congress that manages trade grievances of domestic interest groups.

International Trade Organization (ITO) Conceived as a complement to the Bretton Woods institutions—the IMF and World Bank—the ITO was to provide international discipline in the uses of trade policies. The Havana Charter for the ITO was not approved by the U.S. Congress, however, and the initiative died, replaced by the continuing and growing importance of the GATT.

intervention An action taken on the part of one or more central banks in order to influence exchange rates. Since the move to a system of floating rates, the Group of Five (the United States, Japan, France, Germany, and Britain) has attempted to coordinate intervention in currency markets, usually by buying and selling currency, to achieve target rates.

intrafirm trade International trade that occurs between subsidiaries of the same corporation.

intra-industry trade Trade that occurs across national boundaries but within the same industry. For example, when country X sell auto parts to country Y and country Y sells auto parts to country X. This type of trade is not well explained by the Heckscher-Ohlin theory.

invisible hand doctrine Coined by Adam Smith in his pioneering book, *Inquiry into the Nature and Causes of the Wealth of Nations* (1776), the term is used as a rationale for laissez-faire as the best economic policy. The doctrine argues that individuals, in their quest to advance their self-interests, are led, as if by an invisible hand, to achieve the best good for all. Accordingly, government intervention in the economy would distort the automatic, self-adjusting nature of economic life. Competition among individuals inspired by their selfish motives will automatically further the best interests of society as a whole.

isolationism A foreign policy doctrine that calls for the curtailment of a nation's international relations and the avoidance of

entangling alliances. Isolationism constituted a key plank in the U.S. foreign
policy approach, with a few short periods
of aberration, between the Revolutionary
War and World War II. This foreign
policy of nonentanglement was made
possible mainly by the geopolitical
detachment of the United States. The
ratification of the United Nations Charter
by the Congress in 1945, which inaugurated an era of internationalism in U.S.
foreign policy, brought to an effective end
the era of isolationism in which the United
States avoided incurring any binding
political obligations to other nations. In
fact, modern trade, communication
technologies, and military weapons make
isolationism a virtual impossibility for any
nation in our time.

Jackson–Vanik amendment An
amendment to the 1974 Trade Act that
denied most favored nation status to the
Soviet Union (and other Soviet bloc
nations) because of its restriction of
emigration rights.

J-curve effect When the impact of a
currency devaluation is initially an increase
in the trade deficit as the cost of goods
already contracted for import rises, but
later, the deficit decreases as demand for
imports decreases and demand for exports
increases.

joint venture A business enterprise that
is partly owned by two or more parent firms.
For example, a 50-50 joint venture involving
IBM and Toshiba would be owned in equal
proportions by the two firms.

keiretsu Japanese business confederations
composed of allied financial and industrial
companies. As part of their *keiretsu*
obligations, Japanese companies usually
hold each other's stocks. The *keiretsu*
system can be an effective barrier to
foreign investment by making it difficult
for a foreign firm to acquire a firm that is a
member of a *keiretsu*.

Keynesianism A school of economics
inspired by the theoretical contributions of
John Maynard Keynes (1883–1946), an
English economist. Keynes argued that
government spending and investment
function as means of disbursing purchasing
power into the economy and, hence, affect
the demand for consumer goods in the
same way as private investment. He
suggested increasing government expenditures during deflationary periods and
decreasing them during inflationary
periods as a means of manipulating
aggregate spending and income. By
prescribing governmental intervention to
maintain adequate levels of employment,
Keynesianism paved the way for the
growth of the welfare state in the wake of
the Great Depression.

land use rights During the period of
economic reforms in China, instead of
granting full property rights in the form of
private land ownership, the Chinese
government offered land use rights that
were temporary and could be withdrawn
at any time.

learning curve A graph that represents
the learning of an actor over time. A
learning curve with an initially steep slope
implies that learning must occur quickly
and often at high cost. A shallow learning
curve implies that learning can be slower
and more gradual.

leveraged buy-out (LBO) A method
for converting a publicly traded firm into
a privately held firm by purchasing a
controlling interest in the firm.

liberalism A school of economics that
relies primarily on a free market with
the minimum of barriers to the flow of
private trade and capital. Underdevelopment
in the Third World, according to this
school, stems from certain domestic
economic policies of the developing
country, which tend to accentuate market
imperfections; reduce productivity of
land, labor, and capital; and intensify
social and political rigidities. The adoption
of market-oriented domestic policies is
the optimal way to remedy these weaknesses.

licensing A firm's granting the right of other firms to employ its intellectual property (e.g., patents, copyrights, and trademarks) in exchange for a fee.

liquidity The availability of sufficient amounts of currency or of some highly valued substance (like gold) sufficient to allow countries engaged in international exchanges to settle their accounts.

loans-for-shares program Under this program established in 1995, the Russian government auctioned share-backed securities to Russian banks and other institutions. In return for these loans, the banks were to receive an immediate voice in management and a commitment to receive equity shares of the companies three years down the road when the value of the shares was expected to have increased dramatically. The program was strongly criticized for giving too much power to the banks.

locomotive theory An economic theory calling for a coordination of national economic policies and advocating that countries with payments surpluses follow expansionary policies that would serve as engines of growth for the rest of the world. This theory was adopted by the Carter administration in the late 1970s as the basis of the U.S. strategy for global economic growth.

Lomé Convention An agreement originally signed in 1975 committing the EU to programs of assistance and preferential treatment for the ACP countries. The Lomé Convention was replaced by the Cotonou Agreement in June 2000.

London Club An informal group of commercial banks and other private lenders that seek to coordinate the rescheduling of sovereign loans owed to members.

Long-term Textile Arrangement Established in 1962 as a way of resolving a series of trade conflicts over cotton exports from Japan, it was replaced in 1974 with the Multi-Fiber Arrangement.

Lorenz curve a graphical representation of the cumulative distribution function of a probability distribution; it is a graph showing the proportion of the distribution assumed by the bottom $y\%$ of the values.

Louvre agreement Agreement negotiated in 1987 in Paris, in which government officials announced to the world that exchange rates had come into the proper relationship and that they would oppose further substantial shifts and would cooperate to stabilize exchange rates at prevailing levels.

Maastricht Treaty on European Unity The 1991 treaty among members of the EU to work toward a monetary union, or common currency. This ultimately resulted in adoption of the euro in 1999.

macroeconomics The branch of economics that analyzes patterns of change in aggregate economic indicators such as national product, the money supply, and the balance of payments. Governments attempt to influence these indicators by implementing macroeconomic policies.

managed trade Managed trade regimes arise when industrialized countries adopt industrial policies domestically—forms of government intervention designed to shift comparative advantages within countries toward high value-added and/or high technology production—and then attempt to modify existing international trade regimes to prevent the use of such industrial policies from becoming a new form of protectionism. An example of this is the U.S.-Japanese Semiconductor Trade Agreement of 1986.

Market Access Group (MAG) A group within Asia Pacific Economic Cooperation that focuses on market access issues.

market forces The dynamic occurring when competition among firms determines the outcome in a given situation, and a supply-and-demand equilibrium is reached without government intervention.

Market Opening Sector Selective (MOSS) talks Talks between the United States and Japan in the 1980s that dealt with removing Japanese barriers to trade and investment in specific industries. An agreement on this was signed in 1986.

Marshall Plan (European Recovery Program) An American program of grants and loans instituted to assist the recovery of Western Europe after World War II. The program had two main objectives: to prevent the occurrence of a collapse in the international economic system similar to the one that occurred during the interwar period and to prevent the formation of communist systems in Western Europe. It eventually became the tool of U.S. leadership in Europe as it allowed the United States to play a key role in financing international trade, encouraging European trade competitiveness, and fostering regional trade liberalization in Europe.

Marxism (and neo-Marxism) A school of thought inspired by the theoretical and philosophical formulations of Karl Marx. The fundamental component of the economic dimension of Marxism is predicated on the surplus value theory. Marx argued that under a capitalist system the value of commodities depends on the labor that is put into producing them. However, workers are paid only a small proportion of that value, sufficient to enable them to pay only for the goods necessary to maintain their average consumption. The difference between the actual value of the labor exerted by the workers and the wages that they receive is the surplus value, which is the source of all profits, rent, and interest income that goes to the owners of capital. The system inevitably produces poverty by under-paying workers and overpaying capitalists. The capitalist system also is vulnerable to periodic economic depressions and unemployment, which exacerbate poverty. Marxism and neo-Marxism also maintain that the imperialist drive to dominate and exploit Third World countries is intrinsic to capitalism. Accordingly, the theory argues that Third World countries are poor and exploited because of their history as subordinate elements in the world capitalist system. This condition will persist as long as they remain part of that system. As such, the only appropriate strategy for Third World development is revolutionary: the obliteration of the world capitalist system and its replacement with an international socialist system.

mercantilism A theory originating in the seventeenth century, when certain trading states made it their goal to accumulate national economic wealth and, in turn, national power by expanding exports and limiting imports. Some analysts and policy-makers have charged that countries pursuing protectionist trade policies in the twentieth and twenty-first centuries are following a similar strategy, which they termed *neomercantilism*.

Mercosur A common market among Argentina, Brazil, Paraguay, and Uruguay, known as the "Common Market of the South" ("Mercado Comun del Sur"). It was created by the Treaty of Asunción on March 26, 1991, and added Chile and Bolivia as associate members in 1996 and 1997, respectively.

microeconomics The branch of economics that analyzes the market behavior of individual consumers and firms. The interaction of these individual decision makers creates patterns of supply and demand that fix the prices of goods and factors of production and determine how resources will be allocated among competing uses.

Millennium Development Goals (MDGs) Eight goals for economic development adopted in 2000 at the United Nations Millennium Summit. They reflected a new and fuller approach to poverty alleviation at the global level.

monetary policies (monetarism)
Policies designed to manage the size of the nation's money supply in a manner that fosters investment and economic growth. These policies are usually inspired by the monetarist theory, which attributes economic instability to disturbances in the monetary sector. Monetary policies, therefore, attempt to influence variables like the balance of payments, currency exchange rates, inflation, and employment by increasing or decreasing interest rates and controlling the money supply.

monopoly A market structure with only a single seller of a commodity or service dealing with a large number of buyers, which results in closing entry into the industry to potential competitors. Consequently, due to the absence of a competitive supply of goods on the market, the seller usually has complete control over the quantity of goods released into the market and the ability to set the price at which they are sold. This results in a lower level of production and a higher price than would occur under more competitive market conditions.

monopsony A market structure with only a single buyer of a product who is able, therefore, to set the buying price. The classic examples include the demand for labor in a one-company town and the purchase of all output from certain mines by a large manufacturer.

moral hazard The risk that a contract will change the behavior of one or both parties. If one party covers the other for all of its mistakes, then the second party will likely assume more risk than is optimal for both.

most-favored nation (MFN) principle The GATT and WTO principle stipulating that "any advantage, favor, privilege, or immunity granted by any contracting party to any product originating in or destined for any other country shall be accorded immediately and unconditionally to the like product originating in or destined for the territories of all other contracting parties." This principle is a guarantee of nondiscrimination or equal treatment in trade relations.

Multi-Fiber Arrangement (MFA) An agreement among developed country importers and developing country exporters of textiles and apparel to regulate and restrict the quantities traded. It was negotiated in 1973 under GATT auspices as a temporary exception to the rules that would otherwise apply, and was superseded in 1995 by the Agreement on Textiles and Clothing.

Multilateral Agreement on Investment (MAI) An agreement to liberalize rules on international direct investment that was negotiated in the OECD but never completed or adopted because of adverse public reaction to it. Preliminary text of the agreement was leaked to the Internet in April 1997, where many groups opposed it. Negotiations were discontinued in November 1998.

Multilateral Debt Relief Initiative (MDRI) An expansion of the preexisting HIPC program established by the G-8 in 2005.

Multilateral Investment Guarantee Agency (MIGA) One of the five institutions that comprise the World Bank group, MIGA helps encourage foreign investment in developing countries.

multilateral trade negotiation This is the principal method of reducing tariffs and nontariff barriers under the GATT and the WTO, also called a "trade round." The GATT and the WTO are authorized to convene periodic negotiations for this purpose.

multinational corporation (MNC) A business enterprise that retains direct investments overseas and that maintains value-added holdings in more than one country. A firm is not really multinational if it just engages in overseas trade or serves as a contractor to foreign firms. A multinational firm sends abroad a package of capital, technology, managerial talent, and marketing skills to carry out production in foreign countries.

national champion A firm that is protected and promoted by a specific national government. An example is the efforts of the French government to promote the growth of France Telecom.

nationalization The seizure of a firm by a national government that results in its becoming a state-owned enterprise. Nationalization is not illegal under international law if compensation to the original owner is prompt and adequate.

national treatment A GATT rule designed to prevent discrimination against foreign products after they enter a country. It requires countries to give imports the same treatment as they give products made domestically in such areas as taxation, regulation, transportation, and distribution. It also requires them to treat foreign-owned enterprises no less favorably than domestically owned ones.

Neo-liberalism a term referring to a reemergence and redefinition of classical liberalism and often stressing the need for deregulation of the economy and reduced trade barriers.

New Arrangements to Borrow (NAB) Arrangements, which became effective in 1998, under which twenty-five member countries or their financial institutions stand ready to lend to the IMF under circumstances similar to those covered by the *General Arrangements to Borrow* (GAB). These new loan funds were made available by a decision of the IMF executive board in the wake of the Mexican peso crisis for countries with short-term adjustment problems.

New International Economic Order (NIEO) The view advocated by the less-developed and developing countries mainly in the 1970s that argued that the open monetary, trade, and financial system perpetuated their underdevelopment and subordination to the developed countries. These countries called for the dismantling of the Western-dominated international economic order and its replacement with a new international economic regime that would better serve the interests of Third World countries. These countries also sought a North-South dialogue on issues ranging from transfer of technology and capital, to redistribution of global economic benefits, to rapid economic development in the South.

Newly independent states (NIS) the 15 independent nations that split off from the Union of Soviet Socialist Republics after its breakup in December 1991.

newly industrializing countries (NICs) Countries that have a high level of economic growth and export expansion, outpacing the less-developed countries but not as industrialized as the developed countries. Middle-income countries like Mexico, Brazil, and Portugal are considered NICs, as are the Asian tigers (Hong Kong, Singapore, South Korea, and Taiwan). Government policies played a central role in the initial stages of industrialization in the NICs. Targeted industries were promoted through import protection, tax incentives, and subsidies.

nomenklatura A communist institution that was designed to preserve the dominant role of the communist party by giving out responsible positions to those loyal to the regime. Started by Joseph Stalin, *nomenklatura* included a list of positions in all levels of government and society that the government or the communist party controlled. It was used as a reward system to attract people to the communist party and to maintain party discipline.

nonconcessional loans Loans offered on terms set by the market, so that interest rates and payment schedules are determined by the relative supply of investment funds; also called "hard loans." *Concessional loans*, or "soft loans," are offered on terms more generous than those prevailing in the market.

nongovernmental organization (NGO) An organized actor in domestic or international politics that is not a government: for example, a labor organization, environmental group, political party, or private firm.

nontariff barriers (NTBs) These are measures designed to discriminate against imports, without levying taxes directly on merchandise, or to offer assistance to exports and thus have trade-distorting consequences. These measures include quotas, by which a government determines the amount of a commodity that can be imported, procurement policies, customs procedures, agricultural policies, health and sanitary regulations, national consumer and environmental standards, *voluntary restraint agreements* (VRAs), and a broad range of other laws and regulations that insulate the domestic economy from international competition. The success of the GATT in removing quotas and tariffs had the unintended consequence of the emergence of "the new protectionism" through an increase in the use of nontariff barriers. Unlike the regulation and removal of quotas and tariffs, NTBs do not lend themselves easily to international control. They are usually an integral part of national economic and social policies and, as such, are considered national prerogatives beyond the scope of international regulation.

North American Free Trade Area (NAFTA) The agreement to form a free trade area among the United States, Canada, and Mexico that went into effect January 1, 1994.

North Atlantic Treaty Organization (NATO) An alliance of Western nations formed by the United States and other nations after the emergence of the Cold War and in opposition to the Soviet-led Warsaw Pact.

obsolescing bargain theory A theory advanced to explain the dynamics of the activities of multinational corporations. The theory contends that the firm's initial good bargaining position, stemming from such advantages as superior technology vis-à-vis the host country's government,

encourages it to invest in foreign countries. However, once the firm has made an investment, the bargaining advantage may slowly shift to the host country. The host country will then attempt to negotiate more favorable terms with the foreign investor. This happens because the technology may mature and become more easily accessible to the host country's firms, and the host country may learn how to gain better access to global capital and final product markets.

offshoring The relocation of some business activities overseas.

OLI model OLI is a theory pioneered by John Dunning about the foreign direct investment where O stands for ownership, L for location, and I for internalization.

Oligopolistic structure a market form in which a market or industry is dominated by a small number of sellers (oligopolists).

oligopoly A market structure in which a few companies dominate an industry. This concentration often leads to collusion among manufacturers, so that prices are set by agreement rather than by the operation of the supply and demand mechanism. For an oligopoly to exist, the few companies do not need to control all the production or sales of a particular commodity or service. They only need to control a significant share of the total production or sales. As in a monopoly, an oligopoly can persist only if there are significant barriers to entry to new competitors. Obviously, the presence of relatively few firms in an industry does not negate the existence of competition. The existing few firms may still act independently even while they collude on prices. In an oligopolistic market, competition often takes the form of increased spending on marketing and advertising to win brand loyalty rather than reducing prices or increasing the quality of products.

oligopoly rents Economic rents that accrue to members of an oligopoly. Oligopoly rents are similar to monopoly rents but generally lower because the limited competition within an oligopoly makes it impossible for firms to agree on how to restrict overall supply.

oligopoly theory A theory proposed to explain the genesis of multinational investments. The theory argues that firms are prompted to move abroad by their desire to exploit the market power they possess through control over such factors as unique products, marketing expertise, control of technology and managerial skills, or access to capital. The oligopolistic competition for global market shares makes firms match each other's moves in entering new foreign markets.

Organization of Arab Petroleum Exporting Countries (OAPEC) The Arab members of the *Organization of Petroleum Exporting Countries.*

Organization of Petroleum Exporting Countries (OPEC) A group of countries that includes many, but not all, of the largest exporters of oil. The purpose of OPEC is to regulate the supply of petroleum and thereby stabilize (often by raising) its price. See also *cartel.*

ostpolitik A German policy of cooperating with the Soviet Union and Eastern Europe that began under Chancellor Willy Brandt. This policy helped to bring about the détente between the United States and the Soviet Union in the 1970s.

outsourcing The use of contractors to perform some of the tasks originally done inside a firm.

Overseas Private Investment Corporation (OPIC) A fund created by the U.S. government in 1961 to insure U.S. firms against some of the risks involved in foreign direct investment.

parent country The home country of a multinational corporation with subsidiaries in other countries.

parent firm The headquarters of a corporation that owns a subsidiary or joint venture elsewhere.

Paris Club An informal group of governments whose role is to find coordinated and sustainable solutions to the payment difficulties experienced by debtor nations.

parity The central value of a given currency relative to the currency to which it is fixed or pegged.

patent A type of intellectual property right in which an inventor is guaranteed the right of a temporary monopoly in exploiting his or her invention. Patents are granted to create an incentive for innovation. See also *copyright, licensing, and trademark.*

perestroika **(restructuring)** An economic initiative launched by Soviet president Mikhail Gorbachev in the mid-1980s in an attempt to move the Soviet economy in the market direction and to open up trade, finance, and investment relations with the West. The initiative envisioned the decentralization of industrial decision making from central planners to individual firms; the creation of financial markets to determine capital flows; the scrapping of the system of centralized supply and replacing it with a wholesale distribution system; and the improvement of trade and financial interactions with the West. Because *perestroika* was implemented in a halting and ultimately unsuccessful manner, it had the unintended consequence of hastening the decline of the Soviet economy and ultimately helped bring about the breakup of the Soviet empire.

performance requirements Requirements imposed by governments on foreign subsidiaries of multinational corporations that include, among others, minimum levels of exports, minimum levels of employment of national citizens, and limits on profit repatriation. MNCs generally oppose these requirements.

piracy The seizure of private property without compensation for private gain. Traditionally, piracy referred to the seizure of cargos on the high seas by colorful ocean-going robbers, but increasingly the term is used to refer to the seizure of intellectual property in the form of illegal copying of artworks and copyrighted entertainment products and software.

Plaza agreement Agreement negotiated in 1985 at the Plaza Hotel in New York, in which the United States pledged to narrow its budget deficit by reducing spending, and the other participants agreed to pursue economic policies that would help ease the imbalances in the world economy and promote healthy growth with low inflation.

population control Policies to reduce the rate of growth of population.

portfolio investment Investment that does not involve direct control over the management of a firm. Portfolio investment is arbitrarily defined as ownership of less than 10 percent of the outstanding equity of a firm.

posted price The official price of oil used to calculate the taxes paid by the oil companies to host-country governments.

Poverty Reduction Strategy Paper (PSRP) A document prepared by potential participants in the HIPC program to demonstrate how they would use the funds made available by debt relief to reduce poverty.

predatory pricing The practice of allowing the prices of goods produced by a firm to decline to unprofitable levels in order to underprice other firms and, in turn, increase the firm's market share or drive its competitors completely out of the market. This unfair practice is usually characteristic of a large multiproduct or multimarket firm that can offset its losses in one product or market with profits made from other products or in other markets.

price supports A form of government subsidy for the production of commodities. The market price of certain goods is fixed at a level that guarantees the producer an adequate return on investment. That price is not determined by the free interaction of supply and

demand but rather by government regulators, and often the government purchases surpluses that remain unsold at an artificially high fixed price. See also *subsidies*.

primary products Unprocessed or partially processed goods, often used to produce other goods. These products include agricultural commodities such as grain and vegetables, and raw materials such as iron ore and crude petroleum.

principal supplier procedure A GATT negotiating rule that requires negotiations to take place among actual or potential "principal suppliers," which are defined as nations accounting for 10 percent or more of a given product in world trade.

private equity Shares of businesses that are not publicly traded on a stock exchange.

private equity fund A fund that invests in exchange for private equity ownership: for example, a fund that provides start-up capital for new ventures or invests in leveraged buy-outs.

privatization The selling of state-owned enterprises to private owners.

privatization vouchers The distribution of vouchers representing partial ownership of a state-owned enterprise to citizens of a country for the purpose of compensating them for forced savings.

producer cartel A cartel of producers. See also *cartel and Organization of Petroleum Exporting Countries (OPEC)*.

product cycle theory A theory advanced to explain the tendency of multinational companies to move from exporting to undertaking foreign direct investments in overseas production to service foreign demand. The theory argues that firms invest abroad when their main products become "mature" in domestic markets. As the initial high-growth stage of domestic product commercialization ends and the domestic market becomes saturated (growth in demand slows down and new competitors arise), the firm begins to look for new sources of demand abroad in order to maintain its growth. This is achieved by establishing foreign subsidiaries with lower costs so that the firm can remain competitive in its home market while also improving its access to foreign markets.

productivity The amount of product created by one unit of a given factor of production over a stated period of time. Productivity expresses the marginal relationship of inputs to outputs and measures the economic efficiency of production. Productivity indicators ordinarily relate output to a single factor of production, creating measures like *labor productivity*, *capital productivity*, and *land productivity*. Measures of *multifactor productivity*, in contrast, combine productivity indicators for multiple factors of production (labor and capital, for example) to produce a single overall measure of productivity growth.

productivity growth Change over time in productivity. See *productivity*.

Profit and capital repatriation The return to the home country of profits derived from foreign investment.

protectionism The use of import tariffs, import licenses, quota restrictions on imports, and other nontariff barriers to protect local industry from competition with imported goods and services.

quad Multilateral negotiating group consisting of the United States, Japan, the European Union, and Canada.

quantitative restriction See *quota*.

quota A quantitative restriction on imports of a particular product.

race to the bottom Allegedly a consequence of globalization, the general tendency of firms and therefore of governments to seek the lowest level of government restriction on their activities. According to proponents of this view, globalization will lead to very low rates of taxation, lax enforcement of laws protecting the environment, lax labor

standards, and a general retreat from welfare state policies.

recession A short-term decline in national business activity, usually lasting for at least three consecutive quarters of a fiscal year. Recessions are characterized by rising unemployment rates and falling rates of production, capital investment, and economic growth, but these declines are not as severe nor as persistent as those that occur during depressions.

reciprocity The practice of offering trade concessions, such as tariff reductions, by one country in return for similar concessions by other countries. Reciprocal agreements help countries to avoid any likely balance-of-payment deficits inherent in unilateral tariff reductions. These agreements also have the advantage of being politically feasible, because the trade concessions can be billed by the government as being more advantageous to its country's interests than to those of the other country.

regional integration The reduction of barriers to trade and investment within a group of countries that occupy the same international region. Regional integration can take on various forms, such as free trade areas and common markets.

rent Earnings that can accrue to a unique factor of production in excess of the amount that that factor could earn in its next best alternative employment. An example of this is a trained doctor who can earn $100,000 per year. If he could not earn his living practicing medicine, his next best alternative career, for example nursing, would earn him $24,000 per year. His economic rent, therefore, is $76,000.

repatriation of profits The transfer of profits of a multinational corporation from one country to another, usually from a host country to the home country.

research and development (R&D) The systematic or organized efforts aimed at the formation or advancement of knowledge and the application of that knowledge to the development of new products and production processes as well as to the improvement and refinement of existing products and production processes. R&D encompasses activities that can be divided into three groupings: basic research, applied research, and development. *Basic research* refers to efforts aimed at expanding knowledge in the sciences, both natural and social. *Applied research* aims at the formulation of engineering concepts and methods as well as the invention of machines and techniques that can be used as inputs in the process of production. *Development* is the process of refining and perfecting a new kind of product or activity to facilitate its mass production or commercialization. Usually, both governmental and private (business as well as nonprofit) institutions share the responsibility of undertaking basic research.

reserve currency Currencies held by governments and institutions outside the country of issue that are used to finance international economic transactions, including trade and the payment of debts. Stable, easily convertible currencies issued by major trading nations like the United States, Germany, and Japan are generally included in national reserves.

revaluation A change in the official rate at which one currency is exchanged for another or for gold. *Devaluation* reduces the relative value of the currency and creates a mechanism for adjusting balance-of-payments deficits, because it lowers the price of exports abroad and raises the price of imports at home. This mechanism will not function during periods of competitive devaluation when the devaluation of one currency causes other nations to follow suit.

right of establishment The right of foreign citizens or companies to undertake and perform economic activities necessary to conduct business under the same conditions that apply to domestic citizens or companies.

safeguards Emergency restrictions on fairly traded imports that the GATT or WTO permitted governments to impose if an unforeseen surge in imports caused or threatened serious injury to a domestic industry.

screwdriver factory A factory where the workers simply assemble products from parts or subassemblies. Critics of foreign direct investment often accuse multinational corporations of setting up such plants instead of investing in research and development and more complex manufacturing activities.

Secondary debt markets Markets that permit creditors (holders of debt) to sell that debt to others.

seller's market A market that favors sellers, usually because demand exceeds supply. The opposite of a *buyer's market*.

services Economic activities that are intangible, such as banking, tourism, insurance, and accounting, in contrast to goods that are tangible, such as automobiles and wheat. Services account for an ever-increasing part of the trade of industrialized countries.

seven sisters Seven oil companies that used to dominate the production and distribution of oil worldwide: Exxon, Mobil, Gulf, Socal, Texaco, Shell, and British Petroleum.

Shanghai Communiqué The first of three joint U.S.-China communiqués issued in 1972 in which the United States established its "one China" policy by acknowledging that "all Chinese on either side of the Taiwan Strait maintain there is but one China and that Taiwan is a part of China."

Short-term credits Loans that are made that must be repaid within a relatively short period of time.

Single European Act (SEA) Signed in Luxembourg and the Hague in 1986, it came into force on July 1, 1987, committing the members of the European Union to more thorough forms of economic integration, including the creation of a "single market."

Smoot-Hawley Tariff Act Legislation passed by the U.S. Congress in 1930 that raised tariffs on many items. This legislation may have deepened and accelerated the effects of the Great Depression.

socialism An economic and political system in which private property is abolished and the means of production (i.e., capital and land) are collectively owned and operated by the community as a whole in order to advance the interests of all. In Marxist ideology, socialism is considered an intermediate stage in the inevitable transformation of capitalism into communism. A socialist society is envisioned as being characterized by the dictatorship of the proletariat; the existence of a high degree of cooperation and equality; and the absence of discrimination, poverty, exploitation, and war. With the nonexistence of private ownership, the private profit motive is eliminated from economic life. Consequently, market forces do not play a role in organizing the process of production. Instead, large-scale government planning is employed to ensure the harmonious operation of the process of production.

South-South trade and investment Trade and investment that flows from one developing country to another.

sovereignty The principle that the state exercises absolute power over its territory, system of government, and population. Accordingly, the internal authority of the state supersedes that of all other bodies, both inside and outside its territories, and the state emerges as the ultimate arbiter of its grievances vis-à-vis others. Theoretically, sovereignty preserves the territorial inviolability of the state and its independence from outside authorities. In practice, the sovereignty of smaller and weaker states is limited and even the larger and stronger states confront a world in which various forms of interdependence, economic and otherwise, diminish their

claims to a territorial monopoly of control. In addition, international law and international regimes (like the GATT) limit the exercise of sovereignty by those states that recognize their utility. This does not prevent governments from cherishing the idea of national sovereignty, however.

sovereign wealth fund (SWF) A state-owned fund composed of financial assets such as stocks, bonds, property, and other financial instruments (including derivatives).

special drawing rights (SDRs) Artificial international reserve units created by the IMF in 1968 that can be used to settle accounts among central banks.

special economic zone (SEZ) The Chinese version of an *export processing zone*.

speculative attack In any asset market, the surge in sales of the asset that occurs when investors expect its price to fall. It is thought to be a common phenomenon in the currency exchange market, especially under an adjustable pegged exchange rate.

spillover See *external economy*.

spontaneous privatization The theft of state assets by managers and workers in state enterprises and local government officials in the Soviet Union after the economic reforms introduced by the Gorbachev administration undermined central planning without privatizing or deregulating the economy.

spot market A market in which commodities sell at prices fixed by supply and demand at the time of sale. The forward market, on the other hand, exchanges promises to buy or sell commodities in the future at a preestablished "forward" price.

STABEX Part of the Lomé Convention, STABEX was a compensatory financing scheme set up by the European Union in 1986 to stabilize the export earnings of ACP countries.

stabilization programs Deflationary policy packages designed to reduce a country's trade deficit as well as imbalances in its balance of payments and domestic resource use by cutting down the levels of public and private expenditures.

stagflation An economic downturn characterized by the simultaneous existence of stagnation and persistent and intractable inflation. In the light of conventional economic theory, the condition of stagnation is puzzling because each of the above two conditions (i.e., stagnation and inflation) is considered a correction for the other. For instance, inflation, which is caused by the existence of an excess of money pursuing too few goods in the market, is usually considered a spur for slack demand. The simultaneous existence of slack demand and rising prices is usually explained by the rigidity of prices in modern economies. The downward inflexibility of prices in modern economies, occasioned mainly by the attitudes of resistance on the part of workers and company management to lessened growth and to cuts in wages and prices, makes any economic slowdown less effective in curtailing price rises than is expected by conventional economic analysis.

stagnation The utilization of an economy's resources below their potential. Stagnation might occur for two reasons: (1) the growth of the rate of output below the rate of population growth; or (2) the existence of insufficient aggregate demand that may prevent an economy from achieving its potential despite its capacity for sufficient growth.

state-owned enterprise A firm owned by the government.

strategic alliance A generic term used to encompass the many forms of interfirm cooperation that occur in the world economy. It includes all the possible varieties of joint ventures but also less formal cooperative arrangements among firms.

Structural adjustment a term used to describe policies implemented by the International Monetary Fund (IMF) and the World Bank) in developing countries

that are designed to reduce trade and budgetary deficits and to stabilize the economy, often involving the imposition of austerity measures such as reduced government spending for health, education, and welfare.

structural adjustment program A set of policies that are imposed on an indebted country by the International Monetary Fund in order to qualify for an injection of new capital. A structural adjustment program often includes austerity measures, such as reduced government spending, along with other economic reforms such as currency devaluations and reduced barriers to trade and investment flows.

Structural Impediments Initiative Talks between the United States and Japan that occurred in 1989–1990 and concluded with an agreement on reducing the U.S. bilateral balance-of-payments deficit with Japan by opening Japan's market to U.S. exports and investment flows.

structuralism A school of thought that contends that the international market structure perpetuates backwardness and dependency in the Third World and fosters dominance by the developed countries. As such, unregulated international trade accentuates international inequalities, due to the declining terms of trade for the South, and creates a dual economy by giving rise to an export sector that has little effect on the rest of the economy. Foreign investment in the South leads to a net flow of capital to the developed North and tends to concentrate in export sectors, thereby aggravating the dual economy and the negative effects of trade. However, unlike Marxism and neo-Marxism, which argue that the international system is immutable, structuralism argues that the system is amenable to reform. Rather than prescribing a socialist revolution, the structuralist prescription for promoting economic development in the South focuses on four types of policy changes: (1) import-substituting industrialization; (2) increased South-South trade and investment; (3) regional integration; and (4) population control.

subsidiary A firm that exists within another larger, parent firm. The parent firm owns more than 50 percent of the voting stock of the subsidiary. A subsidiary can be domestic or foreign. Only multinational corporations have *foreign subsidiaries*.

Subsidies and Countervailing Measures (SCM) An agreement within the GATT that governed the employment of subsidies or measures designed to counter the effects of subsidies or trade barriers in other nations.

subsidy A grant of money made to either the seller or the buyer of a certain product or service, thereby altering the price or cost of that particular product or service to the recipient of the subsidy in a way that affects the output. Governments usually make payments to domestic producers to offset partially their costs of producing and selling certain goods and services. Subsidies commonly are used to support infant firms just entering a new market and to bail out older firms suffering from intensified competition. Subsidies also are used to promote the development of high technology industries, even when these are questionable candidates for "infant industry" status.

Supplementary Finance Facility An IMF trust fund financed by the sale of IMF gold, it was created in 1979 to help alleviate serious payments imbalances.

supply inelasticity A situation that exists when the supply of a good or service does not respond to changes in prices.

supply-side economics A school of economics that holds that decreasing impediments to the supply and efficient use of factors of production, such as reductions in the tax rates, increases incentives and shifts the aggregate supply curve. Hence, supply-side economists argue that since taxation and government regulation crowd out investment, taxes and government regulations ought to be reduced in an effort to stimulate savings, investment, and growth.

surveillance An essential aspect of the IMF's responsibilities associated with overseeing the policies of its members in complying with their obligations specified in the articles of agreement in order to ensure the effective operation of the international monetary system.

tariff A tax imposed on commodity imports based either on the value of the good or on a fixed price per unit. The tariff usually is levied by a national government when the imports cross its customs boundary. *Protective tariffs* attempt to shelter selected domestic industries by restricting the quantity and raising the price of competing imports, while *revenue-producing tariffs* are enacted mainly to increase government income. Some tariffs comprise fixed duties on a variety of imported products. However, in most cases, tariffs are ad valorem duties—that is, they are a percentage of the imported products' value.

tariffication A pledge made by countries engaged in the use of nontariff barriers to replace these barriers with actual tariffs that can be reduced in future trade negotiations.

tariff-jumping hypothesis A hypothesis that explains foreign direct investments. Its proponents maintain that firms resort to foreign direct investments in order to jump over existing tariff or nontariff barriers in host countries.

technological dependence The dependence of a country on another country or a foreign-owned enterprise for access to a technology or group of technologies.

Tequila crisis One of a series of crises that occurred in Argentina in 1994–95 in the wake of the Mexican peso crisis of 1994.

terms of trade The relationship between the prices of a nation's imports and those of its exports. Nations face declining terms of trade when import prices rise faster than export prices, while rising terms of trade occur when relative export prices grow faster.

Tesobonos Mexican Government bonds denominated in pesos, with coupons and principal indexed to U.S. dollars.

Tiananmen Square A square in Beijing that was the location of a major student demonstration for freedom and enhanced political participation in 1989 that was brutally suppressed by the Chinese government.

total factor productivity The portion of output not explained by the amount of inputs used in production. It represents the residual effect of changes in technology, political institutions, and other unmeasured or immeasurable variables, which is often greater than the effect of changes in labor and capital inputs.

Township and Village Enterprise (TVE) Firms established after 1981 in China that could act more or less like private enterprises.

trade barriers Government restrictions on the free import or export of merchandise. These restrictions include tariff and nontariff barriers, which attempt to shelter selected domestic industries from international competition.

trademark A symbol or name representing a commercial enterprise, whose right to the exclusive use of that symbol or name is, along with patents and copyrights, one of the fundamental intellectual property rights that is the subject of the WTO's TRIPs agreement.

trade preference system The practice of offering lower tariffs on imports from a specified country or group of countries. A trade preference constitutes a violation of the most-favored-nation principle of nondiscrimination among trading partners in the setting of tariff levels.

trade-related aspects of intellectual property rights (TRIPs) This was the term used for bringing intellectual property protection into the Uruguay Round of trade negotiations under the pretense that only trade-related aspects of the issue would be included. In practice, this action did not constrain the coverage of the resulting agreement.

trade-related investment measures (TRIMs) Any policy applied to foreign direct investment that has an impact on international trade, such as an export requirement. The Uruguay Round included negotiations on TRIMs.

transaction costs The costs other than the money price that are incurred in trading goods or services.

transfer prices The practice of inflating the price of imports or decreasing the value of exports among the affiliated companies of a multinational corporation to enable a subsidiary to evade national taxation in a high-tax country.

transparency The clarity with which a regulation, policy, or institution can be understood and anticipated. In practice, it means asking government agencies to make public various kinds of information that can help the public hold the agencies accountable for their actions.

trigger price mechanism (TPM) Adopted by the Carter administration in 1978, this policy established a "fair value" reference price for steel prices in the United States based on Japanese production costs.

twin deficits The budget and balance-of-payments deficits that occurred in the 1980s in the United States.

unfair trade practices Under the GATT this refers only to exports that are subsidized or dumped. This term also is used to refer to almost any trade that the speaker objects to, including trade based on low wages or weak regulations.

Union of Soviet Socialist Republic (USSR) a constitutionally socialist state that existed in Eurasia from 1922 to 1991.

Unitary tax A state corporate income tax on the worldwide income of a given firm.

United Nations Code on Transnational Corporations An attempt by developing countries in the

United Nations to establish a code of conduct for MNCs during the 1970s. Originally conceived at the time of the NIEO, this idea languished and became increasingly irrelevant. As attitudes toward foreign investment changed, Southern interest in the code declined.

United Nations Commission on Transnational Corporations (UNCTC) This commission acted as an intergovernmental forum within the United Nations for considering issues related to multinational corporations, for conducting inquiries, and for supervising the work of the Center for Transnational Corporations.

United Nations Conference on Trade and Development (UNCTAD) An intergovernmental body established in 1964 within the United Nations, responsible for trade and development. Historically, it has often been the international voice of developing countries.

upstream A business is upstream from another when the former provides input to the latter.

U.S.–Canada Free Trade agreement A free trade agreement between Canada and the United States signed in 1989 and superseded by the NAFTA agreement in 1994.

U.S. Export Control Act of 1940 one in a series of legislative efforts by the United States government and specifically the administration of President Franklin D. Roosevelt to accomplish two tasks: to avoid scarcity of critical commodities in a likely pre-war environment and, more notably, to limit the exportation of war materiel to pre-World War II Imperial Japan.

Value-added tax (VAT) a consumption tax levied on value added, similar to a sales tax.

Value chains A progressive chain of activities that enhance the value of a final good or service. Examples of activities that progressively enhance value are research, design, manufacturing, and commercialization.

Venture capital a type of private equity capital typically provided to early-stage, high-potential, growth companies in the interest of generating a return through an eventual realization event such as an initial public offering (IPO) or a sale of the company.

vertical FDI Foreign investment that fragments production across countries so that different tasks are allocated according to differences in the relative abundance of factors of production. Vertical FDI occurs primarily to reduce costs of production.

vertical integration The attempt to own and control activities that are both "upstream" and "downstream" from the core business of a firm. A good example is the petroleum industry, in which multinational petroleum firms tend to own oil production facilities, refineries, and retail outlets for refinery products—the entire chain of activities from production to commercialization.

voluntary export restraints (VERs) See *voluntary restraint agreements*.

voluntary restraint agreements (VRAs) Bilateral, and sometimes secret, agreements stipulating that low-cost exporters voluntarily restrict exports to countries where their goods are threatening industry and employment, thus forestalling official protective action on the part of the importing country. VRAs usually are used to get around the GATT restrictions on quantitative import restrictions. Because of their ostensible "voluntary" nature on the part of both the importer and the exporter, VRAs are considered consistent with the GATT norms of reciprocity. However, in actuality, VRAs result in the same outcome as that resulting from unilaterally imposed quantitative import restrictions. That is, the price of the goods subject to VRAs in the country of destination tends to rise because demand remains relatively constant while supply diminishes.

Vredeling proposal A proposed directive for the European Commission that called for greater consultation between management and labor regarding company policy and plans. Proposed in 1980, it came under strong opposition from European business leaders. The idea has been revived in various alternative forms since then.

Washington Consensus A set of principles that informed economic liberalization policies in the developing world from the 1990s on. Some of these principles were forced on developing and emerging countries by coercive actions of the U.S. government, the World Bank, and the IMF, but others were adopted voluntarily.

welfare state A nation in which the government undertakes large-scale action to ensure the provision of social goods and benefits. Welfare programs usually are provided at public expense with little or no cost to the recipient of the services. Policy prescriptions advanced by proponents of the welfare state emphasize securing a minimum standard of living for all citizens so that no one is denied an essential service that might be available to others; the production of social goods and services; the control of the business cycle; and the manipulation of total output to allow for social costs and revenues. Among the instruments of the modern welfare state are progressive taxes, social security, unemployment insurance, agricultural subsidies, and government-subsidized housing programs.

World Bank group A group of five closely associated international institutions providing loans and other development assistance to developing countries. The five institutions are the IBRD, IDA, IFC, MIGA, and ICSID. As of July 2000, the largest of these, the IBRD, had 181 member countries.

World Intellectual Property Organization (WIPO) The United Nations organization that establishes and coordinates standards for intellectual property protection.

World Trade Organization (WTO) an international organization designed to supervise and liberalize international trade that came into being on January 1, 1995, and is the successor to the General Agreement on Tariffs and Trade (GATT).

Acronyms

ACP	African, Caribbean, and Pacific
AFL-CIO	American Federation of Labor–Congress of Industrial Organizations
AFTA	ASEAN Free Trade Area
AID	Agency for International Development
AIPAC	America Israel Public Affairs Committee
ANCOM	Andean Common Market
ANWR	Alaska National Wildlife Refuge
APEC	Asia Pacific Economic Cooperation
ASEAN	Association of Southeast Asian Nations
BIS	Bank for International Settlements
BIT	Bilateral Investment Treaty
BP	British Petroleum
BRIC	Brazil Russia India China
CACEU	Central African Customs and Economic Union
CACM	Central American Common Market
CAP	Common Agricultural Policy (European Union)
CARICOM	Caribbean Community
CEAO	West African Economic Community
CED	Committee for Economic Development (United States)
CEPS	Center for European Policy Studies
CEPT	Common Effective Preferential Tariff
CFIUS	Committee on Foreign Investment in the United States
CIEC	Conference on International Economic Cooperation
CIPEC	Conseil Intergouvernmental des Pays Exportateurs de Cuivre
CIS	Confederation of Independent States

CMEA	Council for Mutual Economic Assistance (Comecon)
CNOOC	China National Offshore Oil Company
CoCom	Coordinating Committee
CRB	Commodity Research Bureau
CTC	Center on Transnational Corporations (United Nations)
DAC	Development Assistance Committee
DLF	Development loan fund
DM	Deutsche Mark
DPW	Dubai Ports World
DSU	Dispute Settlement Understandings
DTT	Double taxation treaty
EBRD	European Bank for Reconstruction and Development
EC	European Community
ECB	European Central Bank
ECCAS	Economic Community of Central African States
ECO	Economic Cooperation Organization
ECOSOC	Economic and Social Council (United Nations)
ECOWAS	Economic Community of West African States
ECU	European Currency Unit
EEC	European Economic Community
EFTA	European Free Trade Area
EMI	European Monetary Institute
EMS	European Monetary System
EMU	Economic and Monetary Union
EPZ	Export Processing Zone
ERM	Exchange Rate Mechanism
ESCB	European System of Central Banks
EU	European Union
FDI	Foreign direct investment
FDIC	Federal Deposit Insurance Corporation (United States)
FINSA	Foreign Investment and National Security Act
FIRA	Foreign Investment Review Agency (Canada)
FOGS	Functioning of the GATT System
FTA	Free trade agreement
FTAA	Free Trade Area of the Americas
GAB	General Arrangements to Borrow
GATS	General Agreement on Trade in Services
GATT	General Agreement on Tariffs and Trade
GCC	Gulf Cooperation Council
GDP	Gross domestic product

GKI	State Committee on the Management of State Property (Russia)
GKO	Gossudarstvennye Kratkasrochnye Obligatsii (Short-Term State Treasury Notes, Russia)
GNP	Gross national product
GSP	Generalized system of preferences
GSTP	Global System of Trade Preferences
G-3	Group of Three
G-5	Group of Five
G-7	Group of Seven
G-8	Group of Eight
G-77	Group of Seventy-Seven
HIPC	Heavily Indebted Poor Countries
H-O	Heckscher-Ohlin
HST	Hegemonial stability theory
IBA	International Bauxite Association
IBRA	Indonesian Bank Restructuring Agency
IBRD	International Bank for Reconstruction and Development (World Bank)
ICA	International Commodity Agreement
ICAO	International Civil Aviation Organization
ICSID	International Center for the Settlement of Investment Disputes
IDA	International Development Agency
IEA	International Energy Agency
IFAD	International Fund for Agricultural Development
IFC	International Finance Corporation
IFG	International Forum for Globalization
IITSA	International Investment and Trade in Services Act
ILO	International Labor Organization
ILSA	Iran-Libya Sanctions Act
IMF	International Monetary Fund
INF	Intermediate-range nuclear force
ISI	Import-substituting industrialization
ITO	International Trade Organization
ITT	International Telephone and Telegraph Company
JEI	Japan Economic Institute
JETRO	Japan External Trade Organization
LAIA	Latin American Integration Association
LBO	Leveraged buyout
LDC	Less-Developed Country
LTA	Long-Term Arrangement (for international trade in textiles)

LTCM	Long-Term Credit Management
MAG	Market Access Group
MAI	Multilateral Agreement on Investment
MCA	Millennium Challenge Account
MDG	Millennium development goal
Mercosur	Southern Cone Common Market (South America)
METI	Ministry of Economy, Trade, and Industry (Japan)
MFA	Multi-Fiber Arrangement
MFN	Most-favored-nation
MIGA	Multilateral Investment Guarantee Agency
MIT	Massachusetts Institute of Technology
MITI	Ministry of International Trade and Industry (Japan)
MNC	Multinational corporation
MNE	Multinational enterprise
MOSS	Market opening sector specific
MTN	Multilateral trade negotiations
MYRA	Multi-year rescheduling agreement
NAB	New Arrangements to Borrow
NAFTA	North American Free Trade Area
NATO	North Atlantic Treaty Organization
NBER	National Bureau for Economic Research
NGO	Nongovernmental organization
NIC	Newly Industrializing Country
NIEO	New International Economic Order
NIS	Newly independent state
NNP	Net national product
NTB	Nontariff barrier
NTR	Normal trade relations
OAPEC	Organization of Arab Petroleum Exporting Countries
OAS	Organization of American States
OAU	Organization of African Unity
ODA	Official development assistance
OECD	Organization for Economic Cooperation and Development
OEEC	Organization for European Economic Cooperation
OLI	Ownership, location, and internalization
OMA	Orderly marketing agreement
ONGC	Oil and Natural Gas Corporation (India)
OPEC	Organization of Petroleum Exporting Countries
OPIC	Overseas Private Investment Corporation
PEPFAR	President's Emergency Program for AIDS Relief

PNTR	Permanent normal trade relations
PRI	Partido Revolucionario Institucional (Mexico)
PRSP	Poverty Reduction Strategy Paper
R&D	Research and Development
RTAA	Reciprocal Trade Agreements Act (United States)
SAARC	South Asian Association for Regional Cooperation
SADC	Southern African Development Community
SALT	Strategic Arms Limitation Talks
SAS	Scandinavian Airlines System
SCM	Subsidies and Countervailing Measures
SDR	Special drawing right
SEA	Single European Act
SEIU	Service Employees International Union
Sematech	Semiconductor Manufacturing Technology
SEZ	Special Economic Zone (China)
SII	Structural Impediments Initiative
SIMEX	Singapore International Monetary Exchange
SWF	Sovereign Wealth Fund
TNC	Transnational corporation
TNE	Transnational enterprise
TPM	Trigger Price Mechanism
TRIMs	Trade-related investment measures
TRIPs	Trade-related aspects of intellectual property rights
UAE	United Arab Emirates
UMA	Arab Maghreb Union
UN	United Nations
UNCTAD	United Nations Conference on Trade and Development
UNCTC	United Nations Commission on Transnational Corporations
UNDP	United Nations Development Program
UNICE	European Employers' Union
UPEB	Unión de Paises Exportadores de Banana
VER	Voluntary export restraint
VLSI	Very large scale integrated (electronic circuits)
VRA	Voluntary restraint agreement
WHO	World Health Organization
WIPO	World Intellectual Property Organization
WTO	World Trade Organization

Index

CPSIA information can be obtained
at www.ICGtesting.com
Printed in the USA
FFOW01n1715231215
19880FF